The Biggest Book of Yes

49 Short Adventure Stories

Edited by Jon Doolan

Contents

Foreword

At the time of publication, the YesTribe will have crawled past its fifth birthday, and looking back, there is so much to be proud of. Everyone who has joined the community, attended an event, joined our ever growing volunteer team or contributed to one of the many projects to have blossomed from a small idea, has done so because they said yes.

This was our aim from the start. To create opportunity, to nudge folks towards accepting that chance, and to celebrate their act of doing so. Hundreds of people have plucked up the courage to stand on their first stage, to share a previously untold story, to brave a first act. In a world ever dominated by stats, it's more important than ever to remember that each of us is more than a figure – we are a living, breathing, walking story.

This is the final act (or so the word 'Biggest' would suggest) of a splendid trilogy. The opportunity for people to become authors and to share their real-life stories and for so many more to be inspired to dream up, act on and share their own.

The tales in this book are not opinions, memes or rhetoric. They are heartfelt, personal and true. Words have never been so important.

I've been moved to tears by the chapters I've been lucky enough to read so far. Each one is a reminder that we're onto a wonderful thing.

A huge thanks to Jon for bringing all of the Books of Yes to fruition, and to every writer for sticking their hand up despite the nerves, doubt and worry that putting yourself out there naturally brings.

If there's one thing that bonds all us, it's that we shouldn't underestimate each other or ourselves. In these times, this feels like as good a foundation as any to start from.

Dave Cornthwaite

Founder of **SayYesMore** and the **YesTribe.**

Davecornthwaite.com

Introduction

All it takes to create a book is one word. YES!

In January, I put a message on the YesTribe Facebook page asking for authors for the third and final book in the Book of Yes series; The Biggest Book of Yes (because, once you've used the other superlatives, there's only one way to go, right!?)

I got so many positive responses that I worried that I wouldn't fit them all in the print book. I couldn't say "No!" to anyone. That's not really in the spirit of the book, is it?

And that's the secret I've been keeping these last few years. I never asked for 'good' writers. No one had to jump through any hoops or pass any qualifying tests.

Every single author is only here for one reason – because they said, "YES!"

That's not to say the chapters are terrible! We've spent a lot of time making sure these stories are told in the most exciting way we know how. We really hope you enjoy them!

I also want to take this moment to thank the incredible Tom Napper. Not only did he design the awesome cover (and the image for chapter one), he also coordinated forty other artists who drew the pictures that you'll see in this book.

And guess how they managed to get in this book? That's right. They said, "YES!"

A big thank you must also go to all of the people who helped promote this book (especially Zoe Langley-Wathen, Claire Jenkins and Esther Zimmer who led the team). Without your efforts this book wouldn't have reached as many people, or made as much money for the charity as it has.

All royalties go to the Teddington Trust. Every single author, artist, marketer and editor has given their time and effort for free. If you want to learn more about the Teddington Trust, check out the last chapter written by their founder, Nicola Miller.

This book is full of Yeses. It's a celebration of everything that that one little word means, what it can create and what it can become.

If you want to write a book, just do it. Say, "YES!"

If you want to become an illustrator, there's nothing stopping you. Say, "YES!"

If you want to go on an adventure… you guessed it! Say, "YES!"

And it's not some half-hearted, "Yeah, alright, maybe." It's a fully formed, lung-busting scream! "YES!!"

What will you say, "YES!" to?

Jon Doolan (Editor)

Jondoolan.com

Founder of **The Adventure Writers' Club**.

Chapter 1

If Not Now, When?

by David Altabev

Prologue

Running is my meditation. A space to break away from life, reconnect with myself and nature. Movement in its simplest sense. Time where my mind can gather my thoughts. A moment to breathe. What follows therefore is not perhaps a traditional account of an adventure, but more a series of vignettes from my journey, thoughts and ruminations that percolated through my mind as the ground passed beneath my feet.

Start at the Beginning

I strode purposefully up the medieval steps, worn smooth by the passage of thousands of pilgrims before me. My head down following the blue dot on Google Maps guiding me to the start point, my heart beating a nervous flutter.

I was looking for the Lisbon Cathedral from where I would collect my passport for the Camino. As I walked into the square I looked around at all the buildings and thought, 'But any one of these could be the cathedral. They all look old.'

After circling the square, I eventually stumbled across a large side door. In this little opening sat an old man behind a very old wooden desk. On the desk was a hand-written ledger for all pilgrims to fill in, some tourist leaflets and a sign indicating that I was at the right place. That and a massive Virgin Mary on the wall behind him said that I might just have found the cathedral.

I handed over my €3, and as the man handed me my booklet, I inspected its empty pages that would, in the days to come, be filled with a myriad of stamps from as yet unknown destinations. Places like pilgrim hostels, cafés and so on would give my Camino passport a rubber seal of approval to show that I had walked through their village. If I collected enough of these, then at Santiago, I could prove that I'd travelled the entire length of the route and could get my certificate. I don't know why it mattered getting the certificate. I'd almost never show it to anyone or do anything with it, but symbolically, it felt like something that I should do, almost as a rite of passage along the Camino.

Getting a stamp in my passport was one of those simple pleasures of travelling that I used to love, each stamp an insight into the culture of the country I was visiting. A silhouette of Everest on a Nepalese visa or tribal spears on the Ugandan stamp.

Looking back at the portly gentleman with the ledger, I asked, "Where do I start from?" A genuinely innocent question as I had no clue.

"You follow the signs," he said.

"What signs?"

"The arrows."

"What arrows?"

"The yellow arrows. You follow the yellow arrows," he said, sounding slightly exasperated.

'Uh huh!' I thought. 'Just follow the yellow arrows. Simple enough.'

He looked back at me, his dark bushy eyebrows furrowing as the exasperation gave way to the improbable realisation that I was as clueless as I looked and really didn't have any idea what I was doing. For a start, I was starting the Camino late in the afternoon, and I'm guessing most pilgrims that cross his path arrive early in the morning to start their first day, prepared and knowing where the route is.

I looked back at him, my face revealing an almost embarrassed smile that said, 'Yes, I have no idea what I am getting myself in for. And yes, I read the guidebook on the plane over three hours earlier.'

It was a Tuesday afternoon, and until last Friday, I'd never even thought about running 250 kilometres along the Camino di Santiago.

I stood on the start line at 2.30pm with twenty-seven kilometres to run to the first monastery. I knew I could run twenty-seven kilometres. I'd worry about the other 223 kilometres once I got to the monastery. All adventures start with the first step.

I eventually arrived at the monastery in good time for dinner. It was, as you would expect, basic. Metal bed frames, plastic mattresses, faded pictures of Jesus Christ on the cross. There was both nothing memorable about the place yet a place full of memories. Time had stood still for decades. The furniture was old but well cared for by its inhabitants, blessed with the luxury of time to concern themselves with the small but important tasks.

What it lacked in luxury, it made up for in its iridescent splendour, from the ornate architecture across its exterior, to the vantage point it held across the farms and towns below, offering a view over the valleys that I would be running across the next day. I watched as the sun set over the hills and smiled. Day One was done!

Day Zero

It's 5pm on a Friday and I'm sat in the office trying to get the last two emails done so that I can leave for the weekend. I look up from my desk around me to see that nearly everyone else has left already.

I write an email and click send. It's that non-committal sort of email whose subtext reads, 'Sorry, I've not got around to it this week. Can we look at it next week?' Just one more email to go.

My heart isn't in it, and I just want to get out and go. 'I need a break,' I think to myself. I'd been working for myself for about two years, and in a story that's familiar to anyone who's started up working for themselves, I'd taken just about every piece of work that had been offered to me without taking a break.

Part of the appeal of working for myself had been the idea of taking large chunks of time off. When I was working, I would always plan them in my head for when the next project or contract was due to end, dreaming about the places I would go. Inevitably, contracts would get extended, another piece of work would come in that I had to say yes to, you know, just in case there's not another piece of work after that. The end result was that I'd taken less holiday in the last two years than when I was employed. Maybe there was something to be said for having a standard nine-to-five job?

But this time, work had definitely slowed down and I reckoned that if I managed my workload, I could squeeze a ten day break into the next couple of weeks. But what to do? I can't believe I'm asking myself this? How ridiculous is this? Normally I'm full of ideas, but suddenly having to come up with an adventure that I can plan and start in three days was causing a monumental mind block. Torn between going on an adventure and having a proper holiday to relax.

I log on to Facebook, procrastinating to avoid making a decision, a vain hope for inspiration. Apparently the average person scrolls through 180 metres of updates a day. Or the height of Everest every year. I'm going to do a 5k at this rate as I distract myself and look for ideas.

As I scroll down the infinity loop of mindless updates, I stumble across a post from my friend Fran. She'd just come back from doing the Camino de Santiago from Porto to Santiago, jogging the route over twelve days. Fran and I had been speaking a lot over the last few months about running as she had been training for her first London marathon. I looked at the post as it looked back at me.

My initial reaction was to recoil at the scale of the challenge, far beyond anything I had done before. I only had nine to ten days. Would I have the time? Could I run that far? Every day, day after day? I log off Facebook, write the last email, close the laptop and leave the office.

On permission to fail

What would you do if you knew you could fail? I recalled a conversation with my friend, Fiona Quinn, when we'd been taking some promotional photos for her then upcoming stand-up paddleboard expedition from Land's End to John o'Groats. It had never been attempted before, nevermind completed, and if she completed it, she would be establishing, not setting, new records for others to follow in her footsteps. It was one line in our conversation that had stuck with me that I now recalled:

"If there's no risk of failure, then it's not really an adventure for me. It's just a holiday."

I paraphrase slightly but you get the gist. Failure is a very misunderstood concept in Western culture. We revere success, celebrate the successful, yet rarely hear stories of failure that precede success. For what is failure but measured learning? Do. Fail. Repeat. Learn. This is how we grow as individuals, as communities.

When I stopped to really analyse the fear of failure, the 'what if I didn't make it', I realised that the probability of failure was in fact extremely low. Barring any big injury, as long as I kept putting one foot in front of the other, I would eventually arrive at my destination, many thousands of steps later.

It may take me longer than I had planned for, but by choosing to run the Camino specifically, I had already drastically improved my odds. There was no route planning or wayfinding as the route was already set and lined with yellow arrows and markers that were pointing the way. It's almost impossible to get lost. Pilgrims hotels, *albergues* and cafés had all sprung up along the route to cater to the whims of weary pilgrims, meaning food and accommodation were easy to come by. I was travelling outside of peak season and never had to worry about booking somewhere. So really, it was just one foot in front of the other, and repeat.

But more importantly, the actual fear of failure was irrelevant. If I never stepped into the arena and tried, then I would be destined to a life of frustrated failure. Failure not because I had given it my all and tried, but failure because I had chosen not to step up and show myself. That sort of failure was not failure I could honestly live with. Exploring my edge was a core value and so I had no choice but to honour my values, step into the arena and show myself.

And hey, at worst, if I fell short, I could take a taxi the rest of the way and enjoy a couple of days off. I didn't realise it at the time, but in that moment, I had given myself permission to fail. This was not a race, it was a marathon – or six back to back to be accurate.

On finding your why

I sat in a concrete bus shelter peeling away the skin of a tangerine I'd stolen earlier; an overhanging tree from someone's garden. Its citrus smell wafting in the rain had proved too hard to resist.

As I peeled back the bright orange skin, I stared out at the grey drizzle that had enveloped me. The rising morning sun that had cleared away the clouds and cheered my spirits had long since disappeared. A puddle had formed at my feet. My clothes were drenched from a sudden downpour. But it's worse than that.

It was official; I was lost.

Somewhere along the way, my mind had wandered, and I'd lost the path. I'd been running around in mindless circles trying to find these elusive yellow markers to take me back onto the trail.

Cold. Wet. Lost. Hungry. Why was I doing this to myself again? It's only day two and look at me; I was a mess.

My sister's voice of reason drifts back into my head.

"When David, when, are you going to take a *holiday* holiday? You know the one where you go away, relax, eat good food, have a warm clean bed, come back feeling more rested than when you went away? You know, the type of holiday that normal people do?"

Why can't I just be more normal, whatever that is? Why do I fill every holiday with some crazy madcap adventure? I mean, what was I thinking running 250 kilometres and calling that a holiday? My mind drifted to quitting. I've got the time off. I could just go back to Porto, rent a room and chill out by the beach eating good food, drinking cocktails in the sun.

Understanding your why of adventure is one of the most intriguing aspects of any adventure. What drives a person to put themselves into unknown, uncomfortable and challenging situations?

The why, the intrinsic motivation driving us to take on these physical or mental challenges, is often what separates us from success or failure. Without a compelling why, it's hard to muster the necessary courage to start, never mind the willpower to continue when the early glamour gives way to the harsh daily realities.

As the cool air around me began to bite and a chill set in my legs, I thought back to my why.

Because I can. To explore what my body was capable of and go beyond my previous mentally imposed limits. Exploring my edge, those self-imposed limits, and discovering what happens if I push them that little bit further has always been an intriguing space for me. What am I really capable of? I'll only ever find out if I keep testing myself, keep exploring. One day I won't be able to do these physical adventures, I reminded myself.

Someone once said that adventure is the freedom to choose. This was my choice, my freedom to take on this challenge. The last few years had allowed little time for adventure. Some family issues that needed my attention, then setting up my own company had competed for my time in varying degrees. Making time for myself had fallen down the list of priorities. I don't regret the choices I had been making, but the need to nourish myself by being outdoors and indulging in selfish pleasures had been neglected. Time to strip life back to its bare essentials and lose myself in the moment, to motion in nature. Because if not now, then when.

I finished my tangerine, strapped my pack back on and headed out into the rain to re-find my route.

On excess baggage

As I followed the trail path along the river, familiar markers of an approaching town appeared. The hedgerows became more manicured, benches and other signs appeared, and then without warning, the trail opened up revealing a wide tree-lined boulevard that ran along the river into town. With benches dotted between the perfectly spaced trees, this is, I imagined, where the locals would have come to spend their evenings before the days of television and phones.

I remembered warm evenings from my time living in Perugia in Italy where the boulevards that existed in every town, no matter how small, were filled with the old and young, wandering up and down, bumping into neighbours and friends, and catching up on everyone's gossip. Dripping in sweat, the chafing between my legs becoming almost unbearable, I thought to myself, I'm definitely not going to be impressing anyone with how I looked.

Making my way up the boulevard, I saw the arched stone bridge across the river coming into view. A left over the bridge, and my home for the night was at the other end. The longest day so far at thirty-five kilometres was coming to an end, and I was in fine spirits.

As at the end of every day now, the last few kilometres were punctuated with increasing numbers of pilgrims arriving at their destination. I passed an American family of four, their accents a sharp contrast to the local Portuguese around me. Arriving into the Albergue de Peregrinos de Ponte de Lima to check in, they soon caught up behind me.

"We saw you passing us along the river. How are you running with such a small bag?"

I turned around to see the man, who I assumed to be the father, pointing at my backpack. At eighteen litres, my Montane running pack had been a last minute purchase after my usual one had broken the week before. It was decidedly smaller than his forty-five-litre backpack, and miniscule compared to some of the sixty and seventy-litre monsters I had seen people carrying. What the hell did they have in there?

"It's got everything I need in it. And far easier to run with a small backpack than what you're carrying," I replied, a slight air of superiority in my voice, misplaced pride that I was doing this run with such minimalist kit.

In truth, this encounter belied a more important point that would only reveal itself to me later that evening. Walking into the dorm room that I would share with thirty other people that night (even at eighteen-litre good ear plugs made it into the essentials of my packing list!), it started to dawn on me. People's beds were strewn with their belongings. Makeshift clothes lines criss-crossed the room. Multiple pairs of shoes sat at the end of beds, iPads, Kindles, books, what looked like whole wardrobes. So much stuff to be carrying.

I would notice it more each day, the people with the biggest packs struggling the most under the weight of all of their possessions. Unused to carrying such heavy packs, they would hunch forward to hold the weight, their eyes focussed on the ground in front of their feet rather than the stunning views around them. Shifting uncomfortably as the higher centre of gravity knocked their stride, their feet would land awkwardly, twisting with each stride inside their heavy boots, causing blisters that they would nurse each night.

To be fair, if I wasn't running, I would probably have packed in a similar fashion. A large pack filled with unnecessary possessions weighing me down, preventing me from enjoying what was really important on this journey. A useful metaphor for life. My choice of transport, running rather than walking, had created a necessity to pack lightly, that meant that it was easier to enjoy the journey, to look up and see what was around me each day.

One set of evening clothes, a spare pair of socks and running top, minimal wash kit in a plastic airport bag, guidebook, notebook, chargers, head torch, rain jacket. That was all I needed. Everything else was just extra baggage, stuff that I would have to manage, unpack and repack, clean. Life was so much simpler with less.

On borders

Towards the end of the day I found myself entering the city of Fortaleza, an old medieval walled town typical of the region. Surrounded by fortified walls, large imposing gates facing their neighbours in all directions and ramparts where the cannons would have once sat, it was like a scene from Game of Thrones.

As I followed the path deeper into the city, the streets began to narrow as shops selling all sorts of daily goods and tourist trinkets spilled their wares onto the pavements and the walls behind them. It was a kaleidoscope of colours and sounds as the traders bartered with the late afternoon crowds.

I was making good time and feeling hungry so stopped at a café in the main square to soak up the atmosphere and enjoy a salad. I've always found it odd that in Portugal, a country famed for its food, vegetables can be so hard to come by.

Fortaleza was my last town in Portugal. After my meal, I would be crossing the border into Spain, running over the Avenue de Espanha bridge that spanned the Minho river to another medieval walled town. It probably once had its cannons pointed at where I was now.

I've always found borders fascinating. Arbitrary lines in the sand where, from one side to the other, life could be so vastly different. As I was to discover to my great horror, crossing the border would mean the end of *pastel de natas*, Portuguese custard tarts, best eaten hot with a sprinkling of cinnamon.

You see, by now I had settled into my rhythm for the day. My mid-morning and mid-afternoon breaks would be determined by the local cafés en route and what delicacies they could entice me with. Without exception, I would order a coffee or two, a *pastel de nata* or two (always two) and whatever other local pastries or treats they had.

The sudden disturbance of this routine by Spain's inexplicable rejection of its friendly neighbour's finest pastries reminded me that, whilst the borders may be open these days, old rivalries still remain.

I took my time running into Spain, over the white corrugated iron bridge which gleamed in the afternoon sun. The heat of the day had passed its peak and was settling into a warm breeze for the evening.

This was the year of Brexit, and for me as a British citizen, borders would soon be going up everywhere as my freedom of movement, an inalienable right since birth, was taken away from me. At the time, I had no idea what the situation would be like a year from now and whether I would be able to do these adventures with such ease in the future. It reminded me how lucky I am to live in an area of the world where trust and co-operation between countries is so great that you can simply walk, or in this case run, from one country to the other.

I arrived into Tui, took the obligatory photo of myself next to the 'Welcome to Spain' sign, and ambled into town to find my lodging for the night. It was low season and there weren't many pilgrims on the route, so I always felt comfortable to just turn up and see what took my fancy. I tended to arrive before the other pilgrims anyway so always had plenty of time.

Walking into town, a small building nestled between two others caught my eye. It had the Star of David at the top, the symbol of Judaism, and a small plaque outside that stated that 'In 1492 the ancient synagogue ceased to function', but elected not to say why. I smiled, took a photo and immediately sent it to my mum.

'Ceased to function because they kicked out all the Jews!!!' my text read. She replied with multiple laughing emojis. I knew that she would appreciate the joke.

You see, I'm what's known as a Sephardic Jew, Jews who originate from Sepharad, an area within Spain and Portugal, broadly along the Iberian peninsula. During the Spanish Inquisition in 1492, the Jews were given a choice by King Ferdinand and Queen Isabella in what was known as the 'Limpiesa de sangre', or cleansing of the blood. Convert to Christianity, leave or die. And so began the exodus of the Jews from this part of the world. My ancestors were taken in by the then Ottoman Empire and formed a small community in Istanbul where they still remain. Nearly five hundred years later, my parents emigrated to the UK where I was born.

I stood outside this synagogue, circling over five hundred years of my ancestor's history. At the same time, back home I was applying for Portuguese citizenship. Both Spain and Portugal had enacted homecoming laws to allow Jewish people who could demonstrate that they were Sephardic Jews from the region to return. They had the chance to apply for citizenship and come back to the homes that they had been forced from, to the villages that still bear their Jewish ancestors' surnames. I smiled silently to myself at this unexpected chancing upon this small piece of personal family history.

The title for this story, 'If not now, when', comes from the Talmud, the central text of Rabbinic Judaism that serves as the primary source for Jewish religious law. It refers to Moses passing on his teachings to the people he had shepherded for forty years, prompted perhaps by the urgency of imminent death. For imminent death is our shared common fate, and if not now, then when? If not me, then who?

On stretch targets

When I had first contemplated this adventure, the idea of running twenty-five kilometres a day, day after day, daunted me. I knew I could do it once, but how would my body fare after days of grinding out all these miles? It was perhaps my biggest fear, and the one that nearly stopped me in my tracks.

So when, after three days, Ana, an old friend that I used to work with in London, got in touch saying that she was nearby and that we should meet up, I jumped at the chance. But there was a snag. Ana was visiting her parents who lived in Galicia just off the main Camino route for Easter, still a very important holiday in rural Spain where Christianity is very prevalent. To get there in time for dinner before she left, I'd have to increase my daily mileage from twenty-five kilometres a day, to thirty-five kilometres a day. Yep, a 40% increase on a target that I had already thought might be impossible for me.

But it was too good a chance to miss. What a fabulous anecdote it would make down the pub one day when I regaled my friends of the time I went on a really, really long run and not much else happened.

Four days, thirty-five kilometres a day and I'd make it, knocking nearly two days off my planned schedule. I say schedule, but let's be honest, I was winging it as much as the next person. I believe it's called imposter syndrome?

I texted Ana and said game on, let's do this, because if not now, then when? The chance to meet up, and at her parents' house where she grew up of all places. I said I'd text her in two days to let her know if I was still on target. After four days I took a right, deviating off the Camino route for the first time, and saw Ana down the road outside her parents' house, waving at me with one hand and holding her baby with the other. After the first hello in over ten years, they showed me to my room, took all my kit to be laundered as it was hardening from days of sweat, and then her mum sat me down to the finest home-cooked meal I'd had the whole trip.

Thinking back to four days ago when I had wondered if I could make it this far so quickly, I thought to myself, you never know until you try. Start small and build from there. And above all, take the opportunities that life throws at you, because they may never come around again.

On showing your true self

The rain was intensifying as I rounded each corner, the views of Santiago de Compostela nearing in the distance. I'd given up trying to keep dry and was relishing being in the moment.

My mind and body were working in unison and I felt strong as I glided through the final kilometres smiling and dancing in the rain passing pilgrims huddled under raincoats whilst in my shorts and t-shirt. I darted and weaved between the throngs of pilgrims arriving into Santiago, the emotions of the last seven days burst through, until suddenly…

I was there in the main square in front of the cathedral. I'd taken the final step and arrived, seven days and 256 kilometres later.

Who am I? How had I changed over these last seven days? Who are you? I mean really? It's a question few of us ever sit with, and fewer ever really connect to their truth. We put so much energy into our egos, barriers, adapting ourselves to the world around us, rarely showing our true authentic selves to the world.

There's something about driving yourself through pain barriers day after day that is hard to describe in words. All the energy that you hold inside is drawn up through your body, through every vein in your muscles, driving you forward as the pain takes hold and seeps into every sinew. As you push your body past its normal limits and beyond, the energy dissipates. Spent. Nothing left to put towards your ego or putting up barriers.

As the days wore on and the miles beneath my feet ticked over, I was stripped naked, raw and exposed to the world. Through challenge and hardship and the time to sit and be with the emotions day after day, you gain a sense of who you really are.

The Camino de Santiago is a pilgrimage named after St. James, one of Jesus' twelve apostles. Thousands of people make the pilgrimage to the cathedral of Santiago de Compostela where he is apparently buried.

People make this journey for many different reasons. A pilgrimage is thought of as a journey that an individual undertakes in search a new or expanded understanding of themselves, life and the world around them, often leading to profound personal transformations.

What had started out as a simple run to fill a few days had turned into something much more meaningful. A chance to reset, take time to sit with my thoughts and emotions in the gentle, repetitive and almost meditative rhythm of my feet as they made their way across the Camino. To let go of old grievances and troubles and make peace with my past and myself.

Because for me, that is the true essence of adventure. To discover a truer, more authentic version of myself that I could hold on to and take back into the world.

Website: **www.davidaltabev.com**

Instagram: **@davidaltabev**

Chapter 2

How to be a Rebel

By Clare Ambrose

Step 1 – Embrace New Ideas

I've always been a YES person. Over the years it has taken me on all sorts of adventures: to the other side of the world, buying a narrowboat to live aboard, living as a property guardian, working in the woods at a Bushcraft camp, quitting my job on multiple occasions to follow my dreams and many more.

This is probably the most unexpected YES story so far.

I've always loved reading. I can often be found with my nose stuck in a book, so it seems strange that I never really looked into a book club before. Back in September 2018, I came across the Rebel Book Club. Every month we read a book, and at the end of the month, we meet up (online or in person) and discuss it.

My first meeting was in London, and I was really excited. We had read the book *Wabi Sabi* by Beth Kempton, and she was there to talk about the book and answer our questions. This was a wonderful book on Japanese wisdom. The London meetings were huge with different venues every time, and we'd break out into small groups to do tasks and activities based on the book.

My first meeting in Oxford was much more a traditional book club affair. A lovely bunch of people gathered together over special book-related cocktails in a dark and moody bar with the conversation just drifting to wherever it wanted to take us. I've been a member for over a year now, and we have covered themes including habits, sexism, gender, fake news, fast fashion, environment, AI, adventure and so much more. Even though some of the books have not been ones I would have personally chosen, it's been really interesting to expand my horizons and find out about new topics.

In November 2018, the theme was plastic pollution. We read the book *Turning the Tide on Plastic* by Lucy Siegle. This was a real game changer for me. I have always thought of myself as environmentally friendly and aware of what is going on, but it turns out I had no idea. The book really shocked me in regards to the wide spread impact that plastic has on the environment. Some of you may have seen *Blue Planet* and images of the great garbage patch or *The Effects of Plastic* on the BBC with Hugh Fearnley-Whittingstall. Reading this book was like a light switched on in my head. I was keen to find out more about what I could personally do to help reduce my plastic consumption.

Step 2 – Put the Theory into Practice

My first attempt at a 'plastic free shop' was interesting. It really is everywhere, and once you notice almost everything is wrapped in plastic, it's hard to not see it. My local supermarket didn't really give me much choice about what I could buy 'plastic free', so I ended up with some loose veg, some stuff in glass jars and had to make many sacrifices. I came away feeling somewhat satisfied about how easy it was to make a positive change so quickly but also horrified by the use of plastic surrounding me.

The more I read about the issues, the more confused I felt. It's not quite as simple as just replacing our plastic bags with paper, as one is not necessarily better for the planet than the other. It's about how much planetary resources are used to make the bag in the first place, and how many times it needs to be used to make it balance out. It really becomes a minefield when you start looking into this stuff.

All I knew was that I wanted to do more. Now, 'plastic free' and 'zero waste' shops are popping up everywhere, and it's becoming much easier to get things that aren't wrapped in plastic. It's a great step in the journey to becoming more environmentally friendly with your shopping.

Step 3 – Find Out More

I signed up to all the local environmental groups and decided to head along to some meetings to see what was what.

First, Friends of the Earth; I went along not knowing what to expect. Though a meeting full of strangers doesn't really daunt me, I did feel the dreaded 'imposter syndrome' set in. Why am I here? I don't know enough about the environment? I'm not really one of those environmental types. People might figure out I don't know anything.

As I looked round the room, it didn't ease my fears. The meeting was quiet. There was probably about ten people there. They played very much into the environmentalist stereotype I had in my head, aging hippies with years of protesting under their belt. They had all been doing this for years. The meeting touched on a range of issues including plastic, air pollution, local tree planting and the climate emergency.

My first thought was, 'WOW! I didn't realise things were this bad!' I came away from the meeting feeling disheartened and somewhat confused. This was the first time I'd heard the words Climate Emergency. The realisation of the situation, that the plastic crisis was just the tip of the iceberg, really hit me. I felt overwhelmed by the scale of the problem and saddened by the lack of empathy people had to the world around them. It left me wanting to know more

Two days later, I headed off to the next environmental group. This was a talk dramatically titled, 'Heading to Extinction and What to Do About It.' It was led by a group called Extinction Rebellion whom I'd never heard of before. I don't think many people had back then.

It was a cold Wednesday night in mid-March in Oxford city centre. I headed off to the church where the meeting was held half expecting a similar turnout to the previous night's meeting.

To my surprise, I arrived and the church was rammed. There was probably about 150+ people there. The church actually ran out of space and a speaker was set up so that people standing on the street outside could hear the talk. It started off with a climate scientist talking about the impact that various degrees of global warming would have on the earth. With every degree rise in temperature, it would bring more severe consequences to the planet and the people who live on it including food insecurity, more frequent and extreme weather events and rising sea levels.

This news was upsetting. I felt a crushing sense of fear wash over me as I sat there surrounded by people but feeling very alone. All I was hearing was how bad everything was. It just felt awful. My head was filled with thoughts, whizzing around my brain trying to get a grasp of everything I had heard. What was I supposed to do with this information? How could little old me make a difference? Why had nobody told me it was this bad? Why was no one doing anything about it? The planet was hurtling towards disaster and everybody was just carrying on as normal because we didn't know anything about it.

The second part of the talk was about how I could do something about it as an individual. I suddenly felt inspired and empowered.

The next few days were a blur as my body and brain were in shock processing the information. I felt a sense of grief for the damage that had been done to the planet. I felt worried about what the future would bring. I thought about how it would affect my family and friends. I wanted to talk to people about this but didn't know where to start. There was a great realisation that my world as I knew it would never quite be the same again.

I felt a call to action, to protest, to take to the streets in the April rebellion. An overwhelming compulsion to act overcame me. I wanted to be someone who tried to make a difference to the planet, for the people I love and for future generations. The next thing I knew, I was quitting my job and packing to take to the streets in London for my first ever protest.

Step 4 – Put Yourself Forward

There was only a couple of weeks before the protest but I knew I wanted to get involved. The question was, how? Having never even been on a protest march, I didn't quite know where to start, so the next step was an 'Introduction Evening' where I could learn more about the who, what and why of Extinction Rebellion.

A big part of the Extinction Rebellion strategy was about getting arrested. Although I could see the need, this was not an option for me. I work for a charity and regularly need to get a DBS check. The thought of having to have the conversation about why I had been arrested every time I apply for a job filled me with dread.

Next I attended a group meeting to hear more about the plans for the actual protest. They shared some details but there was also a lot of stuff that was kept secret. It all felt very exciting. As my desire to get involved grew, I still felt a little lost. I wanted to be useful but wasn't sure how. I felt that if I had something to focus on it would help.

Then out of the blue, as if by magic, my question was answered. An email came through asking for stewards to help at the Rebellion. For many years, I have stewarded festivals. This felt like fate, like it was the right thing to do. I eagerly signed up online.

To my surprise, someone from head office got in touch. He was very excited by my years of experience. He asked me if I'd help supervise at one of the locations. I was apprehensive at first and felt a little out of my depth. Was I really the right person to take on this role?

I decided to say, "Yes." I mean, what was the worst that could happen? It just felt like the right thing to do.

Due to security most of the information about the rebellion was kept under wraps until the last minute. This was exciting (I think secretly I've always wanted to be a spy!), but also frustrating. I like to know what's going on so I can be organised and prepared.

Next to think about accommodation. People were needed to camp on the streets. Normally I'd be up for that, but I felt it might be too much. I felt I might need space to escape if necessary. I got in touch with the Rebel accommodation team. I was matched to a house in Shepherds Bush with a local rebel.

Accommodation was sorted, notice was handed in, bag was packed and I had a vague idea what I would be doing. On a sunny Sunday in April I headed to London to rebel.

Step 5 – Warm Up

It started with an opening ceremony in Hyde Park. I arrived and felt a little lost to be honest. As I got off the tube, it just looked like another bright spring day at Marble Arch. People rushing around wrapped up in their own busy little words. Where were the rebels?

I saw some people with tents so decided to follow them into the park. There was a huge number of rebels crowding round one end of the park getting ready for the welcoming ceremony. Some had walked for days from across the country to get to London.

I didn't really know anyone, but wandered around a little hoping I would see a friendly face. I didn't so I sat myself down on the grass and soaked up the atmosphere around me. People were milling around, excitedly chatting in small groups. I could feel the energy of the place, like a volcano that was close to eruption. It was almost a physical thing that I could reach out and touch. It felt electric.

My mind wandered to what the next few weeks would bring? I had no idea what I was letting myself in for, but I felt ready for action.

Later there was drumming, cheering, speeches and a sense of enthusiasm for what was about to take place. While some bedded down for the night under canvas in the park, I made my way to the shared flat.

That night as I lay on my mattress on the floor, I barely slept. The anticipation and excitement kept my mind whirling all night long. This really was about to happen and I had no idea how it would all pan out.

There were three other rebels staying with our host, and none of us knew each other. The people I met were incredibly supportive and friendly. It felt like family. Every evening, when I returned, there would always be food in the fridge and someone to share stories about the day with. They were always there to listen and support.

Step 6 - Protest

I awoke for an early start and headed off to Parliament Square where I would meet my fellow stewarding rebels. The plan was to hang around and wait until someone gave the signal to go, then we'd rush to our stations.

The waiting was intense. It just felt like forever. We were growing in numbers, and people were just hanging around. I was getting to know my fellow stewarding crew, but I just wanted to get on with things, whatever those things were supposed to be. I was excited and ready for action.

At 11am, we got the nod to move and take over the roads. We walked out to stop the traffic, put out banners all over the streets and it began. This happened simultaneously across various locations in London, including Marble Arch, Oxford Circus and Waterloo bridge.

My role was to help establish a base for the stewards. Initially, it was all hands on deck to get the sites established and set up. Infrastructure came in including tents for wellbeing, stewarding, medical, information, training and even a kitchen. I was amazed at the organisation and creativity and just how it all came together. It reminded me of working at a festival. The same sense of loyalty and people coming together as a team to make things happen.

Our rebel stewards quickly got to work and really stepped up their game to make sure rebels and the public were kept safe. It's such an important role. You are the eyes and ears of what's going on.

Our hub of activity was the information tent, which was manned by helpful rebels. If you wanted to know what was going on and where, this was the place to go. People seemed genuinely interested in what was going on. We fielded lots of questions about who we were, what we were doing and why?

By the afternoon, our site was a thriving hub of activity. Throughout the day, news from other sites came in. Oxford Circus had a giant pink boat parked in the middle of it. Marble Arch had been set up as a mini city where people could camp, learn and support each other as rebels. Waterloo Bridge had been turned into a garden bridge with a stage and a skate ramp. We were hearing about arrests being made and creative actions going on.

On Parliament Square, it stayed calm. We had a nice family feel. It was a strange mix of rebels and tourists who had unwittingly strayed into the middle of the protest. They seemed curious and somewhat bemused.

It was an incredible and exhausting day. I met some beautiful people and heard empowering speeches.

I didn't want to leave the site, but my body felt tired and my muscles ached. I knew I needed to sleep and clear my head after the busy adrenaline fuelled day. I just couldn't believe what had been achieved. I felt really amazed at everything that had happened. I also felt a deep sense of loyalty for Parliament Square and the little community we had created. It felt great to be a part of something.

Step 7 – Continue Protesting

As I awoke the next morning, the first thing I did was roll over to grab my phone and look at the hundreds of rebel updates that had come in. Overnight news was sparked with drama around the other sites. Many arrests had taken place. Although this was part of the plan, it still felt unnerving to hear. It was also amazing that we had managed to keep hold of the sites through the night due to some brave and incredible people. This news brought home the reality of the situation we were facing. Soon the police would be heading to Parliament Square.

With this in my mind, I hurried to get ready and face whatever the day would bring. I wasn't supposed to be on shift until later that afternoon, but I was keen to head back to the front line. It was strangely starting to feel like home.

The day passed in a blur of activity. Music and speeches filled the air. The sun was shining. The site was filled with people and many a conversation was had. All in all, there was an amazing vibe going on. It was really nice not having traffic on the roads. It was easy to forget that underlying sense of impending police presence. We knew they would be coming; we just didn't know when.

It was about 5.30pm and I had just sat down to dinner when the atmosphere changed. It didn't feel like a safe space anymore. The police had arrived and arrests were about to begin. I'm not going to lie, when I saw the amount of police marching in lines straight towards our welcome tent where I was sitting, I was nervous.

Although we had had incredible training and support, you don't really know how you will deal with a situation like that until you are in it. I felt an overwhelming sense of panic and I didn't know what to do. My heart was racing as I got up, grabbed my bag and walked away from the action.

I took a deep breath and surveyed the situation. It had all happened so fast, and now I was watching the scene unfold, trying to figure out what to do next.

As I stood there focusing on my breathing, my phone rang. It made me jump out of my skin. Adrenaline was coursing through my veins.

It was one of the other stewarding coordinators. We met on the corner and watched the police invasion. As stewards, we were wearing high-vis tabards and were there to help people. The police weren't targeting us. In fact, they were talking to us and asking us to help. They wanted us to move stuff and take tents down.

Our role then became about looking after the welfare of people being arrested ranging from giving them water to taking their bags and getting them into storage. We slowly started to pack down the tents, gathered up people's belongings and made ourselves helpful as stewards.

As this strange scene unfolded, my personal plan was to stay moving. I had everything I needed on my back, and I just kept ducking and diving around the situation. Watching, observing and helping where I could.

Then, as the evening drew on and the sun began to set, more arrests happened. It seemed to me that the area would be back to normal with traffic flowing through by the time night fell. The police slowly dismantled the road blocks and cars started moving through the square.

I wasn't really sure what would happen, and just as I felt all was lost, something incredible happened. Rebels lay down on the road, one after another. As one person was arrested, another person lay down waiting to be arrested.

Suddenly, hundreds of rebel riders on their bikes arrived like knights on shining steeds. They rode around the square in circles, ringing their bells and playing music on their portable speakers. I think the police looked about as surprised as we were. The atmosphere in the square became electric as people clapped and cheered. I was amazed. I suddenly felt like things were turning a corner. There was hope that the battle was not yet lost.

Then the rhythmic tones of the samba band came rolling into the square bringing with them more and more rebels. The rebels took back each road block and the flow of traffic was stopped once again. It was very touch and go, and we weren't sure what was going to happen.

At midnight, much to everyone's amazement and disbelief, the police just stopped arresting people, got in their vans and drove away. It was shift handover time and the police stations were full. They were done for the evening. Triumphant cheering echoed around the square.

After some much deserved dancing in the streets, it was really hard to leave the site but I dragged my tired body back to the flat and tried to sleep. This seemed like a futile effort as my body was filled with adrenaline. My limbs were heavy and I felt physically exhausted, but my heart pounded and my mind raced. Sleep felt a million miles away.

Step 8 – Protest, Eat, Sleep, Repeat

Next morning, I was back in Parliament Square and it was like the commotion of the night before had never happened. The roadblocks were still in place, and instead of traffic, rebels occupied the road.

It was Easter holidays and unseasonably warm. Tourists were going around doing their daily sightseeing while rebels continued learning and sharing in the streets. Our welcome tent was bustling. The induction tent was overflowing. More people were keen to hear about what we were doing and how they could get involved.

The next few days carried on in a similar way. It felt very much like protest, eat, sleep, repeat. The crazy days blurred into one. Things changed in an instinct. One minute everything ok; the next the police would arrive and start to slowly make arrests. The atmosphere would change very quickly and you had to always be ready. We never knew what would happen next.

It was such an exhausting and exhilarating mix of emotions; so many highs and lows. The people around me were so amazing. Our team at Parliament square had become a little family. I will never forget the people I met and the times we shared.

It wasn't until day six that the site was finally lost. It was early morning on Easter bank holiday weekend and the tourists numbers were high. The police came in heavy. They circled each roadblock and arrested people one by one until there was no one left. It took many hours. It was very calm and serene as people sang, clapped and cheered the rebels being arrested.

I felt heartbroken but also resigned to the inevitable. Once they had confiscated our welcome tents and started surrounding and picking off each road block, I felt that the time on the site was over.

I took off my tabard for the last time. Gradually the site fell before me like a crumbling cliff eroding into the ocean.

A warm sense of pride filled my chest. We'd achieved incredible things both on our site and as a collective. The last few days had taken its toll on me both physically and emotionally. It had been a real rollercoaster and it felt like the time was right to move onto the next phase.

As the last person was arrested, a decision was made to process in a funeral march back to Marble Arch and join the other rebels on the site there.

That night, I slept so much better than any other in the last week. Although my site was lost, there would be more protests with more actions, more arrests, more roadblocks and many more creative actions over the coming weeks.

Step 9 - Regroup and Recover

It's hard to really describe how I felt after the rebellion. My body ached from exhaustion and my mind bustled from the excitement at what had been achieved. I kept thinking back to the memories of the protests; the highs, the lows, the laughs, the people, the fear and the dreams.

For me so much had changed, and there was a real sense of what happens next? It was clear that April had really upped the game, and now people were really starting to talk about climate change in a different way. We had sounded the alarm and changed the dialogue in the conversation.

Just days after the rebellion, parliament declared a climate emergency. This felt like it was the beginning of a positive change.

However, in the coming months, it was clear that although the dialogue had started, action was not being taken, and there was still much more to be done.

Step 10 – If Nothing Changes, Protest Again

Cut to the first day of the October rebellion. I'm sat alone in a small London café nursing a warm cup of tea. My eyes are peeled, scanning the crowds. I'm playing a game I've invented called 'Spot the Rebel'. A girl with long dreads, baggy trousers and a big rucksack joins her friends in the café sitting across from me. I know they must be rebels. It's hard not to imagine her stood at a road block chanting or singing about climate justice, her soprano voice reverberating around the crowd.

For a moment, I catch her eye. There's a twinkle of recognition. A strange sense of connectedness and togetherness.

But I look away quickly. I don't want to give the game away and ruin the plan. Just ahead of us, I can see police stopping and searching people who they suspect to be rebels. We've been warned that the police would be even more vigilant than last time. I've already seen the heavy police presence that is everywhere in London. I glance subconsciously down at my backpack at my feet which is stuffed with food and my high-vis tabard.

My phone sits motionless on the table as I cradle my hot cup of tea in my hands. Butterflies fill my stomach as I mentally will the phone to vibrate. It'll be starting soon, and I can't wait.

Trying to look inconspicuous, I quickly move on. I throw my bag over my shoulder as if I was just on my way to the office even though my heart was thumping like a brass band in my chest.

I wish I had someone to talk to, to distract me. I'm feeling rather alone, like a deer caught in the headlights, dazed, confused and uncertain. I've been to the loo about a hundred times in the last forty-five mins. Will it work this time? Will enough people show up, or will the police would just shut it down instantly? How is it going to be different to last time?

My phone buzzes. My heart is racing. It's time to go.

Suddenly, I can see all of the rebels coming out of shadows, walking purposefully towards their positions. The sense of unity fills me with courage. I stride through the crowds.

Then, moments later, I'm stood shoulder to shoulder with my fellow rebels. This is what I live for. This is why I'm here. I'm here to make a difference. To be seen, to be heard and to enact change.

Being a Rebel

So, over a year later, my journey still continues. I now consider myself an activist and spend much of my time involved in protests, meetings and organising to continue the campaign. I'm still learning and engaging with the complicated issues that face the planet today. If it wasn't for this YES, then who knows where I would be today.

You'll be happy to hear that I'm still in the book club. Our latest topic is fast fashion – another industry that contributes massively to destroying the planet and has many ethical and environmental consequences. It's still a journey which I'm continuing. I'm excited to know where the next steps will take me.

One thing that changed for me was my lifestyle and my choices around my carbon footprint. Individually, these changes mean almost nothing. However, millions of people making changes can make a massive difference. But the issue is beyond that now. We need to come together to push for change from above. This needs to happen fast in order for us to tackle this crisis. The solutions are out there and more will come. We just need the government to implement a change.

For me, I am doing this because I care about the future of this planet and want to protect it for the generations to come. I can't see why people wouldn't want to live in a future that is better for all of us. We need to really look at making the most of the planet's resources, living within the planetary boundaries and sharing in our communities, sharing food, sharing growth, sharing life. It might seem like a radical change but it's necessary and we can do this.

If this story does anything, I just want people to hear about my experience in this movement and what it has done for me. Hopefully, you'll feel like you'll want to take action in your local communities or nationally. There's so many different ways and different organisations to get involved with.

Will you to be the change you want to see in the world?

Website: **justwords13245.wordpress.com**

Chapter 3

Digging Up Dust and Bones

By Kirsten Amor

It was as I was rummaging around the house looking for my work apron that I heard a faint 'ping!' in the other room. "Don't get yourself worked up," I told myself, but my rushing legs betrayed my head's sensible warnings. It was from Birmingham University's archaeology department. I had already received one rejection from them; had they forgotten and sent a second?

I won't lie to you, life wasn't entirely going how I had planned it at that point. Nearly a year after graduating in the middle of the deepest global recession in a generation, I had yet to find a relevant job with my archaeology degree. While my unshakeable optimism had kept me going for the past several months, it wasn't a currency my landlord would accept.

As the pile of rejection letters began to creep ever-higher, my self-confidence waned along with my bank account. I gradually found myself moving back to my hometown and working the same waitressing job from my teenage years. That little voice in the back of my mind, the one I had tried so hard to keep at bay, the one that always pops up at the best and worst moments in my life, began to make itself more assertive.

That little voice took up more space in my head and filled my days with a running commentary of all the different ways I was a failure, or just not *quite* good enough. What that voice was comparing myself to, I never understood, but its methods were effective. Time soon became an immutable blur of scrubbing tables and trying to remove food stains from my uniform.

Months later, that voice had grown to be a constant companion in my life. I was no closer to doing what I wanted to do, and I realised that as the days passed, my goal stretched ever farther away from me. In a moment of tough self-love, I decided to face facts: I could either accept my current lot or try to do something about it.

So, in a last-ditch attempt, I emailed/called over two hundred archaeological organisations in the UK my CV pleading for work. It felt desperate, but so did I.

At first my emails were met with sympathetic apologies, and then as the days rolled into months, silence. I refused to acknowledge my future consisted of polishing cutlery till my fingers were pickled from the vinegar. But the rejection letters, alongside the constant chatter of that voice, had made me come to accept that perhaps people were right; maybe archaeology was the preserve of eccentric English aristocrats with a penchant for khaki.

So you could imagine my bewilderment when I read the contents of the email:

> *'I am currently running an archaeological project in Qatar and am looking for two members of staff that have recently graduated to become part of the team. The work will mostly involve extensive field survey across northern Qatar recording monuments. Some of the work will also involve excavation. In the first instance I would be able to pay £100 a week plus expenses, flights and accommodation.'*

It sounded too good to be true. My heartbeat accelerated faster and faster with each word, my head ballooning with exhilarating images of afternoons spent recording crumbling remains in a remote oasis. As I reached peak excitement however, I sighed. My brain always had a knack for keeping my excitement on pace with its own anxiety.

I knew nothing about Qatar – had hardly heard of it in fact. A quick search revealed glittering skylines and oil. Lots of oil. Even less was revealed about the country's archaeology.

Not only that, but the sparks of the Arab Spring had fanned into a blaze, and turmoil was spreading to other countries throughout the Middle East. I knew little about the region, even less about the work I'd be doing there, the potential political unrest, and all the destruction and uncertainty that followed.

"Stop!" I told myself. "If there's little coverage of Qatar's archaeology, then there's potentially more to discover. You always say you want to travel more, so here's your chance." As for political unrest, well, that sounded like a problem for future Kirsten.

I realised I didn't need to think about this a moment longer. I replied with an overenthusiastic 'YES' and handed my notice in to my waitressing job that night.

*

Weeks later I walked out of Doha International Airport in the middle of the night. My foot had stepped only inches past the threshold of the plane, but already I felt a haze of stuffy, humid heat linger around my cheeks. Despite the late hour, the roads were buzzing with activity. People swarmed across the streets, yelling to each other in different languages. In the middle of it all, a woman adorned in bright floral prints, lots of jewellery and long wavy hair gave me and Naomi, the other archaeological surveyor, a wave.

"Over here! Did you have a safe flight? Are you feeling tired? Don't worry, you'll meet everyone tomorrow after you've had a rest. It's nearing the end of Ramadan, so the city is busy preparing for Eid. I'm Kathryn by the way. Sorry, I probably should have said that first - I work as the team's Publications Officer and Flints Expert. Right. Ready to head out?" Just like that, my Qatari adventure had begun.

After a long doze the next morning, we met the rest of the team: Oskar, Howell, David and Deniz, fellow archaeological surveyors, Gary, the team's maritime archaeology expert, and Richard, the overall project manager. Then there was Faisal, the team's other project manager from the Qatar Museums Authority. Wearing the usual Qatari garb of a *thawb* (long, white shirt), and a *ghutra* (headdress), Faisal possessed a manner of calmness that enveloped everyone around him. We listened transfixed to his stories of childhood days growing up as a Bedouin in Qatar. He grew more animated as he discussed his archaeological research and how various rocks, plants and even slight changes in the elevation of the desert hinted at centuries of human habitation. "You just need to take your time, and look carefully," he explained, checking his watch. "It's time for us to enjoy Eid. Come, I think Mr Richard had a surprise for you."

The surprise in question was a roam around Souq Waqif, the old marketplace in Doha. The ornate bronze lamps softly illuminated the maze of clay structures. Narrow alleyways zig-zagged off the main avenue, the spaces cluttered with various wares on sale. My head repeatedly spun back and forth to take it all in: falcons, their shrewd eyes hidden behind leather hoods, emerald-hued parrots, enormous sacks of fragrant spices, scarves and flags of every colour flapping lazily in the breeze, musicians and dancers performing in the square, the scent of hookah pipes wafting in the air. Wandering through the souk demanded the attention of all your senses to, well, make sense of it all.

Every turn of my head brought something new into focus as Kathryn tried to guide Naomi and me. "So, we are currently in the bird market - lots of parrots and songbirds, plus some falcons – Over here is the spice market. That's quite good if you want to grab some souvenirs for family back home. The gold souq is over that way, and you can find textiles throughout the souq, to be honest. Let's cool down with a walk along the corniche, and then we can find some dinner."

The cramped hive of people and sounds gradually faded as we emerged out onto the expansive harbour. A welcoming breeze flitted around me and caused the sleek hulls of the wooden *dhow* boats to strain against their moorings. My gaze drifted to the dazzling and slightly hypnotic display behind the dhows. Doha's futuristic skyline of glass skyscrapers and edgy towers were putting on a panoramic light show. I was transfixed between the dhows and the skyline, of the juxtaposition of old and new.

"Everything you've seen today was built in the last ten years," Howell's voice broke me from my mesmerising reverie.

"Even the souq?" I asked, perturbed. He gave a shrug.

"Sort of. That was refurbished a few years ago, but there has been a marketplace there for over a hundred years."

The awe that transfixed me a moment ago fizzled out of my sighing chest. "Ah, right."

Kathryn gave me a reassuring grin. "Don't worry, you'll see some archaeology over the next few months - it's just hidden behind all the flashy lights and money."

It wasn't long before I was absorbed into the daily workings of the archaeological team. The Qatar National Historic Environment Research project (QNHER) was a collaboration between Birmingham University and the Qatari Museums Authority to help the country establish a complete database of every archaeological site and findings in the country. With buildings rising every week and commercial interest in the country growing, the government needed to know what was there, and where, before anything else was bulldozed.

Tasked with surveying an entire country and ensuring no sites were left undiscovered for bulldozers to crush, I felt more than a little overwhelmed at the responsibility. 'What if a bad judgement call on my part destroyed the last remnants of an otherwise unknown civilisation?' The little voice said. My shoulders sagged under the weight of these dead or potentially non-existent ancestors.

Each week started with our heads bowed in a huddle over an aerial map, scouring the sheet for potential sites. From above, it is easy to see large patterns which could easily be dismissed as slight undulations when viewed from ground level. At the first meetings, I stared at the map, straining my eyes to decipher what was so clear to everyone else as they chattered away. As the weeks passed and we surveyed more and more maps, my eyes had learnt to read the information hidden behind the squiggles and lines.

The same was true for ground-level surveying as well. While we could hypothesize all sorts of theories looking from the skies, any trace would be left on the ground. Another aspect of the QNHER project was to research the trail of early human migration out of Africa, through the Arabian Peninsula. Millions of years ago, the Arabian Gulf was a lush green river valley, similar to the Nile today. The tiny peninsula of Qatar, which is half the size of Wales, is almost all that is left of this lost valley. This meant that thousands of years later, evidence of our early ancestors can still be found on the surface of the desert.

But our ancestors didn't leave crisp wrappers, keys or old receipts. They left rocks knapped into tools, fragments of pottery, and bones from fish, birds and small mammals. In a desert literally filled with rocks for miles around, how do you tell the difference between 'plain' rocks and rocks early humans have modified for hunting?

The question pulsed in my head again and again, each time returning with renewed apprehension and a previously undiscovered detail to worry over. Luckily help was on hand with Kathryn, who gave us a thorough rundown of prehistoric flints and how they are formed, and the difference between rocks struck by natural forces and those created by humans (yes, there is a difference, I promise!).

After sleepless nights of stomach-clenching nervousness and imagining worst case scenarios for the first couple weeks, I eventually settled into a pattern. Each morning I awoke to the sound of the call of the Fajr prayer reverberating throughout the neighbourhood by the nearby mosque. Under the curtain of darkness and bleary-eyed, we would pile into the cars and drive to some nondescript patch of desert. Before the searing heat of the desert could debilitate us to a dehydrated heap of clothes, the surveying again.

Up and down we walked in invisible lines, eyes fixed to the ground for any signs of human occupation from millennia ago. Often I found myself walking as if in a trance, my mind wondering who was the last human to walk on this patch of earth and what happened to them. Invariably my mind would wander back to myself and what traces might be left of me after I died for others to find. One thing no one tells you about archaeology is how much the piecing of the traces of other people's lives makes you inwardly analyse your own.

Some days our rucksacks bulged under the weight of findings of pottery shards, stone tools and flint knappings. Other times, days would pass before we found anything. Adventurous off-roading trips filled these afternoons, with the sheer randomness of what we might discover part of the allure.

One memorable afternoon we visited an old mock Arabian city on the Zekreet peninsula, its origins no one is still able to source. On another occasion, we clambered up the pair of 19th-century Barzan Towers, where we could view the modern residential neighbourhood through narrow slits that offered the only sunlight in the buildings.

This week we ventured north toward Al Jassasiya, a well-known archaeological site. Compared to Doha, with its constant traffic and noise, the northern peninsula of Qatar had a sedate, almost abandoned atmosphere to it. Desert would stretch for miles on either side, and it felt as though ages would pass before we'd see another person or car.

A whiff of salt caught my attention as I stuck my head out the window of the car. We pulled to a stop and followed Oskar and Howell to a long clump of white rocks.

"Take a look at the rocks over there," they said, gesturing towards the promontories I had noticed earlier.

"O-kay," I said slowly, not entirely certain what was in store for me. Within a few strides however, I could already make out random shapes and patterns in the rock. Leaning close, there was one I recognised straightaway.

"It's boats! They look just like the dhow boats in the harbour!" I exclaimed.

Oskar nodded. "There's plenty more where those came from. There's no exact date for these carvings; they could be several hundred years old or come from the Neolithic era-"

"A footprint! There's a footprint here!" Naomi yelled.

I ran over and gazed at the shallow indentations. Scattered all around it were hundreds of circular marks, flowers, even what looked like animals.

Stepping back, I marvelled at the volume of the carvings. "How many are there?" I turned to Howell.

"Well over eight hundred, I think."

My thoughts turned back, as they usually did when archaeology was involved, to the people that made the petroglyphs. Life must have been hard enough what with finding food and maintaining a shelter.

Why go to the bother of carving random shapes into a rock?

These were all questions I ruminated on in my travel blog, which I had started keeping since arriving in Qatar. Partially to assure my friends and family I was alive and also to recount the places I visited during my time in Qatar, the blog had also led to meeting more people in the country and exploring even more places. Along with Kathryn, who had grown to be a good friend and partner-in-crime for adventures, we found ourselves saying 'yes' to all sorts of adventures.

We had joined a scuba diving club, and explored the Qatari coast for coral reefs and old pottery remains on the ocean floor. Another weekend we decided to try dune bashing, and screamed at the top of our lungs as the car reversed down a steep dune. Another time we went truffle hunting with Faisal and his friends and camped in the desert as they told us cautionary tales of the djinn that haunted the area.

It was following that weekend that I realised the voice in my head had been much quieter recently. Pushing myself with these adventures had given me a renewed sense of self-confidence. My time in Qatar had given me the courage to accept failure as a possibility but not an end-all.

Saying 'yes' to something that doesn't entirely work out the way you think it might does not mean failure. Instead, you learn something new about yourself, or it can take you on a journey that was better than you imagined.

Over the weeks, I gradually felt my anxieties ebb and my self-confidence flow, but the role of an archaeological surveyor wasn't without its challenges. On several occasions, herds of camel approached our site, intrigued and hungry. After trampling the equipment we had set up, they fixed their eyes on our gear. It took some effort to prise the camera strap from the jaws of a gnawing camel. Turns out camels will say yes to eating anything, no hesitations.

The cultural differences also created challenges of their own. Qatar operated around religion and the sun. Days started early, afternoons lulled, and everything stopped five times a day for prayers, which proved tricky for archaeological projects on short time constraints. Eid and Ramadan would see ghost-like stillness in the day to frantic roads and a cacophony of activity in the evening as everyone raced home, ravenous. Although bureaucratic procedures were put in place, in reality things operated more on who you knew. Above all, the city operated on the word 'Inshallah'. This meant anything from, "Tomorrow for sure," to "Not in our lifetime!" I had to learn to go with the flow and find alternative solutions.

And then there were the other geo-political tensions. One morning we rose, before the first prayer calls to drive across Qatar to survey an area close to the Saudi Arabian border. The skies shrouded the landscape in a blue-grey curtain of shadows. With not even the dawn chorus of birds to interrupt the reverie, the air was weighted with an eerie stillness.

Gradually the miles stretched behind us, and Naomi and I settled into a comfortable silence. Peering above, I watched a wave of clouds roll in and dawn fight for every inch across the skies. Yet, the world remained a muted kaleidoscope of shadows.

Suddenly, my rear view mirror burst into a beacon of light. I squinted at the mirror, thinking dawn had finally broken. But no, it was only the headlights of two SUVs behind us.

"Hm, must've pulled out of a hidden layby," I said to myself, trying to ignore the crawling sensation down my spine.

Miles passed, and still the cars remained behind us. In fact, I could swear they were incrementally drawing closer to us as their headlights bulged in my rear-view mirror. My heart paced faster, faster. I turned around to check my eyes weren't deceiving me. By now, they were close to the rear end of our cars. I gave them a hesitant wave to let them overtake me, but they persisted in their position.

My eyes espied a logo on their cars. I squinted to make sense of-*bzzz!*

Naomi's ringing phone cut through my thoughts.

"Hello? Oh, hey Oskar. Yeah, we noticed them too." She didn't speak for several minutes and then turned to me. "Oskar says he thinks the cars behind us are the Saudi border control. They might be following us to make sure we don't try to sneak in."

My hands tightened on the wheel. "Why would we sneak in on a main road? What if we just wanted to visit Saudi Arabia? Loads of Qatari and Saudi people travel back and forth to each other's countries on this road."

Naomi shrugged. I suddenly remembered that Saudi Arabia didn't allow women to drive cars in 2010, which again probably didn't help our situation.

I took a deep breath and loosened my grip on the steering wheel. "Well, we're nearly at the survey site, so hopefully they'll find something more interesting than us once they realise we're just walking in lines."

The road descended around a corner and we turned into the site for surveying only to discover a post-apocalyptic scene. A car graveyard of abandoned trucks and scrap metal protruded out of the landscape with some areas half-sunk in the sand. Left to the elements, the area had a sinister edge, as if it would devour anything that stayed for too long. I tried to ignore the knotted feeling in my stomach.

We knew from the aerial maps that the area didn't hold much promise, but it was another place that had to be checked, regardless. The wind started blowing in great gusts, stirring up small tornadoes of wind in the process. We all looked to the sky in unison. A sand-storm was brewing.I looked up at the road we had been on moments ago, and saw the cars that followed us parked, their gaze on us. The knot in my stomach tightened.

"Let's get this over with," Oscar shouted above the wind. I pulled my headscarf around my face and got the equipment out, still watching the cars leering over us. I forced myself to ignore their surveillance and focus on the task at hand. There wasn't much point thinking about it. So far nothing had escalated to anything more than curiosity, and if there was one thing I had learned from my time in Qatar, it was to take things as they come.

Straining against the screaming gales, I peered inside the hulking shells of metal, the wind voicing their frames with piercing wails at being forsaken in that wasteland of a place. Some spewed sand in our faces. Bits of pamphlets and paraphernalia on the dashboard hinted at the past lives of these vehicles. *Any archaeologists surveying our cars would think we were slobs,* I smiled at the thought. Coming up with nothing, I turned around and gazed ahead. A tree, its trunk bleached white from the sun, beckoned me with its gnarled branches. I drew closer.

The wind had shaped the tree into a hunched, twisted form, its long, sharp tendrils ready to ensnare anyone that came to close. I gave a small shiver. What remnants of nature that existed here had also been warped by the menacing presence in this place. I shivered and gazed back at the site through narrow, gritty eyes. Oskar gave a wave to say he had finished.

We were done and didn't need telling twice. We hopped back in the car and turned around the corner, ready to pass those cars. Adrenaline coursed through my arms. I gripped the wheel, squeezing tighter, tighter and tighter still with every metre we gained on the road. Finally, we could confront the people that had spent hours watching us – and find out what they wanted.

As the car nosed around the corner, I leaned forward over the steering wheel and gasped. The space was empty. The cars had disappeared into the sandstorm haze. Naomi's head spun around as she tried to find them.

"Where did they go? How fast could they have been driving?"

Naomi sank in her seat, confused. I nodded in agreement. We spent the rest of the time sharing outlandish conspiracy theories.

We never did find out the identity of those cars. Whether it was border police, secret police or something more mysterious, we'll never know. Perhaps it is for the best – ignorance is bliss, and all that. To me, the encounter had given me a sort of freedom from my anxiety. I realised I could finally listen to the voice worrying in my head and recognise the fear it came from, but not let it control me.

*

Surveying deserts filled with rocky debris was unsurprisingly a recipe for frequent flat tyres. In the first few weeks of surveying I was terrified of finding myself stranded in the middle of the landscape, but months later I found myself agreeing to off-road adventures into the desert without the ceremonial anxieties about water, snacks, tools and spare tyres. Today was one such day.

We had finished our work for the day, and as the heat did not hold its usual intensity that afternoon, we decided it was ideal conditions for a beach off-roading adventure. Following Oskar in the 4X4, I enjoyed the twists and random turns along the journey. The crash of the waves could be heard over the soft hum of the engine, and the blustering wind revitalised my sunburnt face with a salty sting.

Pale-hued shapes soon appeared on the horizon. My eagle eye spotted the weathered remains of a minaret materialise ahead, a beacon amongst the crumbled shells surrounding it. We parked the cars a short distance away, careful to avoid the nearby quicksand.

I padded around the nearest wall and peered my head around the corner. The walls were bare, with no furniture or decor save the decorative curlicue flourishes that bordered the outer walls.

Despite the afternoon sun, my shoulders gave a shudder. With most abandoned buildings or archaeological sites, some mementos are left behind that indicate the former existence of these buildings. These places, however beautiful, had an eerie, lifeless quality. Absolutely nothing of the people that lived here remained.

"These villages are called Al Jumail and Al Arish - fishermen and pearl divers used to live here, but once Qatar discovered oil on its shores, everyone left and moved to Doha," Oskar explained.

"But they're in such a beautiful spot near the beach! Seems like such a shame to abandon it," Naomi added.

Howell shrugged. "Well, that's life. You can stay here as a poor fisherman, or move to somewhere less nice but with the promise of a better lifestyle."

Not knowing these pearl divers personally nor having any experience in the tribulations of aquatic careers myself, I felt some empathy with the ancestors of these villages. They too weren't happy to settle with the circumstances they found themselves in and had the courage to go into the unknown, with no guarantee that things would be better.

But they were, and I was, much more confident and stronger as a result of it. My writing had gained more traction outside of Qatar. I was even writing features about the project and my travels around Qatar for travel publications. Like those fishermen, I had moved on and found a new groove for myself.

*

After several months of surveying Qatar, we had built up a database of more than four thousand sites and artefact locations. I felt a burst of pride whenever I looked at the database, which was a welcome change from the stomach gripes that had occurred at the start. Those were now saved for the next stage of work on the QNHER project.

Deep in Qatar's northern Al Shamal municipality, we began excavating a nondescript stretch of desert called Wadi Debayan. Around five thousand people were said to live in the area, but so far

I had seen more camels and, bizarrely, emus. My hand paused from trowelling and I spun to look at the arid, flat expanse around me. It was difficult to picture that thousands of years ago in Neolithic Qatar, this would have been a hive of activity. Or so the evidence from the midden was telling us.

Like our modern-day garbage dumps, Neolithic people had middens. They dumped all sorts of organic waste into these pits before moving on elsewhere once it had filled. Rummaging through dead people's garbage might sound gross, but you can learn so much from these middens: what diet people had, what plants and animals frequented the area, even crafts or trade networks based on pottery shards or lithics thrown in as well. Because everything is heaped in dense layers, oxygen is starved from the midden, which gives everything inside impressive preservation.

For weeks we had excavated fine layers of organic material from the sands and sifted through every grain to ensure nothing was missed. Marine shells, operculums, fish bones, even small mammals indicated the people here ate a varied diet, which was supported by an inter-tidal environment with more rainfall and vegetation than exists in the area today.

Further pottery, obsidian and lithics findings also indicated these Neolithic people had established trading networks with people in Mesopotamia, Eastern Turkey and the Central Gulf region as far back as 7,500 years ago.

Archaeology never fails to challenge your beliefs. There's a modern assumption that people hardly moved beyond their villages until recently, but in fact the opposite is true. People have been sailing, hiking, horse-riding and camel-riding across the world for thousands of years. The journeys were longer and more perilous, but people have been saying 'yes' to new adventures since mankind walked on land.

The more we uncover about the past, the more I was starting to learn about the limitations we set ourselves in modern life.

The midden excavation had finished, and there were only a couple of days left before I returned to the UK. We began excavating the wider settlement area, including buildings and hearths, and a skeleton.

"Ah, what?!" Howell and Oskar leaned forward towards my patch of sand. I stopped brushing and drew closer. The tip of a large joint protruded from the desert sands. With a tender flick of the brush, I removed more dust and revealed the rest of the joint.

"I'm no expert, but this looks a bit human, doesn't it?" I turned towards the others.

Howell scratched his belly and stared at the sky, as if searching for an answer. "Potentially, and really exciting if so. We're gonna have to act fast though - the weather forecast predicted storms this week."

Sometimes it can take days to remove a skeleton, depending on -its state and surrounding environment. With a skeleton as potentially ancient as the one in front of me, we would need to take particular care.

Returning at first light the next day, we brought out our miniscule trowels, brush sets and more. Hours passed as the three of us focused on removing every inch of bone from the earth.

The sun was already high in the sky by the time we had the first break, and discussed how to package the bones to send to the lab for radiocarbon dating.

"When will the results be released?" I asked.

Howell gazed off into the distance, his lips murmuring as he counted. "Hmmm, by the time the lab sends us the findings back, it'll most likely be announced in the presentation in London at the Seminar for Arabian Studies. Sorry, it'll be after you have left."

I gave a little chuckle. It seemed fitting that the fruits of my work in

Qatar would be presented in the same place where my next adventure was about to begin – London. Saying 'yes' had me swapping the desert for the city, and fieldwork for office work at an archaeological magazine.

"Don't worry. I have a feeling I might be seeing that skeleton again soon!"

Website: **www.amorexplore.co.uk**

Instragram: **@amorexplore**

Chapter 4

Couch to Kili

By Alun Basten

'Why the hell am I doing this? I could be home now, snuggled up on the sofa drinking a nice glass of wine. I don't even like camping!'

Yep, I was feeling sorry for myself. I was alone in a tent at over three and a half thousand metres above sea level, on only the second evening of a trek to the summit of Kilimanjaro.

I didn't know at the time, but I was feeling sorry for myself as I had caught a stomach bug. I was soon to spend some quality time with our toilet tent over the next thirty-six hours, becoming more dehydrated and weaker by the hour. Not the best condition to be in while trying to hike to almost six thousand metres!

But why was I there anyway?

In March 2017, I finished a long-term IT contract and had planned to take a few months off work. Those few months were great at first. I spent a lot of time working in our garden and enjoying getting off the hamster wheel for a while. However, when I was ready to return to work, several potential opportunities that had appeared disappeared for one reason or another. I was trying to stay upbeat, but I was getting frustrated. My girlfriend thought that my mood seemed to be sinking, and she was starting to worry about my mental health.

For several years, and for no obvious reason, the idea of climbing Kilimanjaro 'one day' had been drifting in and out of my head. We talked about me doing something different. Perhaps making that 'one day' happen would give me a boost and mark my time off work with something memorable.

While on holiday in Norway in late summer, I read an article in a local magazine about a 'crazy Englishman' called Dave Cornthwaite who was using a water-bike to traverse over a thousand miles down the Norwegian coast. I read that Dave had set up a group called Say Yes More. I looked at the website (sayyesmore.com) and liked what I saw. The timing was impeccable, and it made me think – perhaps I really should say yes to this trip...

I asked a few friends if they'd be interested in joining me. Some of the responses were polite. Some were less so!

I decided to go on my own.

*

I read several comments from people who had found ascending Kilimanjaro the hardest thing that they had ever done. Comedian Rhod Gilbert said he was almost broken by it. Former rugby union player Martyn Williams said that he found it psychologically and physically harder than the last British and Irish Lions tour he had been part of. Hmmm... At the point I booked, I was a couch potato whose exercise comprised of playing a round of golf most weeks and as little as possible other than that. Time to get serious...

I decided to hike up Pen y Fan in the Brecon Beacons, the highest mountain in southern Britain, to get some practice. I was fine for the first, oh, let's say one minute. However, I then noticed that my heart rate was increasing rapidly and my calves were starting to burn from the lactic acid coursing through them. After a few hundred yards it felt like my heart was going to break through my chest, so I decided to head back down and build my fitness more gradually. This was going to take longer than I thought.

I had four months to prepare for the trip. I did a lot of walking in the nearby South Wales hills and sand dunes, as well as a weekend in Snowdonia. I also had a few sessions with a personal trainer, who focused on building strength and stability in my legs and core.

I was feeling a lot fitter and healthier, so four weeks before the trip when I went for a health assessment, I was feeling confident that I'd get a clean bill of health. I was surprised when the assessor said that I wouldn't be able to do the more rigorous tests and that the doctor would explain why.

When I saw the doctor, she told me that my electrocardiogram was showing irregular heartbeats. She advised that I would need to see a cardiologist, and definitely before I went up any large mountains!

I booked in to see a cardiologist as soon as I could. In the meantime, *of course*, I did one of the worst things that I could do – I looked on the internet! It sounded (to me, Mr Non-Cardiologist) like a form of arrhythmia, which could be relatively benign, but could also be a sign of heart disease. I tried to put it out of my mind, but I couldn't help but think that the trip could be off... possibly forever.

After about ten days of uncertainty, I met the cardiologist. He ran some tests then told me that the issue was definitely a 'right bundle branch block', which sounded worrying – "What do you mean, I've got a 'blockage' in my heart?" – but he explained that it is a relatively common issue affecting many people, including some very successful sports people, and that it needn't hold me back from living a normal life.

The trip was still on!

*

The weather forecast was sunny and about twenty-eight degrees Celsius in the Tanzanian city of Moshi. However, just a few miles away, at the top of Kilimanjaro, it was due to be minus five with a potential wind-chill down to minus fifteen. Oh, and with a storm due to hit late in the trip. Not the easiest trip to pack for!

On the evening before the trek, there was a welcome dinner to allow the trekking group to meet. I arrived last, so I was looking around the restaurant trying to guess which table I was going to join. I found that the rest of the group consisted of six younger American women. Three of the six were medical students, and two others were already medical professionals. If I was going to become ill, I was with the right group!

We also met our lead guide, called Prosper, and the assistant guide, curiously named Cash Baby. Prosper seemed quite serious on the first night, and I think he was weighing us up for the trek. We soon learnt that he had a fun personality and, as I was the oldest and only male trekker, he named me Baba Simba (Father Lion), a name which stuck all trek. Cash Baby was a couple of years younger but had a very youthful face, hence his nickname, and a mischievous sense of humour.

While considering our hiking potential, Prosper asked us all how high we had been before. The others were saying a few thousand feet. When I said about thirty-nine thousand feet, everyone stared at me, then burst out laughing when I said, "Although that was in an aeroplane!"

"How many times have you climbed Kilimanjaro?" one of the girls asked Prosper.

"I lost count." He scratched his chin and looked thoughtful. "...after three hundred." The group were suitably impressed. "But with me," he continued, eyeing each of us in turn, "every single one of the people I guide reaches at least the crater rim. With me, you will prosper!" He grinned at his own joke.

With my own personal medical crew and a guide who had pretty much guaranteed I'd reach the top, I felt in safe hands.

*

The next day, the trek began gently, hiking gradually uphill through lush rainforest. Moss-covered trees reached through the canopy, climbing vines draped over their branches and seas of ferns and grasses beneath. While we walked, some black and white Colobus monkeys and colourful birds watched us from the trees with occasional interest.

We walked very slowly; it was our introduction to what the guides call *"polé, polé"* or "slowly, slowly", a pace chosen to allow the body time to acclimatise to altitude. I soon fell into a routine of taking the back berth so that I could shout variations on "Three porters coming up on our left!" so that we could move to the side of the track in time; the porters certainly weren't doing *"polé polé"* and weren't slowing down for anyone!

We hadn't met our porters at the park gates, but were welcomed into the first camp, Mti Mkubwa, by our guides and porters, dancing and singing for, then with, us. It was a fantastic welcome and helped to quickly build a team spirit within the group. It clearly wasn't a common event across the other groups in the camp, as some trekkers came to watch and take videos of our group bonding together.

We were still in the rainforest, with tents erected in any available space between trees. Within a few minutes of us sitting down, a monkey appeared and tried to investigate the contents of a rubbish bin that had been set by the mess tent. Soon after, another trekker appeared and asked Prosper how many times he had climbed Kilimanjaro. When Prosper told him, he was blown away. He told us that he had asked several guides in the camp, and the highest number he had been told till then was twelve!

We all went to our tents by 7.30pm. I wondered whether that was it for the night, or if I had misunderstood, and on a few occasions when I heard voices nearby, I looked out of my tent in case I was missing the party. Nope, that was genuinely it for the night. Over the next week, we got used to an early evening and early rise the next morning.

*

After leaving camp the next morning, we trekked through the remainder of the rainforest, then entered the heathland zone towards the Shira plateau. From the heathland zone, we had some great, far-reaching views across the plateau with its open grasslands, dotted with heather shrubs and interspersed by lava flows from historic volcanic eruptions. To the south west we could see Kilimanjaro's smaller brother, Mount Meru, forty-four miles away.

The walk from Mti Mkubwa to Shira One wasn't long, but it was a lot steeper in places than the first day. Some of the group struggled a bit, especially ascending a fairly steep section known as 'the elephant's back' – Lindsay really didn't enjoy it, so re-christened it the 'elephant's butt-hole'. We were again welcomed into camp by the porters, singing and dancing.

From Shira One camp, we could see Kilimanjaro's main peak Kibo more clearly, although it still looked a long way away. Having left the rainforest and with a clear sky overhead, we felt the temperature drop noticeably that evening compared with the previous night. We all snuggled into our down jackets and slipped hats over our heads while watching the sun set over the foothills and eating the seemingly-ubiquitous popcorn. The group was starting to bond well. It had been a great day. But that evening, things took a distinct turn for the worse when the stomach bug took hold.

*

Thankfully the bug hit late in the evening when I was on my own in my tent. I was back and forth between my tent and the toilet tent a few times that night. I came out of the toilet tent at some point to find Bonnie and Tara, waiting patiently to use it. When I said how I was feeling, Tara asked whether I had taken any Imodium. Aaargh! I had packed a box in case I needed them but had forgotten all about them. I took some straightaway and some more a few hours later.

I didn't get a lot of sleep overnight and must have been badly dehydrated. The next morning, I woke up feeling exhausted and was sick straight after trying to eat some breakfast.

While Cash Baby took the girls on the longer route via Shira Cathedral, Prosper and I went direct from Shira One to Shira Two on our own. If I had been feeling like that at home, I would probably have stayed in bed or in front of the TV. Instead, I had to walk over rough ground for about seven miles! I was feeling pretty weak so Prosper carried my daypack for most of the walk, while insisting regularly that I try to eat and drink something.

We arrived at Shira Two camp about half an hour before the girls. There was no singing from our porters today. Was it simply because we had arrived before the main group? Or had the mood changed because they were concerned that I might not make it to the summit?

I hadn't drunk as much as I needed, so Prosper gave me a sachet of what he called "Kilimanjaro cocaine" to help me to rehydrate. It was only glucose powder (well, that's what he told me and I'm sticking to it, your honour!), but it certainly piqued the girls' interest.

Alone in my tent that evening, my mood dipped again, and I was arguing with myself about what to do. I was still ill, dehydrated and feeling weak, and didn't know if I would regain enough strength in time for the summit attempt, which I knew would be harder than what we had done till then.

"Yes, but I didn't come this far to not make it to the top!"

I could also see that it would be a lot easier to descend from the camp that I was in than from any later camp.

"Yes, but I didn't come this far to not make it to the top!"

I didn't want to make it difficult for the group by having to descend with a guide later in the trek, leaving them with only one guide. I wondered if it would be best for the group for me to descend the next morning.

"Yes, but I didn't come this far to not make it to the top!"

My head was all over the place. I didn't know what to do, so tried to push it out of my head until the morning and get some much-needed sleep.

The following morning, I had a difficult discussion with Prosper, to discuss whether I should continue, or if it would be folly to struggle on then have to descend from a higher camp.

"Do you think I should descend?" I asked him.

"How do you feel today, Baba Simba?"

"To be honest, I do feel better than yesterday. I'm not feeling nearly as weak," I replied.

"If you are strong, then the bug that made you sick is weak. Today we try and we see how it goes."

I nodded at his sage advice.

*

Day four was a more difficult walk, but my strength was certainly returning, and I found it easier than I had expected. The box of Imodium had really started working, and it was another three days before my bowels produced anything other than gas again!

We ascended through the moorland zone that morning, past giant lobelias, and through the 'garden of senecios', or giant groundsels, a bizarre-looking plant that only grows on Kilimanjaro. I could best describe them as though someone has wrapped some elephant legs in fur, stuck them together, and then topped them off with cactuses!

By lunchtime we reached a rock outcrop called the Lava Tower. We were told that the Lava Tower is only four metres lower than the highest point in Switzerland. It felt like we were really making progress. After lunch, we descended steeply over our first small patches of ice and down the rock-strewn valley into Barranco camp. After walking seven miles from Shira Two camp, we had gained a total of... fifty metres in altitude! Woohoo!

Barranco camp was incredible, with a patchwork of brightly coloured tents spread for a few hundred metres across the valley. We knew that it would be the busiest camp so far, as it is the first camp after the convergence of three trails. It would also be busier than normal as the full moon was due, when a lot of groups like to summit. However, even Prosper seemed surprised; he estimated that there were around two thousand people there.

Thankfully, I was feeling a lot better so was more aware of the beautiful surroundings. We had seen Kibo from a distance each day, but at Barranco camp, it felt like we were directly beneath it. I felt an understanding of why some local tribes consider Kilimanjaro sacred, with Kibo emerging from the surrounding land like a stone giant's head, draped with glaciers. We also had our first view of the Barranco wall, which is two hundred and fifty-seven metres high and is the steepest part of the trek; it was to be our way out of camp the next morning, and it looked pretty intimidating as the sun set on it.

I managed to make a WhatsApp video call home that evening. After the trip, my girlfriend told me that I had looked awful during the call, and she was concerned that the trek might actually kill me. I'm glad I hadn't called home a day earlier when I'd been at the height of my illness. She would have probably thought I was dead already.

After food, Prosper proposed a change to our plans. He had been walking around the camp, asking guides for their plans to summit and was concerned about the number who were planning to summit in three days' time, at the same time as us. He was very happy with our progress that day, so suggested that we merge days five and six. We'd push onto Barafu camp on day five with the intention of summiting a day early. We agreed with his suggestion so went to our tents even earlier than normal ready for an early start.

*

Day five was one of the highlights of the trek. We were woken at 5am. Then, after a light breakfast, we crossed the camp to the Barranco wall. It still looked intimidating as we walked towards it in the near-dawn darkness, but when we reached the wall, we could see a group in front carefully making their way up. Everyone enjoyed ascending the wall. It is technically a class four scramble, so no climbing gear is needed, but it was a fun hour or two. It made a very welcome change to the long day hikes we had done so far. We were feeling pleased with how we were ascending the wall, holding on to the rocks carefully, until we were caught and passed by porters carrying much larger packs and often without any hands free to help them ascend.

The top of the Barranco wall leads to an open plateau with another fantastic view of Kibo, looking regal in the sunlight. It felt close enough that we could actually believe that we would reach the summit. To the south, the view swept for many miles across the verdant national parks of northern Tanzania.

I could have stayed there for ages, taking in the view, but after a short break we descended into the Karanga valley, walking amongst more of those peculiar senecio trees, then had a steep ascent into Karanga camp for lunch. The cook had a special treat for us – freshly-made chips and coleslaw! We all found it funny that after several days of superb meals, each with several courses, that we were so pleased to be sat there with plates full of fried potatoes! Soul food, indeed!

As usual, Prosper was pushing us to eat as much as possible to keep our strength up, and I couldn't help but laugh when Bonnie threw a couple of chips over her shoulder when his back was turned, just to reduce the portion on her plate.

We should have stayed at Karanga camp that night, but as we were merging two days into one, we continued to the highest camp, Barafu (or Base), for the night. It was the highest altitude gain that we had made on any day, and when we reached the camp, I had probably the worst headache I have ever had; a sure sign of altitude sickness. Prosper gave me three pink tablets. I'm slightly ashamed to say that I've got no idea what they were, but they did the trick!

After food, Prosper briefed us on what to expect during the summit attempt. There would be a steep section as we left the camp, followed by several hours of less steep hiking. This would then be followed by a steep section of scree (loose stones) during which we would need to take two steps for every normal step, as our feet would be sliding down on each step. Most groups try to reach the summit for dawn, to watch the sun rise from the roof of Africa, but Prosper suggested that we try to sleep longer and start a few hours later. It would mean that the sun would rise while we were near the scree section. However, we should have it to ourselves, as most other groups would have left by the time we got there.

*

We were woken at 3am for a light snack, then at 4am we left camp to attempt to reach the summit. Whereas most groups we saw that day seemed to have one guide and one or two assistant guides, Prosper decided to take some porters with us, so that we had one guide or porter for each trekker. The porters were excited as well. Although most of them had portered on Kilimanjaro before, some of them had never been to the summit.

We had walked slowly each day, but this must have been the slowest I had ever walked; truly *"Polé polé"*. We trudged uphill for several hours in the dark, head-torches bobbing slowly as we walked. The moon was almost full but there still wasn't a lot to see. At that altitude, there is no discernible plant life, so I focused on the feet of the person in front and occasionally looked ahead to try to find a distinctive rock or bend in the trail to use as my next mental target.

After several hours, as it was starting to get light, the porter next to me called out "Say 'Yes'!", to which we all agreeably responded "Yes!" This continued a few times, then he called out "Say 'Yes more'!", to which we responded "Yes more!", then my eyes met his and we both burst out laughing. He obviously remembered that I was wearing a "Say Yes More" hoodie!

As we were nearing the top, I realised that we were on the steep stretch of scree that we had been warned about, and we all seemed to be coping well. I turned to Cash Baby who was alongside me and asked whether this was really the difficult patch; he said that it was and we had been lucky that it had rained overnight as the scree had frozen in place, making progress a lot easier. We watched the sun rise over Mawenzi, Kilimanjaro's second peak, while drinking cups of black tea that the porters had carried for us in flasks. The stunning views of Mawenzi with clouds a long way beneath us and the warmth of the early sun gave us all a huge boost. There was no doubt now that we would make it to the summit.

We could see some higher clouds being blown towards us from the east and it was clear that they would get to the summit around the same time as us. While we walked around the crater towards the highest point of Uhuru Peak, it started to snow quite heavily, which meant that we didn't get the views from the top. Maybe next time!

On the 1st March, 2018 (which any true-blooded Welshman would know is Saint David's Day), I stood on top of the highest volcano in the world! We had done it!

There were lots of congratulatory hugs between the trekkers, the guides and porters. I sought out Prosper in the crowd. "Thank you for helping me reach the summit," I said shaking his hand enthusiastically. He smiled back at me. "Thank you, Baba Simba, for helping me keep my 100% record!"

Lots of photos were taken of our happy group, but having spent four and a half days trekking mostly upwards, within a few minutes it was soon time to descend. We were at high altitude (5,895 metres), and Prosper was keen to get us down as quickly as possible. We descended at a speed which I really wasn't happy with, almost running down a bloody big mountain, through snow with rocks underneath. Each step was jarring my feet and knees.

After about an hour, we stopped for a break and Prosper asked me how I felt, I held my hands out a couple of feet apart and said, "If my right hand is perfect health, and my left hand is dead, I'm about... here." I indicated a point much closer to the left. Bonnie was sat next to me and burst out laughing.

I thought that Prosper would also laugh and ask why I felt like that. Instead, he turned around, barked some orders, then headed down the mountain with one of the girls. Before I knew what was going on, the others had left with their guides leaving me with Cash Baby and three or four porters. I didn't understand most of what they said to each other, but I definitely heard someone say "oxygen". When I looked round, I could see one of the porters carrying a package very carefully. I had a very personal and slower descent from that point on. I felt a bit guilty about the whole thing as I was only joking about feeling near death, but I was much happier with the pace that we descended at.

I returned to Barafu camp about thirty-five minutes after the others, at 1.15pm. We had descended from the summit to Base in just over two hours compared with the seven hours that it had taken us on the way up. I was told to try to get some sleep and that I'd be called at 2pm for lunch (Forty-five minutes later? Thanks a lot!), then we would descend to the next camp.

I drifted off and was woken up to find that I had another awful headache. I would have been happy to stay at that camp for another hour to try to sleep it off, but Prosper insisted that it was an altitude headache and that descending would help. I took a few painkillers, and we set off downhill. Thankfully, the headache went away pretty quickly. We trekked for another few hours down to Millennium Camp and arrived just as it started to rain.

A storm had been forecast to hit the region late in the trip. When it hit, it brought probably the heaviest rain that I had ever experienced, drumming insistently on the tents with barely a gap between raindrops and forming floods across any open ground. The storm was clearly directly overhead, with bursts of lightning lighting up the mountain followed by thunder within a second or so. We all had nearly new tents, but none of them remained fully watertight.

If we hadn't changed our plans and reached the summit a day early, we'd have been at Barafu camp in the storm, trying to sleep before the trek towards the summit. We heard the next day that other groups had found the summit ascent that night much tougher than we had.

We woke the next morning to find that the rain had almost stopped. We were due to spend another night on the mountain, but no-one had any completely dry clothes left so we all agreed to push on to the end of the descent path in one day. As we left the final camp, we had another couple of songs and dances from the true heroes of the trek, the guides and porters, this time including a song that appeared to be made up on the spot with lines like

"I miss you mama.

I miss you daddy.

I miss you baby.

I miss my shower!"

We met up that evening with our guides for a celebration dinner and to collect our certificates. While doing the presentations, I saw Prosper move one certificate to the back of the pile. Our eyes met and we both laughed; it was obviously mine.

When it was my turn, he teased me that a few days earlier I had been talking about descending, but he told us how pleased and proud he was that we had all made it. We stayed out for a couple of beers, but having gone to sleep early for the last week, we were all lightweights, so headed back to the hotel – to some very welcome real beds.

*

I have stayed in touch with Bonnie and Tara, and in 2019 we met up in Kathmandu and joined another open group trek around the Annapurna region of Nepal. We are planning further treks amongst the Dolomites with a wider group of friends, then perhaps Patagonia, then…

Hiking Kilimanjaro has given me more confidence to try more things outside my comfort zone, and has ignited a passion for mountains in me that I wouldn't otherwise have known existed. And all because I said "Yes" to getting off my couch once. Go on, give it a try. It may just change your life…

If you'd like to say hi, you can contact me at **alun@babasimba.com** or through **www.babasimba.com**.

Chapter 5

Pacific Crest Trail

By Mariah Boyle

January 2018

My new hiking shoes crunched as I walked past cactus and boulders on the brown-red ribbon of dirt leading me north to Canada. January was not a typical time of year for a hiker to start their thru-hike of the Pacific Crest Trail. At this time of year, most hikers are at home setting up the new ultra-light tent they purchased during a holiday sale, dehydrating food for resupply boxes, or carefully watching the snowfall totals trying to forecast what kind of year it will be in the mountains. I was the anomaly, hitting the trail early during a week's vacation from my job, aiming to complete eighty miles and acquire some desert hiking skills.

I had about six hundred miles of backpacking experience, accumulated in previous years and across many trails, that informed my gear, itinerary and decision-making, but none of that hiking was in the desert. The stories of extreme sun, heat and lack of water made me nervous. I was here, early in the season, hoping the cooler temperatures would be more forgiving.

That morning I had been in the passenger seat, discussing fish with Kenn, a trail angel that I hired to drive me south to the start of my hike. Kenn had discovered I was a marine biologist and was keen on thinking up trail names for me. "What about Swordfish?" he asked.

I liked his suggestion of a marine-themed name, but Swordfish hit too close to home. My job focused on sustainable seafood and I was here trying to leave the stress of work behind, seeking a change of pace from a week in nature. "Maybe," I said. "I'll keep thinking about it."

My calves burned as I hiked uphill with small, quick steps, and I realized that this hike would be the longest amount of time I'd been away from the ocean in my life. The Pacific Crest Trail travels from the border of Mexico to the border of Canada through 2,650 miles of California, Oregon and Washington.

It isn't a coastal hike; hikers stay inland walking along the crests of mountain ranges. I was a water person on a mountain trail. Summits and trails are a secondary love, a high-altitude affair, but I'll always return to the water. And so it felt settled; my trail name would be Ocean.

Feeling alone, I worried about the nefarious people who might be hanging out by the highway underpasses I crossed, about mountain lions and rattlesnakes camouflaged in the landscape around me, and whether I had enough water for another twenty-four hours.

Eight miles into my hike, I looked back at the busy highway I had just passed beneath. *What were those people in those cars thinking about?* They were probably turning up their air conditioning, singing along with a song on the radio, and drinking an iced coffee. *Iced coffee!* Even for winter, it was hot. Day one and I was already dreaming of iced coffee. The self-doubt crept in: *Was I really capable of hiking to Canada?*

My self-doubt abated as I set up camp on a beautiful mountainside. I knew this part of the routine and it comforted me to set up my tent, methodically placing the items from my backpack in their designated spots for the night. I sat outside my tent on the rocky sand; the setting sky ready to put on a show. The broad brushstrokes of red, orange and purple in the sunset seemed to be a message from Mother Nature.

"Good job. You can do this. It will be hard, but you will persevere."

Those who do not backpack ask me why I do. One of the reasons is to do something hard – to remind myself of who I am and what I am capable of. A hike strips away all the complications and conveniences of life to remind you of what is important, life-giving, and comforting. It really was all about food, water, shelter and health. No wonder we hikers can seem a little strange to others. We are living in a slightly altered universe, in the best way possible. When I hike, I make lists of these little joys in my phone. They are a message to my future self, urging me not to forget the bliss of clean socks, fresh fruit, water from a faucet and sheltering in a building during a storm. Without a reminder, these memories fade quickly.

It's not all views and sunsets this first week. I endured a second sleepless night of constant winds, blowing at twenty to thirty miles per hour. My minimalist tent whacked me in the face and made a deafening noise. The one silver lining of windy nights was that I couldn't be paranoid about animals near my tent because I couldn't hear a thing over the Dyneema fabric cacophony. Two nights without sleep left my body unrested and unhealed. My head ached and the lactic acid in my muscles burned.

The first desert snowstorm of the season was approaching. The skies became grey and ominous as the day progressed. Big, fluffy clouds formed daunting, cold masses overhead, dimming the sunlight. I needed to alter my plan. If I doubled my mileage and reached my car a day ahead of time, I would beat this storm.

Cold and snow weren't ideal, but I could endure them just fine. The one unknown factor was how much rain would fall, and what the first real storm of the season would do to the trail. My mind conjured images from the movies where desert landscapes were transformed by flash floods.

Nineteen miles was the day's goal. My grit, enhanced by chocolate and caffeine, would get me there. I hiked and hiked, taking in the beautiful hills and valley below, keeping an eye on the sky. Lizards and birds of prey kept me company and provided some welcome distraction from the long day. In the middle of this stretch of trail, there was an oasis of kindness in the form of potable water. Some amazing souls had forklifted in pallets of water for hikers; we call these acts of kindness trail magic. What a gift! I left with full water bottles and a full soul; reminded that people are kind and good.

The sunset came too soon, and I kept walking by headlamp until I reached my campsite – a flat spot near a switchback that was just big enough for my tent. I crawled into my shelter and felt high after hiking big miles so early in my hike. I knew I would need to work up to consistent twenty-mile days to out-pace winter on this trail, but I was only a few days in and admittedly starting very out of shape, so today was a win. Every muscle in my body ached and I had some bad blisters from sand and dirt in my shoes, however I felt incredibly accomplished.

The following day, the skies opened just as I completed the final eleven miles to my car. A cold rain descended as I gleefully pulled off my shoes and socks, crunchy from sweat and dirt, and slid my feet into a soft pair of sandals. It would be snowing at higher elevation, and I beamed at my perfect timing, the nineteen-mile day had been worth it. I had out-hiked the storm!

My first eighty miles on the PCT were not typical, and I love them for that. This week had planted the seed that maybe, with determination and luck on my side, I could hike the entire trail.

March 2018

The time had come to say "Yes," and I felt like throwing up. I told my amazing, fantastic, smart and loving team at work that I was leaving to hike the entire PCT. I had worked there for ten years; I didn't really know who I was without that job.

I bounced between a self-assured tone: *This decision is perfect. This challenge is exactly what you need. It will unlock a whole new level in your life.* And serious doubt: *You are such an idiot to leave an amazing organization, career and comfortable life. You will NEVER have this again.*

I didn't want to be too greedy; in leaving something that was very good, I worried I was being ungrateful. On the other hand, I needed a change and something in my subconscious was pointing me to the PCT, to this thing that was so big I might very well fail at it.

In one moment, the idea of the hike felt so perfect and freeing that I couldn't believe it was possible. I never thought I would have the savings and freedom to do something like that. On the other hand, I was a planner, a worrier. I've always been self-reliant. This was choosing the unknown over comfort and security. The unknown felt too daring, too risky.

Ultimately, though, I'd always idolized those that didn't follow the well-worn paths in life, and I'd always known deep-down I was destined to not follow them myself. Those who sleep outside often, who go on adventures, who prefer singledom to a less than ideal partnership, or who choose not to have children – those wild people are my people. I had always known it and struggled with that knowing. It was tiring – saying no every time society invites you back in, pointing out the easier, well-trodden path. But saying yes to the trail meant saying no to convention, and so my decision was fuelled by the feeling that this was bound to happen all along.

June 2018

The train rumbled along for hours, ultimately delivering me to Truckee, a vacation town in the mountains of central California, just north of Lake Tahoe. I had committed to a flip-flop of the PCT. On a thru-hike, hikers usually start at one end of the trail and hike to the other, but a flip-flop starts somewhere in the middle, completing the trail in two segments.

I set off on a beautiful day, enjoying the cool pine forest smells as I walked. I soon crunched along several feet of consolidated, melting snow on the trail. I used my hiking poles to keep my balance and stepped carefully in the footsteps left by others. Occasionally, I would lose the trail, but a quick check of my GPS would guide me back. A few thru hikers passed me, prancing and giggling through the snow, skiing down the hills on their heels. Having hiked in snow for several hundred miles, they knew how it would move under their feet. In comparison, it was as if I was seeing snow for the first time, walking a few feet then sliding and falling. *How will I get to Canada if I can't even stay upright?*

I hiked 3.8 miles to the Peter Grubbs Hut, one of the few shelters for hikers on this trail, and it was full. Dirty, wet socks hung from every nail on the wall, steam rising from them as they were warmed by a central wood stove. A low roar came from the hikers' tiny camp stoves, each in their own little effort to heat water for the small pots of dinner being prepared. I sat amongst the crowd, ate dinner and chatted a little but I felt so out of place. They had walked here, some as many as 1,160 miles. This was the downside of the uncommon flip-flop itinerary – you get on trail partway through most others' journeys, and their speed and trail-weathered state can be intimidating. The self-doubt crept back in and I didn't feel like I belonged. *Would this trail ever feel like home?*

July 2018

I spiralled in indecision. I had hiked 344 miles to the town of Dunsmuir in northern California. Helicopters were flying overhead and the news was covering the wildfires non-stop. The forest north of here, and stretching all the way into Oregon, was on fire. Some hikers bailed off the trail and hitched around the trail closure. A few determined hikers forged on via roads to connect an uninterrupted footpath. I didn't know what to do. I wasn't experienced hiking around fires, and this remote area didn't have many road crossings should the fires spread.

For two days, I stayed in town stressing myself out, unsure of what to do. I finally decided I'd just start hiking and see what happened. *The only way out is through, right?*

I climbed through the grey crags, but the views were diminished by smoke. I camped alone and it felt like there was a brick on my chest all night; I couldn't get a full breath. I woke with a headache and decided to do the unthinkable for a thru-hiker. I backtracked. I told myself this wouldn't be fun or safe in the smoke and that I could come back to hike it in October.

This difficult decision was the first time I'd altered my plans. I arranged a ride to Fish Lake, in Oregon, and started hiking north again, leaving a gap in my hike of 272 miles. I felt like a failure. A familiar nagging self-talk returned: *You're skipping miles. You aren't cut out for this.*

Regardless, I stayed the course and resumed walking north. Previously, I had been getting to know hikers in California, but because I had skipped around the fire, I was now in front of most of them. Fortunately, though, I had Hash Browns, a woman in her forties that I met when hiking a section of the PCT a year earlier. We had stayed in touch, and she met me in Oregon to hike north together. *I had a friend to hike with!*

In late July, we arrived at Big Lake Youth Camp in northern Oregon. The incredibly kind folks at this camp had an entire building, camping area and system to feed and host hikers. Other town stops were a long hitch off the trail, so this refuge allowed hikers to rest, shower, resupply and keep hiking without leaving the trail or spending a lot of money in town. I stumbled into the camp dehydrated and sunburnt. The Oregon sun was on full blast, and the charred remains of trees burned in previous wildfires offered no protection.

In the hiker hut, we met Saunter, a hiker in his fifties tackling the trail for the second time. He'd hurt his knee hiking through the snowy Sierra mountains and tried to slow his pace, but his determination and competitive nature kept him hiking big miles. Another woman we had met several times on trail, 3Zs, rounded out the motley crew of kindred spirits. With showers, clean laundry, good conversation and shade, it seemed the oasis of Big Lake couldn't be better. But then the camp served taco salad for dinner – a singular craving Hash Browns had been harbouring for some time. She was overjoyed and even purchased a taco salad pin in the gift shop as a souvenir of the serendipity. The trail provides.

Hash Browns and I hiked out of Big Lake Youth Camp, sad to leave it behind and anxious to enter the very hot and exposed lava rock section of the trail. Oregon's volcanic landscapes were beautiful but brutal. We carried several litres of water and tried not to get sunburned. A few miles in, we found Saunter drinking a beer on the side of the trail with another hiker – they had been gifted a cold morning beer each – another act of trail magic. We joined forces and hiked together at a steady pace, aiming for twenty miles a day, which was the pace he needed to avoid re-injuring his knee. We became a trail family.

We hiked together most of the day and camped together each night. Those days hiking together were the best. I hit maximum endorphins and my body felt strong. Having a trail family made hiking more fun, and the terrain was varied and breath-taking. I felt so good that I started to run on the long downhill switchbacks. How lucky we were to live in the woods! We got to know each other well. We shared the good and the bad of our lives. It felt good to have people listen, undaunted, to all of it. We belonged.

By the end of July, we made it to the famous Timberline Lodge on Mt. Hood in northern Oregon, for the all-you-can-eat buffet, a mainstay of hiker lore. Though this destination had long been anticipated, Saunter and I were unable to fully indulge in the buffet. We were coming down with a virus.

Back on the trail, we pushed on, sick and delirious, for a few hundred miles into Washington. We had to sit down often and stay away from cliff edges, perpetually on the verge of passing out. We were sweating, our bodies constantly trying to outcompete the virus. It took a few weeks until we finally started to feel human again.

Hash Browns had miraculously dodged the virus and she played a key role for us during this time. She helped with the little tasks that felt monumental at the end of the day, like shepherding my electronics to clearings where they could send their satellite messages through the otherwise dense stands of trees.

A trail family pools resources; everyone was a hero at some point. My turn came one night hiking in Rainier National Park. Hash Browns and Saunter were wrecked at the end of the day. I was tired, but had enough energy to take everyone's bottles and slowly collect six litres of water from a single, spring-fed puddle, the only water source for miles.

Saunter was key for water crossings. At each crossing, the rumble of white-water was audible well before we saw the river. Saunter looked at each crossing with glee, trying to piece together the rock hopping puzzle, drawing upon his experience reading rivers.

"I think this is the best path," Saunter said, as Hash Browns and I looked at each other nervously. He balanced on the thin, partially submerged tree trunks that were set up as a make-shift crossing just above the swirling water, an opaque grey-brown from glacial silt. From the other side he yelled over the water, "OK, that's a good route. Who's next?"

"I'll go next," I said, trying to project a little more confidence than I felt. I followed his footsteps, going agonizingly slow across the thin tree trunks, with one foot on each. The churning white-water rushed beneath my feet creating a dizzying effect. My leg shook from the adrenaline and strain, and I laughed at how bad I was at this. "I have Elvis leg. Hold on," I said, borrowing the climbing term and changing the position of my feet to alleviate the shaking.

I stepped onto a large rock and rested, let out an exasperated sigh, then finished the rock hop to the other side, cheered on by Saunter and Hash Browns. "Nice one, Ocean!"

Saunter then coached Hash Browns across while I yelled encouragement from the other side, "You've got this! Nice job! Now move your foot to the next tree." She used her poles for balance and watched her feet as she shuffled across the trees. I took a video of the crossing, a digital souvenir for Hash Browns, her plaid shirt in bright contrast to the grey landscape of the mountain and river.

This was an ideal crossing, we all made it across dry. A few times Saunter would nimbly hop across rocks, keeping his feet dry and point out the path to me and Hash Browns — just to see us splash into the water, soaking our socks and shoes, opting to ford rather than take our chances rock hopping. I still trusted myself more in water than on land. At least by this point in my hike, I had a trail family to help me feel steadier on my feet.

August 2018

I curate a collection of memories of the best night skies I've seen. In Washington, I added a new scene to the collection. I was blown away by the brightness and depth of the stars in the sky when I woke up in the middle of the night. I sat outside my tent in awe. I tried moving my head in a way that could take it all in, but it was too vast. I just had to enjoy pieces of the sky, one at a time.

In the morning, I was tired and slow, but eventually I moved more easily with the promise of spectacular terrain ahead. We hiked across snow fields that hadn't yet melted, then along a ribbon of trail on a knife-edge cliff that dropped dramatically into valleys below us. Clouds against wildfire smoke created a foreboding and dramatic sky. We stopped to take in the view and movement below caught our attention. I started to shoot video on my phone to capture this moment unfolding, thankfully, in a smoke-free valley.

"It's a little herd, man. It's like the fricking nature channel," said Saunter, who had first spotted the group of over thirty fluffy white mountain goats running across a crisp and bright snow field, kicking up the wet snow behind them. The larger goats were moving more slowly while the younger goats ran and jumped playfully with each other, mindful to not stray too far from their mothers. It was our own magical scene from a National Geographic documentary, made even sweeter by the fact that we had hiked here to see it.

He noticed I had my earbuds in, and asked excitedly "You have that nature channel music going and everything?" He knew I had a habit of playing the Blue Planet soundtrack, the big symphony music in my headphones, in only the best landscapes.

"Yeah," I responded.

"Damn!" Saunter replied, excited about the wildlife, then catching on "Oh, is this a video?"

"Yup" I laughed.

"Oh, damn. Sorry," he responded. We all laughed and I kept shooting footage of the goats. We were taking it in, now silenced in our wonder. This seemed like a good omen - we were going to make it to Canada.

Thankfully, we had recovered from the virus before we hit the hypothermia-inducing rainstorms, wildfire smoke, trail closures and re-routes in northern Washington. We wound our way around chair lifts, perfectly still and waiting for the snow to return. We crossed a ski run called Crest Trail and descended to Stevens Pass.

Before we could even set foot inside the ski lodge, someone told us the end of the trail was closed due to a fire. At first, we didn't believe him. There was so much fearmongering and misinformation out there that we had stopped believing everything we were told. The trail was a long game of telephone that muddled the messages it carried.

But then the news was confirmed by others. Our hearts sank. It was as if someone said the world was ending, because this little path of dirt was our world. We were ninety-six miles from Canada, and the trail was closed. *What the hell were we going to do?*

After sitting with shock and sadness for a few hours, we weighed our options. This wouldn't stop us. We could wait for the fire to die out and trail to re-open, but there was no telling how long that would take. We could drive into Canada and hike south to the monument for the photo-op, but that would skip a bunch of miles. We looked at the map. To the west of the PCT was North Cascades National Park. There was a long and skinny lake, Ross Lake, that went all the way to the border of Canada with a trail alongside it. It was promising. Others were talking about this route too. We'd make our own trail.

3Zs and Hash Browns planned to return to this section another time, wanting to hike the route that was closed, so Saunter and I headed north from Stevens Pass, a smaller group than before. In Stehekin, our last town on the trail, we finalized our plans. We recruited JZ, a hiker on his fourth PCT hike, and Oats, a trail runner and climber from Germany, to join our group and share the cost of a speedboat ferry along Ross Lake.

It would take four days to finish our last seventy-seven miles, departing from our beloved PCT. We would hike two days north to a speedboat and ferry across Ross Lake to the border and then hike two days south, back to a highway in Washington where we would start our long journeys home. It was a messy itinerary, but it allowed us to reach Canada and that's all that mattered.

JZ planned to hike the PCT, hitch into town to resupply, then meet us at the ferry in two days. Saunter, Oats and I set off into North Cascades National Park and followed the trail, incredibly rough and steep compared to the PCT, towards a mountain pass and into freezing temperatures. Unlike the PCT, this trail was no longer graded for pack animals, and that's exactly what we had become.

We crossed a high pass dotted with glaciers and snow that glistened pink from algae. We struggled to locate ourselves on the map we picked up at the ranger station; it wasn't intended for navigational use. We'd been consistently hiking twenty to twenty-five-mile days on the PCT, but the first night on this alternate trail, we didn't get into camp until midnight, five hours later than usual. We were racing a wildfire to Canada, and there was no guarantee we would make it there first.

The following day, the cool wind whipped against our faces as the four of us took a small speedboat across Ross Lake, the final step in the journey to the border. Large mountains rose on either side of the lake, creating a dramatic landscape amidst the haze of smoke. I was ecstatic. *Boats! Water! Canada!* I didn't need anything else.

I had more miles to go - this was only about halfway on my PCT flip flop - but making it to Canada from California felt pretty damn far. More than that, the others in my group were finishing the trail - 2,650 miles, how incredible!

Our elation dissolved in seconds when we were swarmed by a throng of mosquitoes at the far side of the lake. Their buzzing drowned out any other sound and the itching began immediately.

Despite the hot and humid August day, we desperately donned our rain gear for some protection. We applied bug spray, but the mosquitoes didn't seem to notice. We ran to the border to try to keep them at bay.

At the border monument, a four-foot-high silver obelisk, we took photos and tried to remain sane despite the bites. It was still a celebration, but curtailed by the onslaught of bugs. We hugged and wrote in the makeshift logbook – not the first group to choose this alternate trail – before the bugs drove us quickly to our campsite and the shelter of our tents. It was not the joyous and relaxing last day we had all dreamed of; we weren't even on the PCT! The mosquito attack forced us into the solitary confinement of our tents to contemplate what it all meant.

That night I cried and cried. I was finally releasing all of my worry that I wasn't good enough and all of the stress from the unforeseen obstacles. *I walked here! I can do hard things!*

It was a total catharsis that carried over into the next day, as we hiked south, an utterly foreign direction for us after months of pushing north. I told the group I was going to hike alone and meet them at breaks; I had more feelings to process. I was overcome with gratitude, wonder and awe. The gravity of having hiked well over one-thousand miles since mid-June to arrive here was sinking in, as was the reality that I would be returning to the trail in California in a few days, without this group of friends.

Tiny babbling streams lined the trail on our second to last day. Everything was dripping wet in every shade of green; the rainforest was stunning. The humid air felt heavy in each inhalation and my heart was overflowing. We set up camp early, this trail being much easier than we expected. It was our last night on trail together – yet another set of feelings to process.

As we approached the highway the next day, marking the end of the hike, we became a bit crazed. We started to run down the trail. Our bodies were machines. The endorphins felt great, and well, *why not run?*

Saunter shook dewy saplings to try to drench me in water and I snuck a rock in his pack. At one point, he jumped over a stream and the mossy rock took flight and rose a foot out of his backpack before it landed back in the mesh pocket. The four of us were laughing and running and life was perfect. I felt whole. I belonged. I had hiked back to myself.

Parting Thoughts

At the end of this hike I wrote a letter to my former self, the version of me, in March, crying over this big life decision. Maybe it is also a message that you, reader, need today:

'You are standing on the shore wondering if it is the right move to wade into the unknown water. I have good news. It is. Jump in.'

Website: **www.mariahboyle.com**

Instagram: **@sharks_and_summits**

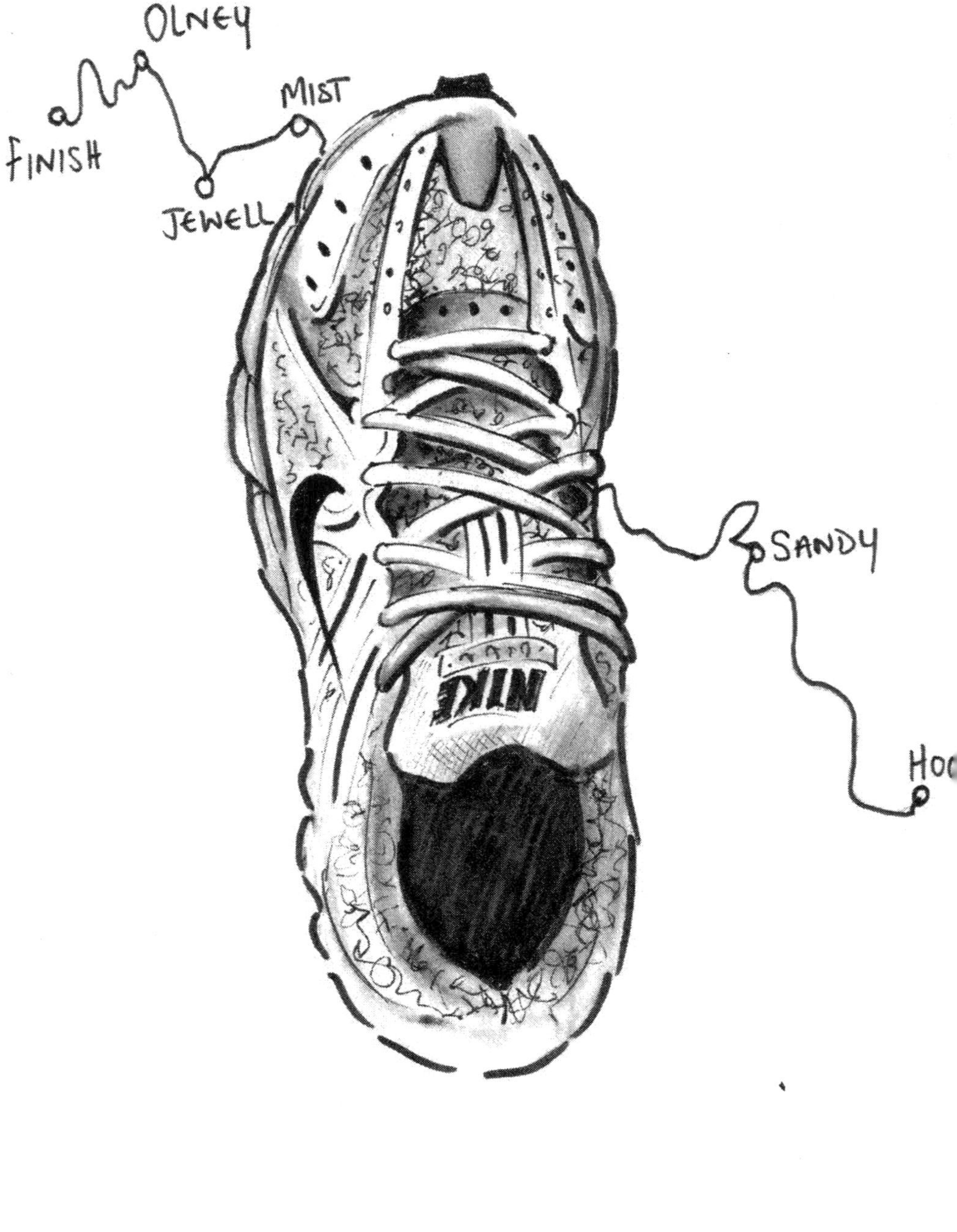
OLNEY
FINISH
MIST
JEWELL
SANDY
HO

Chapter 6

Racing Through My Fear

By Jan Burke

April. 2006

A quiet, grey day in the store. A few customers had called in to buy swimming goggles, tennis balls: things they'd forgotten on their way to the gym. Some had stopped for a chat others were in too much of a rush for more than the basic, "Hi," "Thanks," and "Bye." I decided to make the most of the time by catching up on some emails.

The first was from Head Office:

> *Will those of you who've had trial shoes from Nike please make sure you return your feedback by 12pm on Friday.*

As I was the only regular runner working in the store at that time, I'd been the lucky person to receive the shoes to test so was happy to pass a few minutes by sending the feedback.

A follow-up came on Friday afternoon:

Thank you for your feedback. Would you be interested in taking part in a joint Nike/Sweatshop twenty-four-hour event?

Hmm… It sounded as though it might be some sort of horrible team-building exercise. Extreme short-sightedness and veiled threats about possible blindness meant that I only ever wanted to remove my contact lenses after washing my hands with fresh, clean water, usually at the end of the prescribed maximum wearing time. It would probably involve some product-training with a few games thrown in, so I decided to chance it and withdraw later if it sounded too awful. Meetings were usually enjoyable, and it was always good to put faces to voices we'd heard on the phone.

Monday, and the next email came through:

Thanks for all your responses. We've had thirteen people express interest and unfortunately there are only twelve places. If, after reading this, there are still thirteen people, we will pull names out of a hat. Here are some further details to help you make up your minds. The event will be a twenty-four-hour (I hope my eyes will be ok. I can take specs but don't really see very well with them. Hope it doesn't involve daft games in the wilds at night. I really hate that sort of thing) *race* (Oh good grief – I'm so slow I'll be last. All the other people in the company are really good runners), *with relay teams of twelve runners* (Phew! At least I won't have to do it all by myself and it doesn't sound as though we'll be building shelters from twigs). *It's called the Hood to Coast* (hmm… Robin Hood's Bay to the Cumbrian coast?) *and you will be based at Portland* (But that's somewhere on the south coast. Near Southampton?) *Oregon, USA,* (Woooohoooo!!!). *You will need a valid passport and will need to be available for six days around August Bank Holiday. Let me know if this rings your bell.*

Ring-a-blooming-ding dong! I was ringing like the Bells of St. Clements, Big Ben, jingle bells and all the other bells you can think of too!

*

I'd started running at 7pm on 12th April, 1999, the day before I was fifty. By the time of the emails I'd done a few marathons, none fast, plus a few halves at a similarly slow plod.

The retail work in Sweatshop, a running retailer in the UK, had happened by chance after another job had fallen through at short notice. I'd been in touch with someone at the warehouse about sending running shoes to developing countries and they suggested I tried the local store to see if they had any work 'to tide me over'. After an initial hesitation (*I've only been running five years. I'm quite old. I don't run fast. I'm not really a proper runner*), I contacted the manager, started the following week and loved it!

Meeting customers, learning the technical side of running shoes and the biomechanics of how we run were so stimulating. I also got the chance to test run brand new trainers every other month.

And the chance to enter mad endurance races.

*

The Hood to Coast is the biggest relay race in the world, with over a thousand teams of twelve runners each. It starts near the summit of Mt Hood and travels 198 miles down to the Pacific Ocean. We would each run three Legs (stages) of about ten kilometres each, with a team of six runners plus a driver in each of two vans.

Information soon came through about the race. I started to worry: how on earth would it all fit together? I'd never even completed one relay, let alone one which involved so much planning. We were each allocated our Legs. I looked to see what I'd be doing: Leg Three, an Easy 4.6 miles of gradual downhill, Leg Fifteen, 7.25 Hard miles of 'gently rolling terrain' and Leg Twenty-seven, a Moderate run of 6.36 miles on a rolling country road. The last Leg sounded lovely… if the second one didn't killed me first.

I looked at the recent 10k times of the others. I felt sick: even Rick, who I knew quite well and wasn't at all intimidating, was twenty minutes faster than me – and he'd been injured! My best time had been seventy-two minutes. Two of them could do twice the distance and have a coffee in the time I took. I hoped they wouldn't laugh at me behind my back or think I'd not trained enough or, even worse, that I wasn't trying. All I could do was my best.

I could reasonably happily plod round a marathon in about five and a half hours but speed wasn't usually part of my training. Training schedules don't exist for 'Run three 10ks in twenty-four hours when you're over fifty and the only award you might ever have won would be for hiding in the toilets in games lessons', so I had to develop my own. This amounted to 'run fast for a bit until you can't, then recover' and seemed to be ok for me without inducing an injury. It was new to me: I felt a different sort of fitness growing and very occasionally, felt as though I was running really fast. Stamina improved too and, by the end of August, I had done as much training as I could.

*

We met at Heathrow for our flight. It was the first time I'd seen most of the others. They all looked like runners. They were all younger than me. I was about ten years older than the next person and more than thirty years older than the youngest. Some had even come first in races. Some of them had coached other runners. One had represented Great Britain and had qualified for the Commonwealth Games. I had been running for seven years, never set foot on a running track and this would be my first time ever as a member of a team. I felt insignificant, inferior and very, very nervous. Gavin, from Glasgow, was wearing a kilt.

It was my first long-haul flight in a large plane: three blocks of seats wide, two aisles. I hardly dared move. Patrick, next to me, was reading his racing paper. We chatted about his love of horse racing since a child in Ireland when he'd watch them training on the beach. I don't like sleeping while sitting up, but was entertained by the new experience and watching what was going on around me. Hugh, never far from work, set up his laptop, worked for twenty minutes, closed the lid and immediately fell asleep. It was a skill we all came to admire as the days went on.

We landed slightly late at Chicago. A lurching sprint across the airport with heavy bags for our connecting flight to Portland reminded me how much less fit I was than the others. They seemed to manage it and still be able to breathe. What if I made us all miss the flight?

We just made it! My seat was near a window this time and, with Rick next to me, I could lean across to see the agricultural patterns of the land below. There appeared to be bright green circles dotted around the fields, some separate, some overlapping. It looked like reverse crop circles where, instead of the plants being flattened by UFOs, the circles had been given some rejuvenating power to grow faster than the rest of the field.

Our American neighbour took pity on the two excited, almost-five-year-olds and explained that it was where the fields had been watered with rotating sprays. Obviously.

Our Nike drivers met us with the vans, not the seatless rust buckets I'd imagined but comfortable people-carriers. They whisked us off us to the hotel, which was far more luxurious than the spartan accommodation we were used to. We were particularly impressed by the upholstered walls of the underground car-park and the uniformed doorman, whose outfit was designed with plenty of growing room.

Two days of product training followed: company history, research and development, product testing, topped off by a too-brief visit to the staff shop. I felt like Charlie being rushed through Willy Wonka's factory. There were shelves and shelves of incredible pristine trainers, and all of the training and leisure wear you'd ever need.

Unfortunately, we were dragged away from the runner's Aladdin's cave because we had to leave for the race. Hugh appeared out of nowhere with six large helium balloons explaining that three were to be attached to each van so we could find them easily at the handovers.

Each team piled into their van with kit, food and balloons and set off to the start, stopping at a supermarket en route for more supplies of energy bars, drinks and water. Gavin, wearing his kilt whenever he wasn't running, proved almost too much distraction for a woman parking her car.

Our monkey, sunflower and fish balloons floated serenely to the ceiling, gently nudging each other like children keeping an exciting secret. Portland grew more open. Houses gave way to farms, then woods and we turned off the main road. Nestled in the trees was our start at Timberline Lodge.

The others were chatting nervously, as the van climbed carefully up the winding narrow road, avoiding runners on their way down. Hugh, who had an unarguably impressive running background, reminded us that it'd be very important to keep well hydrated because of the intense heat and to put tights on after our run to help our muscles recover. I sat in the back seat of the van, hoping that the slightly sick feeling was just nerves and not a virus or food poisoning.

BANG!!!

Stunned silence... What had happened? A flat tyre? No, the tyres seemed fine. Drinks bottle exploding? We all checked. Not that either. We were getting increasingly nervous, our voices getting higher and higher.

"The fish has burst!" I squeaked. We all looked at each other and laughed. The tension instantly dissipated like the helium from the balloon. At last, I felt like I'd made a small contribution to the team.

*

The car park at the start was hectic – teams arriving and leaving, organising runners, last minute instructions (*would I ever remember what to do, who to hand to?*). The runners were leaving in waves. The teams with slower predicted times had already started several hours ago. As a faster team, we were in the final wave, starting soon after 3pm. I hoped I wouldn't make us last of all thousand-odd teams.

We are all wearing our team T-shirts printed with our name, Sweatshop Somnambulists, and had photos taken with the snow-capped peak of Mt Hood for the backdrop. Then it was time for Rick to set off on Leg One, downhill for six miles and rated as Hard.

Announcements were blaring out of a loud speaker: "Team 197, the Sweatshop Sohmnab... Sohmnabolsts, come all the way from England. Give them a cheer!"

Gavin was not too impressed that Scotland seemed to have been forgotten. I'm not sure Patrick was either. We gave Rick a rousing send-off then piled into the vans to meet him at the handover point.

Team B in the other van came with us, but it was the only time we'd see them until it was their turn after the Leg Six / Leg Seven changeover.

Another loud cheer and several blasts on the horn saluted Rick as we passed him. He grinned and gave us all a big thumbs up. We drove on to our handover point, worried that we might have a problem and be late for him when he arrived. It was a layby marked by an A-frame, full of cars and runners waiting and shouting for their team mates to arrive.

We piled out and waited for what seemed like an age for him. Had he got lost? Injured? Suddenly, out of the crowd of people, we saw him. He was red in the face and puffing but he was in good spirits and had made it in good time.

Quickly, he handed over the wristband to Hugh who dashed off, still downhill.

I was third to go and started to prepare at our next handover stop: running shoes carefully laced, reflective tabard, head torch, route map. The last three are a requirement by the organisers. It was late afternoon and still light but would be dusk when I finished, later if things went wrong.

The map, far from being reassuring reminded me that, after the last four hectic days and very little sleep, I hadn't got a clue where I was. I'd once been awarded a prize at my running club for getting lost. One time, I'd even managed to go the wrong way on a very well-marked and well-marshalled marathon course. Navigation was not my strong point.

I waited by the handover funnel, wondering if I had time for a(nother) pee before I needed to run. Oh, I hoped it would all go right. I didn't want to let them down. "Do NOT drop the band, Janet!" I said sternly to myself.

I needn't have worried. Hugh handed it expertly to me, I slapped it on and ran off as fast as I could go while they watched and cheered, feeling like a proper runner. Adrenaline carried me along for a couple of hundred yards then my breathing caught up, tapped me on the shoulder and reminded me that I certainly couldn't do that pace for one mile, let alone another five.

I slowed to a more sensible pace and mustered enough energy to give them a wave as they passed me a few minutes later. Everyone cheered me on and I started to believe that it might be ok. I finally started to relax, mainly because it was too late to change anything. I was in this race whether I liked it or not. I decided to start enjoying myself.

A small river meandered through the valley to my right, trees growing along its banks. I started to imagine that water flowing downhill all the way to the ocean, just like our team was doing. The sky gradually morphed from a soft blue to a gentle pink. I settled into my running rhythm with the mental soundtrack of The Ballad of the Easy Rider running through my head.

Then my random running thoughts jostled their way back in: *How far is it to the handover? What if I get lost? I've got previous on that one.* These free-wheeling mental meanderings usually only happen after eighteen miles. At this stage I'd only done three. I added another sort of nervous worry to the rest.

A runner passed me. Then another. We'd set off with the fastest teams so I knew I was going to be passed more than I'd be overtaking others. They all said something as they went but I couldn't quite make out what it was.

More runners. What on earth were they saying? Eventually one phrase became clear: "Way to go."

Way to go? What does that even mean? It wasn't in general usage in the UK at the time and I worried that I might be going the wrong way. But I hadn't seen an alternative route since I started the Leg. No junctions. No side roads. Nothing. Which way should I go?

The runners seemed to be heading the same way that I was. I tried to ignore the niggling doubt in my head and to keep the other competitors in my sights as I plodded on.

Suddenly, I noticed a noise in the distance, drifting on the wind but getting louder with each step: a loudspeaker and cheering. It was the handover!

"And here comes the runner from Team 197, come all the way from England: the Sweatshop Soma... Somnah... Somnahb... Come on, Sweatshop Somblists..."

I had a sudden horrific thought. What if I couldn't find my team? They could well think I'd got lost, I'd taken so long.

No, there they were, waiting for me at the finish funnel, cheering me in. I think it was the first time I've ever been cheered by so many people. Usually everyone's gone to the pub by the time I finish.

I took a deep breath, gulped back tears and passed the band to Rob, sending him on his way.

Immediately after Rob had disappeared from view, I headed to the van for food and warm clothes. I could rest now until my next run, which would be sometime in the night.

While Tim, runner six, was out on the course, we headed for the van exchange at a supermarket car park so Team B could start their Legs. We were looking forward to the comparative luxury of a longer break before we had to run again.

We continued to Portland to find a place where we could rest for a while. Andy was driving. Rob was navigating. The others were asleep but I was wide awake in the back of the van. Their conversation was entertaining, if a little worrying, as we seemed to be very lost and going round in circles.

Eventually, we found a large car park in downtown Portland and made ourselves relatively comfortable. Andy found a bench to lie on but came back soon after, unnerved to have woken to find he was being watched by a raccoon. Others ventured out to see the wildlife which seemed to consist of more raccoons and several rats. Hardly David Attenborough.

We found Team B and Rick set off silently through downtown Portland. The handovers during the night were quiet so as not to disturb the residents. It was strange after the razzmatazz of the previous relay stations.

I hoped Rick hadn't heard some of the conversation about the areas he'd be running through. It wasn't the most reputable neighbourhood, let's put it that way. The road junctions were well marshalled so we assumed he'd be fine.

Soon it was my turn again. I had 7.25 miles to run, described as 'Hard' and 'gently rolling terrain.' Those two things don't go together at all in my mind.

I would be running in the middle of the night on the hard shoulder of an unlit road. To say I was apprehensive would be an understatement. I was trying not to think too much about it for fear I might cry. Left with no choice, I took the band and set off, outwardly confident (I hope).

In the event, it wasn't too bad running by the road: the shoulder was tarmacked and wide, the head torch gave enough light, vehicles gave us a wide berth and drivers called encouragement through the early hours.

I was passed by another runner and finally worked out what "Gdjaaaaab" (or "Gjab" if they are going fast) actually means: "Good job." An interesting demonstration of the Doppler effect. All encouragement was very gratefully received.

I did manage to pass one runner, and spurred on by my amazing success, I decided that I would start counting 'road kill'. Some of the vans had numbers painted on them: the number of runners each team member had passed and 'killed'. It was excellent motivation. My sights were now set on the runner in front who by now had almost disappeared over the horizon.

I gave myself a 'start' of twenty. Keep on keeping on. Seven miles are long in the night and I searched my head for a motivational song. Salt'n'Pepa pushed me up the next hill to my finish.

When I handed over my wristband, my road kill tally was minus fourteen. I'd done better than I'd expected.

It turned into a night-time blur: run, food, drink, warm clothes, drive, stop, back in van, repeat. It developed its own rhythm: fifteen minutes of bustle, activity, subdued noise followed by the gentle rocking of the van, silence interrupted by occasional snoring.

We worried about Tim, who was taking longer than expected. He arrived with a badly bleeding leg having had a nasty tumble. It was a van exchange so he had time to have his leg cleaned up while we watched, and dawn crept over the horizon. The faint lightening of the black night sky. Streaks of orange on the clouds. Then the whole of the east was lit by a glorious blood-red sunrise.

We wished Patrick well for his run, groaned as we saw the first steep section of the rollercoaster Leg he had to face, then piled back in the van and headed off.

The next stop was at a place called Mist, and as we drove along, I wondered what it would be like and how the name came about. Settlers hundreds of years ago, wagons camped in a circle, horses quietly eating grass, a pot boiling on a camp fire...

Other place names had been intriguing, too: My first Leg started at Kiwanis Camp, which made me think of flightless birds but Kiwanis International is a 'service club founded in 1915'. The Leg had passed through Rhododendron (didn't notice any) en route to Weigh Station, which had several options for meaning and derivation. Other sections went through Zigzag (bet that part wasn't straight!), Sandy (bet that part wasn't muddy!), Apiary Road (look out for bee hives) and Scappoose (haven't a clue!).

As we neared Mist, we weren't disappointed. It lived spectacularly up to its name as we crept along slowly, visibility at ten yards, to find a parking spot in the field.

The organisers had suggested sleeping bags and tents as there'd be plenty of time at our van exchange. This didn't appeal to me: even though we wouldn't actually be moving, it still seemed like travelling and I couldn't sleep. The tiredness after the drive had been replaced by excitement and general bewilderment: everything had moved so fast: the training, the travel, the running. I didn't even bother trying to nap.

As the sun burned the dampness away, my run-with-no-sleep brain wondered if the place had now changed its name and was called Sunshine instead.

I opted for stretching my legs and wandered around looking at the vans. Most of them were decorated in some way (thank goodness for Sunflower and Monkey!). Some of the runners had been in fancy dress and we'd all enjoyed the van lit up like a fairground ride at one night-time halt which had played non-stop Elvis. Gavin's kilt drew comment from those who were awake to see it.

One van belonged to, so they said, the North American Drama Society and was topped with two large spheres and a sign massive sign screaming "GO, N.A.D.S!"

The handover sites were well managed and equipped: this one had long lines of Porta-Potties, clean and with hand sanitizer gel, rather than water. After eighteen hours on the road, we seemed to be developing a fine layer of sticky grit on our hands. My contact lenses were gritty too, but I didn't want to touch them, sanitized or not.

Team B arrived. Rick ran, then Hugh, then I had my third and last Leg. It was nearly midday, the temperature was 28°C and I spent the next 6.4 miles trying my best to stay in the shade. Fortunately, there were plenty of trees, though not always where I'd have liked. The van had air-con, and I looked forward to when I'd be back in it.

After the impressively accurately named Mist, I was looking forward to the end of my run in Jewell, surely a place sparkling in the sunlight, dazzling with its bright colours? In the event, it was a disappointingly drab place with clapboard houses and a field of dry stubble where the vans were parked behind the school.

I handed the band to Rob for the last time. I had run my last step in the race and hoped I hadn't let them all down. They'd been so supportive and kind and treated me like one of the team. I hadn't been fast but I'd done my best and was happy enough with that. Now, back in the coolness of the van, I felt exhausted and wanted to sleep but didn't have the chance for that.

Further along, Andy, who was driving, realised just how much fuel the air-con was using. There were a few worrying miles before we found a tiny store with fuel pumps on a deserted country road.

Then it was our last handover. The guys on the Red Bull van were begging everyone they saw for water. They had been drinking Red Bull since they started yesterday and were in an extreme state of jittery dehydration. Deals were soon done, and we were glad of a boost of energy. I'd not tried the high-glucose energy drink before and soon handed it over to someone who had a sweeter tooth than me.

All we had to do now was meet Team B as they finished. Seaside, like Mist, lived up to its name but nobody had expected otherwise. We parked in town and headed to the beach. Music guided us the last few hundred yards and at last we saw the Pacific Ocean. It shone, smooth in the sunlight, welcoming us with a cooling breeze. It was another thing that, at least on this occasion, seemed exceptionally well-named.

I was so tired I found it hard to speak. I wanted to lie down and sleep but soft sand is surprisingly hard, the sun was scorching and we needed to meet Team B.

Gail, the last runner, was approaching. The announcer, voice nearly gone by now and sleep-deprived like the rest of us, told us Gail was coming through town. Then a hundred yards away. Then coming onto the beach. Then, "Here she comes for team Sweatshop Somnamambububobolists, come all the way from England." Sorry, Gavin and Patrick.

Medals received. Photos taken. Time for a quick dip. Then, for almost the last time, we headed back to the vans. Gavin, of course, was wearing his kilt and as I followed him through town, he was spotted by two young American women.

"Hey, it's a guy wearing a kilt! Is it true what they say about what you wear underneath it?" He flicked up the back of the kilt to show them that he is, indeed, a true Scot. They'll remember the day for a long time.

If there were various degrees of blur, I was definitely at five-star. Added to the lack of sleep, I had physical tiredness (eighteen miles running as fast as possible, plus a fair bit of walking), stiffness (even at my height of five-foot-two the back seat was cramped) and post-run adrenaline drop.

Back at the hotel, it was wonderful to have a shower after the heat and dust of the two days, but it was followed by another whirlwind (eat, pack, sleep, coffee). We left for the airport early the next morning. We found out while we were on the way that we were 32nd of all 1037 teams. I was relieved – I couldn't have held them up too much. Hugh was pleased that we beat the German and French teams.

*

I was physically and mentally exhausted, a mix of tiredness and excitement. It hadn't all been good. I'd cried once and wanted to quit several times, felt worried, nervous, insecure but also happy, excited, strong and proud. So many new experiences, places, people and so much to remember. I carry the memories with me still, not always at the front of my mind, but there should the moment arise.

And The Ballad of Easy Rider always plays to the memory of a soft pink and blue sky and a lazy river meandering ever onwards to the sea.

Facebook: **jan.burke.142**

Chapter 7

How to Dance Like Nobody's Watching

By Claudia Colvin

Step 1 - Decide you want to dance

If you're reading this book, you might be looking for adventure inspiration. Maybe you know what it feels like to be stuck in a job that isn't right for you, daydreaming of doing something different. You might also be struggling with the idea of doing only one thing five days a week, year after year after year. What about all the other things you love to do?

In many ways, my job was pretty good. I was working in the charity sector on a project that had a positive impact on people's lives. It challenged me, I learnt from it and I had a good team. I spent most of the week in Parliament or the House of Commons, surrounded by people in serious clothes, trying to solve serious problems and taking themselves seriously in the process.

Heads would turn to stare at me when I laughed out loud in the cafeteria, and eyes widened in bewilderment when I told people about my interests and hobbies. Greek folk dancing, camping outdoors in late October and laser tag competitions seemed like a universe away from the carpeted open-plan offices with long corridors and even longer layers of bureaucracy. Everything felt so serious, and that was the problem. I wasn't comfortable being myself at work. The stuffy carpeted corridors were suffocating the goofy, playful and creative side of me.

I decided to embark on an adventure, in search of a career that allowed my different passions and personality traits to coexist, without having to choose one and neglect the others.

Step 2 - Show up

There are two things you need to know about me. The first is that I'm full of ideas. The second, and harder to admit, is that I struggle to execute, commit to and complete the vast majority of these ideas. I love the rush of having a new idea, daydreaming of what it would be like for that idea to come to life. When it comes to starting, I freeze. And when I start, I don't always get round to the finishing part.

Sometimes it's choice overwhelm: torn between too many ideas, I don't know which one to pick. Sometimes it's perfectionism and blank page fear: If I start, it has to look good, it has to be perfect. I have to read every book, listen to every podcast on the topic and speak to every person I know who can teach me something about it.

And so I've lived my life swimming through this simmering hotpot of ideas and interests, a notebook always at my side in case a new one turned up. Some ideas stayed with me for years before being set aside. Some got lost forever, on days with no notebooks and plenty of "I'll remember this. No need to write it down!" I never bought my round the world flight ticket. I never completed my PhD proposal. My ukulele lies abandoned after a three-month course I took two years ago.

The most persistent type of idea that ended up on my notebook was a business idea. I'd been immersing myself in the London start-up scene for years, in awe of founders who boldly turned their ideas into action.

For all those years, perfectionism and self-doubt had stopped me from making a move. But in November 2016, I'd had one stuffy corridor walk too many. I wanted to stop daydreaming about being an entrepreneur and start actually being an entrepreneur. I wanted to finally tackle the self-doubt that for all those years had been telling me that my ideas weren't good enough, that *I* wasn't good enough, that I didn't know enough, that I needed to wait just a little bit more because insert excuse here.

I had spent the past five years filling notebooks with business ideas. It was time to say yes to one of them.

Step 3 - Confront your fears

In the autumn of 2016, five different business ideas were pulling me in different directions,

which was as exciting as it was unhelpful. I loved all of my ideas equally. How was I supposed to pick?

I started exploring what each idea would look like as a fleshed out business. I did market research and put myself out there. I met people, asked questions and soaked up all the learning I could get my hands on. I read books, listened to podcasts and went to events. And I started to develop assumptions about my different ideas.

I started believing some would be easier than others; some more profitable; some more likely to succeed; some more sensible and within my reach. The least sensible idea of the five seemed like the one that would be hardest to set up, that would make the least money and be the most likely to fail.

As I sat, researched, took notes and wrote ideas, thoughts would take over.

Most likely to fail.

*Most likely to **fail**.*

Fail.

You will fail.

That F word was my biggest fear and it persistently buzzed around my mind like a summer fly that won't get the difference between the window pane and the opening you're directing it towards. Those thoughts were the soundtrack of my research process. My mind gremlins heckled me all the way through, making sure I never got comfortable imagining myself as an entrepreneur. They told me I wasn't going to make it, that my ideas sucked and who was I to start a business anyway?

I could research as much as I wanted: I would never actually start anything if I didn't address that first.

I turned to my notebook. This time, instead of writing down my ideas, I wrote down my fears. All of them, one by one. I numbered them and drew a line under the last one. I started a new numbered list below the line. Next to each number, I wrote down each fear's worst case scenario. When I finished, I looked through those worst case scenarios and thought "what then?". In most cases, the answer wasn't that bad. Some of my fears, like "what if people will judge me?", didn't even have a worst case scenario because they just didn't matter. Others, like "what if I run out of money", could be worked around with enough forward planning, like saving methodically and getting a part time job.

After this exercise, I took a deep breath and noticed how my mind gremlins had gone quiet. They seemed satisfied now that they'd blurted everything out on paper. I looked out of my window at the

London skyscrapers, glimmering from a distance through the dark. Their quiet light nudged me on.

I thought back to the assumptions I had made about my different ideas. I thought back to all the conversations I'd had in the past months with other entrepreneurs. Every single person I'd spoken to, regardless of age, business type, amount of entrepreneurial experience or any other variable, had told me a story that included struggle. The gruelling struggle to set up; a large obstacle they walked right into later on in the journey; a setback they had to bounce back from. If I started a business, I would also experience these challenges.

The assumptions I'd made about my ideas were incorrect. I could find a way to make all of them profitable; none of them would be easy; none of them were particularly sensible; all of them were a little mad and so was I, in the best possible sense of the word. My business ideas now had a level playing field.

I thought about what had motivated my decision to be bold and experiment with entrepreneurship. It came from a desire to do more of what I love and inspire others to do the same. It came from a belief that life is better when we take it a little bit less seriously and find more time for play; when we do things because we want to, not because we're expected to, or we're scared of being judged. So I picked the idea that allowed me to stay closest to this.

I decided to start a business called Nobody's Watching, and propose silent disco freestyle dancing as a fitness alternative.

Step 4 - Dance in your own way

During the research process, I'd told people about the different ideas I was playing around with. When I shared this silent disco idea with people who knew me, most would say, "You want to do *what*?"

At the time, I had experience working in English teaching, peacebuilding education, project management and recruitment. My degrees were in Middle Eastern Studies and Languages. This business idea stuck out like a sore thumb.

When I told strangers, they would ask, "Are you a DJ? A professional dancer? A fitness instructor?"

"I am none of these," I'd reply, laughing nervously. "I'm just someone who really loves to dance, wants to do it more often and wants to inspire others to do the same. You don't need a degree for that. You just need passion, an ability to bring people with you, make them feel comfortable and included, a (questionably) good taste in music, and the entrepreneurial spirit to go out there and make it happen."

But people who **really** knew me said, "Oh, of course!".

Because people who really knew me had seen me dance. They'd seen a smile circling my face while dancing to my signature animal moves: the shark, the crab, the t-rex or whatever else inspired me that day. They'd seen what happens when I'm suddenly hit by an unexpected great tune: I'd excuse myself and leave a conversation mid-sentence; I'd start dancing in a food queue; I'd be unable to focus until the song was over. They allowed me to drag them onto the dancefloor, because they knew I was happy to dance alone but always happier when I danced in company.

They also listened to my nostalgic 'I miss dancing' sighs. I was really struggling to find places where I could dance this way.

Clubs weren't doing it for me. Inebriated, overdressed and often judgemental crowds left little room for my dance moves: the shark, crab and t-rex weren't welcome here.

Dance classes weren't doing it for me either. I'd go to the class looking for fun and leave feeling like a failure, having spent most of it cramped in the corner, tripping over myself and forgetting the moves. I didn't want to learn something. I just wanted space to goof around to feel-good music and have like-minded people to share it with.

In 2016, I attended Yestival, a microfestival for people who want to live their life more adventurously. One of their early morning activities was a silent disco, with a 7.30am start. Back in 2016, I wasn't a morning person, and the prospect of waking up so early did not excite me. But I was curious and wanted to try.

The alarm went off as the sun was rising. I reluctantly pulled on the zip of my sleeping bag and groaned as the cold air slapped my warm body awake. I ran to the silent disco tent and grabbed a headset, eager to start moving and shake off the cold. As I put on the headset, everything changed.

We were still in a field, it was still dawn and I was still freezing cold, but all of these three things suddenly entered a new dimension: one with a cheerful soundtrack. It felt like being immersed in the happy ending scene of a movie. It was exactly what I'd been missing from all my recent dance experiences. One hour of dancing to uplifting tunes. No right or wrong moves, freedom to dance however you wish, plenty of room to move and other smiling sober faces to share that with.

Something about the headphones made it easier to dance. They created a safe bubble that cocooned you into a musical microworld, whilst leaving you connected to the other dancers. As I danced, my many layers started coming off; by the end I was left in a t-shirt, covered in sweat, a big smile spread across my face. I washed off the sweat, but the smile didn't leave my face all day.

I left Yestival thinking, 'If this isn't a thing, someone needs to make it a thing, because everyone needs to feel how I felt that morning.'

This idea was profoundly out of my depth. All I knew was how to dance like nobody's watching. I would have to teach myself everything else.

But that night I was determined and I was fearless. I knew what I wanted to do. It was time to start planning how to do it.

Step 5 - Don't hold back

I started saving money from November 2016, and saved enough to get by during the summer months without an income. The plan was to use the summer to test the idea, do a few events and get feedback. By the end of the summer, I'd know if Nobody's Watching was something worth pursuing. I planned to get a part time job in September so I could have some regular income whilst building the business, or whilst experimenting with another idea if Nobody's Watching didn't pick up.

In May 2017, I purchased my kit. I started small with ten headsets and one transmitter and therefore only one music channel.

My first test event was in June. There were five people, including me, and it was painfully awkward. It was in a makeshift meeting-room-dance-floor, with stacked chairs and tables on the side and a carpeted floor under our feet. We were at Business LaunchPad, a social enterprise that provides free business support for people under thirty. My business counsellor, Caesar, had helped me recruit my first guinea pigs, who were Business LaunchPad staff or mentees. My four participants were shuffling from one foot the other while eyeing each other suspiciously, as if they expected a Britain's Got Talent buzzer to go off and to be booed out of the room.

The mind gremlins felt empowered and started heckling again. "See? Your idea sucks. This is terrible. You've only got four people here and they hate it!" But as the playlist churned out more songs, they started loosening up. Their awkwardness shifted, smiles and sweat emerged, and I started to recognise the familiar glow of someone who's having a boogie and loving it.

I ran this first test session as I had experienced it myself at Yestival. Here's a great playlist; here are the headphones; off you go, have fun.

This worked for me: I don't need much to start dancing, just a great song and enough room to move.

But that doesn't work for everyone. Many people have never danced sober. All of a sudden I was asking a room full of sober strangers trying to dance like nobody's watching.

I talked about it with Hasmita, one of the guinea pigs. She asked me about my background and helped me see how I could use it to my advantage. As an educator and facilitator, I had learnt to create safe spaces, to work with icebreakers and create trust in a group.

"Why don't you do this in the event?" she suggested. "Do a warm up. Set the scene. Give us permission to dance around like goofballs and get comfortable dancing."

And that's how the format was born.

I start all my events with a playful warm up. Picture a room full of people doing a T-Rex dance move to Le Freak, crawling along the floor pretending to be Tom Cruise in Mission Impossible, or flailing their right hands in the air as they sing "Single Ladies". The warm up gives people permission to play. It shows them this is a space where we dance to feel good, not to look good. They realise no one will judge them, so there's no need to hold back. Once they realise this, they're ready to dance unguided.

The rest of the event is freestyle dancing, with two channels to pick from: 60s/70s/80s on one channel; 90s/00s on the other. The songs are all feel-good greatest hits that you can sing along to.

My summer of testing was over. The result was a format and enough evidence to suggest I was onto something. It was time to get a part time job, and take Nobody's Watching to the next level: a first official event.

To do that, I needed to write event copy to put on a public page for any random person to read and judge. I knew my events were something worth going to, but I didn't know how to communicate it. I didn't know if I'd be able to convince a stranger to turn up simply by reading the event page. I can't count how many times I rewrote that copy.

My mind gremlins were wide awake and there was a whole team of them with different opinions.

"This is terrible!"

"Nobody's going to come anyway. Why are you even bothering to write this up?"

"Commas. More commas."

"No, bullet points work better."

"No, it needs to be shorter, but longer, with less words, and more bullet points, no less bullet points. You need to start again now."

I was learning to ignore them now. Learning to push through the self-doubt and just get on with it.

I finished and published the page, posted it on various Facebook groups and held my breath. Two days later, I had gone over capacity by 200%. In a rush of validation, I bought ten more headphones and crossed all my fingers in the hope that not everyone who reserved a ticket would turn up on the day.

The kit was just about enough; the videographer didn't have a headset and told me he'd had a surreal afternoon filming people jumping around to what, from his perspective, was absolute silence.

Twenty people came. The group size made it feel real, like I had finally created the 'thing' I'd set out to create. They were smiling, playfully dancing around, having a great time. At the end, they all asked when the next one was and how could they sign up.

I was in total elation. I took everyone to the pub and spent far too much money buying everyone a round. It gave me the kick I needed to officially launch Nobody's Watching in January 2018. My launch party got featured on Time Out London and the hype was exactly what I'd hoped for. It was game time now. The events were published, tickets on sale, dance studios booked. I just needed to wait for people to show up, once a month.

Step 6 - Don't be scared of making the wrong move

What followed were the ups and downs I knew were coming but had no idea how to prepare for. Attendance was highly unpredictable. Sometimes I'd have a full room; others, I'd have zero sign ups, but a dance studio rental fee to pay. Even the most supportive of my friends grew tired of my last minute 'Please can you come tonight I need a few more people?' texts. The struggle was profoundly real. I had no marketing budget and filled events exclusively through organic traffic and word of mouth. I had a small group of fans but it wasn't enough to fill events every time. This knocked my confidence and put me on an emotional roller coaster with ups of, "This is great, I'm offering real value here!", and downs of, "My business sucks, nobody wants the solution I'm offering."

By December 2018, I had decided to stop doing open to public events. I was going to hold one last public event in January and stay open for private bookings only.

Then something extraordinary happened.

My 'last event' in January was two tickets away from being sold out. Only then did I realise that I had forgotten to remove the February and March dates from the ticketing link. I'd already sold six tickets for February and five for March. Maybe I should listen to the signs.

I decided not to cancel the February and March events. They were well-attended and a success. I collected some more five-star reviews.

It felt like I'd finally made it. Somehow, I'd broken through. So I kept going.

Things changed again in the summer. I made a mistake choosing a venue in an inconvenient location; it tanked my ticket sales and my confidence wavered. I injured myself at the end of June and couldn't dance for a month. Autumn came; I was ill and had to cancel an event; the following event had a venue complication and my events became homeless. I found a last minute solution for the November event but I'd have to find somewhere new if I wanted to keep going. Whatever had made the ticket sales spike last winter wasn't working now. Last year I'd decided to stop. What should I do now?

I stood in my bedroom staring in bewilderment and alienation at the silent disco kit scattered across the bed. The rain was lashing outside; a veritable storm of emotion was brewing inside. "What have I done? Why am I doing this? What was I thinking?" I asked myself. The kit stared back, unapologetic. I'd been using it for the past two years and it had become part of my everyday life.

"What's the matter, love?" it seemed to say, in a language I couldn't understand anymore. Suddenly the kit seemed out of place, like the letter "w" in the word answer. So familiar, but once you stop to notice it, you wonder why it's there.

I couldn't bear to look at it, so I slumped to the floor, staring at a spot between my feet for what felt like hours. Why was my kit there? What was I going to do with it?

I eventually dug deep, packed my kit and made my way to the venue. People had booked tickets and were expecting me to show up. I wasn't going to let them down. I was going to run that event and then decide what to do next.

At one of my events in the summer, the one with the poor venue choice, I had met Rick. Rick came to the first event in that venue because it was round the corner from his house and because he believes in doing one thing that scares you every single day. He loved it and has since shown up to every single event I've held. He's my first true super fan. He's American, soon to be sixty and has lived a colourful life in many countries around the globe. When I ask him how he's doing at the start of an event, he often replies with, "I'm way too old to be partying like I partied yesterday," but it doesn't seem to stop him. He loves a salt beef bagel and really doesn't care what people think about him.

After the event, we had a chat (and a bagel). He told me that every time one of my events is coming up, he holds his breath and wonders, 'Is she gonna do it? Is it gonna be the last one?'

I opened up to him and confessed my struggles, how hard it was to fill an event and that I wasn't sure whether I should keep going.

"Everyone had a great time this evening, Claudia," he said. "I think you should do these more often. If you're only doing them once a month, you're not giving people a lot of options to come back. If they're busy on that day, you've lost a customer for another month. With everything that's going on in London, you need something more regular than that."

But how could I justify moving to weekly when I was struggling to fill events once a month?

Two hours later, I got this review from a customer called Natalie:

> I finally got to dance in a space where no one judged or cared as everyone else was dancing freely. And there was diversity, all ages, races and body types and afterwards I felt a lot more confident. And for that hour I felt like it was a Friday!!! Wish there was more regularly as I would go.

There was another nudge. I start remembering past conversations I'd had with various marketing partners like Time Out, Groupon, ClassPass. They'd all ended in, "We'd love to work with you but we can't justify it if your events are once a month. Give us a call when you have more events."

As weekly events from January started to look like a real possibility, new thoughts rang loud in my head. There were marketing opportunities but who was to say they would work? What if I couldn't cope with the increased workload, since I wasn't going to reduce the hours of my four day a week job? What if moving to weekly turned into week after week of me and Rick and nobody else in the room? I love dancing with Rick, and it would still have been fun. It just wouldn't have been a sustainable business.

In the meantime, the other ideas I'd discarded were coming back to distract me. Those ideas were all at early stages: the stage that's easiest to be excited about and find energy for. I found myself wondering the same thoughts I'd had when I first started my research. "What if I'm just not cut out for this?" This "What if" sounded very familiar. "What if" was how many of the fears I'd written down in my notebook had started.

This entrepreneurship adventure had been uncomfortable, painful, difficult but also rewarding, empowering and educational. I thought about how I felt at the end of each event. The dancing made me glow, it made my customers glow, and seeing them glow made me glow even harder. I knew I was offering something of value, and all the five-star reviews I was collecting validated this. Increasing to weekly was a possible solution to my marketing problem. The "What if" worries were fear of the unknown. Every time I started an event, I told my customers to not judge themselves, to dance to 'feel good' not to 'look good'. If I believed so strongly in not being scared of making a wrong move, who was I to not take my own advice?

I decided to see things through with Nobody's Watching. To go big instead of going home. I launched weekly events from January 5th.

Step 7 - Just keep dancing

I'm writing this at the end of January and I have a feeling it will work out. It's possible that it won't, but if it doesn't, at least I'll know

I didn't let my fears stop me from trying. I'll know I did everything I could to go big before going home.

And I'll know that going home doesn't mean the end. It means, "Well that didn't work. What's next?"

Epilogue

Step 8 - Don't Give Up

I wrote this chapter in January. I'm editing it in May and the world is a very different place now.

As the virus engulfed Italy, I saw what was coming in the UK. On March 11th, I decided to cancel all upcoming events for the foreseeable future.

This pandemic's growth curve avalanched straight into Nobody's Watching's growth curve. Because, guess what? It did work out. January and February were my biggest months. 80% of my events sold out. The ones that didn't sell out had enough people to fill the room. I'd been working towards that for three years if you count from launch, four if you count from the start of this story.

It did *not* feel good to stop.

But if there is one thing I learnt from this whole process, it's the subtle art of not giving up. This art is made up of resilience, focus, determination and creative problem solving.

Whilst silent disco events are cancelled, I've not stopped creating spaces for people to come together and dance. I'm doing this online, through Zoom.

The purpose of Nobody's Watching doesn't rely on silent disco. The purpose is to use sing-along dancing to lift people's mood. Silent disco was the 'How' of my business idea, not the 'Why'.

The online events are the same format as my silent disco events: a playful warm up dance routine to start, freestyle dancing till the end. I've added an open mic karaoke for the last song. We need the mood boost now more than ever.

I'm not sure what the future holds. Perhaps a YouTube channel with my warm ups; perhaps I'll just need to wait a few years to pick things up again. But the lessons learnt will stay with me forever. The risk I took in January worked out. It worked out because I didn't give up.

Website: **nobodyswatching.co**

Instagram: **@claudiacolvin**

Chapter 8

Mentality Mountain

By Karl Coppack

"Take a seat, Karl."

It's January 2015 and let's just say that things had been better.

I didn't want to take a seat. I didn't want to be in this room. I didn't want to be in this postcode. My bed was less than a hundred metres away and that would have everything I needed, but no. This had to be done.

"How can I help you?"

It was fortunate at least that my GP is so close to me. Had I needed to drive to her that day I would have summoned up some ludicrous excuse not to be there, but there I was — sat mournfully on a rickety chair, not making eye contact and talking into my armpit.

2015 had not started well.

2014 though had been a hell of a year. In the January I published my debut novel which, thanks to the occasional bout of laziness or fear, took about twenty-one years to complete. Joseph Heller took the same time to write *Catch-22*, but at the end of that he had *Catch-22* to show the world. I didn't, but I was pleased with what I'd done.

It went down a storm too and, though it didn't make me rich or famous, I'm proud of it. The year was only a few days old and I was already a published author—something I'd dreamt of since I was about eight-years old. A good start.

A few months later I was cajoled into leaving my job as an Account Manager for a large publishing firm. That sounds negative, I know, but it led to better things.

I wasn't sacked as such, but the company had had their hand in the small of my back for a while and was pushing me ever doorwards with growing severity. I'd first had a verbal warning then a written one for no real crime other than cost cutting. I wasn't alone in this purge and several people made the same journey as me around the same time.

Two weeks before my tenure was about to expire, I landed a job at a charity. I was delighted. Not only because I had a new job, but because it was an area I'd long wanted to enter. I'd done some fundraising a few years earlier and enjoyed every moment of it. I duly resigned.

My old lot weren't especially pleased that, thanks to my notice period, I would be there for four more weeks instead of the two they'd hoped for. They made me an unattractive offer of two weeks paid leave and two unpaid if I left that day. Given how they'd treated me, I dug in my heels and refused. I then stopped wearing a suit for work.

Despite serving four and a half years there I left without a gift, card, leaving speech or leaving do. That's how bad things had become.

This was still a plus though. I now have the best job I've ever had. I'm making a difference and the people I make money for, know my name. In my last place a director frequently mistook a friend of mine for the man who came in and sold sandwiches. He'd been there three years and sat twenty feet from her every day. They sacked him too.

So, a published author and working in a sector whose door I had been tapping on for a decade with little success. I was getting on.

Things were moving quickly elsewhere too.

It was around this time that I had a drink with another mate who edited the football section of *The Times*. I told him I would soon be unemployed, and he offered to help. He knew I could write so promised me some shifts as a sub-editor or even as a match reporter for the lower leagues. Nothing elaborate. The odd 350-word review for the Monday paper.

A few months later I entered Griffin Park, for a game between Brentford and Brighton. I was wearing a press badge. I was ushered into a press room where I fell into conversation with John Salako, the former Crystal Palace player. I was suddenly a football writer for *The Times*. Talk about landing on your feet. I'd been dreaming of that gig for even longer.

Yes, that was quite a year.

I apologise if this sounds like, in Del Boy's words, 'the parable of the lucky git,' but a crash is coming, I assure you. Never fear.

I was also given the opportunity to work on the Monday paper so on Sunday afternoons I would head to London Bridge and sit at a desk surrounded by screens showing football. I was given only light duties — one of which was to ghost-write a column for a former international footballer. I'd phone him, he'd offer his views and I'd put them into words. After a while my name started appearing under headlines. I failed English at school, so I hope the poor swine who was charged with teaching me got to see that.

Author, charity employee, football journalist, sub-editor, friend to retired footballers.

2014 was the year I thought about every night before I went to sleep. The year where things took shape.

So why the trip to the doctor?

"Well, it's like this …"

Sat in that surgery, I paused after those words. I mean, how do you describe what's wrong with you in concise terms? Where do you begin? It's like explaining the plot of *War and Peace* in three sentences.

See, I've always been prone to melancholy. It's a natural state and though I like a laugh as much as the next man, I've always been the sort of person who enjoys the journey away from a party more than the one to it. The word 'dour' was recently used to describe me and I'll concede that it fits perfectly. Oh, I have my passions, but they're mostly solo pursuits. Crowds aren't always for me.

Bearing in mind that was when I was fine!

There were other times when I really didn't want to face anyone at all, when I don't want to talk to anyone or even be seen. If I absolutely had to be somewhere, I could put on a mask and get through it, but I'd soon be craving my cell again.

For some reason it got worse if I'd been praised and there was a bit of that in 2014. The feedback for the novel was extraordinary. One woman told me that it was her favourite book of all time and that she read it on a loop. The second she ended it, she'd start again. Anyone would be flattered by that, but not me. I felt like I'd cheated her somehow. I considered sending her a list of a hundred books that were superior. Good job I've never worked in marketing.

That's a common feeling. If I've performed well in a meeting or been funny or done something good or worthwhile I'll pay for it afterwards with some vicious self-flagellation.

That phase didn't last too long. A few days later, I would wake up feeling fine with no hint that I'd had that doubt.

Things came to a head in December 2014. I was discussing these darks spells with my friend Caroline as she'd noticed that they'd increased in number and were lasting longer than usual. I shrugged this off and said it was just me being me. It was when I told her that I'd half-heartedly googled suicide techniques during yet another sleepless night that she stepped in. She told me to go to the doctor to at least share this development with a medical professional.

My response was, in direct contradiction to the theme of this book:

"Nah!"

I knew what this was. I'd be fine. It was one of those things and I always came back from them. Surely everyone gets this way from time to time.

But, then she did something clever. I'm not sure if she knew it would work, but it did.

She asked me to go 'for her' rather than me.

That made it different. I've known Caroline for years and though I was more than happy (if that's the word) to deny my mental state, it's impossible for me to let her down. The thought of so much as disappointing the people I love sends me into a spiral. I made the appointment.

So, there I was, sat in Room Number One with my GP, reading the warning posters Blu-tacked to the walls and trying to keep my voice even as I shuffled my feet and spoke in a dreary monotone.

One thing I was keen to emphasise was that I didn't have depression. Oh no. Nothing like that. I listed my feelings — stress, anxiety, a sense of worthlessness, a zombie-like approach to emotion, a downright fear of emotion, crying fits and an urge to disappear. I wasn't suicidal as such. It would just be a lot easier if I were not around at all. The sperm who narrowly missed out on the egg.

But it wasn't depression. I knew what that was, and this wasn't it.

I wonder how many people tell their doctor what it is that they don't have. It's like a departing tenant telling their landlord that everything is how it was when they moved in, but please don't go into the spare room.

She asked me if I were to write those feelings around one big word, what would that word be?

Ten tortuous minutes later I was diagnosed with high-functioning endogenous depression.

I had depression. I have depression.

Let's look at those words.

High functioning means just that. As I've said, at my lowest I can still operate from behind a disguise. Depressives are actors when they need to be. I could be feeling like the lowest piece of excrement on the lowest floor of the lowest well. I could have had ten minutes of solid sobbing for no reason and you'd have no idea. I'd be Normal Karl. The same person you'd see when I'm fine. When it comes to hiding this thing, I'm Robert de Niro.

Only once have I been discovered and that was at Wembley in 2015. I'd been out with my friend and mentor from *The Times* along with a gaggle of journalists. I wasn't feeling great and the match didn't help, but I 'briefly put on manly readiness' (Liverpool FC and Macbeth tended to go together in 2015) and played Normal Karl. On my way home he rang me and said that he knew I was struggling and was I okay?

I was stung by that and it took me a year for me to ask him how he knew. It transpired that one of our party that day has similar issues and noticed that I behaved differently when I thought no one was looking.

But, in the main, I can get by when my every fibre of my being wants to crawl under my bed and not come out.

'Endogenous' is something different and means that my depression comes from within me rather than, say, an event. I'm not depressed because my dad died in 1996, nor am I down because life threw up some giant hurdle or other which prevents me from being happy. No, I'm depressed because there's something inside that makes me this way. Grief and loss don't help, obviously, but my condition has nothing to do with that. It's just like being born with a club foot or a big nose. It's just there. A biological quirk.

You'd think that that diagnosis would have me snapping my fingers and shouting, 'Yes! That's it' before heading home, relieved that it can be treated. Nope. It opened Pandora's Box. The next few months were the worst of my life as the evil genie flew from the bottle and told me that it was all my fault.

Oh, I knew it wasn't, but try telling my mind that.

I told my family and friends and they were, as you'd expect, supportive. My then girlfriend merely said, "Well, obviously!" when I told her. She'd always known. It seems I wasn't as adept at covering my tracks as I'd assumed.

My late sister was a Pharmacy Lecturer back then, so I asked her about medication. You see, I was given a week to decide if I should be medicated at all as it's a big step. I said I would, and we went through some options. At the end of that exchange she said with her usual cheery voice dropping a little: "This is all very sad." I think about that every day.

Is this going to become upbeat at any point, Karl? This is supposed to be a celebration of positivity. Well, yes, but I'm not done with you yet.

I was given a drug called Mirtazapane. I was told that it took a fortnight to get going and that one of the early side effects was suicidal thoughts. Nice.

Luckily, I had a different reaction. I took my first one at 11am and nodded off. I woke up at 5pm with the day half gone. I then walked around for an hour or so and sat down at 7pm. I awoke at 11am the next day. I had slept for twenty-two hours in twenty-four. Clearly that was no good.

I'm now on something called Venlafaxine. I can now stay awake and the only side effect is the odd bout of nausea. They haven't cured me as such, but I think they've been the wet tea towel dropped onto the burning saucepan of anxiety.

The effects are lessened but the underlying cause is still there. That's not a bad thing necessarily. At least I can now recognise when a 'dog day' is going to strike. I can even alter my social diary when the clouds descend. Also, my friends know why I act like I do. A while ago I suggested to my football mates that we go for a curry after a pleasant night in a pub. By the time we got there I said I just couldn't go in and needed to be home. Each and every one of them shook my hand and patted me on the back without any judgment or sign of annoyance. They know now. Normal Karl had gone on holiday but would be back soon.

So, how do I live with this? How do I say 'Yes' more?

Well, I was recently asked by my therapist if I had any hobbies that may distract me when my mood sinks. Here goes.

I write a weekly football column for a multi-award winning website, I blog, I'm writing a collection of short stories, I'm writing a play about a famous killer, I'm a runner, I have a Second Dan black belt in Taekwondo, I also teach Taekwondo, I play guitar, I play chess online every day, I appear on a weekly football podcast, I host my own podcast, I attend a huge amount of football matches, both home and away and I do all this with a full-time job.

Oh, and I'm a contributor to *The Ripperologist* magazine, part-organiser of the annual East End Conference, occasional host of *The Whitechapel Society* meetings and talks and conference host.

I say 'Yes' an awful lot.

I do those things because I must. I cannot be bored. Boredom is the worst thing in the world. Boredom, for me at least, is a very dangerous thing.

Of course, there's a medical need for all this. They go together to build a wall to protect me from the truth. I am petrified of looking at myself and my condition. I have to distract at all time. Distract, distract, distract.

In some ways that's a good thing. It keeps me busy and I achieve a lot. I wanted to start Taekwondo. Then I wanted a black belt. Then I wanted to teach it. The black belt took five years—quite quick. Fundraising? Easy. I raised some money with my friends for my all-time hero. We changed his life. I'm proud of them. Less so for me as I need the next thing. Now.

But that's all about the mental. What about the physical? What about the adventure? The lifeblood?

Well, here's an example.

In October 2019, I decided to walk up Snowdon.

I'm not sure how that came about, but one day I wasn't going to do anything like that ever and the next I was looking at maps. As you do.

Could I do this alone? No chance. I'd chicken out and go back to watching drone videos on YouTube instead or, worse, bottle out of it the second the track got too tough. No, I needed a companion. Someone unusual enough to agree to such things.

I've known Reenie for six years and we met in unusual circumstances. It sounds terrible when you say, 'we met on Twitter,' but Sharon Horgan and Rob Delaney did just that, and they wrote CATASTROPHE together, so maybe it's not that weird. Anyway, we made each other laugh one day and instantly became mates. Over time, she's both learned of and helped me with my bouts of depression and I've cackhandedly done what I can for her and her own issues. There's a nice feeling of mutual help along with our childish sense of humour.

She agreed to the Snowdon hike and we made our way to North Wales at 5am.

The plan was to arrive at Pen-y-Pass car park in time to find a space and then set off once we strapped on the correct footwear etc. Fat chance. By the time we turned onto the final road, the A4086, the place was alive with luminous tabards and complicated sock/boot arrangements. The car park was full so we were forced to head past it and onto Nant Peris (later to be renamed Nant Perishing) and get a bus back.

I loved being there, but at the same time I wandered what the hell I was up to. I get this feeling a lot.

There are numerous ways to climb the mountain. The Llanberis path is the longest one and starts lower down while the 'Miners' Track' winds around the beautiful lakes underneath Snowdon before climbing rapidly. However, my mate Matt knows a few things about climbing, and he suggested the 'Pyg Track' as it's 'short'. It starts behind the car park and climbs steadily before a right turn reveals the lakes down below and Snowdon towering overhead. A wrong turning there could see you up the infamous 'Crib Goch' route which involves a knife edge ridge with a sheer drop either side. Sod that.

The Pyg it was then.

We walked.

At first the climb was easy enough. The only real problem came with trusting the stones beneath our feet in the damp. We learned that black ridged rocks were our friends as they could take a walking boot, but the lighter, smoother stones were to be viewed with suspicion.

A walk then, not a scramble. You'd need your hands at some point, but it was hardly a climb.

I had my first rest at half an hour and felt a bit ashamed of it. The website said that anyone can cross the Pyg if they had 'a reasonable amount of fitness'. I'm overweight but I run a fair bit and have done Taekwondo for thirteen years. I'm nothing like athletic, but I don't need a rest at the top of every staircase.

She'll deny this, but Serena is way fitter. She told me at this point that her Obstacle Course runs stood her in good stead for this sort of thing. Her credo is always 'move your feet and keep going' so she was fine. Taekwondo students have a similar catechism in our Tenets – 'indomitable spirit' and 'perseverance'. I was fine. I just needed a nice sit down and if someone wanted to bring round a nice high-winged armchair and a tea that would all be better.

We walked further.

Finally, we came to a level section and a right turn. The whole area was now covered in cloud and mist, but there came a welcome sight—a stile. I explained that I'd seen this on YouTube, and it marked the point where the track crosses into Crib Goch. One look to the right confirmed this. Up above was a huge brown-green ridge topped by cloud. It looked wonderful. It also looked like a bad idea. This was no temptation. We continued on the Pyg.

I was having real problems with my specs now. I was sweaty though it was still cold and raining. A fresh layer of condensation formed as fast as I could wipe another away. In the end I had to simply carry them. I'm glad I did. Without them I could not see what was below.

Llyn Llydaw is a natural reservoir about a third of the way up the mountain. The Miner's Track snakes along next to it. It's rumoured to be coldest natural lake in Wales and, from high up on the Pyg, it looks utterly beautiful. The water is a perfect navy blue, contrasting with the browns of the bleached stones which surround it. It was one of those moments where you have to stop dead and take it all in.

Oscar Wilde once said that 'beauty is the only thing that time cannot harm'. Llyn Llydaw isn't just beautiful; it is peaceful, and just the thing you need to see when you're exhausted and a bit worried.

We crossed the stile and came across some walkers on their way down from the summit. I jokingly asked if we were five or ten minutes away from the peak. They snorted and said, "You've got a fair bit to go yet." They were right. Two and a half hours to be precise.

Here the path is fairly level. It even drops a little so you can get a bit of pace going. It's certainly less strenuous than the earlier path up to the stile. Serena and I began to relax. We talked about the view and how much fun it all was rather than worry about that big mountain which stood in the distance.

Fools.

The next bit—somewhere between one hour to two hours into the walk—was tricky.

The websites tell you that the Pyg is the easier of the routes. Easier, not easy. It's here when you realise you've been duped. You're no longer upright for much of this but stooped in expectation of the next scramble. Oh, there's no worry about falling or anything like that, but there's no real path here. Just a gentle suggestion on where to go. The next bit involved walking uphill while water from broken plastic pipes tests your boots' waterproofing capabilities.

And the strangest thing is that you don't mind. At this point we had other people around us, and we'd share rueful grins or grimaces.

There was a sense of camaraderie in all this. Every now and then you'd take a photo or have a chat about what people were doing there. At one point I found myself sat in the middle of a school party having my picture taken.

As we walked on, we'd pass people coming down from the peak. "Only an hour to go!" they'd offer cheerfully.

But it was tiring too, and I was aware of Reenie, now resplendent in a bobble hat scampering away ahead of me while I stared at the next section trying to work out where my feet would go next.

After a while we came across an obelisk which marks the spot where the Miner's Track meets the Pyg. There's still no sign of the peak at this point, but that meant another bit of the walk was over. When you're tired you just walk to the next marker.

Sadly though, this also meant that the hard work was about to start. Though it's nothing like sheer, the terrain became steeper here as Crib Goch reaches its highest point above. Now the track is at its busiest as you're joined by the Miner's walkers. The scramble continued.

One man patted me on the shoulder and told me that we have about thirty minutes to go. Invigorated, I put a little more energy into my scramble. Ten minutes later I asked a passing walker how long we have.

"About half an hour, I reckon."

I slowed down.

The mountain was messing with my mind.

A nice woman from Yorkshire told me that it's going to be hard for bit and then it eases off. There's a right turn called 'the Horseshoe' where the path levels out. That intelligence reached my ears like an oasis does to the eyes of a desert wanderer. I can picture it now. A level path. Maybe sanded roads with ice cold sparkling water on tap for us all to sup. I even began to envisage palm trees and drinks housed in half-coconut shells.

There is indeed a turn to the right. It's sharp and it's ANOTHER BLOOMING CLIMB! It also got weirder. Some of the rocks were covered with bin bags and I had no idea why. There was even a rail to hold onto as the path narrowed as it turned to the left again. Someone told me that there was a turn left coming onto the Ranger's Path which comes with a huge wind 'though not dangerous'. It sounded wonderful as I was hot and sweaty as well as cold and wet.

It really does mess with your mind.

But we got there, and it was a bit flatter though not quite as heavenly as the woman portended. I promised myself a good scowl in the direction of Yorkshire if I got to the top and I could work out in which direction it was. We were walking in cloud now and didn't know where anything was, least of all the summit which, we were told was anything from five minutes away to a couple of months.

But this was the final straight. No question of that. For a start there was now a train track next to me and the path was wider. People appeared with dogs or with bicycles over their shoulders. What's more, they were smiling. I was smiling too. The end was nigh. Just around this next bit. Or the one after.

There were steps now too rather than boulders. Sure, it was tiring, but there was more of a spring in my step now. So close. Just behind that hill, I reckon.

Serena and I were together now and, finally, three hours after we left the car park, we arrived at a final spiral staircase with a queue of people clinging to it. Atop the summit cairn is a circular plaque with names on it. Apparently, it's an orientation device and tells you which country you can see in what direction.

HA!

We could barely see the café fifty yards away, never mind Ireland! Everything was cloud. Everything.

We'd done it though. Every single person in England and Wales were below us at that moment and though a man nearly hit me with his bike as, for some reason, he absolutely had to show it to that curious gold plaque, there was an overall feeling of pride. Though that could have been exhaustion.

I won't go through what happened on the way back. I won't mention my willingness to wander off the track and take fifteen minutes to find a path which was ten metres to my right nor will I relate the time on the final stretch where Reen was looking for me and found me thrity to forty feet above her with a look of confusion on my face ('How the hell did you get up there?') Best of all, I won't tell you about my fall which resulted in a smashed knee and bent finger — an act which Serena witnessed from about fifty feet away yet couldn't hear due to the howling wind and occasional bout of hailstones.

Three hours up, four hours down. Four, long and painful hours.

So that was Snowdon. An achievement. An adventure. Something worth living for.

As we climbed into my car, we both swore I'd never do that again. I started looking at Ben Nevis routes when I got home.

You see, I want to cram in as many experiences as I can before I expire, whether that's through natural means or self-inflicted ones. My sister died at forty-eight. My dad at fifty-one. I'm fifty-one now and genetics aren't on my side.

My mind is a constant battle between emotion and logic. I know that on my worst days, I'm a decent human being. A bit of a prat at times but basically good. That's logic talking. However, my emotional side goes wildly off kilter. It crushes me into the darkest spot in the darkest room and hides me there. Emotions win most of the time, so I have to take advantage when I've got them on the ropes.

Get out there. If you've ever wanted to write, then draw up a notepad and get started. If you've always fancied playing a musical instrument, then the only thing that's stopping you is you. Fancy doing a parkrun but have never run before? Go along and walk one. Then try jogging a bit of it. You never know where it can take you.

When are you going to be here again?

Say 'yes' more.

Twitter: **@TheCenci**

Chapter 9

The Beauty of Being Indecisive

By Emma Karembo Cornthwaite

There's one question that I beg that you never ask someone when you first meet them.

There are three reasons why you shouldn't. The first is because it is just really boring. Use that glorious mind of yours. The second is because for some people (like me) it's really difficult to answer. And the third, most important reason, is because people aren't defined by their jobs or careers.

The question is of course, "So, what do you do then?"

For me there is no short answer.

My answer is normally a sigh followed by a deep breath and then... "I'm a house and pet sitter, massage therapist, expedition leader, wilderness first aider (yep, that's a job!), event organiser, fundraiser, bushcraft instructor, field cook, housewife, occasional blogger and co-manager of SayYesMore. I coordinate a team of volunteers, organise multiple events and run a global social enterprise from a converted double decker bus in the countryside!"

Most people, normally after a few seconds while they mentally digest what I've just told them, follow this up with, "So, how did you get into all this then?"

It all comes down to being indecisive. Throughout my teens I had a complete inability to choose one thing that I wanted to be. To most people, that might seem non-committal or lacking in direction. How can someone spend all their formative years not knowing what they want to be 'when they grow up'?

Well, it all started at home.

My Mum inspires me. She's an absolutely incredible human being. She's had many different careers and been brilliant at all of them.

When discussing the future, Mum would always say, "Do what makes you happy. The rest will sort itself out." That sounded simple enough, so that's what I set out to do.

When I was in school, I always wanted to be on the stage. Singing, dancing and performing was my thing. Acting didn't feature though, as I had trouble reading and speaking to an audience aloud. (I still do, usually ending up trembling and close to tears). Sadly, I was not the whole package. When auditioning in London for anything and everything, I'd often be told I was average. I was never going to make it on the stage because I was nothing special.

At that point I was thankful as ever for my practically minded mum, who always fully supported my dreams but also believed in a good backup plan. Well done, Mum!

I had already started nursing training in London, mainly so I could audition in my spare time. My mum was a nurse. Her mum was a nurse. I'd always cared for people and volunteered in my spare time;

it made sense to train in something that came so naturally to me.

I loved nursing and being surrounded by people, especially those who needed compassion and comfort. I felt like I was making a difference. I excelled at the practical 50% of the course, but struggled to keep on top of the theory side of things. I had dreams of working for Medicins Sans Frontiers (MSF) in Africa; to live with nothing but the clothes on my back, the meds in my pack and a tight knit team who worked from dawn until well into the night, powered by passion and comradery.

Then the dream crumbled. In my second year of nursing I received a letter. I had been discharged from university for failing an essay by two points. Two points! I'd retaken it with guidance from my tutors but still got the same mark. I appealed along with seven of my classmates, strangely all in the same circumstance. It was a losing battle; the faculty was striving to raise standards, and in the end we all lost.

I was beyond devastated. The ground disappeared from beneath my feet. My chest and stomach felt hollow. My brain couldn't compute what was happening and I was in shock – and this turned to panic.

What was I going to do now? Who makes a backup plan for their back up plan?!

The career I was born to do had just rejected me. I curled up on my bedroom floor surrounded by my helpless and outraged best friends, clutching the letter in my fist, sobbing so hard it hurt. We're talking full on, don't care who hears it, ugly dribbly crying, until several days later, my tears ran dry.

Eventually, my uncle came to the rescue. He gave me a job as his assistant at his recording studio, which helped to cover rent. He also gave me a kick up the butt and told me that only I had the power to control my future, that I shouldn't leave it to chance or let other people tell me that I can't make it.

Sulking got me nowhere, but I still dreamed of Africa. It was nursing that rejected me, not Africa. Nobody there even knew I existed. I owed it to myself to try it from a different angle. I looked into relief work, charities, agencies like the United Nations and World Health Organisation (WHO) but they all required a degree, even at entry-level.

I plucked up what was left of my courage and applied for a BA in International Relations and Development Studies at Westminster University... and got in. Faith in humanity and in myself restored, I was back on (albeit, a different) track to making a difference.

I continued to struggle academically. I understood my classes but had trouble translating thoughts into words and retaining facts and information long enough to impress during debates. It seemed like I didn't know the answers nor had anything to say. I was fed up of feeling stupid all the time so decided to get tested. My fears were confirmed: I had Dyslexia.

Along with most of the population, I associated poor maths and spelling with being dyslexic, and given I was average at both, I never considered that I might be. It turns out, a large part of having dyslexia is issues with memory, in particular when reading aloud or transferring words between the brain and mouth in the correct order. If only I had known during my first university attempt!

Overwhelming relief came next – I wasn't stupid, a failure or slow; I was just dyslexic. Everything was okay because now I had an explanation for my performance. It does nothing to help my head always being in the clouds or off dreaming that I was staring in a Disney movie, but it gave me confidence that I was capable of achieving the same as anyone else.

In order to get good grades and produce my best work, I had to be really passionate about the subject otherwise I wouldn't retain the information. So, I turned all my assignments into passion projects. I was aiming for Africa but had never actually been, so decided that for my final project I needed qualitative data... I needed to go there.

I researched and found a small local youth volunteering project in Kenya and asked if they needed extra hands during the summer.

Having only exchanged a couple of emails with Beth, the leader of a project in a tiny village called Bombo, and without knowing who I was meeting or where I was going, I sent Beth £400 and booked a flight. This was back in the days of chunky Nokia 3210s and internet cafes – I could hardly turn on my GPS SOS device or go on Facebook to be rescued if it all went wrong.

As I gazed out of the window on our final approach to Mombasa airport, I suddenly got fidgety. What was I doing? This was the most naïve and dangerous thing that I'd ever done. I was literally flying across the world to meet a woman I'd never met. I just trusted Beth was a good person and jumped in with both feet.

The wheels screeched on the tarmac and I was soon passing through the terminal, a rucksack bigger than my entire body slung over my shoulder and my valuables safely tucked into the security belt my Dad had insisted I wear under my clothes. I was like a sheep in a pack of imaginary wolves, feeling like a young Bambi exposed, heart pounding, sweaty palms out in a grassy meadow, consciously trying to appear as if I was 100% confident.

And then suddenly I saw a smiling lady striding through the crowd with open arms. "Emma?" she said grinning.

"You must be Beth," I said, returning the friendly smile. I was immediately at ease in her company. Beth was everything that I hoped she'd be.

Together with eight young Kenyan volunteers, we built two new classrooms for a village school using the local sticks and mud bricks method. We camped among the mud huts with no electricity, a twenty minute walk to the water well and sharing one long-drop loo between the entire village. I was accepted and protected by that community, most of which had never seen a foreigner (making babies cry by doing absolutely nothing was my specialty). I even had an initiation ceremony by the elders of the Guilliama Tribe, ensuring that I will always be welcomed back. It's how I gained my Kenyan name, 'Karembo'.

I made lifelong friends during that trip and one of them, Silas, later named his daughter after me. I still visit their family in Kenya, and we enjoy weekly video exchanges via WhatsApp. Had I never said 'yes' to volunteering with Beth, I would never have met the beautiful souls in Bombo who taught me so much. I wouldn't have enjoyed a picnic on red sand with a family of adorably curious wild giraffes, learnt Swahili or taught first aid around a campfire.

It was my initial experience of saying yes before I was ready that got the ball rolling. It led to a whole lifetime of adventures.

I achieved a First for my dissertation, which I actually loved working on and I graduated with honours, something I never thought possible.

From then on, I had the travelling bug. I wanted to get out and experience the world but also carve out my own place within it and make a difference.

Having backpacked through South East Asia and only once volunteered overseas, I still didn't have the experience needed for my dreamy job in Africa. I then landed a full-time charitable fundraising job with a UK healthcare organisation. I liked the medical link; I raised money for specialist nurses, a soft spot for me.

But after a couple of years, the magic faded. I was stuck in the work cycle, working for the weekends, many of which were spent working a second job just to keep up with rent in London. I couldn't save any money, my colleagues left without being replaced and I felt alone with my dreams of adventure slipping further and further away.

It was around then that I serendipitously discovered Escape the City, an organisation specialising in finding interesting jobs for those tiring of the city hamster wheel.

One morning I sat at my desk, surrounded by empty chairs and office tumbleweed, and updated my profile with the roles I was searching for. Within twenty minutes of clicking submit my phone rang; an invite to go for coffee. Two hours later, I said yes to quitting my job, giving notice on my flat and becoming one of the new event directors for an educational charity called Street Child. Their main fundraising event was the Sierra Leone Marathon and I was flying out in five weeks.

After googling where Sierra Leone was, I was on cloud nine! Finally, I was heading off to volunteer in West Africa, expenses paid, cost-neutral and for a charity small enough to show true financial transparency and impact.

In February 2013, I happily set off for a four-month placement in the town of Makeni. Back then Street Child was a small, haphazard machine and the in-country team weren't 100% aware of my arrival. Rather than remaining stranded at Lungi airport, I proceeded to hitchhike through this new and unknown country with a 4x4 convoy of burly Welsh miners who happened to be on my flight and vaguely heading in my direction. Eventually, after taking two days to do a journey that I later found out would normally only take four hours, I made it to my new home. I was warmly welcomed by the open arms of a chatty and excitable, blonde Belgian girl called Marie. She was a hugger, like me, so I instantly knew we'd be friends.

The Street Child compound in Makeni used to be an orphanage and school, once occupied by rebels during the civil war. They had looted the water pump and generator, which left us with no running water and sketchy electricity. We hauled water up from the well each day using a cut open jug tied to a scrawny piece of rope and carried it across the compound to shower using a cup and bucket. I had a rat living in my bedroom, which I had to name Jeremy in an attempt to make him less intimidating after weeks of failed evictions.

Also living with us were my two fellow marathon musketeers, Tracey Bravo and Mark Maughan. Both quickly became my family out there and we did everything together. We made an awesome team and working with them alongside the Sierra Leonean Street Child team was everything I imagined for my African dream and more. Working and living in Sierra Leone required constant adaptation, often being a challenge to get things done. With each hurdle, we encountered fun conjuring up creative solutions. We cried laughing every single day and were well on our way to pulling off the second ever Sierra Leone Marathon.

My life became very surreal very quickly by regular home standards, but to me it felt perfectly normal. I felt safe and at home in Makeni, more so than I ever had in London, and I wasn't ready to leave. With only three weeks left of my placement, I built up the courage to approach the CEO whilst he was over from the UK visiting our projects. With research and a practised speech to make me sound convincing, I told him where the gaps were in the organisation and how I could fill them… and why he should take me on as a full-time member of the Sierra Leone team.

I held my breath as he pondered in silence for what felt like forever, giving absolutely nothing away. My heart was pounding in my throat - would this be my dream coming true?

Being a man of few words, he simply said, "OK".

I was having the time of my life and I had just won the chance to continue living it. I bounced back to my hut, blissfully high on life.

By that point, I was making regular trips to the capital, Freetown, and building my network there. By joining the local Hash House Harriers running club, I soon found my way into most businesses in Freetown, meeting delegates from all over the world. Then I somehow wound up joining His Excellency the President of Sierra Leone for regular squash matches on his private court… a totally bonkers everyday life, but it worked.

I lived simply (the way I loved to), I had incredible friends to share weekend adventures with and every day I could actively see where my work benefited the communities around me, both at the grassroots level and further up the chain in the Ministry of Education. Street Child was becoming a force to be reckoned with and I was proud to be part of that team.

Life went on like that for a couple of years. We had struggles and triumphs as any regular lives do. We saw volunteers come and go, and we even went to neighbouring Liberia to set up Street Child there too. I was so sure of my future in Makeni that I adopted a puppy. I was the happiest I had ever been and proud to have earnt my place.

Then the unimaginable happened. In the Spring of 2014, as marathon time approached again, we started hearing reports that the Ebola virus was spreading beyond Guinea and across neighbouring Liberia. We were next.

I wished I'd kept a diary account of the months that followed. Everything moved so fast. See it as a glitch or a superpower, but my dyslexia has its perks. For example, my brain has an automatic ability to 'forget' or lock away hurtful experiences, guarding myself against harmful memories. This might be responsible for my cheery demeanour, but it can be incredibly inconvenient when trying to recall something important, no matter how awful it was. All I can say is that this period was so harrowing, so horrific, that at the time I just couldn't face writing it down or committing it to memory.

When Ebola struck Sierra Leone, it was beyond heart-breaking. When I say it 'struck', it devastated communities, wiped out entire families and suffocated every corner of the country that had become my home, shutting down any remnants of normal life.

I had numerous arguments with my Dad about 'him putting me on the next plane home'. I couldn't even consider leaving just because I was an expat and had the ability to escape. I felt I needed to stay and help in whatever way I could. Besides, I knew I could mitigate the risk by avoiding contact with everyone.

Fear was everywhere; I wasn't scared for me but frightened for my friends, my colleagues and their families, and the thousands of children under our care around the country. It was a terrifying unknown virus, which developed far faster than we were able to fight it.

In a region of the world where many people had never had a biology lesson, many couldn't comprehend the notion of bacteria and how it spreads. Understandably, rural communities rejected the people in alien-looking hazmat suits who came to forcefully quarantine their family members. School and public gatherings were banned for months. With no end in sight, Street Child came up with a way that teachers could deliver the curriculum over the radio so that children could still attempt to learn.

Eventually, Ebola reached Makeni, striking two streets from ours and that's when it felt a little too close. It was a confusing time listening to the clouded lies from the local press (mostly in denial) and, on the other side, international reports heavily sensationalising everything. Luckily, a friend of mine, a lead advisor to the President and WHO during the outbreak, was able to let us know what the reality was.

The government began closing district borders in an attempt to contain the virus so we needed to leave Makeni. We arranged transport home for eighteen international volunteers and relocated to Freetown where we could still work.

It was usually such a cheery drive to the capital. Today was very different. We passed deserted streets and towns on lockdown. On the rare occasion we did see people, they were sobbing on their knees in the streets or working in hazmat suits. I felt numb. It was immensely surreal, as if the car was our bubble of protection during this immersive fly-on-the-wall nightmare of a reality.

Eventually, we were told that expats not working in direct response to the crisis, whether clinically or within the government, had to evacuate not only for their own safety but because for no reason other than their nationality: if they were to contract the virus, they'd drain resources from hundreds of others to repatriate them home. It would have been irresponsible and unfair to stay.

I returned to London with my colleague, Grace, and we lived week-to-week in a short-term let waiting for any positive news to indicate things were improving, hoping to return home soon. We watched from afar, completely helpless, hearing of friends and colleagues who lost the battle, lost family members, children becoming orphans and parents to younger siblings. The best we could do was campaign for more funds from the UK, Europe and the USA to be sent over for all those in need. I became fundraising manager for Street Child and we worked around the clock to raise over £6m towards the recovery effort in the aftermath of Ebola.

Personal experience mixed with passion made returning to fundraising a natural step. It only helped that my natural response to public speaking nerves mingled with my emotions over the trauma. It always resulted in tears on stage when appealing to crowds of bankers!

Things eventually began to improve in-country, and I was finally cleared to go back for visits. Having carved out the fundraising job in London, the CEO didn't want me to go back permanently. I was making a difference from afar, but that satisfaction was marred with depression. I had lots of friends around me, but they couldn't possibly understand what had happened. Sierra Leone was on its knees due to this crisis and I was utterly devastated for the country and for the people that I loved and left behind.

To add to that angst, I was dealing with the loss of eleven dearly loved family members and friends in quick succession that year so I really wasn't in a healthy headspace at all. My heart felt like it was heavier than a lead balloon while at the same time being as brittle as a poorly formed eggshell. Any more tiny cracks in its surface would cause a fault line so big that it would bring the whole thing caving in, crashing down on itself.

I felt guilty for so many reasons: for leaving Sierra Leone to suffer so deeply, for still being able to draw breath and feeling sorry for myself because of it all. As a penance, I worked long hours in the office and at home on the weekends. My work became my life. I had tunnel vision, and that tunnel was aiming south with no exits.

I needed change, something to snap me out of the downward spiral. Just at the right moment, I was introduced to a crazily over-positive group of rainbow-coloured exercise unicorns called Project Awesome (PA). They saved me and brought me back to life a little.

A PA friend, Kate Davis, told me that the guy who started the Sierra Leone Marathon had given the blueprint to another group wanting to start a similar project in Uganda, so I went along to show support at their launch party at Escape the City in 2015. I still really wasn't in the right frame of mind to be surrounded by people but it was the first time I'd been out for months. It felt good but also overwhelming.

That was the first time I properly met Dave.

I had vaguely followed his adventures online and thought he was devilishly attractive, so when he offered to walk me to the tube, I blushed, stared at the floor and (of course) said yes.

Only when we were walking did I realise that I was on the verge of tears with a lump in my throat. Everything, all the emotions that had been building over the last few months, was weighing heavily on my mind. I couldn't have been very good company, so I was very relieved that it was a short distance to the station. It took all my strength not to burst into floods when I melted into one of the best hugs I had ever received.

I was content for a while, working all hours and slowly clawing back some 'me time' thanks to the influence of fun and happy people in my life again. I didn't see Dave again for months.

Through Project Awesome and my continued friendship with

Tracey, I discovered The YesTribe. At first, I was hesitant to join because I felt I wasn't cool enough (go figure!), but I was exponentially ecstatic when I finally did. I had found this wonderful collection of humans who were just there and always said yes to doing things together. People of all backgrounds and ages who didn't judge, didn't ask questions and accepted who I was on any given day. People who just wanted to make the most of what they had, make good memories and who were just inherently good. I had found my tribe.

The Sierra Leone Marathon was moved from May to October in 2015 due to Ebola, so I was away during the first Yestival. Things really took a turn for me when Casey, a YesTriber in Scotland posted she had a free house over New Year, and she and her lovely mum invited the Tribe to fill their home to celebrate.

Sixteen strangers travelled up and it was glorious to be out in the open air on the West Coast in the middle of rugged nowhere. Icy winds whipped hair around my face and my fingertips turned blue from the cold, but no one had any expectations other than to give out the goodness they had brought with them.

Those few days in Scotland were magical. They helped me to start thinking clearly and more positively. It was also where Dave and I shared our first real conversations (he couldn't escape as he had his leg in a cast after breaking it on his latest expedition) and I started to see that there was a life beyond this two-year funk I'd been living in.

I stayed at Street Child for a further nine months after Sierra Leone was declared Ebola-free in March. By the time I handed in my resignation, in the year since meeting Dave, I had said yes to an impromptu adventure in Bali, ran my first ever marathon (my last Sierra Leone Marathon), and attempted my second marathon at altitude in Nepal. I became Tracey's birthing partner (read about it in The Bigger Book of Yes!), helped create Yestival 2016 and I moved into a houseboat with the man beyond any dreams I ever had. I was making a plan to be a forever kind of happy again.

I felt I needed a new challenge and had done all I could for Street Child. I didn't have a clue what was next but knew I needed space to figure out what it was. Ever the fan of a good back up plan, within a week of becoming unemployed, I enrolled on a course to become a qualified massage therapist. It was a fall back while I searched for my next solid 'thing'.

Expeditions were on the calendar with Camps International again, taking teenage groups overseas. The YesBus needed a crowdfunding campaign to fund its conversion so I managed the project. As time went on, I kept saying yes to opportunities that brought about new experiences, and over time, I accumulated random jobs and skills.

In the Spring of 2017, Dave and I went on our first big adventure together, following the Danube River from Germany to Budapest on a random tandem bike called a Hase Pino. Five weeks of cycling on a tandem through storms and camping together was definitely what some people would call a 'make or break' kind of trip. But we had so much fun laughing our way through every day and falling even deeper for each other.

This was Dave's thirteenth thousand-plus mile adventure, whereas I had never done any long-distance endurance anything, except for hobbling through a marathon, which isn't really on the same scale, is it? He supported me through it, and I loved him more for pushing me to achieve such a massive journey with him.

I assumed he was glad with how it went because on the day we hit the thousand mile mark, he got down on one knee and asked me to be his husband... Nope, that's not a typo!

So, to return to the original question of how I got into all this, the short answer is, "Definitely not by design!"

I wouldn't be where I am now and living this life if I hadn't failed all those times and been forced to find a new path. Each one has shaped me, delivering me to this point.

The easiest way to describe what I do is, "I am a freelancer." I just happen to freelance in more things than there are days of the week. I have never been a career junkie or money-focussed, not because I have always had money (I've been great friends with my overdraft over the years), but because I am motivated by happiness and a drive to help. Whether it's helping people, animals or the planet, I am happiest when I am doing good.

I've learnt to live within my means and spend less than I earn. Having the freedom to make and take opportunities as they come is what enriches our lives. I am constantly learning from the best - my husband inspires me with what he has achieved and continues to accomplish. He's definitely the most hard-working and time efficient productivity ninja I have ever met.

I'm still working things out and probably forever will be, but for now my 'full-time job' is looking after all things SayYesMore, from managing the YesBus to helping our voluntary team on a daily basis. From developing the website to applying for financial grants, from curating Yestival to designing artwork for merchandise – the list goes on. It doesn't matter if the 'job' doesn't come with a salary, it produces awesome outcomes spreading plenty of joy and confidence for people who least expect it.

My 'holidays' are when I take time out to wear one of my other hats and actually earn some money. It's not a perfect system, but for now, it works. Every day is different by choice and I am so happy with the variety it all brings. I'm grateful for what it is constantly challenging in me.

Who knows what the future will look like. There are still a bunch of jobs I have always wanted to try and hopefully still will. This year alone I hope to become a paddleboarding instructor and up my bushcraft game by learning to whittle more than just a tent peg. We are selling our adorable houseboat and searching for a spot of land to call home and develop into a camp/glamp site and new home for YesLand. Among a long list of ambitions, I would still love to become a mum, farm alpacas and bees, start a plastic-clever business, become a scuba instructor and oceans advocate, teach forest school and become a travel writer. That should keep me busy for a while!

One thing that I have learnt is that just because you fail, it doesn't make you a failure, and neither does having multiple vocations. If one path doesn't work out, it's ok because there are always other options to say yes to.

I suppose that is where the beauty of being indecisive really comes into its own.

Website: **www.sayyesmore.com**

Instagram: **@emkarembo**

Chapter 10

Ticket to South-East Asia

By Sue Crawley

We arrived in hot, steamy Bangkok. Despite it being late in the evening, the streets were buzzing with people. Mopeds and tuktuks darted in and out of the traffic peeping their little horns erratically. Locals and tourists funnelled along the pavements dodging street vendors. Steam rose from the roadside cafés as all manner of foods were being cooked under the open sky.

I watched all this from the inside of my cab, the window rolled down and the exquisite, exotic cooking smells drifting in with the car fumes. We were on our way to a five-star hotel, a present from a good friend and the only night of luxury we would have on this trip.

I looked in amazement at the city as it whizzed past my window and wondered how on earth I had got here. I'd had a full and interesting career in Education for over forty years spending much of it as a Special Educational Needs Advisor. I'd been working eighty-five-hour weeks for the last two years and it had just about finished me off!

I looked over to my husband, Dave, as he sat in the other side of the taxi, his gaze fixed on the lights and sights of the city.

A couple of years earlier, Dave had had a heart attack. Subsequently we had talked about changing our lifestyle and making the most of every day. Our three children had grown up, left home and all had their own careers. So why not realise my dream of taking off with nothing but a backpack and a plane ticket? I could retire NOW and say YES to the adventure of a lifetime! It just felt that it was the right time and if we didn't do it now, would we ever do it?

Little did I know that the adventures we were about to experience would change my outlook on life forever! Friends, who thought I was crazy to do this and had tried to put me off this adventure, may have been right. But I am so glad I came!

I had thought about taking a trip like this for many years. I had seen our children take gap years and explore Europe, Africa and Asia. I had enjoyed their adventures vicariously, but now it was my time to live my dream!

Dave turned to face me and gave me an enthusiastic little smile. He hadn't initially jumped at the idea of backpacking around South East Asia. This was going to be so very different and completely out of our comfort zone! But now we were here, I could see he was really going to enjoy it.

We'd actually visited Thailand before when, for our 50th birthday, Dave and our three girls, Lauren, Hannah and Nicky, had taken an adventure tour around the country. I'd loved it and I couldn't wait to be back.

But this was going to be a trip with a difference. Last time we'd been here, we'd planned every last little detail. I didn't want that this time. I wanted to experience a real adventure off the beaten track. The whole point was to just go and see where the adventure would take us!

I laughed as I pictured us; two sixty-two-year-olds taking off with just a backpack and a plane ticket to the other side of the world!

Would my arthritic knees be up to the task? Would Dave, with his bagful of medication, be ok? Should we really set off with no plans at all? Where would this trip take us? At this point I had no idea! This was madness but if we didn't try, I would probably regret it for the rest of my life.

We decided, as Thailand was renowned for beautiful islands, we would start by travelling around some of these. Countless Instagram accounts showed images of white sands with beach bungalows and hilltop huts snuggled on the edge of the jungle. It looked like heaven!

As we arrived on the jetty to board the boat, it was chaos! Ferries, longboats and speedboats filled every open patch of quayside. Hundreds of people were milling around looking for their vessels. The sweltering sun beat down on us as we queued to buy a ticket. After over an hour of frustrating disorganisation, being moved to several different queues, we eventually purchased a ticket and were given stickers to put on our T- shirt and rucksack indicating which island we were going to.

We were herded towards the jetty, and amid the shouting and pushing, with locals trying to sell their wares and the stifling heat, we boarded a small ferry.

We made our way to the top deck and just prayed that our rucksacks would follow us onto the boat from the massive pile of luggage that was on the quayside. We really just had to put our trust in the local men who were throwing luggage onto different boats.

The breeze on the deck, as we sped across the water past limestone rocks jutting out of the sea, was a welcome relief after the intense heat on the land. The wind lifted my hair, and the splash of salt water on my face made me feel happy and relaxed.

After an hour and a half, we started to slow down as the colourful boats moored in the island port came into view.

We disembarked along with around fifty other travellers. With bated breath we waited. Finally we saw our rucksacks fly through the air and land on the quayside. PHEW! How could we have doubted that their system would work?

There were over twenty songthaews outside the port waiting for the passengers as they disembarked. These vehicles are a combination of truck and minibus; an open truck with bench seats and a cab for the driver. Again there was chaos as everybody tried to find the songthaew that was to take them onwards to their accommodation.

We had checked the map and seen that our accommodation, that we had booked just the day before, was about two miles away. We could walk it. It was only a short distance, and it would give us a chance to see what was around the area. We slung our rucksacks onto our backs and trudged down the road, Dave leading the way.

It was a fairly flat walk, which we appreciated. With sweat dripping down our foreheads and T-shirts sticking to our back, we sauntered along the beach. Crystal clear, azure water lapped the beautiful clean sand. Alongside the beach there were many cafés, bars and restaurants. The buzz of people chatting and the smell of delicious noodles filled the air as we made our way to our homestay.

There were a number of stalls advertising snorkelling trips, and as we had decided to stay here for a couple of days, we booked one of these trips. This adventure was full on, no more than three days in any one place, so that we could cram as many experiences as possible into the trip.

The next morning we got up early, walked to the port, grabbed a noodle breakfast and caught the excursion. It included stops at some of the 'most beautiful snorkelling spots' in Thailand. We couldn't wait!

We were given a safety briefing and were ready to board. As we snaked along the path to the boat, I noticed the lady in front wearing bright pink water sneakers with, whom I assumed, was her daughter. She stood out as most people were wearing flip flops. I took no more notice as we all set off on the boat to the first snorkelling site.

As we arrived at the snorkelling site, the boat was rocking while waves aggressively slapped the hull. Not what I expected! The captain said, "You've got half an hour and make sure you came back to *this* boat!"

Once in the water I could see what he meant. There were so many boats, all looking similar, and around a hundred snorkelers in the water.

I swam off looking for fish but found it difficult to keep an even keel. The waves were choppy and buffeting me around. I consider myself to be a strong swimmer, but even I was uncomfortable. I looked up and trod water, lifting my mask to see if I could catch a glimpse of Dave.

I couldn't see him! My heart was pounding as I glanced about. By now most of the other snorkelers had swum back to the boats. I could see three boats left but wasn't sure which was ours. What if I got on the wrong one? Would our boat leave without me? Would they have to send a search party to find me?

Then, miraculously, I saw Dave's head bobbing in and out of the waves just ahead of me. I shouted to him, but the sea was choppy and he kept disappearing from view. I shouted again. He obviously couldn't hear me. I lost sight of him again, but I'd made a decision. Dave was on a course for the boat on the left. I decided to follow his lead and just hope that it was the correct boat.

It seemed that I was swimming against the tide. As I battled my way through the water, I could feel the current pulling me back. My anxiety was growing by the second. I had to get out of this! I used all my stamina and swimming technique to fight the swell, but as I moved a little nearer to the boat, I seemed to be pushed back again. The boat seemed to be moving further away!

The saltwater crashed over my head and filled my mouth as I coughed and spluttered it out. My eyes were stinging as, again, I tried to look around to see if Dave had made it to safety. After what seemed an age of swimming with all my strength, my legs and arms aching like I'd done a workout, I eventually made it to the boat, weary and worried.

As I heaved my tired body out of the water, I was relieved to see Dave's face smiling back at me. He offered me a towel and I sat on one of the benches, completely drained.

All of a sudden, I noticed a commotion on the boat next to ours. All I could see was someone with pink shoes being hauled out of the water. I joined Dave who was in conversation with a French couple we had met. As we tried to speak in the little French we knew and they tried to respond in English, we discussed the uproar.

Suddenly, a young girl of around fifteen ran to the bow and tried to leap across onto the other boat. We reached out to stop her. We were concerned for her safety.

"That's my mum!" she cried. "She's unconscious!"

At this point, amid the hullabaloo, the crew lifted the lady with the pink shoes and transferred her to the stern of our boat.

An English lady, Gilly, who we had spoken to briefly, and another French lady took the girl to her mother.

After what seemed like an age (it was probably nearly an hour) the French lady returned from the stern. Tears poured down her cheeks and she gabbled quickly, apparently trying to explain what had happened. We tried desperately to work out what was being said, but we couldn't make any sense of it at all.

It was at this point that Gilly sat down near us, her ashen face completely drained of colour. I moved over to sit next to her and asked if she was okay.

"I've been a nurse for thirty years," she said, her voice weak and quaking. "I've given resuscitation to many people. This is the first time I've ever failed."

I put my arms around her shoulders and held her. "You did everything you could."

I wrestled with my conscience. Why didn't I notice the pink shoes in the water? If I had seen her in trouble, maybe I could have done something to help. The crew and passengers tried to comfort her daughter. The boat turned back to port and, as we arrived, doctors, medics and nurses were waiting to put her mother on a trolley and carry her to the hospital.

The captain made the decision to continue with the trip! "What? Surely not!" Nobody really wanted to snorkel after what had happened. The mood was very sombre. Everybody felt so upset and so sorry for the lady and her daughter.

The time passed but I can't really remember much of the rest of the day. It was all a bit of a daze. I think we were all just thinking about what had happened and wondering if we could have, should have, done more.

When we eventually disembarked, we saw the daughter with the rest of her family. As she saw us, she burst into tears. "My mum's died!"

It was such an awful tragedy in such an idyllic location. How fragile life is. If I hadn't realised before, I knew now that I must make the most of every second of my life and be grateful for everything I have. Life is so unpredictable and vulnerable that we should make the most of the precious time we have to live.

This accident could have happened to anyone of us on that boat. I was reminded of a saying I heard recently, 'Leaving your home and getting back safely is such an underrated blessing', and in that moment it was so true.

*

The road to the jungle village in Sumatra stretched for miles. There must have been at least thirty-five miles of palm oil plantations. Hundreds of thousands of palm trees were planted in straight lines. They'd replaced the natural habitat. This was a real concern as wildlife, including orangutans, monkeys, rhinos, tigers, sun bears and pygmy elephants, were becoming extinct as a consequence. But this wasn't solely due to the palm oil plantations. Farmers were burning down trees to plant crops and shooting animals that took their crops. I guess it is the world-wide problem of getting the balance between protecting these wonderful animals and allowing local people to farm and survive. Nothing is ever black and white!

The drive to the jungle village was a little hairy to say the least. It seemed the drivers just put their foot down and overtook anything; cart, scooter, lorry, car, buffalo, regardless of any vehicles coming towards them. The roads were full of pot holes, the likes of which we had never seen in England, but our driver didn't bother to slow down as we bumped and jolted our way towards the village. A number of times, I thought we would collide head on with a lorry only to stop inches away from a catastrophe.

After a number of near misses, we arrived. I had never felt happier than stepping out of that jeep.

The jungle was inhospitable. The rainforest was dense. The rain had started a few hours earlier and we were now soaked through to the skin.

We climbed up hills and down ravines through the jungle looking for orangutans. Our guides, Ibo and Jimmi, had spotted some movement in the canopy above. "There! There they are!"

I couldn't see anything!

"Look over there to the right of the giant Dipterocarp tree!"

And there they were, a mother and baby orangutan sitting in a tree eating fruit. This was what we had come for. We spent some time watching the two orangutans interact. We were the only ones around and this was a special moment watching the mother and baby.

The guides said we really should be moving on if we were going to reach camp before dark. Ibo asked, "Do you want to take the easy route or walk the longer route along the river to the campsite?" As I was determined to experience this adventure to the full, I asked which route we were more likely to see wildlife.

"The longer route will have more wildlife," said Ibo before he sucked his teeth and looked down at my legs, "but with your knees, maybe you should take the easier route to camp."

I was determined to ignore my arthritic knees and opted for the second, more challenging, route to see these beautiful creatures.

By this time the rain was torrential. I couldn't see in front of my face. My glasses were steamed up and the terrain was becoming even more slippery. The ground was lethal and my feet slipped as we made our way down the steep gullies. I clung onto tree roots with one hand and Ibo's hand with the other as we descended down the ravine towards the riverbed.

Suddenly, my feet gave way and my grip on Ibo was no more. The root I was holding was wrenched out of my hand and I plummeted down the ravine and fell on the rocks. I was winded and stunned.

I looked back up at the rest of the group. I must have fallen around twelve feet to the bottom of a gorge. The guides rushed to my aid and, concerned for my welfare, asked if I was okay.

I wasn't! I was in agony from the sharp pain in my ribs and the dull ache in my shoulder. I asked for a few minutes to regain my composure. I knew this was really my fault as I had gone against their advice to take the easier route, and this was the result! I said I was fine as I certainly didn't want to cut short this adventure and I didn't want the guides to worry. I took a double dose of painkillers that I had in my backpack for my knees and carried on.

Eventually, we arrived at our camp, a piece of tarpaulin stretched over some bamboo; our bed for the night. We bathed in the river fully clothed; our bathroom for the night! It was such a relief to be at the camp. The smell of the supper being on cooked on an open fire was very welcoming.

I took some more painkillers as we changed into some dryer clothes. Then we moved under the tarpaulin to enjoy the meal that had been prepared; a real feast. The guides had cooked rich, aromatic vegetable Rendang, Nasi Goreng and creamy Bubur jagung, a corn dessert, followed by fruit bursting with freshness; bananas, mango and dragon fruit.

After the meal, we played what Ibo called 'mind games'. What did this involve? Not what I had imagined thankfully! These were a series of challenges based on lateral thinking that Ibo and Jimmi gave us to solve. "How do you make fifty-six out of five matches?"

Dave was showing his mathematical prowess and getting most of the challenges right, but I really couldn't focus on the tasks. By now, the painkillers were wearing off and the excruciating pain was throbbing across my shoulders, ribs and side. Not wishing to be rude and not wanting to admit how much pain I was in, I stayed until Ibo and Jimmi had finished their quite considerable repertoire before crawling onto our rubber mat and trying to settle for the night.

I don't really know how I got through that night. I took another double dose of painkillers and hoped I could get at least a little sleep. Not a chance! The pain was agonising and every time I tried to move I was reminded of my fall. The rain was still torrential and the noise on the tarpaulin was deafening.

As I lay there, trying to ignore the pain and blank out the noises of the rain and screeching jungle sounds, I eventually drifted off to sleep... for about twenty minutes, through sheer exhaustion. But that was about it. As soon as I moved, I was woken up by the sharp stabbing pain across my back. How was I going to get through the next few days trekking?

After what seemed like an endless night the sun rose and we were up and on our way again along the river through the jungle. I couldn't just pop into a chemist so I had to manage the pain in the best way I could.

Three excruciating days later we were out of the jungle and I managed to find a local doctor who gave me a remedy that helped me to manage the injury for the rest of our trip.

A couple of months later I had a proper diagnosis: I'd survived the whole trek with broken ribs and torn shoulder ligaments.

*

After a very peaceful journey on a slow boat along the Mekong River through Laos and into Thailand, we decided this was enough relaxation. We needed more action!

We chose to indulge in Dave's passion for motorbikes. Dave knew of a route called 'The Golden Triangle' in Northern Thailand that linked Chang Mai, Chang Rai and Pai.

We picked up the hefty beast, a Honda CB500 early one morning, and as I rode pillion, we made our way through the busy traffic out of the city and into the countryside. The breeze on our face was most welcoming after the stifling heat of the city. The smog caused from farmers burning the fields had given Chang Mai the ignominious title of 'most polluted city in the world' on this particular day!

We enjoyed the freedom of the open road and arrived at our homestay in good spirits. After a delicious meal of Pad Thai and

Massaman curry, we slept until sunrise, exhausted after the first day's ride.

And then we were off on the road again. We had looked at the map the previous night and had decided to divert from the recommended route. Instead we took a road along the Myanmar boarder of northern Thailand and down into Pai. I say we, but really it was me that wanted to get off the beaten track and have an adventure within an adventure! Dave was very sceptical. But the road was definitely there marked on the map!

Later in the day, we would question this decision.

The road was fairly good to begin with and, apart from the predictable pot holes, we were making good time. Passing paddy fields and forests we saw literally hundreds of temples and Buddhas that would suddenly pop up along the roadside. It seemed that around every corner there was another Wat. The warm breeze on our faces and the wonderful aroma of the roadside stalls, selling all kinds of spicy delicacies, made for a very pleasant ride through the hills and valleys of northern Thailand. It was extremely peaceful despite the regular jolt as we hit another pothole.

After a short time, the road changed from concrete and potholes to stone and shingle. The bumpy ride became difficult as we tried to keep our balance. The bike's tyres were slipping around dangerously on the lose surface.

Suddenly, the road became a hundred times worse! The road surface had disappeared and was now two feet deep mud! We stopped and looked at the map again to check we were on the exact route. Yes, it seems we were on the right road but our craving for adventure and trying to take a route high in the mountains meant we were now on a road that was almost impassable.

We had two choices. We could either turn back and take the long route round to Pai. We'd risk riding in the dark and arriving late into the night. Or we could continue and hope that this road would improve drastically. We decided to plough on.

Big Mistake! The road turned up a steep incline and the mud deepened with ruts and a ravine on either side. We tried to get a run up the hill and went for it. The wheels became stuck in the deep mud and the bike fell over with us underneath. We couldn't move for a few minutes as we lay there taking in what had just happened.

Slowly, as we pushed the bike off so that we could free our sore bodies, we realised that the back box had broken off and the passenger foot plate has completely sheared through. We checked ourselves for any serious injuries, but we were just cut and bruised.

We retrieved the box, managed to fix it back on and decided to push the bike up the hill. Like a guardian angel appearing out of nowhere, a Good Samaritan suddenly stopped in his 4x4 truck and helped to push our bike to the summit. We were grateful to this kind man as, by now, I realised I had injured my shoulder again trying to lift the bike, seven weeks after the first injury in the jungle.

It was difficult balancing on the back of the bike without a foot pedal and with the bike continuing to slide around through the mud. We tried to make it down the next hill but the back wheel slid away, and again, we fell off the bike down the side of the track and into the trees lining the road. This time the front pedal broke off and Dave was stuck under the bike as I was thrown against a tree.

We lay there unable to move, but then very slowly we heaved the bike up. Dave's shirt was torn and his shoulder was bleeding. I had fallen on my ribs, which had exacerbated the previous injury. Things weren't going well!

The third fall occurred as we tried to take a run up another hill. By now we were battered, bruised, sore and more than a little anxious that we would not make it to Pai.

The light was fading fast. The evening jungle noises had started and the shrieks and howls were getting louder. I was concerned that we would have to spend the night in the jungle when all I wanted was to lay my weary, sore body on a bed.

It was just as we were in our most desperate moment that we came to a police block. We were stopped and questioned. The kind police officers informed us that it was only a few kilometres down the valley to Pai. The lights of Pai were twinkling in the distance. What a relief!

The last kilometres, with only one foot pedal each, was a skill in itself, trying to balance and keep the bike stable. We arrived in Pai exhausted, our clothes torn and bodies bloody and bruised. The dust was thick in our hair, and we were covered in mud. We must have looked like we had come out of a war zone, judging by the reaction from our hosts at the homestay, who rushed out with first aid kit and cooling towels. The welcome sight of this lovely couple, who greeted us and offered us hot tea, was the best feeling, a mixture of relief and ecstasy. We were safe and had made it almost in one piece!

*

This trip involved travelling 29,000 miles through eight countries and twelve islands. It took me outside my comfort zone and inside some amazing countryside and challenged me in so many ways! We took planes, trains, boats, tuktuks, ferries, songthaews, motorbikes, coaches, scooters, slow boats, buses, speedboats, minibuses, bicycles, taxis/Grabs/Gojecs and walked hundreds of miles. We visited islands, mountains, jungles, beaches and inner cities festooned with rats and cockroaches, and all in very basic accommodation. We experienced many fantastic moments.

Truly this was the trip of a lifetime, and the memories will remain with me forever. But what stood out was the amazing, friendly people who had shown so much kindness. People who had much less than us but who were willing to share everything with us; food and water shared by a group of local women on a train through Malaysia; the guy in one village who took over an hour to fix our scooter and offered us cold drinks and food whilst we waited but charged us less than a bottle of beer for his troubles; the lovely lady at one of our homestays who got up at 4.30am to take us to the port on the back of her scooter but would not accept any money; the gift carved by the guide to remember our trek through the jungle; the ethnic groups in Laos who had very little but appeared so happy as their children played in the dust with no toys.

We learned a lot from these wonderful people. They had nothing but they may have had more than any of us! I will always remember the lovely man we met on our trip who told us that if it doesn't affect your health and doesn't leave you out of pocket, then just help someone. Be that person that does the good deed. Make someone smile!

This experience has shaped the rest of my life. I learnt that you can overcome difficulties because your difficulties are often nothing compared to others' hardships. I learnt that you can be kind and it makes such a difference to how people feel. I learnt that you should try to go about your life with a smile, even when things become difficult. I learnt that you should certainly make the most of every second of life as you never know when it may be your last!

Life is fragile, unpredictable and precious, so make the most of every opportunity and don't be afraid to say YES even if it is outside of your comfort zone!

I am now living this life trying to do what I can to help others on a daily basis and volunteering when I can. And do you know what? It feels good to help and to try to put a smile on other people's faces.

Instagram: **@backpacker62**

Facebook: **sue.crawley.560**

Chapter 11

Ama Dablam

By Jason Day

Life gets in the way. It's a truism, but occasionally you reach a point where you get the chance to say 'yes' and alter course. This is the story of how things came down to a choice like that for me. I have always been a climber, first trees and walls, then rocks, then mountains. My first visit to Nepal was to trek in the Himalayas in 1992. It was a chance to walk the paths of my heroes of the 70s and 80s, people like Doug Scott and Dougal Haston, who I had seen on Blue Peter climbing Everest. Nepal lived up to all my expectations, the colours, the people, the smells, the smell of the people. It was as if I had stepped back into a mediaeval world, all set in a shining land of snow and mountain peaks flooded with sunlight under a pure blue sky. It was intoxicating.

My stand out moment on the trek was rounding a corner to be confronted with a view of the *most* beautiful mountain. Ama Dablam is in the Khumbu, not far from Everest. It is a lower summit (6848m) but that central pillar rising from the outstretched arms of the South and North-West Ridges is genuinely breath-taking. I stood there with my mouth open. I promised myself I would come back and climb to that fluted, symmetrical summit. I was already a competent rock climber, and beginner alpinist, but I needed more experience in the mountains.

As I said, 'Life gets in the way'. As much as I wanted to climb, I wanted to have a family, and back in the UK I fell into relationships with non-climbing girlfriends, who said they'd travel the world with me, but really wanted to settle. I got married. I had a job I didn't really enjoy, but it paid the bills. Marriage and children was an absolute joy, but over time my climbing withered. I became a teacher, which I loved, though not the preparation and paperwork that goes with it. More time passed, I had a wonderful family, but I saw too little of them beyond the demands of school.

Eventually it all came crashing down. I became separated from my wife and was threatened with not being able to see my children, my ability to work collapsed. I burnt out – I was at my lowest point. What I desperately needed was a sense of achievement again, a sense of self. I was approaching forty, trying to mend emotionally, but fragile and with a very low opinion of myself.

Climbing came to my rescue – on a UK climbing website I found a wanted ad: "Partners sought to climb Ama Dablam" in the autumn of 2006. This was a scratch team using up spare places on a climbing permit. We would use Base Camp facilities and food on a guided expedition, but as far as the climbing went we would be on our own, carrying our own loads and our one tent from camp to camp on the mountain. A short meeting was arranged. Sadly we couldn't schedule any training climbs, but we were good to go... Did I want to go? I said yes.

There is a golden rule of adventurous climbing – know your partners. Know their interests, abilities, strengths and weaknesses. Know that they will back you up, or talk you out of a foolhardy situation. Know that they are capable. Know that they have your back. Did I know that about the other two guys in the team?

No I didn't.

That omission would have consequences on the mountain, but still – the expedition was a ray of hope for me. My mental wellbeing improved now that I had a goal to work towards. I got fit. I climbed more. I saw the children when I was allowed. And I worked as a supply teacher to raise the necessary cash. September rolled around and I flew out to Kathmandu to meet up with the others. We immediately set out on a four week round of acclimatisation trekking. This was a blessed time for me, a reset to 1992 and the beginning of my dreams of a life more firmly based in the mountains.

Mountain life is hard when you have the tourist choice to visit or go, but the people who make their lives there don't have that choice. The environment breeds openness to cooperation backed up with steely resolve. The Sherpa people have this and more, for their society is founded on Buddhism. It's an eminently practical religion – you will be reincarnated, but Karma is the spiritual payback for how you have lived this life. In a mountain environment where you depend on the kindness of others, and the selfless support of your community, Buddhism promotes and supports these ideals. Being in the mountains with these people was heaven.

We spent a few days in Namche Bazaar, which had expanded considerably since I had first been there, and then set out to acclimatise. Climbing high in the day and sleeping at a lower altitude in the evening forced our bodies to produce more red blood cells. Over time we became more able to cope with the reduced pressure of the oxygen in the atmosphere. Headaches, dizziness and nausea caused by low oxygen saturation in our bloodstream abated, and we found we could walk faster and longer between rest stops.

We climbed up to Donag Tse, a jagged peak of 5,500m altitude north of Gokyo, pushing our altitude limit. From there we crossed the Ngozumpa Glacier, heading East over the Cho La (5,400m) towards Dzongla. This was an emotional moment for me, the site of my first view of Ama. I stood in a biting wind, skinny flakes of snow swirling around me, staring at the route we would be climbing. Then I had dreams; now those dreams were possibilities – nothing was certain. Ama Dablam was the highest peak I would ever have attempted and to make a mistake there could very possibly be fatal. I would have to make good choices. As I thought this, I looked at my climbing companions and wondered if I had made good choices. No doubt they were doing the same for me. Getting cold, we turned aside from Ama, with her glittering fluted dress of snow and the massive jewel at her throat, and trudged on down to the tea houses of Dzongla.

After three weeks we descended the Khumbu valley to Namche. The air became scented with rhododendron and wood smoke and thick with oxygen. In the Everest bakery in Namche, we ate cinnamon rolls and talked over the expedition members' experience and expectations for the trip. Our group aimed to be as self-sufficient as possible above Base Camp. The re-ascent to Ama Dablam Base Camp through the Khumbu valley was another one of scent filled air, chanting, incense and colour. Arrival at Base Camp was followed by a puja ceremony as the sherpas set up a shrine and prayer flags. A monk chanted and blessed us with handfuls of smoking herbs, throwing rice into the air as an offering to the spirits of the mountain. With all that as a prelude, and the sherpas to provide endless smiling encouragement, how could anything go wrong?

We settled to the routines of Base Camp life – checking on the weather, further acclimatisation walks and eating. The food was excellent. The sherpas had a cook tent and turned out plenty of filling food around the theme of potatoes, eggs and onions. The weather was clear – biting cold in the pre-dawn, but as the sun reached our camp, steam spiralled off frosted tents and the sherpas came round with breakfast tea.

We were keen to press on and it was agreed that we should set off a few days after arriving in Base Camp. The route leads up and over the glacial moraine ridges, and despite our month long acclimatisation, we were soon puffing in the rarefied air.

Doubts seeped into my mind – would I go as slowly higher up? Surely we had been higher before? But your body loses acclimatisation faster than it gains it, so we just had to do the work again.

The altitude worked differently on each of us. I puffed and panted, like a leaky steam train for the first part of the morning. The others struggled in their own ways, one with headaches, the other with nausea. We spent the night at advance base – halfway between Base Camp and Camp One. Inhospitable and uncomfortable, it is full of boulders deposited when the glaciers melted. We shifted things around and eventually settled in for food and rest.

I say rest – the noise of the wind on the tent, nausea and headaches, and a rebellious digestive system, all resulted in brief naps interspersed with an open-eyed questioning of my own sanity. We were still evaluating each other's performance. I was the oldest, and was very aware of my laboured breathing. Other than that I was in good shape, but one of the others was struggling – and had a really bad night of headaches and nausea. He was worried about the effect of altitude and couldn't rest. This was something that would alter the shape of our climb later on.

The next day we climbed to Camp One – the first real climbing that we had done, as the angle imperceptibly changed from walking to requiring the use of hands here and there, to the point where a fall was possible.

There were fixed ropes here, strung up on the mountain by the sherpas to provide a lifeline. The idea was that you clipped your harness onto the rope and hence the mountain. If you should slip, a one way clamp would grip, preventing a fall. The main point here of course is that these are not ropes that we had put in place – they have been placed by previous climbers and sherpas. The ropes may be worn, battered by the winds and constant contact with rock, bludgeoned by ultra-violet rays in the high altitude sunshine. Sunlight is death to nylon ropes, and death to ropes is death to you too if you happen to pull desperately on the wrong strand.

Typically old ropes are left in place, so it isn't uncommon to come across cat's cradles of nylon in various states of decay. I looked up at the icy tower hanging above the camp and imagined how I was going to feel perched over the vertical drop to Base Camp, when it came to clipping onto some wind blasted skeleton strands of rope.

Camp One did have one great advantage; as a rabbit warren has holes, the hillside here had been levelled into tent platforms by successive expeditions, so we found a relatively flat platform on which to put the tent. This was a glorious spot – the tent door opened to the North East, framing the mountain above us. The camp was secure, there was nothing above us that could fall and wipe us off the mountain. The weather was still, and we had ample food and fuel for the climbing above.

That night I slept deeply, secure in the knowledge that we had accomplished the first part of the plan and that the team was working well. We still weren't fully acclimatised, but we had achieved our aim for that day. Acclimatisation means climbing high, sleeping low, so the next day we descended to Base Camp, secure in the knowledge that we were sticking to our plan. The next climb would be to Camp Two, followed by descent to base before an attempt on the whole climb.

Leaving Base Camp for the Camp Two climb was harder than before, perhaps it was the weight of expectation we imposed on ourselves, perhaps the extra 'just in case' food in our packs, or the extra gas canisters. Light snow began to fall this time as we reached advance Base Camp and set up our tent again. I was relatively happy this time, but our companion again struggled with the altitude.

In the grey light of dawn, before the sun had got to the tent he had come to a decision – his climb was over. Our teammate had been showing signs of altitude sickness, but we hadn't known how much the altitude was preying on his mind. He had a new job and a fiancée to return to, lots to look forward to, and had decided not to risk the climb. It wasn't a discussion but a reasoned explanation of his decision to leave and we respected it.

It meant we were down to just a pair of climbers. In one way this was good – we would be more efficient climbing as a pair than a group of three – it is simply faster. Decisions would also be easier, but that very simplicity came at the price that we would be fully dependent on each other. Remember I said that you shouldn't climb with someone whom you haven't fully tested? A climbing partnership is full-on life or death, you are looking for the other person to have your back, and you do the same for them. It's one of the most rewarding things about climbing.

We set up our tent again at Camp One, and settled to the tasks required to function at altitude, most importantly re-hydration. There is no running water on the mountain, it's frozen as ice and snow, so any drinking water has to be melted on the stove. This requires gas and care as the stove is inside the tent during bad weather. We were lucky though. We had enough gas canisters to sustain the two of us for the next two days up to Camp Two and back. Our plan was simple and incremental – the next day would involve a climb to Camp Two to look at the route, then descent to Camp One. A nights rest there, followed by a descent to Base Camp for rest and food that should see us well acclimatised for an attempt on the mountain proper.

Early morning is prime time for climbing as overnight freezing holds fast the loose rocks above you reducing the threat of rockfall. Fortunately the route from Camp One to Camp Two is along a rising crest of rock – exposed to the elements and predations of vertigo, but not to danger of rockfall. It was a superb day's climbing – brittle light flashing off specks of mica in the rocks, steel cold air and the exhilaration that comes with being high on a mountain. We threaded our way round the pinnacles of the ridge and realised that the technicality of the climbing was fairly easy. Climbing can sometimes be a brute struggle to haul your body upwards or else be an intricate puzzle solving game where you have to examine the rock closely to work out how to distribute your weight to best advantage and move sloth-slowly upwards.

Our ideas of a pure rock climbing approach ended when we got to the Yellow Wall below Camp Two. This was a section of overhanging, rotten rock, stained and dripping with water, down which hung an assortment of fixed ropes hanging vertically away from the wall. It is not that high, but there are only two ways to get through this obstacle – climb it with hands and feet, or use two jumar clamps attached to slings on your harness to inch slowly upwards.

A short discussion led to the decision to use the ropes. Full on technical climbing at this altitude would require better lungs, and for me better ability, than I had that morning. We simply had to choose the best looking rope, and then hope that it would be securely fixed at the top – that's two big If's – *if* it is not damaged, and *if* it is secured then we won't fall. Falling was not an option – we were above the altitude for helicopters at this point, and no one was going to come and get us if we were injured.

We knew that others had climbed this section, and we found a strand of fixed rope that was pretty new, so up we went. My partner went first – this had been the pattern for the day, and when I got to the top I couldn't see him – he had already moved on to the camp. This was odd, we were supposed to be moving as a pair, but in the excitement of getting to Camp Two, I put it aside.

Some mountain camps are exposed. Camp Two on Ama Dablam is definitively so – perched on the very tip of the ridge before it swoops down to connect to the central column of the mountain. There is clear open air and thousands of metres of drop on both sides. A few small tent platforms are spread along the ridge at odd angles. The effect is like a group of ladybirds on a blade of grass.

We went to the far end of the camp and stared up at the route, the summit hidden from us by the foreshortening effect of the mountain. The hanging serac (ice cliff) that gives the mountain its name bulged out from the West face above what we knew to be the location of Camp Three. Above that, the snow ran in fluted grooves to a square cut top. This had been a great day, but we still needed to race the gathering clouds back to Camp One. The reconnaissance was a success, and the best news was that the fixed ropes were well-attached.

The down-climb to Camp One went smoothly and we set about re-hydrating and fuelling up on food. I was in high spirits. We knew the route would be fine to Camp Two and then we could set about the harder technical climbing above. The following day we would descend to Base camp, rest, fill up on food and get more gas canisters in preparation for a full climb to camp three and the summit.

But in the morning there was a second bombshell, casually enough delivered, but devastating: My partner was going to change the plan. He'd thought it through, without my input. He felt he only had enough energy for another couple of days, he told me, so instead of descending to Base Camp again he was going to Camp Three that day, and the summit the day after.

This was definitely *not* the plan – I was counting on another round of Base Camp acclimatisation. We had time in hand and the weather was settled, so why should we rush? But there wasn't any debate, and he made it clear that his mind was made up. The full import of this decision was that he was intending to climb on to Camp Three and the summit – take it or leave it; suddenly it wasn't a climbing partnership. Worse than that, he was taking the tent, one of the stoves and the spare gas. You can't just take half a gas canister, so I was left with one part used canister and no tent as he packed up and left the camp. At least I still had a stove.

Why didn't I just accept the new plan and go with him? I'm still not sure about that one. Was he justified? I had a suspicion he thought I wasn't strong enough to get to the summit. Maybe 'pulling me along' with him on a slower acclimatisation plan would impact his chances of a summit, and he wasn't about to give that up. I believed that in hurrying we might miss out on the summit through inadequate acclimatisation, so I wasn't about to change my position. The end result was that I was stuck. I would need a tent for the night, and I only had one day of gas left. My only option was to return to Base Camp. Even there I wouldn't be able to just collect a tent and return up the mountain, without the tent, my climb was over.

As I sat at Camp One trying to process what had happened, I remembered I had a radio and could communicate with Base Camp. Some of the other expeditions had tents set up by climbing sherpas at Camp Two so there might be a chance of a spare place. I called it in, and the expedition leader asked around for me. There was a maximum of one night's use of a tent available at Camp Two. That was fine, I only had one day of gas anyway, so I set off for Camp Two to enjoy my last day of ascent. On my own there was no backup. This was soloing. I had no intention of adding flying to my skill list, so I clipped onto the fixed ropes where possible.

I found the tent described by Base Camp and moved in, watching the sun dip behind the mountain and along with it my hopes of climbing to the summit. I went through the drills to eat and re-hydrate, finally preparing myself a bottle of hot water to go in my sleeping bag – this is a great trick, providing warmth and also non-frozen water to drink in the morning.

When all is going well on a mountain you climb in the morning, rest in the afternoon and endure the night, but no one moves late on in the day unless they really have to. At around ten o'clock that night there shouldn't really have been anyone moving between camps, let alone coming down the mountain and talking in weary agitated voices. But there was definitely a pair coming into camp that night, late, and struggling. In the circumstances they would be looking for shelter and to re-hydrate. They had obviously been on the go for a long time. I poked my head out of the tent and offered up my bottle of water, at least they could drink as they were melting more snow, and it was gratefully received. They were OK for a tent, as they had left one set up in Camp Two.

The next morning was my last on the mountain, and I used the remaining gas to melt snow to fill my other water bottle. I took a last look up the tower towards the summit and turned sadly downhill. I met the team from the night before in the last tent before the ropes. We talked about their climb to the summit from Camp Two the day before. Starting the descent late they had become increasingly cold, pelted with rockfall, tired and thirsty. They were very grateful for the water and handed back my bottle.

The sherpa looked at me as if sizing up my chances "Are you going down?"

"I have to," I shrugged. "My tent is up at Camp Three. My partner went on ahead. I have food but no gas." I would be lying if I said I was badly off. After all there was no unknown ground between me and the Base Camp, I knew I could climb it safely and the summit was only a part of why I climb. No problems right?

The truth was more complicated – I had invested a lot into the climb, emotionally, in preparation time and in money. The only reason I couldn't go to the summit was that I was out of gas. I could get more at Base Camp, but that meant descending half the mountain to come back up, and now that our one tent was at Camp Three that wasn't going to happen. I had no team, no backup and was basically out of luck.

The sherpa grinned at me while his partner dug around for something in their tent.

"Why don't you take our gas? We have spare and we're going down anyway." His mate handed me two gas canisters.

My mind took a second to adjust – no longer was there the fig leaf of logistical difficulty. The decision now came down to me – climb on alone or descend for good.

This was my big Yes moment on the mountain, not joining the climb, or even keeping on when the team fell apart. Downwards lay safety, certainty and security. Upwards lay who knew what? Could I really climb the rest of the mountain solo?

"That's... awesome, thank you!" We hugged – we all understood what that moment meant. I stowed the gas away, turned back towards the summit and pulled out the radio to tell Base what I was planning to do. I think that was a defining moment of my climbing career. I had asked the other team about the route and judged it was within my capabilities and the weather was good. You cannot rule out accidents and I would have no backup, but at least now I had the chance to complete the climb.

That day went by in a blur of decision, move, decision, move. Each small section of the route above me, I scrutinised in the light that I *must not fall* onto the ropes. I'd like to think that I never over-reached myself, but couldn't swear to it. There were vertical sections of gullies with shattered rock held together by the ice. At one point, I stepped onto a traverse across a sweeping snow ledge under hanging ice cliffs and above a simply huge drop down the West Face.

After finally climbing the side of what is called the Mushroom Ridge, I came in sight of Camp Three. As I approached our tent I could see my partner descending the side of the Dablam serac towards camp. He trudged over to our tent where I stood. I wanted to know how he'd got on. "Alright? Been to the summit?"

"Yeah, yeah. Good day," he said matter-of-factly. "Wind's getting up though. Thought you weren't coming?"

"I had a bit of luck getting some gas. You staying or going down?"

"Down. Camp One tonight then base tomorrow – you?"

"Summit tomorrow - I'm a bit bothered about the wind though. I've only got a fleece and my duvet." I had been expecting to pack my shell layer at Base Camp before the summit ascent proper, but I hadn't taken it on what was supposed to be a reconnaissance to Camp Two.

He handed me his windproof jacket – we were about the same size.

"Take this. I'm fine from here on down." And then he left.

People have asked me why I wasn't angry with him for going off ahead – but it's not that surprising. We had no emotional investment in each other, barely knew each other in fact. I'd had a great day's climbing. I have had arguments on mountains with people whose judgment I didn't trust, but this wasn't one of those times. When you have so much physical and emotional energy tied up in simply getting enough food and drink, a hissy fit is an unnecessary luxury. I moved into the tent, dozed and drank tea, ate as much as I could and tried to suppress the altitude nausea.

Morning came slowly, and I could hear four others in the camp gearing up. I stayed in my sleeping bag, willing myself not to start early. Camp Three is in shadow until after breakfast, and you would only get cold waiting in line for others on the route. I set off soon after the sun arrived and within three hours was approaching the summit.

I passed the others as they descended, and so when I stepped up onto Ama Dablam's flat summit and looked over at Everest peeking over the Lhotse wall. I was on my own. I sat down in the snow and radioed down to Base that there was 'no more up'. They had been watching my final approach to the summit through binoculars, so they were ready for the call – their radio reply was the opening blast of Blur's *Song 2*, and I remember falling backwards onto the snow and singing along, as much as my breath allowed.

"Wooooooohoooooo!"

It wasn't a feeling of exhilaration I felt, more the satisfaction of a job half-done. Half, because the descent is the most important part of climbing a mountain. None of us wants to stay up there.

I climbed down from the summit in only two hours, spent the night at Camp Three and then the next day descended all the way to Base Camp. I had achieved my summit and was full of a sense of a job well done. I don't remember feeling angry about the team falling apart. We all had our reasons for what we had done on the mountain and I was no better than the others. I haven't stayed in touch with the others, or they with me, so I suppose we were three individuals simply there for our own reasons.

The important thing from my perspective was that I took the challenge of the mountain and met it on my own terms. I could have backed down when it became difficult, but everyone has their own challenges to overcome. I tried on the idea of saying 'yes' to continuing with the climb when I was given a chance. I am so glad I did because it had a massive restorative effect on my self-confidence.

Soon after returning from Ama Dablam, I met a wonderful woman who shared my passion for the mountains. Three years later, she became my wife, and we qualified as International Mountain Leaders together. We moved to the Alps to lead other people on their journeys in the mountains.

Life gets in the way, but sometimes all you need is a chance to change course.

Website: **daysawayadventures.com**

Email: **daysawayadventures@gmail.com**

Instagram: **@daysawayadventures**

Chapter 12

An Alphabetical Adventure

By Paul Donaghy

So, what would it be? A Half Marathon or a Duathlon? A ride on a Segway or Indoor skydiving? An attempt at the Speed Golf world record or a 10k Tough Mudder? Decisions, decisions, decisions! How was I going to celebrate my 50th birthday? My predicament was that I had decided to do them all and then some more!

My Mum, Pat, died from breast cancer, just nine days after her 50th birthday in April 1989. That number had never really resonated with me until I was hurtling towards the big five-oh myself, my half century, fifty not out. As I started to think about how young she was, it struck a chord with my own life journey – I was shortly approaching the very young age that she had reached. So, in the run up to my 50th birthday I decided that I was going to go on an adventure (or twenty six), to say YES to as many opportunities as I could and to complete my 50th year in remembrance of my mum - to complete the year that she hadn't and to have as much fun and excitement as I could along the way.

So began the year when I would try to attempt as many new sports as possible – from axe-throwing to zip wire with some kayaking in between, an A to Z of sports that would take me to Scotland (twice), the Lake District and North Sea, Southern Spain, up hills, over ice, through mud and even via Hogwarts!

Now obviously, it would have been a lot more of a challenge to complete them in the correct alphabetical order, but I had a full-time job. I'm also not that organised. So weekends and school holidays were taken up in pursuit of my challenges, and they were ticked off in any old order. I've only got a chapter to squeeze them all in, so I've picked some of my highlights. I'd set up a fantastic excel spreadsheet (did you know there is actually a world championship for that?). With some help from friends and family, I was getting plenty of ideas for upcoming events. I started to plan ahead with certain letters and book entries. For others I just did a quick Google search and turned up five minutes before they started.

WINTER (Park Run, Bowls, Dip in North Sea, New Year Sprint, Escape Room, Olympics in the Bar, Fives, X-Country, Indoor Skydiving, Curling)

Xylophone racing apparently isn't an officially recognised sport- as yet! However, X-Country is one of those glorious, sepia filled memories from secondary school where everyone has a story or recollection of hiding behind the bike sheds or catching a lift on a milk float up a hill. I know it's stretching the alphabet a bit but apart from playing on an Xbox or buying a skateboard and entering the X-Games, I was really struggling to find an event for this letter.

I am a long-standing member of Durham City Harriers and much prefer short bursts of sprinting. I train, and have been known to compete, over shorter distances usually between sixty metres and four hundred metres. I find if I go more than once around a running track my legs start to go wobbly and I need to sit down!

In the North East of England there is a very popular Harrier League with six cross-country fixtures taking place around the region during the winter months. This, of course, guarantees the best chance of mud, rain, wind, snow and ice – the perfect combination for plodding around a farmer's field for six miles!

Now, I do possess a pair of sprinting spikes for running on the track but do not have the equivalent footwear for muddy cross-country courses. I decided that one X-Country run was more than enough so picked the closest venue to home and put my name on the list of entries at the last minute to avoid any fuss or questioning from fellow runners. I managed to borrow a pair of middle-distance spikes – although they were one size too big for me – fine I thought, just stick an extra pair of socks on, they'll be great.

The Junior races had all been and gone. The Women's races were done. All that was left on this very cold and breezy February morning was the Senior Men's race. Now, that's not men who are seniors – no! It's anyone who is not a junior i.e. eighteen and above – lots of young whipper snappers, and to be fair, a lot more experienced runners as well! It certainly brought back memories of school fields, that particularly strong smell of Deep Heat, the biting cold wind, very short shorts and a lot of worried looking faces as the starter calls us all to the start line.

The Senior Men's race is set off in various 'packs' – us slow lads set off first and are given a two and a half minute head start followed by the 'medium pack' and then the super stars in the 'fast pack'.

'What am I doing here?' I thought to myself as I huddled into the back of the starting pen.

"What are you doing here?" laughed one of the officials I recognised from the summer track and field circuit.

Just as I was about to explain the relevance of my A to Z challenge, and that as I was planning on trying curling later in the year, I couldn't count cross-country as the letter C, so was going to be creative and claim this for letter X, a gun went off.

"BANG!"

That was it. No more time to chat or prepare myself. The starter had officially said we could head off into the mud. "Well, here goes nothing."

The course was two laps of Thornley Hall Farm, up and down fields and through puddles of thick mud. It was going to be a real tough slog. The organisers of these events obviously have a sadistic streak; there are no flat, verdant fields and babbling brooks adjacent to the route.

No sooner had I reached the first incline out of the starting paddock and into the neighbouring field, then the 'middle pack' came flying past me, seemingly floating across the mud. Just around the corner and through a gateway into another series of boggy hills and I could hear the 'fast pack' approaching rapidly. These guys could actually fly; their cross-country spikes had little wings on them and their feet glided across the ground like a flat stone skimming across a still pond. They whipped past me with the greatest of ease and were soon out of sight, never to be seen again. Well, not quite! Due to their incredible speed, athleticism and all-round fitness they managed to overtake me a second time and completed the two-lap course before I had even finished my first circuit!

Meanwhile, I had happily found my position in the race, was comfortably in the last twenty-five to thirty runners and we still had another lap to go! As my shoes grew heavier and heavier, the miles ticked off and my legs felt like lead. At least the two pairs of socks were keeping my feet dry.

Back up the same hills, passing the ever encouraging marshals, through the even muddier fields I plodded, as the finishing line slowly began to creep towards me. I knew the final half a mile was a downhill section through a couple of fields and then onto an undulating open stretch. The last few remaining spectators were cheering on the tail-enders as the drizzle arrived. I found a small reserve of energy from deep inside and managed to speed up over the final hundred metres, over-taking a couple of my fellow competitors and finding the strength to lift my head and even smile as I crossed the line.

"Great sprint finish, Paul," whispered the friendly official as I was bent double getting my breath back.

"Cheers! "I mumbled.

It took me over sixty-one minutes to plod round the course and I finished 393rd out of 414 runners – a season's best performance! Yes, those gold-tinged school memories should definitely remain locked in history. It definitely doesn't get any easier with age!

*

Come on, who doesn't love the Olympics? Could be the Summer or Winter, certain sports just have a mesmerising effect on me – a couple of weeks of live sport on television, sports that have strange rules yet after a few hours of watching we all suddenly become experts! One of these sports is Curling. I'd stay up late watching Canada v Sweden to see which team would qualify for the knockout stages and play GB if we beat Japan! However, if you've ever tried Curling, or even find a local club, you'll realise that it is quite a localised sport. I.e. unless you live in Scotland, you've got a very slim chance of ever having a go.

Due to the success of the GB (Scottish) Ladies' team at the 2018 Sochi Winter Olympics, there were plenty of 'come and try' sessions on offer to try and reach a new audience. After jiggling around our busy diaries, the family managed to find one on a Saturday morning that we were all available to attend. Off we went, crossing the border to the small village of Kelso for a two-hour session of Curling.

What an amazing place! Curling is a very seasonal sport and the Kelso venue is only open from October to March. The building is pretty non-descript from the outside: a grey, square-ish building that blends in with the surrounding terrace houses. However, once through the front doors it was like walking back in time into an old-fashioned history museum of ice sports. There were old-fashioned skates and wooden sticks strewn all over the walls; doors and notice boards were adorned with black and white team photos and the trophy cabinet overflowed with all shapes and sizes of shields, cups and awards from way back when.

However, once you get out onto the ice you step into a modern, crisp, clean and very fresh ice rink. The only noise was the comforting clacking of stones as they bumped into each other on their way down the ice. Four lanes were set out with dividing lines and red and blue circles at either end. The ice was brushed, the stones were lined up and we took our first tentative steps onto the surface (I was also hoping I could have ticked off "Z" at the same venue by riding on that big ice resurfacing machine, the Zamboni, but I'd just missed my chance!).

We were taught how to hold a stone and launch ourselves from one end of the rink by pushing off on one knee, how to spin the stone slowly so it curled in the right direction as it slid along the ice and then, the highlight of the day – how to sweep with the broom, whilst sliding down the rink backwards and avoiding tripping over the stray stones. What a buzz!

After practising for a while and getting acclimatised to the cold air, we had a quick game against another family and managed to release the stones before the hog-line so they rested near the button of the house. Hammer time indeed! So many technical terms and specific rules; they make it look so easy on TV. I'm sure that if I'd been born slightly closer to Scotland this would have been a sport I would have taken up; I absolutely loved it.

SPRING (Speed Golf, Zip Wire, Helicopter Flight, Ultra-Marathon, Gymnastics)

Zooming across the water – I had decided to raise some funds for St

Oswald's Hospice during the year – setting up a fundraising page and putting a target of £1967 (the year of my birth) as the goal. St Oswald's is a very well known and loved charity in the North East of England and was the place where my mum was treated during her illness. They organise a wide range of sponsored events each year. As luck would have it, they announced that in the Spring they were doing a zip wire challenge across the River Tyne starting from the Tyne Bridge on the north side and heading over to the south side in Gateshead. Back in 2012, Bear Grylls had carried the Olympic Torch on the same route as it toured the country on its way down to London for the Games.

"Did I just push my daughter off the Tyne Bridge?"

I had persuaded my eighteen-year-old daughter, Lauren, to join me on this escapade (always a good idea to have someone to hold your hand if you're a bit scared). Bright and early on a clear Saturday morning in April, with our snug harnesses checked and then doubled checked, we headed up the never ending steps on the Gateshead side of the river.

A feeling of intense excitement mixed with a sense of tremendous trepidation filled my gut as our group headed across to the north side of the iconic Tyne Bridge. In a few months' time we would both be plodding down this same route in the Great North Run (H for Half marathon, anyone?).

But this morning we'd found a much quicker, if slightly more terrifying, way to get across the mighty River Tyne. I had decided to wear one of my birthday presents for the challenge and so was resplendent in my black and white football shirt with a red number fifty on the back. Hooped Newcastle United socks, pulled right up, and black shorts completed the outfit. I looked like a slightly older version of Kevin Keegan (albeit with less of a perm) ready to step onto the hallowed turf of St James' Park.

Our group were the first to arrive at the take off point and we lined up looking over the edge of the bridge. What a mistake! My stomach flipped and my voice suddenly got higher as I asked Lauren if she was okay. My mouth became dry and the joking and merriment were instantly replaced with serious glances and nervous laughter. One by one we had to climb up onto the chest-high railing and sit with both legs dangling over the edge. Directly below was the river (I kept humming the words to Jimmy Nail's iconic hit 'Big River' over and over to myself).

We had decided that Lauren would go first, so that we could chat to each other at the start, keep ourselves calm and then she would not be left by herself. This seemed to be the right decision, but I did feel slightly guilty as I gave her a gentle push and set her off on her way. The high-pitched scream (of joy?) was also slightly off putting, but I'm sure I could see a smile on her face as she disappeared down the wire.

Rather disconcertingly, just as I slid myself into the ready position and hooked my harness onto the steel wire, a water rescue boat came into view and headed down the river to position itself directly underneath me! It was like they were preparing for my impending doom. 'That's actually quite reassuring,' I thought to myself. 'If I do plummet into the freezing water below, at least I won't have to swim too far to be rescued!'

One final look ahead. What a fantastic view down the quayside: the Millennium Bridge seemed to be giving me a reassuring wink; the Baltic Art Gallery, standing strong and straight like a life-guard; the Sage building reflecting the still water from its gigantic glass windows. And on the other side of the river I could spot little dots where my family were watching on in encouragement.

Three, two, one and jump – literally, I jumped off the Tyne Bridge. The harness took hold and the belay fed the rope as fast as could be as I hurtled down to the Gateshead side. A black and white blur? A flying zebra? A fluttering barcode? I let out a whoop of delight as I flew across the river.

Suddenly, I came to a rather groin-squeezing halt as the ropes were stopped abruptly and I was lowered down to terra firma. My heart was still racing, the butterflies from my stomach had dropped a few inches and I gave my daughter a massive hug. Absolutely magic!

*

Undeniably, this was the really big one, a challenge that actually required proper training sessions. What could be easier than a forty-six-mile ultra-marathon? I did run the London Marathon in 1999 and have plodded along the Great North Run (albeit dressed in an assorted array of fancy-dress costumes!) but this was a ridiculously long distance in anyone's view.

This was a proper challenge that I had somehow persuaded schoolteacher pals, Steve and Deon, to accompany me on. Steve has been the other half in our pantomime camel outfit escapades on several occasions. Deon has put up with me on speed golf days and very slow swimming in the North Sea during a sprint Triathlon at Whitley Bay.

Now, we are all busy people, but in order to cover forty-six miles in under twelve hours (before they close the finish line and the officials pack up all their stuff) you do need to do a serious amount of training. To be fair we did a couple of sixteen-mile jogs and one that was about twenty-four miles when we got completely lost on an old railway line in the pouring rain. But it was more the short sharp stuff that we had time for.

And, of course, the gear! I wasn't planning on this being a regular occurrence and although I had no idea, I didn't have the flash gear either! A decent pair of trail shoes, leggings, plenty of layers and spare socks and jacket would suffice. Plus, a cheap runner's daysack loaded with Mars Bars and Jelly Babies.

Now, I should really have had no problem with the route as my dad literally wrote the guidebook! No, he actually did. My dad, Peter, and his friend, John, enjoy walking and have written several walking books – Northumbria Church Walks, Tyne and Wear Metro Walks.

He's also written a guidebook called Discovering Newcastle-Gateshead and was asked by Brian Burnie (founder of the Daft as a Brush Cancer Patient Care charity) to write a walking guide along the length of the River Tyne – from the source to the sea. I've got the book in my house, so should have no excuse for getting lost.

The River Tyne has two sources (North and South). This year the ultra run was starting at the southern end at Garrigill in the hills of the Cumbrian moors. While thinking we were taking up a massive challenge ourselves, we were in fact ONLY merely attempting the half-ultra as the real hard-core runners continued on and completed a ninety-five-mile super ultra-marathon!

As April was coming to an end, we got ourselves to the start line in Garrigill for 9.30am and checked out the opposition. There were only about sixty or so competitors – the majority of whom looked like seasoned 'ultras' with all the equipment and in a wide range of shapes and ages. As we eyed up our fellow runners, we spotted several athletes that we were highly confident of beating and we couldn't wait to get going.

The start was a steady procession out of the village and, actually, in the opposite direction to the finish as we had to run up to the marker stone that signalled the official source of the South Tyne. It was quite overcast as we headed off, and it took us an hour to reach the stone. By now the three of us were dead last and everyone else was out of sight so our navigational skills would be vital.

Despite having a copy of the route in my pocket and my dad's wise words of wisdom in my head, it was almost inevitable that we would get lost early on. It only affected us once really but probably added another needless mile to the forty-six we were already signed up to do.

The night before the run was the inaugural Durham Adventure Festival and the guest speaker was a certain Dave Cornthwaite. I listened intently as he described his many thousand-mile challenges and adventures on skateboards and paddleboards. He talked about his next Waterbike challenge picking up litter around the canals of England which sounded like lots of fun (hmm, that could tick the W box!). This mere forty-six miles seemed quite insignificant.

I can't say we ran the whole way. There was a mix of jogging, fast walking, a bit of clambering, some hiking up hills and then a lot of shuffling over the last few miles. The route alongside the River Tyne is beautifully scenic and, as it twists and turns through valleys and fields, you really feel like you are miles away from civilisation. There are incredible inlets, wonderful waterfalls, small streams and babbling brooks constantly moving in the same direction towards the sea. I even recognised the odd ox-bow lake as we headed through Haltwhistle – I knew those Geography lessons at school would come in handy one day!

The first checkpoint at twelve miles was at Alston Railway Station. Never have cold salted potatoes been so inviting. The smell wafted along the platform drawing us in. The taste was incredible; the salt really hitting the spot and as we were in last place, we were able to finish the lot! Also on the menu were Jelly Babies, Jaffa Cakes and flat Coke. This first pit stop came just at the right time. We'd been going for about three and a half hours and we were beginning to realise the enormity of the challenge. The weather was pleasant – cloudy skies, no wind or rain. We were in good spirits as the route took us along the old South Tyneside Railway line from Alston for about five miles.

We reached the halfway point, crossing the river under the towering Lambley Viaduct (an impressive Victorian structure 110 feet in height with nine semi-circular arches). It was a great opportunity for another selfie of the three of us (as if we needed an excuse to catch our breath). As we staggered past the twenty-five mile mark, we stumbled upon the next support point, the back of a little white van with a cheery volunteer again offering flat Coke and even more Jaffa Cakes.

We were parallel to the A69 for a short while and then climbed up through several woods, passed a couple of ruined castles and then crossed a few farms to descend to Haydon Bridge for the final support stop and a welcome toilet break at the Anchor Inn. We were almost there. There were only six miles between us and the finishing line.

The light was fading as we shuffled up the final hill and through the final forest. We got out our head-torches to see the path in front of us and Steve had both hands on my back as he pushed me uphill to keep my legs moving – this was definitely unchartered territory for all of us. A couple of sips of water and the final few Jelly Babies just kept us going in our final descent towards the Boatside Inn at Warden – where the North and South Tyne meet. It was a wonderful moment to see Donna and Lauren and Ben standing there. We were officially the final competitors to arrive at the concluding checkpoint and crossed the forty-six-mile finishing line at 9.20pm. However, we were not actually last, as during the day eight people had dropped out and did not finish.

I was absolutely shattered; I couldn't even bend down to take my shoes off. I was poured into the back seat of the car and lay there for the whole journey home. I couldn't actually walk. I had to crawl up stairs to bed. eleven hours and fifty minutes to cover forty-six miles. Unbelievable!

Maybe I should have done unicycling or ultimate Frisbee instead!

SUMMER (Axe Throwing, Quidditch, Via Ferrata, Waterbike, Triathlon, Yoga-cise, Rowing, Javelin, Mud Run, Lyke Wake Walk, Kayaking**)**

Quite what sport I was going to do for this letter was never in doubt! Ever since watching a short piece on the local news about the Durham University Quidditch team, I was hooked. Like most people, I've seen the Harry Potter films and read the books but I definitely needed to do a bit of homework to remind myself of the difference between a bludger and a beater, and a seeker and a keeper! I contacted the University team (called Durhamstrang) via Facebook and they were very keen to assist me with my quest. Unfortunately, we would have to wait until early summer as they were currently training for the British Championships – I kid you not!

So, one Saturday morning, an expectant and excited group of us (I'd somehow persuaded ten friends to join me!) headed down to the Sands in Durham and were taught how to fly! Well, almost. The brooms were actually one metre long drainpipes!

To distinguish the different roles and positions we all wore various coloured headbands. The oval arena was about the size of a football pitch and at each end there were three ring-shaped goals. The overall aim was to get a ball through one of these hoops while trying not to get hit by a different ball from someone with an alternate coloured headband. To end a match, as you Muggles will know, someone must catch the golden snitch – which was in reality a tennis ball in a long sock tucked into the back of a random player's shorts!

It was a weird, yet fantastic, mix of rugby, basketball, netball and dodgeball with a bit of primary-school-yard-pretend-flying mixed in! I absolutely loved it. It was right up there in my top three challenges and I've been tempted to actually join the team!

*

Right down by the River Wear in Durham is the Durham Amateur Rowing Club and every summer they organise an All-comers Regatta for people with little or no experience on the water. I definitely fit into the latter category having only had a few turns on the indoor rowers in the gym at school. Three colleagues from the PE Department joined me for a couple of practices, although we never got all four of us together at the same time. We quickly learned the difference between bow and stern, port and starboard but never found out what a rigger, a button or a sweep were.

On the actual day of the regatta, one teacher fell ill so my daughter, Lauren, stepped into the boat at the last minute. The races were only two hundred metres each and, despite our PE background and love of sport, we were absolutely rubbish, losing all three races and officially finishing last. This naturally gave us automatic qualification into next year's regatta but for all the wrong reasons.

That's it I thought – much to the family's collective sigh of relief, all done, a complete A to Z of challenges ticked off. However, there was to be one final twist.

AUTUMN

It was about four weeks into the first half term at school. I was getting bogged down by Year Eleven GCSE Maths books (I'm a PE Teacher and not used to marking quadratic equations and fractions). Out of the blue I received an email from a friend I had worked with previously. She was putting an advert out at the end of the week as a colleague had suddenly decided to change career and had left their post.

I wasn't massively happy at work. I mean, you'd be hard pushed to find a teacher who was deliriously happy in the first term back after summer, but I wasn't actively looking for a new job. However, as soon as I read the message, I thought maybe now is the time to change, to find a job I'll really enjoy doing, a job doing sport everyday (and NO probability or angles!). Despite not explaining the exact role, working hours or even the salary, I agreed to take it.

I had just found a bonus letter – **Y** for saying **YES** to a massive change and just like that I decided to stop being a teacher after twenty-five years!

The next day I handed in my letter of resignation and told the Headteacher that I would like to get off the bus! A strange corporate analogy that had been used to encourage the staff to travel in the same direction. Well, my form of transport was going on a completely different route and I'd just arrived at my stop. I worked until the half term then just as my 51st birthday approached, my new adventure began, and I haven't looked back since!

To conclude the connection with my Mum, my daughter and I were invited to the St Oswald's Hospice Life List Awards for our efforts in raising over £2,200 over the year. That year was for you, Mum x.

As for me, I'm really loving my new job. Turning fifty undoubtedly gave me the chance to have some fun adventures from Axe Throwing to Zip Wires and to really challenge myself (and my family)! It also gave me plenty of ideas for new and exciting challenges to pursue in my new job. We've already had an indoor Curling competition which was very well received and I'm busy sawing a load of drainpipes in half for the inaugural Primary Schools Quidditch Challenge. Now then, I just need to find my Quaffle...!

Facebook: **paul.donaghy.39**

Chapter 13

Third Leg Meg

By Meg Dyos

Meg Dyos was a part of The Coxless Crew, a team of six women (Laura Penhaul, Emma Mitchell, Natalia Cohen, Isabel Burnham and Lizanne Van Vuuren) who rowed unsupported nine thousand miles across the Pacific Ocean raising funds for Breast Cancer Care and Walking with the Wounded in a twenty-nine-foot pink ocean rowing boat called Doris. They left from San Francisco in April 2015 and rowed into Cairns, Australia in January 2016 stopping off in Hawaii and Samoa to swap the fourth rower of the boat and restock supplies (Izz Leg One, Lizanne – Leg Two, Meg – Leg Three).

Their documentary *'Losing Sight of Shore'* tells the story of their journey. Produced by Sarah Moshman, it can be found on iTunes and Amazon.

Will I, Won't I?

Whilst writing my dissertation for my English Literature degree I often visited the website 'Escape the City', exactly what I planned to do once I finished University, but to do what? I had already taken three gap years before finally getting my head down to do my degree, but I wanted more adventures, a challenge and definitely not a nine-to-five life; something to escape to so that the prospect of 'real life' could be avoided for a little longer.

Whilst scrolling aimlessly during one of my many study breaks, daydreaming and procrastinating about my future, I stumbled across an advert that said: 'Are you woman enough to row the Pacific Ocean?' I scrolled on, but kept coming back to the advert; something was drawing me to it. I digested all of the information, researched and researched; questioned and questioned; dreamed and dreamed until the prospect of rowing the Pacific Ocean haunted my every waking moment. A team of women to row from San Francisco to Australia unsupported in a pink boat called Doris, aiming to set two world records in the process. This is something that hadn't even been done before – who knew if it was even possible! I had to send off an application for this. I had to at least apply because really, what was there to lose?

I sat in my sister's kitchen in Hampshire overlooking the rolling fields. April – a funny old month that each year gets me itching for an adventure. With a steaming cup of tea in one hand and my iPhone in the other, I recorded the video that I sent off as a part of my application to row the Pacific Ocean. I was nervous. I was tired. Was I just procrastinating and avoiding finishing off my dissertation? Did I really want to do this?

We laughed together at my recording, a piercing in both sides of my nose, my hair flicked over to the right, a denim dress and no script to follow. I wanted it to be natural, conversational and to show them who I was right at that moment in my life – the idea that I would even be considered was just downright ridiculous. There was just no way. I knew that.

I'm Meg: hummus connoisseur and lover of all things involving the sunshine! I had never rowed, never been in the deep ocean, never had proper biceps and am terrified of sharks – and I had just applied to row across the deepest, largest, sharkiest ocean in the world where there was NO hummus.

The visions and excitement of being selected as a member of the team took over my dreams. The anxiety and the fear of being selected to row the Pacific bombarded my nightmares. Could I really be chosen?

To my surprise, I was selected for the first stage of the recruitment process. I went down to Christchurch with Laura to see our pink ocean rowing boat Doris being built and sat in her to visualize what life on her would be like. She was small and the cabin where we would spend 50% of our time was only comparable in size to a two-man tent or a larger bath with a lid on it. A tingle of exhilaration mixed in with absolute fear travelled down my spine and the small hairs on my forearms stood on end.

But I'd been offered a job that I thought I really wanted. This was one of those crossroads moments. Do I choose adventure and the chance of a lifetime or do I settle down with a job I knew I would be good at?

I made the decision and I said, "No," to adventure. My life was just too unsettled to be on a boat in the middle of the Pacific. I wasn't in the right headspace to be at sea. Unresolved issues remained unresolved both mentally and physically and I believed that I needed to spend time focusing on them.

The chance to be on a record setting adventure passed me by and from that day forward I wasn't sure if that was to be the worst decision of my life.

Imagine my surprise when one year later, hours after just handing my notice in on the job that I had so desired, I received a phone call from Laura Penhaul, the powerhouse behind the all women Pacific row attempt. After exchanging pleasantries, Laura got down to business – It went something like this:

Hey Meg,

Are you still keen to be a part of the row? We're leaving in just over a month and we're looking for someone to join us on the third leg of the journey from Samoa to Australia? Are you up for it?

This time, I jumped at the chance.

The Journey from Land

On 21st April, 2015 at 2.30am, the girls of the first leg on Doris left San Francisco rowing under the Golden Gate Bridge and into the unknown ocean towards Hawaii. Whilst they began battling waves the size of houses and seasickness, I was on land hitting the gym hard and getting as many calories on board as possible.

Across another ocean from Lizanne in South Africa (second leg), in separate gyms and separate countries, we trained, building our muscles and communicating only through Skype. We'd still yet to actually meet in person. In order to be an ocean rower, we needed to not only put on weight, but also build masses of muscle. I quickly entered into a love triangle with the leg press and the chest press under the arches of Bethnal Green station whilst she built muscle in Cape Town. As someone that had only really ever swam in a pool and run outside, standing in a gym did not give me the same emotional kick. Seeing muscles begin to develop that I didn't know I had felt good, but it was hard, slow work and boy did I ache.

In addition to the increase in muscle mass, I had to put on weight too. Every day I sent our Strength and Conditioning coach my daily food intake to ensure that I was consuming the correct amount of calories to reach my goal weight. Much to my disbelief, beans on toast did not count as the diet for an aspiring Michelin Man.

Eating the large amount of calories and sustaining a steady rise on the scales was weird. I'm not an obsessive dieter but I do like to keep an eye on my weight. It was a strange phenomenon to train my brain into being happy about a higher number.

Lizanne and I continued to Skype and I really began to feel like I had known her for years despite never meeting in person. Below is a snippet taken from one of our blogs:

> *Meg and I are fast becoming best buds. We're having weekly Skypes, comparing notes, reviewing each other and generally just chatting about how much our muscles ache :) The reviews have gone something like this...*
>
> *Liz: any concerns this week?*
>
> *Meg: I don't like weights*
>
> *Liz: you should really learn to rant better*
>
> *Meg: eat more doughnuts*

I obsessively watched the pink dot of Doris as she traversed (very slowly) across the GPS tracking page on our website. Every movement forward was a bonus, a day closer to the day when I would join the crew in Samoa.

But then, something changed. The dot wasn't moving westwards any more but south down the coast of America until it stopped at Santa Barbara. We received an email informing us that due to problems with the batteries Doris was heading back to shore. Five days on land and batteries sorted the girls set off again but all planned dates in our timeline were being pushed back. Everything was a few weeks behind schedule. In April 2015, when the girls left for the first leg of our journey, we were due to arrive in Australia for October/early November, so an approximate six months. This was looking more and more unrealistic.

With a vague idea of when Lizanne would be leaving and an even vaguer idea of when I would depart for the third leg, I moved back home to my mum's house to save money. I worked for a local company on the basis that they understood my timeline of not knowing when I would need to leave, and I kept trying to maintain a life whilst mentally rolling amongst the waves of my impending adventure at sea.

I found it difficult listening to other people who constantly projected their fears about our journey onto me. Their fears sometimes then became mine and it made me feel uneasy. I started to love spending time with people that weren't shocked by what we were doing and were predominantly excited about our endeavours.

Anna McNuff's words stuck with me from her blog that she wrote at the end of her incredible running adventure around New Zealand:

'Our conscious world is constructed of false bottoms and imaginary ceilings. Our limit for the bottom is governed by fear, fear of what will happen as we stumble into the unknown. And our ceilings are defined by what we believe ourselves to be capable of. As it turns out, both boundaries are entirely imagined'.

We *were* going to get to Australia. I just needed to focus on getting myself fit and ready to join the team when my time came.

Our psychologist, Keith Goddard, worked tirelessly with us all as a team ensuring that our mental strength was where it should be; he prepared us mentally for situations that we might face at sea. For me, my fear of sharks and the fact that we may well encounter them at sea had me waking up in sweats.

Prior to the girls' departure, I can count the number of times that we had met as a team on one hand, so Keith did a lot of work introducing me to each and every one of the team member's personalities. He wanted me to be as prepared as possible for when I stepped onto Doris and to slot into the team dynamics with ease.

Keith was also there to help with any communication with our families if anything happened when we were at sea. Did I want to know if something serious had occurred at home when I was a thousand miles away from any land and powerless to help? Likewise, how I would like people to be told if anything happened to us was an equally hard decision to make. What we were doing had its risks and we all knew it.

Blogs were written each day on Doris and were uploaded via our portable satellite system that provided us with email and then sent over to us on land. Our wonderful on-land social media support, Ella Hewton, uploaded these to our website and social media. In the early days, it didn't seem to matter so much when the blogs were posted as long as they were put up before we went to bed. But as time went on and the following of our blogs grew and grew, if the blog wasn't posted by 7pm we would start receiving messages about the girls' whereabouts and whether everything was okay! It was a big commitment to be religious with the timing, so we shared it out between me, Ella and Lizanne. We were the 'on-land' crew and it really felt like, just as much as the girls were rowing their butts off to get to Hawaii, we were also working hard to make sure that everything was running smoothly from land.

It was our job to keep up momentum, continue fundraising for our chosen charities Breast Cancer Care and Walking with the Wounded and keep informing people of what we were doing. By the end of our commitments to the row we had raised in the region of £70,000. Due to the longevity of this journey there was concern about people's interest fatiguing, so with the help of our PR company Carver PR, Lizanne and I took part in a number of media interviews to keep people informed that the girls were still rowing, day and night – twenty-four hours a day. It was an exciting but also relatively daunting prospect being the voice of radio and face on the TV when we hadn't even been on Doris rowing with the girls yet!

When I finally got to meet Lizanne for the first time, it was like meeting someone that I had been friends with for years. After hours of Skype calls where we'd been comparing our growing muscles, it was quite surreal! The girls were due to reach Hawaii in a number of days so Lizanne flew over to the UK before heading on over to Hawaii to meet them and take her place in the rowing team. We completed all of the necessary UK jobs that we needed to do, and then off she went ready to start the second leg of the journey.

I felt slightly sick that the next time the girls were approaching land it would be me climbing into the boat alongside them.

When Izz returned to the UK after her leg of the journey, she joined the on-land support crew. She was so full of rowing and ocean knowledge and I loved listening to her stories of what it was like being on Doris out at sea. Within a few weeks of her return, she offered to complete a twenty-four-hour row-athon with me. Not only would this help psychologically to prepare me for what the routine of two hours on the oars and two hours off felt like, it would also set me up for the sleep deprivation I would feel on Doris. We had so much fun, raised a lot of money and it was so awesome getting to know Izz!

I still hadn't been on a rowing boat, and I still hadn't done any rowing. As much as Keith had told me again and again to get myself on a boat, I was so worried that I would sit in a rowing seat and hate the prospect of rowing an ocean. Instead, I dealt with my lack of rowing experience when the Pacific Ocean was staring me in the face and had a twenty-minute lap of Apia Harbour in Samoa with Ems.

I was ready, I was mentally prepared and I was officially bulked – my turn had arrived.

Third Leg Meg

I remember that feeling of total fear; the kind of fear that makes your legs weak and your stomach feel like it's in a washing machine; the kind of fear that makes you unsure of where the balance lies between complete hysteria and total uncontrollable laughter.

Five days before the girls made landfall in Samoa, I said goodbye at Heathrow Airport to my mum, her incredibly supportive partner and my boyfriend who I'd declared my love to just weeks before. I didn't know it then as I stepped away through into the airport security, but his support towards our journey before, during and after our return made me sure that he was 'The One'. We now have a beautiful daughter together and I'm so happy that despite stepping into the unknown for four months, he decided to wait for me.

This was it – there was no going back.

Based on our predictions, the second leg of the journey was due to take sixty days so it was expected that I would have been heading off at the end of August/beginning of September. However ninety-seven days later after being what can only be referred to as 'stuck in the doldrums', the girls made landfall in Samoa. It was the end of October. We were going to be spending Christmas and welcoming in 2016 on Doris.

Tired, very tanned and beyond happy to have finally reached land, the girls wonkily stepped onto shore – they had made it and I was in absolute awe.

How could I be a part of this team? Why had I been chosen? I felt so small right in that moment, star-struck and completely and utterly out of my depth. I didn't know what to say to these incredible women who had fought waves bigger than houses; these super humans that had been followed by sharks; these crazy cats that had now rowed over six thousand miles unsupported but still had a whole three thousand miles to go! How was I here, in this moment, ready to undertake the final leg of this journey with them?

I rung home and cried – I couldn't do this.

After seven days on land, unpacking and packing Doris, organising supplies for the final leg of our journey, saying a teary goodbye to Lizanne and getting fully integrated into the rowing team, we were ready. A lovely send off from everyone who had supported us on land, another goodbye to Tony Humphries and the film crew (Our on-land support and weather man) and off we went into the unknown.

I could do this.

I took the oars alongside Ems for my first proper stint at rowing. I was excited, completely and utterly terrified but so grateful to finally be a physical part of the rowing team. Months of waiting, watching, training and eating were over. I'd absorbed all of the calories and advice that I could like a sponge absorbs water. I was ready.

11.30am on 11th November, 2015, we rowed out of Apia harbour and the curves and smells of land slowly shrunk into the distance. Eye of the Tiger played from the on-board speakers as the girls soaked up the adrenaline of it being the last time they would ever row into the unknown. I, on the other hand, tried to focus my mind away from the fact we were actually leaving land and instead tried to engage my core muscles whilst also focusing on rowing – not as easy as it sounds... With each stroke of the oars I felt calmer. With each stroke of the oars I felt more a part of the team. With each stroke of the oars we were further and further away from land until we couldn't see it anymore – I was rowing the Pacific and there was no going back.

I lay in the cabin after my first two hour rowing shift and listened to the waves, enjoying the feeling of the swell pushing us along in the direction of Australia. The sounds of laughter echoed from Laura and Nat on the oars and the smell of beef curry flooded my nostrils. It was absolute bliss.

However, by the time my second rest shift came around (eight hours in) I was feeling the swells of nausea in my stomach. My body was preparing for a night's sleep whilst my mind was processing the idea of rowing throughout the night in a week where the moon was nowhere to be seen. Crystallized beads of salt stuck to my skin mixed with the day's sun cream residues, and I had found it hard getting into the swing of relieving myself in a bucket. There and then I knew for myself, lying there in the tiny space of our twenty-nine-foot ocean rowing boat bobbing along under the starlit sky, that this challenge was not going to be easy.

It was dark – very dark. Like the darkest shade of black, but mixed with waves and stars and more waves and more stars and on this particular night I wondered what on earth had possessed me to apply to undertake such a challenge.

I continued to be shocked by just how much water we could see. Our 360-degree horizon just seeped and rolled all around us everywhere for miles and miles. Some days the waves moved in the same direction. Some days there was not even a ripple and the ocean showed the reflection of four girls in a pink boat rowing along.

All different shades of blues, mesmerisingly beautiful, the Pacific was not always scary and angry. She had a personality of her own and the power to control anything that is brave enough to venture on and in her almost as if she is a living being.

On nights where she was angry and the waves were big, we knew who was in charge. We were a floating coconut bobbing up and down each wave, being pushed around by each new current. Waves often ended up on our heads and sometimes we were pushed off our seats. It was scary and it was adrenaline pumping.

We used our oars to propel us forward, but a lot of the time the efforts of our rowing just held our position to stop us moving backwards, the currents clawing and dragging us the wrong way. It was a mental challenge on days like these when it didn't feel worth it, when it felt like we were rowing through treacle just to hold ourselves in one place. It was a fight to head in the direction of Australia.

By day seven, I had become more accustomed to life on the ocean. The rules of the sea were becoming clearer and I was able to steer Doris in the right direction if Mother Nature also played ball. The act of rowing itself had become the norm and the system of our loo with a view or 'bucket and chuck it' was just beautifully simple. Our shifts were split up into two-hour chunks with two hours rowing, two hours resting – day moved into night and sunsets became sunrises. Eat, sleep, row, repeat.

However, one week in and my bottom had already become cross (the stage before angry) meaning that salt sores had developed and sitting was becoming more and more uncomfortable. Nothing that Sudocreme and a bit of talcum powder couldn't assist with, but this was only the beginning of the relationship my skin had with salt.

I also really struggled getting around Doris. At the end of each shift I couldn't seem to manoeuvre my body around our twenty-nine-foot expanse without doing a half crawl, half moving squat position. Much to the girls' amusement, I then couldn't fit myself in or out of the cabin through our human sized cat flap in a very effective way. Despite all efforts to watch the three cabin door entrance and exit pros perform this task, I tried and tested as many different positions as I could get my body into. One must note that I was at least double the size of the other girls at the beginning of the leg so this also didn't help the matter.

The light reflected off the waves in so many different directions, each ray being refracted as the sea moved up and down, up and down. You became fixated on one particular wave watching it peak and trough and you'd lose yourself in your own thoughts.

Yet avoiding boredom on Doris was a constant battle. With so many hours of sitting on a seat looking at blue day after day and week after week twenty-four hours a day, we had to come up with ways to entertain ourselves – and oh we did. We told each other the stories from films we had seen, sang songs as loudly as our vocal chords would allow, had deep and meaningful conversations that went off in so many tangents they could last for a day, and we constantly watched for wildlife. However, most of all we laughed and we cried. Tears of laughter and tears of frustration, even the two combined.

As we continued to roll with the waves, my tan deepened and I began to look less like a non-rower who had been kidnapped by three super humans and their pink boat. That's when I officially decided that I did not like rowing. I had experienced fleeting moments of dislike towards the repetitive movements forwards and backwards, forwards and backwards from the start. But as my bottom had become angry, and my seat bones developed pressure sores I decided that I *hated* rowing.

However that being said, rowing continued to be the easiest part of a day. Being on the oars was the place where your mind could drift away, it was where you could have space, and it was the seat that you would see wildlife from.

However, on the oars was also the position you would be most subjected to splashing, the soaking of salt water on those salt sores again aggravating them. You remained the victim of flying fish attacks and you had to stay awake at night, especially when steering.

There were definitely lots of moments I would've much rather have been at home but they were fleeting and few and far between. As difficult as things were, the beauty of seeing a mahi mahi fish jump up in the air and flop its belly back down into the water or experiencing a whole 360-degree sunset was just too much to ever want to miss. I had moments of absolute total euphoria, and I honestly do not think that there was one single day that I took for granted on Doris.

We focused on staying in the moment as much as possible and not projecting too much into the future because everything was so variable at sea. Nevertheless, no matter how hard we tried, looking at the stickers that counted how many days we had been at sea versus the mileage count on our satnav, it was impossible not to make predictions as to when we would hit land. Each shift differed so dramatically in terms of our speed and direction that you could almost make a new prediction every couple of hours. This made it particularly difficult for all of our parents that planned to fly out to Cairns to welcome us in when the day finally hit.

We celebrated Christmas on Doris opening presents and singing songs together. Ems and I made sure that the girls felt as Christmassy as possible by beginning the day with a Christmas Carol concert. At the state of our singing, you would have thought that it would have scared off the wildlife. However, it seemed to have the opposite effect! Doris became the Noah's ark of the Pacific with not just one boobie bird landing on her but four!

Then we spent New Year toasting the ocean that had got us close to Cairns and toasting each other for rowing us there.

But we still had miles to go, food supplies were running low and we were at risk of being in danger if a cyclone struck when we were in the shallow waters of the Great Barrier Reef. So we rowed, harder than I most certainly had ever rowed before, putting 100% into each stroke that we pulled to get us to Australia. It wasn't fun, it was tiring and we were in pain. The three girls that I shared Doris with had spent over 250 days on-board compared to my seventy-something, but our bodies were exhausted and we were tired. We drew on our team values SPIRIT - Strength, Perseverance, Inspiration, Resilience, Integrity and Trust. We rowed hard, we rowed strong and we rowed together.

In those last hours together rowing, we were focused. We rowed harder with every stroke pulling us one wave closer to the land that we could now see and smell. It is hard to write in words what land smells of when nostrils have smelt only salt water and body odour and dehydrated food sachets for so long. It smelt like heaven. It smelt like life, like breath, like fresh fruit and a shower, like hugs and family and space to stretch. As we looked at each other with love and fondness, there was not a moment that we had not relied on each other to undertake and complete this challenge. The enormity of what we had achieved was too overwhelming to feel so we kept our eyes on the prize and rowed over the Great Barrier Reef towards our end goal.

On 25th January, 2016 we finally reached Cairns, Australia. After nine months at sea, Doris made landfall setting two world records in the process. Our final approach into Marlin Marina, Cairns saw us being escorted by a fleet of sailing boats and other small craft. As we got closer, we saw the crowds of people awaiting our arrival. As soon as we saw our parents cheering us in, we all became overwhelmed with emotion and I can still remember the feeling of my mum's arms wrapped around me as if I had been lost and she had found me – it felt like home.

Our legs were drunk as our bodies swayed to the non-existent swell of the ocean on land. We were dazed and overwhelmed and hungry and beyond exhausted and yet full to the brim of adrenaline. Cameras flashed around us and furry microphones asked us questions. The cacophony of noise was almost overwhelming. It was as if the time together at sea, just the four of us, had dispersed into thin air, a distant memory.

We were on land. We had completed our journey and what a journey it was. We were just ordinary women doing something extraordinary; there to show the world that you really can do what you put your mind to.

Everyone has a Pacific to cross.

It really was an adventure like no other, with girls like no others. I have no words to describe the way that I feel about each of these awe-inspiring women that I shared this journey with both on and off land. On Doris with Laura, Ems and Nats or on land with Izz and Lizanne, to the very bottom of my heart I love you all. I want to thank you, each one of you for what we have shared: the sights, pains, laughs, fears, tears, moons, stars, sunsets, sunrises, all of the colours of the rainbow, countdowns, sleeps, eats, waves, sores, pains, smiles and the list goes on…

Laura, thank you for giving me the chance to join The Coxless Crew and teaching me how to row hard – really hard. Ems my fellow Christmas fairy, I thank you for teaching me to row using my legs and to grunt through the pain with me. Nats for making me laugh like I have never laughed before, for twerking and for keeping me in the moment. Lizanne thank you for comparing our muscles over Skype in the build up to our legs of the row, for telling me everything would be ok in Samoa. Izz for supporting me through a twenty-four-hour row-athon after your return from the Pacific, and for embracing my family's craziness in the process. Last but not least, thank you to Doris for keeping us afloat and always pushing us forwards.

I love you all, in my heart forever.

Meg

X

Email: **Megdyos1@gmail.com**

Instragram: **@megdyos**

Chapter 14

One Tribe

By Alejandra Eifflaender-Salmón

Have you ever felt lost and alone, even when you're surrounded by people? Have you ever felt isolated, unwelcome, unwanted?

That's how I felt.

But then I found my tribe.

Peru

Over forty years ago, I was born in darkest Peru, just like Paddington! Fifteen days later my parents had to move to a different country for work.

Years later, we came back as a family and got lost in the beauty of the country, the culture, food and music. I had an amazing childhood full of sunshine and joy. We lived in a beautiful house in a safe suburb in Lima. The capital of Peru, Lima sits on top of a cliff overlooking the vast Pacific Ocean. Panoramic views stretch out over the crashing waves, down to the beaches below and up to the broad blue sky. This stretch is often called Costa Verde (Green Coast) because of the hanging green vegetation that covers the otherwise barren cliffs.

In our neighborhood, Miraflores, we could ride bicycles and play outside, appreciating the perfectly manicured gardens, with vibrant flowers and swaying palm trees gazing down at us as we rode by, the wind in our hair and not a care in our hearts.

We went to a good private school, my brother and I, where we had great teachers. I used to perform at a well-known theatre and built sandcastles with my brother at our beach house south of the city. Life was incredible growing up in such an amazing place. Lima has a lot to offer and yet most of the tourists skip the city and head straight for Machu Picchu or the Amazon. However, for those who visit Lima, the reward is great. It's the food capital of Latin America!

But unfortunately, terrorism was like an ever present shadow in the background of my life. In the 70s and 80s, violence wracked the city through selective assassinations of political opponents. Peruvians lived their lives under siege, not knowing where the next bomb would explode or who would be the next target. Ask anyone what it was like to live in Peru at the time and they will have at least one story of a bomb, a murder or a kidnapping involving their family or friends. It was an especially difficult time for my family as both my parents were diplomats – prime targets in this particular war.

One day, my brother was kidnapped by the terrorists. He was only seven years old. I came home from school and everyone was sitting in the living room being unusually quiet. No one told me what was going on. They just sat in silence staring at the floor. I asked for my brother. That's when dad told me.

I thought things like this only happen in movies. One thousand thoughts went rushing through my head! I can't believe this is happening to us! Can the same situation happen to me? How do I answer the phone if it's about my brother?

I felt scared, confused, worried. I was angry at the people who took him and angry at myself for not protecting him better! It felt like my heart was being ripped in two.

Luckily, one anxiety filled week later, he was dropped off in an isolated park in the outskirts of Lima. He was unharmed. We'd paid a large ransom for his release, but it was worth every penny. When he got back, I felt happy and angry at the same time. I was glad to have my brother is back with us. I picked him up and just screamed, 'My brother, my brother is back!'

My little brother has always been my best friend, and no one can replace him, I felt very proud to be his older sister and his protector. I just hugged him, breathing in the smell of his tousled hair, and told him that I loved him and that I'm proud of him and so happy he was safe.

My parents had developed close bonds with their friends at this time. Perhaps it was the fear and dread that brought them closer together. They'd pulled a tribe close around themselves, like a protective force field against the horror of the terrorism.

But suddenly, when I was twelve, my parents packed our bags and off we went to another destination. In their minds we had to leave, move forwards and heal the wounds of our past. A time I remember as mostly idyllic was also full of pain and terror for my parents. They'd lived for years in constant fear for their lives and the lives of their children.

We left my beloved Peru. I was lost, adrift without a tribe to call my own.

Michael

I was twenty-four years old and in London when I decided to go back and rediscover the countries in Latin America.

Latin American food is very special. Their cooking styles have always fascinated me. The diverse land holds cuisines which are a fusion of many cultures. Criollo cuisine is a blend of ingredients, cooking techniques, spices and flavours from all over the world. It's an eccentric fusion of indigenous, Asian, West African, and European cooking that makes Peru's food irresistible and unforgettable. The variety of the food changes from place to place. While away in other countries, every time I tasted the Latin American food, inhaled the smells of ceviche, seafood or quinoa, it brought back memories of my happy childhood. Ceviche is an explosion of flavour in your mouth: an appetizing sensual dish prepared by curing raw fish in marinated freshly squeezed lime juice, with crispy onions, chilli peppers and coriander that gives the scent of freshness to the dish. It's simply exquisite!

I met Michael, my husband, in that magical time when I returned to Peru in search of the tribe I had left all those years ago. We had both lived and worked very near each other in London. We'd frequented the same places, walked in the same parks, drunk coffee in the same cafés, danced at the same parties, but we didn't meet until we were both in South America.

We grew up in very different worlds, yet much of our childhood was similar — the music, the fashion, the travel. However, whereas Michael used to listen to music and play guitar and video games, I loved to dance and adored the sea. Where Michael lived in a safe environment in the North of England, I was used to seeing the destruction of bombs. Michael loves the mountains, Joni Mitchell and travel and, thankfully, I love all that too! We were both young with so much passion for life. We wanted our own adventure, to create and discover a parallel world outside the city where we could help others.

Michael and I met through friends while traveling and fell in love almost instantly, one night we were on a bar and the owner told us he had a special drink for us. He took a big glass jar from a high shelf. Inside swirled some pale yellow alcoholic liquid. And inside the liquid curled a huge and very dead snake. He told us the drink was called 'snake juice' and had a special way to put together souls (of course we laughed at him). After dinner, we decided to try the magic drink. The snake juice was bitter and strong, the flavour of the unfortunate reptile masked by the intense burning heat of the alcohol.

But it worked. We spent the rest of the week in our shared house cooking, eating, talking and laughing and thinking how beautiful it was that this snake juice had brought our souls together.

This is also when we had the idea for the Voodoo Café.

Voodoo Café

The Voodoo Cafe was a small coffee bar in San Blas – Cuzco. The walls were orange and it had round wooden tables covered in old erotic comics that we found in a vintage local market. San Blas is a lovely part of the city, well known as the artisan quarter. It has many cobblestoned paths, quite like a hipster hangout, with lots of pretty cafés, galleries and the most amazing views over the Cuzco skyline. We wanted to create a small space of fun, adventure, information and equality.

We started the café to support the local orphanages and a local home/hospital for children with disabilities. Rather than just giving money, we wanted to be personally involved in the solution for our local community.

In Cuzco, we lived many stories. We had the best English breakfast with 'authentic' Heinz beans (made to a secret recipe invented by blending local beans with ketchup and mustard! It was so convincing that our breakfasts were very popular).

The funny thing was that, wherever you go, food always connects people. One of our specialties at the Voodoo Café was our homemade brownies. Oh MY! They were yummy! Our brownies were super thick, fudgy, a bit chewy and chocolatey with the perfect crust on top that just melts in your mouth! They were there to make your life more delicious.

We had days of karaoke with great and bad singers, days of poetry and open mic where the stories varied from amazing prose to desperate cries for attention. The café also had a day dedicated to the small local gay community as they were not many places for gay local and non-local people to go.

Looking back, it was certainly worthwhile. With the money we earned, we used to go to the local children's hospitals and orphanages to help in as many ways as we could. Fundraising for the children's needs brought much happiness, like celebrating the kids' birthdays with cakes and entertainment for the whole day.

When I was a child, I remember the cruelty and impact terrorism left in those communities, and one of my dreams was to give back to the country where I was born.

Would you do the same? It doesn't have to be much – maybe a present for children in hospital at Christmas or a donation to a local food bank. Maybe you can offer some time to volunteer at a local wildlife reserve?

Every plate eaten at our cafe was going to help others. Our small tribe of two soon became a vibrant tribe of hundreds – all supporting each other and bringing joy to each other's lives. I found a new type of strength in dealing with human atrocities, in knowing that, although I couldn't change the world, I could play my small part in making a difference.

The Amazon Jungle

The good thing was that we were able to leave the café in safe hands to go travelling. We travelled along the Andean Cordillera through the Altiplano (the high tableland of central South America) and deep into the Amazonian jungle.

That's how we arrived to Pilcopata. Pilcopata is also known as the valley of Kosñipata (land of the clouds), a humid place where the sun rose every day, There was only a few houses, a local shop with the only telephone in the village and a small police station. We had to stop in Pilcopata because it was one of the last towns before reaching the Amazon jungle.

The day we arrived at Pilcopata, we spent hours making two handmade bamboo boats with Américo, our young guide, and Ciro, the local shaman. We made quite an eccentric team.

The scale of the Amazon is hard to comprehend – it's estimated that 2.5 million insect species inhabit the rainforest, as well as at least forty thousand tree and plant species and many thousands of birds and mammals. It's also an endangered part of our planet. The problems with deforestation are well-known, and illegal mining and oil extraction are also big issues in many areas.

My main concern about the Amazon was flesh-eating piranhas. I was so wrong! The place was peaceful and the river roared loudly into my soul.

Millions of butterflies surrounded us like an enchanted paradise. The trees where so green and tall stretching towards the sky like powerful ancestors, protectors of the land but also vulnerable to the will of humans. The sky was blue and bright and full of elegance. The luscious green all around made me speechless to witness such life, such beauty. The deeper we were navigated down the river in our handmade boats, the more often we caught a rare glimpse of remote animals skittering, startled through the undergrowth. The place was mind blowing. You can feel the so calm and frightened at the same time when you are in the jungle.

On our way, we encountered the screech of birds and croaky roar of the howler monkeys. It was like being shouted at by an army of King Kong's! Howlers have the distinction of being the loudest land animal in the world. Their territorial calls can be heard up to three miles away. They were all hiding on top of the trees, out of sight but well within earshot. Funny creatures!

We had many amazing encounters on our journey: giant otters, piranhas, hoatzin (also known as the reptile bird), South American tapirs and the famous black caiman. The first time I saw this mottled, grey reptile basking on the banks, I excitedly thought, 'Congratulations! You've just seen a wild black caiman.' It just stared back at me with large uncaring, unblinking eyes. The black caiman is the largest predator in the Amazon, and it can grow at least five metres (sixteen feet) and possibly up to six metres (twenty feet) in length. The one I saw was a little titchy but I still felt a chill of danger as I watched it from the safety of our boat.

While we were on our way, Américo told us about a young American man that used to visit the area and had recently been eaten alive by a black caiman while swimming in a river pool nearby. For a moment, all I could see were caiman. Every log on every riverbank was suddenly a scaly lizard. After that story, I wasn't even brave enough to go for a swim!

Suddenly, around another bend in the river, we saw two large boats crammed with half naked men. They wore feather belts made of plant material and had painted their bodies with tattoos. Their eyes were black and they wore crowns of toucan and curassow feathers. In their hands they brandished a selection of stone spears and bows with arrows notched. They did not look happy to see us.

I thought we were in a scene from the movie The Mission. We were ready to say our goodbyes, AMEN!

These guys were part of the Machiguenga tribe, many of whom live without contact from the outside world. The Machiguenga people are like other indigenous Amazonians and tend to be short, strong and slim with broad, pleasant facial features.

I don't have a Peruvian accent. Because of all my travels my Spanish is quite well spoken, with a twist of Mexican or Argentinian. I was worried whether the tribe's people would even understand me, especially in this situation of life and death! How could I explain to these people my life story in a minute or two? How could they know anything about the Western world if they'd lived most of their lives in isolation?

They pulled their boat alongside ours and one man began talking in short sharp sentences. He told us that we weren't welcome here. That we should turn back now. The threat from the pointed spears and arrows was very clear.

I took a deep breath. In Spanish, which I hoped they would understand, I told them that many years earlier my dad had come to the area. I told them his name.

The old tribal chief's face suddenly split into a massive smile of recognition. He remembered him! *'Gracias a Pachamama!'* We were, for the moment, safe. Phew!

So we climbed into their boats and we were on our way as welcome guests of the community. The Machiguengas are renowned for usually being non-violent and for their warm reception of visitors. But they have become suspicious of strangers as they have had many encounters more recently with aggressive people searching for gold.

The first day we spent in their community was great. They had heard of England and asked if our king was David Beckham! They even invited Michael to play football for the afternoon. They were very proud of the way they played. Poor Michael was horrified of their tactics and decided that the way to make friends was to let them win!

"Did you enjoy the football match?" I asked the sweat-covered Michael as he hobbled over to get a swig of water from the flask I was holding.

"You're kidding?" He laughed and rolled his trouser leg up to show a purple bruise that was expanding across his shin like a snake bite. "Bunch of foulers, if you ask me. I suppose I should let them win, though."

I gave him an encouraging pat on the back and a kiss on the cheek and sent him back into the fray. My brave husband on the front line!

I sat with the ladies and elderly of the community, laughing and learning to make handmade bags with natural yarn which they picked from trees. I would occasionally look up to cheer my husband and laugh with the ladies at the funny way the *gringos* (foreigners) run; a bit like a quirky duck, we agreed.

After football, they took the time to teach us how to catch the food we would need to survive. We went to the edge of the river to turn over every single stone in a search of river crawfish, or river langoustine as they called it. We had to lift quite big stones and catch the lobster-like creatures with our hands before they slipped away or gave us a nip. I think we were pretty good at the job as we managed to fill a bucket full of river langoustine while others went on a hunt for catfish.

That evening, we had a delicious meal. They had prepared rice and a yummy catfish soup. We were so grateful for the beautiful food and felt proud that we had collected it to share with the community. Within a few hours we felt part of their tribe!

Later, we had a ceremonial ritual. The natives had prepared *chicha* especially for us. *Chicha*, is a fermented drink made of cassava. It has a pale, straw-yellow colour with a slightly milky appearance. I must admit, *chicha* tastes more like a melted popsicle, with a nutty aftertaste. It's horrible, but we had to drink the special homemade brew. Quispe, the chief of the tribe, gave us two necklaces with jaguar teeth to protect us from the *chucanchaki*, the malicious spirit that haunts in the forest.

This first magical trip holds many memories for us. Our month with the Machiguenga tribe was the start of an amazing friendship. Michael and I felt both amazed and intrigued by their culture. Traditionally, the Machiguenga believe in the divinity and sacredness of the nature around them. They believe the forest is there to nurture them, its plants, herbs, animals and fish, and that the earth is working in harmony to sustain everything in the world.

Over time we dedicated ourselves to helping them in many ways. We brought the resources they needed to work on their plantations, basic materials like pens and books for their education and I used to bring medicine and help cure the wounded.

In return they gave us the knowledge of how to survive in the wild. They taught us the simple way to life live at its fullest, and they gave me the acceptance, the feeling of belonging, like part of the family in their tribe.

However, it was not all joy. I saw how global economies were hurting my tribe. We have seen the impact that big companies have had in the Amazon; the chopping of their wood and the impact on their communities and the wildlife. Many of them are living in extreme poverty. We have rescued children from the hands of bad people, and even helped children and adults that had been shot when loggers were hunting natives. Recently, loggers and miners have been clearing new roads to infiltrate the Amazon rainforest inhabited by these uncontacted groups of Machiguengas, putting their survival in jeopardy.

We saw so many problems with deforestation, mining and oil extraction that it is very difficult for me to describe. The scars, both physically in the landscape and emotionally in my heart, run deep. However, the one thing I have learned is that when a problem seems insurmountable, there is always something you can do – and the benefits are mutual.

Fortuitously, due to the impenetrable Amazon rainforest, some small groups of Machiguengas have survived to this day and remain living in voluntary isolation from Western civilization.

Back in the UK

Years later we came back to Britain, young, poor (because we had given all our money to the poor), but with lots of energy and love to give!

Michael and I came to the UK charged with so much energy, thinking we could do something positive in a new tribe, in our new community in Cheshire. Sadly, reality hit me and left me broken into a million pieces. I could find no one to give my love to, no one to teach, no one to help. I'd ask myself where my empty life was going, feeling no sense of direction. What was stopping me from doing the things I wanted to do? Maybe it was the anonymous buzz of urban life? Or a lack of interest people had in improving their situation? Maybe I was not 'one of them' and therefore not accepted into their 'tribe'.

I watched from a distance as my parents, my friends and loved ones passed away on the other side of the world. I felt so impotent. My days became nights and my nights became days. All that I felt was a mess. I became the shadow of my life, feeling lonely, depressed and sad.

Throughout history it has always been difficult for outsiders to integrate into a new group of people in a foreign country. Yet it has been proven, time and time again, that these new arrivals can not only integrate, but also become productive and valuable members who contribute to their adopted country.

My grey days turned to hell. I couldn't cope with the cold weather, the indifference of the people in the town. I was feeling broken like a jigsaw puzzle, split into a million pieces. Maybe the negativity converted me into an anonymous face in the crowd instead of a useful member of the community. The worst of it was that I felt unwelcome and unwanted.

When I was eight months pregnant, I was looking in a shop window in my new hometown in Cheshire. I was pushed and beaten on my back by a man with an umbrella, yelling at me that foreign people had no place in the town. Was it about my skin color? Or maybe I don't belong here? Should I go to the police? Is he going to attack me again? Should I be silent? That day when I arrived home, I cried all day and felt trapped in a place where I was not welcome. I missed the old me, the happy person I had been! I thought if I could read my own mind then all I would read was tears. I felt like a waste of space.

I have always had dyslexia, which made me feel a bit different and isolated, but now I found myself slipping into postnatal depression. I even shaved my hair and threw my clothes into the rubbish, not realizing the next day, I would have to go out in the clothes I was wearing as that was all I had left. Everything in my life became negative.

Have you ever felt you were in a place where you don't fit in? That's how I felt. I felt lost, not knowing who I was. Was I a wife, mother, colleague, foreigner? Who were my tribe? I didn't know the answer. I had been 'Alejandra' but now they knew me as 'Alexandra'. Maybe this small change would help me fit in, I thought, but it felt as though part of me was lost. And it made no difference to how I was seen.

Part of me felt as though I was living a clandestine life, hiding from everyone and everything. I was lost in a strange town. Although I was captivated by my surroundings in the Cheshire countryside, I felt scared and alone. I wondered what was not to love about where I lived but something was missing.

What did I really want for my life? I was sick of not knowing who I was, I was sick of being unhappy, of not having a smile! I was afraid of the town, of the people, of the darkness, of my life.

I just wanted to feel accepted, integrated, and to develop connections. I craved togetherness, community and to belong to a new tribe.

Sometimes just reaching out and taking someone's hand can be the beginning of the journey to overcome our fears and sense of loss.

Light came from the darkness when, one day, my husband and I decided to join a sailing club. Water had been always been my passion and my inspiration. Back in Peru I was once a surfing champion, but now I was living in a beautiful village surrounded by hills.

The sailing club instantly brought back my fighting spirit and my love for water. I made so many friends who today I consider as family - the community I was looking to find for so many years. This was a new tribe! We connected through our love of water. I think that to be connected by water is a way of life. It represents a people and community, a tribe so tightly bound by their love and passion for water, be it oceans, bays, rivers, lakes or streams. Water can always make a strong connection. Just like the Amazon tribes all connected though water.

Months later I was offered a position on the sailing club committee, and I brought the first stand up paddle board to the club. It was an instant success. So many people, both experienced sailors and people that didn't sail, became interested in paddle boarding. So, I decided to train as an instructor to teach people free of charge. I wanted to share my love of the water through paddle boarding, and it has been an inspiration for me to help them. I started to find myself again and the darkness started to disappear.

Something else that connected me to my new tribe was not just the passion for water but also food. I spend many days at the sailing club in summer helping to cater for people around the UK. I love food and I believe it has the power to make connections and help integrating communities. It nourishes me spiritually and I get excited sharing my knowledge and recipes that I have picked up from around the world.

Today we have regular gatherings with paddle boarding friends from different clubs and groups all over the UK. I have taught over a hundred people and my life could not be happier.

I am now able again to continue to support people and charities worldwide. From Latin America to Africa. All these give me the strength to look back and reflect on my positive and privileged life here in such a wonderful and safe place. In the name of my parents, my husband, brother, sister and I decided to support the people who were at the beginning of my life, never forgetting the beautiful land where I was born, by supporting local communities in the UK and throughout Latin America in the form of charities in all the ways we can. In Latin America, we provide food and resources for the poor, the elderly and children, helping local fisherman in small fishing communities, lifeguards and doctors in rural places, and bringing help to people in jails and rehabilitation centres for alcohol and drugs addiction.

I also feel very privileged to help and support few charities around the world from Latin America to Africa. I feel that is important, Because "Giving is not just about donating. It is about making a difference." I feel that my mission is beyond borders.

My message today is… Like the people of the Amazon, we all need to find a place in the world, our own tribe. If you are feeling lost or alone, ask yourself what has stopped you from finding togetherness, community and belonging?

Wherever you're from, whatever your background, if there's something you want to do then there is a way. We all have good days and bad days, but don't forget that the embrace – the hug – of our tribe can always bring light. Human beings are not designed to live in isolation. 'No woman/man is an island' as the old saying goes.

Sport, music and, most importantly, food could all be the catalysts to finding your tribe. Find your tribe and find the people who make you feel good. Say Yes More and make your life meaningful. Everything is possible and positive when you Say Yes More!

Website: **our-tribe.co.uk**

Chapter 15

The Chemotherapy Chronicles: Hiking the Trans-Catalina Trail

By Charlotte Fowles

I peeled off my sock and surveyed the damage. The flies immediately congregated on the bits of my foot that were oozing – it was disgusting but also fascinating. I had heard that the chemotherapy treatment might make my skin more susceptible to blisters, but I hadn't realised exactly what that would mean for me on this hike.

Although I had used Compeed plasters to try and prevent blisters, I hadn't been expecting just how destroyed my feet would be. On the heels, on the toes, under the instep. There didn't seem a part of my feet that wasn't bleeding or blistered or both – apart from, thankfully, the soles of my feet.

Despite having hiked for many years with barely a blister, it was definitely different these days. I'd bought decent boots and been fitted properly for them, including insoles, but due to the necessary operation and the subsequent treatment programme, I'd had limited time to break them in. This probably wasn't helping.

In some places (perhaps from the heat) the Compeed had started to ooze its substance, rather than staying stuck to the foot. This mixed with the blister fluid and blood to form a hideous, sticky mess. This was why I changed my socks at lunch every day; I really didn't want them to get infected. I had deliberately chosen this route and this time of year – the Trans-Catalina Trail in California in October – as I wanted it to be a little cooler. But a heatwave had swept in and the temperatures were punishing.

I cleaned my feet up as best I could, re-dressing where they needed it, and pulled on the clean socks. I attached the first pair – wet with sweat – to the outside of my pack and put on my sandals. I took some weird comfort in the little ritual, feeling the air on my feet and the relief of sitting down, knowing that it wouldn't be long before I'd put my feet back into their hot boot-hell ready for the afternoon section of the trail. Having the socks hanging there like a pair of sodden rats made me think of pictures and films I had seen where people do this. I felt a little more like a 'real' hiker.

*

Back in January, before I had been diagnosed with stage 3b skin cancer, I had set myself the goal of a solo, multi-day hike. I had no idea where or how long or what that would look like. I just knew I wanted to do one.

I had spent the previous two years doing a lot more things independently from my husband in order to increase my confidence when I was alone. We'd done many outdoors adventures together, from crossing the Australian outback for months in our four-wheel drive, to hiking in Nepal. But it was because we did so much together that I thought it was important to do more by myself.

People tend to get into a routine when they spend lots of time together (including on adventures) and we were no different. We knew what our strengths were and played to them. I knew that I relied on him for some things, and I wanted to be more self-reliant. I also lost self-confidence as the years went by. I needed it to change.

I'd had conversations with people who said "Oh, that's just what happens as you get older," and I couldn't accept this, not for myself. And especially not at aged thirty-nine! I knew that if I did accept it, then it would prevent me from accomplishing things that I really wanted, and I couldn't live with that. I needed to fight against this.

I also had more fear as a result of suffering a horrific leg break four years before, which had left me unable to walk for three months. I hated this new, more fearful part of me. I understood it – my body's reaction to the accident was designed to keep me safe – but it didn't feel like me.

We had originally planned on coming to California together but now, in another twist, after fifteen years together, we were getting divorced. So here I was, alone on a solo hike that I had wished for but with significant things in my life having shifted in major ways.

*

The Trans-Catalina Trail itself was described by most people that wrote about it as 'tough'. It is a one-way, 38.5 mile trail traversing the length of Catalina Island, twenty-two miles off the coast of Southern California. With over 8,600 feet in elevation gain/loss, most blogs and guides advised walking poles as a must and described how challenging parts of it were, particularly navigating the extremely steep downhill sections. With a lack of shade on the trail, it can be very hot and dry. It would feel hotter still as there is no water stops between the campgrounds.

I wasn't particularly ego-driven in choosing this trail despite its descriptions. Choosing it had depended on fitting in with other logistical factors. I didn't feel the need to prove anything to myself or others. I wanted this as a learning experience for me. I eventually want to do a much longer, months' long hike, and so this felt like I was testing the waters.

I knew I could do challenges of various descriptions. Two months before this, I had completed a challenge to hike the length of Dartmoor in two days, and had done this with a small group of women. I had learnt extra skills and tips from our excellent group leader. I learnt what it was like to carry a heavy pack long distances. I learnt that having strict time-pressures, covering certain distances in a set amount of time and pushing ourselves at a pretty sparky pace was very do-able, and I was capable. But I wouldn't do that again. Why not? Because I had now shown myself that I could, and I had learnt more of what I enjoyed and what I didn't.

I love being outside, and I also love being in places that *feel* quite remote. Where you don't see many people at all. Where you can enjoy moments of deep stillness. Where you can marvel at the natural surroundings. Where your rules are your own. I love the slower pace of hiking and kayaking, and I love the smaller details that you see which you can miss in a car or a faster boat. I love the early morning freshness and the smells and sounds when you're camping – like the wafts of wood smoke from a fire and the noise of the insects in the trees at night. I love the feeling of enjoying a beautiful spot in solitude because you made the extra effort to get up earlier and go a little further.

And I also loved having the time to enjoy these things and not be in a constant rush or under pressure. So, I had taken on board some of the hiking blogs' advice regarding this trail and decided to spread the distance over five days rather than three.

*

I started the hike from Avalon Harbour after catching the ferry from San Pedro. Due to arriving around 5pm, I wouldn't be able to start the trail that day, so I walked the one and a half miles to the Hermit Gulch campground so I could be up early and ready to start properly the following morning.

Even in that short distance, I could feel the weight of my pack. Despite this, I felt my shoulders loosen. I took deep breaths in and reminded myself that there was no rush. I whispered my new motto to myself as I went: "Slow down to speed up." As I relaxed, my chest rose and fell slowly with these deep breaths and I felt at peace with the path I was about to walk.

As I arrived at the site, I was relieved to find the warden still there... just! I took my map, my instructions for the site and headed towards my pitch. I could have chosen anywhere as I was the only guest. Despite Catalina Island being a real tourist hotspot with many visitors from L.A., on a Monday night out of the high season, I already had some of the solitude I was craving.

I set down the pack on a bench, already relieved to have it off my back after even a short walk, and momentarily wondered how I would carry it for so much longer over the five days. Undoubtedly, I was carrying a bit too much and that was one of the things I had set out to learn. In my relative naivety and generally being fairly strong, I had wondered how much difference a few grams here and there *really* made. This was how I was going to find out!

I had accepted that I had too much but there were good reasons for most of the extras. In the normal world, I would never have dreamed of taking trainers as well as my boots and sandals, but my cancer and chemotherapy world was not normal. I was quite wary of how my feet would be in the new-ish boots if my skin really was bad, and wanted a back-up. After the Dartmoor hike earlier in the year, I was already missing three toenails, and I was hoping not to have a repeat of this with these boots. The rigid fabric made me nervous.

As I contemplated my enormous bag, which weighed just under fifty pounds, I told myself the same thing I normally did when faced with an issue, "Well, you'll just have to get on with it, won't you?!" I found this vaguely reassuring in a weird way! Knowing that there wasn't any choice but to get on with it felt immensely freeing.

I started setting up camp – a ritual that I really enjoy. Simply opening up the tent bag and releasing the smell – the tang of the tarpaulin – is enough to cause a rush of happiness and, if you're not on an adventure at the time, the yearning to embark on one as soon as possible.

As it was approaching dusk, I kept my eye out for wildlife. Being so close to the town, I wasn't expecting much. Suddenly, my eyes caught a movement and looked to my right. An island fox was slinking out from under a hedge. Native to the Channel Islands of California, I was excited to see one. I've seen literally hundreds of foxes in my life, but there's always something much more exotic about even a relatively common animal when you're overseas! As a herd of deer started to graze through the campsite, I remembered the dolphins and whale I had seen from the ferry trip over. I was feeling pretty smug about my wildlife encounters so far.

I was not feeling smug about my tent pitch, however. Being October, and after the usually very hot, dry summer, the ground was extremely hard. I had wisely eschewed the extra weight of a peg hammer, so I found a large rock to bash the pegs in with. As it (inevitably) glanced off and grazed my knuckle, I made a mental note: 'Trail Injury Number One'.

I decided to keep a track of various happenings that I suspected would be quite regular. It was 'Hiking and Camping Bingo'. When you're by yourself for days, you need to make your own entertainment! And after stubbing my toe on one of the pegs and tripping on a guy rope, I felt well on the way to having a full house.

After a quick re-hydrated meal dinner, I got ready to settle in for the night. As I was packing away my tiny stove, a young couple joined the campsite. They pitched far away from me, and I started thinking more seriously about the fact that the ranger had now gone home and I was alone with them. What if they disturbed me? At best, that would be through being noisy and disrupting my sleep. At worst, they could choose to interact with me aggressively, perhaps if they got drunk. And I wouldn't be able to do anything about it. I thought that I was safer when there was no one else around.

As I sat there in the dark inside my little tent-sanctuary, looking at the canvas surrounding me, I pushed the thoughts from my mind. What could I do? Whether or not I saw other humans on the trail, I would have to deal with it. Worrying about who might be out there – potentially psychopaths as well as normal people – would not serve me in any way. I could do nothing to change this, so, as with all other aspects, I would just have to get on with it.

Before I zipped up the tent I spent some time looking at the stars. Out here, on this island, far from the insanity of L.A., I thought that the stars glittered so much brighter and called out to me so much more than the city lights ever had done.

A frog chorus started and I smiled. This. This was what I had come for. Me, the natural world and nothing else.

*

I was excited as I set off in the morning – my stomach was tingling and I was smiling broadly. Obviously, I took the obligatory selfie, and with a wry smile, wondered what sort of state I'd be in a few hours' time if I took another one! This first day was to be the longest. It also started off straight up a tough hill. I knew this and had decided that it was better to get it out of the way earlier. All I had to do was just keep going.

Wow! So much easier said than done. Tough didn't even come close. Even at 8.30am it was baking hot in the sun. Walking up and up and up continuously with no shade. I knew there was a lookout at the top of this first horrible stretch, so I bargained with myself that I would have a proper stop then as it probably wouldn't take me all that long.

I tried not to look up – which was a good job as I would have found it nearly impossible to! Alongside paying attention to the ground because rattlesnakes were one of the dangers of the trail, I could only really look at my feet. Perhaps by looking at them I could will them to move a little faster and make it a bit easier?

I started counting my steps in sets of twenty. Every time I got to a hundred steps, I let myself pause and lean right forward on my walking poles. I sucked in a few deep breaths just for a few moments before I began the trudge upwards again. What on earth was I doing?! This was insane! This became my next item on the Hiking and Camping Bingo – how many times would I question my own sanity?

One advantage of hiking by yourself is no one can hear how totally mad you sound talking to yourself. Over the course of the trail, I often spoke out loud to myself. I encouraged, cajoled, chastised, insulted, apologised to and laughed at myself. Sometimes I would speak only to some parts of my body; "Come on, feet, *move*. You're never going to get this over with unless you blooming well MOVE!"; and sometimes I would talk to my whole physical being together; "Come on, body. You're doing *so* well. I'm sorry. I know you've already been through a lot, but you can do this! Yes, you can. Look how much you've done already! It's literally just one foot in front of the other. Keep going. Slow and steady wins the race!"

Being by oneself whilst doing something challenging is a type of double-edged sword. When I've been with companions before, it's great to help pass the time, encourage each other on the harder sections and have a good laugh after a stressful bit is over. But there are also those times when you can't talk to anyone and just need to get your head down and keep going. Those moments when it's really tough and you need to ignore everyone and shut everything out. When you're with someone and you're trying to encourage them, it's hard to know what stage of this mental state they're at. Whether they're at the 'I need encouragement' phase, or the 'if anyone talks to me or tries to jolly me along, I may well stab them' phase.

I think it was fortuitous that I was alone on this trail for, as I told myself in one of the harsher moments, there was no one else to blame but myself!

After arriving at the first campsite a lot later than I thought I would, I was saved from mentally beating myself up about that too much when I met two guys hiking together, Chris and Jack – the only other two people there. I had seen them ahead of me earlier that day and presumed they had arrived at the campsite ages before me. As we got chatting, I learnt that one of them had done a few of the really difficult hikes in the U.S. and he reminded me that we had climbed over three thousand feet of elevation today. Apparently, the rule was to add one hour onto your expected time for every thousand feet gained. That, along with the wisdom that it usually takes a couple of days into each hike to find your 'hiking legs', helped reassure me that it wasn't only me that found these things really taxing.

He also remarked that a sadist must have designed the trail route considering that, at the end of a very tough elevation day, the campsite that you had to get to was situated up another hill!

*

I hadn't appreciated before I started the trail that, in fact, each and every day would begin by going uphill. I don't know why I didn't pay more attention to that, or if I had done, it would have made any difference. Like many things in life, once you're in the middle of it, you keep on keeping on and potentially don't appreciate the significance or impact of certain details until you look back.

Along with the daily hill starts, the days fell into a rhythm of sorts. Carlos was right. After two days, it wasn't exactly easier, but my had body adapted in its own way. Which also wasn't in the way I was used to.

What I found especially difficult to get used to since starting the chemotherapy was that my body was not my own. It behaves differently with many unpleasant side effects, and the fatigue was tough. No matter how much sleep I had, even if there had been twenty-five hours in the day, I would have slept that long and still been tired. Not tired as we usually know it, but a bone-deep, utter exhaustion that required the utmost effort to get up and out of bed, and caused me to yawn constantly throughout every day. A physical challenge like this was bound to be extra strenuous, but it was as if my brain had just not accepted that.

What was utterly wonderful about this hike was the *different* feeling of exhaustion that I had at the end of each day. Instead of utter weariness and a leech of energy from deep inside, my body felt used and really achy. I was almost delighted with this physical sensation – to feel as if I had moved my body and expended my energy in an honest, hardworking way was so much more welcome. I slept better every night than I ever had when camping before.

*

The trail traversing the island, and including so many steep hills, meant that I very often had incredible views. One section of the trail which took me through the highest point in the island and across a ridge rewarded me with views of the ocean on both sides. The terrain was generally (after a blazing Californian summer and current heatwave) fairly barren and dusty. One blog I had read had said that, at times, although the trail is well marked, it seemed to disappear in the new growth of grass. Well, that wasn't a problem for me! Much of the vegetation was brown and dried and I could clearly see the trail snaking its way across the ridges for miles in the distance.

There was greenery, in the form of the plants that thrive in such dry environments. It reminded me of what I'd seen in the Mediterranean including a lot of cactus. Many of these were sprouting prickly pears, and the bright red fruit added some much-needed colour to the landscape. The sea was the deepest of blues, and when I could see the small harbours, the lighter turquoise and jade waters sparkled invitingly. From up on the ridge, I longed to be down on the beach plunging my throbbing and shredded feet into the cooling ocean.

I did get the opportunity to do so on a few occasions. One of the real highlights of the hike that made the strenuous, sweaty and shadeless trudging worthwhile was the fact that a lot of the campsites were next to picture perfect inlets and beaches.

One afternoon I arrived at the campsite at 2.30pm. This was an occasion where I was delighted with my decision of not only spreading the hike out over more days, but getting up and setting off as early as I could each day. This had the double benefit of doing much of the uphill sections before the heat got to its most severe and finishing that section earlier in the day. With the ocean to yourself and a beach to enjoy, it is infinitely preferable to have time to sit and watch the waves crashing softly on the sand to turning up at 5pm and racing to get the necessary tasks done before the light goes.

I was extra glad that I had this to myself on this occasion. I set down my pack on the beach that had a slightly wild and remote air about it. Driftwood was strewn across the sand in places, the waves gently fell against the shoreline and seabirds were circling and calling to each other.

Taking this all in, I burst into tears. This wonderful, peaceful place was so reminiscent of somewhere my (now estranged) husband and I would have been on one of our adventures together. All the reminders that my mind was tuning into were from a time when our life was full of hope and everything was so different. But that was no more and could no longer be.

I dried my tears, found myself a rock to sit on and watched the waves. I had always found water very calming and almost meditative, and so it was today as the small waves rolled in and out, in and out. As my hair blew across my face, I began to taste the salt carried on the breeze and I stretched out my legs in front of me – the fresh air relieving my hot, hardworking feet. My leg muscles enjoyed the feeling of the stretch, used but not completely spent.

Sitting there, immersed in one of natures' most vital rhythms – that of the waves and the tide – my mind drifted back to the events leading up to this moment right here.

My diagnosis had come in February.

After surviving many traumas already, I'd decided that 2019 was going to be my year. I was turning forty in December and I had a great deal of adventures planned, culminating in an epic trip over my birthday to celebrate.

But cancer had other plans. I'd had surgery to remove some lymph nodes and a large patch of skin from my back where the dodgy mole had been. And now, stage 3b cancer, the oncologist explained, meant that it had spread into my lymph nodes and I would therefore need chemotherapy.

I remember feeling an odd, slightly out-of-body sensation, as if I was watching a scene unfold below me, hovering above, observing. It's such a cliché, but as the doctor continued to explain the diagnosis, I sort of watched the scene with my mind gently floating.

I knew the language of cancer well – my dearest Dad had died eight years ago from bowel cancer, and then, at the age of just thirty-six, my best friend Mel died from aggressive breast cancer. I couldn't help but think of them as I'd listened to the words, and I'd felt a deep sadness again for Mel as her suffering had been – in my opinion – so much worse than what I would go through.

Which was why, six months later, as I sat listening to the soft rush and drag of the waves, I was still managing to feel incredibly lucky – despite the pain of my torn feet and the sadness of the past.

*

No matter how far into the trail I was or how used my body got to the activity, some things didn't appear to change. One constant source of almost morbid amusement to me was the mile markers on the trail. It was incredibly well signposted with a marker at each and every mile. Except for two of them quite early on. But this was a problem, because, what had been a source of elation back then ("Oh, it's mile five. I thought I was coming up to mile four because I hadn't seen that marker. I've actually gone further than I thought... YES!"), occasionally tricked me with a sense of false hope.

Whenever I had considered that I hadn't seen a mile marker in a while (which was fairly often!), I found myself saying, "Ah ha... maybe that's because that one is missing and I've actually done TWO miles... oooooh, that would be excellent." And it never was. Not once after those first early missing two. And when I was plodding up my very slowest, hardest mile, up what I'm *sure* was an almost vertical track, which took me *one hour and fifteen minutes*, I became obsessed with where the mile marker was. PLEASE, could it just be soon?!

I realised that because of this, I had started to talk to the mile markers in advance. "Come on then. Where are you, you horrid little thing?" I did this with pretty much every single one. It became one of my little rituals... and I took photos of the view at each marker.

Despite the demanding nature of the trail, there were many times I felt enjoyment and – above all – a sense of deep gratitude. Focusing on the positives of many bits helped me through. Finding the smallest patch of shade mid-hike (a *huge* victory!); having climbed up so high meant that I had a cooling breeze and a slight mist when I finally made the top; the feeling of really earning the magnificent views; when I was at the bottom of the hills, realising that I could swim in the cold, rejuvenating sea; the flawless sunsets with their beautifully rich colour; and, overall, a deep sense of gratitude that my body was still – just about – able to do this. In the words of the hashtag that I had been using throughout the year; #FUcancer.

If it wasn't exactly positives I was focusing on, it was reminding myself how much worse it could be. I thought as often as I could about real adventurers.

I had recently heard Sir Ranulph Fiennes speak on his book tour. He told a story about one of his team mates on one of the polar expeditions who had suffered greatly with his feet. He said that the feet had gotten so bad that the skin had torn off the bottom and he was walking on raw flesh and nerves.

So, whenever I felt remotely sorry for myself about my feet or considered the pain, I reprimanded myself. "Get on with it, girl. It's not even remotely close to half as bad as that. It's manageable. Just ignore it and keep going."

*

As I almost stumbled into the town and arrived at the marker that indicated I was finished, I was so relieved. I'd done it. I'd DONE IT! I'd plodded my way up and down the punishing trail in the fearsome heat, and I had made it. There had been many times when I wondered what I had let myself in for and if I really could. My knee had started to be very painful at one point, and I'd be scared I would have to give up.

I yelled out, "I am titanium!" not caring who saw me or thought I was mad. And I smirked to myself at my joke – since my horrific leg break, I was literally titanium, with a rod and screws inside my leg, knee to ankle. Despite this, and all the other hurdles, I'd made it.

As I sat at the bar and treated myself to an ice-cold cocktail to celebrate while waiting for the ferry, I thought about what this meant to me. I thought back to when I was waiting for my scan results (to see where cancer was in my body) and had a lot of time to contemplate the worst. I'd been surprised that I wasn't more scared.

I had the odd moment of dread, but when I properly thought about it, it wasn't death itself that I feared. It was loss of life – meaning loss of making the most of life. Of wasting opportunities. So, I had pushed myself.

I didn't know if I could do this hike, but I'd wanted to try. And how

I felt on completion was the epitome of a piece of wisdom I'd recently heard: 'Confidence is a result, not a requirement'.

Whatever else life throws at me, I've got this.

Website: **charlottefowles.com**

Instagram: **@fowles.charlotte**

Jen THE ULTRA Runner

Michelle Robyn

Chapter 16

The Accidental Ultra Runner

By Jen George

It began, as all good adventures do, with a pint in the pub.

It was the hottest weekend of the year so far. Wales was dry. Unbelievably dry. I had never experienced this phenomenon before.

The fire tracks through the mountain forests surrounding Talybont-on-Usk were barren in the heat. It felt more like attempting to cross the Gobi Desert rather than run a half-marathon. Small clouds of dust rose with every laboured stride, choking the air. Stupidly, I had worn leggings. Whilst they were protecting me from the worst of the sun, I was desiccating faster than a coconut.

When I caught up a group of struggling runners, I latched onto them for dear life. United in our suffering, we cajoled each other into continuing. It was now a question of survival instead of finishing with a good time.

It was a relief to return to the shade of the trees half-an-hour later as the path turned to follow the Brecon canal. Passing a pub, all four of our heads suddenly turned in unison. A waiter had just stepped out from the cool interior. The heavy wooden door was gently framed by a flowering wisteria, its gentle fragrance light in the air. The waiter had a tray expertly balanced on one hand and our eyes immediately became fixated on the drinks it transported.

Ice clinked as he set the first drink down on the table. I licked my cracked lips with a dry tongue. Tantalising beads of condensation sparkled in the sunlight before running down the glass and pooling on the wooden bench. It was too much for my parched body to bear. I didn't trust myself not to run over and snatch it.

Unintentionally, I caught the eye of a lady called Emma who was part of the group I had caught. We came to a silent agreement that it would be poor etiquette to be barely a kilometre short of the finish line and get distracted by a pint.

Exactly thirty-eight minutes later, we were back in the pub garden. I ordered a berry cider, keen for something fruity to quench my thirst. It was agony waiting for Emma's drink to arrive. I dipped a finger into mine to distract myself and drew a line with the liquid across the wooden table. It evaporated almost instantly.

When Emma's drink finally appeared, I gulped mine down within a matter of minutes. Now knowing the significance of this beverage, I regret rushing to drink it, but was desperate for the refreshment.

As is totally normal with runners, we spoke almost solely about running for the next forty five minutes.

I ordered a second pint.

We arrived at the subject of race entries.

"Do you fancy joining us for Race to the Stones?"

"Race to the what?" I was beginning to feel a little bit fuzzy round the edges.

Emma spun her phone round to show me the website.

"It's an ultra-marathon. I'm doing it with a friend if you want to come?"

I'd like to say that I jumped at the chance. But even under the influence of alcohol, present Jen was looking after the self-preservation of future Jen and this sounded pretty full-on, even by my usual standards of crazy.

"I'll have a think about it." Three and half marathons back-to-back sounded like torture.

At this point, some friends joined us at the table. I forgot about the race and ordered a third pint.

*

The next morning, surprisingly, I woke up without a headache. I had eaten a decent dinner and had somehow managed to rehydrate myself too. The only problem was that I was now desperate for a wee.

I had camped for the night and so wriggled my body out of my sleeping bag, stretching my stiff limbs. Hitting a button on my phone, I could see that I had new emails. I wandered across the field as I opened my inbox.

A wave of dread washed over me, and I stopped dead in the doorway to the toilet block.

Three emails sat in a row, each of them beginning with a variation of 'Thank you for entering...'

My mouth opened in horror as I remembered the three entry forms that I had enthusiastically filled out the previous evening.

Race to the Stones, a hundred kilometre run. The Wiggle Cheddar

Sportive, a hundred mile cycle. And The Swim Serpentine, a two mile swim.

A noise behind me brought me back to my senses and I realised that a small queue of impatient campers had formed. I pocketed my phone and then sat in a cubicle with my head in my hands.

What had I done?

My bank balance later confirmed my commitment. At this point, I considered just removing my entries on the spot and cutting my losses with the cancellation fees.

But something made me stop.

When I got home on the Monday evening, I sat down with a glass of wine and had a look at my diary. I did a few calculations and then very rapidly put the glass of wine back down.

Ten weeks to train for Race to the Stones. Or rather nine to factor in rest days before the event. Oh, and my sister's wedding was a few weeks beforehand too...

Eight weeks. *Eight.*

I picked the glass of wine back up.

*

I was in a deep sleep the first time my alarm went off at 5am, the noise jarring me awake in a panic. Sitting bolt upright, heart pounding, I struggled to catch my breath as the primitive part of my brain scanned the room for a non-existent danger.

I laced my shoes, purposefully taking my time. Leaving the house, I felt that my first few steps should feel significant as I began this momentous journey to becoming an ultra-runner.

In reality, my first strides were to dodge the bin lorry that mounted the curb as it swerved to avoid the speed bumps.

With only a rough idea of which direction to head in, I probably should have checked the distance or even a route before I set off. In the spirit of this challenge so far, I made it up as I went along.

The first few days were horrendous. The problem with running to work in the morning is that it meant that I had to run home again afterwards. Covering twenty-four kilometres a day whilst teaching science for five hours in the middle, in hindsight, was not particularly smart.

On the fifth day, I had worked out that I didn't need to leave quite so early in the morning. This backfired when I then bumped into two of my favourite year nine reprobates in the middle of their paper round.

"Miss!"

I ignored it to start with, expecting a torrent of abuse, but on the second shout I chanced a sideways look in their direction. To my surprise, they weren't about to throw anything at me and were instead cheering me on, pulling some impressive wheelies on their bikes.

Day after day, I laced up my shoes. With three weeks to go before the event, I decided that I should at least attempt to run over twelve kilometre in one go to give myself a shred of confidence.

I needed an incentive. My housemate, Matt, offered to drop me off in Weymouth at six o'clock in the morning. On doing so, he then left the county so I had no choice but to find my way home to Bournemouth.

As the first rays of sunlight danced on the surface of the bay, I could feel their warmth against my skin as I ran along the seafront.

The first hill nearly broke me. It was steeper than anything I tackled between home and work. As it flattened out, I took a few minutes to enjoy the solitude high atop the cliff.

Suddenly, something small and powerful crashed into my foot. Confused, I looked down. A tiny creature was attacking my running shoe, it's furry body writhing from side to side hissing with determination.

It was a weasel.

Recoiling in surprise, I lost my balance and staggered backwards into the fence. The force of hitting something solid launched the poor creature into the air. It soared deep into the long grass between the coast path and the edge of the cliff.

Slightly in shock, I bent forward to catch my breath, warily surveying the flattened clump where my attacker had disappeared. A few seconds of silence passed. A seagull drifted by. I inspected my shoe and found to my amusement that there was now a hole in the fabric.

A volley of angry squeaking erupted from the undergrowth, and the rodent once again threw itself into ferocious battle.

I didn't need telling twice. I sprinted as fast as I could until I was sure I had left it behind.

I ran up. I ran down. I ran up again. The Kimmeridge cliffs presented themselves as a special version of hell reserved for people making questionable sporting life choices.

When I reached Swanage, I realised that my energy levels were dipping dangerously as I began to fantasise about food. A foraging mission to a local store rewarded me with sufficient calories to satisfy my needs. A rowing regatta was taking place in the bay and so I sat amidst the spectators on the sea wall. With my legs dangling, I took a few moments to refuel. My tired brain became transfixed by the methodical synchronisation of each racing team as they drew their oars through the glittering water.

Shaking myself out of my stupor, the final miles brought me round Old Harry Rocks and into Studland Bay. I'd completely forgotten that the far end was a nudist beach. Let's just say that I unintentionally experienced a whole range of views along the coast that day.

Finally, reaching the Poole Harbour ferry, I felt an enormous relief as I slumped in my seat. The horror began when I attempted to stand up again the other side.

My legs felt as though someone had clamped them in a vice. Shuffling onto dry land, it took everything I had to drag my feet into something resembling a run. It was more of a controlled stumble. An elderly couple tutted loudly as I careered violently across the slipway, struggling to keep myself in a straight line.

When I eventually staggered through the door, Matt, back from his travels, greeted me with a pizza and a sports massage. In that moment, it was the best sight in the world.

Lying in bed that night, I knew that if I could successfully run that distance alone, I stood a good chance of completing a hundred kilometre with friends.

*

Three weeks later, I was stood on the start line of Race to the Stones with Emma and her friend Jason just outside the town of Lewknor. I already felt like a bit of a fraud wearing the event t-shirt with a hundred kilometres stamped across the back as I hadn't exactly earned it yet.

Despite the thousands of people participating in the event, the start line was pleasantly uncrowded, with groups of friends and individuals nervously milling around. A stand was handing out transfer tattoos featuring the event logo. I quickly grabbed a couple, using my own spit to stick one to my arm and one to my cheek so that I did not have to waste any of my water.

We joined our start wave and gradually moved forwards. Dance music was blasting out from enormous speakers, accompanying the warm-up routine that was being staged for each wave of runners setting off. The adrenaline had kicked in and I was grateful when it was our turn to churn out some star jumps to release some of my pent-up energy.

All of a sudden, we were off. A klaxon sounded and we found ourselves swept along at a rapid pace. As the route narrowed, there was some jostling for position, with elbows knocking, a blur of coloured t-shirts flashing by and the sound of a hundred pairs of feet pounding rhythmically along the trail.

We were going too fast. After the first couple of kilometres, we made the choice to rein in the pace before our enthusiasm got the better of us. There was a long way to go.

Sat in the pub the previous evening, myself and Jason had devised a strategy for entertaining ourselves throughout the run. At each kilometre marker, we would all take it in turns to ask a question that was compulsory for us all to answer. No topic would be off limits. Life goals, worst dates, shoe sizes, wildest dreams... I'm pretty sure that, by the end, I knew more about Jason, Emma and John than I knew about anyone else in my life. It gave us a focus, a routine distraction from the aching limbs and sore feet that were to come.

The onset of a searing headache within the first ten kilometres was a harsh reminder to rehydrate more thoroughly as we arrived at checkpoint one on the very edge of the Chiltern Hills. After finding some well-needed shade and swallowing a couple of paracetamol, I entered the food tent.

I couldn't believe my eyes. Pies and cakes and crisps and energy bars stretched the whole way along the marquee. Enormous tanks filled with electrolyte drinks and rehydration agents were being continuously refilled by the support crew. Acres of sandwiches and wraps, pasta and bananas stretched as far as the eye could see. It was like going into Spar as a kid and being told that everything was free for the day.

Anyone who is familiar with my eating habits will know that I follow the nutritional strategy of the Everest mountaineer George Mallory. Why do I eat the mountain of food in front of me? Because it's there. I stashed as many jelly beans as I could in my pockets and crammed some flapjack into my mouth, hamster-like, before we continued on our way.

The sight of the Thames twenty-five kilometres in was a welcome relief as the trail reached its banks just south of Wallingford. Jealousy got the better of me as I watched a disobedient Labrador defy its owner and launch itself between the reeds, landing with an almighty splash in the middle of the river. I couldn't resist. Weighing up the disadvantages of continuing with wet shoes, I jogged into the shallows, plunging myself into the murky water. I closed my eyes and took off my fluorescent pink running cap. Dunking it in, I poured the contents over my head and neck to relieve myself from the heat. Within an hour, both my hair and trainers were completely dry again.

It was around this point that Jason's turn at asking a question led to us adopting John. Overhearing us talk about the last TV program I had watched, (Poldark, in case you were curious), we discovered that we both came from Cornwall. This shared trait was deemed more than enough for him to qualify as part of the team.

Climbing high up onto The Ridgeway, the searing heat was reflecting off the eroded paths. The exposed chalk was painfully bright in the midday sun. Lots of people had already made the sensible decision to walk. We paused briefly to speak to an American man with hiking poles who had come all the way over from the States for the event. A river of sweat that had once run down his face and back had long since dried up, leaving salt tracks staining his yellow charity t-shirt. Reasoning that the quicker we descended to the cool of a wooded valley beyond, we excused ourselves from the conversation and continued.

I received a text from friends Harry and Mike to ask what I needed at kilometre thirty where they would be meeting us.

Lilt. I wanted Lilt. In vast quantities.

I discovered throughout my training that whilst it is possible to spend huge quantities of money on expensive energy gels, fizzy drinks and Swizzels Squashies seemed to do the job just as well for me.

Decanting the cloudy liquid straight into my rehydration bladder, I didn't really think through the consequences of continuing to run with a carbonated drink in a confined space bouncing around my rucksack. I quickly discovered that this was a terrible idea. At kilometre thirty-seven, I went to take a sip from the mouthpiece of the hose and the pressurised jet that escaped shot straight to the back of my throat and out of both nostrils. Spluttering, I sprayed myself with a combination of sticky, tropical fruit residue and congealing phlegm.

Unfortunately, this was not destined to be my only nutritional disaster. My body began to scream for salt to replace the amount it had lost through sweat. Trying to avoid consuming too many sugary electrolyte gels, I managed to eat nine packets of Walkers' salt and vinegar crisps by kilometre forty.

As a science teacher, I should have known better.

Vinegar is an acid.

I became acutely aware that I had a blister developing on my tongue and that blister was BIG. It was already beginning to occupy its own hemisphere in my mouth.

At the checkpoint, a concerned event medic approached. He crouched down, gently placed his hand on my back and asked if I was okay. No, I wasn't okay. Bent forward with my hands on my knees, I was quietly salivating into the bushes. Swallowing with the mega blister had become increasingly difficult. I gave him a unconvincing thumbs-up whilst simultaneously attempting to wipe the Lilt snot that had crystallised in my eyebrows. He recoiled at the sight and backed away, satisfied that the condition I was in was obviously not life-threatening.

The fifty kilometre-checkpoint reminded me of an artist's impression of a medieval battle site, with banners and flags silhouetted against the evening sky. The hordes of runners queueing for food, showers and toilets could easily have been mistaken for cavalry warriors waiting to collect their steeds and charge boldly into war. Even the drumbeat blaring out from gigantic speakers was rhythmic, almost march-like in sound.

On closer inspection, we discovered that a more accurate comparison would be to the aftermath of a violent skirmish. Casualties of the first half of the event were limping their way around the site, seizing up from staying stationary for too long. Unreliable knees and ankles were bandaged up or strapped with supports. Sports tape every colour of the rainbow could be seen holding various body parts together.

A menagerie of tents for the competitors choosing to stay for the night were already spaced out across the field in neat rows. The idea of a cosy sleeping bag and soft pillow was enough for my eyes to begin to droop. Yet in silent agreement, we all rose to our feet from our table in the food tent. The rays of the falling sun settled momentarily on the power station tower in a distant Didcot as we joined the dwindling number of competitors committing themselves to the night.

The sixty kilometre-checkpoint came and went. Kilometre after kilometre passed. As we began the approach to Uffington Castle, delirium began to set it. Shapes and colours danced across my vision, vibrant constructions of an imagination addled by exhaustion. The sun dipped behind the horizon and the temperature dropped within seconds. The hairs on my arms stood on end as I shivered, gently at first but escalating violently. Sentences were no longer coherent as I began to slur my words. It was all I could do to put one foot in front of the other.

With my world narrowed to the small circle illuminated by my head torch, I stumbled on the uneven path. I felt someone catch hold of my elbow to steady me.

Jason's hand was outstretched, offering his running jacket.

"I can't."

"You need it more than me."

This simple act of selflessness was enough to reduce me quietly to tears. I gratefully accepted, zipping myself up into the folds of fabric, pulling it high on my neck. Feeling slowly returned to my icy fingers.

A short while later, the open hillside descended into gently undulating fields. In the absence of a breeze, the stillness of the night felt comforting as we passed through the dense corn that blanketed the landscape. Scatterings of stars adorned the dark skies, vivid and welcoming in their presence.

I became aware of the distant thumping of a heavy drum and bass beat echoing through a shallow valley. It was faint at first but grew stronger as we crossed through a gate in a brambled hedgerow. The source of the noise was a small team of slightly worse-for-wear spectators who had set up camp on a tartan picnic blanket. There was cider. And cheese. Throwing ourselves into the revelry, we danced together, gleeful and foolish. It was a challenge to drag ourselves away back into the darkness.

We reached a village, our spirits lifted by our impromptu party. Our pace had quickened and conversation was flowing again. Suddenly, I realised with a horrified jolt that I hadn't seen a marker post for some time.

Standing on a footpath at the side of an empty A road, we debated the issue for a few minutes. Continue along the road and we may find ourselves wildly off course and lost in the darkness. Turn back and we risked adding an unnecessary half an hour to our moving time. Eventually, we came to the decision that turning back to confirm the route was the only sensible option. It was a relief to finally spot a sign that had been hidden behind a parked car, pointing us along the low wall of the village church.

The midsummer night was short lived. The pink glow of the first light of dawn soon evolved into a glorious sunrise in the East.

On reaching the ninety-kilometre checkpoint, I dared to believe that we might just complete the run.

I staggered off to the port-a-loo which, by this stage, was quite a challenge to get into. Twenty-two hours straight of being awake had begun to take its toll.

I'd just rest my eyes for a few seconds...

BANG.

As I drifted off, I must have gently rested my head against the door. When another unsuspecting runner came to open it, he got the shock of his life. I pitched forwards, barely conscious, head-butting him straight in the nuts. The poor guy didn't stand a chance. As I sprawled on the floor with my shorts still around my ankles, he dropped to his knees in agony. With dignity left in tatters all round, at least he was distracted as I hastily scrambled to make myself decent again. Mortified, I crawled back round to where the rest of my team were waiting for me on a picnic bench.

With less than two kilometres to go, the faint strains of music could be heard coming from the finish line. It was torture – to finish the race we had to pass the turn off to the home straight and run to the namesake of the race, the Avebury stone circle, another three hundred metres further up the gravel track.

A one-way system was being operated around the stones to allow the race photographers to work their magic. Posing for a few group shots together, we were smiling, knowing now that whatever happened, we would be crossing the line together.

One kilometre to go. We retraced our steps to turn the final corner. We attempted a jog and promptly stopped – running at this point had become so painful that sustaining anything faster than a crawl for more than three seconds wasn't going to end well. Having made it this far, it wouldn't be very good etiquette to be stretchered off this close to the line.

Five hundred metres to go. The finishing funnel in the distance felt like an optical illusion, a mirage never quite within reach.

Fifty metres to go. We linked arms for the final time. The moment of solidarity went beyond team morale and emotional support for each other. I'm pretty sure that the only reason we were still upright was because eight legs were better than two.

A small crowd was assembled, cheering loudly as, with hands held tight, we raised our arms in victory and took our final steps across the line.

A combination of euphoria and exhaustion overwhelmed me. Barely able to lift our heads to receive our medals, we embraced as a four for one final time.

*

Back at home that evening, I surveyed my face in the mirror. Despite my best efforts in the shower, I still had a visible ring of dirt round my neck where the dust from the trail had mixed with sweat. I realised too that, now the transfer tattoo had washed off, my face had caught the sun and I now had the outline of the race logo faintly burnt into my skin.

My phone pinged – my colleague Caroline had sent a picture of the chocolate brownie cake that she had baked for a celebration in the office tomorrow. In bright pink icing, '#UltraRunner' was written across it. I'd take that.

I looked back in the mirror to catch my own eye, a grin spreading rapidly over my face.

Instagram: **@jen_george_adventures**

Facebook: **Jen George Adventures**

Website: **jengeorgeadventure.com**

Chapter 17

Snow Ahead

By Aliza Goldberg

I followed the fresh footprints in the snow. I stretched my natural gait to match the path before me, stomping down the top of the slushy imprint. My legs were shaking with every step. The wind pushed at my buckling knees and made my eyes water. Snowflakes whirled around me, sticking to my glasses and making the mountain even fuzzier. I did not know where I was or where I was going.

My two layers of gloves clamped down on my hands, stiffening in the cold air. I gripped my hiking poles, stabbing them into the mountain slope as I climbed up, holding on to them like they were nailed into the earth and could sustain my weight in case of a fall.

My hiking partner and boyfriend was ahead, following the map to piece together a path out of the storm. Whenever I saw a cluster of footprints, that meant he had stopped and turned his body around to look for me, shuffling his feet before turning back around and continuing onwards. I smiled as I added my own step into those muddled footprints.

I was wearing all the clothes I had, but all that fabric was hanging heavy with moisture, stale from yesterday. Yesterday was when the storm had begun. It had followed me from Southern California to

Oregon, where I had driven north in a rental car to escape it. Sometimes that feeling of helplessness, of knowing your own small size in the face of a storm, is freeing. It is a release.

Why was I here, wandering around a mountain, stuffing fistfuls of snow into my mouth, and trying not to let my heavy backpack turn me over? How did I end up on this path? Should I bother continuing?

When setting out on the Pacific Crest Trail, common thruhike wisdom passed down from one year to the next recommends figuring out your 'why'. When the going gets tough, having that answer of why you started hiking in the first place will keep you pushing.

My rationale was simply, 'why not?' It was not my intention to complete the entire 2,652-mile journey from the United States border with Mexico into Canada. I have never considered myself an athlete and, as a city dweller, never had much opportunity or experience camping and backpacking. But I needed space to think through what I wanted in my life and how to reorient myself to get there.

Any time I mentioned that I was leaving to thruhike the Pacific Crest Trail, the people I was talking to shifted their weight from foot to foot and tightened their grip on their pint. "Erm…" they would start, "but why?" There was an assumption of past trauma, of something I needed to escape. Was I a drug addict or alcoholic? Heartbroken or suicidal? In mourning? Had I just survived a terrible car accident or long bout of chemotherapy? All of the above, perhaps?

There was no singular moment I decided to hike the Pacific Crest Trail. The decision came in a trickle. First, a school friend hiked two hundred miles of it and came back to Brooklyn, where I lived, with blisters and stories about what she saw in the desert and who she met along the way. Then I watched as another friend quit her job, sold all her belongings, and hiked alone all over South America for fifteen months.

In September of 2018, I bought a tent, a sleeping bag, a backpack, and proper hiking clothes. "I can always return these," I thought to myself. Two months later, I was on the South Downs Way for my first and only test run, a one-hundred-mile trail in southern England. I completed it in five rainy days at the end of November. I not only survived, but I also wanted more.

Throughout literature and film, when a woman cuts her hair, that means she is going through a transformative period in her life. Almost always it is coupled with her life falling apart, but nevertheless, it is inspiring. Chopping off her hair is her first small act of bravery, before she even acts. She has willingly shirked societal norms and expectations of her. She no longer ties her worth to her beauty. She is free.

So there I was, sitting on a swivel chair in front of a mirror, staring at the ponytail of scraggly blonde on the metal tray. It was ragged and held together with a hair tie that I would not need anymore. And more hair was falling in front of my face, behind my head. Little ringlets all over the floor.

I was not even at a hair salon. I was at a beauty school, letting a student hack at my hair for free. I was going to hike from Mexico to Canada and I didn't care what I looked like. I just wanted a buzzed neckline so my hat would fit better. My hair would not get tangled and knotted from weeks without showering, because there was barely any left.

The concept of 2,652 miles broke my brain. I had to break up the journey into small chunks. Setting out from the southern terminus in Campo, California on April 8th, 2019, I did not have my sights set on Canada like everyone else I met on the trail. I was just wondering if I could make it to Warning Springs, a small community in southern California around mile hundred on the trail.

With my tendency to envision worst-case scenarios in such clear detail, it seemed an inevitable certainty. I assumed I would fail to complete the journey because of a severe leg injury, the kind where the bone punctures the shin or thigh and shards of white peek from crimson flesh. Or I would lose my footing in a river crossing, get pushed by a strong current, and strips of my clothing would wash up onshore years later. Or a blister would get infected and turn into a case of gangrene. Or a camouflaged rattlesnake would lunge from a shrub to bite me and I would not find a way off trail in time before the venom stopped my heart. There are many ways to die on the Pacific Crest Trail.

The day the storm began on Mount Ashland in Oregon, I was not inventing new ways I would die hiking. In the morning, the woods were silent and pure. The white sky and white ground made the neon lime green moss even brighter on the tree bark. The forest felt like it was mine, empty except for my boyfriend and the wind.

As the day wore on, the snowflakes grew thicker. There were puddles in my shoes. My body skidded into numbness. I kept sinking into the snow or falling down onto my knees or hip. The thought of slipping and catapulting down a slope then entered my mind again. The only escape was to walk to lower elevation. A full retreat back to the trailhead and into town had not yet occurred to me.

Wading through snow up to my knee, I slowly made my way down Mount Ashland. I stopped under a rare cluster of trees to spoon peanut butter into my mouth and catch my breath. It had been seven hours since I woke up and unzipped my tent to a charming layer of frost and little glittering flakes whirling about. Without any breaks or anything to look at, it felt like I had been on this one mountain for years, but since there were no distinguishing markers, the setting looked so unfamiliar I must have only just arrived ten minutes ago.

At the first gurgling sound of a creek, we stopped moving. I could see a snaking path half-buried under snow. Two tall trees watched over the creek, their arms allowing for the first glimpse of brown dirt I had seen all day. I have been calling myself a creek creature ever since the first water source on mile five, because I plan my entire day around water sources. But instead of plunging my hands into the strong icy flow to hydrate, I peeled off my gloves, threw my backpack down off my shoulders, and rummaged through the contents to lift out the tent.

I stomped the snow to harden it for the tent stakes. Unzipping the sagging rain cover, I shimmied out of all my clothing, piled them into the corner, took my dry pyjamas out of its Ziploc bag, dove into my damp sleeping bag, and fell asleep at 3pm. Opening my eyes hours later to the same scenario of bleak sunlight, the tap tap of snow hitting the roof of my tent, the wet heap of clothes in the corner, the mesh tent hanging heavy just above me, filled me with dread.

I turned over onto my side and looked over at my boyfriend. "Are we going to get hypothermia?" he whispered to me.

"Not yet," I replied.

I scooted over my inflatable pad to overlap with his, nestling my head under his jaw, trying to absorb his heat.

"Let's go back to Ashland and try again in a few days," I heard him say, the sounds vibrating from his chest, mixing with the beat of his heart. I nodded, tapping his face with my wool beanie. Tears fell onto my sleeping bag. It was taking us so many days to go such few miles. Thruhiking is a constant race against time, as we try to traverse a variety of climates before the changing seasons make them impassable. I had not accounted for blizzard conditions in late May.

I rummaged through my backpack for my coil of rope, strung it across the inside of the tent, and hung up our socks, buffs, and hats. They swayed as we slept that night.

Icicles fell on my head as I crouched under the tree the following morning to pee. I did not want to pack up and move, but I did not want to stay either. Pain shot up my forearms from my palms as I folded up the tent. My hands were red and raw.

After shoving feet into stiff sneakers, we started back up the mountain.

On the retreat back to Ashland, I stumbled across a line of footprints. My heartbeat sped as I hoped to come across another hiker, who could give us intel about the trail or help us think through a plan. I then realized the prints were mine from the day before. Despite our best intentions to go straight across the ridge of Mount Ashland and pass the Oregon-California border that was only twenty miles away, we had instead zigzagged and looped, putting in steps and expending calories without anything to show for it.

I had given the footprints a character and personality, shaking my head at them and their naiveté. So much was clearer now, with the benefit of hindsight and a calm sky. The horizon was literally visible, even if I was still uncertain about my plans.

We veered off trail again to a shelter one mile away. The stone structure was more of a gazebo than anything hospitable, with picnic tables and a fire pit in the open air. My boyfriend opened the valve of his stove and tried to torch branches and pinecones. As we leaned against one of the columns of the structure, it started to rain. It was too cold to stay still in a place with no walls.

In the near distance was a National Park Service pit toilet. They are made with concrete walls and a door that locks. The toilet does not flush, but a plastic dome covers the pit. A white plastic lid covers the smell.

I unfurled the orange tent cloth and laid it out on the bathroom floor. The tent poles clacked against the corners of the outhouse, pressing up against the ceiling spotted with dust and dead flies. The placement of the toilet prevented the tent from lying flat. We hung the tent cloth on the handicap railing on the wall and covered every ledge and handle with a wet item to dry. We wrung out socks into the toilet so they wouldn't make puddles on the floor.

The thick cement walls cut the wind and shut out the precipitation. I blew up my inflatable pad, shook out my sleeping bag, changed into my still-dry pyjamas, and curled up for an early 'night' at 11am. I hoped the force of the rain pattering would wash away the snow, making it easier to walk without sinking down with every step. We could be in town by the following morning, hitching a ride from the Interstate that passes by the trailhead.

My face was level with the air vent in the wall, making me shiver. My boyfriend was spooning the neck of the toilet. I took out my iPhone to distract myself and realized I had an Internet connection for the first time since we left town two days prior. I sent a message to the Trail Angel community page on Facebook. Trail Angels are locals who live near the trail and find joy in helping out hikers with rides, hot showers, a place to sleep or even just snacks and water.

I asked if anyone could give us a ride into Ashland the following morning, in case no one wanted to spontaneously stop on a highway shoulder and let two soaking wet strangers dirty their car. A photographer and mushroom forager who has lived in Oregon for decades said he was on his way now. He gave me directions to a nearby fire road and he said he would be waiting four miles away in his Subaru.

We swatted our belongings down from the ledge and off the railings and back into our bags. Trudging four miles on a slushy paved road used for fire trucks in the case of a wildfire, our footing was more sure, as was our evening.

In the beginning, I had certainty. Since the best time to hike in the desert is in April and May, when the frigid winter nights have ended and before the scorching summer heat has begun, I hiked in a horde. When I took a break in a trail town, known as a zero day, we would see fellow hikers in the grocery store or camped out in a Trail Angels' backyard. We had the same plans and were on the same schedule. These hikers hailed from all over the world, mainly Germany, Sweden, France and New Zealand. The reasons for our dream were different, but we all shared the same vision.

*

They say that stupidity is repeating the same action over again and expecting different results. After waiting a few days at a hostel in Ashland, Oregon for the storm to finally pass, reading books in a bunk bed and eating brie on fresh baguettes, leaving only to pretend to shop for crystals, we returned back to the Pacific Crest Trail to try again.

"Oregon is trying to kill me," I cried as I slipped off the trail and hit a tree for the second time that afternoon. I also fell on my butt, my elbow and my knees. It is easy to slip in snow, especially with thirty pounds on my back. My bag was laden with food for the next week, with a few days' extra in case of another storm. The hand warmers and extra layers I brought in post-storm wisdom lay at the bottom of my pack, dragging me down. Hanging onto my trekking poles stopped me on several occasions from sliding off into the valley below. By the end of that first day, my poles were irreparably bent.

And yet, there I was, shuffling alongside a wall of snow twice my height with a curved top like a surf wave about to break and rush to the sandy shore—over my body. An avalanche risk if ever I saw one. I wanted to touch it to keep my balance, but didn't want to disturb the pile. I did not even want to speak.

That surfer wave of snow was the top of the mountain. The wind had pushed all the snow from the other side up like someone had deliberately shovelled it there. After the top, the elevation and snow flattened and my muscles relaxed.

We continued battling snow until evening, when the snow patches became smaller and more manageable due to lower altitude. At the first pine needle crunch, I ripped off my microspikes, hopping on one leg as I grasped each foot. I stripped off all my clothes and walked around camp naked so my clothes could dry on a boulder. The cool sunset air soothed my bruised legs. My boyfriend boiled snow potful by potful.

He and I were the only ones in these Oregon woods. The past few months, in the desert of southern California, we would always camp amongst a gaggle of new friends. Marching away from the Mexican border mile by mile, the group compared the caloric value of our granola bars and shared handfuls of M&Ms. We would swap recipes: put powdered potatoes in ramen, mix boiled rice with dehydrated green beans, sprinkle popcorn on your tortilla slathered with bean dip. Hiker culture feels stuck in the 1960s, though we rarely listened to the Grateful Dead and most of the group had probably never heard of Janis Joplin. Everyone had a ridiculous trail name like Rampage and Spice. Once the storm first hit, though, we all scattered.

I knew there would be still more snow ahead because we had been analysing the NOAA snow accumulation maps that updated in real time. But I did not know when.

It dawned on me then that there was no one to blame for my misery. I put myself on this mountain and I was the only one who could get myself out. No mundane complaints about train delays or bad traffic or a loud neighbour or extra charges on my phone bill. I was just as in control of my situation as the situation was out of control.

When something bad happened on trail, I still had to keep going. Maybe I could take a break or even set up my tent early. But there was no escape. I was still in the middle of nowhere. At a pace of two miles per hour, the situation would never change drastically. I was only covering so much ground in a day or even a week. The next day, I had to wake up early and go do it all again. The only way out was through.

As the sun set that night, I stared up at the tent roof. I could not sleep and would have trouble sleeping for that whole stretch and beyond, falling asleep at 11pm well after the moon had risen and waking up at 3am with two hours to think before it was time to eat breakfast, pack up and start moving again.

I saw Oregon through this sleepy haze.

"I don't like hiking, as it turns out," I confessed to my boyfriend during breakfast.

"Huh," he responded. He looked around, surveying the trees, the fluffy brown leaves in the dirt, his toe sticking out of a hole in his sock.

"I'm going to quit. I just don't know when. But..."

It felt like a break up. I did not know if I was breaking up with the Pacific Crest Trail or my boyfriend, or both.

"Well, let me know before you just leave me behind."

I nodded. "You can still use my tent," I offered.

My face was red, sunburned from staring down at the snow. The Ziploc bag I had been using to store my food had torn down the side. Ziploc bags were precious cargo on the Pacific Crest Trail and now I had to throw one of mine away. I had others, of course, but I would have to shift everything around and reorganize my possessions, my life.

Whenever something went wrong, as small as a Ziploc tear or as large as falling down thirty times in one day, I would think, "Why me? What have I done to deserve this?" Though I am not a religious person, I would feel personally attacked by some higher power seeking to punish me. I would then attack myself for feeling victimized and not having the correct attitude about hiking, creating a loop of hatred and self-loathing that only peanut butter and the right podcast could dispel.

I roused myself, shivering, ready to keep doing the activity I decided I no longer enjoyed for the next ten hours. I bundled up to walk over to the bear box, a metal latched container to keep food away from animals. A flash caught my eye. My clothes were glittering.

Everything I had washed the night before was stiff with frost. Defeated, I shook off the snow and shoved everything back into my pack to dry at an undisclosed date and time.

The steepest incline of the entire trail stood between me and the deepest lake in the United States, Crater Lake. With heaving breath, slipping in the snow mounds, wishing for switchbacks, I put in the steps to rise up to the vantage point of the lake. The deep cobalt water contrasted with the red rock canyon, all surrounded by slate, snow-covered peaks. Wizard Island lounged in the middle of it all, dotted with pine trees. Gazing down from the edge, I wondered if the views were worth the pain and exertion to get there. For this, it was.

"Excuse me, the trail up ahead has been deemed unsafe for hiking, so you cannot continue," a park ranger stammered as we made our way around the crater rim, craning our necks to view the lake below from every angle.

'If only you knew what the trail behind looks like,' I thought to myself. But I was relieved someone was stepping in to tell me what I already knew, that hiking in snow is dangerous—especially at the edge of a crater with an eight thousand-foot drop. Though his red chubby cheeks and nervous pacing made him look like a child, the park ranger was being the adult I could not get myself to be. He was telling me to stop the nonsense.

"Are you planning to camp around here?" he continued. I nodded, proud that it wasn't obvious that I had been sleeping in the dirt for almost four months.

After checking my permit, he told us he did not feel comfortable with us roadwalking around the cordoned-off trail. "Let me radio in to ask if I can drive you," he said. "Unless you're a purist."

A purist is someone who feels the need to hike every inch of the Pacific Crest Trail, in the right order from north to south or south to north, and in a timely fashion. I had skipped over seven hundred miles of the Sierra Nevada mountains to return to later or risk imminent death. I had walked on roads in Northern California to avoid parts of the trail other hikers were warning each other about, even though they were never officially closed down. I did not snack on beef jerky I had made myself. I had never even weighed my backpack. I was not a purist.

I had walked over a thousand miles, which felt like enough. Since I had flipped over the Sierra to come back to after the storms had subsided, I had to do some advanced calculations to determine at what point in my journey I would reach the thousand-mile mark. Every milestone came with delirious markers made out of pine cones or rocks, whatever hikers could find to celebrate a triumphant three hundred or four hundred miles walked. Once you stop walking in order from border to border, those markers become more personal.

At mile 1773.4 from Mexico, I gathered wisps of neon green moss from the side of the trail and laid out the one and three zeros. I added "mi" for clarity and because I had moss left over in my palm. Hikers behind us must have had a moment of panic as they neared two thousand miles of the trail from Mexico, but passed a thousand-mile marker.

After a twenty-minute detour on the highway around Crater Lake, I was back on trail, stumbling through sun cups and wishing the park ranger had driven us just a little bit further or maybe to Washington.

"We were just kidnapped by a child," my boyfriend said when we stopped for lunch. It was true. I never saw his driver's license. I was not even sure he was a park ranger or just dressed in khaki. I climbed into people's jeeps with no hesitation now, ready to sacrifice anything and everything for a chance to sit down.

Sitting had become my definition of luxury. Any time I passed a picnic table, it was mandatory to pay my respect with a little sit down. Eating in a chair instead of cross-legged in the dirt with my back curved to reach my plastic cup of cold couscous on the ground was bliss. When Trail Angels had picnic chairs set up and fresh fruit or potable water to give out from the back of their van, nothing could be sweeter.

Crouching by a trickle of water to then squeeze it through a filter just to hydrate was exhausting. My calves would burn as I waited for my two litre bladder to fill. My biceps would burn as I forced the water through the plastic tube. My hands would burn as the frigid water lapped my fingers. The locals who stashed dozens of gallons of water in the bushes were miracle workers. They were known as Water Angels.

Kindness was the most abundant aspect of nature I found on the Pacific Crest Trail. I certainly felt relief and awe at the top of a mountain or under a roaring waterfall, but when every other moment was so wild and rough, it was soothing to be cared for.

From the free car ride from San Diego to the southern terminus at 4am, to the snack exchanges amongst hikers, to the cold beers under a bridge in the rain, I was rejuvenated time and time again. One Trail Angel gave me a new pair of shorts and rash cream when she saw my chafing, along with a hot shower, warm bed, and a scrambled egg breakfast complete with mimosas. Another set up a grill just off trail and lured hikers to come over with promise of pancakes. When he heard I was vegetarian, he led me to his camper van and gave me a one-pound bag of raw carrots, which I happily crunched on during my snack breaks over the next few days.

During a hailstorm that lasted for five hours, I veered off trail as the sun started to set. The trail had become a river, my rain jacket had stopped functioning, and I was so cold that I was having trouble forming sentences. We were not planning to leave the trail, but also we did not plan for so much hail. A local was waiting in the parking lot with his heat on high. He had noticed there was a storm an hour away in Bend, thought there might be hikers in trouble on the trail, and figured he would wait and gather them all until he could not fit anyone else in his truck.

An injured hiker who had to quit the trail rented a jeep and roamed the nearby highways looking to pick up hitchhikers. She brought me to town, bought me dinner, and gave me her shoes since she was not going to be using hers anymore and mine were getting holes. Other drivers picked me up from the side of the road even though I had not showered and my clothes were covered in mud, politely putting newspaper down in the backseat before gesturing me to hop in.

I was surprised by all of the generosity and did not expect it. My assumption was rather that I would be murdered. But having anxiety makes you numb to fear. Having rational fears and irrational ones, to the point where they were indistinguishable from each other, I felt free to do what others would probably have the good sense to avoid. I cannot escape the anxious thoughts, but I can ignore them and dive headlong into dangerous situations like climbing into the back of any car that stopped for me on a highway and sleeping in the beds of strangers I found on the Internet. Anxiety has never stopped me.

This is not a story of resilience. It is a story of waiting for the moment to quit, but also wanting to see one last sunset, one more turquoise lake glittering with white ripples of reflected light. The above-average precipitation levels led to snow, yes, but it also led to a superbloom of wildflowers in every colour. The moon was so bright I had to sleep with my buff over my eyes like a mask. The rodents in Washington were inquisitive, adorable, and hungry for Oreos. The sound of silence was a joy and a treasure, so vastly different from the chaos of city life. The mountains were so magnificent, making me want to get back out there for one more day just to see what would come next.

I did not find myself on my thruhike. I came home with more questions than ever and no solutions. The hike was just a hike, not a conduit for epiphany. But I finished.

Instagram: @pctshewrote

Chapter 18

Saying Yes More Because of Crohn's Disease

By Thomas Hough

'Why won't it just go away?' Camping in the Olympic National Park in Washington State should not have been like this. Unable to sleep because of the pain, continuing to retch even after I had nothing more to bring up. Roaring through the forest like a bear was in the camp. But there was no bear. It was just me and my stomach going through pain like I had never experienced before. Like someone had taken a clamp to my bowels. This wasn't how it was meant to be. I was meant to be exploring the unique ecosystem of the rugged Pacific coastline, alpine areas and temperate rainforest.

I hardly slept through the night so, in the morning, I had to be left behind to recover whilst my friends went on their day's adventure. It was understandable but also deeply frustrating.

Lying there staring at the tent roof, willing my stomach cramps to pass, I had to try and be content with myself. As bad as it was in that moment, so far up to that point, my travelling around the world for five months had been the best days and experiences of my life. Living every day to its fullest and taking advantage of every new opportunity and experience. I truly felt I was being the person I was meant to be in life and was determined to carry on this adventurous feeling when I returned home in October of that year.

It wasn't meant to be.

After returning home, the symptoms came back and basically wiped out November. At times I was pretty much housebound, switching between the couch, the bed and the toilet due to the pain, fatigue and stomach issues. It was all consuming and would be like this every few weeks. I saw two different GPs who just put it down to a virus and said it would pass. But it didn't.

It carried on for a few months and eventually I realised that the only way to stop the pain and vomiting was to not eat anything when the agony struck. This obviously wasn't sustainable, so I saw another GP. He thought it might be Irritable Bowel Syndrome (a common misdiagnosis) and prescribed me peppermint tablets. But still it continued, only now with fresher breath and less time between bouts of sickness. And now I started to get pain in my stomach whether I ate or not.

By the time summer came, I decided to go on a group camping holiday to Alaska, trying to keep the adventurous spirit alive. I don't know how I managed it though, as I was ill for most of it. I'd eat very little to get me through the day. Spending some evenings just lying in my tent listening to music to try to zone out from the stomach pain whilst the rest of the group partied with the locals, swam in the lakes or just simply sat outside and soaked up the majestic scenery as the sun set.

When I came back home, instead of interest in my once-in-a-lifetime trip, all I got was "Bloody hell, Tom! You've lost so much weight!" At first I didn't know what they meant, but flicking through the pictures of me jumping into the Arctic Ocean, I could see. I was almost skeletal.

It was around this point that it finally dawned on me. Something was very wrong. The signs had been there all along, but it's amazing what you can get used to. I'd brushed the symptoms under the carpet, trusting the GPs knew best, but I knew something had to change.

It was October now and my health really began to spiral. The pain became unbearable. A new level I'd ever experienced. Like someone was grabbing my bowel with barbed wire and not letting go. I couldn't stop it or stop being sick. I just had to ride it out until it subsided. I could only eat a little amount and not very often. Good days - I could manage breakfast and dinner but this was becoming rare. Bad days - I was eating sugar pills to get me through the day at work. Whenever I tried to eat normally, i.e. three meals a day, I'd soon regret it, but it's hard not to eat when you know you're underweight and always tired and hungry.

I went back to see another GP who referred me to a gastroenterologist. The only problem was that I had to wait six weeks to see him, and by then, it had really started to affect the quality of my life. I was starting to take days off work, and whenever I was home, I would just lie in bed because either I was too tired or too sick to do anything else.

I held out hope that the doctor would give me an answer. It was the only hope I had. However, to my incredible disappointment, when I eventually saw him, all he did was book me in for a colonoscopy. All I had to do was wait another six weeks!

Leaving the hospital, I just broke down in tears and was in such a panic that I threw up in the car park. I didn't know how I could last one more day like this let alone forty-two of them. All my hope had gone. Sitting in my car, I was an emotional and physical mess. I'd never felt so helpless. I was done with life.

I needed this to be over with. So I went back to the GP and demanded, "Sign me off work." The doctor sat there in stunned silence looking back at me, his patient, white as a ghost and much thinner than before. By the look on his face, I could tell he now had serious concerns about me.

Gathering his thoughts, he replied, "Before I sign you off I just want to weigh you."

'Fine,' I thought. 'If that's what I need to do to get my sick note I'll do it.' I slipped off my shoes and stepped up onto the weighing scales. I watched the scales jolt up but not as high as I was expecting. I knew I must have lost a bit of weight, but I didn't expect it to be that much.

"You've lost two stone in a year," his voice now reflecting his concerned demeanour. He pulled my records up and rather matter-of-factly announced, "And you've got a low blood count too. Are there any other symptoms?"

"Yeah," I said looking over my shoulder to check the door was shut from prying ears. "My... er... my stools are kind of black too."

"Really?" said the doctor looking me deep in the eyes. I felt like he was composing himself, like he was about to tell me some grave news. I just wanted to know what was wrong. "Your symptoms could be pointing to internal bleeding. Signing you off work won't do. You have to go straight to hospital. Today."

That was not what I was expecting. So I clarified. "To see who? A gastroenterologist again?" A sense of dread was sitting heavy on my shoulders.

"No. There's no time. You'll go straight to the surgeons."

Once at hospital, I stayed there for the next three weeks because, after one x-ray, they had diagnosed me with suspected Crohn's Disease and had found a stricture (narrowing) in my bowel that was so small I needed surgery to remove the badly inflamed section.

For those who don't know what Crohn's Disease is, it is a chronic (lifelong) condition that causes inflammation to the digestive system and is a form of Inflammatory Bowel Disease (IBD). Imagine having a wound that never heals – only it's your bowel. The inflammation can cause diarrhoea, ulcers, bleeding, sickness, scaring, fatigue and intense pain. Pain that feels at time like someone has trapped your bowel in a vice and at others like you're constantly being stabbed but can't fight the attacker off.

There is no cure for Crohn's Disease, and although the symptoms can be managed through medication, this isn't always the case. Sometimes surgery is required to remove badly inflamed sections of the bowel. When the symptoms are under control or the disease is in remission, people can live full and active lives. However, when the disease is active or treatments aren't working, it can have a real impact on someone's quality of life, both physically and mentally.

Due to the delay in diagnosis, there really wasn't another option besides having surgery. Even if there was, I don't know if I would have taken it. I just wanted this hell to be over. I'd had enough of the constant pain and being sick. I wanted my life back. Having been diagnosed with Crohn's Disease, I didn't know what my future life was going to be like, but I knew anything must be better than the last year.

I could have been operated on straight away as an emergency case, but due to my health being in such a bad state, the surgeon wanted to wait for the fear of complications resulting from my anaemic and underweight body. They also didn't know how much bowel I'd need removing and whether or not I'd have to have a temporary stoma created if my bowel was too damaged to be re-joined straight away. A stoma is where the intestine is brought to the surface of the abdomen, and an opening is made so that digestive waste (liquid or faeces) drain into a bag rather than through the anus. To try and give me the best chance in surgery, they fed me intravenously twenty-four hours a day for ten days. They couldn't risk me eating any more for fear of a blockage.

Sitting around in a hospital for days on end would probably frustrate most people, but I was just happy to have an answer and to know things would get better. The time allowed me to finally read Dave Cornthwaite's book, *Board Free*, about his life-changing adventure of skateboarding across Australia. Reading it made me very glad that I'd managed to go travelling for five months before I became ill instead of putting it off like so many other people do. Looking back now, I can see that the inspiring and motivational qualities of the book actually planted a little seed in my head that would eventually grow into my own adventures. It made me wish I did more with my life and followed my dreams. However, this seed did take a year or so to grow.

At the time, I depressed myself by telling myself that this was it for me. With Crohn's Disease, my life was over. There was no way I would be able to follow my dreams of living abroad or going to New Zealand, was there? I'd been diagnosed with this horrendous lifelong illness. I may as well throw my life on the scrap heap.

I must admit that my knowledge of Crohn's Disease was very limited at this point, but I couldn't get these ideas out of my head. Sometimes it was all I could think about.

The surgery itself went well, and they had to remove a sizeable amount of bowel. Thankfully, they were able to re-join the remaining healthy sections back up.

Recovery was slow. I never realised how much energy the surgery would knock out of my already weakened body. By 18th December, I had almost lost hope of being home for Christmas. I still had about four different wires going into me; to feed me, give me hydration, for pain relief in the form of morphine and another for the last dregs of my epidural.

It did get better though. Eventually, I got more comfortable looking at my twelve centimetre scar on my stomach. The doctors were amazed at how well it was healing, and I had also started to go to the toilet again which was the biggest milestone to pass. I never knew this simple achievement could make me so happy. Due to this success, the doctor wanted to try me on soft foods, and a few days later, as there had been no real issues with eating, I was told I could go home - the day before Christmas Eve!

When my sister visited me that night, I told her the news but I couldn't finish the sentence without crying. The crying kind of stunned her as she wasn't used to seeing my tears. She squeezed my hand and just recited, "Don't cry. Don't cry. You're okay. Don't worry." I felt so stupid to be crying about just getting home for Christmas, but I guess all the stress of the previous three weeks had been bottled up. Now I knew I was going home I could finally release it. It was a great feeling, I was finally going home to start the next stage of recovery and I would be able to celebrate it with my family at Christmas.

On the drive home, my sister turned to me with a smile. "There's no need to worry about getting me a Christmas present this year. I've already got the best present I could ask for. My brother is coming home!" As cheesy as it was, I had a warm glow rising up within me.

I grinned and punched her playfully on the arm. "That's good. I didn't get you anything anyway!"

Coming out of hospital with physical and mental scars and with the diagnosis of Crohn's Disease, I thought that, at the age of twenty-four, my best years were behind me. All I'd be doing from now on would be yo-yoing in and out of hospital with flare ups. Thankfully, after another admission to hospital, by the end of 2012, my health started to settle. I thought, 'This is it. My last shot at one last adventure before this disease takes over again.'

The pessimist in me was afraid that being adventurous was too much of a risk to my health. The realist kept telling me that I have a chronic illness and I needed to respect that and just accept a less adventurous life. Thankfully though, the optimist in me won as he knew I had to try. If being diagnosed with Crohn's Disease had taught me anything, it was that you needed to make the most of your health whilst you can, and that trying and failing was better than not trying not at all.

But where to start? All the ideas I came up with got the same response. 'I can't do that. I have Crohn's Disease stupid!'

I had the same thoughts when I decided to go to a talk in November 2012 held by Exodus about their cycling holidays. Adventure cyclist, Mark Beaumont, was giving a talk. Walking to the venue I kept asking myself, 'Why am I here? I can't go on a cycling holiday. That sort of thing was for healthier people, not me. Why waste my time?'

Something in Mark's talk did stick with me though. A few weeks later, I saw an article in the Evening Standard newspaper about RideLondon, a hundred mile bike ride on the London 2012 Olympic Road Race route. Reading it awoke the optimist in me again, and I was reminded how Mark completed his round the world cycle by just cycling a hundred miles a day which, with enough planning and training, he felt was in the reach of anyone.

So I entered the ballot not thinking I'd get a place, just mainly to satisfy myself that at least I tried something. I could have aimed at something smaller, like London to Brighton which is fifty-six miles, but sometimes I like to jump into things and then see if I can swim.

To keep the optimistic spirit alive, I added Mark's cycling books to my Christmas list and got one signed with the added message: 'get busy living'. Three words that I hoped would keep the pessimist's voice at bay and keep reminding me that now was the time to try and do more.

As predicted, I failed in the ballot which is where it could have ended. I mean, I still had loads of negative thoughts and doubts about it anyway like; 'What am I doing? I have a chronic illness. I can't cycle a hundred miles. That's what healthy people do! You won't finish it, so why start?' And the biggest fear of all – 'Will I make myself more ill by doing this?'

But the answer to all these were, 'I won't know unless I try, and goddamn it, I need to at least try.'

So I applied for and got a charity place with the MS Society, bought a bike and started training. And boy, did I need to train! I mean, I couldn't even cycle my bike the few miles home from the bike shop without getting out of breath. All I could do was just laugh and keep telling myself that at least I was trying.

I knew that with Crohn's Disease, getting to the RideLondon start line was not guaranteed. I needed to make sure my training was fun and at least had a few destination rides included. Within a week, I had even cycled the thrity-five-mile round trip to Hyde Park. Not that I enjoyed the slog of the return journey, but at least I did it.

It was all about setting little goals and seeing the bigger picture. After every long ride, I was knackered to the point I didn't know how I could cycle one mile more let alone another sixty. But then, the next time I got back on my bike, I could feel the improvement. So much so that I agreed to cycle with Dave Cornthwaite and Squash Falconer on the London to Brighton section of their three thousand-mile journey on ElliptiGOs across Western Europe in aid of CoppaFeel!

However, when Dave posted the event on Facebook, I didn't say yes straight away as I was nervous about how my Crohn's Disease would handle such a distance. The social aspect of the ride was also a worry, as I didn't want to slow them down or, even worse, for my Crohn's Disease to embarrass me in front of strangers.

The worries kept going around in my mind until I realised that, although I was only three weeks into my training and yes I did have Crohn's Disease, this was too big of an opportunity to turn down. I decided to borrow one of Dave's phrases and started to 'SayYesMore' and signed up!

The ride itself was, in fact, a breeze due to the leisurely pace of the group as we rode out of London and into Surrey. People would stop and stare as we passed by or come up to us and ask what the unique contraptions Dave and Squash riding were, experiences I'd only read about in his *Board Free* book while convalescing in hospital eighteen months before. This fact reminded me not only how far I'd come, but also how surreal this whole ride was.

A small section of the ride was along a road I'd driven down countless times before, when I used to work in Burgh Heath. I started to think about all the things that had changed in my life since then, most notably acquiring a chronic illness and losing part of my bowel, thoughts that dampened my mood somewhat. Then I realised that, back in those days, I wouldn't even have imagined I'd be cycling from London to Brighton. It made me realise that it hadn't all been negative changes.

Arriving on Brighton beach, the whole surrealness of the day was complete. I'd only ever been to Brighton twice before, once via a train and once via a car, never by bike! To christen my achievement I dove into the sea, an act I didn't think twice about until I stood up realising that this was only the third time I'd gone topless in public since my surgery. I knew the six-inch scar on my stomach was still visible or at least to me it was, but after that split second, I realised I didn't really care if someone noticed. Despite having Crohn's Disease, I'd cycled the fifty-six miles from London to Brighton. I felt untouchable at that moment, like a superhero with a hidden power. As much as I was on cloud nine for what I'd achieved, I internalised it all. "Why are you so happy?" someone might ask. And then I'd have to explain the whole story. I wasn't ready for that yet. For now the success was very personal and that was enough.

At this point, my mentality was to be adventurous *despite* having Crohn's Disease, a mentality I felt still held me back, mentally and physically. However, that was all about to change. I was soon to start being adventurous *because* I had Crohn's Disease. It was a whole new way of thinking about it.

It was May now, and World IBD Day was coming up, a day where people aim to raise awareness of Inflammatory Bowel Diseases. I really wanted to do something to mark it but I didn't want to paint my Facebook page in awareness pictures like other people were doing. I wasn't yet comfortable talking publicly about my Crohn's Disease. I knew I wanted to do something though, but what?

Somehow I stumbled across the cycling event, London Revolution, which was a two day event that loops around London. Coincidently, the second day was on May 19th, World IBD Day.

It seemed like a great thing to do, training and a personal way of challenging my IBD. It was perfect! The only problem was it was going to be an eighty-mile ride over some very hilly terrain. I'd cycled the fifty-six miles from London to Brighton a few weeks earlier, but that was at a leisurely pace. This would be completely different. eighty miles was a distance I knew I wasn't fit enough for. It was simply too early in my training to attempt. I should do it next year. However, my determination to do something to mark the day took over, and I convinced myself that it was too good of an opportunity to back away from. I couldn't take the risk of waiting until I was ready. Who knew if I'd be well enough to cycle it in a year's time anyway? Now was the time to say yes to the challenge, and to say yes *because* I have Crohn's Disease.

When I arrived at the start line at Windsor Racecourse, the feeling of being out of my depth was rammed home to me in the form of a throng of lycra-clad people on their lightweight road bikes. I glanced down at my t-shirt, trackie bottoms and trainers on my heavy hybrid bike. What had I gotten myself into?

The first challenge of the day was Box Hill, and although somehow I got up it without stopping, my energy levels were flagging and, by mile forty, I hit the wall. I could feel my energy reserves being depleted, and no matter the terrain, my legs were like lead. Each mile seemed longer than the last. If I could have stopped, I would have done. I trudged on, but I knew the worst was yet to come.

The North Downs was where the real hills start to bite. I tried my hardest to summit the first big hill without stopping, but I soon gave in. Sometimes when cycling I feel like a steam engine, mentally shovelling on the coal when I need to go faster, but by now I'd run out of fuel. I was empty and not even running on fumes. I'd become so tired that, as soon as I saw a big hill, I slowly got off my bike and walked it. I was physically beaten, and even when I got to the top of the hills, I didn't have the energy to pedal down them. I would just glide enjoying the short rest periods they gave me. The scenery of lush rolling green fields and small country lanes were a highlight of the route, it was just a shame I was so tired and unfit to enjoy them.

Why had I signed up? This was no fun at all. Now even the half miles ticked past slowly in my head.

When I saw the signs for ExCeL London, which was near where the ride was to finish, I was so happy. It had been such a struggle, but I was going to make it.

Crossing the finish line wasn't as euphoric as I'd expected. I knew the gravity of what I had just completed, but I was too mentally and physically beaten to enjoy it. I was just simply overjoyed not having to put myself through any more torture. I called my Dad to come pick me up and lowered my aching body tentatively onto the kerb at the side of the road.

Sitting there I told myself, 'I'll NEVER EVER do something that stupid again!' I started to replay the day in my head. I couldn't believe I'd actually done it. Sure, I was worried about how badly I'd struggled to ride the eighty miles in ten hours (especially when RideLondon was going to be a hundred miles and had a time limit of nine hours). I'd definitely bitten off more than I could chew.

However, I tried to put those thoughts to the back of my mind and focus on the present. I'd just cycled the furthest distance in my life. I was incredibly exhausted yet my Crohn's Disease was fine. I had to remind myself that I was sitting at ExCel London where, only a few months previously, I'd watched the Paralympics. If you'd told me that the next time I'd be there it would be after cycling from Windsor, I wouldn't have believed you. I'd have told you that's something I could never do, especially because I have Crohn's Disease. Boy was I wrong! I had indeed cycled eighty miles from Windsor for that exact same reason - *because* I have Crohn's Disease. That was when the euphoria set in!

When I started training for RideLondon, I never knew how many miles I would have to put into my legs just to be able to cycle a hundred miles in a day. Now I know why they say the hardest part is just getting to the start line. The thousand-mile mark came in a cycle from London to Oxford. One of the many rides I never imagined I'd be able to do. Oxford is somewhere I'd drive to but never ride to.

There was a slight hesitation in signing up to the ride as it was on Wimbledon finals day and Andy Murray was the first British man to get there in seventy-seven years. It was a moment I didn't want to miss witnessing live on TV. It's some years on now and I do regret not watching the tennis but still not as much as I would have regretted missing out on the ride. I can always watch a tennis match from a sick bed, but I can't cycle seventy-five miles to Oxford from it!

By now in my training and my life, saying yes more *because* I had Crohn's Disease took over so much of my decision making.

Of all my worries with aiming to complete RideLondon, my biggest worries came from whether or not my health could be stable enough to allow me to train for it and then be well enough on the day to complete the hundred miles.

I'd spoken to friends who had had similar challenges, but their IBD had flared up and stopped them doing their challenges, marathons, etc. Yet here I was waking up at 4am, fit and ready to ride my cycling Everest.

There was a great buzz of anticipation as I made my way to the Olympic Park to join the thousands of other cyclists who were doing the ride. I tried to soak up the atmosphere as much as I could. I kept telling myself to treat this as my last adventure, because with Crohn's Disease, it could be.

Cycling on the closed roads of London was a very surreal experience. The only things I had to look out for were my next photo opportunity and the other cyclists whizzing past. I was getting overtaken quite a lot, but I was used to that by now being on a much heavier bike. It was never a race for me anyway. I just wanted to get around the route however long it took.

I'd always thought crossing the finish line would be the highlight of my ride. I'd even used this mental image as motivation to train when I didn't want to. However, the highlight of the ride came at the eighty mile pit stop.

It was then that I realised I was going to make it. Mentally the finish line was in sight. At the start of the day I knew I was capable of doing it but I never allowed myself to get carried away as I still had a hundred miles to go.

But now, with only twenty miles to the finish line, I knew I was going to do it. This realisation got me quite emotional. I was overcome with the sheer joy of finally being able to release the emotion I'd built up through my training, never allowing myself to believe this moment was possible until it was. The emotional high made the last miles some of the easiest of the whole day, recounting all I'd gone through with the training and the physical and mental lows Crohn's Disease had given me. Lows that were now my fuel for adventure.

I was so happy that I'd proven the negative part of me wrong, the part that said my Crohn's Disease would never allow me to complete RideLondon. Yet here I was, so close to the end.

I turned past Trafalgar Square and into The Mall, and there it was, the finish line. I took a few more pictures before composing myself for the sprint to the line, and before I knew it, it was over.

I'd summited my Everest, and all that was left to do was get my medal, something Crohn's Disease will never be able to take away from me.

Facebook: **TheChronicAdventurer**

Instagram: **@thechronicadventurer**

Twitter: **@ForEveryIBD**

Chapter 19

Driving a Tuktuk across India

By Claire Jenkins

"No, Claire."

"No, that doesn't appeal."

"Why would you want to do that? Why would anyone want to do that?"

"It's too dangerous!"

"It's not my kind of fun."

For a long time (almost a decade!) I had wanted to do the Rickshaw Run across India, where you race point-to-point in a tuktuk with tens of other fellow adventurers.

Between 2010 and 2012, I had worked in India for BT and fell in love with tuktuks. With their crazy colour and their cartoon toy shape, they became my symbol of adventure just from the sense of fun you get from weaving through traffic lanes and dicing with death on your way to work. There is something so invigorating about taking this roller coaster journey each day, arriving at work with a 'Phew! Made it! Hurrah' type feeling. I loved being in motion, being able to see different things, the hot air against your face and the closeness to the local community. You didn't get that feeling from being behind a window in an air-con work taxi.

When I left India, I was presented with a plastic tuktuk by my team. It became my pride and joy until Barty, our family Jack Russell decided that he liked it more and it became a chewed plastic mound on our living room floor.

At the start of 2019, I wrote my first ever 'Yes List'. This was a big step for me; I hate plans. I break out into a nervous panic at the thought of committing to things more than forty-eight hours ahead. One of my best pals has the rule that *'Claire must give me five days' notice to things or it's a no'*, after getting increasing frustrated with my usual organisation:

"Hey, Zoe. Do you want to do this."

"Yes sure. When?"

"Tonight at seven?"

"No, Claire…"

So doing my 'Yes List' was a pivotal life moment for me. In the years prior to this, I had all these things that I wanted to do but never seemed to get round to doing them. The power of writing / typing something down was revolutionary to me. I am target orientated, so saying that I was going to do these things mean that I had to do them. These things included saving money, to a watch a TED Talk a day, keeping a gratitude journal… and the big one, driving a tuktuk across India.

I had written it down, so I started to think, 'Ok. Let's make this a real possibility rather than just something you joke about with your friends.'

I had decided that as this was such a dream trip for me, something I had wanted to do for so long, I didn't want to share it with a random. I had also dreamt of doing this with a fella... but no one from Tinder or Bumble seemed to have made the grade of adventurous co-pilot yet. So it looked like it was going to be me solo.

I started looking at prices, and at £1500 for the Rickshaw Run plus flights and expenses when I was there, I started to have doubts. More than the money, I wasn't so sure about travelling on my own in India, despite having lived there on and off for two years. I knew that it wasn't really safe. Two of my pals had even said, "*Claire we just don't want you to go on your own, please don't.*"

For which my response was, "Come with me then."

"No, Claire."

A few days later, I happened to read one of the emails that comes out from Explorers Connect, a UK adventure group based in Bristol. They shared an advert for:

> '*Co-drivers to join a global round the world trip on a solar powered tuktuk, starting in India.*'

The project was led by Julian, a social entrepreneur and engineering professor at a University in Melbourne. He had challenged his students to convert a tuktuk to use solar power as part of their final year project. After this Julian had a light bulb idea of driving it around the world. Thank you Julian. The world needs inspirational creative thinkers like you!

I emailed Julian and that was it. I was on the team with an Australian called Talia who was working in Nepal. Talia and I made arrangements to chat via WhatsApp.

After the initial pleasantries, she got down to the nitty-gritty.

"Soooo... how do you feel about museums, churches and temples?"

'Eeek!' I thought. 'Am I letting myself in for a history tour here?' So I gambled with honesty, fully prepared to give up on the trip if it meant seeing every church, museum and temple between Chennai and Mumbai.

"Gee, please no! They bore me to tears!"

I had struck travel buddy gold! PHEW! We shared a passion for food, chatting to people and a contempt for museums, churches and temples. And of course, we both wanted the achievement and bragging rights of saying "I've driven a solar powered tuktuk across India."

One of the things that many people asked us was, *"Aren't you worried? What happens if you don't like each other?"* This hadn't really occurred to either of us, logic being that if you're up for something like this then you're going to be pretty interesting.

A couple of days later, I landed in Chennai with all of the confusion of a tech spoilt Londoner. *"What? No Wi-Fi at the airport? How do I book an Uber? Darn it, going to have to turn on the expensive data roaming. Eeek!!"* Which went totally against my Jenkins genes of being tight. I gave in and, £35 later, I had found my Uber and was on my way to my Airbnb. I arrived at said Airbnb to find out I can't check in until 4pm. It's 7am. I curse myself for not being one of those organised types who checks this kind of thing in advance.

I faffed about for a while and decided that I just want to sleep so I checked into the Marriot with its lush white duvets, air con, floor to ceiling windows and room service.

I briefly considered if I was a fraud. It's India. everyone knows you're meant to stay in dreadful accommodation when you travel here. It's part of the experience, the typical stories people have. Dare I break away from what people expect?

Yep!

So I spent a lush few days carrying on doing my day job from a plush leather chair and beautiful wooden desk with views across the river, whilst running up an expensive room service bill for delicious but overpriced curry. It was a romantic view showing the Tetris landscape of spangly new buildings, ugly, old, concrete buildings and various brightly coloured road side shacks serving up food and selling brightly-coloured, plastic household goods. I'm very glad that I had this romantic version of India, safely up on the 7th floor away from the dirt, pollution and foul smelling rubbish in the actual river.

Talia and I met in my hotel room at 2am in Chennai. I opened my door and met the coolest lady you could meet; confident, driven, and smart, one of those people that has effortless charm and wit. I knew I was going to love travelling with her. Talia started her day with taking full advantage of our four-star hotel buffet breakfast. She had been travelling through rural Nepal for three months so she sampled EVERYTHING. We had an amazing array of juices, coffees, Western and Indian food before heading off to the port with Talia's big bag of paperwork to get our tuktuk out from customs.

A complex pattern of paperwork, port authorities and middle men started. It turned out that Talia's big bag of paperwork just wasn't enough. The long and short of it was that we couldn't get the tuktuk without Julian (the named owner) being there (after having considered bribes, forgery and a considerable amount of eye fluttering).

But he was back in Melbourne lecturing a new batch of freshers. There was no way that we could ask him to fly out. And why would he even want to? I mean, who does that kind of thing? The flights would be so expensive and who could or would just drop out of work? It seemed like this would be the end of our trip before we'd even started, we'd already wasted a ton of money on a nice hotel in Chennai and had achieved zero bragging rights. So close to achieving a dream of nearly a decade and for it to be ruined by darn paperwork.

I hung my head, feeling numb, my stomach feeling like a deflated ball of lead. How would either of us react to not going on the trip? Surely someone should have realised that we needed Talia's name as the owner? We'd both been quite pragmatic about it and discussed the options of actually having to go home without having achieved anything. Talia was so apologetic about it. I could sense and see how guilty she felt as she had been part of the organising team. As the traffic noise of Chennai honked and tooted around us, with a face full of anguish and a body tensed with fear, ready to accept the inevitable disappointment that was heading our way, and slumped on a chair, Talia called Julian.

Then, suddenly, she flashed me a smile and gave me the thumbs up!

What a fella! The exact kind of person that I love and admire. With cancelling and rescheduling some of his lectures at the University, Julian was set to arrive a week later. I was so full of admiration, joy and respect. I hadn't even considered it a possibility that he would even consider coming let alone actually doing it. You have to love a person who says "YES!" My adventure was not going to be over. I hadn't wasted money on flights and accommodation. And my adventure dream was going to happen, and now we had an even better story to share.

The down side was being stuck in Chennai for another week, which is a bit like being stuck in Milton Keynes and not able to leave. It felt so frustrating. But, hey, nothing we could do about it so we got on with it! An extra week in an industrial city... what do you do? We had looked at leaving and going hiking but felt that we should stay just in case we were needed. We briefly considered one of the local museums, or one of the temples, but went for Chai instead.

By this time we had moved out of our swanky hotel and into something cheaper, a lovely rundown old colonial building turned into a hostel. We had a room with a couple of ceiling fans and en suite bathroom with a concrete floor rather than a marble one. I loved it. It reminded me of the Best Exotic Marigold Hotel.

Our days passed with chai drinking, eating biryani and the occasional meeting (and a stint on a film set as Talia appeared in a Tamil movie – true story!) We even woke up one morning to find our hostel had been turned into a TV set for an Amazon Series and our veranda was the production set. One day, we went to a local technical university to talk about solar power. Talia was a great speaker in front of hundreds of female students and most definitely a great role model for these young women engineers.

On Wednesday morning, Julian eventually arrived. For a brief moment, I wasn't sure how I felt about a fella joining our girl's road trip but how could you not love and be inspired by a chap who hops on a plane to ensure an adventure continues? I loved Julian instantly. It was wonderful to meet the man behind this awesome vision.

Even with Julian, the tuk owner, it took a further two days to get the tuk out and all of the electrics re-connected. Luckily Julian and Talia were electrical engineers!

The day before lift off, I woke in the early hours poorly, vomiting and diarrhoea, dripping in sweat and just generally feeling awful. I loved our hotel room with its wooden ceiling fans, wooden shutters, plastic covered mattresses and cement floor, but I still like a luxurious hotel room. So I ordered a tuktuk on my Uber account and went back to the Marriot. I hopped into a white bed, cranked up the AC, piled on the lovely, fluffy duvets and went to sleep whilst begging the security staff for some ibuprofen.

Day 1: Chennai to Vellore (150km)

Talia turned up with my suitcase. I had left at 2am in my bed shorts and t-shirt with my laptop and passport. Definitely not the most sensible thing I have done at 2am.

"Oh no, Talia. I don't think I can make it," I moaned from under the duvet covers.

"CLAIRE!!! We've waited two weeks for this. There is no way this tuk is leaving without you. Get up and get dressed!"

Ok good point. I dressed slowly, and we hopped into a taxi to finally get our tuk from the port customs authority.

It was a beautiful red machine, like a kids cartoon toy but for grownups. Three wheels; black solar powered panels on the side and on the top; plastic curtains; cream leather, comfy seats; enough room for six passengers; and the cockpit for the driver, and with some flower garlands from the local market stall hanging off the wing mirrors. It was a machine of adventurous beauty.

Finally, we were off on the 1500 kilometres to Mumbai, Julian at the wheel, Talia and myself in the back amongst our backpacks, suitcases and a big box of driving snacks, with me desperately hoping that I didn't need the loo on route.

Driving out of Chennai was immense fun. It became the opposite of a bowling game, driving a tuk down a narrow alley whilst not knocking over parked motorbikes, pedestrians, cows or market stalls. After two weeks we were off (plus the previous eight years of wanting to do this trip). Would it match up to my dreams of what I wanted the experience to be? Was it going to be worth the eight years of pining to do it?

Being in a bright red tuk covered in solar panels driven by Westerners attracted a lot of attention. Everywhere we went we had a curious entourage of motorbikes, trucks and cars all waving, honking and asking for selfies and even trying to run us off the road to get said selfies after any refusal. After a while there was a pattern of the same questions.

Where from? *Australia and London.*

Where going? *Mumbai!*

Why? *Because it's fun!*

The bemused faces and subsequent laughs were fun. They were always followed by a request for a selfie and for a coffee at the next stop. Out of curiosity we always wanted to stop for a natter but we had flights to catch. Literally.

After a few days, we realised we could shorten the conversations by just shouting at every motorbike driver, "We're from Australia and we're driving to Mumbai because it's fun". It was interesting to think that something so amazing and exciting for me was unfathomable for not just my family and pals back at home, but also most of the Indian population we met.

Arriving into Vellore was going to be our first challenge of seeing if hotel owners would be happy to let us charge our tuk, as this doesn't tend to be covered in any hotel reception's operating manual. Fortunately, a quick call from the hotel staff to their boss gave us permission and we started unwinding the hundred-metre extension cord to the local socket, whilst explaining to the local crowd that had gathered what we were doing.

Day 2: Vellore to Hosur (200km)

I am known within my family and friends as being a terrible driver, I have a very short concentration span and am very easily distracted by anything new and sparkly. I hadn't really driven since I wrote off my car going round a bend back in Ross-on-Wye a few years before. The responsibility of not crashing our beautiful tuk and keeping two other co-drivers alive weighed on me. Perhaps I should have thought about this before signing up?

Julian was leaving that evening to head back to Chennai to fly home to Melbourne, so it was time for me to learn. We headed off down a side road and I jumped into the cockpit. At first it is weird; no circular steering wheel just what looks like a coat hanger on its side; you only have one pedal for a break; no clutch; and all of the speed is controlled by the accelerator with your right hand. Forwards for quicker and backwards for slowing down. And you sit like you're manspreading, which is weird. After a week on the road, I found that not only did I end up with claw hands but I also had splits down the bum of all of my trousers.

My first turn of the accelerator on the coat hanger was sooo exciting but also nerve racking. I had visions of pulling off too quickly and sending Julian, Talia and our luggage flying out the sides. But it wasn't and it was so smooth we glided down the road. And then I went full throttle (well, to fifty kilometres per hour). It was mesmerizing and darn exhilarating!

Looking out of the windscreen, the wind rushing by feeling so close to the local environment, yet at the same time feeling really peaceful, I instantly fell in love with it. It is a combination of feeling total freedom and awe of your stunning, colourful surroundings.

Arriving into Hosur, we attracted our usual crowd, and some young engineering students, Santhosh and Abilash, who were fascinated to chat techie engineering with Talia and Julian. They even went to get some new plug convertors for us. That evening we were invited to their parent's home for dinner, which was an incredible experience meeting the mum, learning about the home shrines they have for their religion and of course a delicious plate of curry, naan and rice... in exchange for a few hundred selfies.

Day 3: Hosur to Tumaku (150km)

Our day started late. Talia had had little sleep as she had been checking our little tuk every two hours through the night to make sure it was charging. It takes a full ten hours to charge. At some point, the evening the security guard had unplugged it as it had tripped the hotel lights. Oops!

My Granny Jenkins was always fastidious about hitch hikers and me not ever picking one up when driving. Talia and I hadn't discussed our hitchhiker policy until waiting at a toll bridge. A chap asked if he could hitch a ride with us. Quick assessment - he seemed smart in a shirt, trousers shiny shoes and cufflinks. Interacting with local people had been part of our plan, so why not? It'd be more stories from our adventure.

He hopped in to join us on our way to Bangalore. In very broken English, he explained that he was an IT project manager, and then he started to chat about his recent massage course. He asked me if he could massage my feet. I refused for a while and then gave in. Who doesn't love a foot massage? And anyone who wants to touch my feet after walking around Chennai for two weeks in flip-flops is welcome.

A foot massage became a calf massage... and then I was asked if I wanted my chest massaged as it would relax me. I calmly declined whilst fighting the inner desire to smash his face in and then spent the next thirty minutes trying to get him out of the tuk whilst being frightfully English and polite. I didn't want to antagonise the situation but I also wanted to throw this chap out at fifty kilometres per hour onto the motorway.

After eventually getting rid of him, we agreed that it was only women and children that we would pick up. From that point onwards our 'emergency' word became 'Broccoli' for any time we felt alarmed. Reason for this, one of our many conversations was around misunderstanding how to pronounce words. Mine being the word 'stoic', with painful memories back to my A Level French class when everyone else laughed at my pronunciation 'Stoike' rather than 'stow -ic'. Talia's equivalent was 'broccoli' pronounced 'brock o lie' rather than 'brock-o -lee' She was twenty-five when she realised that this wasn't just how Australians pronounced it versus Europeans, and it was in fact only her family, in the entire whole world.

I was disappointed that we never got to shout 'Brocolli' for the rest of the trip.

Day 4: Tumaku to Davangere via Bangalore (200km)

As I work from home most of the time in recruitment, I decided that I could do this from India. The time difference meant that I could drive local time 8am to 1pm and then hop in the back of the tuk from 1pm for an 8.30am UK start. Each afternoon I would bungee cord down my laptop, and water bottle onto the seat in front of me sit on the floor and get going. It was amazing driving through the Indian countryside with the plastic side curtains open, watching the cows in fields whilst coaching grads to interview success. I had a local sim card, the internet was fantastic and hardly anyone could tell where I was unless Talia shouted 'BUMP' or was particularly loud on the horn, which was most of the time.

"Ok so tell me what do you know *BUMMMP* about the company you're *BUUUMMP* interviewing with?"

"Are you ok?"

"Sorry. I'm driving a tuktuk across India and we're just going over a bump."

"What? I thought you worked in London?"

I love what I do but there was something even more enjoyable about working when you can combine earning money with living an adventure driving in a tuktuk.

One of the many things I love about travel is the folk you meet along the way, and the kindness that is extended to strangers. One epic person was Sushil Reddy, an Indian IT graduate and holder of a Guinness World Record for the longest solar electric bike ride for seventy-nine days and 7424 kilometres across India. He had seen our social media posts and got in contact to hook us up with his network along the way to meet him in Mumbai. The first person we met was Mr Madan from Volta Automotive India in Bangalore. He has a dream of converting all existing tuktuks in India to electric ones to reduce pollution and provide a healthier work environment for the drivers. We spent a fun morning comparing tuktuks and solar powered specs as well as driving round the suburban outskirts of Bangalore in each other's tuks. Ours was beautiful and bright red but their turning circle was so much easier.

We then headed to Davengene and stayed with Mr Aakarsh. Well, we stayed at his home, but we never actually met him as he was away. We were welcomed to his house by his staff and also his Grandma. The area was a beautiful suburb with painted white walls, roses and manicured gardens. I was struck by the international love for dogs here. Typically when travelling Asia and Africa I am used to dogs being treated as pests. Here, morning and evening, we saw handsome and beautifully groomed mini fluffy dogs prancing along being walked by the family servant. I felt very lucky to have had an insight into a part of India that we would not normally have seen. The usual portrayal of India is dirt, poverty and shacks, so it was wonderful to see other parts of Indian life. Mr Aakrash had developed a solar powered light that was affordable for shack owners to buy. Typically these shop owners are limited in the opening hours they can work. With a light they could stay open longer as well as diversify income by providing mobile phone charging.

Day 5: Davangere to Hubli (160km)

With limited time we typically had to stick to motorway, but today we decided to go off-roading and just turned left to see where we would end up. Driving the tuk over potholed muddied roads was fun! Especially when I forgot the golden rule about shouting, "BUMP!" at each pothole. Talia was not impressed as each time she scrambled to ensure our luggage didn't fall out of the sides.

We decided to turn into a local primary school and spent a fun few hours driving the children around their playground and letting the teachers drive whilst talking about the potential for solar power.

It was here that I discovered Talia's love of climbing, we stopped at a water tower, which are these large UFO concrete structures on fifty-metre stilts towering into the sky. And she just had to climb it. We scrambled over the gates and up the steps clambering onto the top of the water tower with some of our snacks to see the view. Soon it started to rain, and we had to hurry back to the tuk to cover up the electrics.

After a few weeks in India we had become accustomed to unusual sights, but one of my highlight surprises was coming across a gypsy convoy. Fifteen cows pulled wooden caravans with hay strapped on top, huge painted wooden wheels, buckets hanging off the side and a group of goats tied on the back, with men walking at the side and women inside tending to a small charcoal fire. I have never seen actually gypsy caravans beyond the ones I have stayed in via Airbnb back in England so it was a real cultural delight. We asked for a photo but were shuttled away.

Day 6: Hubli to Kolhapur (210km)

Our next stop was Kolhapor to meet with Mr. Mayank Gupta. He sent his house keeper to come and let us into his two bed penthouse apartment with floor to ceiling glass walls and views over the countryside. Arriving sweaty, dirty and with crazy hair we were let into this stunning apartment, fed chocolate and left to rest before Mayank came back. He was Co-founder of Zilingo, a hugely successful fashion tech company based out of Thailand kind of like ASOS here in the UK. I love to talk entrepreneurship and business and was in the presence of tech royalty so the dinner conversation was epic.

In the morning, he took us to his latest business venture; an aquaponics farm an hour from his home. My first career was in produce buying at Tesco so anything agri-related is a dream topic for me. We had a fascinating tour of his farm, learnt about fish farming, and saw all of the salads and herbs that he was growing. There were a number of women harvesting produce and it was such a beautiful sight. The green crops contrasting with the brightly coloured pinks, reds and orange saris, with their jewellery glistening in the sun.

Day 7: Kolhapur to Pune (250km)

Ten years before I had lived on and off in Pune whilst working for BT. I was keen to see some of the old team that I had worked with. We parked the tuktuk with some of Sushil's friends, Neha and Preshant on the outskirts of Pune and hopped in a taxi tuk into the centre.

One of the things that we had noticed whilst travelling was we had not seen or come into contact with any other Western folk apart from a few in the Chennai hostel we had stayed in. I liked this because it made the experience that much more unique. So meeting some Australian women, suited and all made up for their evening business meetings, was unusual. There is something exciting about chatting about your adventures when people are in work mode and you're slightly sweaty, grimy with frizzy hair, in baggy comfy driving clothes and full of the joys of adventure, rather than the frustrations of cross cultural working in the IT world.

We met Simanta, who was one of my former managers, at Bar 101 on top of the Marriot hotel, one of our old business networking haunts. It has one of the best night time views and plays funky Ibiza background music against a silhouetted mountain back drop. So beautiful. It was strange for me to bring the travelling fun side of me into my old corporate life. It was a chapter that I had left behind whilst I had loved my experience of working professionally in India as a young woman and all of the challenges that gender brings, I had felt bored, trapped, suffocated and uninspired by my company and the people that worked there. Stepping back in time and merging an old life with a new life was unsettling for me for sure.

However, it was fabulous to see Simanta, and great to see that he had moved on and up to manage a larger team with a different company and now had a baby. When you haven't seen someone for eight years and you only knew them in a work context, how would it be? Sharing some food together more as friends rather than boss and team member was great. Simanta, like most local people we had met, was like, "Why Claire?" with utter bemusement screaming from his face. "Why didn't you just take a plane, it is much safer and quicker."

Later, he dropped me 'home' and I snuck into another house where I had not met the owners. In the morning, we woke up to a beautiful breakfast made of steamed rice dough pancakes called Idlis with different dips, chutneys and dosas, thin crepes made of lentils. It was lush and gave us a kick ready to get us on the road to Mumbai. We had a presentation to give at the University of Pune at 9pm to some sustainability students. Twelve hours to make a five-hour journey.

Day 8: Pune to Mumbai (200km)

The drive from Pune to Mumbai was one that I had done many times on the high-speed highway. Simanta had said that we would not be able to drive the tuk on this highway but trying to avoid it had been impossible. We *somehow* ended up on it speeding past signs that said 'no three wheelers' and lorries honking at us. To be fair, lorries had always honked at us so this was nothing new. Driving down this road I was Facebook Live-ing, and a number of my old team were watching started to ask, *"Are you on the Pune highway? What! No, Claire! You can't be on there! It isn't allowed!"*

Suddenly, we arrived at a checkpoint. And were immediately escorted to the correct road by a policeman as this road was apparently too dangerous. Having driven through Bangalore traffic, it really didn't feel dangerous in comparison. Nonetheless, it was fun to have a police escort. After a while, we were asked to pull over for what we wrongly assumed was some sort of fine. Nope. He just wanted a selfie.

Driving in India is epic fun. The roads are dangerous, no one adheres to any rules and it is a deafening yet exhilarating cacophony of musical horns, motorbikes and yelling. All this against a backdrop of luscious green landscape, brightly coloured trucks and ladies in twinkling saris.

The drive over the Sahyadri mountain range, through the Bhor Ghat pass, upped the dangerous driving exhilaration levels. Whilst I was safely in the back on some coaching calls with candidates, Talia had to navigate down a narrow mountain pass, through a horizontal hailstorm, high winds and contend with Google Maps not working due to the rain. She did an incredible job steering a tuk semi-blind with a windscreen steaming up as we needed the sides up to protect the internal electrics from the rain outside.

Hitting Mumbai was a whole other experience of crazy insane slow moving traffic. Reaching the edge of town around 2pm, it took another five hours (with a confused Google Maps which kept giving us last minute directions to turn right across eight lanes of traffic) to reach the University. Arriving at the University, we finally met Sushil, the electric bike world record holder who had set us up with all of his friends.

He invited us for dinner in the staff canteen before the presentation. So wonderful to meet someone who had made such a difference to our journey. To hear more about his solar powered passion and trips across India in a tuk and on an electric bike was inspiring, I hadn't met a Guinness Record holder before.

With his contacts, we had seen a totally different side to India which we would not have seen on our own. We had met incredible entrepreneurs in amazing suburbs with amazing homes all doing something to assist the poor or the planet in their spare time.

So this was it, we had driven 1500 kilometres across India, and only had to drive across Mumbai towards to the airport to a nearby hostel. There we would meet the next crew who would take the tuk north around India. We persuaded Sushil to join us and drive the tuk to help relive his adventure of the previous year. Arriving at the hostel, we said our goodbyes to Sushil and then, while waiting for the boys to arrive, used their hotel room for a shower and change.

The boys had never been to India let alone driven a tuk so Talia and I bundled one of them into the driver seat to go for a scoot round some narrow streets, just to get the practice of reversing, stopping and, of course, honking the horn.

Then that was it, a brief hour together and then into an Uber to Mumbai Airport for a direct flight home. Talia was flying off to another adventure with her brother hiking and climbing in Kazakhstan. We hugged and said until the next time.

So what does it feel like to have completed a dream after so long?

It took some time for me to assimilate the experience, and realise that it had actually happened. From seeing the advert to hopping on the plane, to being stuck in Chennai for two weeks and then eight days on the road and arriving back to my London flat had all happened within the space of a month.

If I hadn't have written 'tuktuk adventure' into my 2019 Yes List, I don't think I would have even have seen the advert with Explorers Connect. Or if I had, I am convinced that I wouldn't have taken it up. I would have found too many barriers and just kept my dream as something unobtainable and oh woe is me.

I had the best time, feeling like I was truly living, being inspired, feeling alive and feeding my desire for learning. I was doing the things that I love, meeting new people, learning lots of new info. I really felt freedom and alive at being open to all of the things that journey threw at us.

With the power of social media, I loved being able to include my friends back home through my daily Facebook Live chats and sharing my adventure with them. And guess what? When the Tuk gets to Europe, so many of them want to join me.

"Yes, Claire! That looked so much fun. I want to join next time!"

Email: **claire@tablecrowdtalent.com**

LinkedIn: **claire-jenkins-26495936**

Chapter 20

Ushuaia to Lima by Bike

By Emma Karslake

Day 1: Ushuaia, Argentina

I manage to stab my calf at Ushuaia Airport when cutting the protective wrapping around my bike. Very silly but, in my defence, it turns out that our camping cutlery is very sharp. We finally put the bikes together and take off. Damn it is heavy! Is my wheel caught in something? It feels like I am trying to pedal a motorbike.

Maybe it would have been a good idea to practice a bit on this bike before leaving Europe to cycle across South America for six months.

None of my teammates lived in the same country as me during our few months of preparation. We had Skype meetings to discuss fundraising and training, but no opportunity to train on the bikes that arrived a week before our flight. Oh well, I will get used to it.

I met Agnès at university. She is a calm force of nature with a majestic mane of golden locks. Agnès and Astrid are childhood friends. Any meeting with Astrid ends up in laughing fits.

When they asked whether I would like to travel around South America, I said, "Yes!" without batting an eyelid.

"By bike?" they added.

"Erm... Sure." They then proposed that Julie, a friend of theirs, joined us. I had only met her once but thought she was nice enough. And so, the four of us found ourselves at the most southern point of Argentina about to embark on an eight thousand-kilometre bike trip for charity.

Day 5: Ruta Nacional 3, Argentina

Windy, with gusts of eighty-five kilometres per hour according to the weather forecast, but more according to me.

We can barely stand and decide to hitchhike to the Chilean border. After a long wait, we finally get a lorry driver called Augustin to take the four bikes and us. He says he will be stopping before the border, but that he is going there in the morning. He later adds that we can sleep next to him in his lorry, which we politely decline, preferring the tent.

We finally drive off, one of us in the passenger seat and the three others squished behind on his small one-person bed. Four hundred metres later, he enters an asphalt mine, loads off some bags, drives another few metres into a quarry and stops, telling us it is forbidden for us to be there but that we can spend the night anyway. He points to a pit and says we could pitch our tent there, again mentioning the possibility of sleeping in his lorry. We say good night after having unloaded the bikes as he is scared that his boss might see them.

The four of us will have to squeeze into just one of the two tents tonight, since flat ground is scarce. We realise that even though Augustin looks friendly, this is potentially an unsafe situation. If I read the headline 'FOUR 22-YEAR-OLD TOURISTS ATTACKED IN

AN ASPHALT MINE AFTER ILLEGALLY ENTERING IT TO CAMP', I would think that the people were idiots. This was not the plan, but now we are here.

The lorry drives off. Around 11pm we hear it coming back, a door opening, then nothing. At 3am I think that if Augustin wanted to harm us, he would have done so already, so I fall back asleep feeling safe.

Day 6: Ruta Nacional 3, Argentina

In the morning, Augustin tells us that he can pick us up in one hour, on the road, not in the mine, and that we have to make our own discreet way out. We climb the fence with the bikes, cross a field, and end up at another entrance of the mine. We have no choice but to continue, so we scramble under the barbed wire. Workmen resurfacing the road opposite stop to watch us with eyes wide open, but saying nothing.

Augustin never came to pick us up.

Day 7: East of Porvenir, Chile

After a long rainy day on a mud track, we are staying in what other cyclists have called 'the old bus shelter'. We are sharing the space with three French cyclists who were there when we arrived. Thomas sweeps the floor with a makeshift broom. Ghislain and Xavier are reading in a corner, wrapped up in their duvet as the temperature has dropped, aggravating the feeling of dampness.

Coming back from outside, Agnès notices the clear wooden floor and the broom in Thomas' hand. "Oh!" she stops at the door. "Shall I remove my shoes?" I look at the heap of muddy gear near the door. Thomas looks at my dirty hair and face, I look at his, and in the middle of our laughing fit, Agnès still seems to be wondering whether we are a no-shoes household.

A kind soul in a pickup truck left us a pack of dried ravioli and a bottle of olive oil. As the number of ravioli goes down in my plate, I add a bit of oil. Three ravioli left, better top up the oil. One left and I feel a lack of oil even though the lonely pasta is currently floating. We decided not to carry salt or oil, because they are heavy and messy, disregarding any basic nutrition advice. After seven days of effort, my body is craving fat. I pour more oil in my plate and carry it to my lips. Never has oil tasted so good.

Day 8: Travelling into Porvenir, Chile

We set off at 6.15am to avoid the wind. Agnès and I ride at the front with Thomas and Ghislain. One of them compliments us on our speed, which I was both hoping for and expecting, since we are currently pedalling faster than we would on our own. The guys have to dash off ahead to catch a ferry, and we resume at a more sustainable pace.

Day 14: On the Ruta Provincial 7, Argentina

We spend another joyful morning cruising at thirty-five kilometres per hour on average, not bad for a twenty kilograms bike carrying its weight in panniers and water.

We then face a choice: two hundred kilometres of asphalt, or seventy kilometres of unknown surface in the desert? We feel optimistic about the shortcut. We fill our water bottles at a police station, thinking we will be on the other side by teatime.

Day 15: On the Ruta Provincial 7, Argentina

I am not sure the thing going through this desert can be called a road. There is a large trail of rocks in the middle, on which about two cars a day drive at a very low speed. To make matters worse, as we turned to take the shortcut, so did the wind.

We stop after fifteen kilometres of track because my knee is sore, I am exhausted and scared of losing focus. Our joints are the only suspension on our bikes, and with every rock I jump, I feel an invisible hammer hit my kneecap.

I get off my bike longing for that dry grass on the side. As I put my hand down to ease my hundred-year-old body onto the ground, I let out a squeak. I do not know what this thing is, but it is not grass.

I check whether any of the tiny needles got stuck in my palm and lie down on the rocks.

Day 16: On the Ruta Provincial 7, Argentina

We are still on the 'shortcut'.

The quality of the path improves but the wind is blowing us to the right and off our bikes without respite. One, two, three, I am moving! As long as I maintain a bit of speed, I can keep going, at least until the next gust.

I see Agnès topple ahead of me, and I follow shortly after. Nothing about this is fun.

On the plus side, this ride is so unpleasant that I cannot even feel my bra scratching my sunburnt back like I did at breakfast. We got burnt through our long sleeve shirts yesterday, and I am now wearing more layers than comfortable, just to protect myself from the UV rays.

We see water. Bikes are dropped to the side and we are waist deep in the river, finding every bit of this sheep-dropping-filled river absolutely delightful. We decide to call it a day after our meagre fifteen kilometres.

A little house with closed shutters offers us its shade. Certain we will not bump into anyone here, we are nearly done pitching the tents when a car pulls in and a man steps out, house key in hand. Astrid and I try to act natural while talking to him in our coats and boxer shorts. He has obviously noticed that we are wearing dotted knickers for trousers but is kind enough not to mention it.

We spend the night inside. The man offers us dinner and pastries. He does his grocery shopping over two hundred kilometres from here, at the closest large supermarket. Like many Patagonian people, he is welcoming and makes sure that we have what we need, sits with us, but speaks very irregularly. Space and time are different here. No question requires an urgent answer, as most of the days are filled with silence.

Day 17: Travelling to Rìo Bote, Argentina

Today has to be our final day in this hellhole because we are running out of water and are short of food. I power through the remaining forty kilometres huffing and swearing because my knee is very painful. We exit the rocks onto brand new tarmac. I am so happy I could kiss the black surface.

Now for water. The map indicates nothing for another sixty kilometres. A burst pipe by the side of a building is letting out a small but steady stream of water. Agnès and I look at it, smell it, agree that we have no choice, and fill up our filters.

We camp at an oasis. The owner comes to chat and mentions that he shoots everything he sees apart from cats. Astrid later tells me I have misunderstood. He shoots everything apart from *his* cats.

Day 18: El Calafate, Argentina

Today we cycled to El Calafate. We camped at a campsite where I flooded the bathroom.

Day 20: Santa Margarita, Argentina

We spend the day taking turns to lead the single file, shielding each other from the wind, one kilometre at a time. A cyclist cannot fight Patagonian winds, only endure them.

When we finally arrive at a farm, Agnès lies down. Now that the wind is not hitting her face anymore, I can see the tears roll down her cheeks. I put a handful of raisins in her mouth as Astrid holds her thumb up by the door: the signal that we have been given permission to pitch our tents.

Astrid let her bike fall on a puppy but he is OK.

Day 25: Rìo Bravo, Chile

After doing a bit of accounting, Agnès declares that our consumption of manjar (a sort of caramelised condensed milk) is digging into our budget. We are generally keeping to our food budget of three euros per person per day quite well, but considering that we eat half a pot of manjar each on most days, we are pushing dangerously close to our upper limit of five euros.

The deal is that when we manage to stick to three euros a day for a few days, we can afford to treat ourselves to say, a box of the cheapest red wine and a couple of fresh vegetables. With heavy hearts, we agree to halve our consumption of manjar, as sacrificing boxed wine is off the table.

Day 32: Puente Manso, Chile

As sick as can be.

We stayed at the same camping spot and I suffocated in the tent all day.

As midday approaches, the fleece I was shivering in this morning becomes unbearable. Unfortunately, the thought of having to pull up my body to remove it is even more unbearable. I just about manage to push the sleeping bag away from my shoulders and overheat in silence.

Two hours of slow cooking later, not having moved an inch although desperate to lie on my other side, my bodily functions catch up with me. There is no way out of this now and my painful limbs will just have to do what they are told.

The tent is a few metres from a river. The only other place I can go is on the other side of the bridge and I would have to climb a fence.

Too bad!

The tent is between Agnès and me as I empty my bowels once, then twice and three times within the hour. I give strict instructions to Agnès on where she should not venture, which leaves her with few options when her time comes.

I now know that I can get up, so I roll out of the tent, this time with determination, and join Agnès near the fire where she is boiling our underwear. Those babies have not seen hot water in a month. We then make soup, which I manage to drink. Agnès agrees to read me a story. When she opens the tent to go to bed, her eyes turn into big white and green beads and her nostrils quiver.

"This tent should not have been left closed."

Day 37: North of La Junta, Chile

Staying in a shed on a farm, sheltered from the rain. Half a skinned sheep was hanging above our heads till the farmer came to drag it away, leaving some of its blood on Astrid's pannier in the process.

Fun evening.

Day 39: Lago Lonconao, Chile

The rain will not stop but we got to stay in a lake house. The water made its way through Astrid's pannier and into her sleeping bag: a camper's worst nightmare. There is no way our stuff will dry, despite our best efforts at redecorating the lake house by hanging up our gear.

A miracle occurs as the owner mentions a tumble dryer. Astrid's eyes widen and she instantly takes up the offer. The man asks us twice whether we are sure that we do not want to wash our clothes too, since he also has a washing machine. He does not understand that if we wash our clothes, we have nothing left to wear. I suppose we could wash some of our clothes, but my daily underwear-washing rota is on schedule and I recall having washed my leggings ten days ago, so surely it is too early to submit them to the washing machine.

Day 53: Concepción, Chile

As get to Concepción, I still have scabs on my elbow and knee from a fall three weeks earlier, but they are now much puffier. Astrid had commented early on, saying I should pull them off to clean the wound. What an unpleasant prospect! I poke at the main one and pus spills out. I pull the side of it, and it is too painful.

Despite the cool night, I am flushed and sweaty. Enough for today. I will go to see a nurse tomorrow.

Day 54: Concepción, Chile

The nurse declares that all scabs need to come off. She takes out sterile compresses and tools as I relax into the seat. Here, it will be done professionally and it will not be painful.

Wrong! I clench the leather chair while she tugs at the hard bits. Thank god it is over. She will just give it a wipe now.

Wrong again! She takes out a new tool and lands it into the big white pool in the middle. "Don't forget to breathe, OK?"

"Am I still hurting you? I'm being as gentle as I can, but I can try to go lighter." The more careful she is, the more I think this will never end, but I cannot muster the courage to ask her to go harder and faster.

The bandage is on and I breathe a sigh of relief as she grabs my elbow, ready for part two. I watch the nurse on her impossible mission not to hurt me, and I can feel Astrid's gaze from the corner of the room. She does not need to say "I told you so" and is compassionate enough not to.

Day 94: Santiago, Chile

It is now just three of us leaving Santiago. I am relieved that Julie decided to quit. Even though I am carrying an extra tent, I feel lighter already.

Hanging out with someone over coffee is one thing; sharing four square metres with them is another. Deep down I knew this was a likely outcome. I remember my parents' tone as they expressed surprise when there were quibbles within the team two months before our departure. We had already bought our plane tickets, so what were we supposed to do? 'It'll be different once we are there,' I thought. 'Once all we have to do is cycle seventy-five kilometres a day and camp, everything will be easy.'

We knew the ideal preparation would have been to do a two-week trip somewhere in Europe. But we all had jobs, no bikes and no money. Squeezing fundraising and planning into six months was hard enough. We had some rough moments when planning, but what was the alternative? Throwing the towel in before we even started?

If I had to do it again, I would want to know all of the teammates better than I did then, but I would take up the offer of such a trip again even if uncertainties arose. Will the great people you meet on the road be outweighed by a fight over who should do the dishes? Will you regret having seen the desert for the first time because the conversation took a bitter turn at lunchtime?

Is it unwise to embark on a trip you are not sure of? A little. Is it worth it? Probably.

Day 96: San Felipe, Chile

It does not look like we will find a place to wild camp before nightfall so we stop in town at a big church.

There is a queue for the parish office. I get in line. Ten minutes later, the door opens and a lady comes out. There is only one person in front of me but at this rate, if I wait for my turn and the parish person cannot help, it will be night by the time I get back to the bikes. I ask the lady ahead of me if she minds me "asking a really quick question" to the parish clerk. She kindly accepts and I proceed to ask much more than a really quick question.

The parish lady rings the priest. "He can't help you. He says if he houses three women, locals will talk. I'll try to ring some people."

Three phone calls later, the queue has got longer and the woman behind me starts fidgeting. "Look," she says, "this is taking a long time." She is right and I am so sorry but I need a place to sleep. "Why don't you just come to mine?" she continues. Phew!

I give her my spiel about how all we need are two square metres for the tent and a couple of litres of water, definitely the most polished phrases in my otherwise broken Spanish, and she nods.

We cycle behind her car, following her one functioning rear light. Once we are at hers, we are at home. "OK girls, so what's your deal?"

I explain that we are cycling from Ushuaia to Lima and that we are stopping three times to volunteer for charities in Concepción, Santiago, and near La Paz, where the money we raised will fund various projects.

"Let's shower, have dinner and then you'll sleep in the spare room", she says in a very matter-of-fact way.

We then have a ten-minute debate on whether we should eat the carrots I got out of my pannier since, in our host's opinion, that is a lunch food and not a dinner food. We share a meal with her family and meet the neighbours, who seem positively horrified at the thought of anyone willingly cycling eight thousand kilometres.

Our host, Lucy, explains that the Mapuche, indigenous people of Chile, have been blamed for some of the devastating fires in recent months, but that it makes no sense because so much of the burnt areas are Mapuche land. She says that there is a lot of prejudice against her people, and I believe her.

Further South, we had been told that the Mapuche are lazy people and do not try very hard to earn money. Lucy tells me that she thinks people accumulate too much stuff. She has a microwave, a TV, a roof over her head and her daughter is doing well at university. Why should she care about getting fancy clothes or a new car?

As always, we mention that our hosts would be welcome to visit us in Paris. Lucy shakes her head. It will never be possible for her, but it would be nice for her daughter to do so after university. It is not awkward to hear this, even though it is sad, because it is true. We 'had no money' after university but managed to save €2,000 each in six months and raise another €22,000 by appealing to European firms and relatives. Lucy will not have that luck. She knows it and is not envious. She says it is nice to hear about France through us, as it is a bit like travelling herself.

Day 101: Combarbalá, Chile

We arrive in town and ask the firefighters and police for a place to stay. The latter make a rape joke.

In the end, a policeman seems to understand that we are just looking for a place to pitch the tent for free, but then takes us to a holiday camp where the owner starts haggling with us. We explain that there has been a misunderstanding, we cannot pay. Bored of the discussion, the owner gives up and disappears on his motorbike.

I am tired of begging, which we have been doing a lot in this populous region where wild camping is difficult. We have some money, but not enough to pay for camping spots more than twice a month. Are we taking advantage of locals? We have great prospects ahead of us. We can choose to do whatever we wish with our lives and careers, wherever we wish to do it. That is not the case for many people here, yet we essentially end up asking them for compassion. Sure, we never ask for more than tent space and water, but still, it is a strange dynamic.

I conclude that we cannot change things now, that we simply owe a lifetime of kindness and dinners to strangers who may knock on our doors.

Day 104: San Pedro de Atacama, Chile

In San Pedro de Atacama, we visit salt caves and mines, and it is tough to actually comprehend that the hills covered in white are salty, not snowy. I wonder if a kid who grows up here finds it difficult to comprehend that the Alps are snowy, not salty.

Day 117: Machuca, Chile

We slept at 3,200 metres of altitude. It was so cold in the night that we are now melting ice for breakfast. Astrid tries to wash up but the water on the sponge and plate freezes before she can put soap on them.

Despite my dusty cotton shirt and my forty kilograms of bike and bags, I feel like a professional cyclist on the last stage of the Tour de France. Two steep climbs lead to a prized viewpoint where a tourist bus is stopped.

A man points at us while elbowing his friend, and people turn their gaze from the mountains to the crazy cyclists appearing from the bottom of the dirt track. One starts clapping and whistling while others cheer.

A favourable wind on the plateau gives us the speed we need to look much cooler than we are. I feel pretty good, cruising at 4,100 metres at firty-two kilometres per hour on that flat part of desert from which the surrounding snowy mountains look like they might topple onto you at any time.

Never mind that we hated ourselves for putting our bodies through that freezing, restless night; we feel (and pretty much are) on top of the world.

Day 123: South of Uyuni, Bolivia

As we contemplate some unappealing and expensive tins in the shop, we spot a mound of blood oranges that cost next to nothing. We also know that bread is cheap. After further enquiry, the shop next door has even cheaper oranges. Today is 'naranja y pan' day, because why not, and rice is boring.

I have an absurd and hilarious discussion with a toothless woman who keeps adding and removing buns from my bag. I am close to giving up when we figure out that when we say we want to buy forty, meaning forty buns, she understands forty Bolivianos worth of buns, in which case we would also need to purchase her wheelbarrow to lug them around.

Three delicious identical meals and a lot of heartburn later, we pitch the tent in the desert behind an earth mound. Three people come out of the bushes, two of them on a motorbike. I check on the map and there is absolutely nothing in the direction from which they came.

Day 132: Caracollo, Bolivia

We are spending the night at a school with Rodri and Caro, two Argentinian cyclists we met in Uyuni and Jeremy, an American cyclist we had met in Patagonia and ran into again in northern Chile.

In the evening, we play football with some school mums. The goalkeeper keeps losing her sandals but her many layers of long skirts make her a valuable team member, as she stops the ball by just standing with her legs apart. It is technically cheating, but it is very effective. After the match, those who were wearing football gear wrap fifteen skirts over their shorts and leave with their kids.

Day 133: Lahuachaca, Bolivia

We are staying at a school again. We waited an hour and a half soaked and obviously freezing for the person in charge, who then decided to chat outside instead of letting us in.

When he finally shows us where we could stay, followed by four other teachers and five kids, we hint to him that we are cold and need to change, to which he replies that in Bolivia, everybody changes in front of everybody. Absolute nonsense. As if he would expect a Bolivian woman to get undressed in front of ten staring men. Nice try, head teacher.

Day 154: Copacabana, Bolivia

We are about to cross the border into Peru and will no longer need our Bolivian coins. We head to the village shop, empty our purses and pockets onto the counter to produce a small pile of metal, looking like we robbed a piggy bank.

"We'd like to buy everything this can get us, please."

The lady behind the counter raises an eyebrow. "Would you like about fifteen buns? Or I can fill a bag of sweets."

No team consultation needed as we point for the sweets. When the last coin matches the last sweet, the lady shovels in a few extra while giving us the type of endearing smile I thought was reserved for cute ten-year-olds.

Day 156: Between Puno and Juliaca, Peru

A farmer called William offered to let us stay in a spare room. In the morning, he gives us warm milk straight from the cow. He is intrigued by our powdered milk, and asks whether we can prepare our usual breakfast for him. We mix powdered milk, peanuts and oats in a tin plate. He gets through it slowly as we eat the delicious warm rice he and his wife have prepared. He claims that it is very tasty and that the powdered milk is great. We tell him he does not have to pretend. He smiles politely and puts down the plate.

Day 169: San Pedro de Cachora, Peru

After a three-day trek, we arrive at a village wanting nothing but a good night's sleep, only to discover that there is a huge village party tonight.

If you cannot fight it, embrace it. We drink punch with 'caña', 90° alcohol, and dance with the villagers. They dance in a circle holding hands and moving mostly their feet, with little movement from the knee up. It is actually quite difficult to do and they make fun of our moving hips and upper bodies.

Day 182: Lima, Peru

Our faces are already black with dirt and pollution and we are not yet in inner Lima. We are stopped on the side of the road as Astrid and I try to reason with Agnès who wants to ride the equivalent of the M25 because "it's the simplest route".

We are mere kilometres away from our destination. Our return flight is in three days. Now is not the time to be reckless. "It's a four-lane high-speed road, Agnès. No one in their right mind would ride this!" I say gesturing at the non-stop traffic.

Swish, swish, swish, goes a guy rollerblading past us on the Peruvian M25, hands behind his back, looking like he is thinking about his shopping list. My point is very much weakened and my finger is left hanging meaninglessly in the air.

A year later: Epernay, France

I meet Agnès at a train station near Paris, excited to get to cycle all the way to Prague with her. Before leaving for South America, I thought I might sell my bike when I got home. That idea seems ridiculous to me now. I feel most at home when I am in the saddle.

Website: **waterwheels.jimdofree.com**

LinkedIn: **emma-karslake**

Facebook: **waterwheelsprojet2017**

Chapter 21

Leaving Point Pedro

By Pete Lamb

"Please keep going," I say, almost laughing through the words. My companion has just begun a rant about our predicament. I want to capture it on film.

"Keep moaning about it?" Marc queries, also laughing, but more of an exasperated, tired and irritated laugh. I have known him for a little over two weeks, but I feel his pain, I know his struggle, and yet I cannot resist asking the question.

"How are you feeling?"

"How am I feeling? Well, we're almost there. The weather is fine. I should probably feel pretty good. But the thing is..." here it comes...

"There is absolutely no point in doing this. Why should we run two more kilometres to come to a town which is full of tourists who all look the same as us, and everybody will think that we're tourists as well." I hold back a giggle. I don't want to run the final two kilometres either. But I want *him* to say it.

Now Marc speaks with incredulous laughter intertwined in his words. "What we are doing here... is just celebrating mental toughness. Except for today, because this day is not about toughness at all."

For sixteen days we have run strong, rested well, not succumbed to petty bickering or moaning about insignificant things, until today. We cannot see reason in subjecting ourselves, tired and irritable, to the crazed tourist town below us.

I pan the camera around to myself, content that Marc has expressed my feelings perfectly, and mutter, "What he said."

*

We're on the outskirts of Ella, a tourist town in which we will blend in easily. But those down below won't know we've run here from the shores of northern Sri Lanka, negotiating four hundred kilometres to this point on roads with no hard shoulder, through a military zone; along barren coastline; through bustling tourist towns and the insanity of Kandy's city streets.

They can't appreciate what we're doing *surely*. They would just ask *why*. Like everyone else. *Why are you doing this?* Them, with their coiffed hair, oriental parachute pants and Lonely Planet guide books. *Would they get it? Would they care?*

There is no Lonely Planet guide for running through this chaos. Marc and I are forging a path along an untraveled road. To our knowledge, no one has run the length of Sri Lanka before. We are in this together, yet alone.

Frustrated office worker seeks adventure

It had begun almost two years previously while working in Bristol training to be an Actuary. By day I would work hard and chase promotion. In the evenings and at the weekends, I would study towards my exams.

By the summer of 2017, I had burnt out and I was seeking a new challenge.

At about the same time, I underwent the first of two open-heart surgeries in the Bristol Royal Infirmary. For the last ten years, I've been an Outpatient at the Bristol Heart Institute. Having overcome Congenital Heart Disease, I thought it rather a waste to be sat at a desk, squandering my second chance and not taking advantage of being as fit and capable as everyone else.

That summer I receive a letter from 'Above and Beyond', a charity supporting Bristol city centre hospitals, asking for a donation. I immediately saw an opportunity to raise money for the hospitals that had treated me so well by taking on a big physical challenge away from the office. I decided to run my first marathon in 2018. And then... well, things escalated.

"So Pete, I hear you're running two marathons for us? That's incredible! And you're going to cycle to them!! That's crazy!" Faye, the head of marketing for the charity, and Amy, in fundraising, were wide-eyed and suitably impressed.

"Actually... it's seven now." Eyes explode open opposite me as I sit smiling, wondering what on earth I was doing. I had never run a marathon before, and yet I had entered into seven races over seven months, all over Europe. Even worse, I'd told them I was going to cycle between them all.

I later set my sights on running across a whole county. The country I selected was Japan. I planned out a three-thousand kilometre journey on foot. But I also decided the sensible thing to do would be to run across a slightly smaller country first, to test the waters, test the theory, to see whether I am capable of such an outrageous solo adventure.

That country was Sri Lanka. And as it turned out, it will not be a solo venture at all.

Message from a stranger

Hey Pete, My name is Marc, and I'm from Germany. I just got to Sri Lanka. I was wondering if I can accompany you on this adventure? I have done two IronMan triathlons and several marathons. Please let me know whether you're up for having a chat about it. I look forward to your answer. Best regards. Marc

PS. I can imagine that sharing this terrific adventure would be an awesome thing. And as I'm a studied TV journalist, we could create amazing movie content as well! Take your time to think about it.

It takes me a week to respond. I am instinctively an independent traveller. I'm more than comfortable in my own company and wary of sharing plans with another, largely in the hope of avoiding confrontation.

In the spirit of seeking out new challenges, I reply, *I'd never really considered doing it with anyone else before, but I can see a lot of positives to sharing the adventure! Yes, let's do it.*

*

Our journey together begins in Colombo, the day after I arrive from India, in a plush vegan cafe that feels somewhat out of place. It would be the last time we sit comfortably in clean clothes for a while.

Marc is a tall blonde German, softly spoken and warm-hearted unless provoked by idiotic tourists or extreme heat, much like me. Just two hours after we meet in person we are on a train to Jaffna, two-hundred-and-fifty miles north.

We jump off the train early and take an auto-rickshaw to the most northerly point in Sri Lanka – Point Pedro.

Leaving Point Pedro

I stir briefly in the night and check the stars above my head to confirm it is still night-time; the moonlight is so bright it might have been midday. I sleep in my bivvy bag, the night punctuated by flutters in the mosquito net above me and a few nudges from the wild dog sleeping at my feet. Come morning the dog's watch is over and, as I rise, he returns to wandering the playing field we are camping on, checking his mangy fur and sniffing the ground for clues as to where the next meal is coming from. *I wonder where our next meal is coming from.*

As the sun rises, the colour in the sky grows from mottled pink to burning rose and finally a fierce blue. We pack up our tent and bivvy and wander up the narrow path from the playing field to the 'Northernmost notch in Point Pedro - Sri Lanka'. My legs tremble slightly as I tentatively make my way across the coastal rocks to wet my hands in the ocean. I want to dip my hand into the sea in the north and (hopefully) later absolve myself of all the pain and sweat in the sea at the southernmost point. Our eventual arrival at Dondra three weeks later is just a distant dream.

Just four kilometres down the road, we pitch against a pillar, our rucksacks weighing heavily on our shoulders. We are drenched in sweat and sit on a dusty stone step outside a shop. I find a food market upstairs above the corner shop and buy two coconuts and a bunch of bananas.

"Is this is it? Is this all we've got?" We're only half an hour into our adventure, and already the heat has drained us.

Ten kilometres later, we are in the woods. A small shrine shelters us from the sun, and we heave ourselves onto the cold concrete. Thoughts turn readily to how hard this is going to be. We're not even close to halfway today, and the heat is oppressive, the need for water relentless, the weight on our backs like a millstone.

We follow the sparsely populated coastal road south and happen upon a small temple where we can wait out the midday sun under a huge, gnarled tree. My body appreciates the respite. Under the towering tree canopy there is the sweet relief of not being drenched in sweat for the first time today. After drying out, I feel almost human. It is short-lived, this blissful comfort of being cool.

The promise of food and shelter later sees us walking in the dark along the beach after thirty-five kilometres and a sunset ocean swim. It is *still* over an hour to walk to town to find dinner.

The sand rises up through my blistered toes, wearing away dead and dried skin. It falls away beneath my heel, arranging itself into a momentary crevice for a curious crab to negotiate. It is quite a surreal end to a brutal first day.

I am not sure what I have gotten myself into as I am initiated into the mind shatteringly noisy production of 'Kottu', a bread-based dish diced up with meat, vegetables and spices on a large metal grill with two enormous cleavers. The clang of metal-on-metal shakes me awake from a hunger-induced near-coma. The food is greasy, stuffed with fried bread and chunks of chicken and vegetables. It is simply divine.

We only just make it up the road and onto a concrete slab to lay out our camping gear before sleep comes for us, deep and satisfying.

*

Our second day begins and ends with pounding club music. Before sunrise, rickshaws pull alongside us and offload wares for the morning market. Unbeknownst to us last night, we have managed to camp in the marketplace.

We find a quieter spot in the evening but again struggle to get to sleep. Fireflies dance overhead, their flickering lights are mesmerising against the jet-black sky.

Yet again, we are not alone. I am beginning to realise that solitude doesn't truly exist here. In the middle of the bush, beside a secluded reservoir, a house party begins, and drum and bass music rumbles all night long only metres from our wild camp.

*

We swap the thunder of music for the internal storm of unquenchable thirst.

"I'm out of water, how far to the next town?" I question of a similarly desperate Marc.

"Nine K!".

"Oh, oh dear." We won't make it.

Forced into extreme measures on our third day, we induce a family to take pity on us. A man scales a coconut tree in the garden and retrieves two of the biggest coconuts I have ever seen. From these, he expertly slices the tops off with a machete and pours out two litres of water.

We sit with the whole family, dripping sweat on their porch and sipping the heavenly coconut water. We leave with a bottle-full to keep us going to the next town.

The following day, we leave a roadside stall with two plastic chairs dripping above two puddles of sweat on the concrete. Several empty juice bottles are stood in this mess. The pools merge into one large sweat pond, obstructing the doorway to the shop.

We apologise, put on our socks and shoes that had been drying in the sun and run away as fast as we can, still thirsty.

This is becoming one of many daily rituals for us.

Progress

We settle into routines during the long, hot days.

In the mornings, I tend to my blisters and repeatedly find plasters, tissue and duct tape from the previous day at the end of my socks. For the first week, I also require heavy lashings of nipple tape to prevent uncomfortable chafing. On the one day I forget I come close to drawing blood from an extremely raw left nipple.

Every ten kilometres we stop for coconuts at the roadside or freshly squeezed juices at ramshackle fruit stalls that have to be told in strong terms not to add three tablespoons of sugar to each glass.

We nap during the day, usually after a huge lunch, seeking a patch of trees to string up hammocks and sway in the breeze.

After dinner, we hunt for ice cream, cookies and chocolate milk.

Towards the end of each day, I carefully place my headphones in my ears, select 'Africa' by Toto and begin four minutes and fifty-six seconds of utter joy. I bound along ahead of Marc, screaming the lyrics in my head.

But none of these little rituals is as obsessive, (or necessary), as that time of day we seek out six magic letters:

'B U F F E T'

Oh the food! That's what we've come for! We eat our way through Sri Lanka, dotting from cafe to restaurant, from coconut stall to vegetable market, from banana wagon to bakery van, hotel canteen to beachside hipster vegan hangout. But it is the buffet restaurants that steal our hearts, our stomachs and our money.

Large terracotta pots sit in a line on a white linen cloth along a wide table. Taking the small lid from each, I find enormous piles of steaming basmati rice, spicy chicken curry, green beans in fragrant spices, silky takka daal and red-hot shredded beetroot. My stomach is already rumbling, thunderous, as I approach the buffet table, my hands shaking in anticipation. The wafts of spice and sweetness are intoxicating. Mounds of aubergine, chutney and coconut roti, fiery coconut sambal, cooling raita and creamy potato are waiting for us. After second and third helpings, we sleep deeply, before rousing ourselves to run on to the next buffet restaurant. *This is our life now. This is adventure.*

Breakfast is less indulgent. We eat iced buns and sickly sweet bananas from the abundant roadside rest-stops. Coffee fuels our early morning sessions. It is weak, tepid and bitter.

Exciting place names tick by - Parantan, Kilinochchi, Mankulam, Vavuniya, Dambulla, Kandy, Nuwara Eliya, Ella and Udawalawe. They provide pit-stops and bouts of fevered attention from locals. In the larger of these towns, we find sweet relief from the searing heat in air-conditioned cash machine booths.

A week into our adventure, Marc's ankle swells to double its usual size - the recurrence of an old running injury is untimely but not unexpected. At dinner, on day ten, we have an awkward conversation. Marc doesn't want to quit but feels he is slowing me down. I don't want to leave him behind but think he needs to stop and rest properly. The swelling is moving up his leg and probably needs some medical attention.

We agree to reach Kandy, somehow, and reassess but I really don't see how he can complete another 350 kilometres after that. I'm worried this will turn into a solo adventure after all.

Things are looking up

Outside the maelstrom of Kandy's city streets, we pose in front of the 'Welcome to Kandy' sign. We do not linger; the city is overflowing with auto-rickshaws and taxis. It's roadsides spill over with tourist tat being flouted by over-confident salesmen. The city is a wall of noise. The petrol and diesel fumes choke us to the point we cannot run through it without gasping for breath.

We find a room for the night and sensibly take a taxi to the edge of the city in the morning. We are about to enter the most remarkable stretch yet.

After the gradual incline from Dambulla to Kandy, the road explodes skywards, and we are thrust into two days of thigh-burning ascent. Amazingly, Marc's ankle has steadily improved over the last couple of days. His pain has primarily gone, and the swelling has disappeared.

Struggling to find somewhere to wild camp after leaving Kandy, we walk into the Pussellawa police station. They warn us of guns in the town below and of wild boar and snakes in the surrounding wild country. With a combined effort of British and German charm, we get what we came for. The police sergeant agrees to let us camp on the parade ground but we must be gone by 5.30am sharp to ensure the ceremonial stage can be set up for the high commissioner's visit in the morning, *of course*.

Unfortunately for our thighs, the first day of climbing is merely an introduction to the mind-boggling switchbacks and hairpin bends, the absurd gradients and quite unbelievable vistas that lie ahead.

The next day my journal entry is titled: *'The holy **** look at that view day'*. Three kilometres down the road from the police station we are sipping a tea and looking out over tumbling green hills, vast rivulets of land intersecting each other in diagonals. Rows and rows of tea plants line the mountainsides, and a large estate sits in the valley surveying its empire. This is tea country, and we milk it for all it is worth, repeatedly stopping at hairpins and hill crests to take photos and shoot video.

We push on towards Nuwara Eliya - a further twenty-one kilometres with around 1500 metres of ascent to conquer. We run hard after lunch and exhaust ourselves. Marc hitches a lift on the back of a lorry at one point as its clutch smokes and the engine screams at the incline. We take many breaks as the road leads us relentlessly upwards and the tea plantations begin to sprawl out beneath, beside and above us.

Eventually we reach the peak and the sign for Nuwara Eliya, feet burning, brain dead, and soaked through. We are ready for the day to end but, my word, what a view!

I blitz it down the final stretch into the oasis below, feeling that rush of adrenaline that usually strikes in the last mile of a marathon. Descending into Nuwara Eliya is a beautiful end to a tough day in which we have climbed more than the height of Ben Nevis. I feel like we have broken the back of this run. We are only 230 kilometres from the finish line now.

The following day I title my journal: '*The shredding of the knees day*'. And, to be blunt, it is excruciating. We have risen to Nuwara Eliya; this great bowl in the mountainous central region, a long way from the harsh and arid north. We must now descend steeply from it, towards the verdant surrounds of the national parks and the pristine beaches of southern Sri Lanka.

The diversity in the landscape provides a beautiful distraction from the discomfort of the punishing downhill from Nuwara Eliya. But it isn't just the landscape that is changing dramatically. I notice the hip belt on my pack becoming ever tighter as I shed the excess pounds of accumulated weight from gorging on Indian street food the previous few months. I feel the steadily increasing confidence in my body's abilities. The blisters on my feet become callouses; the bag on my back becomes part of me.

Yet all this time, two constants plague our run. One is wild dogs, whose viciousness gives us a regular adrenaline-filled turbo-boost of energy, leaving us exasperated. I imagine them to be our cheerleaders instead of our pursuers, supporting us to the finish line as they gnash their teeth at the roadsides.

The second constant is Beethoven. *Für Elise* is one of classical music's most recognisable compositions. It is revered and delights music-lovers the world over. But for two battered and exhausted runners, in the searing heat of southern Sri Lanka, it is a hellish refrain, composed by the devil himself. It is played out by bakery vans in a high-pitched siren at all hours of the day, but most often before sunrise. It sends shivers down our spines as the wail disturbs our sleep, and provides a therapeutic target for any displeasure we feel during the day. We would hear it once more on our final day.

Running Sri Lanka

The early morning is sticky and humid when we set off from Udawalawe national park. We ran close to a marathon distance yesterday, seeing wild elephants at the boundary as we pounded the concrete. Today we barely scraped ten kilometres before capitulating, our legs screaming and our bodies pouring with sweat, more so than any other day.

I later find myself at a corner shop scoffing samosas and spicy potato rolls. Sitting outside the shop, I am set upon by two-hundred school kids who giggle "Hello," stare or simply laugh at the sweaty white man on the plastic chair in another puddle. It is a lovely interaction despite the language barrier.

As the day rolls on, the clouds gather, at first just teasing brief respite from the sun, and later filling the whole sky till sunset when they're lit up in shades of orange and pink. I find myself every day looking up and willing the clouds to move faster to blot out the sun. Every time one does so, it feels like a little victory. Sadly, the relentless heat finally breaks us on this day.

We find a large rock on a cricket pitch outside a school and attempt to sleep for a couple of hours, just like that first day under the large swaying temple tree. The sounds of traffic and monkeys swinging through the branches overhead mean neither of us sleep for any decent length of time. We conclude that we cannot run during the daytime heat any longer, and an overnight ultra-marathon is therefore a logical conclusion to our adventure. Marc had joked about finishing the remaining distance in one hit when we woke up this morning, and I had laughed it off - well I wasn't laughing any longer. I'd never run an ultra-marathon before but was facing a total of eighty kilometres for the day. It will be brutal, yet beautiful.

*

Around midnight I stop on a narrow strip of road that passes over a series of large ponds. When Marc catches up, he is ecstatic. I'm doubled over, panting for breath and can't understand his joy.

"Yeah buddy! We did it! Our first marathon!"

We have just hit forty-two kilometres for the day, the first time we have covered a marathon distance in a single day. Standing tall again, I take in the surroundings. Above, the stars are impossibly full and bright, and the moon lights the road sufficiently that both of our broken headlamps are redundant. Fireflies flicker above the water while in the pond reeds, the chirp of tens of thousands of crickets breaks the silence of the night. The diesel chug ruins this blissful scene. The bus does not expect to find two semi-broken runners on the roadside and so nearly runs us down.

Now we enter hell. I stop every five minutes throughout the night, feeling generally awful and delirious. I am grateful to see and hear Marc is in a similar state.

The sun is rising now, and the towns are coming to life. Traffic is increasing. I begin to realise just how long I have been awake and how far I have run.

The previous day feels like a dream. I remember running alongside a young child out of a small village at twilight. I also remember eating a cupcake at the roadside at 4am having run seventy kilometres through Sri Lankan fishing villages.

I think I will remember that cake for the rest of my life.

We are only ten kilometres from the finish when we hear it again. The tinkling arcade 8-bit style ringing that comes to shepherd us to the end of the journey like Hades leading fallen souls across the river Styx. The bakery van idles by, blasting and butchering in equal measure Beethoven's masterpiece, *Für Elise*, as I am slumped on a kerbstone.

"I haaaaate it. It's the worst song in the world!" Marc just laughs; he is past the point of complaining and is instead filming my rant just as I filmed his on the outskirts of Ella.

We have been running through the still hot and humid night. We've been awake for twenty-four hours, and we're now ready to tumble into the ocean at Point Dondra and finish our adventure.

We decide to walk the final hour after sunrise, only managing ten minutes before we can no longer continue; Marc's leg chafing having reached excruciating levels and my legs no longer working as intended.

So we cheat, after 610 kilometres of running we take a tuk-tuk into Dondra, walking the last kilometre to the coast, filled only with relief and no regrets.

The final day has been mentally, physically and emotionally exhausting. Arriving at the coast in Dondra, we are so ruined we miss the actual finishing point. I instead find a small piece of rocky bay to film the final flourish, running the final ten metres for the benefit of Marc's film.

I stand on a rock and scream with delight, then jump into the sea and slip on the sea floor, stepping on a sea urchin and causing my feet more pain than six hundred kilometres of running had inflicted. I am in a daze, all of a sudden none of my limbs work adequately, and I can't even celebrate, save for a lazy high five with Marc.

I am broken.

It is over.

People power

Sri Lanka holds a special place in my heart these days. I felt so welcome, so safe. It felt so wild, and I truly revelled in this *wildness*. Marc and I made our home in various corners of Sri Lanka. We camped on playing fields and the banks of a reservoir; we strung our hammocks up beside a military school, rivers and inside a Buddhist temple. I bivvied in the long grass beside a petrol station and the empty shell of a building. We were woken up by market traders and military drills, by calls to prayer and drum'n'bass. I almost forgot the fact we were running each day.

In traversing this diverse and beautiful country, I discovered a joy in running I'd never known before in those marathons or hours of training. I am yet to complete my planned run through Japan due to injury; it matters not. Sri Lanka turned out to be that grand adventure that I was looking for, and helped me raise over £5,000 for Above and Beyond and the Bristol Heart Institute in the process.

In the end, the blisters on my feet healed, but I can still feel the crush of the ground beneath my feet. The skin on my shoulders has regrown, yet I can still feel the comforting weight of my pack. The stupid tan lines have faded, but I can still feel the searing heat of the midday sun.

It would have been such a different experience had I been solo. I am incredibly grateful for Marc sending that message, and I will always look back and delight in the fact I said *yes* to his request, to sharing the adventure.

I suspect if our roles had been reversed, I would never have had the guts to message a strange German and ask if I could film him running across a country. Social media gets a bad rap, but it brought us together for a genuinely epic three weeks.

In truth, this could never have been an outright solo project. The people of Sri Lanka would never have let it. It is *people* that made this time so memorable. The policemen that took us into their station and allowed us to grace the hallowed parade ground; the coconut sellers with their breath-taking machete skills; the market traders and the family that gave us emergency coconut water – all contributed to a beautiful, collaborative effort to get us to the end.

Some advice then, to would-be adventurers, or those looking for something out of the day-to-day routine. This advice relates not necessarily to saying a big fat *YES!* to adventure, for you probably have that idea well and truly ingrained by now.

It is saying yes to *people*. To offers of help, of free food and beds to sleep in, or patches of grass to sleep on. Say yes to all those lovely people and their kindness and generosity, to those humble and warm-hearted enough to give more than they expect to receive.

And one day give back, as a host, as a kind stranger, as someone giving a lift to an unfortunate sodden hiker on the roadside. Even for shy and introverted travellers like this one, all those chance meetings and stories of genuine selflessness by people I do not know have been so worth it. All those people out there are *fantastic*. Believe me; I've met a lot of them.

And some of them even want to join you in your adventures and make them all the more memorable. And maybe you should take that ball and run with it too.

But please don't ever say yes to driving a bakery van near me with a repeat of Beethoven's *Für Elise* on a loudspeaker. I never want to hear *Für Elise* ever again.

Blog: **pete-lamb.com**

Instagram: **@petelamb_**

Facebook: **petelambontherun**

Twitter: **@petelamb_**

Film: Search *'Chasing the Lamb'* on YouTube for a short film by Marc Bernreuther.

Chapter 22

Rowing the Pacific

By Cazz Lander

Getting to the Start Line

I blinked as a cold sweat began to creep across my forehead, trying desperately to keep my expression neutral.

"I guess I'll see you in Monterey then," I blurted out, breaking the awkward silence.

Five minutes earlier, I had opened my laptop and logged on for our weekly crew Skype catch up expecting to discuss the trivial topics of 2k erg times, companies we thought might sponsor us, and most importantly, what colour the boat should be. Instead, two of us had found ourselves rather unceremoniously removed from the crew due to the skipper deciding they wanted a boat of highly skilled flat-water rowers. It appeared my recent learn to row course, completed on the idyllic Leicestershire canals, didn't quite tick that box. All the other skills I bought to the crew were apparently deemed unimportant, discarded on the side-lines due to my lack of flat-water rowing experience. I took a deep breath, said goodbye and clicked on the large, red end-call button, a fake smile plastered on my face. I exhaled and let the smile fall, my stomach beginning to tie itself in knots.

I was angry that someone else had decided whether I was capable of rowing two thousand four hundred nautical miles across the Pacific Ocean. I was angry that, two months previously when I joined the crew, my lack of flat-water rowing experience hadn't been an issue. I was angry that, just a few days before, I'd been asked to email the women we weren't able to offer a spot to, thank them for applying but let them know they hadn't been successful.

The only thought that kept running through my head was 'I've failed'. How could I tell friends and family that I'd been kicked out the crew and that I would no longer be rowing the Pacific Ocean? As it stood I had no boat, no sponsorship, half a crew and less than nine months until the cannon would sound in Monterey Bay signalling the start of the Great Pacific Race. My social media accounts were plastered with posts explaining what I was going to do, and it had become part of my identity. As the likelihood of me being on that start line started to dwindle in my head, tears started to streak down my cheeks.

The thing is, I understood performance and I understood what makes a successful athlete and team. I worked full-time as a Sport Scientist with British Olympic and Paralympic athletes, identifying the 1% margins for gain to turn a silver medal into a gold medal. I was adamant that being a good flat-water rower wasn't the most important factor in being a good ocean rower.

Everyone wants to win gold in elite sport, but the biggest lessons are often learnt in defeat. An elite athlete's mind-set has some unique qualities, often able to block out everything that doesn't equal success, but equally open to learning from mistakes. What others might perceive as failures are looked upon as learning experiences, with the performances analysed in depth, understanding what can be taken and built upon to ensure future success. Calculated risks are taken, the impossible is seen as possible and 100% effort is exerted to achieve the goal.

Working daily in this environment, it's difficult to not let that attitude define how you approach problems. I found myself wondering if, in just eight months, I could form my own crew and be on the start line.

At this stage, I hadn't told anyone what had happened. Friends and family had just come to terms with what I was setting out to do, albeit constantly projecting their fears onto me, questioning what made me think I could do something like row an ocean. Their fears were robust – I had never crossed an ocean by boat, I had never rowed, I was five-foot-three and jokes about whether I would be able to reach the oars were aplenty, but I had an unwavering belief buried deep inside me that I could. I'd completed several 100-kilometre ultra-marathons, two relay swim crossings of the English Channel and undertaken numerous multi-day paddling and hiking expeditions all around the world. I'd spent years instructing sailing, windsurfing and kayaking in the crystal clear waters of the Aegean Sea and the slightly murkier, colder waters of South East England, understanding every ripple on the surface of the water and every cloud in the sky. I knew I was both physically and mentally tough enough for the challenge. I might not have had the rowing pedigree, but I had a whole toolbox of skills that would set me in good stead to succeed.

With a new outlook and feeling positive that perhaps I could get to the start line in just eight months, the next morning bought me crashing back to earth. My phone began to buzz, my crewmates name lighting up the screen. We hadn't scheduled to speak, but I was excited to tell her my thoughts about how we could still do this.

As soon as I answered, I knew something was wrong. Over the next few minutes I listened as she explained that she wasn't able to continue, with circumstances outside of her control removing her from the race, at least temporarily. That familiar feeling in my stomach returned, a cold feeling of dread spreading across my body and my eyes beginning to well.

I called Chris, the race director, and, after a deep breath, told him simply, "I don't think I'll be on the start line." I was sat slumped on the cold tiled floor of my kitchen watching small tear droplets smash onto the hard surface feeling entirely defeated by the whole thing.

"Don't be silly," he replied, snapping me out of the puddle of pity I was beginning to drown in. "You've got eight months. That's plenty of time."

I sat for a moment in stunned silence and let his words sink in. Eight months felt so short for the mountain of tasks that needed to be completed, but the reality was I just needed that outside confirmation that it was possible. The twisting sensation in my stomach disappeared as quickly as it came on, replaced with a tingling chill that swept over my body as I realised the dream was still alive.

Within a day of advertising online and being inundated with emails from prospective new crew members, Megan came on board. A fellow non-rower with a background in mountaineering, her attitude and skill set ticked all the boxes. Together we spent many long nights re-branding the crew as Pacific Terrific, recruiting a third crew member and then spending the next two months caught up in an ever-changing fourth crew member situation as people committed and then dropped out.

As March rolled around, and the start line crept ever closer, we made the decision to stop searching and row as a crew of three, a feat never attempted on the Pacific before by any crew, male or female.

By this stage we had our boat, 'Danielle', a twenty-five-foot Sea Sabre pure class ocean row boat built by Justin Adkin that had successfully crossed the Pacific Ocean two years previously. It was designed to be rowed by a crew of four with two crew rowing at any one time, and we knew that by rowing as a crew of three we would often be on the oars alone. The usual two hours on, two hours off rowing shifts also wouldn't work well with just three of us on board, and so problem solving the many unknowns of rowing as a crew of three quickly became our go to late night activity over a strong cup of coffee.

We trained hard throughout the winter and spring in the cold blustery waters of the Solent, giving up our warm comfy beds for sleepless nights shivering in the cold bare cabin of our ocean row boat, silently gliding past shipping containers that bore down on us out of the gloom as we logged miles. With each and every stroke, we felt more and more comfortable in our tiny floating home. For the first time, it seemed like everything was on track, the panic and stresses of the previous months fading into the background.

It appeared that the universe wasn't quite finished throwing us our curve balls yet.

Six weeks before we were due to fly to California, our third crew member walked away from the boat. As I put down the phone, instant relief flooded over me, letting out a big exhale of breathe, startling my dogs from their peaceful slumber and causing them to tumble over each other as they sought to see where the noise had come from. Tension drained from my body, and I knew it was clearly the right decision for the dynamics of the crew.

It left Megan and I in a predicament. Unsure if we could handle the boat as a pair, we had just eight weeks until we were supposed to row to Hawaii and were floundering on a solution. Unable to sleep, I made camp under a mound of blankets as my eyes glossed back and forth over the list of potential team mates we had written, with my gaze being drawn back again and again to one option at the bottom of the page. Eleanor, a twenty-eight-year-old Australian had emailed some months previously, but at the time we had a full crew. She had a long CV of previous expeditions including a solo cycle tour through Europe, bundles of enthusiasm and I remember being particularly gutted that she hadn't originally emailed a few weeks earlier.

"This is ridiculous," I told myself. "No one in their right mind would be able to join an ocean row that starts in six weeks' time."

Megan agreed that it was a long shot but worth a try to see if she would be interested. After a flurry of emails back and forth, my phone buzzed and the screen lit up with the words 'Yes, I'm in!'. For the first time in eight months, the warm tears rolling down my face were matched with a smile and a little giggle of delight.

Crew dynamics are perhaps the make or break of any team expedition, and bringing on a new crew member, particularly one we had never met, was a risk. But it was one that paid off. We each brought something different to the team and six weeks later, by the time we arrived in Monterey, California, it was hard to believe we had only been a full crew for a matter of weeks.

Monterey was an intense two-week period of sorting equipment and food, packing the boat and getting in our compulsory pre-race hours out on the ocean. An eventful prologue race in Monterey Bay gave us our first real taste of what the ocean had in store. The forecast of low winds in favourable directions whirled into ferocious gusts. One oar plunged into the water as a wave would tip the boat, leaving the other oar exposed. As darkness hit, all crews had ended up on para-anchor. We were unceremoniously towed back into the marina, soaked to the bone but feeling more prepared than ever for June 2nd.

The Pacific had other ideas.

The race was delayed by four days due to swirling black storm clouds that hugged the horizon and bought with them unseasonably cold wind that snapped at your face from precisely the wrong direction. I'd been raring to go on June 2nd, but with every delay, apprehension set in, my chest feeling tighter and the thud of my heartbeat becoming more noticeable.

On the third evening, we were summoned with the other crews into the yacht club, where the race committee and safety officer announced an eighteen-hour weather window had been identified. We would leave tomorrow afternoon, which should give us enough time to make it out of the bay and away from the jagged rocky coastline before the weather closed back in. Silence filled the room as everyone took in the news. A few nervous smiles crept onto people's faces as we closed into a circle and Chris gave a rousing speech. I felt my eyes begin to well and my palms turn clammy as the reality hit me that we were leaving tomorrow. Conditions were far from ideal, but any further delays would put us at a much higher risk of experiencing hurricanes in the later stages of the row.

The Race: Surviving

The official start line was out in the bay, so we paraded in a flotilla of ocean rowing boats out of the marina, music blaring from our speaker system and smiles plastered on our faces like a mask hiding the nervous apprehension. Finally, it was just us, the other boats, a few supporter yachts and some inquisitive sea lions. The supporters who had lined the marina were now just diminishing hazy dots on land, already heading back to their normal lives, and out at sea the swirling grey storm clouds still hugged the horizon. The cannon sounded with a loud bang and bought us back to reality as we pulled hard on the oars, echoes of whoops and whistles bouncing through the air as we all cheered with glee.

Ten hours of battling the currents and the wind later, we finally made it to the headland of the bay. Our confidence had been steadily dropping over the course of the evening as we struggled to make forward progress. The enthusiastic cheers of the start felt like a distant memory. They'd been replaced with honest, quiet conversations as to whether we were going to have to be rescued because we couldn't get out of the bay.

"What's that there?" piped Eleanor, pointing into the darkness and interrupting the conversation.

A small twinkle of artificial light caught our attention on the starboard side and we realised we weren't alone. In the darkness, we could see the twinkling red navigation lights of Cockleshell Pacific Endeavour and Team Attack Poverty, the two male pairs boats bobbing just above the horizon and playfully reflecting in the white capping waves. Relief flooded through me, and I kicked myself for doubting our ability so early on.

As daylight broke, fog blended into the grey gloomy skies making it difficult to see where the sea ended and the sky began. The particularly nasty weather system we had been warned about was firmly overhead bringing thirty-five-knot winds and twenty-foot waves that dwarfed our boat. We were tossed about like a child's toy as the waves rose up like mountains and then cruelly crashed down on us, ensuring not one inch of our bodies stayed dry. With every stroke, we were flung from our seats, thankful to be attached to the deck by a safety line, our shins already mottled black and blue from the oars.

Megan appeared in the cabin hatch. "Call from safety officer," she reported. "All crews have to go onto para-anchor."

One day rolled into the next and for seventy-two hours we bunkered down in the tiny main cabin, the waves sounding like a never ending line of trains thundering towards us with a sudden jolt as they smashed into the boat and the para-anchor pulled tight. Periodically, we would open the hatch to be seasick, and then return to staring at the names on our cabin ceiling of every person who had sponsored us. Elbows and knees pressed into faces as we played Tetris to fit three bodies into a space about the size of your bath.

As the first week came to an end and the weather calmed enough to be back on the oars, news filtered through to us that the other female crew and one of the male pairs' crews had been rescued and were out of the race. My heart sank for them, and I was overcome with an overwhelming sense of disappointment for those crews.

"That could have been us," mused Eleanor, her eyes glazed and focused on one point as she battled with severe sea sickness.

"But it wasn't," Meg replied.

"We're going to make it to Hawaii, you know,' I chipped in. We all shared a small knowing smile of quiet steely determination.

We quickly settled into a routine, each rowing three hours on, three hours off in a rotating seat pattern, meaning the boat was kept moving at all times and we each rowed for a total of twelve hours a day. In our three hours off, we spent the time sleeping or doing boat chores, desalinating water to drink or boiling water to add to our dehydrated food packs.

For twenty-nine days we didn't see the sun and instead woke to the same moody grey cloudy skies that never cleared and pitch black nights where the moon struggled to shine. Our clothes were drenched and encrusted with salt as the boat was ruthlessly tossed around and waves flicked up and fell on us like shards of glass, rubbing our skin red raw.

Conversation on the boat often turned to what people missed.

"Mountains," Meg would say without missing a beat. "And green. Grass, trees... you know, all the colours you never see out here."

"I miss Lamb Roast," El would quip at least twice a day whilst tucking into her freeze-dried food pack. "Oh god! Imagine the gravy and the potatoes and the lamb and the veg and the... ahhh, I just miss all of it."

I didn't really miss much. I feel much more at home on water than on land and I was loving every moment of being on the boat.

During that first month, we were close to shipping lanes so radioing cargo ships and tankers became a frequent activity. The conversations would often be to check a passing ship had seen us on AIS, and politely ask them to ensure they gave us a wide berth. We were quite the tourist attraction out on the Pacific but the ships made me nervous. We had worked hard to ensure that we could control as many variables as possible, but ships were uncontrollable. We had heard stories of boats being run down, and I was acutely aware that despite being bright orange, we were barely visible between the waves.

One morning, our worst nightmare appeared to be coming true as a fishing vessel appeared on the horizon. It was a small forty metre vessel compared to the three hundred-metre container ships we were used to seeing, but still big enough that it could do some serious damage to our boat. The AIS alarm beeped, showing it to be on a direct collision course, but still around two miles away. Plenty of time to radio and ask them to change their course. As El and I rowed on, I heard Meg on the radio.

"Fishing vessel, fishing vessel. This is ocean rowing boat Danielle, ocean rowing boat Danielle over." Silence.

Fifteen minutes later and despite repeated calls, we had had no response on the radio. The vessel was now less than a mile from us, and there didn't appear to be any sign of life. Could it be an abandoned boat drifting in the same current that we were in? The mood on our boat had visibly shifted and everyone was tense.

"Grab the foghorn, El, and just make loads of noise," Meg suggested, as she continued to call on the VHF.

I was in the rowing seat with the footplate to steer, but was struggling to get us out of a strong current we were stuck in.

"I'm going to try and steer down the starboard side of it," I told the others, the fear in my voice visible as I desperately fought with the footplate and oars. The bobbing vessel rocked slowly side to side in the rolling swell, and still it bore down on us.

Suddenly, as it was no more than seventy-five metres away, it dramatically changed course and two smiling crew appeared on deck, enthusiastically waving. I stopped rowing as adrenaline coursed through body. Meg waved our handheld VHF at them and one disappeared inside.

"Hello," came an American voice over the radio. "We saw you on AIS and came to see what you were. Are you really rowing all the way out here? Surely you have an engine?"

We sat in stunned silence for a second, all breathing deeply with relief splattered across our salt encrusted and wind burnt faces.

"Um, no," replied Meg slowly. "We've been trying to radio you for the last twenty minutes."

"Oh right," the cheerful male voice on the radio replied, completely oblivious to the stress he had caused us. "Sorry girls. We had the radio turned off."

As Meg rather unenthusiastically partook in a little more conversation over VHF, I felt my heartrate start to subside and breathing return to normal. I exhaled, and caught El's eye, a smile and laugh escaping across my face as I shook my head. What on earth we were doing out here?

The Race: Thriving

A few days later, I woke to find the sea deadly calm, the sun creating magical streaks of glittering light across its surface.

"We should clean the hull," I told Meg and El when they woke, realising immediately I had just volunteered myself for the first swim.

Armed with a snorkel mask, ice scraper and constant reassurance from Meg and El that they would warn me if they saw a shark, I slowly lowered myself off the side of the boat.

"OMG!" I gasped, as the water reached my stomach and instantly stole all the air from my lungs. "It's freezing!!"

I wiggled my toes and stretched out into a starfish position as I got my breathe back, embracing the opportunity to move my limbs and float. As I dived under the boat I was startled by a few fish who had taken up residency and blown away by the beauty of the sea, columns of sunlight cutting through the water and extending as far down as I could see. The glittering water turned from turquoise, to dark blue to black.

From then on we stopped having to row in thermals and the sun began to shine. Night skies became littered with stars, planets and satellites and the sea glowed with phosphorescent algae. We spotted dolphins, whales, sharks and sunfish. It almost seemed too good to be true.

It was... we received a call from Chris, the race director.

"Hurricane Fabio is heading directly for. You aren't going to be able to out row it, so you need to slow down and let it pass ahead of you." This would put us in the outskirts of the storm's wrath. We prepared for the worst and limited our mileage to twenty miles a day.

Fabio came and went like an old boyfriend. He kicked a few waves our way but the conditions were no worse than those we had experienced in week one. Back in full wet weather gear, we rowed for the majority of the time and spent just one uncomfortable night all squashed in the stern cabin, limbs entwined, as the hurricane tossed us around like a cork bobbing in the waves.

We eventually found the trade winds and our daily mileage dramatically increased, often rowing between fifty and sixty miles a day and surfing the big waves. As I watched the bright orange sun rise above the glistening horizon one morning, turning the sky a multitude of purples, oranges and pinks, I felt something slap into the back of my head. Two seconds later, there was a thud on the deck and then another slap against my thigh. I looked around to see hundreds of squid diving back into the water, like tiny fifteen centimetres missiles. On Danielle's deck, a few stranded squid wriggled about excreting ink. I let out a yelp loud enough for Meg to stick her head out of the cabin.

"I've just been attacked by flying squid!" I exclaimed. Was I hallucinating from lack of sleep?

"You've what?" laughed Megan, her mouth dropping as her eyes darted back and forth over the deck.

As the wildlife sightings increased, so did the amount of rubbish. Every day we would see at least one large piece float close to the boat. Sometimes it would be a wine bottle, sometimes a clump of abandoned fishing gear, sometimes a large plastic crate. The scale of destruction we, as humans, are having on the planet was clear to see, even in one of the most remote locations on earth. Distressing, disappointing and overwhelming. It became the norm to see more rubbish in the ocean each day than wildlife, floating on the surface and below the waterline, waiting to be ingested by a curious fish or bird.

Of course, as land got nearer, the amount and type of rubbish increased and so it wasn't a surprise when, as the sun rose on the morning of day sixty, El stopped rowing and stared at the clouds on the horizon behind us. "I can see land!" she said, excitement rising in her voice. I turned around to look, and sure enough, rising out of the cloud, were the faint outlines of the mountains of Maui.

"Megan!" we both screamed. "We can see Hawaii!"

The last time we saw land was fifty-eight days ago. It's hard to fathom not seeing land for that long, but instead our days had been spent looking at a distant horizon of blues and greys which often became the most incredible hues of pink, orange and red during sunrise and sunset. Maui wasn't our final destination and, as such, it stayed a distant blur on the horizon for most of the day, disappearing and then reappearing behind the clouds, a dark brown shadow against the backdrop of blue.

Every glance at land bought on the realisation that the row was almost over. Part of me wanted to turn the boat around and row as hard as I could back out to the open ocean, but the knowledge that we were just a mere one-hundred miles away from completing our goal kept us on track.

As Maui passed us by and the sun began to set, lights began to twinkle on the horizon from lighthouses and, closer to the boat, from buoys. The flashing lights pierced through the darkness, blinking on and off at given intervals, interrupting the vast horizon of darkness we were so used to seeing. Realisation set in that we were almost there, but we were adamant to not begin celebrating early. The ocean was still toying with us, even close to land the waves were choppy, large storm clouds were circling overhead and our second hurricane of the crossing was threatening the southern Hawaiian islands.

In the early morning sunlight on what would be our final full day at sea, we could clearly see the island of Molokai about ten miles away from us. We were close enough to see the large green forests reaching down to the ocean, buildings dotted across the green and brown mottled landscape and the cascading contours of the hills. Our mobile phones, which had stayed silent for over two months, began beeping fervently, reminding us with a jolt that we were re-entering civilisation.

The excitement of seeing land soon wore off, and we endured a final day of sweltering heat beating down on us. Every stroke felt lethargic as we slowly rowed towards O'ahu, which at times would make itself just visible in the distance behind our bow.

It seemed the ocean was determined to make us finish as we had begun, and so we spent the final night in full wet weather gear. Crashing waves from the Molokai channel drenched us to the bone as they powered straight through the boat like an express train. Raindrops blurred our vision and pounded our skin relentlessly.

O'ahu

As the sun rose to our east, the silhouette outline of Diamond Head was visible ahead of us, the large white lighthouse and red buoy marking the end of the journey. A large sea turtle swam up to the boat, raising its head and making eye contact as if welcoming us to Hawaii. The sea turned to a beautiful shade of aqua blue, the sunlight glistening on its surface as though infused with thousands of specks of glitter. The rain clouds and winds, that had made our last night at sea one of the most testing, faded away and reality began to sink in.

We had done it. Two thousand four hundred nautical miles. Two World Records for the first crew of three, male or female, to row the mid Pacific Ocean and the youngest crew of three to row any of the world's oceans. Sixty-two days, eighteen hours and thirty-six minutes.

As we glided over the finish line, my eyes stung with tears and I desperately blinked them back as a wave of relief sent shivers across my body. I grabbed El and Meg, wrapping my arms round them, a beaming smile breaking out across my face making the corners of my eyes crinkle.

"Woooooooo!" we all screamed, a mass exodus of emotions that had built up inside of us exploding out as the reality of what we had achieved set in.

"So," I said, leaving a long pause as a sly grin plastered over my face. "Shall we do the Atlantic next?"

Website: **cazzlander.com**

Instagram: **@cazzlander**

Chapter 23

630 Miles Braver

By Zoe Langley-Wathen

I was desperate. I was alone. I had a tell-tale tingle in my bladder warning me of my impending predicament. I knew I needed to unzip the door and just go for it. But I was afraid.

Following hours of risk assessing, sweaty palms and tiresome bladder-squeezing, I finally faced my fears. Slowly, carefully I pulled down the zip of the tent door and ventured out into the inky blackness.

Instant relief. For the first time, I encountered the life-changing experience of peeing with a view and realised in both awe and acceptance that I should have stepped out of the tent sooner – in fact, I should have stepped outside YEARS ago.

My story begins with a moment of divine intervention. For fifteen years I had been telling myself, "It's not possible! I could never do that!" I wasn't strong enough, I wasn't fit enough, I wasn't quick enough or perhaps I simply wasn't brave enough. So believing that I wasn't enough in any capacity, I didn't try. That goal I had dreamed of for so many years was not attempted, because I had crushed the idea from the moment it had begun to bloom.

The rite of passage into middle age is often a milestone to be acknowledged. I wanted to mark it in a manner that was both personal and demanding. For around eighteen months, I had been searching for ideal adventure inspiration. The Inca Trail and Kilimanjaro had both been on my bucket list but for this celebration, they lacked any significance. They didn't sit right with me at that moment in my life. I wanted to *feel* my choice.

It was around May 2009 when an impromptu decision to wander into the small branch of Waterstones led to my epiphany. It would prove to be the demise of my stalwart 'not tough enough' belief system. As I entered the shop, a shaft of sunlight shone gloriously onto a single book on the shelf in front of me: *The South West Coast Path Handbook*.

It immediately struck me that this was both the book and eureka moment I had been waiting for. It was like the church scene straight out of The Blues Brothers movie, where Jake and Elwood receive a message from God. Okay, so I didn't somersault down the bookshop aisle proclaiming, "I have seen the light!" but I did have an extra skip in my step as I turned to the counter to pay for this book that was about to change my life.

As I said, divine intervention.

Or perhaps it was simply an excellent example of great product placement. Either way, one of us was in the right place at the right time and now it was down to me to use this gift well.

The 630 miles of the South West Coast Path, England's longest National Trail, resonated with every part of who I am. I had grown up in North Somerset, close to the start of the path and holidayed around Devon for years. Ancestors had once been tin miners in Cornwall, before taking off up to Northumberland to the coal mines. Lulworth Cove in Dorset was my home for over three years and I had lived on the Isle of Purbeck for seven years before moving to Poole, the end of the trail. I was even employed in the Art department of a school when a commissioned artist worked with some students to design the base of the start/end marker. The whole trail fizzed with multiple connections and was exciting in a way that no other adventure had yet touched me. The spell had been cast and the magic had worked. I was committed to seeing this through.

There were mixed responses from family and friends when I shared my plans to challenge myself by walking solo with my backpack and tent. My parents were naturally concerned about the safety of a lone female. Many of my friends just thought I was bonkers and didn't really understand my need to do this. Everyone, however, supported me from start to finish and when I announced that I would be fundraising for three charities, they all stepped up to help raise sponsorship money.

Concerns grew that time was too short to make this epic journey. I only had the six weeks of my summer holiday as a teacher. That seed of doubt that I was incapable stuck, although thankfully my determination remained unfaltering. I would not be beaten. After a discussion with the governors, the headteacher of my school gave me permission for two and a half weeks of unpaid leave. Now I was reassured it could be achieved.

Although planning had begun, my challenge didn't actually feel real until I delivered an assembly in June 2010. I talked to the students about my plans. The effect on both the school community and me was massive. From this point on, I had announced my intentions to the world; there was no backing out now. In this girls' grammar school, students constantly asked questions about how I would face certain obstacles, fears and expectations. Parents would stop and ask me about the adventure during parents' evenings and school productions, with many claiming they wished they were in my shoes. My hair-brained plans were the topic of conversation in the staff room, as teachers and support staff would quiz me over the tea trolley about how my training or preparations were progressing.

Over the year, the fire in my belly burned constantly to ensure I raised enough money for my charities. I also needed something resembling a success story to bring back to my next assembly in September 2011 and had to ensure I trained for strength and endurance. I worked constantly to keep the community informed of my progress and kept my finger on the fundraising pulse, including organising a ball and charity auction, dubbed The Glitz and Grammar Ball. I had so much energy and never seemed to stop.

That is, until April 2011 when the mother of all coughs set up residence in my chest. It didn't let up; I coughed all night, retched in the morning and hacked constantly throughout the day. I felt lousy at my fortieth birthday in May and went through various tests, antibiotics and chest x-rays. For a time, I truly believed that my walk would have to be postponed until the summer of the following year. My family, friends, teachers and students all rightly thought the same.

The doctor I visited in June concluded that he would send me on my walk with an inhaler. I had never used one before this illness, but it was a tough bug and not quick to leave. I too was a tough cookie however and decided to step out on July 3rd regardless and see how I fared. I sincerely do not remember using that inhaler once and by the middle of July, twelve weeks after the cough had started, it left me. I still believe that walking and the fresh air was the best cure; my outdoor medicine.

Nevertheless, as bold as I might have seemed to head off on my journey, it did not make avoiding my Nan any easier. It's not that I didn't want to see her. She'd been suffering from post-stroke ill health and was in hospital. Due to the acuteness of my cough, I had made the hard choice to stay away for fear of passing on my germs.

Striding out along the South West Coast Path that first day in July felt alien to me. 'A fish out of water' springs to mind. What on earth was I thinking? How could I possibly have believed that this was a feasible challenge? I should never have come and I so far out of my comfort zone I couldn't even see it on the horizon. You get the drift.

With a deep breath, I headed westwards along a standard tarmac path. The sea ebbed and flowed on my right, waves crashing ceaselessly onto the soft sand. I felt hugely conspicuous with my equally huge rucksack perched unnaturally on my shoulders like a builder's hod. Each time I saw people walking towards me, I puffed myself up as much as the weight of the pack would allow, just enough that they might be hoodwinked into believing my façade as a seasoned adventurer. That was until, less than half a mile from the start, I stood on a cast iron manhole cover and did my impression of Bambi on ice as I tried to keep my balance. My imaginary status was in tatters.

Imposter syndrome still veiled me. In those early days, I had constant doubts that I should never have embarked on the walk, though I enjoyed the welcome and support I received from the people I met. And I totally devoured the scenery.

The trees seemed to be so precariously planted on the sides of these impossibly steep cliffs, reminding me of an image I had once seen of a landslide capturing a collection of trees on a hillside. They were still vertical and yet mid-slide downwards after a storm. The sun was shining, however, making a great start to my adventure. Every few steps, the light peeped between the thick canopies of leaves above. It shaded me from the sun and created an enchanting effect, backlighting the variegated shades of green along these leafy, woody tunnels I had now entered.

The holloways soon opened out onto high moorland between Minehead and Porlock Weir. The route towards Selworthy Beacon was filled with the purple haze of summer heather, punctuated every so often with a lone tree, bent and worn with tired complicity towards the northeast. My regular, sharp intake of breath was not due to the tight chest and persistent cough that I reluctantly still carried. It was at each new visual excitement that cropped up. The coastline on the horizon, which was now visible, faded into a pale, watery palette that, although lacked the vivid sharpness and colour of the landscape in the fore and middle ground, gave me a good idea of what to expect in the next day or two.

As I dropped down into Bossington, I spotted a character with blonde-grey, rock star-style curly hair blowing in the wind, riding a motorbike across the lowlands towards me. Or was it a wheelchair? On second glance it definitely was a wheelchair. I couldn't quite make it out but was completely taken by the similarity between this hairy figure and the giant hairy dog that lolloped alongside this motorbikeywheelychair. Frankie stopped and, after showing an interest in what I was doing, he introduced himself. I quizzed him as to the nature of his vehicle and then spotted the plastic boot, strapped around his right leg and foot. He informed me that he had had Achilles surgery but was also dog-sitting the friendly Frankie look-a-like they called Nonny, so he had needed to create something to allow him to 'walk the dog'.

Frankie talked me around his Heath Robinson affair for a trike. It was actually pretty ingenious, if a little crude. He had taken the seat and large wheels of a regular wheelchair, joining it to the front fork of a motorbike. Ahead of the handlebars sat two large batteries, generously gaffer-taped and nestled neatly in a welded basket overhanging the front wheel. I appreciated it for both its engineered beauty and comical value. Not to mention that Frankie wore the smallest suggestion of shorts and when I asked to take his photograph, it truly appeared as though this sun-kissed hairy-goatee guy was sat on a motorised contraption, wearing nothing but his curly locks! He somehow plucked a crisp twenty-pound note from those tiny shorts and became my first on-trip sponsor. He could never have known how much that gave me a confident spring in my step for the rest of the day, particularly now feeling credible as a genuine backpacker.

Carried into the second day by my new-found conviction in my capability as a solo hiker, I strode off without allowing myself to begin the destructive self-talk of doubt. Instead of feeling alone, which I believe deep in my heart did actually concern me, I absorbed and appreciated the wide variety of quaint cottages adorned with climbing roses and thatch. There were grand gatehouses, cleverly engineered chimney pots and a remote church topped with a petite, semi-truncated spire, tucked away in a valley inaccessible to most four-wheeled transport.

I wondered how I would ever finish the walk in time if I kept stopping to 'absorb', take photos and take pleasure in the sights being offered to me around every corner. This day not only filled me with the need to pinch myself to ensure I was indeed walking my dream path, but it also came with the realisation that, although I was following a coast path, it wasn't simply a case of keeping the sea on my right all the way to Poole. So many people had joked that at least I wouldn't need a map and that, "There's not much chance of getting lost then."

There were many occasions where I had to refer to the map and the guide book. I would study it closely, and then study it some more just to be sure. With no hiking buddy to confer with, it was my own decisions that counted now. Increasingly, I became aware that the sea was disappearing and the views across the twinkling water and craggy coastline were being replaced with over-sized rhododendron bushes and tall, delicate ferns. Gunnera patches spread with their tightly-packed army of wide, umbrella-like leaves. Steep banks dominated these dense, almost sinister woods. My over-active imagination began to take hold and I experienced my first moment of 'real fear'. In hindsight, this was not truly warranted. It was simply li'l ole novice backpacker me, a never-ending wood... and a man.

The estate management had cordoned off an area of trees with red and white tape. In my head, I began to question why, though it didn't occur to me that it may be to mark an area for proposed cutting back or tree-felling. Instead, I continued my silent storytelling to imagine a crime scene, a grisly murder perhaps. I soon sensed I was not alone – in this wood where it had been only me, the trees and my thoughts. I turned and saw a man a few minutes behind me. I am not sure why but I felt uncomfortable. To my knowledge, it certainly wasn't the body language the man was presenting. Being enclosed within a wood, with miles left before returning to open space and not a soul around me, except this guy, was unnerving. Like a learner driver, I was still learning about this solo walking malarkey. Then came a diversion due to a landslide and I felt the alarm of being lost.

After much internal debate about how to handle the situation, I decided to slow down and stop trying to race towards the end of the wood. Carrying nearly eighteen kilograms meant that I was incredibly slower than my usual walking pace and slower than any two-legged being I met on the path! I would let the man catch up, say hello and let him pass. As it turned out, he was not wielding an axe and turned out to be a normal, friendly man who was interested in my adventure. After a few minutes of discussing the diversion and then strolling together, I think my snail's pace was too much to bear, he bade me farewell and I heaved a sigh of relief while scolding myself for being fearful.

As I stepped out into the open moorland once again, the views reappeared along with the severity and close proximity of the path to the cliff edges. My thoughts soon took a new focus. Following nearly two full days of slow walking, I was learning that my back and shoulders were suffering greatly. The sixty-eight-litre rucksack I had crammed full of necessities for my six-week expedition was laughable. I wobbled a little on the narrow tracks, feeling vulnerable and unsteady, partly due to my issue with heights but mostly owing to my inexperienced insistence on packing gear that I thought would be essential for such a long trip. I would monitor my kit use and aim to begin the culling of items from my pack if my body had any chance of surviving the next 610 miles.

I think the first items to leave were my yellow plastic, two-egg caddy and a miniature frying pan. I'd had this dreamy notion of calling at farmhouses to buy freshly laid eggs to cook my own breakfast or supper of Eggs Benedict or Scrambled à la Coast Path. Some ideas, as lovely as they might seem, are simply not practical.

The desire to capture and experience picture-postcard views

continued. Day three brought me much in the way of rugged beauty, through the Valley of the Rocks; packaged complete with a family of posing mountain goats with long horns and even longer goatee beards grazing the land.

The level of ascents and descents were increasing and I could feel my body working ever harder, particularly as the cough I mentioned earlier was still with me at this point. For the first couple of weeks, my (then) partner had agreed to drive my Bongo campervan, so I would have somewhere familiar to sleep for a while. After that, I would be on my own for the last five weeks. That evening, we met at Heddon's Mouth where the duty manager in The Hunter's Inn kindly agreed to a discounted room for the night for us. It had begun to rain hard and it was a fair distance back to the campervan. As events unfolded, it would appear that serendipity had played a large part in us staying under a roof in a lovely room that evening.

Following a well-deserved, hearty dinner and a quick update to family and friends as to my location, I received a call at the inn from my daughter. Laura by now was sixteen years old and for the first time was 'home alone' and doing a great job of being independent. The task then sadly fell to her to inform me of the death of my dear old Nan. At ninety-two years old, her struggle with health was finally over. I wept for her. I wept for my birth mother, Lorraine, who was due to fly back into Heathrow four days later to move back to the UK after nearly forty years in the States. She had missed her farewell. I also wept selfishly for me. My decision to stay away had prevented me from saying goodbye, although I had hoped in my heart that Nan would hold on until the end of August when I returned and I would surely be well again. My resolve was now to dedicate the following day's walk to the memory of Mary – my longest-serving grandmother who inspired me with her ability to say, "Yes!" to so many opportunities; such as visiting and walking part of the Great Wall of China, solo and seventy.

As I ascended the steep valley towards the hill known as Great Hangman the next morning, it poured with rain. Enormous blisters had formed on my heels and I continued to weep. I sniffled and wiped my wet face. Picking up a rock that was shaped like a heart, I called into the sky, "This is for you, Nan!" A skylark directly above me replied to my call with its majestically repetitive, high-pitched notes. I reached an enormous cairn at the top of the hill and set my stone into the pyramid-style structure. From this point on, whenever I hear a skylark it brings Nan to mind and it makes me smile.

My bravery levels were being tested a little more each day. I now approached campsites and talked to proprietors about my charity walk and found that, nine times out of ten, they were keen to support my cause by allowing me a free or extremely cheap pitch for the night.

Total strangers stopped me to ask about my adventures as it seemed unusual to them to see a female walking and camping solo. I received so much positive energy and help from every person I met. A taxi driver gave me a free ride from a campsite to the start of the day's walk. A campsite owner collected me in her car at the end of a long day hiking. People stopped me to give sponsorship money or buy me drinks when I had finally started to feel comfortable going into a pub alone.

It still bugged me, however, that I had yet to face my two innermost fears: wild camping solo and tackling river crossings, specifically those that required wading. I was too nervous about pitching my tent outside of the safety of a campsite. I seriously did not understand how I could do it but knew I had to. Much of this was almost certainly projected fear from others, although I had not recognised this at the time.

By the time I reached Falmouth, I had continued to be treated like royalty. Although I'd only planned for a one-night stop, I had stayed on at the home of old family friends for a further eight nights and Lea and Steve, who were now retired, ferried me to and from my start point and destination each day between Redruth and Falmouth. They lavished me with a comfy bed, amazing food, foot massages and such heartfelt generosity. I can never be thankful enough for their encouragement and help. All this and yet something was missing which I was unable to pinpoint.

During my hike, I had periodically met with other walkers. I never felt lonely, as I had once thought I might, due to the constant stream of tourists and locals wanting to stop and chat. Walking alongside other hikers was different, however, as they totally understood the need to challenge oneself and the acceptance of pain and endurance that is likely across such an epic distance. I maintain to this day that I have never met with such a special and connected group of individuals who made this journey so extraordinary. It is common to meet with others but perhaps not so usual to meet and keep in regular contact post-walk. I confided with individuals within this group about my need to conquer my solo wild camp fear. I was actively encouraged and given various personal hints and tips from each of them during those times we walked together; their positive messages were gradually sinking in.

Every day I continued to walk and assess possible suitable camp spots but kept finding excuses, like other places to camp or stay. Finally, by Day Thirty-one, I knew avoidance was pointless, so I took the plunge. After searching for an hour or more, I pitched my tent in the place that I thought looked the most sensible and safe. I look back at my photographs now and roll my eyes, as pitching snugly between a five-bar gate and a kissing gate clearly was not the best wild camp of my quest! Had I wandered a few more metres ahead I would have found a spot on Gribben Head, with a wide vista and a day mark tower emblazoned with red and white horizontal stripes. I maintain that I subconsciously chose the gates for the security of a boundary, rather than a wide-open space in which I might feel vulnerable.

After the lengthy bladder-squeezing described earlier, stepping out of the tent was a pivotal moment in my adventure life. I gasped at the sheer volume and beauty of stars decorating that sky. Never in my life had I come across heavens like these. I felt liberated and once again found myself being scolded by the other me… the new, braver me.

As I breathed in the splendour, at last I understood what had been missing that previously I was unable to identify. Unlike when I was staying indoors being treated to all manner of luxuries, I was now outside, free and grubby, connected to the wildness of the natural world. Earlier, I had experienced a sunset, and a few hours later I would encounter a sunrise, first hand and intimate – just me and the magnificence of the spectacle. I guess I perceived it as a meditation, a means of being in the moment. I promised myself there and then that I would not pass up the opportunity to solo walk or wild camp ever again.

Thankfully, this eventual 'yes' to find my courage filtered into the rest of my South West Coast Path adventure. There had been many river crossings but none so scary as the River Erme, my nemesis. All the other rivers were served by footbridges, ferries, tidal causeways or, at the very least, stepping stones. Erme was an estuary of wide proportions and required careful planning. I had spent months reading about it and fearing the worst – me being carried out to sea on a raging tide. Arthur, Mike, and Steve, all solo hiking the path, had met up on the bank of the river. We decided to wait for low tide and make the crossing together. For this I was grateful, as the mouth of the river looked as terrifying to me in reality as it had done in photographs. I kept thinking of young Jinni, another walker we had met who was a day or two ahead of us. She must have conquered this unaccompanied. I was both in awe of her courage and a little embarrassed that I had not insisted I go it alone. In retrospect, I realise this would not have been practical or polite as my new tribe and I had a great rapport and we did well supporting one another.

It was a wait of seven hours on the west beach of the River Erme. I could see the slipway on the far side, diagonally across the water. We set up a little camp while awaiting the low tide window, due around 9.15pm. A small fire was lit and the guys poked sticks into the sand, hanging their socks over to dry. We shared stories, drew in the sand and ate our flapjacks and free pasties donated to us by the lady in the local tea shop. But all the while we were eager to get the crossing done and dusted.

I knew from my research to expect to wade across knee-deep. I put my waterproof sandals on and tied my boots to my rucksack. Arthur left to begin the crossing, perhaps a little too early. Mike soon followed, concerned that Arthur had stopped dead in his tracks and was looking out of his depth. Steve followed, so I took a deep breath and coached myself across.

No amount of reading and researching prepared me for the experience of crossing the Erme. The tide was receding fast and as it ebbed, it pulled with such force I felt it would pull me off my feet. I could sense the water depth was increasing as the river bed banked away and anxious at the rushing of the tide, I dug my walking poles into the bed to give myself the chance of a double anchor point against the pull.

As the water suddenly became deeper still, I fought my poles in and out of the water and my stomach knotted with fear. I felt a strong grip on my arm. It was Mike – he had reached and held onto Arthur for a short part of the crossing and now reassured me too. He could see that I was battling with the strong current and though I would never have asked for help unless it was an emergency. I was genuinely appreciative of that gesture.

It took around half an hour to cross and was dark by the time we set foot on land. I heaved a sigh of relief and once again felt liberated at the conquering of yet another nightmare. The effect was to change my approach to life forever.

I sang, 'Somewhere Over the Rainbow' as we plugged on for another two and a half kilometres before pitching. Spotting six glow-worms going about their nocturnal-illuminating business on the way up to Scobbiscombe simply held my moment of triumph higher and longer.

Forty-seven days after beginning my first ever long distance path, I walked the final seven miles from Swanage to South Haven Point; the end of the South West Coast Path. Students, colleagues, family and friends all rallied together to make the final stretch of that 630 miles special.

The welcoming party waiting for me at Swanage, along the sands at Knoll Beach and Studland are all moments I will cherish, as I crawled comically to the finish, two dress sizes smaller.

Strangely, for a big birthday challenge event that was only meant to be a one-off, I have found myself incorporating new challenges into my annual calendar every year since. Every year then extended to every day, where I now find myself confronting fears and pushing myself to say, "Yes" to those activities I would normally say, "No" to. You could call it a 'micro-bravery' couch to 5k; stepping out and taking daily risks on a smaller scale. Increased removal of my comfort zone culminated last year with a move away from the security of my thirteen years in permanent contract teaching. Instead, I now walk into the unknown, stepping into different schools most days.

Ultimately, I have reclaimed my spare time and am devoting it to being outside more by embarking on a one hundred day map challenge and setting up my new venture 'HeadRightOut'. I aim to encourage others to HeadRightOut of their comfort zone, do something that scares them every day and use every opportunity to help build their resilience and self-belief.

100MappyDays and 100ScaryDays seem far removed from a big birthday trundle along a coast path, yet the journey has evolved into something far more than simply ticking off one hundred walks or scary activities. I have discovered a true passion for fostering a love of the outdoors in others. I could never have known how my own wellbeing would be affected so positively, simply with that decision to say "yes" to an impossible dream that carried me along a profoundly long path.

There's a number of ways to follow Zoe's Head Right Out journey or to find out about booking her as a speaker:

www.headrightout.com or **@headrightout** on Instagram, Facebook, and Twitter.

Facebook Group: **HeadRightOut Hub** (all women welcome to join)

Email: **headrightout@gmail.com**

Chapter 24

Rome to Home Alone

By Chris Lansdowne

My friend, Sam, used to work in the British Army where he had the intimidating role of 'bomb disposal'. During his first tour of duty in Afghanistan, he was attacked by a wild dog. His colleague shot the dog. The bullet passing through the animal's body, ricocheted off a wall and passed through Sam's left eye, stopping in his brain. He was given a five percent chance of survival but, following a dozen operations, is now the proud owner of two impressively large scars, a false eye and a poor short term memory. Thankfully Sam is otherwise very well and has a new appreciation for waking up in the mornings, alive and healthy in a warm, safe bed.

In recognition of Sam's sacrifice, and all the sacrifices that men and women in the armed forces make, I wanted to do some effective fundraising. I also wanted to complete a challenge, something that would push me outside of my comfort zone. I wanted something tough but memorable. I wanted to take on an adventure that would really stretch me, physically and mentally.

I decided to cycle from 'Home to Rome Alone'. A 1500 mile journey across Europe from London to Italy, with nothing but a bike, a tent and myself for company to raise funds for the charity Help for Heroes.

I enjoyed cycling but at best, I would have called myself a summer cyclist, enjoying Sunday rides with friends often followed by a few drinks. I had cycled a little the previous year, building up to a respectable forty miles in one go, but I hadn't sat on a bike since the previous Autumn. In January, I began cycling again in earnest. Before long, I was completing sixty-mile weekend rides, panniers loaded with tins of beans simulating my touring weight. However, mentally I was still not fully committed to my ride until I unexpectedly received my first donation. It was £50 from Sam's father. There was no backing out of this now!

Training had gone well but six weeks before 'D-Day', I began my test ride - a cycle from London to Yorkshire. This involved three successive eighty-mile days carrying all my equipment, clothes and food. It would give me a good idea of how fit and prepared I was.

The first day went well, as I progressed through the beautiful home counties' rolling countryside. This day felt wonderful, my legs feeling strong, effortlessly climbing hills and enjoying a sense of freedom as I passed gold and green fields, slow, easy rivers and babbling brooks, the road marshalled by wind protecting trees and hedges whilst the sun warmly shone down on me.

In contrast, the second day involved riding north across a relatively barren and pancake-flat fen countryside, dulled further by a miserable grey sky, whilst the roads, arrow straight, pointed directly into a strong, cold northerly wind for the entire eighty miles. I often cycled at a walking pace, feeling like I was pushing through treacle, hoping for a bend in the road to offer a moment's respite.

At the end of this second day, I climbed off my bike, my legs like jelly, my entire back and neck stiff, seized in the shape of me leaning forward into the wind. My mind was dazed from the unremitting brutality of the effort that day. I made a cup of tea, sat and ate a packet of ginger biscuits and wondered if I really was up to the challenge. I had so many questions - How would I cope? Surely there would be harder days than this? What about the Alps...?

The following day, my legs sore and tired, I slowly pedalled a further eighty miles through beautiful but tough rolling Yorkshire countryside. The sky thankfully was once again blue and sunny, the landscape now dramatic with fast, sweeping descents followed by long, tough draggy climbs through pine trees now making my burning thighs cry out to me to stop. Thankfully these hills alternated with flat wide open green landscapes, an endless patchwork quilt of farmers' fields. I finally crawled into Newton-on-Rawcliffe, where I was met by my mother and risked being crushed by her worried embrace.

The three days had been very tough, but I had survived my 'practice' run and knew I was more or less where I needed to be. Looking back, the second and third days of my training ride taught me my most valuable lesson on a bike. I could keep going when it was tough. I didn't need to be amazing or set records but if I kept chipping away at my target. I could achieve what I had previously thought was too difficult.

Having said that, I was also realising just how challenging my ride would be both physically and mentally (albeit not yet emotionally). After all, my practice run was most of the length of England, something that would have felt impossible to me a few short months ago.

A handful of weeks later, after a tearful and nervous goodbye to my family and friends, I found myself standing on the ferry to France watching the British coast disappear in a haze of fog. I was suddenly very aware I wouldn't see anyone I knew for several weeks. I felt a deep sense of loneliness sitting in my stomach like a heavy stone of anticipation. I was on my own. This was it. But I also felt an exhilarated thrill, the anticipation of meeting the challenge I now faced that I recognised from each time I was about to play rugby. I was ready for this, even though I didn't fully believe it.

I find it far easier to progress when I'm taking some form of action. The action doesn't have to be huge. Rather, I find it helpful to just do *something*, and in doing so I feel I am moving in the right direction, both physically and metaphorically. Instead, sitting on the ferry and waiting allowed my brain far too much freedom to focus on my worries, which at this point, I had plenty of. Can I climb the Alps? Would I find campsites and food? Could I fix every problem with my bike? Will I sleep okay? Will I get injured? The worst question of all was 'What if I can't finish this ride?'

Whilst ruminating, I spoke to a man who was sharing a phone charging socket with me. When I told him my plans he looked at me with envy and said, "You have no idea how much I'd give to swap places with you!" And, at that moment in time, I thought he must be even crazier than me!

Two hours later, we docked in Dieppe and I waited on my bike at the front of the ferry, butterflies fluttering in my stomach. Finally, the doors opened and I cycled onto French soil. Full of energy fuelled by the last few hours of worry, I cycled to a roundabout with two exits, both marked Dieppe. With no idea which way to go, I turned left, racing up a sharp hill.

It was a dead end.

Meekly, I turned my heavy bike around and headed back down the hill smiling to myself, having learned the French word for 'loading bay'. I had mistakenly headed for Dieppe port, not Dieppe town!

Coming from the UK where cycling is at best tolerated by drivers and pedestrians, it was wonderful to see cycle paths everywhere and to be greeted by people's smiles, their hands raised in a wave instead of a raised rude gesture. I often found when I stopped cycling an interested French person would talk to me. These conversations were a welcome distraction from a sore bum and the hamster wheel of worries in the back of my mind.

On one occasion, whilst I was sat eating some bread and butter in a car park, an older man said, "*Bonjour,*" as he walked past looking at me with interest. Moments later, he returned with a jar of his homemade olive tapenade, passing it to me as a gift simply saying, "*Bon mange*," or "good eating." With a nod of his head and a smile, he turned and left to continue his day. Simple, kind acts like this really show me the amazing good in humanity, and were not infrequent on any of my travels, then or since.

My first unwelcome surprise emerged over the next few days and became a feature of the entire ride. Many people had assured me that French campsites were common, and they had seen dozens every day. Looking back, I doubt they travelled much in northeast agricultural France. Consequently, I cycled around ninety miles each day with a gradual building concern that I would have to camp in the wild and wake to an angry French farmer sticking his shotgun up my nose. Thankfully, that did not happen and eventually every night I spotted an oasis of a campsite in the middle of nowhere.

As my route steadily passed through northeast France, skipping north of Paris, I received various supportive texts from home such as, "Could you just pop into Dijon for some mustard, it's not far". Some of these, as my sense of humour ebbed and flowed, did grate, and I had to hold back from replying with a sarcastic response as I knew they were intended to make me smile. Despite the worry over camping, a few things became clear; the ride was physically challenging (cycling ninety miles carrying ten kilograms up and down rolling hills would never be easy), but it was clearly achievable, and my fitness would improve as I progressed.

The days quickly fell into a strangely reassuring routine:

Wake with the sun and rise around 6am. Dress and take the tent down.

Enjoy four to six cheese rolls and a mug of tea as the tent dried.

Pack and head off around 8am.

Cycle until 1pm. Eat lunch at a cafe or restaurant.

Stop at around seventy to eighty miles to buy food for dinner and the next day's breakfast and snacks. Then stop again around ninety miles to find a campsite.

Put up my tent, shower and wash cycling clothes. Then cook, eat and wash up.

Look at the next day's maps, send some texts and fall asleep.

Physically it was hard, but the memory of what my friend, Sam, had endured helped put my struggles into perspective. In a way, it was quite simple – I just had to keep cycling! Thankfully, there were very few day-to-day problems, just the discomforts of my derriere and my legs, which wasn't pleasant but it steadily eased as I became more conditioned to life on the road.

Where I had expected lots of little physical and logistical problems, there were none. I slept very well. My bike had no punctures or mechanical issues. I always found campsites, shops and restaurants, and once off the bike, there were no real aches or pains.

I hadn't expected my emotions to be a problem, but surprisingly found this to be the hardest part. I realised I had never spent more than a whole day completely on my own and now found the evenings very lonely, longing to speak with people. It wasn't that I needed advice or affirmation. I missed sharing the experience. This may well have contributed to naming my bike Lance (pre-drug admission of course!). I occasionally found myself talking to 'him' about "that bloody hill", or asking, "How can there still be a headwind?", much like Tom Hanks' character did in Castaway to a football named Wilson.

Time inevitably passed and I continued cycling. The days and nights rolled past and I enjoyed seeing many beautiful parts of France - long tree lined boulevards, wide sweeping fields, crops swaying in the breeze, endless green vineyards and medieval villages.

One highlight of my ride came after a very long and frustrating hill. I turned to the left, relieved to let my bike start to roll down the gentle slope. Suddenly, I noticed that I'd disturbed a huge eagle, which took flight then flew alongside me for fifty metres or so. We both watched each other closely, intrigued by what we were seeing before it banked and flew off.

I often wished I had the time to stop and see more of the scenery and towns but soon I arrived at the foothills of the Alps. I discussed my route with one very experienced looking cyclist at a campsite who pursed her lips, sucked in air and looked concerned. Her immediate, stern advice was, "*Mange, mange, mange!*" – "Eat, eat, eat!".

I set off the next day, and after an hour hit my first hill. I had cycled up some steep hills in the UK, but they plateaued after very short periods. In France, I was in my easiest gear and struggling. Various expletives went through my mind and the horror of imminent and embarrassing failure felt like a very real possibility.

I stopped with my heart beating like a train, sweat sliding down the side of my face and off my chin, and I began to panic. I momentarily considered my options – go back and get a train home which would have been humiliating; or walk up the hill with my bike which would have felt like a betrayal of what I was trying to achieve. The third option was to try again, and again, and again.

About an hour and several stops later, I had a much better idea of what I was about to go through in the Alps as well as a much-improved knowledge of what I could achieve on my bike. As I reached the top, a truly spectacular view materialised as the hill turned into a stunning vista of tall Alpine pine trees interspersed in the rich verdant green grass, bright coloured flowers scattered in all directions under the deep blue sky with the magnificent snow peaked Alps in the background. That night I slept well with a slight smile on my face – I'm going to make this!

The next day marked another milestone as I passed from France into Switzerland. I cycled proudly to the checkpoint, slowing to a halt and anticipating a thorough interrogation from the guards. I certainly expected a stamp in my passport which I had prepared and ready, an excited grin affixed to my face.

The border guards, however, had other thoughts. The lounging, cigarette smoking French guard briefly glanced up, then with an irritated tilt of his head, motioned for me to continue cycling onwards, past the equally stereotypically immaculate and upright Swiss guard (though neither as perfect as the pizza-eating Italian guard whom I would meet later). It hadn't occurred to me that cyclists here were as common as flies at a picnic.

I cycled onwards, arriving as planned at Lake Geneva, seeing the old and picturesque 'Chateau de Chillon' sitting on the edges of the blue, sparkling lake that marked the base to the Alps proper. The relatively small mountain edge dwarfed the enormous French castle.

The campsite here paired me with an expat English lady running the campsite, who was pleased to have someone English to speak to. A rare and pleasant evening followed involving wine, cheese and a lot more talking than usual. These occasions lifted me psychologically, and I set off the following morning feeling much more upbeat, into the glacial valley that marked my route for the next two days.

These two days were shorter and I gradually approached the Alp that I was soon to cycle over, which I had now unhelpfully labelled 'The Wall'.

On the first night, I stopped at a town called Sion. Whilst setting up my tent, I spoke with an elderly lady who was walking her dog. In her strong French accent, she told me she had always lived in this town, and proudly informed me, "You won't need a tent. The air is trapped in the valley. It stays warm in winter and spring, and cool in summer and autumn. Because the air stays the same temperature, it doesn't rain, and this valley is the driest part of Europe. It hasn't rained here in twenty-seven years!"

Three hours later I sat in the tent ironically smiling, facing a deluging thunderstorm that lasted most of the night, making me question whether all elderly women really can predict the weather or if I had met the local prankster.

The following day I arrived at Brig, in the shadow of my nemesis – 'The Wall'. I made camp, took it easy for the rest of the day and enjoyed an uneventful evening with an extra-large dinner as I prepared for what I was expecting to be my hardest challenge yet.

I set off in glorious sunshine, fuelled by my 'reserved for special occasions' porridge breakfast, and headed towards the Alpine pass. At twenty-one miles, the climb wasn't that long but was unbroken with an average incline of six percent which would take me from an elevation of five hundred metres above sea level to 2005 metres. This may not sound excessive to a fit cyclist on a carbon bike. However, to a thirty-year-old slightly chubby chap carrying ten kilograms on a heavy steel framed bike, it was my personal Everest.

During these tortuously slow few hours, I cycled determinedly, and slowly but surely edged forward. I cycled through a long pitch-black tunnel, getting intermittently soaked by icy meltwater pouring through cracks in the tunnel roof and stopping when there were no car headlights to light the way. I watched sweat drip from my chin every second in the baking heat of the lowlands before the icy coldness of the snow-covered peak later took over. I witnessed countless stunning views down the wide, deep and ancient glacial valley, spotting towns I had cycled through over the last two days.

All these events happened at what felt like a glacial pace. I cycled level with ramblers at times and enviously watched as school children overtook me with practiced ease on their bikes. Finally though, after five hours of constant effort, I couldn't have been more elated when I climbed off my bike at the top of the Simplon pass knowing I had cycled to the top of an Alp! I allowed myself to luxuriate in several selfies with the huge commemorative stone eagle to record the moment.

Fortunately according to the laws of physics, 'what goes up must come down' and so I enjoyed the next thirty miles of descent without pedalling once. Instead, at times, I found myself desperately braking in wet, skiddy and filthy conditions.

I arrived at the bottom of the mountain looking more like I had played rugby in the mud rather than cycled. I showered, put my tent up, then sat down to eat at the campsite restaurant. As the sun began to set, the orange light glistened across the wide calm lake and house lights beginning to twinkle on the other side as the evening began to take hold. I ordered a pizza and a beer, then took a deep breath, reflecting on my day and sitting down to enjoy my first Italian meal in a campsite restaurant.

This should have represented a highpoint of my emotional and physical journey, but it turned out to be the hardest of all evenings. After the euphoric highs and achievements of this day, spending the evening on my own seemed somehow sad and cruel as I absorbed yet another tough lesson in life – the value of sharing life's experiences with the people you like and love. Tiredness eventually trumped sadness though and, after a few very unhappy minutes in my sleeping bag, I once again slept well and woke to face another day, emotions thankfully settled.

Cycling in Italy marked one very welcome change in my evening routine. Northern agricultural France is not known well for its restaurant or cafe culture, so I had cooked every evening. Entering Italy changed this. My path now headed south to the Mediterranean, then down the west coast of Italy, avoiding some of the Tuscan hills. This brought me in contact with a lot more tourist-friendly towns and, consequently, pizzerias! This was a considerable improvement on my cooking, which could have been charitably described as basic.

The next day started well. However, my mind was becoming more entrenched in the need to camp at absolutely all evening stops and not use a hotel or B&B. On this particular day, after around ninety miles with no sighting of any campsites, I very reluctantly looked to find a hotel, and a further five miles later, stopped in a town called 'Vaggiano'. By the time I stopped, my pedal had developed an irritating squeak, so I went to a bike shop and met a man I was about to become very grateful to.

The bike shop owner, a gentle looking fifty-ish-year-old man, still clearly very fit and clearly passionate about everything 'bike' in his shop, turned out to be an ex-professional cyclist who, after listening to my planned route, told me to go next door to the cafe and return in two hours. I did as he instructed and ordered a couple of drinks at the cafe. To my surprise, the café owner brought out bowl after bowl of food, followed finally by a bottle of beer. As the two-hour mark approached I went to pay, intrigued how much this would cost, but the café owner smiled and flatly refused to take any money. Instead, not sharing the same language, she literally pointed me back to the bike shop.

Back in the shop, the cyclist/bike shop owner had obtained maps from his friend, photocopied them and drew the best route to Pisa. By his reckoning, cycling this route was shorter and avoided several climbs thus saving me a day.

I set off the following morning having enjoyed life's little luxuries such as sleeping in a hotel bed, having a hot shower and a full stomach. My bike pedal had been well oiled and my heart was genuinely warmed by the kindness of the bike shop and cafe owners.

I kept the receipt from the bike shop and, six months after I returned to England, found the shop online and emailed the owner a Merry Christmas. He replied returning my season's greeting and said he still occasionally thought of me. Knowing I made it apparently gave him great pleasure.

It transpired the bike shop day's good fortune was just as well as the following twenty-four hours consisted of 105 miles, four smaller mountain passes and my first puncture. But I was rewarded the following day. I cycled up to a huge body of water, slowly breaking into a massive grin as I realised this was the Mediterranean sea. I had actually crossed Europe on my bike. As milestones went, this was a major one!

I gradually realised Italy had three major differences to France. Firstly, the temperature was a lot hotter, usually around thirty-five degrees Celsius which I enjoyed. Secondly, it was significantly hillier. Lastly, lunches and dinners now consisted of pasta, pizza, Coke or, on special occasions, beer.

Having conquered my nemesis, 'The Wall', I was beginning to enjoy this second half of the journey now that I was fully expecting to complete it. One lovely part of Italy I cycled through was a town called La Spezia just south of Pisa. This long flat stretch of beach had a tailwind, a lot of cyclists and many good looking people who were headed to the beach. It was here, at a traffic light where I had my only accident of the trip. I *may* have been watching the women cross the road as I slowly halted at a traffic light. The camber of the road was making my bike tilt to the right. Unfortunately, as I always unclip my left cycling shoe, I continued to fall to the right, causing a moment's panic followed quickly by a crunching sound of my knee hitting the tarmac. Embarrassingly, I was perfectly positioned in the middle of the road in front of fifteen women, ten cyclists and a few cars. Once again, I had been taught a lesson I wouldn't forget, although my consolation was that I got a smile from the lady who had caught my eye.

Despite the improved food, the Tuscan and coastal hills took it out of my legs, and I steadily grew increasingly tired. The Italian roads also lacked a certain smoothness, and at one point, after a particularly unbearable stretch of road, I was forced to purchase a pack of washing sponges to soften the relentless rough vibrations from the saddle.

A few more memorable moments punctuated the days, such as cycling past my first roadside sign for "Roma", spending two days cycling down the hard shoulder of the Italian equivalent of the M1 (legally) and stopping at Pisa to see the famous leaning tower.

Most campsites in Italy were quite straightforward, but at one I thought a lady kindly asked if I wanted help as the ground was very rocky and the tent pegs didn't go in very easily. I declined but she returned with six men. Unsure of what to expect, I continued pitching my tent pegs. The men stood with their arms folded and watched me. When I finally stood, they all looked at each other and walked off appearing distinctly unimpressed. To this day I'm not sure what they were expecting or looking at!

By now, having spent nine days getting to, up and over the Alps, and a further seven days in Italy, I was enjoying the reality that I would get to Rome on time. I had covered about 1400 miles, and although punctuated by funny, joyful and satisfying moments, the majority of this time had been a tough and uncomfortable experience requiring gritty determination.

This changed completely with two days to go. Firstly, I was a day ahead of schedule, so with eighty miles to go, I cycled a short and easy forty miles each day. Secondly, I noticed my perspective shifted from 'coping' to 'freedom'. I developed a deep joy in what I was doing and a slight sense of melancholy that I was about to finish this short but significant chapter in my life. One of the most unexpected feelings was a sudden strong desire to slow down and savour every moment.

These last two days passed far too quickly, and I found myself arriving in Rome. However, there was still one puzzle and one surprise to come. I approached the city from the top of one of its seven hills surveying the view that I had been planning to reach for almost six months. I felt an enormous sense of pride in what I had achieved. After five minutes of savouring this moment, I headed off to find the Colosseum which was the agreed meeting point with my partner.

Thirty minutes later, I returned to the top of the same hill after having cycled in a big circle. The tantalisingly close view of Rome became a mocking scene, laughing at my ability to navigate across a continent, but not into a city.

A further thirty minutes later, I eventually found the road down to

Rome which was very steep. With about fifty metres to go (although I didn't realise this with corners in the way), my constantly braking wheels changed their noise from a normal rubbing sound to a squeal. The friction rich brake pads had worn out to reveal the almost frictionless metal base. Now unable to slow down, I was ejected from the hill and unwittingly accelerated round the corner on to the main road filled with fast-moving traffic.

My mind was numb with the sudden danger. I gripped the handlebars and clenched my teeth as if this could magically protect me. I rigidly pointed my bike along the road trying not to swerve into a car or lorry expecting a huge impact at any moment. A likely combination of the Italian drivers' Formula One reflexes and good fortune intervened to avoid causing a fatal accident.

My final wonderful discovery on this trip was that a few spare hours with a bike is a great way to see a lot more of a city than can be seen on foot. After two or three hours of pleasant meandering around Rome, seeing more than I had seen on foot in several previous visits and enjoying a couple of local beers, I slowly and quite reluctantly cycled to the Colosseum.

My adventure came to a delightful end with meeting my other half and, to my wonderful surprise, my family. They found me lying on a stone bench, looking up at the sun-drenched pillars of this historical wonder of the world in front of a perfect blue sky dotted with occasional crisp white fluffy clouds and birds flying around the top. It is a memory I can still see years later with perfect clarity.

Few days pass without being reminded of a memory or a lesson from this eighteen-day adventure and it remains an achievement that I am very proud of, including the £6000 I raised for Help for Heroes. This was the first adventure that opened my mind to realise I could achieve so much more than I thought I could, and since then I have been far better at taking on challenges.

When life presents tough or seemingly insurmountable challenges, I would advise, say "yes". Succeeding against a struggle takes guts and perseverance which is how we grow in both abilities and spirit. Pushing ourselves with new and exciting challenges stretches us and redefines our limits allowing us to do more in life. And what could be wrong with that?

Email: **chrislansdowne@gmail.com**

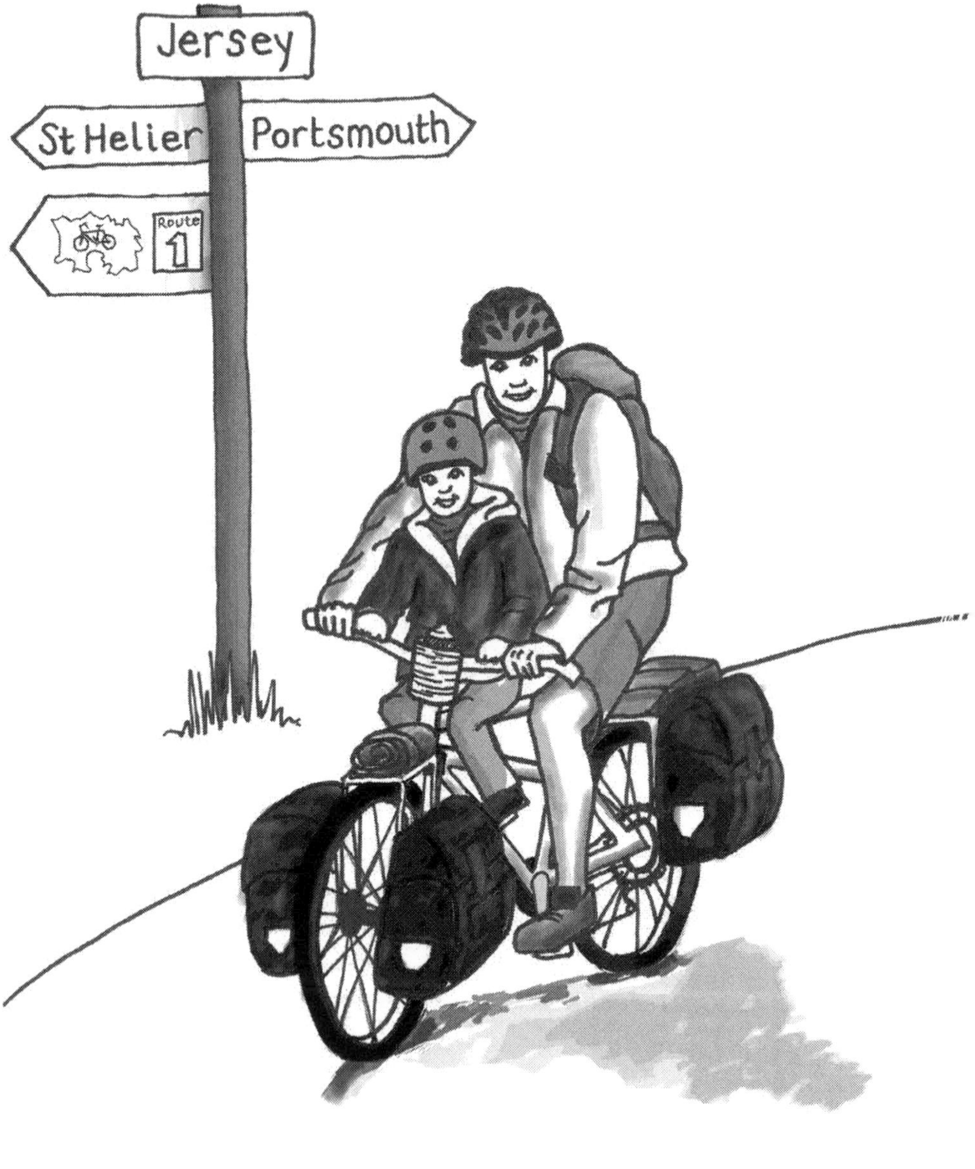
Jersey
St Helier
Portsmouth
Route
1

Chapter 25

Go Daddy!

By Geoff Long

They say that true love is catching the vomit of your own child… Well as I stood on a ferry in front of 150 or so passengers, with puke dribbling through my fingers and strangers passing me tissues to help deal with the situation, I guess I was proving my commitment.

These poor people had paid extra for the privilege of 'stunning panoramic sea views' as they 'relaxed in the reclining seats of the Horizon Lounge'. Instead, they got me dealing with my five-year-old boy's lack of sea-legs.

So there we were. Not the most auspicious start to our last minute, leap-of-faith, bike-packing trip – but it is one of the memories from it that we still laugh about years later.

Josh had not long turned five when we found ourselves on that ferry – I'd split with his Mum when he was only a year or so old. Even with a good few years of 'single-Dadding' under my belt, I still held onto a massively strong fear of getting it wrong and nursed a deep desire to make up for the imperfect mess that I'd created by breaking up our family.

Let's go back a while…

Josh's Mum and I had been together about eight years when he was born. As can often be the case, the view of us from the outside may well have presented a fairly rosy picture. A young professional couple, recently returned from a big trip, travelling and volunteering around the world for eighteen months. Returning to the UK full of new experiences and wild stories of Easter Island, the Galapagos, living in the Himalayas and diving with whale sharks and hammerheads. All that, plus we were coming home to a decent house, were financially comfortable and had a couple of lovely cats to complete the picture of domestic bliss – what could possibly be wrong...

Unfortunately, the reality wasn't as simple or as positive. In addition to making a break from the rat-race and escaping from the daily office grind, part of our original reason for travelling was to get our relationship to a better place. I'd been away back-packing and cycle touring on a number of occasions before, including a big thirteen-month trip. This created quite a mismatch in our past life-experiences, which we hoped might be smoothed over somewhat with a massive dose of shared memories in exotic places.

Well, the sad fact is that it didn't quite work out like that. Travelling is a stressful business. In some ways it taught us to get through difficult situations together, and for sure, we gained some pretty amazing experiences and memories. But memories in themselves can't resolve those underlying cracks within a relationship.

There's a huge lesson in itself right there – don't waste your emotions, dreams and desires, voyeuristically drooling over that photo of the 'perfect' couple on a tropical beach, longing for *their* life. Even if the image *is* real and the couple genuine and not staged, Photoshopped click-bait marketing. The fact is, life isn't about looking gorgeous on a beach for that $1/250^{th}$ of a second as the shutter blinks. It's about the real, less than glossy, messy moments and the perfect collection of imperfectness that we all are.

Suffice to say that when we came back, it felt like things hadn't really changed too much at all. There was no doubt that there was a bit of 'back to the real world with a bump', where the everyday nine-to-five felt a little flat compared to life on the road. Lingering doubts about our relationship were surely amplified by these post-trip blues.

Having said that, my misgivings remained fairly well hidden – by me.

You know when something isn't right in your life, but you don't really confront or acknowledge it? Let alone sort it. We push this stuff down, keep the awkward stuff in our subconscious, slightly out of focus... We're so often masters of 'not going there' when it comes to facing the dark and difficult stuff. And hand in hand with that stuff comes the shame. I had an intense feeling that I *should* keep the relationship going. I *needed* to be in a happy family. I *had* to make this work – I couldn't contemplate the alternative. My successful brother was happily married with kids. My sister too. And aged thirty-eight, I felt like I really should be settling down and doing the right thing... this just had to work.

So things carried on as they were, and despite my underlying misgivings, my partner and I continued as a couple and even decided to try for a child.

Within eighteen months of returning, we found out we were expecting a baby, and this is where life took a new direction. No surprise there... there aren't many bigger events in your life than becoming a parent. But whilst the recognition of that was definitely going on, there was another painful realisation that punched me right in the guts. All those suppressed emotions surfaced, they were laid bare, unavoidable and hit me right between the eyes: I didn't want to be in this relationship.

This moment initiated a new and horribly painful stage of my life. Wow! Why the hell wait until now to acknowledge that I didn't want to be with my partner? In the midst of what should have been joyous news, this felt like madness – but I couldn't deny it. It was like someone had switched on a light to illuminate a sign which announced the fact.

I must clarify here that I'd always wanted kids. I'd never understood people who didn't. And whilst not denying the inevitable shock of finding out that I was to be a father, it was quite obvious my feelings of being unsettled were not simply related to the news of us expecting. The issue was not becoming a father. The problem was of feeling that I was *with* the wrong person to raise that child.

Again, despite my now clarified doubts, I didn't have the courage or strength to step away from the situation. I might have realised that I still had serious doubts about our relationship, but I still didn't want this to be the way it worked out – it wasn't the family dream I had in my head – a broken family surely couldn't be my destiny…

Thoughts of loyalty, duty, comfort and familiarity became mixed with and amplified by fear – fear of the shame and abuse I would endure if I walked away. Shame I imagined directed at me by others, and probably more powerfully, shame that I would aim at myself.

We became immersed in the progression of scans and checks that are part and parcel of pregnancy and we remained together. The fact was that, right now, I still wanted to support my partner and I still wanted a child. Part of me tried harder than ever to keep things on an even keel – we *can* make this work. We *must* make this work.

Maybe, as you read this, I come across as weak, someone unable to direct his life in a clear and mindful direction. Indeed, there's plenty of evidence of me not dealing with various situations in the best way over the years… so sure, in part you're probably right. But similarly I'd wager, it's not an uncommon situation for people to get themselves into. We are so often doing the best we can. Life is messy and quite often there isn't a 'right' answer where everything comes good. Often, we are facing situations that we have little or no experience of. All too frequently we are emotionally incapable and uneducated to handle the feelings and circumstances we find ourselves in. It's less true these days, but during my educational era, school focused on facts and figures – not the elements of emotion, the mysteries of mood and the riddles of relationships.

And so Josh was born, and it gave our relationship a new found focus. To go through the experience of child-birth with someone can't help but bring people closer together, and at some level, provide a permanent connection. But, once again, this milestone didn't remove the existing issues I had with our relationship.

It wasn't until another two years had passed that we split properly. Over that period, we slowly divided our lives financially and emotionally. A trial separation was followed by the decision that things weren't reparable, and that we must make the move to live in separate houses permanently, agreeing to share the responsibility for our son fifty – fifty, both financially and time-wise.

I've been told by many over the years that this is still not the norm. More often than not, a child spends the majority of time with their mother, with the phrase, "I only see my dad every (or every other) weekend," being a common one. But, this wasn't what I wanted. I needed to be near Josh as much as I could, and it was irrelevant now whether the fault of my failed relationship lay with me, or was just a simple case of the wrong people getting together. My ideal family vision was in tatters, and all I could focus on was doing everything I could to give Josh the best life possible.

*

And so I set out as a co-parenting single Dad, with a heady mix of fear and excitement clouded by a still strong sense of shame and sadness about how I'd got here. The emotional baggage generated by my journey so far was surprisingly heavy. And for some reason I decided that I needed to carry it all with me...

So it goes without saying that the first few years weren't so easy. There was obviously a significant amount of re-adjustment required to living on my own, and this was compounded by the usual practical, logistical and emotional challenges of raising a toddler.

With a full-time job, it was a case of juggling the shopping, cooking and cleaning when I could, and to be honest, keeping my head above water.

In truth, I find it difficult to recount this time with great clarity – something that I think isn't uncommon in parents of young children! The cloud of sleep deprivation adding to the blur of what happened and when. What I do recall is the ever present desire to be with Josh and do things with him. Read – sing – dance – laugh…

We developed little habits which would make us both giggle, like saying goodnight in as many different ways as possible – "In a while crocodile!", "Take care polar bear!", "Bye bye butterfly", "Be sweet parakeet!", "Out the door dinosaur!", "Too da loo kangaroo!" and so on! These moments, often silly, but far from meaningless, began to build a stronger and stronger bond between us. And due to the nature of the single parent, there is no one else to dilute this connection.

Of course he had his Mother when he was with her, but when he was with me it was just us, it was our time, one on one. This brings an intensity to a relationship that you don't get in a 'normal' two-parent arrangement. Inevitably, there is the possibility of downsides to having the undivided attention of a parent, but there are certainly some serious upsides too.

Given the traumatic path that I took to get to this point with Josh, the existence of these positives took a while to dawn on me. There were still days when I would walk out of the house with Josh and it would feel like everybody was staring at me with critical and accusing eyes. It was as if I had a whole bunch of signs over my head saying "Failed his family!" "Bad parent!" "Struggling single Dad!"

Of course no one was thinking this – no one knew my history or would necessarily have said those things even if they had. It was purely a projection of my own self-doubt and anxieties. But with that ugliness still rearing its head at times, it was even more crucial that I started to acknowledge the positives. I needed to begin to shed some of the shame and the idea that I'd destroyed everything, and replace it with thoughts that I was actually doing OK.

In fact, not just OK. I was actually creating something special. It didn't happen overnight, but slowly a wonderful realisation began to come over me... this little human, as well as growing himself, was making me grow and healing me. Something I'd not really given a lot of thought to previously. He was teaching me stuff every day, making me reflect on my own behaviour and giving me purpose.

With every giggle, every sparkle I saw in his eyes and every smile that he sent my way, I got a shot of unconditional love that was like an intravenous injection of hope and redemption. A child's innocence and their ability to experience pure joy is a delight to observe. Where an adult's reaction is too often tainted by a lifetime of learnt responses, filters and 'appropriate' conduct, a kid reacts intuitively, from their gut. Sure, this means sometimes you get some pretty direct and not always reasonable or balanced behaviour, but you also get a refreshing honesty that has a fantastic ability to help sweep away, or at least bring into focus, some of the baggage we collect as we 'mature'. The cynicism, sarcasm, suspicion and all those other delightful feelings that we can end up relying on rather too much as adults. Watching a child's elation about the simplest things is a precious antidote to low mood or depression.

As the months and years went on, I began to feel myself settle into being a father. It was 2015. Josh had just turned five and summer was fast approaching. I was trying to work out what we could do together for a holiday. This always brought back the sadness of the split, memories of my own family holidays and a tendency to feel sorry for myself as I reflected on the fact that it was still just Josh and me. It brought up those self-conscious feelings of being 'the single Dad', conspicuous amongst the happy families on the campsite or playing at the beach.

I decided that I wasn't going to let these lingering reservations control me. Maybe there was an element of wanting to prove that not only were we going on holiday, but we were going to do something pretty cool...

I'd always loved to travel, explore and take the less orthodox path (quite literally) wherever possible. If the well-worn route went left, I'd veer right and fight my way along the overgrown assault course of a track if there was one. If there was no track to find, I'd scramble my way through the scrub just to avoid the feeling that I was following the crowd. So the idea of adventure wasn't new to me, but it was a different thing to tackle with a young boy in tow. The responsibility for his safety added to the questions whizzing around my head about what was possible, sensible and practical.

I'd done a reasonable amount of cycle touring in the past, including surviving on some pretty hairy roads in India, getting lost in Norway, and a fairly major and icy jaunt around New Zealand. But cycle touring... we're talking a pair of shorts, half a tooth brush, porridge oats and a tiny lightweight tent... how was that going to pan out with clothes for two, child friendly food and other kiddie paraphernalia?

As it was, the thing that spurred me on was that Josh and I had already spent a lot of time on a bike together. He did ride himself, but since he was very small (six months plus), if we ever had to go anywhere around town, we'd always go together on my bike. The seating arrangement was one that put him in front of me, between my arms and where he held on to the handlebars as well. Thankfully, he had grown out of the phase where he thought it was fun to grab the brakes or randomly try to steer us into the bushes!

We'd done hundreds of miles like this, and in all weathers, so I was confident in the set-up, but it would be a different ball game with a full set of panniers and a tent. Would the bike handle the weight? Moreover, would I?

I never lacked faith in Josh's ability to cope. I knew he was strong enough for it. By this point, he had survived a few years of being cycled to nursery in the face of horizontal rain as we made our way along the seafront into the prevailing south-westerlies. I remember a number of occasions where I noticed he was looking to the side and realised that he was trying to avoid being pummelled directly by the raindrops, which he used to call, "bullets"! I would hold a hand in front of his face in an attempt to shield him and kids in passing cars would stare aghast as they cruised passed in comfort on their way to school. But this was all character-building stuff, and having spent so long on the bike together, I knew we had an innate ability to balance and ride as one.

And so I went for it and booked one adult, one child and one bike on a ferry from Poole to Jersey. After a frantic few weeks attaching racks, packing and repacking panniers and thinning-out kit to a bare minimum, we were ready to go. Or as ready as we were ever going to be.

*

It can be a little intimidating walking or cycling onto the car-deck of a ferry – but I think Josh's main feeling was already one of pride. We were off on an expedition together! We had everything we needed – a tent, sleeping bags, cooker and food. All strapped to the bike that was going to help us explore Jersey. It's a pretty thrilling feeling as an adult, so I'm guessing when you're only five it's really quite something.

For me, I had a stormy mixture of emotions – in parallel with the relief that we'd made it on board with hopefully everything we needed, I had a heap of anxiety about what I'd got us into... Was it sensible to be cycling across Jersey with a fully loaded bike and small child on-board? What if it was super windy? What if a rack broke on the first big bump with so much weight? What if it was too hilly for me to ride? Was I just being supremely irresponsible putting a small child in this situation?

As a parent you spend a lot of time trying to look like you know what you're doing, answering questions to which we really aren't qualified to respond, acting like everything is under control in order that our offspring feel safe, whilst inside you are grappling with problems and wrestling doubts. I was definitely battling with such feelings on that ferry. But ultimately, having Josh with me was a help not a hindrance. His presence gave me strength and courage to tackle whatever came our way.

Putting ourselves in challenging situations like this is what builds us. For sure there are easier options, but they don't come with the rewards you get for trusting in your own legs, lungs and mind to physically and mentally get you somewhere.

And so we arrived in Jersey, having survived the vomiting incident that started this story off. We witnessed the kindness of strangers who came to our rescue, giving me some much needed positivity and a bit of calm to my unsettled thoughts about the trip. We were off!

Two-up on the bike with a full set of four panniers, handle-bar bag and two-man tent. From the glances of onlookers as we cycled off the ferry, it was obvious we hadn't chosen the most conventional transport option, but we wouldn't have wanted to be anywhere else. OK, so we weren't stepping onto Antarctica or some other wild location, but it really felt like we were setting out on a great adventure together.

At times like this, the phrase, "It's about the journey not the destination," ring particularly true. Just travelling as we were had made the trip special already, without 'doing anything', without ticking the obligatory tourist experience boxes, which we are often made to feel are compulsory if want a good holiday.

Being so physically close on the bike meant we could chat all the time, talking about what direction we should go and the sights we were seeing. When we hit the first big hill Josh was like an on-board motivational coach! "Go Daddy! You can do it! Go! Go! Go!" I can't imagine that there is a better form of inspiration out there than your own child between your arms shouting encouragement – the hills weren't going to be a problem.

In a couple of hours, we'd made it to the campsite and set about sorting out our base. It's surprising how much stuff you can cram into four panniers. Unpacking, we created a scene that looked a bit like our bike had simply fallen over and exploded.

Once we'd got things ship-shape, we started on dinner. In itself, this was an exciting business, as we were using a multi-fuel primus-style burner, which sounds a bit like a jet engine taking off and has flames to match. This contraption is slightly terrifying to work with but a small child's dream, and soon enough, our neighbour's two young boys were over to investigate. They were fascinated by how we'd arrived by bike, how we were cooking and why such an inferno was involved.

Their camping arrangements were a world away. Along with their two parents, they were travelling in style. A gargantuan inflatable family tent sat alongside a huge four wheel drive vehicle, surrounded by a collection of bikes and other toys strewn around everywhere you looked. The contrast with our minimalist camp was striking, but the boys seemed more than happy to abandon all of their toys to join Josh and I sitting on our bike helmets, slicing stuff up with a big Opinel camp knife and cooking up dinner. As we got to know the family better during the week, the difference in our lifestyle was to become even more apparent and it was to be a great lesson about how 'less can be more'.

In the meantime, it was just great to arrive, to be there and feel like we had everything we needed however minimal our possessions. We had a week ahead to be together just the two of us and explore.

*

The next morning, we set off for a trip along the north coast. We went down to two rear panniers for day trips. Even with the loss of the bags, we were still quite a unit – full kit for the day, plus eighty kilograms of me and another eighteen kilograms of five-year-old.

Wherever possible, we were going old-school – navigating by map, land marks and road signs. That combined with being intimately immersed in the countryside on the bike, makes for a fantastic way to really engage with where you are and appreciate the sights, sounds and nuances of a place.

Travelling under your own steam also gives a true perspective of scale and terrain. You notice distance, you notice hills and your brain naturally keeps track of where you are far more innately than when whizzing along in a car.

Cruising quietly around the back lanes, we could hear the birds, farm animals and the wind in the trees. We stopped wherever we wanted to take photos, investigate fields of Jersey's famous potatoes and inspect beetles as we spotted them crawling across the road. It was lovely to travel together like this and our first trip swept away any lingering doubts about whether this whole thing had been a sensible idea.

As the week progressed, we refined our camp, making use of discarded camp chairs which we brought back to life with some old cable and string. The crook in the trunk of a nearby tree became our natural cooler for milk and butter. We also made some small refinements to the bike set-up with Josh making himself a water bottle holder from an empty baked-bean can bungee-corded to the handlebars just in from of him.

More porridge and pain au chocolat powered trips around the island followed over the following few days. They included a low-tide ride out along the causeway to Elizabeth Castle off St Helier, which didn't do wonders for the bike's gears, but was a lot of fun. Josh was lapping up the sense of adventure created by heading off every day and finding our way to new coves and harbours, enjoying a gadget-free, basic-living lifestyle. He also revelled in simple achievements that are huge from the perspective of a young kid, like cooking his own bacon breakfast on the mildly terrifying MSR stove.

As our week progressed, we got to know our neighbouring campers better, and they offered to give us a lift to the far side of the island for the day. It was doable on the bike, but wouldn't leave much time to enjoy the beach and would probably involve cycling back in the dark, so I accepted. It was this trip that actually did a lot to highlight exactly what we had and maybe in the moment hadn't quite realised.

Finding ourselves in the back of a top-of-the-range leather seated 4x4 'spaceship', we might well have been expected to feel like royalty. But as we sat there dashing across the island, all we felt was a bit claustrophobic and very detached from where we were and where we were heading. Our neighbour's two kids were even more removed from their immediate environment – staring at screens in the back of the headrests, Bluetooth headphones isolating them from everything other than the film playing twelve inches from their faces. It was a world away from our relatively slow, but engaging pace of travel on the bike together, and with both of us feeling a bit cooped-up and queasy, we were very pleased when the journey was over and we reached our destination.

I hope this recollection doesn't sound ungrateful – it isn't meant to and it was lovely to share the day with the other family on the beach. But it really helped me see what I was able to give Josh without many tens of thousands of pounds worth of car, a plethora of toys and all the latest gadgets. Maybe I was actually able to give him a whole lot more.

Josh is ten now. He still has a Jersey sticker on his bike helmet five years on and when I told him about writing this story and asked him for his recollections of the trip, a bunch of enthusiastic memories came pouring out. I guess that must be a good sign.

In addition to my story of being a single Dad, I'd also like to emphasise that it is *totally* possible to have adventures with kids. People are often surprised about how much I've done with Josh, and sometimes have the attitude that becoming a parent equates to a loss of freedom and a reduction in the type of activities that can be undertaken.

Of course there are some physical limitations which restrict what kids can do. With some practical adaptations and a change of expectation in terms of things like distance and speed, it is completely realistic to share some fantastic adventures with your children. I'm sure there's no need to labour the benefits of doing this –building confidence, trust and fitness, expanding knowledge through active learning, planning and self-sufficiency are just a few of the positives.

These 'adventures' can come in many forms... from camping in the garden, a bike ride in the nearest forest or a walk up your nearest hill. They don't need to be epic adventures worthy of the Discovery Channel to leave lasting memories in your kid's minds. Start small and build up as your confidence (as well as theirs) grows.

The road back from a traumatic relationship split can be really tough. As I've learnt, any self-criticism that you already have within you is only amplified by feelings of failure and doubt about the future. But anything's possible. I made a commitment to keep getting out there and doing stuff for both Josh and myself. I chose to show up and keep putting the effort in, even when I doubted myself. I now live with a new partner, and whilst I completely appreciate the benefits of living in a two-parent family, my journey taught me about the genuine positives of spending one-to-one time with a child.

When I started out, I imagined that being a single Dad was simply a sign of failure, when in fact it actually drove me to become a stronger person. It has given me a close and meaningful relationship with my son. What more could I ask for?

Website: **geofflong.co.uk**

Instagram: **@bigtriphippy**

Chapter 26

In Search of Simba

By Abigail Mann

As I forcefully ejected the last dregs of bile from my quivering stomach, I vowed to myself, never again. It was 3am and the velvet black night felt just as ominous as the feat I was enduring.

My ribs were on fire from the last tumble on the rocks. My legs were like old, rusty hinges; they threatened to seize up at any moment. My hands were ice and I could barely see ten metres ahead of me.

There was not a single person in sight. An eerie silence enveloped the space.

I was on top of Ben Nevis in some of the worst conditions in almost twenty-five years. I feared danger, but there was a strange sense of calm pervading as if my mind knew that panic would worsen things. For a moment, I allowed myself to retrace the events that led to this nightmare...

*

As a young child, I would often hike with my parents and siblings. My father once made us walk twelve miles from Nottingham along the River Trent to our house in the village of Hickling. I spent my entire childhood outside: climbing trees; making rope swings; building rafts from anything my siblings and I could find. Our only rule was to be back before it got dark. Perhaps, this was the birth of my spirit of adventure?

By young adulthood, my attention turned to what I then considered to be far more exciting 'adventures' with friends. Somewhere along the way, my desire for the great outdoors waned and I, along with every other young adult making their way in the world, succumbed to the routine of work.

At age thirty, I reconnected with the great outdoors. Despite having never hiked any mountains before, I decided to climb Ben Nevis. At midnight. The reason for such idiocy was that I had also booked a knee-jerk trip to climb Kilimanjaro. So what better preparation than having a play around on Nevis? Thus, my story unfolds…

My adventure began at Euston Station. Eager and excited, I was ready to depart an hour before the train arrived. Or so I thought. Anticipation was running high. I sauntered down to the terminal, breezily handed my ticket to the attendant and attempted to sail by.

"Hold on a minute," he declared. "Wrong ticket."

Cue my first error. I'd misread the timetable board and missed my train. My exuberance draining like a punctured balloon, I allowed negative thoughts to creep in. The whole idea was insane. Who did I think I was going off on a solo adventure to climb a bloody great mountain through the middle of the night!? Shackleton I was not. I couldn't even catch a train on time.

Once aboard the next train, my journey became interesting. I met a lovely lady who decided I needed tea before the big climb, endured some apoplectic drunks and a kind soul shared his homemade lunch with me. Finally, one man absolutely insisted I take his window seat as I'd never been to Scotland on the train and in his words, 'Ye'll nay get a better view, lass!' He was right; the views were beguiling.

At Fort William, I was happy to meet other hikers and any nerves I felt dissipated as we discussed the various training we'd done. I came across two young ladies in the toilets. They seemed woefully ill-prepared.

"Do you think we'll be okay in trainers?" one apprehensively enquired.

I uttered a reluctant, "Maybe."

"Oh my God. What have we got ourselves into?" she replied.

If only we knew.

There were around four hundred hikers in total and plenty of guides would be stationed at various points along the mountain trail. Before long, we were informed of poor conditions. There was snow on the mountain at the summit and rain and wind were scheduled. Visibility would not be ideal. Not ideal? What does that mean? I had booked to do this in June to avoid this. Oh, how naive I was! The weather on Ben Nevis is never predictable. Nerves took hold and my insides churned.

"One final safety measure: never stray from the path. There will be areas on top that might feel like solid footing, but in actual fact you are standing on a snow cornice. This is nothing more than a layer of snow at the edge of the mountain. It is incredibly dangerous to be near these!"

Terrifying thoughts of falling through snow swarmed my mind.

"There will be sufficient markers along the way, so be sure to look out for these. They are glow sticks," the lead guide proudly confirmed.

What? Glow sticks? This isn't some nineties rave, I agonised. Where are the proper markers? You know, big bright lights that lead the way? Glow sticks!? What were these people thinking? More to the point, what was I thinking when I decided to do something which appeared to my novice self to be so utterly dangerous?

Our route began at the base crossing a large suspension footbridge. Pacing across this, I concocted a plan. If I was to get through this, I needed to get talking. And so I did. I met a lovely group of older hikers and it soon became apparent that they were much fitter than me! A third of the way up, I was struggling. I felt like I was holding them back and was more than a little embarrassed. Feeling the pressure, I encouraged them to go on ahead. Solo it was.

The first leg was a tough hike up a well-marked path. Bulky steps that resembled giant's toes seemed to go on forever. I pushed on through, keen to keep moving. As darkness claimed the land, I approached the halfway mark.

"Right, get yourselves wrapped up warm and waterproofed. The weather is turning fast," our guide bellowed.

It was here that I began to feel mildly unwell. I ploughed on ignoring the nausea to the next section - a series of zig zags- until I reached the plateau. This section of the hike seemed to be well marked and there were plenty of guides to keep me motivated, but I was spent.

The weather had deteriorated as fast as my energy levels. Rain that had previously lashed down turned to snow and visibility reduced to five meters. To top it off, I kept on stumbling like a new-born giraffe. Ice covered the path; conditions were haphazard and I was a mess. I'm not ashamed to say I had a little cry. I knew I would get to the top, but the fear of getting down saturated all thoughts.

Once I'd reached the plateau, snow had thickened everywhere and I was told later on that it was three meters deep in parts. The lovely group I encountered on the way up were already on their way back down. Sleep deprived and demoralised, I slogged on.

It was about 2am when I reached the summit. I'd like to say I was elated. Truly overjoyed that I'd made it. But that would be lying. I'd made a sign to hold for that precious photograph moment, but the conditions were so bad and my hands so anaesthetised by cold I could barely grip. I took one useless photo and that was that.

The summit guide surveyed my sorry condition and wisely commanded, "Stop dithering. You have five minutes to re-energise and drink tea before leaving."

Suits me just fine, I acquiesced. The only problem was, I was drained. How on earth was I going to get back down? I longed for the support of someone else.

Trudging across the plateau was demanding. I fell at least twice, once bashing my ribs. It was at this point that I realised I was completely alone. I couldn't see a soul. The snow had stopped and a strange silence fell across the mountain. It was almost peaceful. Almost. Where were the guides? Where were the other hikers? Confusion mixed with serenity is an odd combination whilst still in the throes of danger atop a mountain. Resolute that the only way off this thing was down, I continued.

About fifty feet further along, something didn't feel right. I'd lost my bearings. I realised I hadn't seen a glow stick for some time. Heart racing and slowly, as if on a tightrope, I retraced my steps until I found the route again. Then I threw up. Exhaustion and adrenaline were not a great mix.

Two more hours passed before I saw another person. It was torture. A stint in the doctor's tent after throwing up twice more was required and it took longer to get down than up! It was the longest, toughest nine hours of my life.

I was told by the guides that they had stopped around two hundred people from continuing shortly after I had made it. That explained the lack of people! A new found sense of pride washed over me. Still, as I drank a steaming cup of tea, I vowed to myself never to climb that mountain again. At least climbing Kilimanjaro would be better, I thought. I'd have a group of fellow hikers with me there...

When I booked the trip to climb Kilimanjaro, I envisioned meeting other hikers on my tour group, all keen to test out their sparkly new gear. The day before the hike, two men arrived as guides; the first introduced himself as Hosea. His smile exuded warmth, but he seemed so frail; his movements were sloth-like, slow and cumbersome. The second man did not smile at all and said absolutely nothing. It was at this point I was reliably informed that I was the only traveller on the tour 'group' booking and that I would be hiking Kili alone.

Alone! This was not what I signed up for. How could it have happened? I wanted singing, dancing, camaraderie and, at the very least, someone to share the incredible experience with at the end of each tiresome day. Instead, I'd got one man who in all honesty looked like he couldn't hike a flight of stairs and Mr. Mute to keep me company. Perfect. Why had I decided to do this again? To top it all off, I wasn't yet over the previous traumatic adventure.

That evening, my thoughts raced from 'What if I fall ill and no one notices?' to 'Can you actually fall off the edge of this mountain?' The rational side of me wanted to believe it was going to be fine. I'd met two travellers the previous evening who had just completed the climb. They raved about how awesome it was: the changes in scenery, the food, the exhilaration you feel upon summiting. But they had each other to experience it together. Who had I got? I felt completely alone.

Nervously packing my bag, I thought, to hell with it. It had to be done. This was, after all, a charity climb. No backing out now.

The next morning, glorious sunlight flooded my room. I had slept lightly due to monkeys bouncing around on my roof! I'd like to tell you that the monkeys' exuberant attitudes had a positive effect and that I too bounced out of bed with a newfound sense of bravery, vigour and adventure on my mind. But in reality, I was still a bag of gibbering nerves akin to that of a fledgling about to take its first leap into the terrifying unknown.

When Hosea arrived, he introduced me to the rest of the hiking team. There were five in total: two guides, one cook and two porters. I soon came to understand the enormous team effort involved in taking just one person up the mountain and instantly regretted my initial thoughts about my trusted guides. Keen to dissipate nerves, I jumped onto their van.

At the base, the gates were bustling with excitement. I was told that at any given time there are ten thousand people on Kili. What an insane fact! I made a mental note not to leave a shred of waste behind. As a solo hiker, I was allowed to skip the snaking queue and head straight to the gate. Filled with anticipation, I set off.

"Pole, pole," Hosea kept saying over and over again. "Slowly, slowly."

He didn't need to tell me twice. I was in awe at the incredible rainforest scenery. Kilimanjaro has layers of terrain. Each day of the hike uncovered a new and beautiful landscape. Day one was spent hiking through the thick rainforest. Enormous green canopies provided shade as we slowly ascended the mountain. Mist enshrined the magical forest. Surreptitious Colobus monkeys swung through the trees.

Halfway through the day, we came across a tree trunk that had been absolutely savaged.

"Leepud," Hosea remarked. "One of big five!"

So, there were leopards roaming the area? Wonderful. Nothing like a predatory cat to keep you moving!

As we neared the first campsite, I glimpsed my first sight of Kili. A glorious guardian standing proudly over its land. Mesmerising, yet still so far away.

At Machame camp, I signed the log book and was told to rest. This was okay, I thought. Not too bad. I might actually be able to do this.

Camp was filled with other hikers and it was there that I began to notice the kindness of strangers. Plenty of them came to chat. Most couldn't believe I was hiking alone. That night, with Kili in the distance and the sun casting a bronzed light over my tent, I went to bed smiling.

Day two arrived and we set off early, but as the day progressed I began to feel unwell. I had hoped to avoid it, but enter altitude sickness. Dizziness, nausea, lethargy and, for me, an upset stomach. I was feeling sufficiently sorry for myself, not least because the hike had become more physically demanding. Scrambling over large, often deep, crevices and pulling myself up onto ledges, all whilst keeping out of other (much faster) hikers' ways, was proving a challenge. But what a place! We had risen high above the rainforest and were traversing across open, rocky spaces littered with flora and fauna of all kinds. It was breathtakingly beautiful.

Arriving at Shira Plateau that evening felt heavenly. A soft, blanket of fluffy, billowing cloud had settled beneath us for miles on end. Once again, as the sun sank gracefully, the light in camp changed from soft orange hues to dusty pinks and I began to feel truly thankful to be there.

I'd become a bit of a landmark feature in camp as people noticed when I was making it to each checkpoint.

"Hey! Abbie, you made it!" a fellow hiker shouted. "Guys, Abbie's here." Cue lots of whoops and hollers. It felt good to be welcomed.

Day three arrived like a bad dream. Sickness took hold the minute I turned my head. Anything I tried to eat or drink didn't go down. I set off utterly miserable, dehydrated and hungry. The day went from bad to worse and my pace was snail speed. I stopped persistently to double over in an attempt to take away the sickness. Hosea could see I was worsening and took the executive decision to take me down to our acclimatisation camp, instead of up to Lava Tower, a stunning viewpoint about three hundred meters higher. I'd like to say I argued. You know, put on a brave face and demanded to be taken there, but I simply nodded and continued my scamper down resembling an old hunchback from a children's fairy tale.

Once we arrived at camp, I rolled into my tent and cried and cried. It was over. I knew it. Glancing out of the tent door, I could see Kili in the distance. 'Take a picture here as this is the closest you're going to get to it,' I thought. 'This is it. The end of the road. You've failed.'

Hosea could hear my woeful sniffling. With his slow, calming movements, the ones I was so quick to judge during our first encounter, he smiled softly and handed me some welcome tea.

"Be strong, like Simba," he cajoled. "This is normal. Tomorrow, strong like Simba again."

I'd never felt so weak.

Waking the following morning, sure to feel the same way, I decided not to move. A few minutes passed and I felt fine. Maybe I would be okay to drink? A pint of Berocca later and I was utterly relieved. The sickness had dissipated. I had finally acclimatised. Relief washed over me.

That day, we tackled Barranco Wall, a near vertical four hundred metre wall. Alex Honnold, eat your heart out. Scrambling up the wall was thoroughly enjoyable. I watched in awe as the porters navigated each twist and turn like mountain goats - powerful and skilled the entire time, despite only wearing worn, tattered trainers. At the top, we were greeted with an enviable view of Kili. It was finally within reach. What looked like snow from the bottom of the mountain was in fact the overbearing and awesome Heim Glacier, a mountain of ice.

We began the final ascent at 12am the following day. I'd feared this moment, but to my surprise, I felt fine. Four hours in and I was really enjoying the hike. Tiny head torches snaked their way up the trail like a little army of fireflies guiding our way. It was truly spellbinding. But as the temperature dropped, so did my energy and

I once again became slow and sloth-like. A fellow hiker had spotted I was in trouble. He took the time to chat. He spoke of his family in Canada, why he was travelling and enquired upon what had brought me to Africa. Frozen to the core, I couldn't even put my coat on. After assisting, he suddenly stopped me.

"Quick, turn around!" he rushed. "Look, down there."

Right on cue, the blanket of clouds that I had become so accustomed to, parted and for a brief few moments we could see the sparkling lights of Moshi. Overwhelmed with emotion at how far we had come, we shared a knowing smile and he went on his way.

Once again, the kindness of strangers had shone.

After what felt like hours of Hosea saying, 'Almost,' I reached the summit at 7.23am. Ashy, rocky surface surrounded me; the place was other-worldly. The cone of Kili was so deep and vast that it became almost impossible to take in the true extraordinary beauty of the scene. Bursting with relief and happiness, tears fell and froze instantly. Hosea repeated, 'Simba, Simba,' over and over. I had just enough time to take a few pictures of the soul-searching sunrise and the famous Kili sign before my phone completely shut down. It was minus twenty degrees.

Climbing Kili was, at that point, the most challenging experience of my life. A kaleidoscope of emotions embroiled for first position in my mind, but the feeling that remains firmly rooted is that if it wasn't for the kindness of people like Hosea and the team, I would not have made it to the top. The mountain was charming, but the people were more so.

I spent the rest of that summer travelling around Tanzania and teaching English to Maasai tribesmen. I even visited Zanzibar where I met a man who told me all about his climb up the mountain. About how he'd chatted to a young woman who was finding it tough and how he'd helped her put her jacket back on. It took us both about an hour before we realised that I was that woman!

*

Fast forward a couple of years to 2017 and either my brain had complete amnesia or I was a foolish glutton for punishment. I somehow found myself about to embark upon the National Three Peaks challenge. To climb Ben Nevis, Scafell Pike and Snowdon all in under twenty-four hours. Had I forgotten the last time I had attempted Nevis? Or what the gruelling final ascent of Kili was like?

It's funny how the human mind works. Whenever we complete challenges, the brain somehow rewires things, tweaks memories and erases the negative so that you look upon them with nostalgia. A rose-tinted view of what you know deep down to be truly crippling feats. It's only when you're on another crazy hair-brained adventure that it all comes flooding back.

This time would be different. I had a companion for a start. Beka, a long term friend, who'd see me through the tough stretches.

At 10am on the day of the challenge, we set off in groups. Once again, it appeared there were hikers in the group much quicker than Little Miss Average here. Attempts to maintain pace were futile. We wilted like daffodils just shy of the halfway mark. To top things off, Beka fell sick.

"Go ahead without me," she requested. We had both trained consistently for the challenge, so knew we had to go for it. I scuttled on upwards in an attempt to catch my group. Like the runt of a litter, every time I caught up, they would move on and my energy was sapped in this tedious game of cat and mouse. Instead, I chose to go at my own pace and tried not to forget to look up.

Once I'd reached the top, I took a small amount of time to take stock. The summit was unrecognisable. Thoughts of how far I'd come since the last trek here invaded my mind. How different it was this time round.

It was the perfect day for hiking. A Picasso worthy mixture of pearly clouds, ocean blue skies and imposing rocky faces. This time, I saw everything: the lakes, the falls, the sheer number of mountains stacked up like soldiers. Rank upon rank, guardians of the highlands. Awe-struck moments like these are why we hike. The power the mountains have to render you so insignificant and utterly speechless is what keeps you coming back for more.

As the cool breeze tickled the hairs on my skin, I was brought out of my dreamy daze and back into challenge mode. Short on time, there was only one option: to run. With a grin as wide as my ears, I flew down the mountain to whoops and cheers from those I passed. What a rush!

Nearing the bottom, I saw Beka waving and a sense of achievement ensued. I'd made it down in four hours and forty-five minutes. Half the time it had taken me the first time round. I felt truly alive.

*

Six long hours later, our team arrived at Scafell Pike. Filled with the momentum of Nevis and buoyed with hope that this climb would be just as thrilling, Beka and I hopped out of the van and set off. As darkness fell, we ambled our way up the gravel track. At 978 meters high, Scafell Pike is 367 metres lower than Nevis. When you're about to climb it through the middle of the night, these sorts of facts are a welcome comfort blanket.

Lack of sleep is a devilish thing, isn't it? Have you ever tried to do anything at all on zero sleep? The simplest of tasks flummox you. Things like trying to open the front door of your house with the key fob for your car. Or putting the milk in the microwave instead of the fridge. We've all been there. So, it will come as no surprise to you, that my memory of hiking this stretch is hazy at best. What I do remember are two things: being chilled to the bone and getting lost several times.

The track up Scafell Pike is deceptive, more so when it is dark, so whilst the initial climb went well, the final ascent was what you might call a mixture of success. Beka had slipped behind so I was hanging on to a couple of other hikers for company. As we traversed higher, rain began to lash down; a punishment from the heavens for daring to think this might be an easier hike than Nevis. Menacing large boulders of rock jutted out from every angle. Trying to find a route through seemed hopeless. Even our guide had lost all ability to navigate through the scattered rock.

After some strenuous exertion, a number of false turns and an ocean of rainfall later, we finally reached the summit. To this day, I have no idea what that mountain looks like. We couldn't see a thing and the photo evidence of the fact I was there resembles an X Files image of an extra-terrestrial being: blurred, ghostly and terrifying. The elation I had felt on Nevis was a distant memory as I battled through the relentless frozen winds to reach base again. What should have taken me three hours actually took four.

It was 3am when I returned to the bus, the last in my group. The warmth I felt upon seeing my companion's smiley face was just about enough to offset the guilt I felt at slowing the group down. Thank goodness for great friends.

On the journey to Snowdon, a few lucky souls were able to get some sleep. Mine was a broken state of affairs. I drifted in and out of disturbed, hallucinatory sleep. Fall asleep. Wake up. Panic. Fall asleep. Wake up. Panic. As daylight arrived, sleep departed. Full of unspent sugar from the copious protein bars and gels I'd consumed in some kind of woeful attempt to feel prepared for the final push, I sat anxiously awaiting arrival. I'd convinced myself there was no way I would make it up another mountain. Queasiness swished around in the pit of my stomach. Throw up, my brain shouted. That way, you won't have to go up again. My thoughts betrayed me.

"Are you okay? You look pale," Beka remarked. Confession time.

"I'm not sure I can do another one," I whispered.

At that moment, our mountain guide requested silence as we pulled into Snowdon Car Park.

Piercing eyes and a commanding stare were followed with, "Right, listen carefully. A storm is heading our way. Gusts of up to fifty miles per hour are to be expected. Due to safety concerns…" Say it, I thought. Say we can't go up. "…due to safety concerns only some of you are permitted to go. If you think you can make it to the top in two hours, you may go. We will be asking some of you to stay behind."

Pick me. Pick me. Pick me!

As the guide spoke to the last of the team and got off the bus to prepare, I stared at Beka, despondent and resigned to quitting.

"You look like you're going to cry your eyes out," she honestly stated. "You can do this. It's just two more hours. Come on, get your stuff together."

Reluctantly, I began to get organised.

"Abbie, snap out of it and hurry up!" Beka demanded. Tough love at its best.

The first stretch of the Pyg Track begins gently, but pretty soon there are some craggy climbs and larger rocks to grapple. I was entering the gates of Mordor. Nothing about it was enjoyable. The weather was misery personified. It seemed determined to prevent my achievement. Shards of rain whipped my face in persistent malice, leaving behind bitter stings of intent. My efforts were cumbersome. So much so that I had the pleasure of a guide to myself. He chatted chirpily as we approached the half way marker. I knew his plan of distraction. I endured it because I myself had my own secret plan. Another hiker and I had plotted to reach the halfway point and then climb back down to the bus. It felt like failure, and it was, but I couldn't see another option. I was far too slow and nauseous to keep going.

"Almost halfway," the guide buzzed. "Just over those rocks there and you'll have just an hour or so to go."

That's what you think, I mused, sly grin creeping onto my face.

"That's it. Half way. Well done!" he chirped.

My eyes scanned the area. Left. Right. Up. Down. She was nowhere to be seen. Well this is just bloody marvellous, I thought. Tears cascaded down my windswept face as the inevitable crossed my mind.

"You can't go back down alone. There's only one way back now and that's up there," he pointed. Soul-destroyed. Sapped of life. Wrung out like a dirty dish cloth, I dragged my soggy, sorry self, one foot in front of the other, and accepted my fate.

"That's the spirit," he persisted. The next hour was spent avoiding looking up and listening intently to the wonderfully patient guide's instructions about how to preserve energy by staying high and following the path of least resistance. This, I realised, was all preparation for the steeper ascent that was about to befall us. The rocks were alive. Creeping up out of nowhere, shifting in pattern, shape and size like a magical, never-ending maze. Half way up that treacherous section, he turned back, took one look at me and smiled.

"What?" I enquired.

"You'll get to the top. Your eyes have perked up. I knew you had it in you."

And he was right. He'd got me to the top of Snowdon. After another begrudging scramble, a few scraped knees and countless curses to the open elements, I reached the summit at exactly twenty-two hours and twelve minutes after I had started the crazy adventure. I'd finally done it!

Since those tribulations, I've hiked countless mountains amongst other exciting adventures. Although these days I prefer to hike without timed conditions, I will always look back upon each adventure (and everyone I met) as seriously awesome feats that wouldn't have happened if I hadn't started saying yes. So, what are you waiting for? Go on, say yes.

Twitter: **@abbiemann1982**

Chapter 27

YES!tival

By Hannah Miller

Hey Hannah,

Thanks for getting in touch, it's so awesome that you are so local – it would be a crime not to get you along to Yestival!

We totally understand your situation and so glad that you messaged us as we would hate for budget to be the reason that someone didn't come to Yestival. We have a scheme called the kindness of strangers and it is a pot that many people donate to and when it reaches the cost of an adult ticket, then we are able to gift it to someone.

What do you say?

You and Seren can come and go all weekend as you like :)

Come and find me at some point so I can say hi and have a cuddle ;)

Big hugs

Emms x

With nine days to go, and slight trepidation, I replied 'Yes!' I was going to Yestival 2018 and I was going with my five-month-old daughter.

Just a few days before, I had found myself revisiting the SayYesMore website.

> Yestival is a celebration of ideas and inspiration with trailblazing, change-making speakers, tented workshops and a sense of adventure designed to set you on a new path.

Yes. I needed a new path. Or just some direction. Inspiration, indefinitely.

> Set in beautiful West Sussex countryside, this is a place to make new friends and plan for the future in the perfect setting, at a festival designed to recharge and ignite every seed of positivity you've ever felt.

Over and over I read those words. It was everything I wanted and needed right there at that moment. Closing my eyes and imagining where I was going to be in a few days' time was like wriggling my cold toes into cosy, thick socks. It felt nourishing. Just what my soul needed.

I had an aching desire in my chest. I wanted to be part of what these people were part of. I was not enjoying home life and hadn't been for some time. I had a boyfriend, but I was lonely. I was anxious and felt useless. Then Yestival had come along. That was the carrot hanging in front of me. It was going to be the positive thing I needed in my life.

> I would love to camp but I don't think I have the right kit this year for my baby, but we only live up the road so maybe we could come for the daytime stuff.

In my initial email I had already laid out the excuses. I must keep my baby safe. She was only tiny. It was going to be freezing. I didn't have the right stuff. I wouldn't be able to keep her warm enough. Of course, I couldn't do it. Who in their right mind would take their five-month-old baby camping on their own, in October, in a field of complete strangers? I must be crazy I thought. How am I going to go to the loo in the night? They'd be drunk and rowdy. It was a stupid idea.

But I had as much camping stuff as any other scout leader had. I had dipped my toe into cycle touring too so I was sure I could figure out a two-night camp in a field. I made a decision. We were going to Yestival AND camping.

I'd reached out to Mel Findlater, upon a recommendation. The founder of Ordinary Superparents; a Facebook group for parents with an adventurous mind-set. Mel was camping in her campervan with her one-year-old and four-year-old. Mel seemed a bit like me – ordinary, for want of a better word. If Mel could do it, I could do it.

Friday 19th October, 2018 arrived, and I beamed. I jumped excitedly and danced about the sun-filled bedroom. This entertained Seren while I considered packing. By 3.30pm we had to take a pause for probably the 20th breastfeed of the day. Somehow, I filled my estate car with enough stuff for two whole nights away from any mod-cons. But we were now loaded and leaving for Yestival 2018.

Just fifteen minutes later, we arrived at the Brinsbury Campus of Chichester College, the current home of the YesBus and Yestival. Within a couple of minutes of arriving, we were greeted by Lev with a wide welcoming smile. My nerves promptly disappeared as Lev's positive mood and helpful attitude put me totally at ease. One full wheelbarrow and a loaded buggy later, we eventually left the carpark with Seren attached to me in a sling.

A farm track lined with tall trees offered long shadows in the setting sun. It led towards the middle of nowhere. Muddy puddles lapped at the edge where the track met lush green grass. Closing my eyes, I breathed in the earthy woodland air.

'Believe there is good in the world' I read, written in multi-coloured chalk on a handmade, perfectly wonky black chalkboard sign. Then another 'If you see someone without a smile, give them yours'. This was encouraging.

My head was whirring with all kinds of emotions and all those irrational thoughts that join them. Was this place full of axe-murderers? Is anyone going to talk to me?

I gave Lev a sideways glance. With his infectious smile and excitable enthusiasm, he was doing a very good impression of someone who *wasn't* an axe murderer. I smiled back and pushed the doubts to the back of my mind.

As we approached the hubbub ahead of us, I could see the famous royal blue double-decker YesBus peeking through the trees. In front of it was a picturesque clearing with tents set up, smoke billowing from a small fire. Ahead, the spire of a tepee extended above the hedge line, and beyond that, the white arch of the main marquee.

But first a little gazebo greeted us, and Lev waited while we checked in, got our water bottle and paid £5 deposit for our Yestival mug. I balanced these on the buggy like a game of buckaroo and we headed off into the field of dreams. No wait; not dreams, holes! IT. WAS. SO. BUMPY! Du-du-du-du-du-du. Now that was memorable.

I picked my camping spot with care. Close enough to the toilets so I had a clear view of the tent (and potential baby left inside briefly at some point) if I was desperate, but not too close so that the constant banging of doors was going to wake her. I was also fortunately positioned near some other families and one with a baby of a similar age to mine. It wasn't just me that thought that this camping lark with a baby was acceptable in October in the UK. My back was aching, I really needed to take Seren off and put her down somewhere. I found a nice spot clear of the crispy cow pats that were dotted around.

I am not worried about 'outdoor germs'. I grew up on a farm, milking cows from the age of eight. I spent summers roaming my grandad's woodland with the dog and making camps from sticks. Though I was still sterilising the dummies with hot water here and there, I had no fear of the little critters nature intended us to live alongside. In fact, it was the bit about being outside I loved.

I hadn't camped for over a year and the thrill of sleeping under canvas again made me squeak with excitement. Another SayYesMore volunteer came to my rescue, and without actually doing much myself, the tent was up and filled with all the (too many!) things I brought. I set our beds and bed clothes like a stocking, milk and cookies on Christmas eve.

I was eager to get some grub so we soon joined the snaking queue for supper in the fading light. As people noticed my daughter attached to me, we kept getting pushed forward along the queue towards the impending feast.

I meandered my way into the main marquee with our plate over-spilling, tentatively seeing where to settle us down. A woman was sat with her daughter at an old cable drum laying on its side with her baby nursing on her lap. Mel seemed like a very content mum. She looked cosy in her yellow down jacket, despite probably sharing the same experience of cold exposed boob that breast feeding mums endure during the winter months.

Mel and her family were the vision of totally 'got this', super-mum on a mission feeding kids and camping in October. I tried to blend in, settling down on a stool at the barrel too, nursing my daughter and trying to eat at the same time.

The food warmed me to my toes just as the air temperature dropped. 'The Big Yes' marquee started to fill. There was a buzz and eagerness for the weekend to officially begin. The tent was awash with colour, fabric draped from end to end across the top of the tent like a spider's web of rainbows. Balloons and garlands hung like at a Chinese festival, swinging as the warm air from the crowds swirled upwards leaving a cool draught around our ankles.

Seating had creatively encircled a small, somewhat unlevel, tiny stage barely three metres square. Cushions and floor chairs were strewn at the front with bean bags and blankets. These made great fort building blocks for the children throughout the weekend. There was even a wooden wigwam type structure and hammocks. Two table tennis tables were near the giant winged statue towering above us. My cold feet were like bees to honey when I saw the big white boxes of warmth in the corners, although the mulled wine from the bar also helped. Tough blue carpeted matting covered the floor as hundreds of feet with an array of colourful socks and slippers hugged it. Five hundred pairs of wellies and boots were stacked up in the two entrances to the tent, spilling in and out like waves.

Mel introduced me to a few other families who were there with their children.

I put my stretchy wrap on for baby-wearing – a six metre piece of fabric, wrapped around my middle crossed at the back up and over my shoulders, over the front, under the waist bit, cross them over and round the back and back to the front and tied in a knot. Got it?!! I poked Seren's legs through. In her winter suit, she was very cosy, happy and almost asleep. Once we were all seated, silence fell.

I was here. At my first ever festival, in a field at the back of beyond with 498 other people I didn't know, camping on a wintery night with my five-month-old for the first time, four miles from home. But it could have been a million miles away. I just soaked it all up. This was exactly where I wanted to be right now.

Our hosts, Dave Cornthwaite and Laura Kennington, got it going and the audience was full of smiles, laughter – uninterrupted attention for those daring to open up and share their stories on stage. I was mesmerised. There was only one person on the line up I knew of, Alastair Humphreys; his book, Microadventures, has often inspired me! All these wonderful stories, amazing people and sharing this together, in a field – the atmosphere was oddly familiar.

A smile stretched across my face, I don't even really remember the content of the talks this evening, just the way I felt. It felt like one giant hug. The compact stage and its 360-degree view made it a challenge for the speakers, but I loved that beautiful faces provided the backdrop instead of a white emotionless screen.

I dipped outside to go find the Portaloos in the dark, over the ankle twisting, holey muffin tin like field. Seren had successfully transferred to the buggy and was sleeping quietly wrapped up in several blankets under the watchful eye of a stranger. I was confident that she was safe.

The smell of smoke filled the air; there was a fire alight about fifty metres in front of The Big Yes. My gaze wandered around the field. The silhouettes of the other marquee tents, as if a circus was in town, were shadowed in the far corners of the field. I breathed in the cold, damp night sky and my eyes watered a little in the still air.

This was the first moment I had to myself, and I mean all by myself, for what felt like weeks or months. I love being Seren's mummy. That is who I am and what I love about my identity now. We make a great team.

Despite the darkness, the giant letters saying 'SAY YES MORE' were lit atop the field. I felt super proud of myself being here tonight. I had said 'yes', and it was only a little yes, but it is just the first of many in this new chapter.

There was an open mic section towards the end of the evening. Anyone could get up on stage and say their piece, whatever they wanted, in sixty seconds. Many promised yeses for the future and thank yous, as well as tales of yes gone by. Adventure, mental health, questions and singing; it certainly was a variety show. There was no less laughing, crying, shouting and love than any of the scheduled speakers; it was like everyone was meant to be there. It was like being in a classroom of all your mates to do a show and tell. There was a rawness of the emotions imprinted on each of our souls. This is what Yestival creates.

The evening concluded with many good-night hugs with many new friends. It had been a long day for us, and I hadn't had a full night's sleep in at least five months. We bumped and jiggled our way back to the tent. It was a chilly evening and my eyelids were heavy, but I was very much looking forward to getting in my sleeping bag and drifting off.

I laid Seren down and zipped her into her cookie monster sleeping bag. She wore a little pink spotty hat with mini ear flaps and pointy cat ears. I know I am biased, but she looked super cute with her little, wet nose. After a quick feed, she was fast asleep.

I agonised for about thirty minutes. Was she too hot or too cold? Did she need another blanket? Was she going to suffocate? I double checked that all loose bedding was secure. She was fine. We were both fine and so I too slipped into a deep sleep.

I woke to the sound of plastic on plastic as the Portaloo doors thumped closed as each camper met the first call of the day. Phew! She was still breathing. I had to check. I took my baby camping in October and we survived!

I lay there with the biggest smile on my face and felt that this is exactly where I was meant to be. However, this was temporary as nature was calling me. I demonstrated my 'ninja mum' moves by quietly and carefully planking and downward dog'ing my way around and over a sleeping baby and escaped through the smallest hole I could unzip. I made a run for it before anyone could notice or steal my baby.

I returned and, guess what? No one had stolen her!

I jumped back into bed next to her and accidentally on purpose woke her up. She woke sleepily in the bright green light inside the tent. She looked like a little Michelin man in all her layers and could barely move her arms, her nose still bright pink, as she nuzzled around on the hunt for her breakfast.

Strapping Seren into her buggy, we bumpety bump bump bumped our way up the field. The dew was clinging to each blade of grass; the sun made it all shimmer and wave like the sea.

The urns of hot water were waiting for me at the bar. Strong, milky and half a teaspoon of sugar. I cupped my hands around the mug of tea to warm them in the cold air; I could drink it almost instantly while I briefly stood around trying to blend in, discreetly pulling three rich tea biscuits out of my pocket. My pre-breakfast snack. They were dunked and quickly consumed. Seren looked on at them longingly but she wasn't really weaning yet. Less than five minutes later, I was back making tea number two with a further two biscuits. Dunk, Dunk, slurp, Ahhhh. Now I could function a little better.

A noise filled the air like a call to prayer. It sounded just like a metal bin lid being hit with a stick. We assembled outside The Big Yes where a huge beautifully decorated blackboard detailed the day's schedule. This calling occurred at the start of every session over the coming two days where the speakers would get sixty seconds to 'sell' their talk on adventures near or far.

I first chose to go to the Atlantic tent and was inspired by Tanya Noble's tales of determination and perseverance taking on an epic island-hopping mega solo cycling challenge on an Ice Trike (you may have read her story in the Bigger Book of Yes!). It was 10.15am, and Seren was snoozing in the morning sun on a hay bale so I was free to give Tanya my full attention. Seeds of ideas were germinating for adventures of my own.

The DONG rang and everyone swarmed and then split again almost every hour all day to hear, discuss, see and feel what adventure meant or was to someone else. To hear that the impossible is possible. The children were kept so busy at the kids' club, Dream Camp, you barely noticed they had parents!

While in The Big Yes marquee listening to a very inspirational lady who kayaked across Europe, I desperately needed to go for a pee. Seren was cosy cuddled up to me as I considered my options. Leave her on the sofa and run in the hope that she was still there when I got back. Or take her with me (What if I dropped her in there? That thought actually crossed my mind!).

The guy sitting next to me seemed ok and wasn't wielding an axe, so I asked him. I realised I was totally fine leaving my most precious baby with a total stranger. I also went to the tent to get supplies, made a cup of tea and considered another pee. On my return she was happy, and he hadn't kidnapped her, and all was fine in the world. I lost count of the number of solo pees I was gifted on this weekend. I was feeling very relaxed and at ease.

DONG, we stayed in the Big Yes and enjoyed listening to another speaker.

DONG, we gathered, we split. This time, the Bell Tent, 'Speaker Q and A with Dave'. The boss, the head man, top dog, big cheese, head honcho, numero uno. Dave Cornthwaite, the man behind Yestival, the YesTribe and SayYesMore.

I didn't really know much about him, the YesTribe or his adventures. We sat cross legged on the scratchy coconut matting in the 'doorway' with a light breeze brushing through. Dave was sat, feet up on a big brown leather chair like someone about to read a book to a crowd of kids. It was informal, comforting and refreshing. Dave just oozes with inspiration and positivity and epitomises what SayYesMore and Yestival is all about. The YesTribe was born out of Dave's desire to put faces to his Facebook friends. He has several books published, a great blog, podcast and some amazing stories to tell. His grit and determination through difficult and challenging times ignited something inside me. I wanted to do things like that. And I was going to.

When I look back on that day, I see myself sitting in that not so little Bell Tent. Of the strangers I was among then, many are now my friends. The adage goes that 'strangers are just friends you haven't met yet'.

DONG! Lunch time. Seren napped on the floor in the Bell Tent while I got to know Tracy and Isaac, original member of the YesTribe and first SayYesMore Baby. We missed the next session and chilled out with a cup of tea at the back of the Big Yes.

Earlier in the day, Mel had given me and the other parents a piece of string and a challenge to ask for help. Humans generally like helping. If we don't ask, we are denying them that feel good factor of helping. They get a feel-good boost, and we parents have a burden lifted.

"It takes a village to raise a child," Mel quotes. So, we have to build our village, and over the weekend, I built up the courage and asked for help when I needed it and accepted it more when offered, however unnatural it felt. Each time I tied another knot in my string. This world is a good place and mostly filled with good people. The human race really is innately kind and compassionate, otherwise we surely wouldn't have gotten this far.

The Adventure Parents session with Mel and Catherine Edsell was filled to the brim with parents who have experienced adventure with their little or not so little ones. Everyone was dreaming of adventure and whatever that meant to them and their families. I heard great advice and loved hearing stories of adventures with kids as young as Seren. This was my favourite session and I was happy and proud to be sitting there among these Ordinary Superparents on my first mummy-daughter camping adventure!

Suddenly, there was a commotion, so we made our way up to the epicentre of the action.

There was a huge snake of people lined up in front of the Big Yes. Dave was standing there with his arms reaching out like he was about to catch someone. Someone else was up a ladder, another had a stopwatch, and a camera was set up.

Then three, two, one, GO! A chap ran at Dave, penguin like, arms fixed to his side, smiling, concentrating; this seemed important.

Dave's arms wrapped around him, the chap stepped aside and immediately Dave was hugging the next person – and the next and the next, faster and faster, this smiling snake of positive energy was getting hugged. For sixty seconds there was screaming and cheering as the stream of happy hugged people filtered off into the crowd encouraging the next.

"Ten, nine, eight, seven…" the countdown commenced, "Three, two, one!" screams, clapping and cheering erupted and at the centre was Dave, somewhere, being hugged, and the crowd around him grew and grew and bounced and bounced and screamed and cheered.

I'm not sure if anyone knew if it was a success or not, but it didn't seem to matter. The heartbeat of this mosh pit in the middle of a field were happy just to be part of the journey. Dave had hugged ninety-six people in sixty seconds in his attempt to break this world record. It was filmed and logged and submitted to the powers that be to see if it was official. World record or not, this was quite a moment.

Dinner followed, and by 7.30pm, The Big Yes was packed. The boots and shoe mountain had returned to the entrances, and we sat back ready to be inspired. There were some fab speakers. I want to tell you about all of them, Dave, Spike and Andy, Clare and Laura. I don't want to do anyone an injustice, but my absolute favourite guests this evening were the Jones'.

"TEN MILES AN HOUR!"

Tom, Katie, Ruth and Rhoda Jones, cycled Lands' End to John o'Groats, finishing their epic ride on 2nd September, 2018. They completed the 874-mile long journey in twenty-two days, three hours and twenty-six minutes. Rhoda, aged just four years and four months old, broke the world record as the youngest to complete the journey on a trailer bike. Her sister Ruth, aged five, finished just before Rhoda and was the fastest to complete the journey on a trailer bike.

"TEN MILES AN HOUR!" Rhoda exclaimed again as her mum and

dad shared their story. If they could just keep riding at ten miles an hour, they would eventually cycle the length of the country. What an amazing family! Tom and Katie seemed like lovely, normal people. I'd sat next to them earlier in the day in the Bell Tent. Tom there in his bright yellow trousers with extraordinary long legs to go with it, towered over his daughters, but they had the limelight. The whole tent was listening intently, laughing and then cheering at the end giving them an ovation that was highly deserved. Tom and Katie are fab role models to their children and to other parents alike showing us all that if you really want something, and you just keep going ten miles an hour, you can go anywhere you want.

Seren and I retreated at 9.30pm to the campfire outside. There is nothing like a campfire to complete a camping experience. All we were missing was the marshmallows.

We didn't stay up much later. Seren needed to go to bed and I wanted to make the most of sleeping under canvas having not camped for some time. I part filled up a hot water bottle from the urn and we pottered back to the tent. Holding Seren, balancing to get my boots off, get my PJs on, get us both into our many layers and my essential thick socks. I had done this before, albeit last night, and so I felt so much more at ease. I was enjoying this. I wasn't worried and, thinking of that first steaming cup of tea in the morning, I drifted off.

I woke to a babbling baby in the morning glow. That first cup of tea was as good as I had imagined. Breakfast was so good I had two! There were plenty of opportunities to go and hear other speakers again this morning. The DONGs started, and the tribe congregated once again to hear what was on offer. Sunday went by so fast. Seren was asleep by 10.30am in the buggy, and so it was a really laid-back morning. The sun came out again and gave us a glorious day. It was just how a Sunday morning should be.

A little later in the morning, Mel got the parents together to talk about our hopes and dreams of adventuring. We got crafty and made some dream jars with ribbon and we wrote our dream ideas on card, sealing them in our jars. Flat sided with a green lid, I plaited some yellow and blue gingham ribbon and tied it in a bow around the neck of the jar. I ran my fingers along the knotted twine. Twenty-six knots. Twenty-six opportunities that these strangers supported me and helped make my weekend.

Everyone congregated outside by the SAY YES MORE sign. It was a little like herding sheep, but we managed it and the team photo was a success. I saw Eabhnat as we dispersed. I wanted to catch her to say a proper 'hi' and get her details as we had chatted in passing on several occasions. She was one of those who apparently had three kids there with her. I had yet to see any evidence of this. She invited Seren and I to Glasgow there and then. I said YES!

The open mic opportunities continued and each time I was drawn to say something but hadn't. We were sitting on the floor, next to the lovely wee Ged from Glasgow, now a dear friend. The next open mic session began. I didn't know what I wanted to say, but I really wanted to say something. This weekend was life changing.

I don't really remember what happened next, but I am pretty sure I abandoned Seren with Ged, not for the first time, and queued up to join the next session on the mic. I shouldn't have been nervous (I give talks in my day job) but I was, and a little emotional as being here really meant so much more than I could put into words.

It was my turn. "Thank you," I said and explained how I had been gifted the kindness of strangers ticket. It was because of them that I had made it to this life-changing gathering. I was almost in tears. I was rewarded with an applause and my new friends smiled back as my gaze shyly flickered between the audience and the floor. I exited, wiped my eyes discreetly and returned to sit on the floor cushions with Ged, Seren and all my new friends.

Dave and Laura were drawing everything to a close. The Dream Camp kids all stood on stage and declared what was going to be on their Yes List, what they dreamed of achieving. It was very cute and certainly inspired something inside. Fearless kids stood in front of us and were brave enough to declare huge ambitions. If they can, I can.

The Greatest Showman soundtrack song 'This Is Me' closed this little micro-festival. Everyone of course knew the words and sung along at full volume. This really is where I wanted to be, and I was sad it was nearly over. There were so many more people I wanted to meet.

But it wasn't over really. It was the beginning.

We eventually headed back after many hugs and I spent as long as possible breaking camp. I'm sure I wasn't intending to drag my heels but I didn't want this to end. Some kids we got to know were keeping Seren entertained, and I was still figuring out how to get our stuff back to the car. In true YesTribe fashion, someone helped us out.

So, what happened next for Team Hannah and Seren? Well it certainly wasn't the end and writing this more than a year on we have achieved so much already. We had breakfast on the beach with our new friends from Yestival, Ruth and her family; that was our first post-Yestival Yes! I went cycling for the first time with Seren on the Granite Trail and stayed in a Youth Hostel with another friend and her family. We've made it to Scotland twice and stayed with Eabhnat and family and Ged, which was a really big deal for us. It was our first time flying and, while there, we got the train to Bute where it was snowing. We climbed a dumpling, I had a food tour of Glasgow and we ascended Arthur's Seat in Edinburgh. It turned out Ged wasn't an axe-murderer either!

Most days are an adventure with a child in tow. Adventures can be big or small, near or far and the best thing is, we get to define what our adventures are. Yestival has opened my eyes to the possibility that I can achieve something a bit more. Something that before I would never have even considered. Something that would have been a big fat NO.

"What are your next adventure plans?" I hear you say. We have a running and cycling adventure on the Camino de Santiago Spain in the pipeline, which I am both excited and terrified about. I am determined to make it happen.

I'm loving life, parenthood and pushing my boundaries by reaching out and embracing the YesTribe, its values and opportunities. I urge you to say 'yes!' more!

Of all the signs that greeted me on the life-changing festival in 2018, one stays with me every day. 'Be Brave, Be Kind, Be Curious'.

Instagram: **hannahbanana_80**

Email: **hmiller2288@gmail.com**

Chapter 28

I Bought a Bus

By Nick Miller

It was a chilly, breezy Sunday morning in late January and I had absolutely no intention of getting out of bed. My head throbbed from the one too many pints the previous evening. From what I could remember, I'd met a couple of friends at my local to catch up. We'd sat by the roaring fire sinking beer after beer as we talked about anything and everything. Exactly what we discussed, or in fact how the evening ended, would remain a mystery.

The wind had picked up, and the fragile caravan I called home was shaking violently. It seemed my plan of a peaceful day in bed gently nursing my hangover was not to be.

I forced myself out from under my cosy duvet, switched on the kettle and flicked open my laptop lid to take a quick glance at my email inbox. There were a few work-related threads that could wait till tomorrow and a smattering of messages from eBay about something I'd been bidding on. Nothing out of the ordinary then.

I gripped my warm cup of coffee and sat down at my laptop. My head was still throbbing. I must have been very drunk last night.

Without the capacity to focus on anything too serious, I found myself being drawn to one particular email in my inbox. For a while now,

I'd been idly dreaming of converting an old school bus into a new, custom-built home-on-wheels for myself. It seemed a distant dream at best as I had no money, very little practical experience and no real sense of what it would take to complete such a project. But it was a fun distraction from real life, and there was something addictive about looking at potential vehicles online and fantasising about what I could turn them into.

The email in question referred to a fifty-three-seater, 1985 Leyland Tiger Alexander N-Type I'd had my eye on for a while. It was relatively cheap at just £1500, and had been bought and then relisted a couple of times over the previous few months, which made me wonder what was wrong with it! The listing didn't say a lot either – there were just four photos and a very brief description.

But there was something about it that just kept on drawing me back. Immaculately painted in pale yellow with a dark green strip around the bottom, it looked unlike any other bus I'd ever seen. And that gave it a certain personality that appealed to me – different, adventurous, unique – all traits that, for better or worse, had been applied to me over the years. A good match then for a place I might one day call home.

I clicked on the link to have another look through the description, and waste away another hour or two indulging my latest pipe dream. As the page loaded, I took a gulp of my freshly made coffee and briefly closed my eyes to really savour the delicate notes on my taste buds. When I opened them again, I nearly spat the whole lot out over my keyboard! Because at the top of the page, where once it said "You are watching this item", it now said "Congratulations! You've won this item."

What?! When?! How?!

I double checked. No, I wasn't still asleep. This was actually happening. At 2.26am, after what must have been a marathon drinking session, I'd taken the unimaginable step of buying a huge, twelve metre long, school bus – that I'd never even seen. Now I know it's easy to do stupid things when you're drunk, but this was on another level!

Except oddly, this didn't feel in any way stupid. Instead I felt giddy with excitement. For a brief moment, that excitement switched to terror at the magnitude of what I'd just done, but it soon settled as a deep inner peace – that feeling you get when you know that something magical is now within your grasp, and that life will never be the same again.

*

Before embarking on the bus project, what really mattered to me was adventure travel. In September 2013, having abandoned my attempt at a career in the music industry, I was lucky enough to find a job working for a small Oxfordshire-based company distributing Christmas trees in London. This job came with an unexpected perk: I would have the summers off, but still get paid a salary if I promised to come back the following season. Taking advantage of this new found freedom from the year-round grind, I spent the first summer going on a bicycle trip from Edmonton in Alberta, Canada to San Francisco. The following summer, having decided I needed more of a challenge, my friend and I headed to Cape Town and embarked on a 4500-mile mad dash across sub-Saharan Africa to Kampala on a couple of ropey old mountain bikes.

It was on this trip that the idea of converting a bus first began to claw at my brain. While taking a few days off to rest at a campground somewhere in Namibia, I stumbled upon a blog post by a fellow adventurer called Dave Cornthwaite, describing his search for a part-time base; somewhere to call home in between his travels.

Luckily, I'd already managed to secure myself a part-time home in the form of a vintage caravan, but had started thinking about what was next. The caravan was comfortable and cosy and allowed me the freedom to disappear for long periods without having to worry about rent payments or mortgages. I stored it on a plot of land just outside Oxford and lived there in the times between expeditions and the Christmas tree season in London. But it was small and not particularly suitable for more than one person. It also couldn't fit my piano inside, and I was keen to get that back within easy reach.

Dave's post explored a few options including a Tiny House, a boat, and most excitingly to me, a bus. Since my early teens, I'd often dreamt about living on a bus one day. It just seemed like a cool thing to do.

A few weeks after reading Dave's post, having left the magnificent Victoria Falls in our wake, we headed into the hills south of Lake Kariba, following the Zambezi on its way to the Indian Ocean. What started as a glorious day or two's riding through the sun-drenched bush of northern Zimbabwe, soon turned into an incredibly difficult endeavour, as the tarmac road gradually deteriorated into thick sand that became impossible to ride on.

After we were forced to get off and push the heavy bikes for several miles, we soon realised we needed a new plan. In the small lakeside village of Binga, we found out about a bus that was coming by the following day and would be able to take us some way along the unrideable road. This would surely help, and so we set up camp for the night and waited.

It was early morning when the heavily overloaded coach trundled into the village and the crowds of eager passengers began assembling in the dusty square. I'd never seen anything like it. The bus appeared to already be full when it arrived, but nobody got off and lots of people got on, along with bags of produce, clothing and other wares for the market, including a couple of goats and a small flock of chickens. The sun was only just starting to emerge, and already we were feeling the intense heat of the day as we hauled our bikes and luggage up onto the roof of the bus.

We laughed at the absurdity of the situation as we clambered over people in our attempt to find somewhere to sit. Eventually, we managed to find ourselves a seat to share, right at the back of what was already feeling like an oven.

How on earth was I going to survive this journey? I could barely breathe and definitely wouldn't be able to sleep. Of course, I could just read my book. But wait! Where was my book? Ah damnit!

I glanced at the roof of the coach. My bike, with all its panniers and my precious book, was irretrievable now, packed under a crate of live chickens. The old lady next to us gave me a toothless grin as the engines started up with a coughing gasp. Too late now.

Without my book, I was soon very bored. People-watching only got me so far and, without the vaguest chance of getting any shuteye, I desperately needed something to occupy myself. My mind went back to Dave's blog and I realised that maybe this was something I could work on. I began by thinking through the few things I had been living quite comfortably with the past few months while travelling by bike, and in more luxury, in my caravan back home. I didn't need sofas, a dining table or a bath tub like a normal bricks and mortar house. Just the basics.

Once I'd mentally stripped out all the people, luggage and seats, and found suitable places for all the essentials of a home, the task quickly turned to figuring out what to do with all the additional room I had to play with! Even after I'd accounted for the most luxurious kitchen I could imagine, a full size shower room, a king size bed, a lounge area, and room for my piano and guitars, I had still only used up about half of the floor space. Maybe a bus was in fact too large a space for one person to live in? Only time would tell. When the bus finally came to a stop, several long hours later, I wrote down my ideas, determined to revisit them at a later date.

Back from the trip in early August, and before my focus shifted again onto thinking about Christmas trees, I attended a few festivals, including the inaugural Yestival. I went really because it was a chance to meet Dave and discuss this crazy bus idea in person. In fact, I discussed it with pretty much everybody in the field. And, thankfully, they seemed to be as excited as I was.

By the time I left on the Sunday evening, I'd decided this was something I was going to do, one day, somehow. From then on for the next three months, I spent every spare moment looking for inspiration and bus conversion advice. Eventually, I must have realised I'd done enough thinking and talking about it and decided to give it a shot.

*

Soon after realising I'd bought myself a bus that fateful January morning, I received an email from the seller requesting payment and things got very real very quickly. A quick check of my bank account revealed what I had feared, it was almost empty. My heart sank. While my salary was due in four days, which would just about cover the rest of the upfront cost, it would leave me unable to afford food and bills.

Was this such a good idea after all? Maybe I should get a normal house instead. It would only take me... I did the maths... eighteen years. I redid the maths. Yep.

If I wanted to remain living here, in this part of the world where I grew up, where my friends and family were, but in a real house rather than a caravan, I would have to work full-time for almost two decades, at a minimum, before I could even put down a deposit on a 'normal' house. This gave me the confidence boost I needed to take another step forward.

Next, I needed to find somewhere to store it and hopefully work on it. My first port of call was the owner of the land I was currently living on, but his answer was clear: under no circumstances could I park a bus there.

There was a glimmer of hope from an industrial estate down the road. Although they had no room on hard standing, the owner of the estate offered the field opposite where, for £120 a month, he said I could park the bus. It was by no means perfect, but my time was running out so my hand was forced.

I arranged with the seller to deliver the bus the following Wednesday, and on payday, sent them the funds. I would still have to find another £300 cash to pay the driver for delivery and £240 for the deposit and first month's rent on the land, but these were technicalities. The main thing was that I had paid for the bus, found somewhere to store it and had a date set for delivery.

Like a boy who's just been tasked with designing his dream treehouse, I could think of nothing else for the next week. I spent late nights at my laptop looking at other bus conversions, grinning the whole time as the potential unravelled in my mind. I dug out my notes from my Zimbabwean brainstorming session and set about formulating a proper plan. Originally, this just meant a few sketches but it didn't take me long to start accumulating masses of unanswered questions.

There were also a few fairly major problems that I was choosing to ignore at this stage. Namely, I had just blown all my money on buying the thing and didn't have any leftover even to eat, let alone buy tools and materials or employ anyone to help me.

I had almost no practical skills or experience either. What I did have, though, was a vision of what I wanted my home to look like and the determination to get there, no matter what it took. Crucially, I also had a belief that anything could be done if I just put my mind to it. So put my mind to it I did.

I went through my design spec and totted up everything that would cost money, which came to about six grand. To find the money for the bus delivery and storage, I had to sell my caravan, rendering me effectively homeless.

To solve both this and my lack of funds for food, I temporarily moved in with my dad. I also set about the unenviable task of convincing my boss to advance me my next five months' salary!

Finally, after a bit of negotiation, he kindly agreed to advance me three months' worth. While this didn't, in the end, turn out to be anywhere near the amount needed to finish it, it was a good start and funded the pivotal first six months of work.

When the time came to take delivery, I couldn't have been less prepared if I'd tried. I had no idea how to drive such a large vehicle, a rather unsuitable place to park it and no available funds to pay for competent help. I just told the seller where and when to deliver it and waited anxiously. Having not seen it, it could quite easily have turned out to be a complete wreck. I'd bought it from a respected bus operator, and it was coming straight out of service, so had reason to believe it would be in decent mechanical condition. But it was so cheap! There could well have been more to the picture than met the eye, and my eye didn't know what to look for. More than a few people had reminded me of this in the days leading up to its arrival. Boy, would it be embarrassing if they were right.

The industrial estate was at the bottom of a narrow but busy country lane, next to a humpback bridge unsuitable for HGVs, and there was very little room for manoeuvring a big bus in the car park. This was going to be fun!

At 2pm on the 3rd February, 2016, I caught a glimpse of my new abode for the very first time, as it rolled down the hill towards me and swung into the estate. As I stepped aboard, once again mentally removing the seats and envisioning my future home before me, I felt like I just received the best Christmas present ever. It was everything I'd hoped for: beautiful, characterful and in remarkably fine condition, both inside and out.

Getting it into place in the field, though, was not as straightforward as I had imagined! Long story short, the bus got stuck in the mud, and with only a brief (and stationary) lesson on how to operate the controls, I spent many frustrating hours over the following weeks trying to get the damn thing to budge.

Eventually, I went to see a local farmer who kindly pulled the bus out with his tractor. With great difficulty, we got it into a position out of the deep mud, just inside the gate, hidden from the road by a few trees where I could, at last, begin work on it. It was not the best start to my new life as a bus owner!

The first task was to remove all the seats, which I later sold, recouping about a third of the purchase cost. While I managed to borrow a generator and angle grinder, I had no idea how to use them properly. I had to rely on friends and YouTube to teach me. Thankfully, my step-dad is an invaluable source of experience and information, and he helped me put together a shopping list for some basic tools.

With my salary advance finally in the bank and some kind of plan in place, I started preparing for the first phase of conversion: demolition. The goal was to strip the internal space back to its core shell giving me a completely blank slate to work with as I crafted my new home. Before I got started though, I just thought I'd ask my old landlord one last time if I could store it at the Christmas tree yard, which was a much better place to do the conversion (having electricity, broadband, running water, access to a toilet and a small workshop).

Amazingly, now that it was more than just an abstract idea, he agreed! This was fabulous news, and after arranging some insurance and getting the bus back out onto the road, I drove my new home the ten miles back to the farm, where four years later I still am.

By this time it was April, my Christmas tree work had finished for the year, spring was in the air and I could finally crack on. Although the seats were already long gone, this felt like a monumental moment. Sitting in the place where just a few months ago my small, cosy caravan was parked was now the huge, empty shell of a former school bus.

I remember wondering whether I really had whatever it would take to do this project. While I had managed to get to this point without too much trouble (albeit mostly winging it the whole way), I was worried that at some point my luck would run out. I'd be left with an unfinished, unsellable lump of metal, no money and no home. From now on, if I carried on, there was no way back – reverting this back into usable public transport would soon be nigh-on impossible. And I would look like such a fool.

All around me, people were telling me it was a crazy idea – why wasn't I listening? Was I simply too stubborn? I think that was certainly part of it.

But I had been in this kind of situation before, on my bike, preparing to cross the Canadian Rockies in winter, against all the advice from the locals. Everybody told me I was insane, I would die and that I should wait until the conditions were 'more favourable'. But I went anyway and had one of the most exhilarating and enjoyable three weeks of my life, forging memories that I will treasure forever.

Maybe I was just lucky back then? This is different. This is serious. This isn't just some silly bike ride. There is a frickin' giant bus and I'm the owner. I'm the guy responsible for proving to all those naysayers that I can do this, that I can turn this into a beautiful home.

I could just sell it now. Admit I'd made a mistake. Get another caravan. Get back in the rat race. Take the easy way out.

Sod that!

The only way was forward. And that meant hard work. Lots of it.

The luggage racks came down easily. With the ceiling, it was just a case of drilling out hundreds of rivets and levering the panels away from the metal frame. The floor was covered in a disgusting, sticky lino that was glued in place. It could only be removed by tearing it off and scraping away any leftover adhesive with a chisel. At the end of each day, my whole body was caked with dust and all sorts of detritus. It was sweaty, tricky and painful work and I was very glad when it was over.

I was nervous about the floor. Most people doing bus conversions build a timber frame on top of their existing floor, fill the gaps with insulation and then lay their new floor on top of that. I had assumed I would do the same thing. However, I realised this simply wasn't going to work. I could only just stand up in her with my six-foot-two build.

I decided that I would rebuild the floor from scratch and hang the insulation underneath the finish floor level. Little did I know how challenging this would be. To dismantle the floor, which was made from a giant sheet of eighteen-millimetre plywood, I had to cut it into tiny pieces with a skill saw and prize each section out with a crowbar. It took forever but there was no other way.

Then came the rebuild. This involved lining the bottom of the floor frame with aluminium sheeting, fitting new floor joists, insulating the new cavity, laying a subfloor and then finally the bamboo floorboards I'd bought. Each section had to be measured and cut to fit, before being installed.

However, once the floor was finally done, things began to take shape quite quickly. The walls went up in a day or two, as did the stage – a raised platform over the rear wheel arches where my piano and guitars would eventually live.

For floorboards, I used some beautiful, old oak planks that my friend found in a field buried in sheep poo! We salvaged them and scrubbed them down before getting a local carpenter to cut them to size. I spent a day sanding them to remove the poo stains, before installing them atop the frame. The finished result created an elegant and natural divide between the bedroom (currently just a mattress on the floor) and the living room.

Soon I was starting to think about my bathroom layout. First, I realised I'd have to sort out my utilities as a bathroom without a water supply wouldn't be much use. Design-wise, I knew I wanted all the comforts of a normal, modern house but without any of the running costs, and everything needed to work both on and off-grid. As well as a way of connecting up mains water, I would also have to have a freshwater tank and pump on board and be able to heat either supply on-demand. And as well as being able to connect to 'shore power' or a generator, I would need the ability to connect to solar panels and run everything in my house from a battery bank. I didn't want to cut any corners or do anything by halves.

However, it soon became obvious that, if I was going to have such an adaptable and flexible setup, it wouldn't be cheap. Once I'd factored everything in, my electrics and plumbing cost over £3k! And that didn't include any labour. This part of the build was very rewarding though, and over the next few weeks, the bus was radically transformed from an empty shell into a fully functional living space.

The kitchen was the part of the bus I was most looking forward to building. I had been suffering for years without a proper kitchen in the caravan and was excited at the prospect of at last having a decent cooking setup. I bought a solid walnut worktop, a beautiful, old Belfast sink and a full-size LPG cooker too – all for about £150. Lastly, I splashed out on a fancy black and silver fridge/freezer combo. With my kitchen budget virtually used up, I set about building the rest of it as cheaply as possible. Rather than buying ready-built kitchen units, I cobbled together a frame for the cupboards out of scrap timber I had found in some nearby skips. The galley kitchen was still missing cupboard doors and overhead cabinet space, but it was functional enough.

Before I started this project, as you will recall, I'd been spending half my year in an old caravan and the other half on a pushbike, living out of a couple of panniers. I loved this way of living, but to wash or do the dishes I'd have to boil the kettle on a camping stove every single time. It became a bit of a bore. You can imagine my delight when, for the first time in over two and a half years, I turned on my shiny new kitchen tap, heard the burner leap into life and found my hands bathing in gloriously hot water within a matter of seconds. And it just kept coming and coming. I let the water run through my hands as I whooped and hollered and grinned at the sheer luxury of it all. It still makes me smile every time I wash the dishes.

By the end of August, I had almost run out of time and would soon have to put the project on pause and go back to working my normal job for the winter. After a tiring few weeks ticking off major jobs like building a bed, installing a shower and lining the ceiling, I held a bus-warming party to celebrate the progress I'd made so far and mark the moment I moved in. I had come a long way and was incredibly proud of what I'd achieved, but there was still a long way to go.

The following spring, to get myself back in the swing of things, I built an additional front step in my porch, constructed a front door and installed my woodburner, to keep me warm on the occasional frosty night. It helped to have small wins like these to get me going again after a dry spell.

I'd love to tell you that over the next few months I finished off the rest of the things on my to-do list, but life is never that simple. Unfortunately, work was put on hold for most of that year as I battled an unexpected illness. As it happened, this turned out to be a very useful thing – I was living in the bus full-time with the time to properly get to know the space and discover what worked and didn't work so well. For example, I discovered that it was seriously annoying having all the light switches by the front door. Last thing at night when I turned the lights out, I'd have to walk the length of the bus back to my bedroom in complete darkness! I've since added a separate two-way switch on the bedroom lighting circuit, right next to my bed.

When I finally felt able to work again, I found it wonderfully soothing to take the time to finish my kitchen: crafting a functional and aesthetically pleasing space in which to cook. The drawers and cupboard fronts I built mostly from recycled pallets and plywood, and completed them with some attractive hand-forged hinges and handles. The overhead cabinets were made from cheap B&Q pine shelves. Several months later, I put the last touches to my kitchen when I fitted the stunning, handmade tiles I'd had commissioned for my backsplash.

Truth be told, I haven't done much work on the bus since. For the last two years, it has remained in this 'almost but not quite finished' state, where all the big jobs are done but there are still quite a few little jobs I haven't got round to yet. Yet it is extraordinarily comfortable and has everything a home needs.

As I write this sentence, sitting in my armchair on the stage, a gentle breeze is drifting through the roof hatch. The evening sun is filling the room with light giving the pine woodwork a warm sandy glow. I can see that the trim around the woodburner hearth needs finishing and the curtains I've been meaning to hang still haven't made it up. But why would I worry about them? I've got all the time in the world. Right now, I'm exactly where I want to be. I have spent much of my time working on my garden and just living life. Because that's what this whole thing has been about anyway – freeing me up to do the things I most enjoy doing.

*

Buying and converting a bus has had some other unexpected impacts on my life. The subtle anxieties of paying rent, saving for a deposit or repaying a mortgage have completely vanished from my life. I didn't even notice the anxiety disappear until I realised a lot of my friends were working in jobs they didn't enjoy just to keep a roof over their heads. I don't expect it will ever come back. Wherever life takes me, I will always have the security of this home and the ability to retreat here for a while, light up the fire and settle in, without having to pay anyone for the privilege.

This, in turn, has led to financial freedom. When I started, I had no money in the bank and £20k of debt. My debt is now repaid, the bus is a substantial asset worth much more than it cost to buy and convert, and I've managed to carve out a comfortable and rewarding lifestyle where I work only when I want to. This has afforded me the time to discover where my passions and interests lie and continue to chase my dreams wherever they lead me, without needing to continually bring in an income.

Most of all though, this project has changed my outlook on my future. I now feel, with utmost confidence, prepared to take on whatever new challenges life throws my way, both mentally and physically. While I started with zero experience of building and few practical skills, just a few years later I am confident in my ability to use (or learn to use) any tool I come across. I feel that I could build or fix anything I want to. No project seems too scary or ambitious now – if I'm simply willing to take the time.

Building my own home has been about so much more than giving myself a place to live. It has given me the chance to find out what I'm capable of, continuously experiment with my ideas and learn from the many hundreds of mistakes that I wouldn't ordinarily have had the opportunity to make.

Although it has taken much longer and cost much more than I initially forecast, it has also been far more rewarding and positively life-changing than I ever anticipated. I've discovered what makes me most productive, what gives me the most joy and how best to channel my creative impulses.

Every morning, as I clamber out of my handmade bed and make my way past my piano and across the living room to my gorgeous handcrafted kitchen to put the kettle on, I giggle as I remind myself where I am and how I got here. Can you think of any better way to start the day? Other, of course, than waking up to discover you've only gone and bought yourself a bloody bus!

*

For more details on the story of my conversion, and to see photos and specifications from the build, please visit **nickboughtabus.com**.

Chapter 29

Hitting the Wall

Laura Mould

It's 3am on a mild June morning and I've been on my feet for nearly twenty hours. The light breeze is refreshing against my face, salty from the heat of the day and etched in tiredness. The lights of the city in the distance cast an ethereal glow in the sky but, for now, it feels like it's just us. Sunrise is still a few hours away and quietly the city sleeps.

My feet are throbbing with every step, hot and sore against the road, I'm reduced to an awkward shuffle. My world has become the patch lit by my head torch, extending no more than a metre in front of me, otherwise there is only darkness. As I take another ragged step, I feel blisters popping and toenails lifting, the sharp pain shooting through the tired fog of my brain. Not for the first time today, I wonder what on earth I'm doing here.

It feels like a lifetime ago that, alongside 250 other runners, I was watching the sun rise over the beautiful historic city of Carlisle. Hunkered in the square of the castle in the crisp morning air, the muted buzz of nervous anticipation reverberating around its walls. Snippets of conversation floating around shoe options, fuelling strategies, hydration levels and previous events. We were waiting for the start of Rat Race's The Wall 2016, a sixty-nine mile ultra-marathon, and little did I know that this would change the path of my life forever.

Before 2016...

I wasn't a runner. In fact, I hated running. So much so that, when my sister convinced me to sign up to our local Race for Life one year, I couldn't even run the entire 5k and would often arrange to meet her at the gym for training in the morning, only to cancel at the last minute (a fact she still reminds me of to this day). I just couldn't see the attraction – running to me was painful, unpleasant and boring. I didn't want to spend half an hour huffing and puffing, tomato-faced, wearing the world's most uncomfortable sports bra... not my idea of fun!

Sure, I enjoyed the gym and worked out regularly with a Personal Trainer, but I also had a mild obsession with cheesy garlic bread (still do) and loved a cheeky beer. I suppose you could say it was all about balance and I was healthy and happy with that.

In September 2015, during one of those conversations that generally happen in the pub but this time happened in the middle of my second set of leg presses, my PT asked if I would be interested in joining her and a team of her other clients in completing a Tough Mudder. By rights, the obvious answer was no. I hated running, wasn't overly keen on the idea of the infamous electric shocks, didn't fancy being plunged into ice baths and was convinced I would catch some hideous disease from the merest sniff of mud. I opened my mouth to say, 'No', and 'Yes' came out instead. What was I thinking?

October came around and, as always happens, all those enthusiastic yeses turned into excuses and our group dwindled to four. By now though, I was determined not to let the team down. Of course, I hadn't done any running and planned on simply winging the twelve-mile course, based on what I thought was a reasonable level of fitness.

The day dawned, grey, overcast and decidedly chilly. Mudder Village livened us up with a legendary compere, music, splashes of orange and the buzz of anticipation. The Tough Mudder Pledge got us even more psyched, the hairs on the back of our necks on end.

And then we were off… twelve miles of mud, freezing water, hills, monkey bars, walls, electric shocks and more. I was far outside my comfort zone. And it was incredible! I finished with a massive smile on my face and a feeling of elation that I'd never experienced before.

Bundled up in our foil blankets and warm kit with grubby faces, wearing our Tough Mudder headbands with pride, we jumped in the car, turned the heating up on full and headed for home. Our smiles were twelve miles wide, the euphoria indescribable.

In the hours and days that followed, I experienced something I'd never felt before. As the elation faded, I felt a little lost and a little blue. For those moments, life had been high definition and now it felt like I'd returned to a boring world of muted tones. I rambled on excitedly to my work colleagues about how amazing it had felt, but I don't think they really understood – perhaps they just thought some of that mud had made its way to my brain. Thankfully, my partner, Rich, knew what I was feeling, having completed a Tough Mudder before, so at least not everyone thought I was bonkers.

Now, four years later, I know that this post-adventure feeling is not unusual but, at that time, I didn't really know what to do with myself. I moped about for a good week, slipping back into the routine of gym, work, eat, sleep, repeat. Comfortable. Normal. Dare I say it, boring. But a seed had been sown in my mind…

I remember distinctly having a conversation with Rich where I said I wanted to do something else. Something that would push me outside of my comfort zone again. Something where failure was a very real possibility. Something that would challenge me mentally and physically. Something that would take me outside of my routine life.

I didn't know what that something was, but I knew Tough Mudder had started to inch open those floodgates. I turned to the font of all knowledge, Google, and started looking for ideas for challenges. There were the usual things of course: Climb Mt Everest (not a fan of heights so probably not for me); Cycle London to Paris (I didn't even pass my cycling proficiency at school, so could be interesting); Run the Marathon Des Sables (forty degree heat, sand and poisonous creatures... are you kidding?!) but most of these involved spending lots of money that I didn't have and taking lots of time off work that I couldn't spare.

I thought carefully about my comfort zone and what I had particularly enjoyed about Tough Mudder and I realised that it was overcoming the challenging things that scared me. Those were the things that had given me that feeling of elation and achievement at the finish. So, I knew I needed a challenge that was scary – and by that, I mean there had to be a risk I wouldn't complete it or that I might suffer adverse effects. The challenge needed to be difficult – something that I would find mentally or physically hard. And it needed to be inexpensive and UK-based, so I didn't have to take excessive amounts of time off work.

That's when I had a mini epiphany. Running! I hated it, it was difficult both mentally and physically for me. I could do it anywhere and it didn't need to be expensive – a decent pair of running shoes would do. I told Rich about my idea and he looked at me like I'd lost the plot, but I was determined.

The following day, Rich sent me a link to the website for Rat Race The Wall. I'd never even heard of an ultra-marathon before but instantly I knew it was the right challenge for me. I would need to cover sixty-nine miles on foot in less than twenty-four hours, taking me from Carlisle to Newcastle roughly following Hadrian's Wall. At this point, I couldn't even run a mile without stopping to walk so I knew there was some hard work to do.

Seven months later...

The sun is rising over Carlisle and the alarm is incessantly chiming in my ear. I blearily open my eyes, feeling like it's only moments since I closed them. Rich has spent a sleepless night tossing and turning and now beams at me like he's been awake for hours. I blink my eyes slowly and stifle my morning grumpiness. The smell of coffee and porridge wafts from the bedside table. I take a deep breath and throw back the duvet.

Half an hour, a hot shower and some coffee later and I feel vaguely human again. As I'm dressing, my stomach churns in knots of apprehension, my head fuzzy from lack of sleep and body rebelling against the early start.

We pack and re-pack our bags… First aid kit, whistle, food, water, spare layers… the list goes on. We check and re-check our mandatory kit. Check and re-check our maps. Check and re-check our halfway bags.

Eventually there is no more checking to be done and we head out into the crisp morning. The streets are quiet and the city sleeps, other than the steady stream of lycra-clad runners flowing to the castle, acknowledging each other with subdued smiles.

I try to distract myself by looking at their shoes, their race vests, their hats. Anything to take my mind off what is ahead, but it has the opposite effect. Everyone else looks like they know what they are doing and are carrying less than half of what I've stuffed into my rucksack, bursting at the seams. My mind whirrs with worry.

We walk up the cobbled walkway, over what was the moat and into the shadow of the imposing stone walls. We try to relax in the morning sunshine in the courtyard, the quiet hum of conversation soothing my frayed nerves. I can't even remember what we talked about to pass the time but soon we were lining up for the start.

The starting horn sounds and out we flow, a mass of neon floating out of the gates. No one is racing… we all know we have a long day and many miles to cover ahead. The mood is jubilant, and I sense many others are just glad to be moving, in the same way I am. Smiles are exchanged as runners find their own space and rhythm.

We filter out of the city into the countryside, following winding B roads bordered by endless fields, steadily trotting alongside hedges listening to the bird song. The first few hours pass quickly and, before we know it, we reach the first checkpoint. It's like an all you can eat picnic buffet with rows of sandwiches on plump white rolls, crisps in a plethora of flavours, and more Mars and Snickers bars than I've ever seen. I avail myself of a delicious egg mayo sandwich and some Frazzles and we continue, walking and eating as we go.

A little later we catch up to another runner and chat as we climb over a stile. When we tell him it's our first ultra he shares a pearl of wisdom. 'It will hurt', he says. 'It's just how long you can take the pain'. At the time, I didn't know how apt those words were, but I've repeated them to myself at nearly every ultra I've participated in since.

Walltown Quarry checkpoint is both a revelation and quicksand. We arrive in the middle of a beautiful day, warm but overcast. Again, I'm amazed by the sheer volume of food available. This time a whole marquee of cake, sandwiches, peanuts, crisps, fruit….. you name it, it was there.

And tea! Hot, strong tea that was quite possibly the best brew I've ever had. We took our tea outside and sat on the soft grass, looking out over the quarry and listening to the various conversations going on around us. It was enough to lull you softly into sleep. We stayed far too long here, but it was irresistible.

We're approaching the marathon mark, enjoying an off-road section of rolling grassy hills, when I experience my first dark moment. For me, dark moments are when I withdraw, and self-doubt starts niggling at me. That little voice in the back of my head starts reminding me how tough this is, how much things hurt, how far I've got to go, how long it will take me to reach the finish. It starts trying to convince me that I'd be better off just stopping now – of course I can't make it another forty-three miles. I'd be foolish to even try.

I stumble through the grass, deep in my own head now. I try vainly to calculate my pace and how long it will take to reach the next checkpoint. Perhaps I'll just call it a day there I think, I'll still have done well. Round and round these thoughts go, dragging me into their endless black hole. I don't know how long I wallowed in the dark but eventually I came back to the light – it was to be the first of many dark moments in the hours to come.

Five months earlier…

Since signing up for The Wall, I'd thrown myself into training. Initially with the gusto akin to the way many of us approach our New Year's Resolutions, full of the optimism of something new and exciting. But now that novelty had faded and I'd exhausted the limits of my Running for Weight Loss app, I was beginning to struggle. Yes, I'd progressed from barely being able to run a mile without collapsing in a sweaty, red-faced mess, to managing three without stopping (provided there weren't any hills on my route to trip me up). But the enormity of the challenge ahead was now staring me in the face, like a giant Everest lurking on the horizon, constantly casting its shadow.

I decided I needed specialist help, so I set about looking for a running coach. And I was exceptionally lucky to find a local coach who was an experienced ultra-marathon runner himself. The first thing that struck me about Cliff was that he was the first person I'd met who didn't think I was absolutely bonkers. It was quite a refreshing change! And I can honestly say that, without his help, I don't think I could have made it to the start line anywhere near ready.

Not only did Cliff train me to run – improving my technique and fitness, he was also a font of knowledge when it came to all things kit, nutrition, hydration, routes, and so much more. He taught me an incredible amount in those months, and I shall forever be grateful to him. One of the biggest things he did was made me enter races before The Wall. Starting with half marathons and culminating in three marathons in a four-week period in April 2016.

This was invaluable experience as I learned how to pace myself and not get carried away, as well as how to manage myself in the race (fuelling and hydrating properly and so on). I still didn't feel like a proper runner, but I was running more than ever.

The section between thirty miles and Hexham, at forty-four miles, passes in a blur. There are times when it's an effort to simply put one foot in front of the other and I doubt my ability to cover another mile, let alone another marathon. There are other times when I look around seeing the fields and sheep and trees and birds and am so thankful for this experience. Passing the half-way sign feels fantastic and we stop for the obligatory photos. We also see our first (and pretty much only) section of Hadrian's Wall, which is quite underwhelming.

We pass the time chatting and making silly videos for our friends and family back home. We are in our own bubble now and it sometimes feels like we are the only runners on the route, until we see another Rat in the distance.

At Hexham we've designated ourselves twenty minutes for a proper feed up and change of clothes. As we approach, we wind our way through a tree-lined avenue in the park, catching glimpses of the tents and flags ahead. And Porta-loos... never thought I'd be happy to see one of those!

Changing from my sweaty, grubby t-shirt into a fresh top reminds me of the feeling of getting into bed after a bath with clean sheets on. Heaven! I change my socks, noticing blisters forming on the underside of my toes and remind myself to keep some painkillers handy for the next section. Feeling rejuvenated, I head in for food. This time I opt for delicious, soft, moist carrot cake and a vat of vegetable soup. Hot and salty with lumps of potato it makes my stomach smile.

As we leave Hexham, the sun is setting, casting a warm orange glow over the sky. We get to enjoy the entire beautiful sunset as we walk, being passed by the occasional car whose occupants shout words of encouragement. We're even told we look in better shape than others by one driver, which gives me a real mental boost. I hit the painkillers too, which gives me another lift.

Darkness falls quickly as the sun sets and the sounds of the countryside change. No longer the high-pitched warblings, now we are accompanied by the twit-twoo of owls and the soft swoosh of their wings. We see bats circling overhead, flitting madly in the twilight.

We trudge on, and it is a trudge now, our energy levels dropping with the light. We focus on keeping moving – throughout the race our goal has been to reach the finish in time for a shower and change, before we catch the National Express home. This keeps driving us forward, despite every fibre of my being shouting at me to slow down.

In the early hours we reach the final checkpoint at sixty-two miles. Less than a mile earlier I felt one of my toenails detach itself from the nail bed, causing me to yelp in agony, despite the painkillers I've been taking consistently now since Hexham. Rich has some extreme bum chafing despite the copious applications of Vaseline.

We stagger like zombies into the checkpoint area. The light spills out from the marquee, splashing over the grass. Inside, there must be twenty runners all sitting down in the warmth and staring blankly ahead. Some with brews, others with food and a handful who look like they're asleep with their eyes open.

I don't want to go in because I know how hard it will be to leave again, so I sit on the damp grass outside and take off my shoes and socks. I wish I hadn't. Somehow seeing the damage makes the pain seem worse. I'm losing toenails and the bottom of all of my toes are covered in huge water blisters. I don't know what to do to relieve the pain, so I simply tape over them and hope for the best. seven miles to go…

Those seven miles seem to take forever. The ethereal glow of the lights in the city never get any closer. Dawn comes and goes in a blaze of fiery glory and still we trudge. Through the outskirts as the city sleeps, and down onto the river side, hoping with every step to see the Millennium Bridge and the finish. Every step is agony, the tank is nearly empty.

And then I see it, less than a mile, the flags fluttering in the morning breeze. The finish line looks deserted but as we hobble over the bridge a handful of marshals are there to congratulate us. I feel emotional as they proudly present our medals and take a photo of us in front of our time – twenty-one hours twenty-five minutes. I'm vaguely hysterical and don't know whether to laugh or cry. We've done it!

The Aftermath

It's really tough to describe the feeling of finishing – it's something I genuinely don't know how to put into words. It's a combination of so many things; elation; exhilaration; pride; exhaustion; pain; relief; gratitude; happiness. It's a huge amalgamation of emotions and is no doubt different for everyone.

We had time for our showers, some chicken curry (best chicken curry ever), a brew (best brew ever) and even had half an hour spare before we hopped on the National Express back to London and to real life. We treated ourselves to a bottle of bubbles and, of course, plenty of cheesy garlic bread on the sofa.

Within days, it felt like a surreal experience, my medal the only reminder it had really happened.

So, what next? Had this been my one and only foray into ultra-marathoning then I'd have felt pretty happy. I'd read a statistic somewhere that said 0.8% of people will run one marathon in their lifetime, whereas 0.05% of people will run an ultra-marathon. I was feeling pretty proud to be in that 0.05% and I felt like I'd wholeheartedly taken on and smashed the challenge I was looking for.

But I was hooked. Runners talk about that runners high, but this was on another level. I wanted to push my body more and find out what else was out there. Here, once again, Cliff was invaluable in pointing me in the direction of other ultras, run by reputable race organisers.

I threw myself into 2016, completing two more ultras, then in 2017 I tackled eight ultra-marathons. At the end of each I felt such a sense of achievement and I was getting out to see more of the UK than ever before. Each race in a new area made me realise what a beautiful country we live in and how much we undervalue it, often looking for adventure in far-off climes rather than staying closer to home.

All this time, I was working hard at developing my career. I worked in a fantastic business and was gradually moving my way up through Operations Director to Managing Director. Whilst those roles brought added benefits and a higher salary, they also brought extra stress and pressure. My working hours grew gradually longer until working a sixty-hour week became standard. I wasn't getting nearly enough sleep and that which I was getting certainly wasn't good quality. My training suffered, yet still I pushed on.

In February 2018, this strain caught up with me. I was running the Pilgrim's Challenge, which is a fantastic two-day race covering sixty-six miles of the North Downs Way, organised by a company called XNRG. I'd struggled during day one with the mud (this event is renowned for it) and hadn't slept particularly well that night. On day two, I knew as soon as I started that it wasn't going to be a great day. Physically there wasn't anything wrong, but mentally there was. Trudging up the long hill through Denbies vineyard, the floodgates opened and I burst into tears (much to the consternation of a nearby couple out for a quiet Sunday morning stroll, who were discussing the correct tactics when dealing with a chasing tiger).

The actual figure varies depending on who you ask, but it's widely accepted that completing an ultra-marathon is anywhere from 50% to 90% mental (some even say 110% although we all know that's mathematically impossible!) Personally, I am in the 90% camp. I'm not necessarily talking about the racing snakes who are competing, but more those average runners like me, who are there to complete the run. Most times, it's not something physical that lets you down but rather mental. You listen too much to that voice that tells you that you can't do it. You listen too much to that voice telling you your legs hurt. You listen too much to that voice that says it doesn't matter if you stop here. When you lose the power to ignore or subdue that voice, that's when you quit.

And on that day, I didn't have the power. I'd used all that power dealing with the stress of work, not sleeping properly and battling day-to-day life. I didn't have any battle left in me to overcome that voice at the time I needed it. It was my first DNF (did not finish, for those non-runners out there) and I was devastated. Looking back, this should have been the kick up the rear I needed to sort myself out. But it wasn't.

I continued my quest for more extreme endurance challenges, taking on more ultra-marathons in 2018 and signing up for Half Marathon Des Sables in Fuerteventura in 2019. Training for this new style of race, where I'd need to be self-sufficient for days on end led me to more hiking and fastpacking, which in turn helped me discover the joys of wild camping. I soon started to love MREs and scoured the internet for new flavours of these wonderful dehydrated meals.

I felt more adventurous than ever – not needing to go far, or even overseas, but rather enjoying the many footpaths and trails the UK has to offer. A quick overnight here or a weekend hiking there. I started running some shorter distances too, setting myself goals for my 10k pace to keep me committed to training hard.

In September 2019, I set out on my biggest adventure yet – leaving my job and starting my own business, as well as launching my Runnerverse website, with the goal to help others on their running journey. Whether that was like me, from non-runner to runner (of any distance) or to help those who already run find new challenges and enjoy their running more.

After six years in the same business, it was a huge step outside of my comfort zone. It would have been easy to continue in the same job, safe in the knowledge that I would know the answer to 99% of the questions asked of me. Safe in the knowledge that my boss thought I did a great job. Safe in the knowledge that I was respected by my colleagues and clients (well, most of them at least!).

But if running The Wall taught me anything, it's that safe isn't always best. I could easily have failed at The Wall, but I didn't and that made the success all the sweeter.

The Wall was difficult, and I could have not done it just because it was uncomfortable or because I was scared. But I didn't let that fear stop me and yes, it was difficult, but I did it. Now I try to apply the same standards to everything in my life.

Did starting my own business scare me? Hell yes, but I still did it. After all, what is the worst that can happen? Did hopping on a plane to Norway in November with only hand luggage to hike and wild camp scare me? Hell yes, but I still did it and had the most amazing time. I wouldn't have experienced any of these things if it wasn't for The Wall – that day really did change the path of my life and I am always glad it did.

The thing is, when you step outside of your comfort zone, that zone gets bigger. So, to step outside it again, you need to do something else scary or difficult or challenging or new. But the feeling when you do is so very worth it. No matter how big or small, let adventure into your life and it can only ever change it for the better.

Website: **runnerverse.com**

Instagram: **@runnerverse** and **@hike_camp_cook_wild**

Chapter 30

Appalachian Trail – The Path Out of Pain

By Gail Muller

There I was, staring up as Katahdin loomed in front of me through the gauze of my head net while the mosquitoes and black-fly buzzed around me like tiny helicopters. I was finally at the start of the Appalachian Trail.

I never thought I'd be here. In fact, many health professionals had said that I *could* never be here. Astoundingly, they'd said I'd ultimately be in a wheelchair due to the musculoskeletal issues that would arise from the malformation of my feet. When I was born my feet were crooked; bent inwards like tiny cute bananas, so I had to wear casts for the first year of my life.

I gazed up at the mountain, it's long sloping flanks towering above me, it's snow-capped peak gleaming in the sunlight. 5,258 feet of elevation lay before me. Could I do this? Was my body up to it? Would I survive the pain?

I thought again to the prognosis in the doctor's surgery. I was just a fourteen-year-old girl sitting on a blue plastic chair being told that there would come a point in my future when I'd never walk again.

The grim prognosis didn't bother me at the time however – well at least not on the face of it. I internalised the doctor's message because I was young. I felt fine. I was fine.

But then, at about twenty-three years old, the doctor's prediction started to come to true. Chronic physical pain struck and never went away. It crept through my right hip, back and shoulder like a colonising mould through my body.

I tried everything to cure it. Over the years I went through every known medical pain relief and intervention option possible. I was finally told, at the age of thirty-two, that I needed to accept my fate, stop trying to find a cure, apply for a disability badge for my car and prepare for the worst.

I scuffed my feet in the dust of the mountain car park. Carefully stretching my body to test for the familiar rising pain. It wasn't there. I smiled to myself and let out a long breath; a breath that I felt I'd been holding in for most of my life.

I thought back to my realisation that orthodox medicine didn't have the answer for me. The doctors had run out of ideas. According to them there was no cure. This lack of hope brought on significant depression and even bleak suicidal ideation. I was facing a blank wall with no doors or windows.

But I've never really been the sort of person to accept defeat. I refused to stop working. I refused to give up my mission to heal my body. And, despite having to drag my body across the floor to the shower some mornings because I couldn't walk, I was determined to step beyond the hospital diagnoses to find a cure.

So I did. I travelled the world through hippy communes, detox centres, breathing ceremonies and hospitals to heal myself. Finally, I found specialists in Italy who were able to diagnose and treat me and, after some years of rehabilitation, I was able to re-embrace life.

And that's what brought me here. With this mountain to climb and the long trail beyond. I gazed once again at Katahdin, trying to imagine myself at the summit, walking beyond, striding through the Appalachian Trail all of the way to the end. I had to steady my thoughts. If I tried to envisage it all at once, it would become unbearable, unachievable. One step at a time, Gail!

The Appalachian Trail's fourteen States run down the East Coast of the USA, and most people attempt it Northbound from Georgia in the South to Mt Kathadin in Maine. Most prefer to allow their bodies to ease into the terrain as the elevation increases the further north you go. Hmm, not me. I wanted to test my body as hard as I could; I'd waited long enough.

The trail starts in Baxter State Park and hikers are immediately plunged into 114 miles of wilderness with no regular roads in or out. It's tough and tricky terrain, you carry all of your food for ten days. Many Southbounders quit the trail right after the wilderness with still over two thousand miles to go. More people have summited Everest than completed the AT southbound. It's tough, full of privation and can be a real shock to the system. I wasn't sure my body would even make it through ten miles let alone a hundred, but I was ready to try.

I took my first step.

*

I tramped across the bridge and up the mountain path with swelling excitement and anticipation. How hard could this climb be? The answer was, bloody hard.

An initial upward hike on dirt paths seemed simple enough, but once the elevation increased it became much tougher. The sun beat down as I grabbed branches on either side to help leverage my too-heavy body up slick rocks and mudslides.

Next I was faced with a level four vertical boulder climb, hanging on by fingertips over sheer drops. No health and safety here. I pulled myself up and over, again and again, looking down and out over views of pine forests as far as the eye could see in every direction, peppered across the range with reflective silvery lakes.

Finally, I reached the summit. I was overjoyed, buzzing with energy. I'd done it.

I made my way gingerly back down, skidding over shale and scrambling over crags.

Back in the car park, I collapsed on a picnic bench. My heart was filled with elation but I was secretly terrified – day one had already taken so much energy and courage. Tomorrow I would lose all communication and be the furthest from help and civilisation that I'd ever been. Would I be able to handle the physical challenge? Would I survive the mental struggle? I didn't know, but I wanted to try.

*

I had no idea what I expected the terrain to be like underfoot, but I was getting an immediate lesson. No rushing here lest you end up in a crumpled heap with your pack following closely behind to thunk you in the back. Bogs up to your knees which you had to navigate over on slippery logs. Rocks with water gushing over them akin to flume rides. Bugs landing on your eyeballs and constantly going down your throat.

Day after day, I trudged through beauty and pain. The blisters, shoulder aches, pack sores, joint pain and exhaustion were well compensated by the incredible views and natural landscape. I felt utterly tiny and overwhelmed by nature, never before surrounded by such wilderness. Thousands of miles of forest expanded in every direction. I was a mere speck and utterly isolated except for those rare other hikers I passed throughout the day.

Evening comes early in the deep forest, and the twilight glimmers of fading light creeping around rocks and tree trunks gave me a feeling of deep-seated primal fear that I can't describe. It actually made me burst into tears the first time. It was as if the forest was warning me to get to safety and out of its belly, that night was coming and I should be next to a fire, leaving the wilderness for the night creatures.

*

I hiked, noting the miles notching up. I swam in beautiful lakes, washed my clothes with safe products in streams and hung them around my tent in the sunshine like joyful hiker-flags to dry. I made friends with those I hiked with and the first trail families formed.

The wilderness reminded me of the Hunger Games in places. People who had hiked strongly ahead in the beginning would be found stumbling on a pathway days later; tired and overwhelmed. They might have been brought up short by a broken water-filter and be sick from bad water, or have tripped and be nursing an injury, or hungry from not packing enough food. All you could do is offer what you have in your pack (which is often not a lot as you tried to keep it light) and hope they were ok but, ultimately, you'd leave them and move on unless it was an emergency. Everyone out here is genuinely having to fend for themselves and get the miles done, because there's no phone signal, few ways out, and emergency help takes a long time to come. Thankfully, I prevailed and, by dawn on the morning of day nine, I was out.

And so I ploughed further into the Maine Mountains. Ever since I had left the hundred-mile wilderness, dirty and exhausted, all I heard was how easy it was compared to what was coming up in southern Maine and the Whites of New Hampshire.

I broke the elevation down into chunks and mini-goals to make it easier for me to handle. The trail was initially kind to me although still unkempt and full of treacherous rocks that would spin out under my feet, roots to snag me, deep puddles and rivers to ford.

I talked myself up and over the Bigelows and Avery Peak; many thousands of feet of elevation. I didn't experience enough pain to stop me, and was encouraged by the Northbound hikers I passed who were moving towards the end of their hikes. I navigated windy cols between mountain peaks, and learned how to erect my tent on a wooden platform, because there was no soft earth to put tent stakes into so high up on the rock. Mornings saw an incredible sunrises and friends catching up from behind.

Hike, eat, sleep and repeat – we spent the next few days repeating these gruelling challenges without a break; checking elevation and maps; filtering water pulled from some dank pool or mountain spring; grinding ourselves up washed-out and almost vertical mountainsides between pines, roots and rocks as the rain and sun clocked in and out above us on rotation.

I can't actually describe how I managed to get through these days as I don't recall how I coped. I just tried to put one foot in front of the other and not cry too much at the pain and the effort so far from home. I was constantly dirty, injured and bleeding.

On the last night before we hit the next tiny town, we built a fire on a waterfall with our dwindling supplies, and treated ourselves to an icy night-time dip to soothe our bodies. We fell asleep to gushing water and crackling wood.

I didn't realise it yet, but these days would be some of my very favourite on trail. The high, cool mountain tops intersecting with the hot, dusky pine forests were a perfect mix; rewarding me with views, friendships and isolation in nature that wasn't so easy to achieve further down the line.

*

Maine kept delivering challenges, and it felt inconceivable that there were so few miles covered, considering the exhaustion I felt. I was assured that I was actually growing my 'trail legs' and that soon my body would realise what was happening and kick into a higher gear.

As it was, I dragged myself determinedly down the Mahoosuc Arm and through the mile-long glacier boulder field of the Mahoosuc Notch – known infamously as the hardest mile of the AT. The boulders were as large as small houses lying jammed against and atop each other with smaller, car-sized monoliths thrown in the gaps. Then, below this Jenga-style challenge were ice sheets we could slip and slide on – inconceivable after the heat of the day that hovered above. A deep stream ran further below adding yet more depth to this eerie and immense stretch of wild landscape. It would have taken all of my concentration, effort and energy even at the beginning of a good day, and I faced it at the *end* of a brutal day, with jelly legs, scratched and bleeding limbs and near total exhaustion.

It was incredible. It completely rejuvenated my exhausted legs and body with a burst of euphoria as I jumped between boulders, used tiny finger and foot holds to climb, and balanced over crevices to avoid the dark water and ice deep below. I climbed under and into cracks where the temperature dropped by huge degrees, making me shiver.

It didn't take long though for whatever adrenaline spike I had been riding to peter out. I was halfway through as my legs began to jerk involuntarily and feel as though they might buckle. As my vision narrowed, I knew I had no choice; there was no back, only forward, and so I did. Inch by inch.

Eventually the end hoved into view; the elevation rising along with the temperature as I emerged onto a flat piece of dirt at the end of the Notch.

All I could do was lay on the ground. I lay, panting, with stars bursting behind my eyelids. What was happening to me? My legs wouldn't stop shaking and I couldn't speak. I began to cry, which turned into a torrent streaming from my eyes and pooling by my ears into the dust.

These escapades continued apace. I left Maine and headed straight into New Hampshire to take on The Whites; an extremely famous range of peaks also known as The Presidential mountain range.

I managed to fall over on my way up Mount Washington; the biggest peak at 6288 feet and the site of the worst recorded weather in the USA. It was my worst fall yet. I couldn't get my arms out in front of me to protect myself from falling face forward on to the moonscape rocks.

A jagged edge met my chest hard. I was winded, squirming face down, pain racing through me like an express train. But I was glad my chest had broken my fall. There'd been only centimetres to go before my face would have met the next rock down.

I couldn't get up though. My heavy pack pinned me to the floor.

Suddenly, I felt a hand on my back and my pack lifted from behind.

Once on my feet, I turned to thank my saviour – a girl in her twenties with blood under her nose, a cut on her eye and black swelling on one side of her face. "You ok?" She asked.

"Yes. Just." I was clearly not quite ok yet.

"Don't worry," she said. "It's easy to do."

I couldn't stop looking at her face. "What happened to you?" I asked.

"I fell over earlier today, just the same as you. Only, when I did it, it was so shocking and painful that I wet myself. Did you?"

Dumbstruck I shook my head, staring at her and imagining how much it must hurt, knowing that there's no way down this mountain range that's easy and you just have to get through whatever happens.

"Well," she said, "you're doing ok then. Have a good hike and take care." And with that, she walked away.

*

I learned to 'cowboy camp' shortly after the Whites, laying my mat and sleeping bag under the huge dark skies and eschewing a tent to count stars and feel the wind on my face.

I also spent time off trail exploring side trails, especially in the 'Pemigewasset Wilderness', where I wanted to explore some old logging camps from the late 1800s that had lain abandoned for ninety years.

My experienced trail buddy explained that the off-trail Pemi Loop would meander through deep forest for twenty-five miles and eventually take us out of the wild and back to the AT just before the stunning Franconia Ridge.

I hesitated for a while but eventually decided to do it, firstly making him promise that he wouldn't hike far ahead of me and disappear because I had no maps of the area or any idea where I was going – we were going decidedly off-grid.

Stepping gingerly over a deep, wide river and plunging into the wet foggy woods away from the familiar white blazes was a little unnerving, but I trusted him. It was a longer trail than the AT route and much more wild and unused. It was scarily easier to step off and get lost because it wasn't marked well, but between using my basic GPS to get bearings and a paper map, we found our way for twenty-five long miles, weaving past areas where it seemed no one had been for an age.

Occasional old camps loomed into view along the sides of the trail, deep under the regrowth reclamation of the forest. Abandoned cracked cauldrons used for cooking and feeding hundreds of hungry loggers lay on their sides smothered by green blankets of new growth. Old rusted tools leant on tree trunks slowly being absorbed back into the fabric of the wood.

We navigated washed out bridges over big rivers, bushwhacked between unconnected trail ends and followed rotten railway lines, overgrown and long abandoned. I felt completely, safely and happily lost.

*

Weeks later I was to feel very *un*happily lost, as I made my way down one of the last huge peaks I would see for hundreds of miles: Moosilauke. It was on this descent back towards the deep forest that I had my first ever panic attack.

It was a hard day, and my friend had gone ahead long before. People I passed had said he was 'just ahead', but when he wasn't at the windy and wild summit, I was taken aback. He always waited for me at significant spots. He'd looked at my 'Guthook' mapping app earlier in the day and noted a small stream about a mile into the descent, so I imagined he'd probably be there.

On I went, but anxiety had begun to growl in my tummy. Where was he? I had never camped alone and was frightened at the prospect. I was scared because the woods can feel eerie as it gets dark. I always knew there might be a time when I was alone in the deep, dark trees and would have to face some significant fear. I just wasn't ready for it to be this soon.

It was dark by the time I got to the bottom of the mountain and my panic had risen. Here I was, standing in an abandoned camp at twilight with no one around, and dusky shadows playing tricks on my mind.

I started hyperventilating; the panic attack escalated to a point where I wasn't really experiencing reality, but more like night terrors and hallucinations. Eventually I ran blindly, sobbing and shouting through the forest and even stumbling and falling into a river, until I got to a road.

Luckily, I stumbled into three Northbound hikers who took me under their wing; one was a paramedic and was able to talk me down to a calmer state. They got me safely to a tiny hostel, which was serendipitously close, and from there, I reflected on what had happened.

I had never experienced anything like that panic and terror before. Although very scary, it taught me a lot. It made me face my fears and pushed me to a place of understanding that helped me feel safer as I continued the trail. I was alone, I was scared, but nothing bad happened and I was okay.

My friend had taken a wrong turn and gotten lost himself, and we were happily reunited soon afterwards.

*

As I got stronger, the trail sped up under my feet and the states zipped past; sleeping on church steps and swimming in silent silver lakes in Massachusetts, covered bridges in Connecticut and then the bountiful delis full of sandwiches of dreams in New York. All accompanied with a fair amount of drought and water fear as the summer burned up all our streams and springs, and we panted in the ninety degree air.

Our feet inexorably took us on, and New Jersey turned into Pennsylvania in short order. It was a state that NOBO's passing us had complained about for a thousand miles. It's loathed by most hikers because it is filled with the sharpest and most difficult to navigate rocks on the whole trail. Every step is a potential ankle turn. The sharp sides of the rocks cut through your shoes and snag your ankles. We were often crying with pain walking the miles at the end of our long twenty-five-plus-mile days.

This was also where the snakes lived in their droves. They curled up in the heat between the cracks and crannies of the rocks where your feet would slip. We would gasp and shriek through the days as we saw black slick bodies wend across the trail in front of us, or freeze when we heard the warning rattle from just under where we had stepped.

Pennsylvania just wore us out. It ground us down to dust in the heat, and it was here that I first damaged my foot – an injury which wouldn't leave me alone.

I was careening down the mountain slope towards the town of Duncannon, to stay at yet another church hostel in the basement on the floor, and I was tired after a twenty-nine-mile day communing with the rocks. My shoe was in the process of falling apart. The sole caught under a root, and I hit my foot fiercely on a stone. Agony.

At this stage of the day all I wanted was a cold beer, so I ignored the pain and hobbled towards the legendary 'Doyle' hotel where Charles Dickens himself had once stayed.

I hiked and hiked; over three hundred miles with my quiet injury, trying to keep in good spirits. But my foot wasn't healing, and I had a bad feeling about it. I was falling behind my crew in the daytime and limping into camp late. It wasn't good.

Finally, sobbing in tears, I called a hostel from the top of one of the peaks and cried about the agony I was in. They immediately told me where to get to so that they could collect me.

A number of hours later, I limped down to a car waiting for me in a trail car park. My friends had hiked on and didn't know my dire situation, so I was alone. As we pulled away towards the closest hospital for x-rays, I was quietly convinced I was nursing a broken foot, and the end of my journey.

*

I lay in my hospital cubicle listening to the clank and whirr of machines and gurneys around me, waiting impatiently to hear the outcome of the x-rays. No one had given me a clear indication of what they thought was going on but they were all being very kind. A security guard had been tasked with bringing me as many snacks as he could find.

Everyone could see I was ravenous, and the nurses were sneaking me paper cups of their own herbal teas that they'd brought to work for break times.

Finally someone approached. "No breaks," she said with a smile. "We think it's overuse and that you need to rest it for a few days."

This made me ecstatic! I had been sure I'd get a diagnosis of a break and instructions to return home immediately. This news was almost encouragement to continue!

She wrote me a prescription for some anti-inflammatories and bandaged me up, then the lady from the front desk came and scooted herself on to the side of my bed with a warm smile; hmmmm, the bill was coming (and it was enormous).

Joyous as I was, I knew I wasn't healed yet. My foot pain receded slightly with medicine, but I knew that it was masking the realities of the issue. I pretended not to hobble, and I elevated my foot and iced it as much as I could in the trailside motel I chose to rest at.

Still, I soldiered on and hiked the Virginia Triple over a few days with my friends. It was spectacular and well worth the silent agony.

Before leaving town, I bought myself some new, sturdier shoes which helped slightly by limiting the flexion of my foot, and I made sure I hiked alone for most of the time during the day so no one could see me hobble and cry. But my pretence could only last so long, and as I made my way to Pearisburg a few days later, I knew that the jig was up and I was in too much pain to continue.

On my last day, I stumbled about wincing at rocks hidden under fallen leaves. I cried to my Mum on the phone about having to make this difficult choice; trying to process what I perceived as failure.

I passed a mama bear and her two cubs in the woods and spent an hour watching them play, accepting this as a beautiful parting gift from the trail. Then I slowly hiked down into town, biting my lip to keep from screaming against the agony creeping up my leg.

In Pearisburg, my trail family were upset at my decision but had seen me decline and knew it was the right thing. They all took the next day off trail and we spent it together cooking, eating and watching movies in the hostel.

Upon waking, they hugged me goodbye in the cool of the still-dark morning. We knew it would be a long time, if ever, until we'd see each other again.

I stepped into the car that would start my long journey home, and my friends disappeared into the dawn-dusked woods.

*

Returning home was very hard; I felt full of grief and displacement but was determined to get back to trail ASAP. My doctor told me I had tendinitis and would need to rest properly for healing to happen, so I diligently sat with my foot up for two and a half weeks.

I then flew to India for a pre-promised trip and, on my return almost one month after leaving the US, I pivoted off one plane in London and jumped onto another – back to my home in the woods to finish what I'd started. Even if I had to drag myself to the end of the AT on crutches and streaming with tears, I was determined to finish.

It was a long reverse journey to exactly where I had left trail, but I was remembered and welcomed when I arrived. I immediately met a new squad at the Angel's Rest Hostel, but they were zeroing the next day and I couldn't afford to zero with my strict schedule. I set off alone the next morning, hoping they would catch me. Immediately, I was hit with brutally cold weather and the sharp icy air caught my throat as I walked. Time to layer up hard.

Over the next couple of weeks, the usual daily adventures of trail life resumed. I re-joined with my new friends, had a hunter cook me bear meat, stayed in a frigid stone hut at high elevation where many things froze in my food bag, and also passed the ¾ trail sign which I'd seen so many friends pass before me online. I was back in the swing of it!

The weeks bled together in the frost and rain, and I was so very happy to be back on trail that I had to pinch myself to believe I was legitimately nearing the end in Georgia! It was beginning to feel like this had become the place I felt the most comfortable in the world; the simplicity of clear goals to move towards and being surrounded by big, wild nature.

Though November and early December were very cold, I was still awed daily by the beauty around me. There was a part of me that knew I just couldn't go back to my old life after this.

*

I finally ticked off VA – the longest state on the trail by far – and crossed the border into Tennessee. I was absolutely overjoyed. We hiked across the NC and TN borders many times, weaving back and forth as the mountain ranges led us a merry and beautiful dance. We saw fewer hikers and the low temperatures continued to stress our bodies.

Georgia seemed to race up upon us over the next few days and, suddenly, I was close to Springer Mountain and sleeping in the woods for the last night.

I couldn't believe it; so many miles, adventures, friendships and growth reaching the mythical endpoint we'd all talked about and imagined for so long. I chose to walk silently and alone that day, reflecting on my time on trail.

It was mid-afternoon when I walked across some jagged rocks, around a corner and up onto the final white blaze. I cried quietly in the frigid, misty air and touched the rock beneath my feet with both my hands. I had done it.

*

I think that we are all capable of great things. With the right determination and self-belief, really anything is possible. If I, with my broken body and beaten spirit, can will myself to walk 2200 miles across the mountain ranges of the USA and succeed, then you can too.

Whatever it is you dream of, take a step in that direction today and say, "Yes!" Just see where that steady, stoic determination will take you.

For me, it's taken me towards another way of life. I am in the process of writing a book and have four more epic trails to hike. I know I'll be seeing you out there somewhere on those trails, be they metaphorical and literal, because this is when you say, "YES!" and start planning an adventure of your own.

Website: **gailmuller.com**

Instragram: **@appalachiangail**

Facebook: **appalachiangail**

Twitter: **@appalachiangail**

Chapter 31

Tandems and Tribulations

By Marcus Mumford

"NO! No I don't want to go with you!" I shouted at the short Georgian man in front of me. He defiantly stood his ground, a well-worn khaki jacket on his shoulders, a leather flat cap perched on his head and heavy boots on his feet. It was as typical an outfit in this rural part of the Caucasus region as you are likely to find, right down to the large knife tucked into his belt and shotgun slung casually across his back.

He had approached our newly constructed camp just as the last puff of air had been blown into the sleeping mats and the stove was being assembled and primed ready for cooking our dinner. Our menu options for that evening's meal (pasta with tomatoes, topped with an unidentifiable meat product, or rice and tomatoes, topped with an unidentifiable meat product) had yet to be decided. A toss of a fifty tetri coin would have easily solved that problem. Yet for some reason our new acquaintance seemed to be taking exception to our being there.

Although our knowledge of the Georgian language didn't extend much beyond 'please', 'thank you' and 'cheers', his hand gestures and demeanour clearly indicated that he wasn't going to take no for an answer. We got the strong impression that he wanted us to pack-up and clear-off. He shifted the weight of the leather strap on his shoulder that supported the shotgun. It almost took our attention away from his glinting knife.

*

These kinds of things are bound to happen when you go riding off around the world on a tandem. In fact we'd been warned about the risks by lots of people before we set off. Concerned friends and family pointed out that "You might get really ill in the middle of nowhere" or "You might have an accident" or "Your bike might get stolen" or perhaps "You might meet someone with a gun". All this well-meaning advice was being handed out essentially suggesting we should stay at home where it's nice and safe.

There was a problem with that. We didn't want to stay 'nice and safe'. The comfort zone of our nine-to-five office jobs was becoming stifling and we were worried that if we weren't careful we'd be stuck in front of our computer screens until we were ejected, or rejected, into retirement. It's not that we didn't like our jobs, but we certainly didn't love them. There were legitimate risks that we had considered carefully and on balance decided that they were still worth taking. We wanted an adventure after all.

What really peppered our itchy feet was discovering cycle touring. It was Kirsty's idea to try a short trip around the Hebrides by bike, which we took on with lots of enthusiasm, very little experience and a little nervousness - but came away totally hooked. The gentle speed of travel, our exposure to the environment and the absolute simplicity of it were very addictive and we soon looked to do more.

That first trip had been on solo machines which had presented a slight problem. Too much bike racing had instilled an over-enthusiastic competitiveness in me that I found very hard to switch off. Put me on a bike at the bottom of a hill and my default mode is to push very hard on the pedals until the top. Fun for me but not particularly sociable or chivalrous I guiltily remember with an apologetic glance back at Kirsty.

We found a solution during our second cycle touring trip when we decided to try a tandem. It seemed like the logical choice as suddenly the workload was shared and if either one of us felt like going a bit faster, then the other would also enjoy the extra speed. It had several other benefits including experiencing every aspect of the journey together and the ability to chat away merrily as we rode. An unexpected advantage was that Kirsty could easily ride no-handed which allowed for lots of in-flight photography and a large selection of photos featuring the back of my head. It was an unsteady learning curve but that second trip through Norway confirmed our love of cycle touring and refined it further. We now had a love of Tandem Cycle Touring.

*

Back in Georgia we were in a standoff with the armed man. The main issue for us - weapons aside - was that we were really rather pleased with our little campsite. After several months on the road we had become quite adept at spotting good places to pitch our tent. Pretty little woodland clearings, hilltop pastures, beachside dunes with spectacular sunset vistas and even deserted cafes could be made to feel quite homely as soon as we had our tent up and stove on. That skill hasn't left yet, so even on the most innocuous car journey we'll find ourselves pointing to an inviting patch of grass and agreeing that it would have been a good place to camp.

On this occasion it had taken us until late in the day to find somewhere suitable but it was worth the wait. We were nestled in a meadow alongside a small, meandering river with views of the Upper Caucasus Mountains filling the horizon, an imposing, jagged ridge still half-covered in snow. A copse of trees helped to keep us out of view from the road and there was not a single house to be seen. We felt relaxed and comfortable and ready to enjoy our evening in peace after a tough day on the bike. Since setting off after breakfast, we'd winched our way up several long hills through damp forests, made harder with the addition of a relentless headwind and a few showers for good measure.

I was trying to explain all of this to the man but the language barrier was making it difficult to convey our desire to just eat and sleep. "It'll just be for one night and then we'll go in the morning. You won't even know that we've been here," I reasoned. But the more I argued the more animated he became, pointing at the tent then with two hands motioning down towards the ground followed by a sweep of the arm out towards the road. Meanwhile the sun was beginning to set, so if he was going to make us move on then we'd be stuck in the dark with nowhere to stay.

We stood our ground, and he stood his

*

"Won't you end up killing each other?"

Choosing a tandem as our mode of transport introduces a new risk that some people were keen to point out. There's a well-worn saying, "Whichever direction your relationship is going, a tandem will get you there quicker," and any prospective Captain or Stoker should take great heed. Coordinating two bodies to work in total unison takes practice and a complete understanding of how the other person thinks. There are inevitable compromises to be made on both sides to try and ensure that the team works and maintains harmony. Introduce an unjustified criticism or, even worse, any suggestion of doubt that the other person isn't doing what they should be doing, and a tandem crew will very swiftly go their separate ways. Which would be fine if it wasn't for the fact that you're on the same bike.

After Norway, we had tested our tolerance of each other with more trips, even spending our honeymoon on the tandem on the Dalmatian Coast. I wouldn't want to claim that we got on all of the time, but after an hour or two of very quiet riding we would eventually forget what it was that we'd argued about and could carry on pedalling as normal.

Returning to our desk jobs after each tour was becoming more and more difficult. It's not unusual to get post-holiday blues, but for us this felt deeper. There was a sense that we needed to significantly change our lives, but at that stage we weren't quite sure what that change should look like.

To begin with we looked at running a hostel. It seemed to offer the complete shift in lifestyle we craved while bringing us into contact with interesting folk. The rewards would be immediate and directly related to the work that we put in which was very appealing. Best of all was the fact that it could be seasonal so we would have the winter months available to venture out into other parts of the world and satisfy our cycle touring cravings. We explored this idea quite extensively to the point of spending a weekend near Machynlleth with the owners of a hostel that was up for sale.

Michael and Debbie were great hosts and almost convinced us that this was the right thing for us to do until we got onto the subject of travelling. When we explained that, once it was loaded with panniers, our bike could in theory allow us to ride almost anywhere in the world, they were amazed we weren't out riding it right there and then.

"With that kind of freedom available to you, I think you should make the most of it instead of tying yourselves down to something like this," Michael told us. It may not have been the shrewdest business move from his point of view, but it flicked a switch with both of us. Our imaginations started racing, and maps and plans began to unfold.

Life is full of turning points where a decision to take one road instead of the other can affect absolutely everything. Looking back at the moment where we had decided to embark on our trip, I think the most remarkable aspect of it was that we were both ready to take the adventure plunge at exactly the same point in time. A collective and unifying Yes! It would mean leaving everything we were familiar with including friends, family and the security of a job, but together we felt we were ready to take on whatever was in store on the road ahead. How difficult would it have been if either one of us wasn't fully committed? Would one have managed to persuade the other to stay - or to go? It will always be one of the most pivotal points in both our lives and everything that would happen on the journey and our lives afterwards was the result of making that decision together.

The plan took the form of a vague line on a world map linking bits we wanted to visit in such a way that we should (hopefully) avoid getting too cold, too hot or too wet. The theory was that the process of cycle touring is the same whether you're setting out for two weeks, two months or two years, it's just a case of finding water, food and somewhere to sleep with a bit of pedalling from A to B each day. We tried to keep away from planning the finer details to give ourselves plenty of flexibility and for serendipity to play its part in our journey. We had learned on our previous trips that the adventure is far richer if you can allow for the route to be shaped by the people you meet and the things you learn along the way.

When we eventually reached the point of departure from our home in Bristol, we were escorted for the first few miles by a large peloton of friends. The group slowly dwindled as people peeled off leaving us with a final hug and a "Bon Voyage". Eventually we were on our own with nothing to contemplate but the enormity of the task ahead. A sense of total freedom and endless possibilities washed over us with a curious mix of relief, excitement and trepidation. It was as much as I could do to keep the heavy bike upright as thoughts of what we were about to attempt and what we'd left behind spiralled around my head. I reached a sweaty hand down to change gear while behind me Kirsty was uncharacteristically quiet.

We'd committed fully: quit our jobs, rented out our house and packed most of our earthly possessions into storage. Turning around to return to those same friends having got no further than Wiltshire would have felt humiliating but, most of all, we didn't want to let each other down either. Although neither of us admitted it at the time I suspect we were both having the same doubts. The beauty of the tandem meant that so long as one of us was willing and able to turn the pedals, the other had to turn theirs.

And so the pedals kept turning. As we left the English coastline behind us we became more and more comfortable with our new lifestyle. It's not a fast way to travel but that was one of the things that most appealed to us about choosing to travel by bike. It's quick enough to make progress but slow enough to take in all the important details. As we crossed the continents everything changed gradually which helped us make sense of it all. Language, landscape and culture altered bit by bit as we moved east. We also became more and more of a curiosity as we began exploring regions that saw very few foreign visitors, let alone two foreign visitors on one bike.

It was hard not to feel like celebrities when babies were passed to us for photographs or the tribal chief was summoned to welcome us into his village. Parking the tandem would always result in a routine that somehow became universal in almost every country we visited. First someone would turn the cranks to see how the two sets of pedals were joined together. Next they'd inspect our clipless pedals so we'd have to show the soles of our shoes to reveal the cleats. They'd then carry out what we named the 'Calibrated Pinch' by squeezing one of the tyres and giving a thumbs up to indicate that the pressure was exactly right. Finally, and usually after a mischievous look around to see if anyone else was watching, they'd give our horn a hoot. That horn was our most effective anti-theft device because wherever we left the bike, provided we were still in earshot we would hear someone giving it a squeeze every few minutes. So long as we could hear the horn we knew our bike was safe.

*

Accepting defeat to our Georgian challenger, we began to pack our belongings. We were travelling with just four panniers between us, and while this lack of luggage space is one of the drawbacks of using a tandem it's also a benefit because there's a pleasing simplicity, no faff and best of all, no unnecessary weight to haul uphill. Even with so little to pack up it still took us a good fifteen minutes to break camp at our beautiful riverside spot, with the added pressure of the Georgian man watching our every move. He had won the argument mainly because we were in no position to defend ourselves and he had become increasingly agitated that we weren't doing what he asked. As we packed up he was busy on his phone issuing instructions to an unknown accomplice.

Once the bike was loaded we were pointed in the direction of the road while the man had a firm hold of the rear pannier rack, presumably to make sure we didn't try and jump on board and ride off. We rolled out of the meadow and onto a single track road, both of us looking worriedly at each other as the man gestured for us to turn left and follow the road. He wasn't letting go of the bike so we continued to push.

By now the sun had well and truly set and we were following the small pools of light from our head torches and shadows danced alongside us. The twinkling lights of a small village up ahead seemed to be where he was taking us. As we trudged on in the darkness It felt like we weren't getting any closer but the man kept pushing with a look of grim determination etched on his face so we continued on towards the lights.

Eventually our strange little procession reached the outskirts of the village and we were considering our options.

We could try and get on the bike and ride away from him, perhaps using the classic distraction technique of pointing behind him, shouting "Look over there!" then leaping on board and weaving as much as possible to avoid any shots that might be fired in our direction.

Maybe we could yell for help from some of the other villagers? But what if they helped the man to kidnap us, before distributing our meagre possessions amongst themselves? We could bribe him? Try and overpower him and bungee his legs together?

All too risky. We pushed on.

We passed several houses, their shutters closed. Only a sliver of light and smoke from the chimneys betrayed the fact they were occupied. Two or three people moved around in the shadowy streets and stopped to stare at this unusual sight. Our man nodded and waved to them looking pleased with his night's bounty. The man then motioned towards a driveway which we obediently wheeled down into and parked our bike against the cracked, green plasterwork under a wide balcony that jutted out above us.

This was it then. The end of the road. I could see a heavy steel gate behind us that was no doubt about to be slammed shut.

In front of us the front door of the house creaked open and a lady with a rugged face shuffled out in her clogs. She smiled and beckoned us into the house. Something about that smile made us realise that we may have misinterpreted this situation entirely, but then again maybe they wanted us to drop our guard? With very few options left we did as we were told and stepped into the house. We walked into their dining room and in front of us was a huge spread of food laid out on the table. Beef, lamb, gherkins, bread, cabbage, mountains of potatoes. And apparently, an invite to join them for dinner.

Georgians have a reputation for two things: one is their fondness for drinking which is no doubt born out of the fact that they claim to have invented wine around eight thousand years ago. Maintaining this heritage is very important to them so offers of a glass of wine or their super-strength moonshine 'chacha' are almost as common as offers of a glass of chai in neighbouring Turkey. They are also famous for their hospitality, which our hosts Jimali and Nora had taken to a new level by providing dinner and accommodation at gunpoint. Our reluctance to join them was quickly turned into overwhelming gratitude as we tucked into the host of Georgian delicacies they had laid on for us including, of course, plenty of homemade wine and chacha to wash down the food.

As each glass was charged Jimali, as the shotgun wielding gentlemen eventually introduced himself, prepared an elaborate and heartfelt toast to our new found friendship. There was, apparently, an inseparable bond that was being formed between our two countries. "Georgia!" he cried raising one hand, "Anglia!" he signalled with the other hand before bringing them together in a tight clasp "Friends!". This of course was interpreted through his hand gestures, mimes and the handful of Russian words we understand.

During the course of the evening we shared stories via photos on our phones and more miming. At one point I found a photo from our time in Lithuania that showed me standing next to a huge statue of Joseph Stalin. "Ah, Stalin!" cried Jimali before darting off into the depths of the house. Worried that I'd offended him, I called after him with profuse apologies, but he was soon back with a big grin on his face, clutching an enormous portrait of the man himself. "Stalin!" he confirmed. We were near to the birthplace of the infamous tyrant and bizarrely it seems he is still seen as something of a local hero.

After a very cosy night in the spare room, we came down to breakfast to find the leftovers from the previous night's feast being offered up including the dregs of the 'chacha' that we thought we'd managed to avoid. By this stage word about their unusual guests had got round to Jimali and Nora's neighbours, so several people joined us for breakfast. As each new person arrived another round of toasts were presented. Eventually I performed a detailed mime that indicated a pedalling motion followed by a swerving action and me falling over to show we needed to get going while I was still sober enough to keep control of the tandem. "I've had more than enough thank you!". Everyone in the room laughed before Jimali charged our glasses one last time.

These kinds of things are bound to happen when you go riding off around the world on a tandem. In fact all those warnings before we set off on our trip turned out to be justified: we did get really ill in India, we did have a big accident in Turkey, we did get our bike stolen in Kyrgyzstan and we did encounter our new friend with a gun in Georgia. The thing we quickly learned though was that these calamities always resulted in exposure to some of the kindest and most generous human beings we could hope to meet. Out of the bad times came some of the best times, and that made taking those risks all worthwhile.

As for the biggest risk of them all? The tandem took our relationship on a bumpy old ride and during those most difficult times it felt like we were held together by the finest of threads. Emotions seemed to be amplified during such an intense situation where we were rarely ever more than a metre apart.

Yet somehow we managed to ride through it and ultimately came out the other side stronger. Using a different form of transport may have had a different result but the bike made sure we had to work together or else the trip would be over.

What was that old saying? "Whichever direction your relationship is going, a tandem will get you there quicker".

It's absolutely true.

Website: **shesnotpedallingontheback.com**

Chapter 32

Embracing Home Ed, Community and the Outdoors

By Eabhnat Ní Laighin

I suppose this particular YesStory of mine really started thirteen years ago on the birth of my first of three beautiful children. It is a journey that has many years still to go. It is saying yes to being the best parent I can be to the three wonderful children who have graced my life. It's a story of striving to safeguard their future. A story of imperfection, mistakes, growth and love. And in the middle of all that it is a story of saying yes to being the person it feels natural for me to be, not just parent, but me.

In December 2018 my kids and I challenged ourselves to #getoutside every day in 2019 and to share our experiences with the world through a blog (which didn't happen) and social media (which did). My aim was to ensure my kids and I got as much fresh air and outside time as possible for our health and happiness and to inspire other families to do the same. When I volunteered to write my story for the Biggest Book of Yes, that was the Yes I decided on. But as I have mulled it over, written, re-written and deleted, this YesStory has morphed into something broader. And to tell it we have to go back a little further in time.

About four years ago, I was plodding along in my full-time, primary teaching job in Glasgow, trying my best to juggle work and life. In school, I was to be found outside among the trees as often as inside among the desks. Outside school I was quite often to be found at a picnic bench in a local park or encouraging my children to climb the higher tree. Family holidays were either at the beach or in my parents' garden. We loved the outdoors and our kids did too.

One lazy Saturday morning, a good friend of mine sent me a link to an online news article about The Meek Family, who withdrew their two girls Amy and Ella from school, for a year initially, to spend their time edventuring. (Education through adventures) My friend's accompanying comment was "This reminded me of you and Dougie. You two could so do that!"

I devoured the article. Then I went straight to their blog and social media pages to glean as much information and inspiration as I could. I'd never heard of such a crazy, wonderful way to spend your kids' childhood! A seed was sown.

Over the next few years, the seed took root and grew. Its roots tangled in my brain and kept me awake at night. I imagined travelling around the UK and Ireland with the kids. I imagined travelling the world, learning through experience and adventure.

Naturally I was also imagining not having to work a full-time, all-consuming job! A job that was becoming increasingly challenging. I was slowly realising that being the mother I wanted to be and the teacher I wanted to be were becoming less and less compatible. I could be good at both, but not great. And if I tried to be great at one? Well you can imagine the ying to that yang!

During this time, my family and I were living with the knowledge that my father's life was coming to an end. All my holidays were spent trying to cram in as much precious time as I could with my parents in Ireland. Nothing puts your life into sharp perspective like the prospect of losing someone you love. The associated stress also meant I was less resilient and effective at work. As a teacher, there's very little room for being off form.

All in all, I was being drawn to change from all sides.

After many long, sometimes highly charged, conversations with my husband, Dougie, we agreed to offer the children a year being home educated. For various reasons, it wasn't to be a big world trip, or even a big UK & Ireland trip, but a series of smaller edventures around Glasgow with a few bigger ones thrown in. The two younger ones jumped at the idea and wanted to start straight away. They saw nothing but excitement in the prospect. Our eldest however, was less keen. She was finishing primary and already registered for high school with her friends. She wanted to transition to this new, exciting phase with them. This was our biggest stumbling block and took a bit of bribery and persuasion to overcome.

With it all now feeling very real, I applied for a career break and, despite being like gold dust, I was very fortunate to be offered an absence of two years. To have that safety net to fall back on made decisions much easier.

And so, in June 2018, the kids and I heard a school bell for what was to be the last time in over a year.

With both of us parents being teachers, we were used to long summer holidays adventuring together in Ireland, the Western Isles or the Isle of Bute. It was a summer of sunshine and beaches and the idea of home ed was very abstract.

Then one morning in August, I awoke to find my husband back in school and my children gathered in the sitting room of our caravan creating a timetable of schoolwork for the day. My heart sank. I had hoped for a much clearer break from school than that! I didn't want timetables or subjects, schoolbooks or jotters. I wanted the outdoors and picnics, trips and adventure, passion projects and mountains of books.

I spent that first morning facilitating history and maths work and then the afternoon picnicking on the beach. That was a compromise I could live with. (for a while)

I had read books, blogs and a thousand social media posts on home education, unschooling and even wild schooling. I had joined the local Home Ed Facebook Group and knew there were many families who had turned to the dark side! I was sold on the idea of no curriculum and learning through experience, but I hadn't factored in my children's institutionalisation. My husband's, I was well versed in, but I hadn't realised quite how influential school had been on the children's ideas of how we learn and what children 'need' to do. It was a bit scary.

Those first few months were a varied mix of days. August and September often felt like a continuation of summer holidays with long days at the beach or picking brambles and apples. Or sometimes a continuation of school with hours spent at the kitchen table with schoolbooks.

We spent the odd afternoon with the local home ed group, but my children were quite wary of these strange, new people. Their mixed age groupings, lack of strict rules and inclusive activities were alien to them. A sports day without medals and everyone being a winner? What was that all about? At one meet, when it came to picnic time, to avoid sitting with the main group, my children, not only went to the far side of the park but climbed a tree to eat their packed lunch. Joining music and sports classes every Monday, which they enjoyed, meant they were beginning to get to know kids. However, they regularly found excuses not to attend the less structured Wednesday or Tuesday meets.

In October 2018, we all bundled into the car and travelled 450 miles to spend the weekend in a field with a group of strangers, drinking from tin mugs, sleeping under many layers in tents and being inspired by the stories of others. Welcome to Yestival! All of us were inspired. I was amazed by Hannah Miller sleeping in a tent with her five-month-old baby girl and inspired by group chats led by Mel Findlater and Cath Edsell. Their focus was on adventure as a parent and building community. It was refreshing to hear other parents with such a love of getting their kids outside and adjusting the concept of adventure to fit into the new frame of family. I was also amazed by my own children and their utter independence. I was asked by at least three people if I'd come alone because I came to all the family groups but they'd yet to see me with a child! They simply didn't need me until there was sibling friction or a sleeping bag to be zipped up. We all came away inspired, driving away with our heads swimming with ideas and vying for airtime to share them!

For quite a while, I had had the idea of starting a blog related to the outdoors, but I didn't know what on earth the focus would be. I started looking into websites and blog names but still the focus eluded me.

In November, we spent three lovely weeks in Ireland, marking my father's first anniversary and enjoying precious time with my mother. If this year with my children was a gift, this was the ribbons and bows. We helped my mother in her beautiful garden. We read books. We baked and cooked. We played music. We even climbed a hill in freezing wind and warmed ourselves with hot chocolate in the car afterwards. We were relaxed and, being away from home, gave ourselves a break from feeling like we should be 'learning'.

In December we returned to reality. The schoolbooks came back out and we bickered around the kitchen table again. The daylight hours were short and, though we went outside most days, the children were less enthusiastic about each other's company and the weather. We often weren't getting on very well and we found it difficult to agree on what we would do with our days. This year wasn't turning out the way I'd wanted it to. I felt it was being wasted away. The inspiration seemed to have frozen up in the colder weather. I was growing frustrated. I thought by now the children would be less concerned about learning fractions and more concerned with personal projects they'd decided on themselves. How would I possibly realise all those plans I had cooked up in October?

However, something I had joined online was about to change things.

In November, Ruth Blanco from the YesTribe started a group called Every Day in December. The idea was to choose a positive habit we wanted to have in our lives and, instead of just letting everything go because Christmas was coming, doing that one thing every day and not loathing ourselves come January 1st. I joined and decided to exercise every day. My youngest became my coach and did the exercises with me every night.

This group taught me two things. If I model something, my kids are more likely to follow. If I publicly commit to something, I'm more likely to do it.

Inspired by Ruth's group and desperate to get my family outside more, I invited the children to join me in a challenge to #getoutside every day in 2019. They said YES!! This would be what I would blog about. This would be my focal point. We would share our adventures on social media and encourage other families to get outside too. We would build a community of families who enjoy time outside together. We would be healthier and happier. Birds would sing, bees would hum, flowers would bloom and our family would live in perfect harmony!

Around the same time, I promised myself that we wouldn't open another schoolbook until they were back at school. They had no relevance to our lives. Anything we covered had no impact or use to us once we closed the book. It was liberating to make that decision.

I created a beautiful YesList for myself full of edventures, adventures and challenges. It is on the wall beside me as I type. It is now adorned with ticks and handwritten additions and amendments.

Over Christmas, we discussed how we would start our big year of #getoutside. January 1st found us climbing Conic Hill with lovely friends. Everyone was excited about the hills we would climb in 2019, the adventures we would enjoy. We were full of positivity.

That evening, I shared our Day One post on Instagram and Facebook and invited others to join us. One home ed mother followed our page and commented that her family would join us in the challenge.

A few days later, Sapna and I arranged to meet up in a cold Glasgow park with our respective broods. We knew each other a little from home ed meets but this was the first time our two families had spent time alone. The kids explored, played and grew more relaxed in each other's company while us Mums exchanged stories and discovered a shared love of the outdoors and similar views on parenting. I had an ally.

We began to engage more with the home ed group. We looked forward to Monday classes and Wednesday meets as the highlights of our week. We gradually made more friends and discovered ourselves at the heart of an inclusive, supportive and positive community.

I applied to become a SayYesMore ambassador and, not only was I accepted, but I managed to travel the 450 miles back down to the YesBus for a weekend of training and sub-zero camping. Inspiration and motivation was sky-rocketing!

The weather and our home ed experience was really improving. We were enjoying our #getoutside challenge more and more. Because we had the freedom to explore during the day we were discovering new places to do fun, outdoor things for free around Glasgow. We climbed and fell off huge boulders in Cuningar Loop and we cycled oddly shaped bikes at Free Wheel North. We enjoyed den building at Baltic Street Adventure Playground and lots of campfires in the woods. We went foraging for fresh herbs in Pollok Park and went birdwatching in Loch Winnoch RSPB reserve.

We attended Climate Strikes and learned what we as a family could do to play our part in averting the imminent climate crisis. We were surrounded by informed and passionate people and we felt empowered to orchestrate change, however small.

And that's just a little flavour. Some adventures we had as a family and some with our ever-growing community of home ed friends. It was all adding up to an ever-increasing passion for nature and the importance of both being in it and looking after it.

I started wild swimming. I loved swimming as a child but, as a mother, I was more often found holding the towels and keeping the sand warm rather than splashing in the water with my kids, certainly not in deeper than my knees. Inspired by the mermaid Lindsey Cole and all the other amazing wild swimmers she introduced me to through the sometimes-wonder that is social media, I decided to swim more. I realised what a poor role model I had been for my children, especially for my girls. Swimming wasn't just for daddies. The hardest part of jumping into cold water is deciding to do it. Once I decided, the rest was almost easy and always fun.

The great outdoors became an even more important part of our lives than it had ever been. Home ed made it so easy for us, especially in winter, while most people work during the only hours of daylight. But the biggest change was that we had embedded ourselves at the heart of a wonderful outdoor, creative, intergenerational and welcoming community. The ethos was of enabling, encouraging and supporting. The conversations were wide ranging!

While playing in the tree house in North Kelvin Meadow one day, a mixed-age group of kids decided to put on a play to raise funds for the park. My two girls were among this group and enthusiasm was high. Over the next few months, they wrote the script, auditioned for and allocated parts and rehearsed in play parks, on the beach and in the woods. When hiring a hall proved to be prohibitively difficult and expensive, the decision was made to perform it in the woods.

My son, not an actor in the group, decided to hold a raffle and asked local businesses to donate. This was turning into a huge and wonderful project and it was completely child-led. The children had ownership of their learning and, oh my were they learning and developing skills. This was the kind of learning I had envisaged.

And the most wonderful bit about it was the social skills they were developing. Older children were leading the group, supporting younger actors and enabling the inclusion of all. There were moments of frustration and discontent of course, but aren't there in every real-life project?

The big day came and the play 'Once Upon a Bedtime Story' was a huge success, despite torrential rain all day. Tarpaulins were acquired and hung between every available tree. The audience brought their own picnic chairs and head to toe waterproofs. Home baking and raffle tickets were kept dry and sold. The actors performed their little socks off. There wasn't a dry eye in the woods, never mind a dry person. Everyone was full of pride.

I loved home ed. We had discovered a community in which we felt a sense of belonging. A community which supported us with positivity and actions. And we all lived happily ever after.

Except this wasn't a bedtime story.

This was real life.

Our son was missing his school friends and playing football in the playground every day. My daughters, though they had made many friends and wanted to stay home ed, were keen to return to school because of the worry over fractions and times tables and ultimately a desire to be 'normal'. Their Dad, who was working in school every day and only experiencing most of our edventures through stories and photographs, though seeing great value in it, wanted them back in school. The bank balance needed me to return to work. We were torn.

The decision to return to school wasn't one we took lightly and certainly not quickly. We had family meetings about it, chats with school and home ed friends, hours crunching numbers and exploring part-time home ed-friendly work options. We decided and undecided over and over again. There were quite a few tears.

Eventually, all three children decided to return to school. I was heartbroken. I didn't have anything against school as such, my children had always been happy there and they were registered in lovely schools with a nurturing environment. They are social beings and make friends wherever they go.

It was the freedom, possibility and community of home ed that I wanted. I wanted it for them, and I wanted it for myself. I also carried a large chunk of guilt for putting ourselves at the very centre of the community, involving ourselves heart and soul and then leaving. It felt like a betrayal.

But none of our lovely home ed friends made us feel like that. They were sad to see us return to normality but they supported us constantly through our indecision and deliberating, offering advice and a listening ear.

The children settled straight back into school and within a week, realised that their concerns over fractions and times tables were unfounded. They loved seeing friends every day rather than just twice a week and they embraced school life fully.

In true YesTribe style, I gave up the full-time, permanent job that was being held open for me and was fortunate enough to secure a part-time job mostly teaching through outdoor learning. I was never averse to giving up a permanent job, having done it twice before to go travelling, but it seemed somehow a more momentous thing to do with a mortgage and three children to support.

However, if there was one thing I had learned over our year out, it was to embrace change and not to let worry step in the way of what you want to do. I also helped establish a group called Climate Ready

Schools Glasgow and work on a part-time voluntary basis with them. So I've found myself 'working' almost full-time, but doing things I feel passionate about.

With the luxury of hindsight, I can see the benefits of our year. We have remained friends with many in the home ed group and we are booked up to go on our third residential trip with them this month. Those ties won't be severed easily. We join their meets whenever we can.

Writing this, it still makes me teary that our home ed journey only lasted a year. Sometimes it's hard not to dwell on the experiences we could be having with home ed. But that's not much of a growth mind-set.

What I now reflect on is the impact that year had on our lives. We embraced the outdoors and successfully completed our 365 days outside challenge. We have now challenged ourselves to spending a thousand hours outside in 2020. A challenge a little more flexible and hopefully more fitting with our current lifestyle.

The biggest impact I see is our confidence in ourselves and our conviction to safeguard the future. Though never lacking I must admit, all three children have a real confidence in their own skin. We are all really passionate about the environment and all undertaking our own big and small projects to bring about positive change.

Having had a significant break from the stresses of full-time work while parenting, I have had the luxury of perspective. I must be happy in what I'm doing if I am to be the best version of myself I can be. I strive to be the best parent I can be, while remembering that parenting is a completely imperfect art.

I have found that the best way to ensure my children's confidence is to have confidence in both myself and them. The best way to teach my children is to model the lifestyle choices I would wish them to make. I strive to be kind and supportive both to others and myself. I strive to protect the earth I love and depend on. I strive to inspire others to love and protect it too. And all the while I feel supported and inspired by the wonderful friends I made last year.

I still haven't completely shelved the idea of that blog. Maybe one day.

*

Just a few days ago, during a conversation about spreading the word on climate action, my daughter said this to me.

"D'you know what Mammy? I didn't realise just how much I learned last year. I was so worried about fractions and algebra and all that stuff that I wasn't aware of the things I WAS learning."

My heart soared.

Facebook: **isleofwildkids**

Instagram: **@IsleofWildKids**

Chapter 33

Shooting Stars in the Outback

By Brooke Nolan

I unzip my tent and peer through the gap as a blast of cold air shakes the sleepiness from my eyes. It's pitch black, the faded outline of the crescent moon just visible through the thick fog that cocoons my tent.

'So much for Australian weather,' I think to myself. Every ounce of me wants to crawl back into the relative warmth of my sleeping bag and snooze until the sun comes up. 'There's no chance of a sunrise in this weather anyway,' I placate as I lay back down.

Five minutes later, after having a stern talking with myself, I peel back the covers and start to pack up my camping gear. I came here to conquer my fear of wild camping alone and watch the sunrise from the top of the highest mountain in Australia. And that's what I was going to do, whether I could see much of it or not.

Trying my hardest to ignore the voice in my head telling me to go back to bed, I pack up my soggy tent, switch on my headlight, hoist my backpack onto my shoulders and navigate my way through the mist to the faint trail at the top of the valley. A sharp right turn and I know I'll hit the base of Kosciuszko mountain some point soon.

One hour later, and I'm at the top nursing a mug of strong coffee with my fingers crossed that the sun might make an appearance. It's colder than I expect and my hands grasp the metal trying to absorb as much heat as possible.

The fog still hangs heavy, visibility no more than twenty-five metres in any direction. Then, just as I am thinking about cutting my losses and heading back to the car, the fog begins to lift. The first rays of sunshine break through the gloom. And it's glorious.

At barely 2,200 metres, Kozzi – as it's colloquially known – is hardly Everest. But, nestled in the country's alpine region, it's pretty much as close as you're going to get to 'real' mountains. Rolling peaks surround me in every direction in a soft light which kaleidoscopes from pink to purple to shimmering gold.

I stand still, alone, and reflect on how much I've changed. On how far I've come. Go back a few short years and the idea that I would ever have solo wild camped was laughable. That I would have hiked, willingly through the foggy darkness to reach the top of a mountain? Call me a comedian and get me a stage.

A lifelong fear of the physical

Throughout my life, I have feared physical activity of any type. As a child, I was teased (by teachers and peers) for having no coordination, thanks in part to my terrible eyesight and assisted further by the fact that my limbs stubbornly refused to do anything that my brain told them to do.

Exercise had always been a source of embarrassment and shame to me. I was a typical British woman, scarred by the horror of school PE lessons. As for the outdoors? I'm not even sure I knew it existed.

Those formative years spent avoiding exercise shaped me in unimaginable ways. As I got older, when going to the gym or for a run, all I could hear was the deafening sound of my own voice saying 'you're fat', 'you're useless', 'you're letting everyone down', 'you're not good enough.' It was relentless.

Yet despite that damaging internal monologue, here I was, on the other side of the world, living a life where every decision I made was geared towards helping me get out on more adventures – adventures that are inherently physical by nature.

Wild camping alone is just one of the many fears I have faced since moving to Australia and I've certainly experienced much bigger adventures since. But sometimes, it's the small moments that stay with you the most.

By tackling, one-by-one, the misconceptions I have about myself, in this case – my ability to wild camp alone – I've realised that perhaps I might not be as useless as I've been telling myself all these years.

Where it all began

Like most people's stories, mine has many beginnings. A series of moments led me to the top of that mountain on the other side of the world. And not all of them were good ones.

'I just don't think this is going to work.' The email was longer than that of course, but you get the gist. It was over. And he'd waited until I'd boarded a plane to Australia from the UK to tell me. Our plan for me to travel while he was on deployment in the navy was a fairy-tale that wouldn't have a happy ending.

What I didn't know then was that that heart-breaking email was going to change my life in ways I could never have imagined. While it might not have felt like it at the time, it truly was a blessing in disguise. It gave me the freedom to discover a new country without the constraints of having to think about someone else. It freed me.

I'd applied for my Australian Working Holiday visa long before I met Mr I'll-Wait-Till-You've-Boarded-A-Flight-And-Then-Send-You-A-Break-Up-Email.

I was nearly thirty years old and had spent my twenties slaving away for a communications agency believing that 'career' was the most important thing to me.

I drank too much. I hung out with people I didn't even like. I worked far more than I was paid to. I was in debt but could never really work out what I spent my money on. I was anxious all the time and started having body-depleting panic attacks that made me feel as though I'd been kicked in the stomach over and over.

They started from nowhere; first a little breathlessness when I got stressed at work, and then suddenly, I was having them in crowded places like train stations, after tough meetings or whenever I felt like I wasn't good enough. And it never made much sense to me. My life – on the outside at least – was great. To everyone who knew me, I was still the same confident person I always had been. I masked my feelings with the sarcasm and wit that was my M.O.

When the promotion I'd been working so hard towards was finally put on the table, I realised that perhaps I didn't want it after all. It was time to listen to my body, and instead, I headed to South America for a three-month sabbatical to think about it. It changed everything. And as much as I hate the whole 'I found myself' cliché, I really did.

For my 30th birthday, I hiked the Inca Trail in Peru. It sparked something in me I had never felt before; a sense of calm and awe that I didn't even know I'd been missing in life. I changed my sabbatical's entire itinerary after that; switching from tourist-filled sightseeing to off-the-beaten-track hiking trails.

I discovered that my own company was nothing to be afraid of. In fact, I loved being alone. I discovered that I loved hiking, kayaking, camping, exploring. I loved having dirt under my nails and salt in my hair. I loved to wake up in the wilderness surrounded by nature. I loved freedom, flexibility and seeing the stars above me while I was miles from civilisation.

I learned many things on that trip, including never to eat guinea pig from a cart on the side of the road. But above everything else, I learned that – if I was ever going to be happy – I needed to trade in the office life, where my eyes were dead and my smile was false, for a life where I could immerse myself in what made me feel truly alive.

Sabbatical sadly complete, I arrived back home to Bristol in the UK and handed my notice in. I took a four-day-a-week job in another agency; an agency that gave its staff flexibility and autonomy.

I had laser eye surgery; correcting my terrible minus 6.5 eyesight and finally ridding myself of the thick glasses and frustrating contact lenses that held me back from living the life I wanted to. I started hiking locally and tried my hand at abseiling, caving and rock climbing. It was already an improvement to that elusive work/life balance that we all seek. But I wanted more.

I needed a bigger 'yes'

"You should apply for the Australian Working Holiday Visa," Joelle said, the WhatsApp video cutting out as I tried to pick up the words she was saying. In the background, I could just make out the beach where she was currently camping. The bright sun glinted off the phone screen and water dripped from her wild corkscrew curls, still wet from her swim.

I'd met Joelle years before on a walking tour in Amsterdam. Originally from Perth, she now lived in Sydney. It was one of those easy friendships where we'd clicked immediately and we'd stayed in touch ever since.

"It sounds incredible but I think I'm too old," I replied. "Isn't the visa for eighteen to thirty-year-olds?".

But my curiosity peaked and later that evening I started googling. I discovered that you could actually apply any time before you turned thirty-one. With nothing to lose, I applied and my visa arrived a few days before my 31st birthday.

I planned to spend a year saving money, fly a few weeks before my 32nd birthday and then spend the next two years adventuring and working my way across Australia and New Zealand, where I'd also managed to secure a visa.

But it turns out that even the best-laid plans don't always go the way you want them to. After being single for over two years, the idea of romance felt about as likely as me getting the urge to join a netball team. Then, just a couple of days after I'd applied for my visas, I met Mr Email.

I won't dwell too much on the year we spent together, as, in reality, it is nothing but a footnote to this story. I am proud of myself that despite falling in love (or at least thinking I was at the time), I was always certain my trip would take place. Our relationship continued with this knowledge, and we decided to try and work through it. With him being deployed for months at a time, the distance didn't seem like an impossibility. We'd visit each other in-between.

Of course, the email changed everything. After a month alone in New Zealand reeling from the shock – and wondering how I could have been so naïve – I arrived in Sydney and fell into the welcoming arms of friends both new and old, who slowly helped to put me back together.

It was here that I realised that I wasn't broken-hearted about the break-up; I was broken-hearted because I should have known better. And I hated myself for it. My confidence was shattered and although

I'd never dreamt of the white picket fence, it still hurt that I was nearly thirty-two years old and had got it wrong again.

I turned to the one thing I knew would fix me. I spent hours exploring the beaches of Sydney, snorkelling the coral-covered bays, hiking the meandering coastal paths and getting lost in the Blue Mountains two hours west of the city.

"I didn't think I'd like it in Sydney," I explained to my Mum and Karl, my wonderful stepdad, on the phone. My cheeks were flushed from the sun, droplets of condensation sliding soundlessly down the ice-cold beer I held in my hand. It was so hot. "I don't usually like cities. But you don't feel like you're in a city here."

I'd been planning to travel the country, picking up backpacker jobs along the way, but a few short months in Sydney and I knew I didn't want to leave. Not now, not in a year, not ever. I finally felt like I had found my place in the world.

I'd met a circle of friends with whom I could finally be myself. People who were strong-willed, adventurous, kind and curious. And it was so easy to enjoy the outdoors – morning ocean swims, evening coastal walks and weekend camping trips."Maybe I can have it all," I mused. Wondering if perhaps it was possible to balance a steady career in Sydney with a love of adventure.

Shortly after this, I met with a small, family-run advertising agency and secured a full-time job as a content strategist and copywriter. Even more mind-blowing was that it came with full sponsorship to permanent residency. Getting sponsored is no easy feat, but the stars aligned for me. Australia was officially home.

Let the adventures begin

"You don't start till February," Joelle said. "Do you want to join me on the Overland Track in Tasmania first?"

The hundred-kilometre multi-day hike would be the first week of a two-month trip around the country before I settled full-time into my new job.

I wanted to go, but I was plagued by the same-old internal narrative, 'Am I strong enough, fit enough, good enough?'. I nearly said no, but I was determined not to let my anxiety beat me.

Fast forward to the first day of the hike. "We have to go up that?" I said, wiping sweat from my brow. This was my first fully self-sufficient hike carrying a week's worth of food and camping gear. My backpack was bulging and I'd obviously packed it badly as it kept pulling me off-kilter.

Luckily, it was Joelle's first self-sufficient hike too. Day one seemed to last forever. Our packs felt too heavy, our thighs burned with every step and we wondered if we'd made a big mistake.

But the further we got, the easier it became. Our bodies adjusted to the weight of our backpacks. We stopped looking at the ground and instead looked around us. And I discovered the joy of tightening your backpack's waist belt to take the pressure off your shoulders.

On that first day, the sky was azure blue without a cloud to be seen, contrasting with the emerald bushland and the rugged rock formations Tasmania is famous for. I saw my first kangaroo (although I later found out it was a wallaby). Silhouetted against the sunset, it was a foreign yet familiar sight. It had a profound impact on me; that singular wallaby was a sign of just how far from home I was.

Each step of that hike healed me a little bit more. With hindsight, I realise that I wasn't just recovering from a break-up; I was recovering from three decades of trying to fit into a box that I didn't want to be in. I'd been following a path that had seemed so clear that I hadn't even bothered to look around and see what other options were available. But now, I was here, in this beautiful country, and I could become anyone I wanted to be.

Being fully self-sufficient on the hike also enabled me to connect with nature in a deeper way than I ever had before. Even on my South American trip, I'd stayed in serviced huts with a warm meal at the end of a hard day's hike. This was different.

Before a big hike, you think that you'll spend your time deep in thought, reflecting on your life so you can make sense of it all. You think that you will have some kind of revelation. That with each step you take, your purpose in life will become clearer.

In reality, that doesn't happen.

"How far do you think we've gone?"

"Shall we stop for a snack?"

"Tent or hut tonight?"

"Ooh, let's swim in that waterfall."

"It's raining. Should we bother with waterproofs?"

"Is that snake poisonous?"

"I need to pee!"

On the trail, all of your worries from the real world fade a little more with each kilometre that passes. Your brain begins to echo the silence and space that surrounds you. You don't think about anything other than the basic human needs of food, warmth, shelter and sleep. You are nothing but pure senses, punctuated by the occasional burst of joy (or cry of indignation) about the power and beauty of Mother Nature.

It is exactly this lack of thought that makes challenging adventures so worth it. In real life, you never truly get a chance to just 'be'.

Each day of the Overland Track, myself and Joelle's confidence and strength built. By day four we'd finished the official hike and decided to embark on some side trips. Apart from a close call with a highly-deadly Tiger Snake, and one small disagreement about the best way to cross a particularly muddy section, we'd proved ourselves to be far more capable than we initially thought.

After I waved goodbye to Joelle, I treated myself to a solo whistle-stop tour of Australia. I watched the sunset over Uluru in the outback. I learned about the country's Indigenous history; a history that too often goes untold. I snorkelled the Great Barrier Reef, marvelling at the thousands of multi-coloured fish and corals. I camped in the torrential rains of the Daintree rainforest, waking up with my tent floor flooded. I drove the Great Ocean Road, seeing my first ever koala and nearly driving into a runaway emu.

When people think of Australia, they think of the beaches, the kangaroos, the surf. But it's much more than that. It is a country steeped in history and traditions spanning 65,000 years. It is ecologically endless with more diversity than you can begin to imagine. It is wild, vast, untamed. In one blow it can make you feel small and insignificant... yet entirely at home. There was no doubt about it. Australia had my heart.

Returning to Sydney (and real-life)

I returned to Sydney after my travels with a mix of excitement and trepidation. I was happy about the unexpected path I found myself on, but I was worried that I would fall back into the same old habits as home.

I'd said a life-changing, "Yes!" to get me to Australia, but it was the small 'yeses' that I said each day that would make it all worth it.

Could I really live an adventurous life and hold down a 'proper' job?

The answer is yes. But it's not easy.

"I'm tired – it's been a really long week."

"I've got work drinks / a friend's birthday."

"I really need to clean the house / go food shopping."

These are just a few of the excuses I used to tell myself back in England. I'd find myself in a pub on a weekend because that's what my friends did. The faintest hint of drizzle and I'd be snuggled up with a cuppa watching whatever nonsense show happened to be on Netflix that week.

Australia was different. But it wasn't just my location that had changed – although let's face it the weather helped – my mind-set had too.

I realised that if I wanted a life I actually wanted to live – instead of one I wanted to escape from – then I needed to start prioritising the things that mattered to me.

Since then, I've been unwavering in this approach. It's not perfect. I've missed birthday parties, celebrations with friends and my annual leave is spent on adventures rather than going back to England to visit family.

Perhaps that makes me sound selfish? But my friends and family know that getting into the wild is what I need to stay strong. I show my love to them in different ways without ever having to give up who I am. And of course, I love taking them along on adventures too.

"Where are you off to this weekend?" Every week without fail my colleagues would ask me this question. And my answer would always be somewhere different.

Facebook proved a lifeline to me, connecting me with a group of like-minded people who became my go-to adventure buddies. I bought a Honda CRV nicknamed Freeda (for the freeeeeeeedom she gave me), pulled out the backseat to make room for a bed and poured over maps and blogs for inspiration for weekend adventures.

I proved to myself that as long as you are willing to put just a little effort in, the rewards are worth it. Nearly every weekend for three years I have experienced something new, often right on my doorstep.

The moments that matter

"I've never seen a shooting star," I announced to a group of friends as we huddled around the campfire not far from Kosciuszko where I would wild camp alone for the first time a few months later.

We'd spent the day snowboarding, taking advantage of the six-week window where Australia sees snow. It was -5°C and we were the only ones in the campsite. Tomorrow, we'd share the five-hour drive back to the city.

"You must have seen a shooting star before," my friend Em laughed. "It's easy. You just look up."

Together the four of us turned our faces away from the warmth of the fire and looked up into the clear sky. A shooting star soared past and we all sat still, stunned by the hauntingly beautiful timing.

It amazes me that no matter how old I get, I can still feel that childish sense of wonder and excitement. In my twenties, I can't remember a single time that anything truly took my breath away, yet the last few years there's been too many times to count.

The Blue Mountains is another place that stole my heart and I spent many weekends there, hiking and camping in the unspoilt wilderness.

Just two hours from the city, the Blue Mountains are not actually mountains at all. The deep valleys framed by vertical sandstone cliffs were formed thanks to millions of years of erosion. At the bottom lies vast rainforests and one of the world's largest protected areas of eucalyptus trees, the preferred food of the native koala. As the light changes throughout the day, the sky turns a deeper shade of blue, the result of sunlight catching the droplets of Eucalyptus oil that permeate the air.

Keen to make the most of a weekend, I'd drive up on a Friday night, crawl into the back of Freeda and awake as the first rays of sunlight poured across the plateau. I swam in waterfalls, climbed summits, slept in caves and cooked over campfires.

Unlike when I was in England, even the rain couldn't stop me. I'd been lucky to meet a group of adventurous women; Marijs, Linda, Sam and Lindsay and we went away together nearly every month. The wet and soggy weekends ended up being some of our best. It turns out that canyons and waterfalls are even more fun when there's rain.

The beaches never ceased to amaze me either. After work, I'd walk along the clifftop paths that Sydney is famous for watching the sunset illuminate the coastline and surfers compete for the biggest waves. At the weekend, myself and friends would camp, hike and swim at myriad deserted beaches within a four-hour drive of the city.

I saw my first ever dolphin on one of those trips. Actually, make that twenty dolphins. They frolicked alongside the boat in Jervis Bay, taking turns in the slipstream. I'm not sure who felt more joy, the dolphins enjoying the free ride or me, smiling like a kid who's just been told they can have ice cream for dinner.

Even getting stung by a stingray couldn't dampen my joy for adventures. During a weekend trip, we paddled to Resolute Beach, a small yet perfectly formed golden oasis in North Sydney which can only be reached by the ocean or a two-hour return hike.

"Ouch," I screamed, looking down at the water and watching it turn red.

I was walking the kayak back out to the ocean after a stop at the beach when I felt a sharp pain in my left foot. Assuming I'd stepped on glass, I limped from the water. Our guide looked down at my foot, where a perfectly formed circular puncture wound made it clear that glass hadn't been the culprit. Blood continued to ooze out of it staining the sand.

I started to feel a pain radiating up my leg. "Well, look at that," he said in a typical laid-back Aussie drawl. His long, blonde, straight-out-of-Home-and-Away hair brushed against my leg as he leant over to inspect further. "Looks like a stingray's gotcha. Never seen that before up here."

Getting stung by a stingray when you're a four-kilometre kayak from the nearest place to get help isn't great. Let's just say the paddle back wasn't easy, especially as the poison from a stingray gets stronger as time passes. Eventually, back on shore, a kind woman offered to take me to hospital.

"Can you boil some water?" the doctor asked the nurse. Assuming that maybe they thought I wanted a cup of tea to help with the pain (I am British after all), I was astounded to see that the boiling hot water was actually for my foot. A fifteen-minute, searingly hot soak and a few painkillers later and the pain began to dissipate. Three years on and you can still see the scar from that day.

My weekend adventures continued and eventually, my company let me work my five days across four, giving me a whole extra day free. They saw the difference that it made to my productivity and creativity. I think a lot of workplaces could learn from them.

Keen to give back to Mother Nature instead of just taking from it, I spent my extra day volunteering for a charity called Emu Trekkers which takes people on hikes in the Blue Mountains, with all profits going to help underprivileged children.

Old habits die hard

I honestly felt like I was living in a dream. I was earning a good wage in a company I respected, doing a job I found fulfilling. But my job no longer defined who I was; instead, I was known as the free spirit, the adventurer, the explorer.

I began writing for outdoor magazines and publications and even got invited to talk on a panel about how to live more adventurously.

Yet despite finding this new balance in life – and although my confidence in myself and my abilities was slowly building – it turns out that old anxieties aren't easy to leave behind.

Although it doesn't happen all of the time, I still battle imposter syndrome, and I regularly fight the negative internal voice that tells me I'm not good enough.

'Why are you even bothering,' the voice whispers. 'You're never going to be able to do it. You're useless, fat, unfit…'

I've even had a few panic attacks, which with hindsight, I now know were caused whenever I turned my adventure escapism into a competition or a group challenge. I had one during an adventure race in Australia, another on a multi-day hike on the Drakensburg Grand Traverse in South Africa and another during a mountaineering course in New Zealand. I ran my first ever 10k and fought panic the entire way. The harder and faster I ran, the closer the panic got to spilling out of me. It's like I was physically swallowing it.

Write your own narrative

You might be wondering why I've decided to end my tale on a seemingly negative note. It's because I feel it's important to know that things are never perfect. We each have our own demons to battle, no matter what scenery surrounds us. And that's okay.

It's been hard for me to accept that the negative self-talk, anxiety and panic I thought I'd left behind years ago can reach me in the outdoors, my safe place. But I won't let it stop me from living the life I want. I will continue to say Yes.

I have found a life that makes me want to get up every morning. A life where I feel content, where I feel whole, where I can balance societal obligations and the desire for security with a life I truly want to live.

And it wasn't changing jobs, countries or friendships that got me here. It was changing my mind-set. By embracing personal challenge, living by my own values and following my instinct, I am slowly discovering what I am capable of. And each time my negative voice gets louder, I quieten it by proving it wrong.

I acknowledge that while the land I have explored in Australia has deeply impacted me, it holds a much deeper significance to its Traditional Owners. I pay my respects to elders past, present, and future.

Happiest under the stars on top of a mountain, Brooke Nolan is a British-born, Aussie-dwelling, writer, hiker and pun lover. Her next 'middle finger up to the negative inner voice' adventure is her biggest yet – a two hundred-kilometre cross-country skiing expedition across an Arctic Plateau in Norway.

Website: **thisisbrooke.com**

Instagram: **@giveintoadventure**

Chapter 34

East to West...
Barefoot?

By Ian Oliver

"And of course, you're going to do it barefoot."

You know sometimes when you lie in bed and you have idle daydreams about adventures you could have in some kind of fantasy life? For years I'd had this weird thought of walking across Great Britain. In my head I'd start at the furthest westernmost point of the mainland, in the mountains of Scotland, and head south-east... somehow; I guess the details didn't matter. In bed I was only thinking of the concept – before arriving in a blaze of glory at the easternmost point, in Suffolk; West to East because everyone does Land's End to John o'Groats – points with no real geographical notability – and I felt it was a bit 'old hat'. I had no idea how to do this, or even if it was logistically possible, but the idea was there, an unwatered seed in my mind. But I'm a fantasist; I take ideas and talk about them, but never go through with them, partly out of a fear of failure but mainly because I realise they're 'too hard'.

Of course, every seed needs water to thrive. In my case this was provided by Yestival in October 2018 - being surrounded by so many inspirational and motivated people (and not the beer) made me think that, just maybe, I could do this. When I went back home to Nottinghamshire, I met up with my hiking friend, Becky, and talked about it with her down the pub.

"So, Becky, you like hiking. You've done some short multi-day hikes. Ever thought of doing a really long one?"

"Well," she replied, "I'd always wanted to do Land's End to John o'Groats, you know?"

"Hold that thought!". And I took a sip of beer, mainly for effect, it has to be said.

With the hard bit out of the way, over the course of two (or maybe four) pints we bounced ideas off each other and even fleshed out quite a bit of the route. Our intention was to do as much walking as possible on footpaths, ideally long-distance named trails. We'd take any chance we could to go off-road, because road walking is boring and uncomfortable, too much hard surface and close traffic. By road the journey would have been 530 miles. Our rough calculations for footpaths suggested we'd be walking closer to eight hundred miles. Footpaths don't generally follow straight lines.

I say "we" bounced ideas; let's be honest it was about 80% Becky. I'm just the man with the ideas; I have very little organisational sense whatsoever. Becky, however, took the thought and ran with it. By the end of that first meeting she'd got a route plotted out, a rough schedule of timings, tentative plans to get publicity, an outline of a pitch to kit and clothing companies for sponsorship, ideas of getting people to join us along the way, oh and she'd decided to change the direction of the entire hike so we'd do it from East to West (to give us a nice first week through the flatlands of Norfolk and so the sun would mostly be behind us rather than in our eyes).

She knocked up a rough kit-list as well, with food, clothing, and other miscellaneous equipment. She calculated how many calories we'd need to consume daily – over five thousand in my case. While she spent the next few months debating which camera to take and whether or not to pack her laptop (she didn't), I was mostly chatting on Twitter with friends who's initial reaction was invariably the same as Becky's first comment. Would I be doing it barefoot?

You may ask a slightly different question. Why the hell would I even consider doing it barefoot in the first place?

Maybe you're expecting me to say something about how being barefoot allows me to feel a resonance with the Earth, or because I'm channelling my inner hippie, or I don't like following rules or something. It's far simpler than that. My feet just get too hot in closed shoes; they feel uncomfortably warm and stuffy, like I've got two bricks on the bottom of my legs. That said, I do enjoy the freedom that being barefoot gives – the relaxed, casual style and that sense of being unrestricted.

Obviously, it would be unrealistic to hike the whole journey barefoot; it's a long way and I'd no idea what the terrain would be like – I wasn't expecting all sandy footpaths and smooth pavements. That said, the idea intrigued me. While I'd initially not considered it, the more people who mentioned it, the more the idea grew on me. I should at least do as much as I could and take sandals for the tough bits. Becky herself was having no such nonsense; she was straight in with the walking boots.

We estimated the whole hike would take about two and a half months, but that was based on walking fifteen miles a day and factored in a lot of rest days. Since neither of us had ever undertaken a challenge of this magnitude before, we didn't really know what we were capable of. I hadn't camped for many years and Becky had never done a walking adventure longer than a week. We were out of our depth.

As I'm sure you're aware, things always sound more interesting when you're sharing a beer in a pub months before you do anything. Over the course of the next few weeks we made plans. However, predictably, these fell by the way-side as normal life took over.

To get used to the idea, and in part each other, we arranged a couple of 'practice hikes' beforehand. These went... well, not great if I'm honest. The Peak District isn't exactly the easiest place to go wandering about, especially during Storm Gareth with forty-five miles per hour winds, snow, ice, and bitterly cold temperatures. The experience gave me pneumonia and I was on antibiotics for three weeks.

It wasn't long until we set off for real. We caught a series of trains to Lowestoft in Suffolk on Saturday 18th May. A final bag check led to a few things of mine being ditched, to be replaced by the contents of the local supermarket. Mainly couscous.

Monday morning came, and we strolled to Ness Point in warm, if a bit overcast, conditions. This is the furthest easterly point of Great Britain and indeed the United Kingdom, and, well... it's not exactly the most impressive place in the world.

In a sense, it's exactly as you'd imagine – a long concrete promenade, slightly rough underfoot, disappearing pretty much straight into the distance. There is no beach here, rather beyond the dull metallic railings is a short drop to a very rocky shoreline, constantly blasted with grey waves. The point itself is marked only with a huge grey compass monument set into the promenade floor. Ardnamurchan Point – our final destination – was clearly labelled as being 451 miles away in a straight line, but we knew we'd have to walk much further than that.

The compass point was the only real marker that this was anywhere significant. A lighthouse, possibly disused, stood nearby, but rather than this being a busy location with shops, arcades or indeed any sign of life, Ness Point is maybe a mile outside the town centre, stuck at the end of a dour, functional industrial estate whose main landmark is a Birds Eye Frozen Foods factory. With the clouds overhead, the sea a little lively and everything around being metal or concrete, the whole thing felt somewhat grey.

If we'd been finishing here, while it would have been convenient, I can't help but feel that being greeted by Uncle Birds Eye and a big metal statue would have been a bit of an anti-climax.

We finally headed off about 11am, having been seen off by a small group of people (mostly staff from a small Maritime Museum we'd popped into the day before, who were all pretty excited about our adventure).

Was I excited to finally be on the move? I don't know, in all honesty. I didn't really think far enough ahead to ever comprehend what we were doing. I never saw the hike in its entirety, but rather I kept thinking of it in sections, of each little bit separately, and once we'd finish one then I'd start thinking about the next. I guess ultimately I even saw it as simply as 'wake up, put one foot in front of the other, stop at bedtime, repeat till finish'. Our first path was the Norfolk Coast Path, which would take about six days to complete, so anything after that was... too far ahead for me to contemplate.

That first week in Norfolk was a great introduction to the hike. It was pretty good weather, the terrain was mostly flat (the highest point of the week was the sixty-three metre tall 'Beeston Bump', known locally as 'the tallest mountain in the world') and comfortable to walk on (a lot of grassy trails and rather too much sand), and the people were incredibly friendly.

Friendly locals were also how we managed to get camping spots. We'd aimed to do as much wild-camping as possible, which is much easier when you're in the hills and wild lands. It's not so easy when the top of the tent is the tallest thing for half a mile. We did grab a couple of nights in the marshes between Sheringham and Hunstanton, but on those first days we were grateful to people we met in pubs who, when we explained what we were doing, offered us the use of their back gardens.

One of these gardens was the scene of the first of my 'minor injuries'. Before we started, people were concerned about whether we'd get blisters, and one of my over-riding fears was that after a hundred metres on day one, I'd slip on a kerb and break a leg. But no, day three saw me burn my thumb on my camping stove. The resulting blister lasted a week.

Leaving Norfolk, we headed west through the Fens; we met far fewer people but considerably more sheep – the latter were busy trimming the grasses on the Nene Way. This was the only part of the journey I wasn't looking forward to, because of the (lack of) scenery, but we blitzed through it in two days.

After wandering past Rutland Water (one of the largest artificial lakes in Europe at nearly eleven square-kilometres, and as old as I am) and then through the farmlands of Leicestershire and Nottinghamshire, we reached 'home'. It did feel a little weird to wander up to Nottingham railway station after two weeks on the road, even if we knew it was only a brief respite.

Well, a brief respite for Becky.

After two days' rest, we set off down the canal from Nottingham, complete with a blessing from Mark Dennison at BBC Radio Nottingham, and along the Derwent Valley Heritage Way. Except I was back at home the following evening, nursing another, let's say minor, injury caused by dyspraxia.

It was a really stupid and needless injury. We were in the village of Long Eaton, Derbyshire, hiking with two of Becky's friends (Ben and Selena), and I'd stopped to take pictures of the preserved remains of the old railway station; the empty space between two bridge markers, the silent platform waiting for a train that would never come, the mural on the garage of the bright pink station house that showed how it looked in the old days. I looked around to see that they'd all carried on, heading to the village green to have lunch. For some stupid reason, I decided to run to catch up rather than just walk. I was carrying my heavy backpack and was barefoot.

Three steps after starting, I dragged the top of my foot along the pavement. I looked down and there was blood everywhere; one of my toes looked a bit like a strawberry ice-cream. Weirdly, I couldn't feel it, and it didn't seem to be hurting that much, but I guessed something pretty bad had happened. I stopped walking, put my foot on a small wall, and dabbed at my foot to see if I could stop the blood pouring out of it and hosing the pavement. It was at this point I saw my toenail fall off...

We carried on hiking for a couple of hours more, patching up the toe as best we could. Ben had parked up near Ambergate, When we reached his car, Becky said she needed to go to the supermarket, so we all piled in and off we went.

"Do you mind," I asked, "if you could drop me off at home afterwards? I ought to make sure this toe heals properly."

"I think that's probably for the best," replied Becky.

"I hope you don't think I'm bailing out on you."

"Not at all. Come back when you're ready."

I was still concerned that by going back home to rest for a couple of days meant I'd failed somehow, and that I was letting Becky down. We'd already agreed that if one of us suffered a hike-ending injury that the other would continue to the end; she was all prepared to do the rest of the hike without me, as I saw her Instagram Stories saying exactly that... until I turned up at Edale on the following Sunday.

This meant not only did I miss Becky's encounter with a herd of cows that she'll dine out on for the rest of her life, but it also technically means I failed to walk the entirety of the route across Great Britain. Meh. *shrugs*

It also meant, for protection, I had to tackle the first week or so of the Pennine Way wearing proper closed walking shoes rather than walking sandals or in bare feet, which was disappointing. My lodger Sarah suggested I needed to keep it dry. I remembered those words after four days, in a dorm at a campsite in Ickornshaw, having seen nothing but rain for days. My feet were soaking wet.

In truth, we didn't really consider the hike to have started until the Pennine Way, as everything to that point felt like mere preparation. Had we started the whole hike here, I think it would have been a much tougher experience. After three weeks we'd gotten into a rhythm, we'd got used to the bags and it didn't feel as onerous as it does for most people. Indeed, we never felt like we couldn't finish. The most difficult thing I found was the incessant rain and resultant flooding – quite a bit of the trail was over boggy ground and at times the path itself disappeared into deep muddy puddles. Sometimes this was frustrating, but once I was satisfied my toe had healed, it became easier, indeed a pleasure, to bounce along happily barefooted like some kind of stereotypical elven ranger.

Unlike most of the other paths we hiked, the nature of the Pennine Way (a long defined route with obvious stopping points) meant we ended up hiking in parallel with other people. We'd hiked with people before, but usually only for a couple of hours; to be around fellow hikers for so long was quite a change. It ended up not being as bad as I'd feared. We kept in touch remotely to tell each other of conditions underfoot (or, in one case, overhead – a hill with very low-hanging trees. It's hard to judge where your backpack is, sometimes. Or is that dyspraxia again?).

We didn't hike the entire length of the Pennine Way. For a very small section we were driven in a small mini-bus because a bridge across a reservoir was closed. A film-crew had taken it over. They were doing some filming for some Hollywood war movie I'll probably never see. People looking after the minibus thought was going to be called '1917'...

One of my main take-outs from the hike is just how much of my own country I went to – some of it being parts I didn't really know about. For me, the best day of the hike was in the second half of the Pennine Way; a pretty long day (about twenty-one miles) from Middleton-in-Teesdale to Dufton. We walked through some absolutely stunning scenery that I didn't even know existed, including three waterfalls and an incredible vista at High Cup Nick looking down a rounded valley out over towards the Lake District. It helped that it was a sunny day. Even so, this is all in the North Pennines Area of Outstanding Natural Beauty, and you can't help but feel if it were anywhere else in the country, it would be filled with tourists. Yet we had it all pretty much to ourselves. I'd argue that many people don't explore their own country enough – they'll go flying around the world to see something interesting but don't necessarily realise something equally as worthy lies on their own doorstep. Maybe that's something people like me can help to change?

Our 15th (and second-to-last) day on the Pennine Way, in the wilds of the Cheviot Hills, felt very remote and foggy; visibility was negligible and the misty rain was getting everywhere inside our clothing. The terrain was hilly and the path was variable. It was thus a little galling to be passed by people who'd run up the entire trail – 250-odd miles – in less than four days. We finished just as the twice-yearly Spine Race did (won this year by the incredible Sabrina Verjee). This is one of those ultra-marathons that most people go '...but why would you do that to yourself'. People feel the need to challenge themselves in different ways, and it's really good to appreciate that. Still probably wouldn't do it, mind.

After overnighting in a bothy on the England-Scotland border, cooped up with two Spine Race marshals, we had an absolutely gorgeous last few miles downhill into Kirk Yetholm – the skies cleared, the sun shined, the air was dry and warm – it was almost as if the Pennine Way was going, 'Okay, I've thrown everything at you and you're still here. Well done. You win.'

As my toe was pretty good by now, I ditched my walking shoes, which were falling apart – there's a 'graveyard' for boots where people have left theirs – before Becky and I headed onwards into the Lowlands of Scotland. With the weather improving and the hardest bits behind us, we really started to motor. The trails became easier, the scenery clearer and it was an enjoyable saunter through rolling hills and along old cattle droving roads, with much more wild camping in the hillsides and waking up to the sun rather than traffic noise – essentially, this was how we'd envisaged the hike to be all the way through.

On the way, I had another minor dyspraxia-induced injury. We'd met a woman in Newtown-St-Boswells whose friend was setting up an AirBnb and wanted someone to 'playtest' it. We decided to make a proper meal rather than surviving on packet food. It being a new set-up, they had never-before-used knives. I pointed this out to Becky, who said, "Oh, you won't cut yourself. Don't be silly." Reader, you can guess what happened after chopping half an onion. My (un-burned) thumb stopped bleeding about seven hours later… by which time we'd also managed to lock ourselves out, requiring the owners to smash a window at midnight to get us back in.

A couple of days later in Peebles, we had our only instance of illness, and weirdly it wasn't me.

While walking through the Lowlands the day before, we'd stopped for lunch and Becky ate a steak pasty we'd bought the previous day in Galashiels. A mile or so later she was starting to feel a little weak, and at one point had to stop in a small wood, pitch up her tent and sleep for an hour or so. We had a brief discussion as to whether I should walk on ahead or not, but in the end she felt just about well enough to make it along the Drove Road to Peebles, where we overnighted in a campsite.

The following morning, I let her lie in to give her as much rest as possible. She woke up about five minutes before we were due to head off, still a bit tired and queasy, and not altogether 'with it'; we agreed we should have a day of rest. She promptly fell back asleep and I had a pleasant day exploring the quaint and pretty town centre. After sleeping much of the day, she seemed fine that evening, and we headed off North the next morning. We never worked out if that pasty was the cause of her illness, but I don't think she's eaten one since.

Eventually (after a rest day in Glasgow with YesTribe matriarch Geraldine McFaul) we reached the West Highland Way, another of those non-negotiable long-distance paths Becky wanted to complete. Our problem here though was, now we were really into our groove and considerably fitter (and thinner – I'd already had to buy new trousers) than when we started, and because the West Highland Way is mostly old drove roads rather than small windy footpaths, we found it quite an easy hike and, dare I say, a little underwhelming compared to what we'd been through already. Indeed, we walked about a quarter of the entire path on our first day, and made it to Fort William early afternoon on the fifth day. It was a really pretty walk, but I think I'd like to go back one day and take more time to savour it. Or possibly run it, I don't know.

On the last day, we left Kinlochleven up a really steep hill and passed quite a few people with daypacks who were struggling to climb. We, with full backpacks, almost sprinted up it like mountain goats.

The last few days on the Ardnamurchan peninsula were spectacular; we were hiking mostly on either single-track roads or on paths that were only casually marked on the map. Very often we were the only people around. We camped next to a loch, then in a forest and, on the night before our last day, on a beach known for its 'singing sand'; it made a kind of squeak when you walked on it. The weather was fabulous for most of this final section, and it was a pleasure to be exploring such quiet and remote scenery. When we reached the sea on the last day, we had a cliff-side path with the Inner Hebrides clearly visible in the distance.

The remainder of the last day was counting down the distances. At ten kilometres to go I had a little bit of a cry; single figures – I'd regularly walk this back at home each day, so knowing that we only had that much left to do was both exciting and yet quite emotional. At five kilometres (a mere Parkrun) was another wide open beach where we stopped for a rest. It was almost tempting to camp up for the night there as it was getting quite late, but we figured we might as well make it all the way on the day.

In a way, reaching the end was a bit of an anti-climax. The path curled round the rocky headland from the last beach, cutting through hills populated with wild deer. A couple of miles in we saw it, in the distance, set against the slightly greying skies – an indistinct dark tower. This was when we realised we didn't know exactly what Ardnamurchan Lighthouse looked like, but it was in the right place.

After wandering past a caravan park, we reached the final road and headed up the slight hill to the lighthouse. It was about 9.20pm and daylight would soon be over, but we passed the visitor centre, walked to a grassy bank just beyond the lighthouse and looked out to sea. Waves pushing against the rocks below, another headland (the actual westernmost point) just visible to the south, the thin cylindrical tower behind us, the sun setting ahead. A much prettier setting than the start, similarly low-key, but quieter, more thoughtful.

We were also greeted at the end. A group of naturalists live in a block at the lighthouse, monitoring sea life and seals, and one of them wandered up to us and asked what we were up to. She was quite amazed when we told her and offered to take our pictures. She even informed us we could probably camp out just below the lighthouse, by the entrance, as long as we were discreet and had packed up by the time they opened in the morning.

Aside from her, there was no welcoming party, no big celebration, just the two of us and, it must be said, a small bottle of port. But maybe that was appropriate. It was our journey after all, and it was nice to just chill. After fifty-seven days on the road, we finally ran out of land.

One of the most frequent questions we were asked was, "What next?" I'd kind of decided, once we'd got to Ardnamurchan, that because they were close by, I should visit the Outer Hebrides as I'd never been. I'd never get such an easy opportunity again. Becky was less clear; in the end she decided to join some friends of hers who were climbing some of the Scottish mountains so she went back to

Fort William. But they're both stories for another time.

Perhaps surprisingly when you spend two months in the close company of the same person, you'd expect there to be arguments but we barely argued at all. We had one clash in Falkirk to do with directions but it only lasted a couple of minutes and was quickly forgotten.

We're both quite solo travellers though and, while I'm much more of an introvert than her, we both had a feel of when we needed company and when we needed space. There were periods, mainly on the Pennine Way, when she'd be happy walking with friends who had joined her for a day, or people we'd passed on our hike, and I'd be comfortable hanging back or going on ahead. Neither of us felt awkward at this.

We had a couple of discussions afterwards about whether we could have done the journey on our own. We concluded we could (I would have been much quicker, just saying). In truth, I know it wouldn't have been as enjoyable and, to be honest, I might not have even gone through with it . Having Becky on the hike with me made it what it was, fulfilling, fun and incredibly rewarding.

The hike made me realise a few things about what I like on an adventure – rolling hills, sea views and remote grassy paths. I like the feeling of always being on-the-move and not being stationary in one place too long. I kind of knew this instinctively anyway, but going on a hike like this really brought it home.

I also like it when it doesn't rain.

Would I do it again? Probably not.

I mean, I'd do another long-distance hike at some point – indeed, in the lowlands, we walked a few miles on the Southern Upland Way, which is about two days' hike shorter than the Pennine Way but much less well known. The hike has shown that, yes, I can do this sort of thing, but I don't think I'd do another huge cross-Britain hike.

I probably need a different challenge. I think I want to run a marathon next time. I know I can do the distance, but can I do it at speed and without stopping after nine miles for a pub lunch?!

Some stats about the hike:

* We walked 952 miles in total. We did wonder if we'd break a thousand; had we found we'd finish around 980 we would have walked longer routes on purpose, but we felt forty-eight miles was just too much to fudge.

* Our total altitude gain was about 22,000 metres, or two and a half Everests. The highest point we reached was Cross Fell in the Pennines (893m), while our lowest point was a couple of metres below sea level in the Fens. Interestingly, our first day on the Pennine Way saw us climb higher than on the first two weeks combined.

* The hike took fifty-seven days, of which five were rest days (Hunstanton, Nottingham, Edale, Peebles, Glasgow). This means we walked an average of 18.3 miles on every day we walked, compared with our initial estimate of fifteen miles per day with many more rest days. We found we wanted to keep moving; rather than rest days we took half-days with either a late start or an early finish.

* Some of my friends claimed we were on Britain's longest pub crawl as we always seemed to be in the pub – this was more for practical reasons though as it provided a place to rest, charge phones, and work out what to do next. The beer was incidental, honest, though at one point it probably was providing about 25% of my entire calorie intake.

* We wild-camped (as opposed to using campsites) together fifteen times, six of which were on the last seven nights. Our plan was to wild camp more, but the weather on the Pennine Way wasn't conducive to it when we started, then we kind of got into a rhythm

of walking with people and going from campsite to campsite. Other places we stayed included the garden of a dementia care home, a random empty scout camp, two bothies and a couple of friends' houses.

* I probably did about a quarter of the hike barefoot. I did where I could, or at least where I felt comfortable doing so, but oh my god this country is fond of gravel paths. I probably could have done it, but it would have taken maybe three times longer. And hurt. A lot. Most of the rest of the time (aside from the first half of the Pennine Way), I was in minimalist sandals. Bear in mind this was the same time as the start of Anna McNuff's 'Barefoot Britain' series of marathon-length runs across Britain, but she was mostly on pavements/roads and not gravel-covered footpaths.

* One of Becky's ideas in the planning stage was we should raise money for charity, and after a quick discussion we settled on MIND, the mental health charity, for mostly personal reasons. In total, between the two of us, and including money donated en-route from people we met, we raised around £1600.

Instgram: **@barefoot_backpacker**

Chapter 35

Bromptoning

By Anisah Osman Britton

I woke up in the hospital, the fog lifting and the confusion dissipating after a nightmare week. They'd set a hot tin cup of water with turmeric and floating herbs next to my bed with a, now cold, chapatti and a tin bowl of slightly turned yoghurt.

This was one of Mumbai's top hospitals but you wouldn't have known that from what they were trying to pass off as breakfast. I sent Alia, my two years younger and two inches taller than me sister, off on an early morning hunt for a banana pancake, whilst I went stir crazy from the endless needles being shoved into various parts of my arm.

I was here because a mosquito had attacked me, won and left me with a consolation prize – dengue fever.

"I don't get sick in India. I'm Indian," I said. "Plus, if you're really careful, mosquitoes are not an issue. I should know. I lived here for two years." But here I was, proving that life has funny ways of waking you up from your misguided sense of invincibility.

A banana pancake heavier and a few hundred quid lighter, I was ready for my sister to carry me out of there.

A couple of months later, I was sitting at home in London panicking. What if that moment had been it? What if I'd never said the things I'd wanted to say? Or read the books I'd wanted to read? What if I'd never finished the Quran? Or gone to do Hajj? Or learnt to surf? Or scuba diving? Or mastered Italian?

I was headed towards, what my millennial compatriots like to call, a Quarter Life Crisis - a moment in one's life where one questions what the fudge they are playing at.

I was the age my parents married; my friends were shacking up, buying houses, and having children (standard); Alia had a serious boyfriend and an enviable six pack (unrelated but seriously, how?); Athletes on TV were now younger than me; I didn't know what Musical.ly (now TikTok) was, nor did I care. I mean, I wasn't even the holder of a driving licence!

In the midst of this collapse of sense of self, my eight years younger than and same height as me sister, Noor, called me. "I'm going to Dublin to see my best friend. I don't want to fly by myself," she said. Would I fly there with her because I've got no other plans in my tiny life (I may have added that last bit for dramatic effect).

Yes. 100% yes. Everyone knows that Ireland is the land of finding oneself, right?

So that was the plan. I would fly her there. Have a few days on my own. Fly her back. I could spend the week exploring the city that is home to much of my Dad's family history. We'd never visited for one reason or another and now I was going to have a week to trace some of those roots. Maybe I really could find myself.

A call to Grandma later, I discovered that the closest relative lived an hour or so out of Dublin so I was going to need transport. Remember that thing about a driving licence? The closest thing I had to transport was my Brompton bike. That could work...

Family WhatsApp group:

I may have sent this prior to looking at a map though, because as it turns out, I had to go South to get to my family. The East to West plan became The Dublin to South plan, along the sunny South East Coast.

I armed myself with some padding to save my easily bruised peach, a proper helmet, waterproof gear, cycle shoes (not cleats, my nerds), and a bucket tonne of anti-chafing cream. I'd also bought a one woman tent for some wild camping activity.

This list of newly purchased items should show you that I wasn't really a cyclist! My lagoon blue Brompton, Luna, was loved but was a tool of convenience. She was a lifestyle enabler that allowed me to easily get to a tube station or to work, no matter where my boat I lived on and I were located on any given week. But I'd never taken her on an actual adventure. It was time to get Luna out of London.

On arrival, Luna was disembarked and we were reunited. Step one had been a success! I slipped into my cycle gear in the arrivals hall, handed the Brompton case Luna had travelled in to Noor and her friend, and I headed out into a beautiful summer's night in Dublin. The sky was so clear. There was no chill in the breeze that hit my face. My legs felt good and my heart felt happy. I was cycling! I was here! Woo-

...Wait, what's wrong with my lights? Why are they flashing blue?

Sirens.

"Excuse me, can you pull in?"

I'm ten minutes into my cycle and I'm pulled over by the police. Excellent.

"Good evening, Miss. Erm, do you know you're on the biggest motorway in the country on a Brompton?" says Cute (male) Police Officer One.

Beat.

"Erm no. Are you serious? I followed the path the bus driver at the airport put me on. I literally haven't turned. He told me it would be grand," I say, convinced he's wrong. Turns out, surprisingly, they're right. I've cycled along the M1, and merged on to the M50.

"Have you been drinking, miss?" Cute (Male) Police Officer Two asks.

"Drinking? I'm Muslim. I've never even tried alcohol."

At this point, they start to crack up realising that it's even worse that I'm on the motorway and not drunk. I see their point.

"What are you doing here then?" questions CPO1.

I tell them, oversharing out of embarrassment. At some point, I mention I'm from London and that triggers hysterics... for some reason.

This prompts Cute (male) Police Officer Three to get out of the car. They retell the story, at the side of the motorway. I was now surrounded by three cute police officers in tears of laughter.

CPO3 finally recovers, folds my bike expertly, and launches it into the back of the car whilst CPO1 notes the address of where I'm meant to be staying that night.

As we drive along, they ask, "So, what's the craic? Where you meant to be cycling to?" I tell them my plan and they're a mixture of amazed and amused. I mean, I couldn't even get from the airport to the city, how was I going to get anywhere else? I could see this question playing out on their faces, and to be frank, on mine too.

After a few minutes, CPO3 comes out with "Lads, we got some time here. Let's give her a quick tour of the city." And that is how I ended up on a history tour of Dublin in a police car!

As they dropped me off at the hostel I was staying at, CPO2 entered with me and instructed the receptionist to give me a map in the morning and winked at me on the way out. I was desperate to ask for a selfie, but I think I'd embarrassed myself enough for one night.

This was going to be a fun few days if the first few hours were anything to go by.

After a day exploring Dublin, Luna was loaded up ready for day one. On the front, I had my bright mustard yellow Game Bag, a city bag for all intents and purposes. It was loaded up with some clothes, a sleeping bag, roll mat, flip flops, essential toiletries, a Kindle, and a notebook and pen. This was covered by a waterproof because I did not trust the *Sunny* South East.

On the back, attached with bungee cables to the seat post, was my tent. On my back, was my Camelbak, filled with energy bars made by my mum and some trusty TRIBE bars.

There was nothing left to do but start pedalling.

Day 1: 61km

The plan was to just follow the coastline as far as I could for the first day with no end goal.

An hour and a half into my ride, I began cycling along the periphery of Scotsman's Bay – a stunning stretch of the coast with calm waters and views across the bay to a picturesque postcard town.

I reached the James Joyce Tower at Sandycove Point and sat at the highest place I could find on a weathered down bench. As I munched some of my Ma's date, coconut and peanut butter bars, I took in the view of the sea with its blue to compete with the blues of the Mediterranean. Who knew the Sunny South East wasn't an ironic title?

Approaching lunch time, I came across a 241 metre green hill and headland blocking my coastal path. This was Bray Head. According to the waitress at the pub I went to get lunch at, Bray Head had beautiful views and fantastic hikes but I definitely wouldn't be able to cycle it.

I, begrudgingly, ate my green fake Thai curry with its extra servings of salt and oil whilst glaring at this hill. What was I going to do? I had decided I wasn't going to turn my maps on if I could avoid it and I wasn't willing to give in within the first leg of the journey.

As luck would have it, a man with his adorable new-born baby came over and had a chat about Luna. I may have disappointed him with my lack of bike knowledge (I think it has three gears? It's the foldy one in the range. etc.) but he impressed me with his geographical knowledge.

Thirty minutes later I was cursing his name as I hit some thigh burning hills. That third gear didn't exist, I learnt.

My first night led me to Wolohan's campsite at Blainroe. I'd looked for a beach to set up camp but the lack of food nearby made civilisation a requirement. I was exhausted, and my legs were slowly turning into jelly, but I hopped back on my trusty steed to find a town of some kind, maybe with a B&B. As I was picturing myself slipping into a hot steamy bubble bath, a couple in their mid-fifties on proper tour bikes cycled past me. I shouted after them, asking them where they were setting up camp tonight.

An hour later, I was at the site, signed in and pitched up. I was at the top of a white cliff with the most magnificent view of the bay and beyond. The ever-changing colours being thrown off the sky and displayed on the white cliff during golden hour was the light display of dreams. A B&B had nothing on it.

I couldn't wait to get some food from the camp shop to munch on whilst staring out at this view. But the shop had closed. I began to panic. Having eaten nothing since lunch, my body temperature was dropping and I was getting shaky. I scoffed the remaining of my mum's bars and a very squashed TRIBE banoffee bar. It was going to have to do...

En route to finding some water, I bumped into the couple who'd directed me and we got chatting about our journeys. They were from Germany and loved the Irish landscape. This wasn't their first rodeo. We sat around their stove, drank tea and ate peanuts until the stars sparkled and left us all in silent awe.

Day 2: 37km

Cereal, toast, tea, oranges, and chocolate were on the menu for breakfast. The shop still hadn't opened, but I'd been brushing my teeth next to a woman from Belfast and her kids, and they had insisted on feeding me when they heard about my food situation.

I'd been observing this family the previous evening. A mum and dad in their early forties and three daughters under ten. They reminded me of my own family set up. We were three girls too. I watched them chase each other around the site, playing catch, for what seemed like hours – a game the mum and dad seemed to be enjoying as much as the kids.

They took me in that morning as another member of the family. It was like we'd known each other forever as we sat on their camp chairs, swapping life stories whilst the girls played. It's amazing how inventive play becomes away from phones and television sets. Every new game astounded me. When had I forgotten how to play?

We took a walk down the steep rocky steps that led to the beach, raspberry infused dark chocolate in hand. Immersing my very sore legs into the cold salty water did me a world of good.

It was time to say goodbye with the promise of keeping in touch.

The joy of cycling is that you have so much time with yourself and your own mind. I thought about everything that had led to me being on this saddle pedalling up some seriously insane hills (and at times, pushing the bike up them!). What was this crisis about, really? I lived a pretty damn privileged life.

And, just like that, I realised my problem. Maybe it wasn't that I wasn't doing enough. I was afraid I wouldn't be able to do everything. I was terrified that I wouldn't fit everything I dreamed of doing into my brief spell on this Earth.

This realisation hit me right in the chest and I had to sit myself down for a little moment to allow my brain to process...

Eventually, I dragged myself and Luna to a little lunch spot to refuel with a jacket potato.

Looking at a brochure over lunch, I'd seen something about Kilmichael Point Reserve that looked like a, potentially, great camping spot.

OMG, was I wrong?!

I bumped along this endless path that led down to the coast and opened up to wet marshland. It was a miracle I didn't get a puncture.

This was, by far, a less than ideal camping spot. It was super eerie with its abandoned and roofless stone ruins. The dark clouds coming in quickly added to this horror film set I'd just stepped into. I then met two rather intimidating men who told me to be careful as animals get shot in this area, and people have been known to get caught in the crossfire. The worst horror film.

That was enough for me to jump back on my bike and cycle away at the fastest speed I had managed the entire trip! As the dark was setting in, I knew I had to get my tent up, pronto.

The next town up was Castletown where I followed a sign to Clone Strand – a typical tourist beach town, complete with a local ice-cream van that looked like it had just hyper-jumped in from the 80s.

My parched and sunburnt self headed straight there. Nothing quite beats a 99! I won't hear anything against them! On ordering, I mentioned my plan for trying to find a place to sleep on the beach to the ice-cream lady.

"Kilpatrick beach is a couple of kilometres back. You're not meant to but crazy adventurers are always camping up there for the craic," she informed me.

Kilpatrick beach it was then. And, my oh my, was it stunning with its long stretch of golden sand with perfect wind breaking dunes. I'd found my spot for the night.

After I set up camp, I headed out for a little walk up the isolated beach towards the water point I'd seen on my way in. I spotted an elderly woman in a turquoise windbreaker walking towards me, shoulders slightly hunched. We crossed paths and greeted each other. She spotted my tent and asked me what I was doing. I told her.

"Oh love, the beach isn't safe for a girl on her own," she fretted.

I explained that I was okay and I wasn't worried at all.

"Isn't your Ma worried about you out here?"

I realised I am very lucky. Being half Indian, people expect that I would not have had certain freedoms but the truth was, I have. Adventure runs in our blood from my grandparents being some of the first East African Indians to arrive in the UK in the 60s, to my parents quitting their London jobs and leaving for Spain when they had two children under three with no real plan but to live a better quality of life. We've all got that streak in us to be a bit different, a bit independent, a little bit crazy without a care for what others make of it.

Of course, being a woman, and a brown one at that, cycling alone draws attention. I have very little fear, which is my biggest strength and weakness, but I am definitely hyper-aware.

This was a bit much to delve into on my first meeting with a woman in her eighties, who was just looking out for me, of course. She interpreted my pause as hesitation and answered for me.

"Ma's are always worried about their daughters. Even the brave ones," and proceeded to tell me to get my tent and my bike.

Yes ma'am.

This trip was about going with the flow, so I flowed. I followed her back to her car, where her husband was waiting for her in the passenger seat. We threw my stuff into the boot, and I jumped into the warmth of the backseat. I hadn't even realised I was cold.

"Love, this young lady is coming home with us," she shouted. Her husband, with his snow white hair, visible hearing aids, and thin rectangular glasses just nodded. She was holding his hand as she said, yet again, that I was coming home with them.

As we drove along, she asked me what my name was and I found out that my hosts were Margaret and David. They lived in the fairy-tale house at the top of the hill whose sun room had unobstructed views of the sea. Their garden, which overlooked a field of cows, is where I'd like to find myself during an apocalypse because it had every kind of fruit and vegetable you could possibly need growing there. They had a library room with every shelf crammed with books and notebooks. Their walls were covered in photos that illustrated their history. One particular photo caught my attention. It was David with the Queen.

"Margaret, what's this photo all about?" I asked.

"Oh love, David has a CBE." It turned out he was pretty famous for his long and successful army career and for his role in the relations between Ireland and the UK.

They showed me to the spare room and explained that it had been done up for guests for the following day, and would I mind sleeping on my sleeping bag on top of the duvets. I had planned to sleep on the beach. Of course I didn't mind!

Margaret quickly put me to work. She handed me a pair of wellies and we headed out to the garden to pick peas and raspberries for my 'tea'. She talked about how David and her had met, how she'd married and travelled with David for his job, and then returned to Ireland. She told of her pain that David's hearing was going. She recounted that he used to live in India and had fond memories. She was still so in love with him!

They'd already eaten prior to their beach trip. As they made tea and scones, I scrambled up eggs for myself. We placed this all on a trolley, alongside some milk, sugar, honey, jam and butter, and wheeled it out into their sun room to sit alongside the old school gas heater. I had some of the raspberry chocolate left from the family I met at Wolohan's, which I contributed to the spread. David's eyes lit up at the chocolate. Sometimes, the little things are enough.

My unease with many of the beautiful moments I had with kind people on my trip was I had nothing to offer. I discovered though, that sometimes our presence and intentions are enough. Sometimes giving is a gift. Sometimes nothing is expected in return.

Now you may be wondering at this point, what happened to discovering my family history and meeting my relative – my great aunt. As far as I could ascertain, I was within a twenty mile radius of where she lived. Before I'd left, I'd sent a note saying I was coming and I'd contact once in Dublin. Once I arrived though, I heard nothing. Our family history on my Dad's side is one I've wanted to piece together for many years in the same way I'd done with my mother's Indian and Tanzanian routes during my gap year.

But fate wasn't on my side. It turned out, I later discovered, that the phone number I had wasn't quite right. My aunty never received anything from me. Although at the time I felt a bit heartbroken, I know now that things happen for a reason and it was meant for me to return for a longer period of time to put the puzzle together.

Day 3: 50km

I woke up to the smell of porridge from the kitchen and the news on in the living room. My porridge was stirred with salt – a new experience for me – and topped with the raspberries we'd picked the night before. They had tiny little green worms in them, which I'd tried to wash out but Margaret and David were eating them without a care in the world, and they were doing alright in their mid to late eighties, so... Hakuna Matata.

As I profusely thanked them, David came out with a map of the area and directed me to where he thought I should head to next. As I waved goodbye, I got teary-eyed wondering if I'd ever see them again. If I didn't, that day with them had been magical.

The rain decided I'd had my fair bit of luck and poured cats and dogs from the moment I departed. My very sunburnt self wasn't upset by this.

After twenty-six kilometres, I could have kept going but hailstones were my limit. I took refuge in a cafe, with a bunch of other cyclists. It's funny. I hadn't really seen many cyclists, then I walked into this cafe and they seemed to be everywhere. I guess this is how Hell's Angels members must feel when they meet on the road. Aside from the hailstones, I think they were all here because of Kate's coffee shop and deli's reputation.

Let it be known that they serve the best vegetarian breakfast:

Four (!) poached eggs, two hash browns, mushrooms, baked beans, and brown soda bread with a bucket load of salty creamy butter. And tea. Lots of tea. I was gobbling it all up, even ordering more bread. I still dream about this breakfast of champions. I wasn't sure my wheels were going to carry me but it was worth it.

As I was paying up, a cyclist mentioned that they were heading to this campsite in Wexford, and if I made it there tonight, I should join them for dinner and drinks. "Of course," I said. If this trip had taught me anything, it was that saying yes was bringing light into my life.

The following thirty kilometres brought the hills and the rain. I felt like Superwoman though. I'm not sure what it was, but it was euphoric. My legs were doing the work, my lungs were working hard but feeling good, I had cold water in my Camelbak bladder, and the sound of the rain masked my atrocious, 'cat being stood on like' singing. I'd picked up some speed too and some of the downhills were pure shots of adrenaline.

As I raced down a quiet stretch of road, I turned a bend and, shockingly, was treated to a view of a city. Although it had only been three days, it felt like a lifetime since I'd seen a city and... traffic? I couldn't believe it.

The last five kilometres of my journey into Wexford felt like a prettier version of my standard London commute. A couple of drivers swore at me, making me, briefly, panic that I'd made an error and hit a motorway again.

I arrived at the campsite earlier than I would have liked, pitched up as close to the water's edge as possible so I could smell the salt, and dropped all my stuff in the tent. After I gave Luna a quick once over and reassured myself I was still puncture free, I cycled down to the closest beach, Rosslare. I picked up some sweets along the way and sat on the wet sand with my notebook and pen trying to scribble all these emotions. I kept repeating a mantra to myself:

"It's OK if I can't do everything, as long as I keep doing something. This will lead to living without regret."

Evening came and I searched for the cyclists from Kate's café but to no avail. I found a small local cinema instead, took a picnic in with me, and lived my best life!

Day 4: 0km

I stepped out of my tent at 7am in the morning and passed out. I knew that was the end of my cycle... or the beginning of my cycle, if you'll forgive the pun – my period was a few days early.

The first couple of days of bleeding for me are unbearable. I get faint and pass out. The pain was excruciating and left me doubled over that morning. I couldn't focus. No amount of painkillers was going to get me to the stage I'd need to be to feel safe and confident riding. I didn't need to be a liability to myself or others. Plus, there was no pressure to go on, so why risk a miserable ending to a joyous time?

I turned the internet on my phone on for the first time, booked a bus from Wexford back to Dublin for that afternoon, and booked myself into a hotel for that night. There was nothing left to do but to wander the cute little village market in the shining sun with a banana pancake in hand.

*

I was so grateful for my few days cycling. It had altered my entire sense of wellbeing. I knew the dengue fever had been a wakeup call. I knew I needed to take more opportunities to do things I love, and to appreciate and remember those moments. I recalled when I studied theatre at school, we were taught a trick of remembering emotions and feelings:

When you feel a certain way and you want it to be imprinted on your mind forever, you close your eyes and press your index finger and thumb together for five seconds. The next time in your life you repeat the action of pressing those fingers together, those emotions and memories come rushing back.

Good trick, but I thought I'd get my ears pierced instead! So every time I would look at my second piercing on my right ear, I would think of my first time in Ireland, my cycle, my strength, my self-understanding... but mostly, I would think of the love I received with nothing expected in return.

I was here because a mosquito had attacked me, won, and left me with a consolation prize and I was grateful to her for it.

Twitter: **@anisahob**

Chapter 36

Punching My Limits

Noni Papp

Warm up - The beginnings

Sometime in December 2018. It was almost 7pm and I was alone in my classroom. I was sitting at my desk surrounded by a lot of half-prepared resources, unfinished documents and rubbish. The lights were off; only the computer illuminated my surroundings. I had a million things to do, but I was unable to move.

The world outside completely mirrored what I felt on the inside; coldness was spreading from the bottom of my stomach towards my throat; my thoughts were like a storm in my mind:

'There's no way I can keep up with all these demands. I'm useless.'

'It's been another day full of challenging behaviours, but I just don't know what to do. I'm a bad professional.'

'I thought I was a people person, but I can't even deal with my team.'

'Where is all this social anxiety coming from?'

There was darkness all around.

I couldn't hold back my tears anymore, and in my mind I was loathing myself for them. I felt like a kettle; sensing the building pressure, trembling, waiting to explode.

I wanted to release all this inside me. I wanted to scream. I wanted to drop myself to the floor. I wanted to punch things.

'Oh yeah, punching things would be awesome. Punching things hard. I bet I could break things with all this pent-up energy inside me. Maybe I would turn into something like a super saiyan in Dragon Ball Z. I only need to visualise the school's management and all of my frustrations... I don't want to cause any real harm or damage, make others hurt or feel sad. But I hold myself back so much day by day that I don't know how to express myself anymore. I need to find my strength again and feel that I have power... What if I joined a boxing class? That's the place where it's acceptable to do punch things. Boxing is a sport I always wanted to try... Yes, this is the way to go. I need to do this for myself.'

I started to google gyms, but then the janitor came in and reminded me about closing time.

The idea was born but, because of the storms of everyday life, I pushed it aside and almost forgot about it.

Fast forward to 20th June, 2019. After starting therapy in December (one of the best decisions of my life), I left teaching in March and started a new job a few days before where I could be myself again. That day was my 30th birthday and I felt much better than the last few years of my twenties.

As a present, my sister took me to see a show called, *The Sweet Science of Bruising*. It was about female boxers from the Victorian era. The play got into my head. 'These badass women weren't afraid to be themselves. They did whatever they liked even when the culture was so much more restrictive than nowadays. They faced their fears, expressed their power and (if that's not inspirational enough) fought in skirts!'

The evening made me remember a thought from the 'old days': I wanted to give boxing a go.

Although most of the feelings and problems that motivated me to think about fighting in the first place had disappeared or resolved, I still thought that I 'owed' this to my old self.

I did some research but, unfortunately, all of the boxing gym memberships I found were out of my budget. I was a bit disappointed but not shaken. I put the thought back to the 'sometime in the future' box of my mind. I was sure sometime, when the time is right, it was going to happen.

And at the beginning of August I got a sign from the universe…

1st round: The sign - up

In August, scrolling through the story feed on Instagram, I saw an intriguing offer. The name of the advertiser had already started my fantasy. 'The White Collar Fight Club'. Wow! This sounds exciting. It must be similar to the fight club in the movie… although 'white collar', so I assume more rules and less blood?

The offer looked perfect; eight weeks of training with two weekly combat sessions held by professional trainers; one strength and conditioning workout and a big final mind-blowing match at the Troxy on the 2nd November. And the best thing of all? It was all for free. The only transaction they asked for was to fundraise at least £50 and to sell twenty tickets for the finale.

I was especially happy that the programme collected money for the Mind charity. This is an organisation that fights against the mental health stigma. They provide advice and support to empower anyone experiencing a mental health problem. I had people who supported me when I was going through hell, but not everybody is this lucky. I wanted to help in their work and 'pay the good forward' I received: if my effort contributes just one person to feel (even slightly) better it was already a hundred times worth it.

I imagined myself going through this program. I knew it's going to be physically, emotionally and mentally challenging. I knew I was going to have at least one meltdown. I was going to be (hopefully, for my own survival's sake) the fittest I'd ever been and this is going to be the story I was going to be proud of all my life.

I'd been waiting for my YES moment: the adventure that really suits me, a big challenge I can say YES to. It had arrived and I was sure I could do it.

I was unbelievably happy. I could feel my heart pounding in my chest as I opened the sign-up form and completed it with trembling, adrenaline-filled hands. I may have even teared up a little bit. I was overjoyed. This was the opportunity I was waiting for. As I pressed the "submit" button, I felt a tingling feeling spreading through my body: 'This is it... this is the start of my journey.'

*

A few days after, I headed to the Eight Members Club in the City to a sign-up meeting feeling super nervous. I have never been to a members' club. I imagined secret passwords, posh people (White collar means city workers, right? Everybody was going to be in suits and little black dresses and I was going to stand there like someone who got lost.) and a bar straight from a design magazine. I was intimidated even before I got there.

When I arrived, I didn't need a password. The big heavy metal door was disappointingly slightly open. I just needed to sign in at the Reception in front of smartly dressed staff. The meeting room (as I predicted stylish: black walls with silver furniture) was already full.

I didn't dare to look around much, but for me, everybody looked fitter and cooler than I was. As I glanced at the women, I didn't see anybody my size and shape. I started to be worried. I'm an active person but not fit. I thought more participants were going to be beginners like me.

I was wearing a colourful outfit; knee length skirt with flowers, blue t-shirt, red coat and backpack. Surrounded by the people indeed wearing the training equivalent of 'city clothes' (tight lycra in dark serious colours). I felt out of place.

In my head, I was running through my usual 'self-sabotaging' talk. 'Oh my! They must wonder what I am doing here. They must think I am a "softy" and an easy opponent.'

I tried to calm myself down. 'It can be a good strategy though. Make the ladies believe I am cute and harmless then surprise them in the ring!'

During the meeting, the coaches and mentors shared a lot of information from the weekly structure through personal experiences to training tips. My mind was focused on two things: safety and the night of the fight.

I was convinced the training and the final fight was going to be as safe as possible. The organisers told us that they match the opponents by weight, experience and level; the possible opponents spar at least two times before the fight night and the event is going to be led by pro referees and medical staff providing the thickest (sixteen-ounce) gloves and head guard.

The fight night information thrilled me; the match consists of three two-minute long rounds in front of hundreds of spectators (1500 if the house was full!) in personalised fight-wear (with a boxer name printed on and everything!) and I'd have my 'hype track' just like I'd seen at recordings of professional matches.

The location, the Toxy, is also special to me. My sister used to live close by so I spent a lot of time in its proximity. We often had brunches at a cafe opposite and walked next to the building on our way to the tube. Although I have never been inside, I've heard the name many times before connected with events (e.g. it hosts a lot of fabulous drag shows). I always knew I was going to go there someday. How special it is that my first visit would be as a headliner in a boxing match!

After the meeting, a tornado of feelings went through me. I was excited, nervous, inspired and hesitant at the same time. It was a big (ok, enormous) challenge for me: super cool, but scary ('I'm going to get punched in the face... at least a thousand times!'). To push myself and not to get distracted by my 'imagining the worst' thoughts, as soon as I got home, I started telling (some) people.

They had mixed reactions. "Oh, my god, WHY?" (Mum); "Of course, you always do quirky things like that. I'm not surprised." (my brother in law); "That's badass!!!" (one of my colleagues who does boxing). Overall, most people were super encouraging. Their support helped me to start feeling more confident. The gloves are still on. I'll smash this!

2nd round: The training

The time of my first combat session had arrived two weeks later. It was held close to Bank Station in an old underground bank vault. The place looked unfriendly. They used a lot of artificial neon lights but some of the rooms remained dark; the walls were thick concrete without paint and the music was super loud. When I got to the boxing area, the first thing I saw was a crying girl in the door looking at the ring. I hoped she was okay, but didn't dare to ask... what if she said something that got me running out from there?

I sat down close to the ring and started watching the end of the training session that came before mine. It looked super intense; the people were giving rapid punches, stepping and leaning away from attack surrounded by the sound of gloves hitting bodies. I tried to focus on their movements to see if I could learn something before I started but my mind started to wander. 'Am I ever going to be like them?'

Shortly after the coach sent the advanced group away, he gathered the newbies and my boxing journey officially started.

After warm up, I felt like we jumped straight into the middle. We practiced turning away from punches but I couldn't get hold of the techniques. The coach and my training partners showed me how to do it slowly several times. Even if I could repeat the movements, when we sped up or practiced 'freestyle', I was lost. My frustration grew. 'Why can't I do it? In theory it's super easy and the others are fine with it. What's wrong with me? I always thought I had a good sense of rhythm and I'm OK with choreography, but now I'm frozen.'

After the session, I left as quickly as possible. 'Well, that didn't go as I expected. I'm definitely not a natural or a hidden boxing talent. My frustration didn't help either. I thought I'd release all my pent up aggression, like I'd fantasised when I first thought about boxing. I really don't know what happened. I just couldn't get hold on this super easy thing. I know I've never done boxing before and it was my first session, but still, I should have been better. I hope I'm going to improve next time.'

*

The second session was two days later at a different gym. Before the training started, I had a chat with two ladies. One of them told me that she had already participated in this programme once before. She had good experience, which was encouraging. I didn't feel like a complete newbie failure. I realised that not everybody was a beginner as I had expected. I got a bit nervous imagining myself being put together to fight with someone who had more experience than me, but then the session started and I had to focus. I was determined to be better than last time.

The coach pushed us super hard physically from the beginning, but surprisingly, I felt better because his teaching style was much closer to my learning style than the previous trainer's. I felt like we went through the basics more systematically.

The last ten minutes of the training, the 'cool down', was one of the most challenging workouts of my life: burpees, push-ups, sit-ups, repeatedly lifting ten-kilogram disks above our heads and squatting. I was absolutely exhausted. I think I must have sweated at least five litres.

"This is the easiest session," said Coach as I towelled myself down. "From now on it's only going to get harder. You are going to experience how it is to be a fighter. How it is to feel 'done'. Being at the end of your energy and at the limits of your mental strength, but still pushing through and never giving up."

I wasn't able to lift any of my muscles, but I couldn't wait to be back and train again.

The second week came and I was curious to see how I was going to perform on the Tuesday combat session after last week's sense of failure and disappointment. Unfortunately, the sense of 'lostness' happened again. When we practiced the defence moves, I just couldn't keep up. I tried to focus but, as I got more and more frustrated, I made more mistakes. I was annoyed, disappointed and furious with myself. This mood followed me to the fitness session on Thursday. I wasn't getting the instructions as much as the first time. I felt completely low.

*

During the third week I didn't feel any improvement in my performance either.

On the Tuesday I had a revelation. I arrived a bit earlier and, as I was preparing next to the ring, I noticed that a lot of people from my group are already in the ring boxing. I asked someone next to me and he said that plenty of the people do extra: some have one-to-one personal boxing training and some participate more than two combat sessions a week (according to the rules we were only allowed two).

I felt my stomach jump: 'It's not a surprise that they seem to have much more experience than me because they probably do!' I told myself. 'I thought two sessions a week was going to be enough but how can I compete with people who do extra? I don't have money for a personal trainer or to have a gym membership. I'm going to be the worst of the group!' With these negative thoughts floating around my brain, you can imagine how the training went...

On Thursday, I considered giving up. It was hard for me even to leave the house because I felt there is no point. I managed to persuade myself to go to the training in the end, but the thoughts remained in my mind, like dark internal enemies ready to bring me down.

During the third week I was still undecided about the future. The deadline of selling the first ten tickets was approaching (the end of the following week) and I hadn't advertised them, because I was still unsure if I'm going to do it.

I chose to take some weight from my shoulder: I was going to leave it for the Universe to decide. If I could find twenty people who wanted to see me boxing and were willing to pay for it, then I had to fight. If I didn't, then it wasn't my fault if I quit the program.

*

The fourth week marked the halfway point of the challenge and that was when I hit my lowest point. I was close to have a meltdown during Thursday's session. I was exhausted, I didn't have the mental capacity to keep in touch with people and I missed my comfort foods. I knew half of the time had gone and I felt the building pressure. I also panicked because next Saturday was the first sparring and I didn't feel ready.

During the last (as physically challenging as never before) conditioning exercise, I felt tears collecting in my eyes. 'I'm giving everything I can but it's not enough. I want to leave. I can't do this, it's just too hard.' Fortunately, I pulled myself together and after the session my fellow fighters comforted and encouraged me. Their support helped me through.

The day of the sparring came and the first victory arrived when the coaches measured my weight. I lost seven kilograms! I was proud of myself and, although I was still nervous, my mood lifted a little bit.

During the round, me and my first opponent both did our best. We gave and received big punches and were absolutely exhausted at the end. The coaches didn't say who scored more and I couldn't decide; I think we were really close. To be honest, I didn't mind not knowing who had won. I felt relief, pride and happiness. 'I did it! It wasn't as bad as I thought it would be. I can actually do this!'

I felt motivated again and full of energy. I started to imagine that I could not only survive the final fight, but maybe win it.

The second round went much better thanks to my newly found confidence. When we finished the two minutes, I was still exhausted, but I knew for sure that I scored more. I was over the moon!

My mind-set had changed and, although I still hadn't noticed much improvement in my boxing skills during the next week, I was positive that if I tried my best in the ring, I didn't need to be ashamed.

I started to form my strategy. I was good at waiting and assessing the situation. I'd notice an 'opening' and aim my punches there. I didn't really do any pre-practiced combinations consciously. I reacted more than acted. I decided to stand my guard, block whatever I could and use the empty spaces to punch.

During the second and third sparring session, I got paired up with the same lady again so I knew I was going to be with her at the final.

Our abilities were quite equal; she had very big and strong punches, but I was a bit faster than her. The result was going to depend on how we felt on the day.

*

The final week had arrived. Two days before the match, we had the official weigh in. We had to gather to get weighed and then pose fiercely with our opponent (I was paired up with the lady I expected) in front of cameras.

As a boxer name I chose 'Noni Balboa'. I hoped I could be as badass as the fighter I named myself after.

The organisers promised that we'd have our personalised boxing gear ready for the event.

I arrived at the weigh in wearing a casual but elegant, long, floaty, flowery dress. After they measured our weight, my training mates and I were waiting around a bit then they started to take our photos.

"Wait a minute! Where are the tops?" I asked. "I thought I could change for the photo? How am I supposed to look like a badass fighter if I'm wearing this?"

Unfortunately, the organisers hadn't received our gear. I had to pose in a dress. I felt quite awkward, but I put on a brave, fierce face and went for it. Dress, no dress, I am a fighter.

I went home like nothing could shake me...

3rd round: Fight night

And the day had come. 7th December, the Fight Night. Although the coaches told us to rest and take it easy on the day, I spent the morning running errands. I couldn't stay still.

After a bath, packing and dressing up I was on my way. I was listening to my 'confidence' playlist on the bus and tried to imagine the best scenarios.

'I'm going to be surrounded by my family, my partner, my best friends, mates and colleagues. It's going to be super special and the final score doesn't matter. I mean, of course, I want to win, but I'm going to be OK even if I'm not.'

I had to walk about fifteen minutes from my bus stop to get to the Troxy. As I was walking toward it, it became bigger and bigger. I felt my excitement increasing the same way. I couldn't believe it was finally happening.

When I stepped into the building through the staff entry, my mind was blown right away. The interior design of the Troxy was like my dream come true: a mixture of a Disney castle and art deco. The walls and furniture were painted with my favourite colours (pastel minty green and lavender) with beautiful golden banisters. I thought, 'It's another sign from the universe for me. This night is going to be amazing!'

After all the fighters gathered in the changing room, we had a final meeting. The organisers told us about the schedule of the day and reminded us of the rules. After the recap, I had to do a medical check-up and, by the time I got back to the room, the order of the matches was on the wall.

I was number two!

I was thrilled as I didn't have to wait long: 'I can "get it over with" soon and enjoy the rest of the night. Finally, in two hours, I can eat the cake I ordered from my family.

For the warm-up I asked my support coach to go outside to the corridor with me. I didn't want to be in the same space as my opponent. Although she was on the other side of the separated room behind a long white curtain, I didn't want the chance to see her or her to see me. If she was more prepared than I was, I would be super nervous and too afraid. If I would feel 'more advanced', maybe I wouldn't take it seriously enough and be overconfident.

When it was time to go, I started telling myself, 'I am a winner. Anything happens in the ring and whatever the final score, I am a winner. I fought these eight weeks through. I pushed myself super hard and I am here. I am having the experience of a lifetime. I am proud of myself and what I had achieved. I am a boxer? Not really. Am I a fighter? Definitely!'

I did my entry walk 'go big or go home' style. I knew it was my first and last time to do this, a once in a lifetime opportunity, so I gave it my all. I was wearing a fake fur coat, danced in front of my cheer team, kissed my partner and shook all my jelly for the VIP tables at the front as well. I felt confident, adrenaline was pumping in every part of my body and I could hear my name being chanted from my tables. I was ready.

The second I heard the bell signalling the start of the first round, my stomach jumped a little bit. I followed my strategy: react and not act, wait for my opponent to punch and give punches where I could see an opening. I also tried to be fast, to move and lean away rhythmically. I knew that my opponent usually aims for the head, so I tried to punch her body to distract her.

After the first round, I was so out of breath. I thought I was going to faint. The coaches told us from the beginning that we needed to work on our cardio, to run constantly and prepare for the hardships of the three rounds. I only understood the importance until I was actually in the ring. During the one-minute break, I tried to inhale as deeply as I possibly could and try to collect myself as fast as possible. I drank a little bit but I focussed on getting more oxygen into my lungs.

When the second round came, I was still inhaling rapidly. I decided to take my moves even slower, conserve my breathing. This pushed my opponent to take the lead, which was in my favour. I counter punched whenever I could. I remember taking some big punches (at one point my head-guard slid aside and I had to adjust it) but because of the adrenaline, I actually didn't feel pain.

After the second round, I was still exhausted but the thought that we only have one left gave me energy. I decided to push myself even harder.

At the beginning of the third round I started super-fast and gave a series of punches. I continued aiming for the openings. After one and a half minutes, the referee sent me to the corner and talked to my opponent about her defence. She was super tired too so she had let her hands down. It'd given me plenty of opportunities to score hits. When we stepped together again, we only had four seconds left. When she started her attack, the final bell rang.

I couldn't believe it was over. When the referee lifted my hand in the air, I screamed my head off, jumped around and blew kisses towards my cheering team whose screams filled the hall.

I did it! I'd pushed myself through the physical challenges, stayed mentally strong(ish) when it seemed impossible and made my dream come true. I was grateful, proud and overjoyed.

I turned my Yes idea into a Yes project and then the biggest Yes moment of my life. And this was the best feeling ever.

Cool down

I would like to use this space to thank everybody who supported me during this unbelieve experience. I truly couldn't have done it without you.

First of all the amazing WFCF coaches, mentors and fighters. Matteo Albanese, Abdul Yassine, Saj Imran, the Ladies Who Box (especially Charlotte, Cloe, Emily, Dhi, Katie and Felicity) and the boys (shout

out for Frankie, Ayo and Ed).

My wonderful family: Anyu, Apu, Orsikam, Kim and meu bonito Namorado.

The best colleagues: Aliyah, Beth, Dilz, Jordan, Magdalena, Marta and Nabs

My fantastic friends and mates: my bestie Krisztina, coach Dzsinksz, Josephine, Max, Brian, Ian M (The Project Awesomers), Norbert, Martina, Ian P, Tim, Nadege, Georgie H, Monica and Maria.

And the two anonymous supporters on my (still functioning as of August 2020) fundraising page (**www.justgiving.com\fundraising\nonibalboa**).

And a final note for whoever is inspired by this story: If you want to try yourself out as a boxer or Muay Thai fighter, I 100% recommend the White Collar Fight Club. You would be in the best hands and have an experience of a lifetime.

Gloves on!

Instagram: **@nonipapp**

Chapter 37

On the Up

By Mark Perez

I'm going to assume that you may have seen Deadpool and know the superhero landing scene – the graceful arc through the air of the villain, the measured landing striking a heroic pose, nailing it to rapturous applause, (if not, check it out).

This doesn't start like that, much as I would like it to. I always imagined that if I was knocked off my bike, cat-like reflexes would kick in, rolling, protecting vital points, landing in a suitable pose to then stand, dust myself off and walk away unscathed, maybe taking a well-timed bow to any onlookers. Nope – the reality was more of a rush of air, a sickening crunch and then a hazy realisation. Not even a witty one liner from the hero!

So how did we get to this? Unlike me at the side of the road, I hope you're sitting comfortably as we roll back a few years, Wayne's World style (as you will gather, I'm a complete movie nerd so will be dropping pop culture references like they are going out of style) – fade to black…

Create in your mind a picture of complete averageness – wife, child, three-bed semi in the suburbs, secure Council job, two cars, three cats (ok, not so average there). Safe and vanilla, regular and routine and perhaps one that you may recognise. And there's nothing wrong with it. But deep down, isn't there a bit of you just wondering if there could be something more? Do you not feel that little niggly poking, flicking sensation somewhere in the back of your mind, that feeling that up to now you have often just ignored or put off, something for another day. If you've picked up this book, I reckon that you would probably agree; but it's easier just to keep calm and carry on, not to disrupt the routine, not to rock the boat.

So when circumstances came and punched a hole in the hull of the boat, it was frightening and upsetting. It can maybe even be an eye-opener or a kick up the backside – an opportunity? For me that event was the end of my marriage and the subsequent divorce. Things hadn't been great for a while but they had limped along before the obviousness of the situation smacked me in the face and we separated. (On a side note, it was the best thing that could have happened and we remain firm friends, bringing up our daughter and avoiding the legal fights and animosity that make for late night mini-dramas on obscurely named channels. We have both since moved into new relationships and to building new lives).

Describing it as an opportunity might seem cold-hearted to some; trust me when I say that I never thought of it in that way, rubbing my hands at the prospect of sowing wild oats like some shire-born lothario. It was a chance to re-evaluate my place in the world, what I wanted and perhaps (trying not to be too cheesy), who I wanted to be. The worries that drive you in your twenties maybe do not seem so important by the time you reach your mid-thirties; fitting in and not standing out from the crowd, worrying about what people may think of you, having the right car or curtains. At least that is how it suddenly seemed to me. So my grand Yes moment (and that's the reason that you've read this far) was less a Yay-piphany Big Bang and more of a slow burning smoulder, prompting a period of reflection. How very Zen.

However like any recently single man, foot-loose and fancy-free, I did what I thought would be a laugh and bought a tent and a ticket to a music festival – Download 2011, mainly to see a favourite band but more likely to recapture the spirit of youth, (ok, maybe not so zen!). So far so predictable; though at least I had not bought a sports car. I can't lie – I had a great time but something just felt... if not wrong, then more just *not right*. I didn't feel old; there were plenty of people of my age as well as hordes of teenagers. It just felt that this was not me; it felt forced, perhaps what people thought what I should be doing with my freedom. I didn't feel authentic, maybe trying to be someone or something that, deep down, I really wasn't. The boat needed rocking, though perhaps not in this way.

Probably more than anything else, this moment was the one that kicked that slumbering part of my brain into action. While it is quite hard to think deeply about life, the universe and everything on a campsite populated by drunken head-bangers, I did manage it. If I was not being true to myself, then what was the point? Plus – I had a tent now.

Now just add one other important factor to the mix. Though much maligned and blamed for the ills of today's society, social media did show me that there was more to life than I could possibly imagine. People were posting weird things from all over the world about activities like wild camping and obstacle course racing, of getting outside in wonderful ways that weren't big headline grabbing expeditions with teams planning for years or requiring thousands of pounds of kit. This sort of thing had always been something that other people did – athletes and professional explorers, all ripped bodies and sponsorship deals. That little flame of yes got a bit of a fanning and burned a little brighter. The *hmm* morphed into a bit of a *maybe, why not*.

Before we go on, perhaps I should say a little about myself, to give you a flavour of our leading man. I was never a team player at school; not in any cool moody rebel from the side-lines way. More just a "rubbish at games and always last to be picked" kind of way. I did not excel or stand out and am certainly not an extroverted life and soul of the party monster. I am much happier at the margin with a few friends that I am comfortable with. In much the same way that I described that easy secure life earlier, my social life was a reflection of this. Certainly not challenging, so to step out of that little circle of security would be a massive thing for me. But what did I have to lose?

I enjoyed running, having recently joined a local running club (trust me, that decision took ages). I had started to get back into running after a sedentary break away (essentially, most of my twenties and early thirties). At the start, running non-stop for ten minutes felt that I would need a paramedic on standby half way around a nearby park. Then that got a little longer, twenty minutes, then thirty. After getting to this sort of level, I felt confident enough to join the Shropshire Shufflers, pounding the streets for an hour once a week, thankful that it was winter and the evenings were dark. The night hid my sweating beetroot of a face and pained expression as we pushed at my comfort zone. Thankful too that the coaches were supportive and friendly. This felt right – not like school where being at the back was an excuse for some to shout Darwinian encouragement (being anything but encouraging). I wanted to come back week after week and get better. And somehow I soon found myself at the start of a local ten-kilometre race around Christmas.

This certainly was not me. I had never been one of those people. I wasn't then and now, years later, I'm still not. I had always had in my mind the image of the people who took part. These people were somehow apart from the rest of us, set on a pedestal. It does feel weird to look back and think about it, but the thought of taking part in a race seemed as likely to me as being on the start line of an Olympic final. So to find myself at the start of the Telford 10K was huge at the time. I would love to say that I didn't feel like a Spartan warrior at the start line, but I'd be lying. I was god-like as I crossed the finish line, (in my mind at least). The reality was more like a sweaty fifty-five minutes in ten quid trainers and mud to my knees. To the winner, the laurels and for me, the rather generic medal for finishing was the sweetest prize imaginable, (no disrespect to the organisers, the bling has got much better over the years).

The medal was hung by its red, white and blue ribbon in pride of place on a picture frame in my bedroom. Barring a victorious season in prep school sack racing (a staple of sports day for the "just happy to be there" participants), I had never won anything. Ok, so the medal from Telford was their equivalent of turning up and finishing, but that's not the point here. I had completed a distance that just a few months before I would have thought beyond me. And the little yes spark wanted to know "what next?" so I answered, "Lots." I had a tent and some ideas nicked from Facebook!

If imitation is the sincerest form of flattery, then some people out there, posting on their blogs and timelines should be incredibly flattered. With the enthusiasm of a rank amateur, I compiled a list of things that I wanted to do, less of a bucket list and more of an *everything as long as it isn't too pricey* list. More races were a feature, building on the conquest of the 10k distance; perhaps a half marathon or two, some obstacle course races, climbing some local hills with a camp out or two. In retrospect, so much seems tame now but at the time I was riding the crest of that wave. I'm sure that you understand that feeling of possibilities, just if you take a step outside your door. Watching The Hobbit with my daughter a few years ago, the scene of Bilbo racing out of his house to catch up with the company of dwarves captures it so perfectly. That feeling that Anything is Possible and to hell with what people may think! "I'm going on an adventure!"

So I was doing things, the philosophy of experiences over material possessions; yet something still felt slightly out of place. Imagine trying to complete a jigsaw by just emptying the pieces out and trying to fit random ones together in no order. There was a nagging feeling just at the edge of my conscious, a glitch in the Matrix that I just could not see. Find the corners, work on the edges and set the frame for the rest of the puzzle to fit into. I felt that the frame was not complete yet.

The answer came from an unexpected source; work of all places. The powers that be put out a call for expressions of interest in voluntary redundancy. It had not even occurred to me that work was as much an anchor holding me back as providing security. I had great colleagues and easily achieved everything that was put in front of me, but the nature of the job itself had changed. Without being too specific, the focus had shifted away from trying to support clients and it was starting to sit a little uncomfortably with me. From getting the email to making the decision to leave must have taken about fifteen seconds. Pretty much the total mental discussion amounted to "Why the hell not?"

If ever there was time for a leap of faith, stepping off the cliff edge like Indiana Jones, this was it. I'm not a spiritual or religious person, but I do think that sometimes the universe clicks into place and gives you a nudge. This was my nudge and the reply email to put my name forward was already sent. If I had tried to start rationalising and being logical like the old me, I would probably have hesitated and sat on my hands, putting off making a decision before procrastinating into inactivity and staying put. Somehow this felt right, just saying yes and worrying about the details later. Perhaps the universe puts these opportunities under our noses all the time, but we are so busy getting on with the everyday routine that we miss them. Being open to this meant that I started to see the possibilities that had been there all along.

Going home at the end of that first day, the first day of the countdown, I had a funny feeling. I thought that the closer I came to leaving the safety and security of my job, a role that had pretty much defined me for around fifteen years, the more terrified I would be. Yet somehow an overwhelming sense of calm had descended. I didn't have to be defined by my job – again those younger me thoughts were being replaced by older me ones! As long as I could provide for my daughter, not much else really mattered. What actually seemed important now was the role model that I could be for her; it was more important to be true to myself and show her that life was for living. It does seem like a cheesy tag line from a movie, but it actually felt true and right. That puzzle's frame seemed to be complete; time to work on the rest of the picture.

The three months until the big day seemed to drag. Work did not feel so important anymore; five o'clock seemed an eternity away every day. Evenings and weekends became so important as the picture started to come together; time with my daughter and my new girlfriend, who was very supportive of the idea. She is someone who relishes life outside of work, exploring the UK by bike, always planning the next adventure. She helped open my eyes to the idea of grabbing life and it not having to cost an arm and a leg. I also came to realise quite how much stuff had been accumulated over the years, filling loft, shelves and garage to bursting. Having it all had seemed like a comfort blanket; now it just felt like lead weights dragging me down, anchoring me to rocks I had to steer away from. I started to take stock of what was stored up and so much just took my breath away. Crates of my daughter's pictures, pretty much everything that she had ever put onto paper from as soon as she could hold a crayon or brush; hundreds of books, many never read but always soon to be picked up; unworn clothes, still with tags. And videos! So many videos. I did feel that if I had dropped dead at that moment, my life would have been summed up by every episode of Friends on VHS, neatly arranged on shelves behind the living room door. If you have ever had that prickly feeling in your armpits, a bit sweaty and uncomfortable, that shifting nervously in your seat, that would be how I felt then. This was certainly not what I would want my legacy to be.

Life became an intense cycle of Freecycle, car boots and trips to charity shops; almost daily, bags and boxes would leave the house, strangers would knock and walk away with electrical items or pieces of furniture. And with every bag and box that left, that weight started to lift. Feelings that items would be missed never materialised. I kept a few precious pictures, but everything else was photographed and stored digitally, before heading into the recycling bin. Of course there were tears with each opened box sparking up memories. Letting go is never easy, but they were happy tears rather than those of loss or grief. The time was right to say goodbye and thank you. Weirdly, in the years that have passed since, the folders on the hard drive have never even been opened. Knowing that they are there is reassuring in some way, but I have never had the urge to revisit them. Again, that expectation that we should be keeping items, or possess certain badges of success, those trinkets to show who we were, it was all just far less important than it had been those years before. The fewer physical possessions I had, the freer I felt – and this was years before minimalism became trendy.

As for work, the day came to leave behind friends made over the years. No job lined up, a modest payment that would keep me out of the workhouse for a few months and a blank canvas that could turn out however I wanted. I fancied retraining and becoming some sort of financial high flyer, but the more I looked into this, again the less authentic it felt to me, (though it did lead to volunteering with a local Credit Union – file that for later). I checked the jobs out there but nothing felt right until an advert appeared after three months for a part-time role with a local housing charity. Part-time could mean some freedom to be out there, having fun and doing things. Why not, so I applied.

The interview involved delivering a presentation to the panel. I've sat through so many death by PowerPoint presentations so thought that if I had a laugh, I might at least be remembered (and possibly be asked never to contact them again). For a very serious role, the first of the handful of slides I used was a skull and cross bones flag. I do not know whether this was recognised as out of the box thinking or if the panel thought I might appear outside their homes dressed as Michael Myers if I got knocked back; they gave me the job!

Six years later, I'm still here and I genuinely love it. That might be the happy ending, but there's so much more. I know that I'm still on the journey and the fun is to be found by travelling it and not in reaching the destination. I am hugely grateful that when I again decided to hand in my notice a couple of years ago, my new employer turned it into an opportunity for a career break instead. Six months off to say Yes to ideas. Which brings us full circle and back to the start, sat by a road looking dazed.

Amongst a myriad of other ideas for adventures, I had read on Facebook about cyclists on the Avenue Verte. Part of my time out of work was to complete that, London to Paris on an unbroken cycle route (barring the Channel bit). "Yes why not." So plans were made, which entailed buying a guide and booking a spot on the ferry there and back, giving six days in France to complete the circular route. Most of the kit that I had collected over the years would be fine and with various bags and bungies, it all got secured to my bike.

As with most of my plans, the big idea was the easy bit. I'm often a bit lighter on the fine details, trusting that most things will work themselves out for the best. Like leaving a secure job, the big picture is easy to figure out. Just say yes and go. The details can be terrifying, so best to do the minimum and then cross all my fingers. I had the gear and could follow the signs that marked the route. What could go wrong?

As it turned out, not much, though what it lacked in quantity it made up for in quality. Coming down a hill, just outside London a driver in a black Audi estate decided to overtake me on a blind bend. Like some demented extra out of the Fast and the Furious, he sped out behind me into the path of the car coming up and around the bend. Not wanting to damage his lovely new car, he pulled in rather sharply, fully inhabiting the space that my front wheel occupied. Needless to say, he was away before I had completed my second bounce. Until you experience it, you will never understand how hard it is to fire off a pithy one liner as your head does an impression of the bouncing bomb. Another driver did stop and offer assistance but in my dazed state, I was adamant that I was fine and did not want to be a bother.

Being no stranger to injury, I knew that I had broken my jaw (again), though at least this time all my teeth were intact, (the postscript to another 'Why not?' moment!) Everything else seemed ok. And for once, life is not like the movies. One minute I had been cycling quite happily; the next I was sat on the side of the road wondering why my top was turning red – the gash across my chin from a tarmac/head interface could explain it. More worrying was the flat tyre, so I concentrated on that, fixing it and checking everything else was okay. It was not until I made camp in some woodland that evening that I even realised that there were two quite large holes on my right knee, as well as some choice patches of missing skin down my arm. Rather stupidly, I patched myself up and curled up in my bag (note to self – in future, get head injuries checked professionally).

I am happy to say that the rest of the trip was accident-free, wild camping by the Avenue Verte in some torrential downpours snuggled dry under my tarp, cycling 250 miles in two days before deciding to get a hotel in Paris for two nights and catching the train back to the coast. On the way, I met some amazing people who were not too insulted by my GCSE standard French, to the point that one lovely lady paid for my lunch without my knowing, having chatted about any number of random subjects for an hour. How amazing was that! I doubt that if I had been chatting to a stranger in some greasy spoon in the UK, I would have bought them lunch without their knowing – now though, maybe I would.

It was a massive effort to reach the capital, so why not enjoy it? A cheap Parisian hotel welcomed me with hot water and a real bed, giving me two days to explore, jogging by the Seine, soaking in the atmosphere and recharging my batteries. Travelling solo without a strict itinerary gave me the freedom to do that, the only pressure being that of reaching Dieppe in time for the return ferry. It also reminded me of how little one actually needs to have an incredible adventure or even be happy and warm.

The universe has an amazing way of turning and bringing you back to insignificant moments that your whole life will pivot on without you even realising. Quitting my job led to those delusions of financial grandeur, which led me to volunteering with a Credit Union for some work experience, which led to the CEO sending me to a local conference where the keynote speaker was a strange ginger guy talking about the power of Yes. That drew me to Facebook and the YesTribe there and another strange request to submit a chapter in a book. After everything that I have been through to get to here, there was only one answer to that, wasn't there.

Instagram: **@severnwomble**

YouTube: **severnwomble**

Chapter 38

An Unexpected Journey

By Glen Pilkington

As a youngster and aspiring 'wannabe adventurer', I had always dreamed of visiting the Himalayas and seeing the lofty mountain peaks. I was particularly in awe of Mount Everest. One day, I wanted to go to the mountain myself. Just laying eyes on that hallowed peak would fulfil a lifelong dream.

It took over four decades but here I was boarding a plane bound for Kathmandu.

I was already bubbling with the general excitement of the trip and simmering with nervous anticipation for the adventure ahead. However, I was nearly at boiling point when I found out I was to go on the most dangerous flight in the world – to Lukla in the Himalayas. Forbes labels Tenzing-Hilary Airport as 'The Most Dangerous Airport in the World'. Whether this is true or not, I made a conscious decision not to google the flight or look at YouTube. I wanted to make up my own mind. And I also didn't want to scare myself off before I'd even left Britain.

The flights were long but my senses were seriously awakened upon arrival in Kathmandu – I can only describe it like a loud alarm clock shocking you awake from a deep sleep. Bustling with activity everywhere, trying to reclaim bags and finding my transport. Has anyone ever noticed when you go on this type of trip that everyone travels with the same brand of duffle bag?

Two days in Kathmandu before the trek started was an experience in itself. The first thing I noticed was the traffic – complete and utter chaos with vehicles of all types seemingly driving wherever they wanted. There was the occasional minor crash here and there but no one apparently cared. In its own way, it was a magical sight. Imagine a busy M25 motorway in rush hour but with traffic going in all directions with no concern for any rules of the road. Something I will never forget is the noise of the constant honking of car horns.

Arriving in the city centre itself, I had time to visit the temples of Durbar Square in front of the old Royal Palace of the Kathmandu kingdom – a bustling plaza of temples, with tourists and locals mingling in a sea of pedestrians, ebbing and flowing, moving in and out just like the tides. Cars beeped. People yelled. The ocean of people roared and kept moving forward.

Turning a corner, I was rather taken aback. I was suddenly face to face with army trucks filled with soldiers all armed with some serious looking weapons. Not something that I ever expected to see.

'Don't worry!' shouted a distant voice in the crowd. 'There is a possible uprising or something but they like the tourists'. Did the soldiers really care if I was a tourist or not? Their faces didn't seem to register any particular affection towards me. I quickly moved on.

The final visit in the City was to Swayambhunath located on a steep hill west of Kathmandu. This temple complex has been in situ since the 5th century BCE and is known for the immense golden domed stupa and mixture of shrines and temples. Every area is incredibly ornate and beautifully decorated. Prayer flags flutter in the wind and the panorama of the whole of chaotic Kathmandu is visible through the polluted haze from so high up on the hill. The brief but steep walk up was worth it.

This sacred pilgrimage site is also known as the Monkey Temple (easier to say than Swayambhunath) and it was clear to see why. Everywhere you look there are monkeys – on the ground, on the top of the buildings. The monkeys, like miniature clowns, entertain the crowds by stealing food and even the occasional baseball cap from unsuspecting visitors. I was so pleased I had made a trip to this temple – the history, architecture and religious connections are difficult to take in all at once. From the painted meditative eyes representing Wisdom and Compassion that stare down at you from the temple roof; to the burnished gold Bhuddas that seem to glow with an inner light in the sunshine; to the intricately patterned stone carvings that are scattered about. Every time I smell the smoky sweet aroma of burning incense, my mind whips me back to the sights and sounds of Swayambhunath.

Heading back to my hotel, I had a few brief moments to take a final walk through the local streets. Wandering around, I forgot about the dirt beneath my feet, the honks and polluted stench of the traffic, the hustle and bustle of crowds of people bumping into me. My mind was calm – I felt at ease.

Back at the hotel it was time to sort out the kit. My heart was thudding in my chest in anticipation of the days ahead. I felt at once elated and serene, knowing that this was the place I was meant to be. My Everest dream was soon to become a reality and...

Darkness. Silence.

There had been a complete power cut. I stood staring into the blackness. It could have been unnerving but I just grinned to myself. Fishing around in my rucksack, I found my head torch and continued with the task in hand. My roommate was tumbling around the room cursing trying to find his own head torch. I was laughing. Maybe, in the darkness, he couldn't see the funny side!

My sleep was restless as I was consumed by eagerness of what was to come in the morning. Suddenly, there was a loud knock on the bedroom door. A voice whispered, 'Time to get up – we leave in an hour.' I looked at my watch. Really? It was stupid o'clock in the morning but the local transport had arrived to take us back to the airport to board our flight to Lukla.

I stood staring at the decrepit state of the two minibuses wondering whether they would actually manage to take all of us and our luggage – they didn't look like they would make it to the end of the road never mind to the airport.

The small and cramped minibuses bounced along potholed roads and, even at this early hour, the traffic was just as manic as during the daytime. Soon we were standing outside the airport trying to count out money to our tour leader for the flight. My brain still wasn't functioning at this early hour and I still to this day have no idea how much money I handed over. But here I was in a departure lounge with a pass in my hand allowing me on a flight.

The Most Dangerous Flight in the World.

We were hurried onto a bus to take us across the tarmac to our plane, driving past an array of aircraft and ancient looking Russian helicopters. Then, suddenly, we stopped. As is common in the Himalayas, Lukla was closed due to the low cloud and poor weather. We had to wait. Sitting in the minibus, the time went so slowly. There was a mixture of complete silence, half-hearted banter and a sense of nervousness hanging in the air between us. What had I let myself in for?

After what seemed like hours, we moved again and we were told there was a window in the weather. Our flight could leave.

Oh no!

That was when I saw the plane. It was tiny! There was no way it was going to carry the group kit and all of us. I forced my reservations deep down inside and allowed myself to be ushered up a small flight of steps and squeezed into a miniscule corner of the plane. Rucksacks were wedged on our knees. I was squashed shoulder to shoulder with my fellow passengers. Looking ahead, I could see both pilots and out of the cockpit windscreen. The plane was so small it felt as though you were actually sitting in the cockpit. I pitied the beautiful young stewardess who shuffled as best as she could between everyone offering mints.

The pilot fired up the engines and the plane shook violently. Looking around, various strips of tape seemed to be holding things together and as I looked out of the small scratched window, I could see the rubber seal blowing around in the draft of the propellers.

The engines got louder and louder as the plane continued to shake and suddenly we lurched forward and rattled along the runway. We all looked at each other nervously and then we were up in the air – cheers of relief filled the plane. I had hoped I would reach Everest without all of this added drama but I guess that is all part of the adventure.

As we flew towards Lukla, the noise inside the plane was deafening but the sky was a perfect blue and slowly the Himalayas came into view. What a sight! It was everything I had hoped for and more. Jagged, snow-capped mountains filled the horizon.

The flight to Lukla is only about thirty minutes and things were going well until about halfway there.

Suddenly, the plane rapidly lost altitude and my stomach churned with the horrible feeling that something bad was about to happen. The drop felt like an eternity and everyone in the plane was looking anxiously out of the windows, at each other and into the cockpit. The pilots looked in complete control and then, just as quickly as we had dropped, everything was back to normal.

There were laughs from the cockpit. 'Don't worry, it happens sometimes. Just the weather'.

Although this was some comfort, I was glad when the small airstrip at Lukla came into view ahead of us and the plane began to descend. The wheels hit the runway and almost immediately the brakes were applied. The runway is very short and everyone was clinging on. The plane came to a stop and a round of very enthusiastic applause rang out from the cabin.

I was glad to get off the plane but in a weird way had also enjoyed this additional drama. Stepping onto the tarmac, ground crew busied themselves emptying the plane whilst other hangers-on jostled to offer their services as guides.

I needn't have worried about the flight in the end. All those jittery nerves for nothing. I was safe on the ground. I had survived and was ready for the next great adventure - the trek to Everest Base Camp.

I knew a lot of people who had completed the trek before. I had imagined it to be relatively straightforward. I knew it would be physically tough but I wasn't anxious about it at all. It couldn't be that hard.

How wrong could I be? There was no way that I could have anticipated what was to happen on the way back.

After The Most Dangerous Flight in the World, we were led straight to a very pleasant and colourful building where we waited for our bags and had tea. The tea houses and shops surrounding us were painted in wonderfully bright colours – window frames were yellow, green, blue and red. I'm not exactly sure what I had expected to see but this was a stunning sight. It all seemed very civilised for such a remote area.

It is impossible to do justice to an Everest Base Camp trek in one short story but I will always remember the dusty mountain paths with yaks passing by with heavy loads, the long and wobbly suspension bridges over the Dudhi Khosi river and the force of the water crashing down below. I never really knew what to expect from one day to the next as the trail meandered through rhododendron and pine forests as we walked higher and higher. I soon began to understand the sherpas when they said the walk was 'Nepali flat'. They smiled as a mixed group of trekkers from the United Kingdom huffed and puffed their way up steep mountainous pathways which were anything but flat!

From Lukla, the route took us to Chumoa and then on to Namche.

Namche was a real highlight. Set on the side of the mountain, this small and colourful market town is the cultural home of the Sherpa people. At around 3,500 metres, it is a key staging point for expeditions to Everest and other major Himalayan peaks. Looking at Namche is like staring at an ancient amphitheatre carved into the mountainside, rustic buildings nestled together highlighted by bright colours.

After Namche, we walked to Khunde and visited the Hilary hospital set up to help the local people and those on treks. After Khunde, a visit to Khumjung would not be complete without going to see the skull of the yeti at the monastery. I don't mean to be disrespectful but the skull does look like an odd shaped upside down coconut. However, there is something mesmerising about the thought that this might actually be a skull of the infamous abominable snowman.

Moving on to Phunki Tenga, we climbed up to probably the most famous monastery in the area at Tengboche. Here, two brightly coloured and ornate dragon-like creatures stand guard by the main arched entrance. I don't think I will ever be able to properly describe the inside of the monastery other than as a colourful assault on the senses and fascinating religious statues. At the time, I knew this visit would be a key highlight of the trip as we met the monks although I would remember the monastery for a far more practical reason later on.

From Tengboche, our journey continued to Deboche, then Pangboche and on to Dingboche. After Dingboche, we headed towards a lunch stop at Thukla. Reaching the top of this steep climb (Nepali flat again) was surreal. Everything went bizarrely quiet apart from the sound of the wind as we meandered through memorials to the people who had lost their lives climbing in the area including the likes of Scott Fisher, the mountain guide who died in the Everest disaster of 1996. It was odd to be so high and yet everything so quiet. No one was talking. Even the wind seemed to quieten, perhaps as a mark of respect for those that had lost their lives on the mountain.

We moved on to Lobuche at just short of five thousand metres where the overnight temperature dropped quickly.

In the morning, I was told that the temperature had been minus thrity-two. Minus thirty-two what, I don't know but it had been the coldest I had ever been in my life. On day twelve, we had been due to go straight to Kala Pattar but this was changed so that we would stay overnight at Gorak Shep. This was an unplanned stop but it would add an extra night of acclimatization for us all.

On the way to Gorak Shep, we trekked through an amazing route of icy mountain tracks. It was at this point, caught in the bleak open landscape, that the stark reality of being in the middle of nowhere hit and I worried what would happen if anyone had an accident. As we walked, part of the mountain path fell away from below us. I remember looking down at a sheer drop to the valley floor below and hearing the words, 'It's OK. Just jump across'. Okay for them to say. They'd already survived the leap! I could just imagine myself making one simple slip, plummeting down the sheer cliff face and smashing to my almost certain doom on rocks below. Even the slightest injury could spell disaster as we were miles away from medical help.

The extra time at Gorak Shep allowed some of us to visit more memorials – more climbers who had died in the 1996 disaster and it was odd to see gold coloured, weather beaten plaques with names such as Hall, Hansen and Harris.

The two paths up Kala Pattar, the highest point on our expedition, looked relatively easy from a distance. However, after bed tea at 4.30am and some very sloppy porridge, the trek to the summit started at 5.15am and took an unexpected two and a half hours. Not what I had expected when I had surveyed the mountain the day before.

As I reached the summit feeling excited and cold, I punched the air. I'd made it! It had been a long hard slog to get to the top due to both the altitude and the fatigue setting into my aching limbs. The air on the peak was thin and I could feel my muscles screaming out for the oxygen I just couldn't give them.

Gradually, the cloud that had settled on the summit began to clear and lofty peaks came into sight.

The slowly unfolding views made up for all the hard work in the thinning air - I could take in the majesty of Everest, Nuptse and Changtse, which looked like enormous glistening shark teeth in the early dawn light. Behind me I caught glimpses of the northern flank and summit of Lhotse. Looking over my other shoulder, the dome-shaped Pumori filled the skyline. I felt an immense sense of calm descend on me even though my heart was still pounding from the exertion of reaching the top.

All of those mountain books, all of those hours gazing at photos of these famous peaks and now here I was seeing them in the flesh. This was where I was meant to be. This was my dream fulfilled.

Sitting for a quiet moment on the summit, lost in my own little world, I overheard the snippets of a conversation. Someone was describing the lenticular cloud sitting over Mount Everest. The rest of the sky was now clear blue, but my eye was drawn to the large cigar shaped UFO cloud that was hovering over the summit. I had never seen anything like it before.

I found out later that a cloud of this type generally appears as a lens shape and normally develops on the downwind side of a mountain or mountain range. Such a formation occurs when stable, moist air flows over a mountain creating a series of oscillating waves.

An urgent discussion started with our lead sherpa, Tenzing, who said that this was not a good sign. 'There's bad weather coming,' he said seriously. I had no idea if this was right or not but was fully prepared to listen to Tenzing.

I smiled every time I heard that name; our lead sherpa was actually called Tenzing and it made me think of the exploits of Hilary and Tenzing on the first successful summit of Mount Everest in 1953. Even though I was only on a trek to Base Camp and the summit of Kala Pattar, I felt that I could relate to these two pioneering greats.

Little did I know what was to follow.

We were all back at the lodge in Gorak Shep by 9.30am – the descent had been quick although we had all been careful, picking our way down the rock strewn route from the top of the mountain. After breakfast, we headed back through the memorial site at Thukla before dropping down towards Periche.

We woke on day fourteen of our expedition to the first snowfalls of the trip. The plan for the day was to get to Pangboche and head back toward the monastery at Tengboche. That was the goal at least, but it was on this day when I realised how quickly things can change on an expedition.

It was now a lot colder and the wind was blowing haphazardly all around us. It felt as though we were caught in a tumble dryer being pushed in all directions by the ever increasing gusts of wind.

We continued walking upwards (which I found very frustrating as we were on the descent) and the snow began to whirl around us too. Slowly, large snowflakes began to fall and, all of a sudden, we were in a blizzard. The elements were biting cold and it was difficult to see the route ahead as we tried to protect our faces.

The wind was also getting stronger. It was pushing against us, almost forcing us to retreat. But slowly we edged our way forward along the paths and ridges.

The howl of the wind could easily be heard coming up from the valley below. The wind gaining strength, it felt like we were walking one step forward and then being blown three steps back. It was getting harder to walk and soon just standing up became unimaginably difficult. We could hear the wind coming and the sherpas kept shouting at us all to crouch down and cling on to any rock that we could grab.

We were told there was effectively a hurricane and that we needed to keep our heads down, keep going and at least try to get back to the monastery at Tengboche.

I'll admit, I was scared. My heartrate was elevated as the nervous tension increased. This wasn't the altitude, this was fear. Here I was, miles from home in a foreign country, trekking in a remote region and caught in the worst storm I had ever experienced.

We continued our struggle against the wind and snow, step by heavy step, gradually edging our way back to the monastery.

Anyone who has been to Tengboche will know that there are huge wide-open spaces. The snow had stopped but now dust clouds were whirling around us. Grit stung my eyes making it hard to keep them open and see what was going on.

Our guide and sherpas quickly told us to shelter by the entrance gate. Only a few days ago, I had marvelled at the dragon-like creatures but now I was forced to use the stone statues as shelter. There were creaks and cracking noises all around us and soon we realised that trees were being snapped in two and ripped from the ground. We could see sheets of corrugated iron, roofs from the few buildings around us, start to flap in the force of the wind like the razor-edged wings of some violent mythical bird.

We were all trying to protect ourselves, turning our backs against the wind and dust. All of a sudden, we could see in the distance a roof being ripped off the local bakery and flying through the air. Some of our group were a little behind us and still on the trail. We saw them emerge from the wooded path moments before the flying roof smashed across the path. We breathed a sigh of relief for our friends. That had been too close for comfort and we could only imagine what might have happened if the roof had hit them. Fortunately, they were safe and heading to shelter with us.

I remember someone in the group shouting over the wind, 'Well, at least we'll have a lot to tell people when we get home!' Once again on this trip there was nervous laughter.

A small window in the weather allowed us to move on to Phunki Tenga. We sheltered in a small lodge trying to eat some food whilst we listened to the vast array of noises outside. Would the lodge even survive the storm or be suddenly roofless like the bakery in Tengboche? I've never been convinced that buildings were supposed to make so many creaking and groaning noises! It was obvious that the lodge was putting up its own fight against the elements.

After lunch, we were all glad to continue moving on despite the continuing storm. The snow had started again and the wind was not letting up. There was a sense that the sherpas were getting more and more anxious which provided little comfort to the group.

An impromptu overnight stay was quickly arranged in the Thamsherku Lodge in Kyangjuma. The lodge owner had been forewarned however we arrived to darkness. 'He said he's sorry,' Tenzing translated for us. 'He can't light the fires. The wind will draw the flames up the chimneys and set fire to the lodge!'

We sat inside with flickering candlelight playing on the basic stone and wooden walls. We tried to eat but again our attention was drawn to the howling wind and raging blizzard outside. The weather had its grip on the mountain and wasn't letting go.

I was shown into my room for the night and saw a broken window, which was patched up by tape. There was a cold blast coming in through the glass and I was worried what would happen if the window shattered – especially as it was right above my bed!

After a night of disturbed sleep, we woke to an eerie silence. The only sound was the pots and pans being bashed around in the kitchen and the crackling warmth of a fire.

Outside, snow lay on the ground but the wind had stopped and the sky was a crystal clear blue with very little cloud. What a difference to the previous day! We could now have breakfast knowing that today was clearly going to be a much better and happier time for us.

We set off after a hearty breakfast crunching through the snow on the ground. The valley looked like a giant baker had spent the evening icing an enormous white cake. Very quickly, we were stripping layers off as the sun's heat warmed the air.

Heading back to Namche, we were amazed to see that two thirds of the roof of the visitor centre we had visited only days before had been ripped away. Now all that was visible was the rafters. Looking around we could also see that forests had been flattened like someone had driven an almighty bulldozer straight up the mountain. It was strange to see the trees lying horizontal on the ground.

As we continued to descend back towards the small airport at Lukla, huge fallen trees were scattered across the mountain path. The way ahead of us looked like the trees had been stacked up for a giant bonfire. Huge trunks had been snapped and there was debris everywhere.

Our next challenge was to navigate our way through this wooded devastation. The yaks could not pass and our main bags were going back up the track hopefully to follow us down a few days later.

Deciding to be a true adventurer and for some reason feeling very bold, I took the lead and ducked under and climbed over the trees on the ground finding a difficult route through. I was feeling rather pleased with myself until one of the straps of my daysack caught on a branch and for a moment I was stuck whilst everyone laughed and took photographs.

Eventually, albeit very slowly, we had edged our way back to Lukla and could relax getting ready for our celebration evening with the sherpas. I have to be honest, we all drank too much of the local brew but I thoroughly enjoyed the experience of dancing in a dimly lit room and laughing so much – it was certainly a night to remember.

So the adventure was almost over – three flights and I would be back in London. We were then told no flights had left Lukla in almost seven days because of the adverse weather. Great!

My boss had told me (jokingly I think) that whilst I could have three weeks off, I had to return on the date set or I would be fired!

Fortunately, our flight was one of the first to be allowed to leave and as we all had tickets booked, we were hurried through the tiny, sparse airport and onto the plane much to the dissatisfaction of some of the other trekkers who had been waiting for days.

Once again, we were crammed into a Tara Air flight, heading back to Kathmandu. The aircraft seemed to rev its engines forever but then suddenly the brakes were released and we were off down the short runway. The aircraft quickly gained altitude and we were heading back to an overnight stay at our hotel.

I was keen to savour these last moments in the mighty Himalayas taking photographs and videos out of the scratched windows. As a keen photographer, I always take too many pictures but this was a trip of a lifetime and something I wanted to remember forever.

All of a sudden, the small aircraft began to lose a little altitude and seemed to be circling. The pilot shouted that there was bad weather in Kathmandu and that he had to land the plane.

Looking out of the window, all I could see were fields below but we were still being made to circle. My eyes bulged when I saw the reason. A group of farmers were herding their cattle off the small rural runway so that we could land!

Eventually, the plane bounced along what I can only describe as a rough meadow. Thankfully, there were no cows in sight.

We got off the plane and seemed to be allowed to wander anywhere. Quickly, airport staff were wheeling huge plastic containers of aircraft fuel in rickety trolleys towards the plane whilst smoking their cigarettes. Clearly, health and safety regulations aren't quite up to UK standards. It seems this was the World's Most Dangerous Flight for the ground staff too!

After a short while, we were back in the air and then, in next to no time, we landed safely knowing the adventure was finally over.

Never in my wildest dreams had I thought our trek in the Himalayas would see us battling a hurricane to get home. I guess this is all part of an adventure and something I will never forget. Equally, I was happy to have proved to myself how resilient I can be when things do not quite turn out as planned.

In addition, I am now very wary when I see a lenticular cloud formation – can't think why!

Facebook: **glenpilkington**

Instagram: **@gp._everydayadventurer**

Chapter 39

SUP Mallorca

By Phil Plume

This has to be one of the best days of my life.

Quite a statement, I know, but it's right up there with my wedding day and the birth of my kids.

What could I possibly be doing that compares to marrying my childhood sweetheart, or being present at the moment my kids were brought into this world?

Well, I'm sitting on an upturned log in a field eating a dehydrated expedition meal in the grounds of a disused power station.

This probably isn't what you were imagining.

This is a Mediterranean hydroelectric power station; a hidden gem. There are no slag heaps, chimneys or cooling towers. The field is a relatively narrow strip of land about a quarter of the way up huge limestone cliffs. They form a natural amphitheatre facing westwards towards the Mediterranean Sea.

I'm surrounded by a pine forest, immersed in that unmistakable scent of the Mediterranean countryside. There are hundreds of frogs croaking in the crystal clear waters of disused high reservoirs filled by waters flowing from deep within the Serra de Tramuntana Mountains. In front of me is an amazing Balearic sunset with streaks of yellows, orange and reds lying over the sea.

The disused buildings are still there just a few feet below me, but instead of huge hulks of rusty metal and asbestos, they are traditional stone buildings with terracotta roof tiles and green shuttered windows; more like a Mediterranean *finca* than an industrial complex.

As far as I can tell the only way to get here is by sea or by hiking over the mountains. Either way, I have this beautiful place to myself. Sweet isolation.

This campsite is not the only reason I'm feeling ecstatic. The whole day leading up to this point had been pretty awesome. It was the fifth day of my mission to paddle around Mallorca in a week, and it had been full of the type of unexpected encounters I was hoping for when I set out on my adventure.

As an experienced Stand-Up Paddler, the idea of a multi-day SUP expedition had been in my head for many years, but with a young family, taking the time out was just impossible.

In early 2019, everything seemed to come together. The kids were old enough to get themselves home from school and look after themselves for a couple of hours, and I had a week's annual leave left. The time was right.

At £120 for a return flight with my baggage, Mallorca was a great choice and the airport is practically on the beach. In my head, this would be quite simple: fly to the airport and walk to the beach, then paddle around the island and walk back to the airport to fly home.

How difficult could it be?

I made contact with Ruben Salvador who runs El Nino Surf Centre next to the airport. He agreed to give me some advice on the paddle, but I could tell in his voice that he didn't think I had a cat in hell's chance of getting around the island in seven days.

The week before my flight, the weather forecast was showing winds of between seventeen and thirty-nine miles per hour.

There is no way I could have paddled in that!

I jumped on Facebook.

"Hi Ruben. Not looking too good is it?"

"With that wind? Don't come."

A decision had to be made. I dug into my pockets and paid an extra £60 to change my flight to the following week. Even if the forecast was bad, I would just get on that plane with my board and paddle and work it out when I got there.

A week later, my plane touched down on Mallorcan soil at 2.30am. Rather than walk to my camping spot, I accepted the offer of a lift by a couple of guys I met in the boarding queue at Gatwick. They were utterly bemused by my decision to paddle around the island, and even more so when they realised I was going to spend the rest of the night sleeping out in the open.

A couple of hours after they dropped me off, I awoke under a small bush in some scrubland right next to Palma airport, tourist flights in full flow above my head. There were cockerels crowing and dogs barking at the nearby house; they could smell me down there in the tall grass. My borrowed Thermorest had leaked during the night, so there wasn't much chance of me sleeping in.

This was the only sleeping spot that was pre-planned. For the rest of the journey I'd just be scouting out locations as I arrived.

*

I'm well known for being a bit of a faffer, and a planned departure time of 9am rapidly became 10.30am. By this time the wind was starting to build and the millpond sea that greeted me on my arrival at the beach now had a bit of texture on it.

I had to get going.

I left the beach full of nervous anticipation, but so happy that I was finally starting. I whooped as I paddled across the water, wondering what adventures would spring from those first few paddle strokes.

The target for my first day was Cala Santanyí, just around the southern point of Mallorca and about fifty-eight kilometres away. I quickly settled into a rhythm and kept plugging away, one paddle stroke after the other. I rounded the point and left Palma bay at the sixteen-kilometre mark.

I now wouldn't see Palma again for another six days. The adventure had begun!

As the clock ticked past four hours and I passed the twenty-two kilometre mark at Cap Blanc, the wind started to kick in.

I could see the other side of the bay in front of me and could just make out the town of Colònia de Sant Jordi another twenty kilometres away. I decided to head straight there across the bay.

The wind was blowing onshore, which resulted in me paddling solely on my left-hand side for three and a half hours. That's when I started to develop my first blisters; big fat juicy ones on my left hand. Not very pleasant and painful too.

I reached Colònia de Sant Jordi and saw a small island about three hundred metres off the coast. I didn't want to sleep on the streets in town and thought this island might provide me with some privacy. The island was about fifty metres across, consisting largely of rock and small low-lying shrubs. I decided a small sandy beach nestled between two rocky headlands would make the ideal camping spot.

I hauled my board and gear onto the beach and pulled out my stove to prepare the first of my dehydrated meals.

My back was aching, my hands were sore and I hadn't covered the distance I wanted to on the first day. To be honest, as I sat there eating my dinner and watching the sunset, I was wondering if I'd bitten off more than I could chew.

This was my second night on the island and, like the first, I opted for sleeping out in the open. Great for a bit of stargazing, but not so good when the dew started to fall. It was so heavy it looked like rain. My bivi is waterproof and breathable, but it's breathability is reduced when it's wet. This resulted in a very wet sleeping bag and a soggy start to the day. I had learned my first wild camping lesson: find some shelter!

*

To beat the wind forecast, the next morning was an early one. I had breakfast in the dark, packed my soggy kit and set off at daybreak to paddle the fifty-eight kilometres to Porto Cristo. It was a fantastic morning, with flat seas and the most spectacular sunrise over the island.

Sure enough, as I passed the four-hour mark the wind started to build and blow into my face. The wind created some significant chop in the water and my speed started to drop.

Paddling for eight to ten hours a day is a funny thing. There's always the temptation to stop, but you know stopping gets you nowhere, so you don't. You just keep paddling, taking one stroke after the next. Sometimes your legs ache, so you kneel down for a bit, then they ache from kneeling down, so you stand up.

You also have lots of time in your own mind. Sometimes you think about friends and family. Sometimes the sound of the paddle entering the water captivates you and it's all you can hear. Quite often, I found myself counting my paddle strokes. I'd get into the hundreds before I realised I was even doing it. At times, a thought enters your head that you just can't shake. I spent hours chanting the name of a place I was heading to one day. I suppose it's a form of meditation. I definitely zoned out after a period of time.

After another three hours or so I realised that I was never going to make it to Porto Cristo before nightfall so pulled into a secluded little bay to try and find a good camping spot. Jackpot – there was a lovely little man-sized cave just up the path to the beach, perfect to keep the dew off. I was feeling very smug as I settled down to sleep, snug as a bug in my cave with the dew falling outside. Luxury!

*

On day three, the countryside seemed more beautiful and wilder than the previous two days. It started with a small chop in the water and the fireball sun rising out of the sea to my right. As I paddled around the last headland before my overnight stop, I could see the small beach of Cala Mesquida. I'd skipped breakfast that morning, and I needed to stop and get some food.

The previous week's wind had resulted in a decent swell pushing down the Mediterranean from the northeast. This created waves, something I had not expected to encounter.

As I paddled closer to Cala Mesquida, I could see some pretty chunky surf rolling onto the sand – about three-foot – certainly enough for the shortboard surfers to be ripping up the waves peeling off the reefs on either side of the bay. But I didn't have a smooth sleek surfboard like them. I had a thirty-two-inch wide, twelve-foot-six inflatable touring board with twenty-five kilograms of kit strapped to the front. This landing was going to be tricky but fun.

I took a moment to scope out the beach. I wanted to avoid the main break; ploughing over a surfer and ending up on the rocks would not have ended well. The beach was also pretty busy, and I could feel the lifeguards' eyes burning into me through their binoculars.

The probability of me coming out of this looking like a plonker was extremely high.

I stowed away all my loose gear and double-checked that my bag was securely strapped to the board before paddling closer to the beach, looking to select my wave. I switched into surf stance and paddled like hell, my heart pounding in my chest and my jaw aching from the effort.

I could feel the back of the board lift and the energy of the wave start to flow through it. I kept my weight on my front foot to ensure that I was on the wave while keeping the nose just above the surface, treading that fine line between glory and nose dive. I was surfing! I intuitively jumped back on the board as the nose started to pearl and guided the board towards the beach. I was now standing right at the back of the board, with a good eleven-foot and twenty-five kilograms bouncing around in front of me. As the beach drew closer, I assessed my dismount. The waves were dumping and churning up the sand into a creamy broth. My best option was to ride that wave right into the beach and jump off at the last minute.

This manoeuvre was executed with such grace that I even surprised myself. I was on the beach, nothing was broken and my shorts were still dry.

What a surf god I was!

I scanned the beach to survey the hordes of admiring crowds clapping and cheering my epic-ness. Unfortunately, they must have been looking in the other direction as there was no round of applause, no cheers, nothing! Their loss. As I revelled silently in my glory, one of the lifeguards walked over to me. He introduced himself as Marco and asked:

"Where have you paddled from?"

"Palma", I replied.

This was certainly not the first or last time I would hear the response

"What, all the way around?"

Marco looked after my kit for me while I walked into town for a bite to eat. After an hour or so, it was time to leave the beach. The waves were still pumping and it was looking like getting out was going to be a real challenge. Marco helped me to the water's edge and we said our goodbyes. I stood on the beach for quite a while waiting for my moment, my gap in the waves. When it came I ran into the foaming water dragging my board behind me. I spun the board around and jumped on top, springing to my feet and paddling like crazy. I pulled myself over the walls of white water and kept on digging deep. I cleared one, two, three waves and was home and dry.

I'd made it out with my surf god status intact, or so I thought. After turning to give Marco a wave goodbye, I was horrified to look back out to sea to find one more wave jacking up in front of me.

'Oh jumping jellyfish!'

I dropped back on the board and into a low surf stance in an attempt to get the nose over the white water and rescue my pride, but it was all in vain. The wave started to crest, and the front of the board was just too heavy; I was unceremoniously catapulted off the back. I'm sure Marco had a chuckle as he returned to his lifeguard duties.

I was calling Ruben every day for a weather update and some local knowledge on where to stop for the night. Each time I updated him on my progress, I could hear his initial cynicism giving way to a genuine enthusiasm that I might actually make it.

Ruben always gave me three overnight options, one being the furthest and therefore best. On this day I went for option two, a small secluded beach just before Cap Ferrutx. It was littered with driftwood, rocks and wild plants, and someone had built a small rustic driftwood shelter against the small cliffs to the right-hand side.

A pathway lined with pebbles wound its way up the beach to the front door of a large refuge, a hostel available to pre-book by hikers using the trails in the national park. I left my board beside the shelter and headed up to see if anyone was home. I found the doors locked, the bins full and the toilets overflowing. It was out of season so the refuge was closed and the water turned off. This hadn't stopped people using the facilities and it wasn't a pretty sight.

This certainly was a deserted part of the island. The sign by the refuge indicated the closest town was thirty kilometres along the coast in both directions, and a dirt track only passable by a serious 4X4 disappeared inland. I decided it was highly unlikely anyone would turn up here this late in the day so I took the opportunity to bare all and have a wash down in the sea.

Thinking back, this was my first wild moment; the day I went feral. It gave me an immense sense of freedom. I wasn't answering to anybody and had no responsibility for anyone other than myself. I was living life hour by hour rather than having to think weeks and months ahead and, the best thing, it had only taken three days.

During my search around the refuge, I found a tiny campsite surrounded by a dry stone wall and located in a copse of pine trees. Adjacent to the campground was a small stone shed. This door was unlocked and led into a tiny camp kitchen, no more than six-foot by eight-foot with a workbench and cookers to the right and a fridge on the left. It left just enough space for me to sleep on the tiled floor in the middle.

I must admit to feeling a little uncomfortable being alone that night. I could hear creatures scuffling around outside. "Probably goats," I told myself, but, inevitably my mind began to wander to the supernatural. Eventually, tiredness took over and I fell asleep.

*

The next day marked the halfway point, both in time and distance.

Ahead of me, I had the two massive bays of Alcúdia and Pollencia: two bays separated by a rocky headland forming a lopsided W. I had two choices: hug the coast and paddle sixty kilometres, or cut twenty kilometres straight across the bay. This decision could mean the difference in completing the circumnavigation or not. However, cutting straight across the bays would take me fifteen kilometres offshore with no radio and out of mobile range. I'd had a really good chat with Ruben the night before and we looked at the weather forecast together. It showed high certainty of very light winds. I was a bit concerned that thermal winds may develop later in the day, but Ruben assured me that these would blow me into the bay rather than out of it.

I decided that the risk was minimal, checked my board and paddle, charged my phone and went for it. It certainly took some commitment leaving the relative safety of the cliffs and the proximity of the land to head out into open water for at least four hours, but the decision was made. I was heading for Cap Formentera. The mighty cliffs were reduced to a small strip of land in the distance, and they never seemed to get any bigger, always on the horizon. After two hours of paddling, I looked back to the equally small strip of land I had departed from.

I had no mobile signal, no radio and I was alone. Although the conditions were calm, if something had gone wrong out there, I would have been in a bit of a pickle. But hey, that's what makes life interesting.

It was another two hours of paddling before I reached Cap Formentera. I was tired but relieved to be passing under the lighthouse with the tourists looking down on me. Now I was close to land and in relative safety, I could relax. I'd been paddling for almost four days and had just been out at sea for four hours. I laid down on my board in a heap of relief and fatigue and almost fell asleep. But sleep wouldn't get me anywhere. I still had another three hours of paddling in front of me and daylight was running out. I splashed my face, had a bite to eat and paddled around the next headland.

The view stretching out before me was so beautiful that it stopped me in my tracks: a series of huge charcoal headlands, each one more distant and a lighter shade of grey than the first. They were backed by clouds and the whole scene backlit by the afternoon sun. It looked like a scene from the ancient earth, a Jurassic looking world, and I realised I was falling in love with Mallorca.

I arrived at my overnight stop after another three hours of paddling and only forty minutes before dark. I was tired, hungry and in need of sleep. Cala St Vincente is a beautiful but tiny beach set into a steep-sided valley and backed by hotels, bars and housing. Very little in the way of wild camping. I decided that my only option was to wait and find a camping spot under the cover of darkness. I shoved my board and paddle as far into a small beach cave as I could and, taking a gamble that it would still be there when I returned, I headed off into town to find somewhere to eat, charge my electronics and while away the remaining daylight.

One burger and a couple of beers later it was 11pm, and I was back down on the beach. My only option was a couple of straw beach umbrellas propped up on a sun-lounger placed on its side. It sounds basic, and it was, but it was warm and sheltered. I fell asleep that night with the sound of the waves lapping on the beach and wondering if my board would still be there in the morning.

*

At 3am I woke to the sound of goats bleating and bits of straw dropping onto my face.

'Those bloody things are playing on top of my house!'

A bit of shouting and banging on the underside of the umbrellas didn't seem to deter them one bit. This was only going to end one way, so I crawled out of my bed and chased them away. My next rude awakening came around two hours later, with a commotion going on outside my shelter. Car engines, people talking and things being unloaded from trailers and vans.

I was basically sleeping on the streets and I didn't know who these people were, so I lay in my shelter waiting for the bustle to die down. Then came the sound of running water, and the realisation that someone was urinating on the other side of the wall that I was sleeping against!

After a while, it fell quiet enough for me to stick my head out and have a look around. The beach was full of sea kayakers getting ready to head out on the water. I crawled out of my shelter, put it back as I found it and pretended that I'd only just arrived. It was a bank holiday on the island, and Kayak fishing is a big pastime. Turns out I'd chosen to camp right next to the favourite launch ramp.

After breakfast, I started paddling with my goal being Port De Sollier forty kilometres away. My progress this day was very slow. There was just so much to take in. The sea was unnaturally calm and the deepest blue I've ever seen. I paddled at the foot of cliffs towering hundreds of feet above me and dotted with gravity-defying goats. The coast extended out for tens of kilometres without a single place to land, just a solid limestone wall rising from the sea and punctuated by cave systems and secluded bays backed by pine forests clinging to the cliffs. I stopped at one particular bay and explored its nooks and crannies. I really didn't know what I expected to find or feel as I was paddling around Mallorca, but its raw natural beauty had taken me aback. It was simply stunning.

Around twenty kilometres in, I noticed a couple of RIBs moored at the base of the cliffs and heard the irresistible sound of shouting and laughter drifting across the water. I was making slow progress this day and could have just passed by, but curiosity got the better of me. I just had to paddle over and check it out.

As I reached the flotilla, I was greeted by two guys clad in wetsuits and harnesses. They were wearing helmets with torches and had climbing ropes slung over their shoulders. I paddled to their boat and asked what was going on?

What I didn't expect was an English accent from the taller of the two gentlemen. This was Tristan, a slim well-spoken English guy working in the sailing fleet out in Mallorca. The other guy was David, an athletic Spaniard and a bit of a thrill-seeker, an accomplished free diver, climber and gorge runner. They were spending their day gorge scrambling deep within the cliffs.

After the usual question, "Where have you come from?"

And now very familiar response of, "What? All the way around?"

David and Tristan invited me to go with them.

They were dressed for the task at hand. I, on the other hand, was clad only in shorts, a T-shirt and wetsuit shoes, but that wasn't going to stop me. I excitedly tied my board to their boat and slipped into the sea. We swam into the mouth of the gorge and clambered up out of the water. My first challenge was jumping into a plunge pool, holding my breath and swimming through a short underwater tunnel, before climbing up a smooth rock chimney on the other side. There was a reason these guys were wearing wetsuits. It was bloody freezing! It took my breath away and set my heart racing. This water was coming straight out of the belly of the mountain.

I spent an awesome thirty minutes with those guys, scrambling up limestone flows and jumping from ten-metre cliffs into ice-cold plunge pools, but time was ticking by and I had to get to Port de Sollier before nightfall. David told me about a great little spot just before Port de Sollier: an abandoned power station. I said my thanks and goodbyes and, with instructions to, "Head for the white crane on the beach," I started paddling again.

As I travelled down the coast, the wind started to build from behind me, pushing me towards my goal. I was now down-winding, half paddling and half surfing towards my destination. I was wondering if the day could get any better when a dolphin breached right in front of me on its way out to sea. I was like a giddy kid and I actually shouted out loud, "Dolphin!"

A short while later, I was sitting on that log in my disused power station eating my dinner. Life was amazing. I was adventuring, having great experiences and achieving my goals. It felt awesome!

*

The next day I headed to Port De Sollier to pick up provisions, charge my electronics and have a nice cup of coffee. My initial aim for the day was to reach Sant Elm on the western tip of the island, but I'd struggled to tear myself away from the power station that morning and time was slipping away from me. There was no way I was going to make it before dark. I checked my map and decided to head for a little port called Banalbufar instead. I arrived just before sunset, paddling into the beach through the biggest swarm of jellyfish I've ever seen and settled down for the night outside a fisherman's cottage.

I now had only sixty kilometres left of my adventure. If I pushed it, I could complete it in one day, but I had two full days left before my flight departed and didn't want this to be my last night out paddling. I decided to split the distance in two and just enjoy the rest of the trip. I was less remote than I had been for the last three days and found myself surrounded by motor cruisers, sailing yachts and even a cruise ship on its way into Palma.

I paddled through the point at El Torro and, for the first time in seven days, I could see on the far side of Palma bay somewhere I'd already been. That was quite a moment for me. It meant the trip was almost over. I was glad that I'd be able to stop paddling and rest, but also disappointed that the adventure was drawing to a close.

Ruben had told me about a little bay just inside Palma bay called Portals Vells. I paddled in and spotted a small marina to my left. As a visiting 'yachtsman' I thought I might be able to use the facilities. There was a site office, but no-one home. I searched around the marina and found a stone-built storage shed with an iron-barred gate reminiscent of a prison cell. It contained three paddleboards and a couple of sun loungers complete with mattresses. This turned out to be the most comfortable camping spot of the entire trip. Believe me, I slept like a baby on those mattresses.

*

I woke early the next day as I knew that if I arrived back at C'an Pastilla before 10.30am, I would have finished the circumnavigation in seven twenty-four-hour periods, and I make that seven days! At the speed I was paddling, the twenty kilometres to the finish would take me four hours, so I made sure I was ready for departure and on the water by 6am. The morning was fresh and clear as I paddled across Palma bay and into the dazzling sunrise.

A few kilometres out from C'an Pastilla, I spotted a couple of paddlers on their way out to greet me. It was Ruben, the guy I had spoken with almost every day for the past week. What a great feeling to be paddling into the beach together. I landed on the beach to a shower of champagne and a huge hug from Ruben's wife, Sandra.

I was done. I had just completed the fastest circumnavigation of Mallorca by SUP and the only solo self-supported paddle around the island. It had taken me seven days or sixty-three hours of paddling. I had travelled 331 kilometres and made close to 110 thousand paddle strokes. I had also disposed of 25 thousand calories, a fact I could see quite clearly when I looked in the mirror while having a shower. But best of all, I had completed my SUP adventure, something that had been a dream for years.

I had said 'Yes' to myself and it felt amazing.

Website: **caveactive.co.uk**

Facebook: **caveactive**

Instagram: **@caveactive**

Chapter 40

Cycling Solo

By Ian Preedy

"My knee hurts, I don't think I can cycle today." These were the first words I heard on waking.

I was in a small B&B in Foix, southern France with my best friend, Tim. His comment wasn't really unexpected. He'd just spent the last two weeks cycling from London to Toulouse. His knee had been so bad that he'd swapped cycling for taking the train multiple times. But this was just the warm up ride. This was just the journey to get to the start line.

We'd planned to cycle from Toulouse to Barcelona, over the Pyrenees, arriving in time to meet up with half a dozen other friends and spend a long weekend in Barcelona. We would explore the city by day and dance at the Primavera music festival by night. That was the plan, but that wasn't how it happened.

The Plan

Tim started cycling from London on Friday 8th May, 2015, taking the ferry from Newhaven to Dieppe, and then down to Toulouse. I flew to Toulouse to meet him the evening of Wednesday 20th May. We would then spend the next seven days cycling the 240 miles to Barcelona with a rest day in Pas de la Casa, a ski resort in Andorra. We'd arrive in Barcelona on the following Thursday before flying home with our bikes on the Monday. Simple.

The purpose of the trip was to challenge ourselves. This was going to be the greatest challenge that either of us had ridden. The total climbing alone was incomparable to any previous ride. We'd done some bike touring before but this promised to be a much hillier route. There was also the reward for all our efforts of meeting up with friends in Barcelona. It's a far better way to end a trip than getting somewhere and then heading home straight away.

For this trip, I had a Trek CrossRip Comp cyclocross, replacing my trusty old bike which was stolen. Tim had his Surly Long Hall Trucker, which he had for several years and used for all our cycle tours.

To transport my bike, I removed and adjusted a few bits, packing it into a large transparent plastic bag, using my clothes to pad the more delicate parts. I hoped my pride and joy, which was less than six-months old, would survive the flight unscathed.

My solution for carrying this bulky twenty-kilogram package out of the airport was to put it on two big luggage trolleys. Genius! What I hadn't anticipated were the airport doors. Turns out they were not wide enough for my double trolley contraption. I could feel the eyes of the other passengers with their airline-appropriate luggage boring into the back of my head as I attempted to jostle my bike bag through the doors. Sweat started falling from my forehead but, after a bit of shoving and wiggling, I up-ended the bike on just the one trolley and sailed through the door with ease.

Seeing Tim's grinning face was a huge relief. "Struggling with the door?" he asked sarcastically.

"Cheers for the help," I smiled back. Fortunately, after unpacking and re-assembling my bike, it was all intact and we were both quickly on our way.

Day 1: Toulouse to Foix

The day started with our number one priority. Lunch. We had learnt the hard way on a previous tour in France that trying to buy bread and things during lunchtime was nigh on impossible. Many of those kinds of shops closed for a two-hour midday break!

We decided to save weight by posting Tim's tent back to England, so he went to buy something to wrap it up in, something suitable for the long journey with numerous careless handlers. He swiftly returned with his trademark wide grin, a French newspaper and a roll of Sellotape. The post office was perplexed with the makeshift packaging, though after some negotiating, they conceded.

We realised we were a bit rusty on our first full day's ride when my phone blurted out, "Too far from route." We had been enjoying the flat and easy cycling along the Garonne river, south of Toulouse, and hadn't noticed that we needed to turn off and leave the river. Also, I left my pair of sunglasses at a café, when we stopped in the afternoon for a well-deserved ice cream. I only noticed once we were about two miles away. On cycling back, I was relieved to see them sitting there, exactly where I had left them.

The last few miles were all up hill, which I found quite tough. We'd completed almost sixty miles by this point. But finally, Foix appeared ahead of us, the medieval castle standing proudly on the hill in the centre like a beacon welcoming us in.

We found a small B&B and then spent the evening wandering in search of food. This took us along a road lined with cherry bushes hanging heavy with fruit, so we helped ourselves.

Day 1 completed: 59 miles (95kms), 2,200 ft (670m) ascent, 1,300 ft (400m) descent.

Day 2: Foix to Luzenac

When Tim woke with the words, "my knee hurts", I knew that today, and possibly the rest of the trip, was not going to go as planned. It was the first time that either of us had had a serious injury while cycling. We had a tough decision to make.

The deadline of getting to Barcelona on a certain date to meet friends meant that we were not able to simply wait and progress the trip. Otherwise we could have taken more rest days or travelled a shorter distance each day.

"What are our options?" Tim asked.

"We could take the train?"

"No. They don't run very often on weekdays in the Pyrenees, and besides, they won't let us on with bikes."

"We could rent a car?"

"It'd have to be big enough for our bikes and all our panniers. Plus, we'd have to pick it up in France and drop it in Spain. Just too expensive."

For each idea raised, logic made it infeasible. After much agonising and thinking through our options, Tim decided to get the train back to Toulouse and fly home. He'd fly to Barcelona a few days later to meet our friends. "What will you do?" he asked.

I was torn. On the one hand, the idea of the journey was to do it together, having your buddy by your side, cracking jokes and sharing the adventure. We'd be recounting tales of the road, memories we'd created and shared together, for years to come. That is what I'd envisaged.

On the other hand, I didn't want to go home. Given all the effort in both planning the route and booking the accommodation, I wanted to stay and complete the challenge. I felt that, although it was something that was at the limit of my capabilities, I knew I had a chance to succeed. I'd never cycled more than ten miles on my own before but this was a journey that I wanted to experience. And I knew that I would regret it if I threw in the towel.

After a few agonising moments, I looked Tim square in the eyes and said, "I'm going to complete the ride."

Tim just nodded. I think he understood.

We needed a bit of time to work it all out; Tim getting the train and booking the flight; me wanting to alter the accommodation, mainly to save some money, and so they were not expecting two people. The couple who owned the B&B were incredibly helpful, having sympathy for our situation. They were in no rush to kick us out, allowing us to stay the whole morning. They helped with making the necessary phone calls, as neither of our half-forgotten schoolboy French was cutting the moutarde.

We wandered back into town for a proper lunch. On top of everything, my phone's touch screen decided that now was a good time to stop working. My solution was to buy a mouse so I could get a cursor and keyboard up. I must have looked ridiculous standing in a rustic French market in cycling gear, using a mouse with my smart phone. It also highly amused Tim.

When back at the B&B, he handed me his GPS and spare batteries, as it was easier to use for navigation than my phone and mouse. I packed for the day ahead, we wished each other luck and said our goodbyes. Tim waved me off from the porch.

A few miles after setting off, I reflected on my situation. I was joyful because I had not passed on the opportunity of exploring such beautiful surroundings but melancholy on the 'loss' of my teammate. I was following a meandering river as it snaked through a valley. A mixture of grass and wheat fields swayed gently alongside the narrow road. Every so often, the scenery was interrupted by a small village nestled in the foothills like a child towered over by giants. Surrounding me were the rocky mountains soaring and reaching into the clouds above.

I breathed in fresh air deeply. Although I was alone, I was not lonely.

Day 2 completed: 22 miles (35kms), 1,400 ft (430m) ascent, 800 ft (240m) descent.

Day 3: Luzenac to Pas de la Casa

I knew that today was going to be tough. Some years prior to this tour, I had been on a skiing holiday at the same destination to where I was staying tonight, Pas de la Casa. Our bus had taken us on the very same road that I was about to cycle today. What lay ahead was cycling uphill for twenty-four miles, without Tim's company to entertain me. I put the bike into its lowest gear and started pedalling.

While the gradient was steady, I was always able to make progress. All I had to do to reach the top was to keep turning the pedals round. I would only focus on the road directly ahead of my front wheel. This beat looking up and feeling daunted by the numerous switchbacks ahead. Each turn of the pedal was progress towards the top of the hill and the end of the day. From time to time I would look back at what I had accomplished as a reminder of the progress made, each time resulting in a delirious smile sweeping across my face.

I do not mind admitting that I shed a tear of joy when Pas de la Casa appeared in the distance as I turned the final corner. My destination! I had started the day at two thousand feet or six hundred metres altitude and finished it at 6,900 feet or 2,100 metres, having not changed out of the lowest gear all day! It was early afternoon when I arrived and checked into the hotel. Thankfully, they were happy for my bike to be stored in my room. I relaxed for the rest of the day, feeling both proud and exhausted.

Day 3 completed: 24 miles (39kms), 5,100 ft (1,550m) ascent, 200 ft (60m) descent.

Day 4: Rest day at Pas de la Casa

I spent the morning of my rest day wandering around the town. It was quite different to when I had been there previously, being at the height of ski season. In May, it was like a ghost town. The biggest change was the main ski slope. I recognised it from when I was skiing there several years before this trip. In place of snow-covered landscape, whirring ski lifts, hundreds of chattering people and their clattering skis, was a grassy, muddy field with patches of snow. A few dog walkers politely said, "Bonjour," but it was hardly the cacophony of noise that it had been in peak ski season. A songbird twittered sweetly in the tree tops.

As I wandered around the town, it felt like I had arrived at the party much too late, or much too early. Favourite bars and restaurants were closed for the season. Chairs stood on tables in dark rooms. Shutters were drawn. Expecting to watch Eurovision in one of the bars, I was out of luck. Off-season in Pas de la Casa is really off season.

Day 4 completed: 0 miles (0km), 0 ft (0m) ascent, 0 ft (0m) descent.

Day 5: Pas de la Casa to Castellar de n'Hug

Mist and fog greeted me for the first section of the cycle today and it was a very nippy zero degrees Celsius. It was fun riding down part of the hill I had climbed up before (though it quickly became an uphill again!). I enjoyed the following four miles of 6% downhill, the first of many long downhills, and it felt fabulous! No pedalling, just having to stay upright and steady, the cold wind whipping my smiling cheeks, the road flying under my wheels.

The border between Andorra and France was easy to pass through. There's only a small checkpoint though they weren't stopping anyone. It was interesting cycling past several ski resorts, like La Molina, where there was all the infrastructure necessary for skiing, chair lifts and snow cannons, though none of the snow!

Lunch involved sitting at the side of a small road, up on the verge, in the sunshine. Wild horses, their manes and fur matted with dirt, nuzzled the clumps of spartan grass nearby. Some of them wandered into the middle of the road as there was so little traffic. Thankfully, they had moved along when lunch was over, and I needed to cycle past.

Many of the views for the day were of grassy hills under a cloudy blue sky, with snow peaked mountains behind me and long roads soaring into the distance ahead.

Arriving at the accommodation in Castellar de n'Hug, a tiny village nestled in the embracing folds of the mountains, the receptionist informed me that I was the only person staying in the whole place. At 6pm, she would be going home, thus leaving me to occupy the place alone. It seemed to sleep sixty or so people across several dorm rooms full of bunk beds.

While walking me to my room, she pointed at a sign on the wall, with a telephone number on it saying, "If you have any questions, ring this number."

I explained that having a UK phone with me, how expensive it would be to ring an international number.

Her response was to walk me to an open window. She pointed at a house a little further down the hill and said, "Any problems, knock on their door. They work here."

After leaving me in my room, that was the last I saw of her!

I went for a short wander around the village, which is set on a steep hillside. At one end of the village there is a brick bell tower about fifty-foot high with incredible views over the valley below. For the rest of the village, it appeared that no two houses were on the same level. Narrow streets and alleys climbed and dropped at all angles.

Noticing the only restaurant in the village, and armed with my trusty Spanish phrase book, I wandered in. I was a little surprised as there were only three people in the whole place and they were all sitting on a single table together. Not phased I asked if they were serving food.

Blank stares.

I glanced at my phrase book to check the pronunciation. I tried again.

Still nothing. It turned out the guys sitting at the table were the waiting staff and chef. One of them looked at my phrase book and shook his finger. It was only then that I suddenly realised my error. I was in Catalonia. They have their own language, Catalan. My Spanish phrase book was next to useless. Either way, through the international language of mime, they managed to understand me. From what I managed to understand from them, today was a public holiday, being the day after Pentecost Sunday. That's why the restaurant was not serving any food and there were very few people around, both in this restaurant and the whole village!

I continued to wander around the village until I found a bakery and bought some bread.

I reflected as I feasted at the end of the day on bread and sliced salami, which I had been carrying with me for some time. Despite the simple food, despite the fact that I was alone, sitting on my jacket acting as a picnic rug, I was happy. The sun was warm, I was looking out over the valley and I was perfectly content.

Day 5 completed: 45 miles (72kms), 3,700 ft (1,130m) ascent, 6,000 ft (1,830m) descent.

Day 6: Castellar de n'Hug to Moia

Knowing I had a long and hilly day ahead of me, I had breakfast early. When entering the breakfast room, I was greeted by a single table chocked full of a huge variety of continental options. Yum!

At one point, during the late morning, the route turned off the paved road. I was greeted by an unpaved, slightly grassy dirt track. Tim and I had learnt, from past difficulties, to make use of Google Street View to check the route in advance. This was the only section of concern for the whole route as only the entrance to this road was imaged rather than all the way along it. The Google car had obviously not been able to travel down it. It looked OK from the satellite image, and given that it was a rather rural area, I figured it would be fine to cycle along.

All went well until the grass disappeared and instead there was gravel. Then the gravel disappeared and turned into a track of stones about the size of my fist. My pace became akin to a snail and it felt like I was riding over loose cobbles.

It wound around several bends and gradually started heading downhill. It was relatively easy, until the hill steepened and maintaining my balance became my sole focus. I was being careful as I had no mobile phone signal, and I was in the middle of nowhere. I did not want to injure myself. I always carried a simple first aid kit, and thankfully have never had to use it, but I was imagining broken limbs. My basic supplies would not have been much use. Fortunately, it was not long until the surface improved to a gravelly dirt track and became much easier to ride on.

Shortly afterwards, I came to a single piece of fence wire that spanned the track at waist height. Behind it nailed into a tree post was the sign, "ÁREA PRIVADA DE CACA." Noting the word 'privada', I thought this translated to read, 'Private, keep out'.

I paused briefly and considered my situation. I had not seen anyone for some time. I was still in the middle of nowhere. Turning back meant attempting to work out a different route and who knows how much extra distance and time that would add to the day. I was already low on water.

The only thing telling me to not continue was the threat of potentially breaking the law.

I ducked under the fence, got on my bike and continued. Should I need to explain myself, I felt it was better to ask for forgiveness than permission. I'm pretty adept at demonstrating that I'm a foreigner and in unfamiliar territory. The one benefit of being by myself is that decisions were all my own.

Over the course of the next half an hour, I ducked under three more fences. Some of these looked like electric fences. Most were only marked by a single white plastic bag attached to them. For another, I only managed to brake about a foot in front of it because as it was not marked at all, just being a single wire crossing my path.

Eventually, I came out onto an opening. In front of me was a grand looking farmhouse with a gravel courtyard. As I could not see anyone about, I decided to cycle on and follow my route. Turns out it is difficult to cycle quietly on gravel. I was about as stealthy as an elephant walking over dried pasta. I made it onto the paved driveway and then back onto a public road without anyone challenging me – phew!

While researching for this book, I looked up the translation of the sign, 'ÁREA PRIVADA DE CACA' which simply means, 'private hunting area'. I felt relieved not to have been mistaken for game, but also that I had not committed any serious offence.

Before arriving at Moia, there was a great lookout point on the road. This provided a view of flat fields separated by trees, with hills in the background, another ideal photo spot.

Cycling through the village involved some very narrow streets, barely wide enough for a car. Buildings flanked on both sides, a couple of stories high, blocking out the bright sunlight. Getting to the accommodation involved cycling down an unpaved gravel track for half a mile in the blinding sunshine, leading to a single isolated farmhouse outside the town.

Day 6 completed: 56 miles (90kms), 4,900 ft (1,490m) ascent, 7,200 ft (2,200m) descent.

Day 7: Moia to Barcelona

The final day of cycling was not a long one. With the excitement and sunshine, I was up and out of the place by 8am. Friends were flying in for the early afternoon and we had agreed to meet at a marina in Barcelona, where we had booked onto an Airbnb on a boat. Not a plush one at all; simply a small one that could sleep three of us with others staying elsewhere.

Mid-morning, I saw two keen cyclists up ahead. I say keen as they were in full lycra and on racing bikes, in comparison to my heavier bike loaded down with panniers and me in t-shirt and shorts. I knew that if I could catch up with them, drafting them would mean my ride would be easier. It took a couple of miles until I reached them. I was then able to put in noticeably much less effort while going at a faster pace. Delighted that my effort had paid off, I thought I needed to capture this moment so while travelling at speed, I got my camera out my pocket, cycling one handed, took a picture and then put it back. Success! I achieved all that without falling off.

As I descended with these cyclists, the temperature change was dramatic, and I could feel it getting warmer. The temperature was pushing twenty degrees Celsius, while I had been in zero degrees in Pas de la Casa only three days before.

The route into Barcelona took me via the river Besòs, which is to the north of the city. As I got nearer, this turned into a lovely, wide-open space sunk below the level of the roads. A wide lawn spread out beside the paved cycle way. People were playing on the grass and walking their dogs, enjoying the sunshine and the clear blue skies.

After several miles, I needed to turn off to head into the city centre. I had to quickly re-acquaint myself with traffic and increase my focus on cycling having not had to worry about traffic for much of my trip.

Finding the marina, I was overjoyed. I was so proud of what I had accomplished over the past seven days, while at the same time a little disappointed that I was the first to arrive – there was no greeting party, no cheering, no banners… no friends. Despite cycling up and over the hilliest places I had ever covered, I was there by myself.

I took some pictures and sat waiting for them to arrive being entertained with the views of the boats bobbing up and down in the marina. I lay back and listened to the halyards clack in the breeze and the seagulls caw overhead. I felt the warmth of the sun on my skin and could smell the salty sea air. I was all alone but I was happy.

My friends showed up shortly afterwards, full of laughter and smiles and noise. They were keen to start their holiday by heading out to the city to explore. I wasn't so keen. After 241 miles, I was exhausted and all I wanted to do was nap!

Day 7 completed: 35 miles (56kms), 1,900 ft (580m) ascent, 3,400 ft (1,040m) descent.

Total cycling: 241 miles (388kms), 19,200 ft (5,850m) ascent, 18,900 ft (5,760m) descent.

Barcelona and Heading Home

We spent the next couple of days exploring much of the popular tourist sites in Barcelona. By day this involved visiting Park Güell, the beach, watching a beach volleyball competition that was taking place right next to the marina and joining a couple of free city walking tours. One of the walks involved showing many examples of Gaudi architecture and concluded at La Sagrada Familia. By night, we danced at the Primavera music festival.

On the final morning, I left the boat early as I was cycling to the airport and needed time to pack my bike. My friends were using public transport.

The cycle ride was easy going. At one point, while cycling on the pavement in the marked cycle lane, I saw a large concrete block up ahead. This sat completely on top of the cycle lane, and it was impossible to pass. To the right of this was a car barrier on either side of the road and a small guard house. As I needed to get to the airport swiftly, and this was how I was being directed, I simply came off the pavement, went around the car barrier and cycled on.

I heard someone blowing a whistle behind me and assumed it to be the guard. I thought that if I was somewhere I should not be, someone would quickly let me know. It was also at this moment that I thought about what the gun culture is in Spain and if this kind of guard would have a firearm.

I did not have time to ponder for too long as a car quickly came alongside me and asked me to stop. The man in the passenger's side asked where I was going. I pointed at my phone and said that I was going to the airport, showing that Google Maps had directed me this way. After a slight pause whilst he consulted with the driver, he signalled me to carry on. It turned out that I had cycled into Barcelona's freight shipping port. After a mile or so, I came to another car barrier and a small guard house, where I cycled though, nodded to the guard and left.

Once at the airport, it was simply a case of dismantling the bike and checking it in as oversized luggage, which is when my friends arrived and we flew back to London together.

Reflection

Cycling to Barcelona by myself showed me that I can cope with hardship, that I have good judgement and can trust myself to make my own decisions. It also showed me that with a sense of purpose and beautiful surroundings, companionship is an added bonus not a prerequisite to enjoying life. I enjoyed setting my own priorities, to stop when I was tired or wanted to admire my surroundings without reference to someone else's needs or desires. Being in nature, cycling through the mountains, along the back-roads, was liberating and inspiring.

With my new sense of confidence, the following year, I completed a solo cycle tour around hilly Switzerland (though not entirely solo as I arranged to meet up with friends each evening to share the day's stories, as they were on a walking holiday). In 2018, I enjoyed spending three weeks solo in and around Vancouver, kayaking, camping and taking myself on multi-day hikes. Most recently, in 2020, I spent nine weeks travelling solo around New Zealand and Australia.

I can't wait to see where the next adventure takes me.

Facebook: **ipreedy**

Instagram: **@ian.preedy**

Chapter 41

Bamako or Bust

By Arijit Ray

Life changing experiences can stem from the simplest of things. Prior to smartphones and tablets, a trip for work meant buying a magazine before catching a flight. Either that or try and decipher what was happening on German TV game shows.

My magazine of choice was a men's fitness magazine with the cover featuring a headline promising tried and trusted tips for achieving the perfect six-pack. Not something I ever had, but was getting increasingly further away from with a sedentary job with lots of travel - and free alcohol on flights.

So I started reading, flicked through all the exercise routines and then landed on an article about a charity event called the Plymouth to Dakar rally. Odd as it actually didn't go to Dakar, but ended up somewhere called Bamako in Mali (admittedly somewhere I had never heard of).

It sounded amazing - Buy a car worth less than £100 (affordable, tick); drive it from Plymouth to Bamako, via Spain, Morocco, through the Sahara desert (adventure, tick); before finally reaching Bamako in Mali, after a short stint in somewhere called Mauritania and auctioning the car off for charity (doing a good deed, tick). All over three weeks during the Christmas holidays (fewer days off work, tick).

As a friend described it, this was essentially a poor man's version of the famous Paris to Dakar rally... except with no support, no fancy off road cars kitted out to the max and really no hope in hell of getting to the finish line.

Generally speaking, I say yes to almost anything. This monster adventure race, on the other hand, seemed to be a stretch too far.

But I couldn't get it out of my head. What I read about the trip sounded amazing. An adventure of a lifetime. So, as this book suggests, I said yes anyway and sent off an application form half expecting to not even receive a response.

A few weeks later I had secured a place on the rally even though I had no car, no mechanical knowledge, no gear and frankly no clue - I also hadn't told anyone that I had planned to do this.

My next point of call was to find a friend foolish enough to do this with me. I am lucky that I know quite a few fools within my friendship circle. But no takers. Eventually, after a considerable amount of begging, pleading and selling I managed to convince two friends that it was completely reasonable to leave their partners behind over Christmas and celebrate New Year's with me dancing on the roof of our car in the middle of the Sahara desert. I mean really, how was this not one of the many genius ideas I had?

To make it a bit more sensible, my two friends were, at least at the time, as inadequately suited to such an adventure as I was. No mechanical knowledge and clueless when it came to putting up tents - an easy work around as I'd discovered pop up tents, which spring open in a matter of seconds. Putting them back down however, is a different story.

Anyway, now we had a team, it was time to buy a car. Obviously we needed a 4x4 that was capable of tackling the harsh terrain we would be covering in the desert. So we began scouring eBay and soon realised that £100 is not a lot of money in the UK when it comes to buying a car.

So, our search ended at the house of some chap called Colin who was selling a Vauxhall Astra estate for £130. We danced the usual dance of kicking the tyres (it had four of them), looking under the hood (the latch to open the bonnet felt very robust) and decided that the flux capacitor was in good nick. Perfect – we had a car and christened her Veronica (it's worth noting that none of my other rally friends called her Veronica. They didn't feel the love). Who would not feel confident and proud to take a Vauxhall Astra estate into the desert? It even had a fully functioning CD player which we thought we could sell for £30 to bring the value of the car down to £100. Or maybe it was a tape player, I don't remember for sure. Either way, it didn't sell despite our best efforts.

After acquiring Veronica, we went shopping (on a budget). We picked up spare tyres from the scrap yard, which we duct taped to the bonnet and the roof of the car, two of the previously mentioned pop up tents to share between the three of us, a travel kettle that plugged into the cigarette lighter of our car (Oh yes! It had a cigarette lighter. I am telling you this was the perfect vehicle!)

We also decided to bring along a 4x3ft granite worktop left over from my friends new kitchen. It weighed more than the rest of our gear combined, but it would prove to be useful as a platform if we needed to jack up our car in the middle of the sand in the desert. We also took some of his leftover deep pile carpet, which was truly very soft on your feet. This would be used as a sand ladder, should the unlikely happen and Veronica somehow got stuck in the sand of the desert.

A bit more planning over the next couple of months and we were on our way.

On day one we met at my house in North London and said our goodbyes to friends and family and stopped at the supermarket to make sure we had enough food to last us the trip. Six Pot Noodles, bottles of water, a few packets of biscuits and crisps and we were off to the start point in Plymouth. Or were we?

As it turns out we broke down. We were about three miles into our four thousand-mile journey, when Veronica started cutting out. Oddly enough, Veronica hadn't given us any trouble in the months we had her. Now she kept starting up nicely, driving for a bit and then cutting out at really inappropriate moments.

We soon realised it always happened whenever we turned left. Ever the adaptive team, we figured we'll just amend our route and make every turning a right. Not so easy to do in the UK, a country full of roundabouts that you need to turn left onto.

Eventually after breakdown five, six or seven, after we had thoroughly checked that the car still had four tyres, the bonnet release lever still felt robust and the flux capacitor still looked fine, we decided to call in the AA. We had been on the road for about five hours now, and travelled about eight miles in total. And had already resorted to opening some of our crisp packets. Hula hoops if I remember correctly.

I forget his name, but the AA man turned up about an hour after we called during which time we discussed what our plan B was. Should we get to the airport and catch a flight to somewhere and avoid the shame of heading straight home after all the hype we had created amongst our friends and family?

When the AA man arrived, everything seemed fine. He couldn't get his head around what was wrong with Veronica. Eventually, he started clutching at straws and asking us ridiculous questions like, does the car have diesel in it? I mean come on? He could see that the petrol gauge was three quarters full!

Now the thing is, in the three months or so that we had the pleasure of owning Veronica, we never once had to fill her up at the petrol station. Being a diesel she was super fuel efficient, and always had three quarters of fuel in the tank. Amazing really. I have never had such a fuel efficient car. Except, it turns out perhaps she wasn't. Apparently the fuel gauge didn't work and we had essentially been running on fumes. Whoops.

So the friendly AA man towed us to the nearest petrol station, told us we were mad for undertaking such an ambitious trip and that he would probably see us again in an hour on the side of the road. Either that or in a few days on the news.

We weren't deterred. We each had a go at each other for being stupid and not realising that Veronica occasionally needed refuelling and then we continued our journey down to Plymouth. We decided that the best work around of not knowing how much fuel was left in the car, was to simply fill up whenever we found a petrol station, and failing that we had filled up a number of jerry cans with diesel, which should be enough to keep us going when we were crossing the desert. We'd never been to the Sahara Desert but logic dictates that we wouldn't happen to come across a service station with fuel and a Burger King in the middle of the sand dunes. It was only day one and we were already starting to think like real life adventurers! This was going to be great.

We arrived in Plymouth somewhere around 2am instead of the planned arrival of 5pm and tried to check into our hotel room - of course, our room had been given away, so with nowhere to sleep we parked on a side street and made ourselves comfortable in Veronica, waiting for morning to arrive to catch the ferry to Santander. A tough, first day but we had made it to the start point of the rally. We were tired, but not broken.

The next morning we drove to the meeting point for the participants of the rally and met the others who had signed up for this epic trip, took some photos and boarded the ferry. We went straight into our cabin for a little catch up snooze, before getting to know some of the others.

It was a twenty hour ferry journey the highlights being able to get some sleep, have a shower and meeting a crazy haired Frenchman. A night at the ferry 'disco' did nothing but inflate his Gallic optimism - he was convinced if he threw his shoe off the bow of the ferry, the combination of our forward movement and the direction of the wind, meant that his shoe would fly back into his arms. It turns out his calculations were not correct. To this day there is a lonely Timberland boot navigating its way around the North Atlantic Ocean.

We arrived in Santander rested, unscathed and ready to go. The plan was to spend the next couple of days driving the length of Spain to the port of Tarifa, to catch the ferry to Tangier in Morocco. Veronica was running smoothly and our CD/tape player was even able to tune into the delightful local cheesy pop stations. We were flying.

The drive through Spain was mostly motorways, so not much to report, although we did notice that Veronica was leaking and losing coolant on a regular basis. Whenever we stopped to refuel, we decided we should top up with coolant as well. Problem solved. By now however, my teammates were not enamoured with Veronica and I was left being the only one to lovingly call her by her name - the others referred to her using expletives which I will leave up to your imagination.

We also found out that the rain in Spain does not fall mainly on the plain. In fact, it primarily fell on our car. We discovered that this wasn't ideal as the bonnet of Veronica wasn't particularly well sealed... So when we stopped it proved difficult to start the engine up again - apparently wet solenoids on car starters aren't a good thing.

Nevertheless, with a bit of pleading with her and a lot of pushing and the occasional/daily jump start from our new found friends, we were able to get her going again. Again problem solved – we were learning on the fly and made it to the ferry port, full steam ahead to Tangiers.

On arrival in Tangiers, we obliged with the customary pushing of

Veronica off the boat. Fortunately the ramps were downhill so we were quickly on our way. The plan was to make it to Marrakech for Christmas Eve, stopping off for a night in Morocco's capital of culture, Fes, on the way.

The drive to Fes took longer than expected as Veronica struggled with the steep, winding roads of the Rif mountains. This may have been something to do with the weight of the kitchen worktop we were carrying, but being in 'go slow mode' gave us time to take in the breath-taking sights of Mount Zalagh. The land was covered with olive groves and the air had the refreshing scent of wild lavender; a big change from the diesel fumes that had been emerging from the jerry cans in the back of our car.

Fes itself is a wonderful and outrageously colourful city seemingly stuck in time. The main attraction are the medina, which you enter through the archways of the stunning Bab Boulud (blue gate). Inside you share the streets with donkeys as you wander through the souks that sell everything under the sun, all whilst being engulfed by the aromas of the range of spices on offer.

The next morning we were on our way to Marrakech. Progress was swift given much of the route was downhill and we were aided by gravity and the weighty kitchen counter in the back of our car. So much so, that we were pulled over by the local police - wrongly so, I am sure. Apparently, we had been speeding and had to pay a fine on the spot. We argued our case and convinced the policeman that we didn't have any cash on us and that we would drive to the nearest cashpoint and drive back to pay our fine. The policeman kindly provided us with directions, to the nearest ATM and off we went.

And we kept going, all the way to the centre of Marrakech, where we had organised a rendezvous with others taking part in the rally. Here we would have one last slap up meal for Christmas before heading off towards the desert.

It was an unusual but memorable Christmas, the first and last away from home, and the usual Christmas roast was replaced with

Moroccan tagines. Nonetheless, we ate, drank and had a ball - and were there to experience a marriage proposal of a couple taking part in the rally (perhaps the first people ever to smuggle a diamond 'into' Africa!).

Next off we were heading to the Western Sahara. This is where we had expected our adventure to really begin. At this point we decided that safety in numbers was needed so all the participants of the rally drove in convoy in order to help out should anyone become stuck.

After driving through Tiznit, where we stopped for a succulent camel kebab, we continued forward to enter the Sahara desert.

The first obstacle to overcome would be navigating our way through the minefields. Literally.

There are somewhere in the region of 7 million unexploded landmines in the Western Sahara that had been planted by the Moroccan army many moons ago, some of which are kindly encircled by small stones to serve as a warning. However the whereabouts of the majority of these is largely unknown. A fact unknown to me when I invited my friends to take part in the rally.

To be honest, I didn't believe the landmines thing to be true. I'd thought it was a gimmick by the organisers to make the trip sound more edgy than it actually was – that is until I saw the remnants of vehicles strewn either side of the passage we were trying to navigate. At this point we decided it would be wise to hire a local guide.

In the absence of TripAdvisor reviews, we chose a chap called Bumba. He didn't speak English, but he was walking around confidently wearing a shesh, a type of Moroccan turban and, more importantly, he had all of his limbs intact which seemed like a pretty good sign.

Bumba jumped into the lead car of our convoy, and we each followed the route he set out, driving very slowly, radios off, silence in our cars and holding our breaths.

Since I am here writing this you can probably guess that we passed this part of the journey unscathed thanks to the expertise of Bumba. It's a moment I don't think any of us will ever forget and, for me personally, something I ever want to experience again. In fact, over ten years on and it still gives me an uneasy feeling in my stomach.

A few miles down the road was the reward for our bravery. The first sighting of sand from the Sahara Desert. We were elated. Having never been in a desert environment before, the sight of sand dunes in the distance and no signs of civilization to be seen anywhere all around was something truly special. We approached the edge of the sand, took a moment to take it all in and moved forward.

Of course, Veronica got stuck about one metre into the desert, in about an inch of sand. Great. The plush carpet we had carried along to use as a sand ladder didn't really help, but we let some air out of our tyres to provide more traction and with a bit of pushing and shoving we were again on the move. Heading further and further into the vast emptiness of the Sahara aiming for one of the thousands of sand dunes that we could see in the distance. We would camp there for the night and celebrate New Year's Eve.

As expected the sand and rough terrain started taking its toll on each of the cars in the convoy, but this group of newfound friends worked together to ensure we all made it.

Eventually we stopped to camp. Our pop-up tents came out of the car and we were instantly set up and ready to celebrate much to the envy of the rest of the convoy.

New Year's dinner for us involved waiting for the travel kettle to boil powered by our cigarette lighter. It is true that a watched kettle never boils. In fact, a travel kettle powered by a Vauxhall Astra estate never boils. But we didn't care. it was New Year's Eve, we were in the middle of the Sahara desert going strong and looking forward to a chicken flavoured Pot Noodle cooked with lukewarm water. Quite possibly the most memorable meal I have ever had.

It seems the rest of the convoy were slightly more organised than us – they laid out table cloths on the bonnets of their cars, and proceeded to enjoy what looked like a lovely three course meal with wine et al. Luckily we were all friends by now, so in return for a forkful of chicken flavoured Pot Noodle, we were offered wine. And plenty of it.

New Year's Eve was seen in with us dancing on the roof of our cars in fancy dress. Disco lights were provided by our indicators and the brightest stars I have ever seen in the sky. Music came from our trusty cd/tape player and for entertainment we decided it would be a good idea to make human pyramids. I mean why not?

New Year's Day involved rising at the crack of sparrows which was surprisingly easy to get on with as the sun comes up early in the Sahara and our tents essentially became greenhouses. We faffed around trying to put down our pop-up tents, packed our car, filled up the fuel tank and topped up with water to ensure Veronica was all set for the long drive and off we set.

Today's drive had two critical junctures. The first leg of the drive was to get from the middle of the desert where we had camped, back out towards the coast. And secondly we needed to drive across the beach to the border with Mauritania before high tide came in.

Now given this first leg was in the middle of the desert, we would be driving up, down and around sand dunes in the middle of nowhere. This meant that any breakdowns or getting stuck in the sand would result in us being royally screwed. We wouldn't be able to push or pull ourselves out of trouble so it was full pedal to the metal all the way to the beach crossing.

We all set off, slipping and sliding along the sand until we built up some speed. In fact, perhaps a little too much for us. As we were figuratively 'flying' along screaming with the adrenaline rush, we hit a bump in the desert which left us literally flying. Airborne in a Vauxhall Astra estate with a granite kitchen counter in the boot. Has anyone else ever achieved that?

We landed safely, after avoiding hitting what seemed to be the only tree trunk in the Sahara at this time of year, but we had to stop.

With all the rough off road riding, our duct tape manufactured roof rack had come loose and we had lost our remaining spare tyre a few hundred metres back - we had already used the other three spare tyres on our trip and when it came to pit stops we were functioning somewhat like a formula one team by now. But we needed this tyre should we get another flat.

I ran back to collect said tyre, reassembled our roof rack with duct tape and we were on our way. However, our slight delay meant that we were cutting it fine to make the crossing at the beach before the tide came in.

Pedal to the metal again, we were reading the terrain well now and making good progress.

After a few hours we were at the beach, the tide was coming in, but we had just about enough time for all of our cars to get across. So off we set.

Half way through the beach crossing and the waves were bashing against our cars, water seeping through the seals on the windows, but we ploughed on. Until we couldn't. Veronica had her fourth flat tyre of the trip. We were thankful that I had run back to collect the tyre that flew off our roof rack and that we all jumped into our tyre-changing roles like cheetah mechanics. We had to be quick, the tide was coming in quickly.

With the water soaking our backs, we jacked up the car, undid the bolts, took the flat tyre off and put the spare tyre on. Except... it didn't fit! There were four holes for four bolts, but they didn't align.

Now the important bit here is that when we bought the tyres from the scrap yard we didn't actually take Veronica with us. We just went there in another car, eye balled them, said, "Four bolts. Looks about right!" and bought them.

This particular tyre was for a Ford Focus - A lovely car, but not a Vauxhall Astra estate.

So we were finished, the tide was coming in and Veronica was immobile. We would have to call it quits.

With the help of our friends, we pushed her up the shore, to keep her from being washed away into the sea and we set up camp while we blamed each other for the spare tyre fiasco.

Whilst most of us camped on the beach that night, our lead car (a trusty 4x4) continued to drive on up to the border with Mauritania. The plan was to come back in the morning with a spare tyre for Veronica. We weren't out of the game yet!

We kept ourselves entertained by swimming in the sea, playing ultimate Frisbee and then decided it would be a good idea to cook some dinner. Given we had planned our trip down to every detail and had expected to be in Mauritania tonight, we were running low on Pot Noodle. In fact, all we had left food wise was a chocolate bourbon biscuit which reeked of diesel. Even so, we considered whether or not we should share that between the three of us. Luckily our new friends with fancy tablecloths took pity on us and shared their three course meals with us complete with fresh fish, caught from the sea.

In the morning, our rescue team arrived with a spare tyre that fit our car. Now adept at putting down our pop-up tents, we packed up and were on our way to Mauritania in minutes.

We made it across the border into a town called Nouadhibou, home of spare tyres, and continued on to the capital of Mauritania, Nouakchott, where we spent the night.

On arrival, we heard that French tourists had been killed by factions of the terrorist group *Jama'a Nusrat ul-Islam wa al-Muslimin'* (JNIM), and advice from embassies was to avoid the area. We were already there, so we couldn't avoid the area. The next best thing was to leave early in the morning and try to tackle as much of the remaining twenty hours it would to reach Bamako in Mali as possible.

We set off early, feeling refreshed after much needed showers and had no plans to stop other than to refuel.

Of course Veronica had other ideas. We were going along nicely until we heard a terrible screeching sound coming from the bonnet. Then the engine stopped.

By now we had become pretty proficient at getting her going. But this was a step too far. Even with the combined knowledge of the team on the convoy, this wasn't something that we would be able to fix on the side of the road with duct tape and cable ties - We had blown a piston. Veronica wasn't going anywhere.

We towed her to the nearest village where mechanics told us it would take a few weeks to get the part necessary to fix her. Given we had flights to catch from Bamako, and the fact that we didn't want to stay in Mauritania longer than necessary, we unpacked our car and sold Veronica to one of the villagers.

We jumped into the other cars of the convoy and continued our journey. Sad to leave Veronica behind but thankful that we were able to move on and continue our journey.

Again, due to the lost time we needed to spend the night somewhere as it was too dangerous to drive through the night. We stopped off in a barn that a farmer kindly let us use. I am not sure where he moved his goats to, but we were thankful for using their dwellings.

The next day, according to our plan, we would arrive in Bamako. Of course, by now all the cars in the convoy were a little worse for wear. A Renault 5 called Marmite was in particularly bad shape and had no power. We were so close to the finish that we couldn't leave her behind and actually we didn't have enough space in the remaining cars to carry any more passengers as we were already one car down. We had also destroyed all the other tow ropes between us by this point. So the only other option would be to bump and push Marmite the rest of the way with the remaining cars. Of course this meant that progress was slow, so we kept bumping, pushing and driving late into the night.

We entered the outskirts of Bamako and saw a police checkpoint up ahead. Surely we would get pulled over for bumping Marmite along. But no, they didn't bat an eyelid.

The rest of the trip was more or less downhill, so Marmite was able to freely coast down the road requiring only the occasional nudge here and there. In fact, at one point she had picked up so much speed that she was able to overtake slow moving trucks. Given she had no power, lights were provided courtesy of a dynamo torch which my friend was furiously winding from the passenger seat to alert oncoming traffic of her presence.

Eventually we all arrived at the hotel where we would spend a few nights for R&R. Veronica may not have made it all the way, but we had and had made some great friends for life.

We weren't there long enough to truly do it justice as this trip was more about the journey than the destination but Bamako itself is an amazing city. Full of great food, great music, colourful open air markets that sell amazing arts and crafts and of course the impressive crocodile infested River Niger.

I hope to go back again one day. I'm sure the locals will remember us fondly for introducing the human pyramid in a local restaurant. I hope this tradition continues to live on in our absence.

Thanks to everyone involved (you all know who you are), especially Dele and Pran. Thanks for saying yes to doing this with me.

P.S. The granite kitchen table was never used on our trip. It made it all the way to Mali. Perhaps it is proving to be of some use out there?

Instagram: @arijit.x.ray

Chapter 42

The Curious Incident of the AK-47 in the Night-time

By Spike Reid

"KER-CHUNK!"

It was that noise that you really, really don't want to hear in a Ukrainian forest late at night.

It was the cocking of an assault rifle. Somewhere close to us, a bullet had been loaded into the chamber of an AK-47. We could see nothing beyond our vehicle and didn't know who had this gun. Shivers ran down our spines.

Seconds later, the internal light in our Land Rover went out. Our pulses started racing furiously as we stood beside the vehicle. We thought our chances of winning this potential gunfight in the dark were fairly low: we didn't have a gun.

Instead, we decided to try a diplomatic approach.

"HELLO!" we shouted out into the unknown. "Good evening! We're English!"

Our expedition had begun in earnest, and we certainly weren't expecting this.

Yeah, but...

Months earlier, Pete and I were in the Old Station House Inn in London. It was November 2007, and I had learned earlier that day that my grandmother had died. My good friend Pete suggested we go around the corner for a beer or two. Pubs are great places to cheer you up and can be a fertile territory for the best ideas.

"Do you want to do a road trip, mate?" asked Pete.

"Yeah, that'd be cool," I said. "But we don't have a car. Plus we don't really have the money right now, do we?"

Effectively, I was just saying a polite 'no'.

Steadily sipping our pints in the corner of the pub, we talked more about the dream road trip we would like to do; we both wanted to escape the capital and travel overland for thousands and thousands of miles, maybe across Africa or Central Asia. But we still didn't have the money or a vehicle, and although getting hold of a clapped-out banger would have been relatively easy, neither of us was a great mechanic. At the end of the night, we went our separate ways. We had dreamed up some adventures but had no idea how we could achieve them – not even a napkin with notes scribbled on it.

On the tube returning from my grandmother's funeral, I read the newspaper my mum had given me. In the Sunday Times *In Gear* supplement, I came across an interesting article – 'Only the Daring Need Apply'. The Royal Geographical Society and Land Rover had partnered with the newspaper to promote their new bursary.

Beneath the picture of a Defender deep in mud were details of a competition. Entrants needed to come up with an idea for an expedition that started and finished in the UK, and required a Land Rover Defender (which they would lend you). The journey also had to further the understanding or enjoyment of geography.

That night, I called Pete.

"You know that road trip we talked about last week?"

"Yeah?" said Pete.

"Well, how about we take a shiny new Defender 110, and do an off-road trip instead?"

Peter and I had known each other our whole lives. Our mothers were best friends at school. Although we didn't live nearby, we would regularly meet on family holidays. We had also sailed along the coasts of Spain and Portugal and saw in the new millennium in the Alps together.

Over the next ten weeks, we developed our idea further, through various stages of application and selection. After we were shortlisted, Pete invited his friend Dave to join us. We quickly became a close-knit team, working tirelessly on the expedition concept in our evenings and weekends, in both Bristol and London. Our proposal was to drive all the way around the world along the line of 50° north. We would start our circumnavigation on the Lizard Peninsula in Cornwall, the only part of mainland Britain clipped by the 50th Parallel. From there, we would drive eastwards to Sakhalin, north of Japan, before shipping the vehicle to Vancouver and driving across Canada to Newfoundland. Along the way, we would carry out a series of case studies into the social impact of climate change with primary sector workers, mainly farmers. The three of us had never undertaken an overland expedition before; we had never even driven a Land Rover. To convince the sponsors, the application needed to be the best one imaginable.

We were invited for interview at the Royal Geographical Society. When the day arrived, we were led into the daunting Council Room, huge historical globes by the door, the interview panel sat on the far side of the twenty-foot-long wooden table.

The following day the Society asked for further information.

'The committee is excited by your project, but due to the risks associated with certain parts of your proposed expedition, the panel is requesting some further information...' read the email from the Grants Officer, listing eight documents, including a detailed risk assessment, crisis management plan, and revised budget with variances. 'Could you deliver all this by Monday?'

Despite the nerves we were unperturbed, and I raced over to Bristol to thrash out this supplementary information with the others. The Society was concerned about the risks to the expedition organised by such relative newbies; we'd travelled independently to many wild places, but this was a far bigger undertaking. Before embarking upon an expedition like this, you have to be aware of the dangers, and have measures in place to mitigate them. We knew we had to be *risk-aware*, but not *risk-averse*.

The extra effort was worth it. That Tuesday morning in January 2008, we got the news: we had just won the first-ever Land Rover and Royal Geographical Society 'Go Beyond' Bursary.

We knew the biggest challenges certainly lay ahead.

Leaving Europe

Four months later, we were a lot more ready for the expedition. We had been trained in wilderness medicine and off-road driving, and secured a dozen more sponsorship deals to aid us on our journey. Land Rover had entrusted us with a majestic, navy blue Defender 110 with a mere thirty-one miles on the clock. Inspired by the Police song, we named her 'Roxanne' and hoped she didn't 'put on the red light' on the dashboard.

We drove down to our staging post in Cornwall. En route, we popped into my old school and gave a talk about the expedition. After a few talks in other schools, our first case study, and a photoshoot at the Goonhilly Satellite Station, we set out eastwards from the Lizard. Crossing into mainland Europe from Dover, we headed through France, Belgium, Luxembourg, Germany, the Czech Republic and Poland. This was straightforward: we did it by road, and stayed in campsites.

The journey dramatically changed when we entered Ukraine. We thought we could leave the European Union with ease. Oh, how wrong we were! The border crossing was far more complicated and time-consuming than expected. They searched the vehicle and demanded full documentation.

That night, clear of the border, we decided to wild camp.

"That forest on the left looks quite good," I said to Pete and Dave as we drove down the highway.

"Hmm," said Pete, as we turned up the forestry track, "I wonder what that big sign there says?"

There was a billboard-sized sign at the junction, announcing something in Ukrainian. We would later learn it read, 'Government Game Reserve – STRICTLY no camping. STRICTLY no fires.'

We pulled off the track and drove into the woods. Dave got dinner going. As master of our rudimentary camp kitchen, each night he would cook up a feast from whatever we had in our massive black provisions box in the back of Roxanne. Meanwhile, Pete would put up the tents or hammocks and I collected firewood, dug a hole in the ground, and made a little fire. After dinner we enjoyed a game of cards, poking the fire occasionally.

That night, we decided it was time to call it a day and climbed into our sleeping bags.

Suddenly, the peace of the night was broken by the rev of an engine on the forestry track. Someone was driving in our direction. We didn't want to attract any attention at that hour, so we quickly closed Roxanne's door. Frustratingly, the little light inside stayed on.

We heard the crunch of tyres on the gravel. The silence of the engine being stopped. The snap of a twig.

Then the metallic clunk of an assault rifle slowly being cocked.

"Oh dear!" we muttered under our breath.

We shouted out our greeting into the darkness, telling whomever it was that we were English. We didn't know whether that increased or decreased our chances of doom. But it was all we had. We didn't have any guns.

After that, there was silence. It was only a few moments, but it felt like an aeon. Who was there? Why did they cock the rifle? How many guns were pointed at us through the darkness?

Whoever it was with the loaded AK-47 probably wasn't expecting to stumble across three Englishmen in the woods that night. We heard them whispering amongst themselves. Two bright torches walked out of the darkness. We stayed frozen to our spots.

We quickly discovered that these four men were government gamekeepers. They thought we were poachers and well-armed, hunting the elusive *'nebezpechnyy kaban'*. Luckily, they had a German advisor with them that evening and Dave spoke excellent German.

"Not good. They say we're in a game reserve," Dave told us. "It's no camping here and strictly no fires."

"Balls!" said Pete.

We were in a sticky situation and had to find a way out. Relocating in the dark could be tricky, but staying there was not what the armed men wanted.

We decided to negotiate. First Dave told them what we were doing and that we were on our way to Japan. They seemed impressed. Then we asked them to let us stay there for the night. We told them that we couldn't find a campsite anywhere else. They thought we were foolish to camp here, and after we passed Kiev, it would be even more crazy to wild camp.

Pete and I waited anxiously, watching the negotiation between Dave and the German advisor. Would they let us stay? Would we have to decamp in the middle of the night?

After Dave finished talking, the four men started discussing it in Ukrainian. Things didn't look hopeful... but then.

"Sie können bleiben."

"We can stay," translated Dave beaming. It appears the gamekeepers took pity on we three hopeless Englishmen in their woods.

"They need us to go very early in the morning."

"That's cool," I said giving a big thumbs up and smile to the Ukranian men. "Let's just do breakfast down the road."

The gamekeepers and their advisor bade us adieu. We swiftly and nervously went to bed, slipping into our Hennessy hammocks suspended between the trees. Although the hammocks were comfy as anything and should've been gently rocking us to sleep, we were all on edge. It was the first time any of us had met gun-wielding officials in the dark. We were aliens in this country, and the dark forest now felt unwelcoming. All the noises of the night were amplified; every rustle of the undergrowth sounded like a trained sniper scoping our position.

Thankfully, none of us heard any more AK-47s being cocked.

In the morning, we swiftly broke camp, wrapping up our hammocks and throwing everything into the back of Roxanne. We rolled out onto the muddy forest track and drove down to the highway where we turned left and headed east. We later learned that *'nebezpechnyy kaban'* means wild boar; we were pleased not to have our sleep disrupted by one of those rampaging through our campsite.

That was our first night camping outside the EU, and the night that the expedition began with gusto. Many more adventures lay ahead.

Photos for Fish

Four weeks after leaving Cornwall, we entered Kazakhstan. It is the ninth biggest country in the world, more than three-quarters the size of India. The first thing that springs to mind about Kazakhstan for most people is *Borat*. *Borat* is about as realistic a representation of the country as *Mr. Bean* is of Britain!

The west of the country is known as their 'Wild West' and supposedly filled with mafia, corruption, and guns; luckily, we didn't experience any of that first hand. Most of the country is extremely flat. We drove through the dusty frontier towns of the 'Wild West'. The 'nodding donkeys' of the oil industry were omnipresent, bobbing slowly away day and night, sucking the black gold out. Kazakhstan is largely devoid of fences or other boundaries. You can drive across the grasslands that form the vast steppe with ease – or most of the time you can.

After a brief diversion to the ship graveyards and dried-up remains of the Aral Sea – one of the worst environmental disasters caused by man in the world – we decided to follow the 50th Parallel as closely as possible through central Kazakhstan. Away from the road, the steppe was largely featureless. Occasionally, we stumbled upon some derelict farm buildings from the communist era, with crumbling concrete and rusted metalwork. There were no humans around and no animals either. Much of Kazakhstan is empty.

But not all of it.

We stopped the Land Rover when we came across a big river. This one ran north-south and had to be crossed. It was the duty of the team-member riding shotgun to check the best route across, but we all jumped out. We discovered a fording point that had been used by previous 4x4s passing through that area.

Dave was just about to scout the crossing on foot when an olive green Soviet 4x4 pulled up behind us. Out jumped three Kazakh men, two of them with pistols in holsters. We still didn't have a gun.

'Oh dear, oh dear,' we thought.

These angry men in faded army fatigues seemed to want to know what we were doing there. They demanded answers in Kazakh and then Russian, but we had next-to no shared language. The men explained, with gestures, that we had to turn around and head back to the road.

Unexpectedly a boy about eight, who was the son of one of the men, climbed out of their 4x4. In the blue tracksuit he had outgrown, he wandered tentatively over to his dad's side.

It was approximately five hours across the steppe to return to the road; this diversion would add at least a day onto our journey. In an act of desperation, I pulled the tiny globe from where it was Velcroed to the dashboard to 'assist' with our navigation. With this little prop, I showed them where we had started and where we were heading.

The situation suddenly transformed. They laughed, nodding their heads in approval. Pulling out my big camera, I persuaded the men to let me take a picture of them all, with our Land Rover in the background. We were now their 'friends'.

Afterwards, I ran around and pulled our little printer out of the back. By shoving in the SD card I could print out a photo of the men, the young boy and our lovely Land Rover. It was a little Polaroid moment, but with no need to flap and wave the photo around to get it to develop, plus it was a proper size.

"Here!" I said, giving them the photo. "This is a present for you."

They seemed impressed, and asked for two more copies and then a photo of the boy showing off his little ponytail, so I powered up the printer again.

One of them trotted over to their 4x4, pulled out a white plastic bag and presented it to us. Pete, Dave, and I peered inside and found it was full of freshly-caught fish. The Kazakhs said we could follow them across the river and then continue on eastwards. Four printed photos had ensured we didn't need to turn around and retrace our way across the grassland. Presenting photos to strangers can be a steppe in the right direction.

Gobi-yond

After visiting the new Kazakhstani capital of Astana with its garishly-coloured modern buildings, we headed on to the eastern half of the country, where innumerable nuclear tests were carried out in the Soviet era and many spacecraft had been launched over the decades. From there, our route took us back into Russia, passing through the Altai Mountains before entering Mongolia. The wilds of this country amazed us all. Thousands of miles of steppe lay before us, dotted everywhere with *gers* – the traditional white tents similar to yurts that most Mongols live in. All the Mongols we met were friendly and curious, in contrast to some of the people we'd met in Russia.

From the heaving and dirty capital of Ulaanbaatar, we took a little diversion from the 50th Parallel to the Gobi. Beforehand, this vast expanse of desert was almost semi-fictional to the three of us. We drove down there, and after putting Roxanne through her paces in the sand dunes, we set up camp.

It was my birthday. We sat enjoying some local 'Hite' beer and playing cards around the fire, which gently crackled, sending sparks up into a sky full of brightly shining stars. I realised how lucky we had been to win this bursary. This birthday, and the expedition as a whole, were things I would never forget.

As we headed north from deep within the Gobi to return to our line, Roxanne seemed to have lost some of her poke. Driving through soft, dry sand requires lots of revs and the wheels would often spin, kicking up dust. But not that morning, and we didn't know why.

The Gobi is the least densely-populated province of the least densely-populated country in the world. This was not where we wanted to break down. As we followed the winding track sluggishly out of the sand dunes, we spotted some vehicles ahead. They stopped; we caught them up: four orange Land Rovers.

"Good morning," we said in greeting.

"Good morning," the leader replied in perfect English. "What are you doing here?"

"We're driving around the world," Pete said, "and this is on the way."

"Jolly good. We're doing a recce for the Land Rover G4 Challenge," he said. "Our basecamp is just over that dune. Would you like to come back for a cup of tea? We've got some lovely Earl Grey."

"Yeah, that sounds great," I said, already salivating at the thought. "Thank you."

As we followed them into camp, Roxanne crawled up the dune.

"You seemed to be going a bit slowly there," the leader, John Limb, complete with his safari vest, observed after we arrived. "Is everything alright?"

"We're not sure. She seems unusually sluggish this morning," replied Pete.

"OK, we'll get our mechanic to have a look," said John. "ASIF! Can you come over and check this out?" he hollered.

Asif wandered over from the support vehicle in his dusty overalls.

"I recognise this Landy!" he said in a broad Birmingham accent. "It came into my workshop in Solihull four months ago to be kitted out for this expedition!"

He popped open the bonnet, wired up his Toughbook to Roxanne, and set about diagnostics while John made us cups of tea.

"You've got a problem with your EGR valve," said Asif.

"Okay, what does that mean?" Pete replied.

"Ah, well, it's vital for your turbo and the wire to it has got a break in it somewhere. Even if I had all my tools with me in my workshop in Solihull, I would struggle to find it. I'll have a go though."

Asif whipped out his pocket knife and cut into the wire. "AHAH! I've found it!"

"Wow," I said, "That's fantastic."

Within ten minutes he had fixed the wire and closed the bonnet.

"Yeah, if I didn't fix that you might have only gone another ten miles before the engine could have seized up and that would've been it."

"Yikes," I said.

After finishing our Earl Greys, we thanked them all sincerely and headed off in our newly-fixed Land Rover. Roxanne had her revs once more, and we blasted off through the sand towards Ulaanbaatar. We felt ever so fortunate that morning, and on the drive northwards, we chatted about how very awkward it would have been to break down in the Gobi desert. In this remote corner of the world, and in our hour of need, we had stumbled across a Land Rover mechanic who knew our vehicle personally. "As if that's possible," you might say.

Asif was the man who made it possible.

Salmon fishing in Sakhalin

Although we were undertaking a full circumnavigation of the world, the tough part of the expedition was coming to an end on the large Russian island, Sakhalin, which lies north of Japan. Longer than England, it has plentiful oil and gas reserves. After Sakhalin, we only had Japan, Canada, and the US on our route, none of which would push the team and Roxanne to the limit as Ukraine, Russia, Kazakhstan, and Mongolia had.

Due to its symbolic nature, we wanted to reach the exact point where the 50th Parallel plunged into the Pacific Ocean. We reached Sakhalin on an eighteen-hour ferry journey from the Russian mainland, and the next day we drove northwards to re-join the 50th. The roads steadily deteriorated as we got further from the towns and cities in the south. Eventually, we turned off the tarmacked road onto a gravel track to reach the coast. Three miles after a hamlet of wooden buildings, the gravel turned to mud. Then we reached our first bridge.

In its heyday, it had been a wonderful feat of timber engineering, a sturdy crossing constructed from huge logs to take oversized Soviet trucks. When we reached it, some of the mighty piers remained, but a gaping rift had formed in the middle, the result of a flood.

Fording was the only solution, so Dave leapt out to scout it. Following his directions, I drove Roxanne across the rocky riverbed. She lurched left to right as we scrambled over it. The water was halfway up the doors, but luckily, little came in. Thereafter, the muddy track worsened significantly, the ruts left by giant six-wheel-drive Soviet trucks becoming wider apart, and deeper. Roxanne struggled. At one point I nearly rolled her; this route was almost impassable.

After fording more rivers and navigating more ruts, eventually, we reached the Pacific Ocean. The fog rolled in from the wild waters. It was August, but felt more like late autumn on that beach. We clambered out of the Land Rover, our necks stiff from the hours of rut-riding. The three of us stood there in our dirty t-shirts and gazed out into the misty ether. Behind us stood Europe and Asia, and months of overlanding.

We drove three miles south along the beach in Roxanne to camp right on the line.

"Hey, look over there!" said Pete suddenly.

Standing by a river was a small brown bear, its paw swiping enthusiastically at the water. But that river mouth was precisely where we had planned to camp that night. It was exactly where the 50th entered the Pacific Ocean.

When the bear heard Roxanne's diesel engine it ran swiftly inland to the damp, luscious forest. Despite the bear's proximity, we still decided to set up camp on our line. However, that night Roxanne and the camp kitchen were at least fifty metres from our tents. Bears are attracted to the smell of food and toothpaste; but they were unlikely to be attracted to the smell of us that night – we hadn't showered in a while!

This was a moment of triumph. We had crossed two entire continents. Dave started to cook a celebratory curry with some 'danger sausage', the salami of unknown origin that was often the only meat available in Siberia. Pete put up the tents, while I popped the champagne in a bucket to chill. The dark green bottle had sat under the passenger seat since we'd left the Champagne region of France months before. As Pete skilfully opened the bottle, so vigorously shaken over 15,000 miles of overlanding, he didn't spill a drop. He poured it into our version of flutes – big, red, plastic mugs. No, not classy: but that champagne tasted refreshing and fine. We felt we'd earned it.

The following morning, I awoke to a splash.

'This must be the bear returning to fish in the river again,' I thought, and without fully considering the risks, I jumped out of my tent with my camera, to capture it in action.

Looking around, there was no bear in sight, but I wandered down the grey sand to the river's mouth. Glancing down into the waters I discovered what had splashed – the river was *alive* with salmon, teeming with them as they raced upriver to their place of origin for breeding.

I did what any good expeditioner would do in this situation – I swiftly whittled a spear from some driftwood. After finding the straightest stick available, I made three barbed prongs that I bound to one end. It was wildly different from Yemen, but then, I went salmon fishing in Sakhalin.

The abundance of fish made beginner spearfishing simple. Standing in the chilly, knee-deep water I managed to catch our breakfast. Much satisfied by this, I went on to catch our lunch. And then our dinner.

Pete and Dave awoke, and came to see what I was up to. They too whittled spears. Pete subsequently pointed out that instead of spearing the fish, you could simply pick up other salmon that had washed up on the beach as they tried to enter the river, as long as you reached them before the seagulls did. In the waters just beyond the mouth, we spotted seals also preying on the bountiful salmon that morning.

Spearing the fish was more satisfying than scavenging, and the three of us all tried our hand, being rewarded with the freshest salmon you could ever eat. It melted sublimely in our mouths. We felt somewhat primeval, but this river was a mighty reward. If it had been further north or south we would've missed this plentiful resource. Instead, it was bang on the 50th Parallel and we felt lucky again as we caught and devoured eight big salmon around the fire on that beach.

Returning to the Lizard

From there, we drove south to catch the ferry across to Japan. We cleaned Roxanne for two days before sailing, because Japan doesn't allow dirty vehicles in, and then for four more hours at sea, pressure-washing and scrubbing her again. After driving the length of Japan to its industrial heartland, Nagoya, we shipped our now-beloved Land Rover to Canada. Unfortunately, we couldn't accompany Roxanne aboard the ship, so we flew across to North America.

Getting the Land Rover through customs in Vancouver was tricky, and there were a few minor repairs needed at the dealership. Insuring Roxanne properly was very challenging, causing us much frustration, but eventually we managed to do so in Alberta.

With this hurdle surmounted, we crossed the rest of Canada to the island of Newfoundland. On this island, which took a long day to drive across, we reached the point where the 50th Parallel goes into the Atlantic. Alas, there was no river full of salmon here, just a windswept headland with the fog rolling in across the ocean. To ship Roxanne back to England, we drove down to New York, reaching it just in time for Hallowe'en and the election when Barrack Obama won his first term.

The expedition concluded with a drive from Portsmouth down to the Lizard in Cornwall. We revisited the school on the peninsula, and gave a talk about their neighbours due east and west along the shared line of latitude.

In every case study we had done along the route, the farmers told us the weather had become far harder to predict in the previous ten to fifteen years. Despite doubts about climate change, many subsistence farmers in less economically developed countries are suffering its effects already. Some had major pest problems due to the lack of very cold winters nowadays, as in central Kazakhstan. Others, like Munkhtsetseg, the seventy-four-year-old woman in Mongolia, had suffered an incredibly punishing winter following an unusually dry summer, resulting in the loss of 90% of her livestock. From Belgium to Siberia, from the edge of Chernobyl to Niagara Falls, the unifying trend we identified between our case studies was that the weather was less dependable. The planting season now shifted dramatically each year, along with the harvesting times. Crops failed more often and livestock was less productive, or even died. The unpredictability caused by climate change is having a substantial impact on many along the 50th Parallel already.

Those stories, direct from the numerous farmers we met, hang heavy in our hearts, and we will forever remember those people.

Our expedition inspired us. It changed our perspective on the world. We learnt a great deal about Central Asia beyond the travel brochures. Anyone who says, "It's a small world!" has obviously never driven around it. Our world is mind-blowingly huge – the circumnavigation took us seven months. We drove Roxanne over 22,000 miles. The team got on remarkably well – none of us remembers having a single argument on the expedition.

The world is wild and wonderful. If you get the chance to travel far from the beaten track, seize it. If you get offered it, say "Yes," not "Yeah, but…"

If you don't get offered it, make that opportunity. Dream up your own wild adventure, either solo or with a carefully-selected team, and then make it happen. Apply for the grants, bursaries, and sponsorship deals – there are so many possibilities.

Remember, the door to opportunity doesn't open. It only unlocks. It is up to you to turn the handle.

And if that doesn't work, you can always kick the bloomin' door down!

Say "YES!" and go forth.

The Royal Geographical Society/Land Rover bursary is run annually, along with numerous others by the Society. If you are keen to undertake an amazing expedition or carry out fieldwork in wild environments, I recommend you check out the Royal Geographical Society's grants page: **http://www.rgs.org/in-the-field**.

Website: **spikereid.com**

Instagram: **@spikereid**

Chapter 43

Swifty Scooting from Chepstow to St. Just

By Sophie Rooney

As I sat and swirled my second coffee around an almost empty cup, I chanced a look out of the window, hoping that the rain outside was slowing. Huge smears and the occasional flash of colour as a pedestrian ran past told me that the rain was actually getting heavier. Not what I wanted to see but not a big problem for me just yet. The person I was waiting for still hadn't arrived. And besides, it couldn't possibly keep raining like this for long.

I returned to the tiny screen in front of me, eager to finish my Facebook post before Claire got there. I was eight stages through a multi-discipline John o'Groats to Land's End challenge. I'd just finished running the length of the Offa's Dyke National Trail having already kayaked, swum and cycled other legs.

Suddenly, a cold gust of wind whipped through the café as a smiling lady stepped through the door. I recognised Claire and Andy immediately. Though I had only met Claire virtually, she had agreed to join me on a Swifty Scooter for a few days as I headed towards Cornwall. Andy, her partner, would be driving the support vehicle.

Despite only virtually meeting Claire, I knew it was them straight away, and they recognised me too. Though after three weeks of being on the road this was probably less surprising. The smell of my kit was more than likely what gave me away.

Claire made a bee-line for me. "Sophie!" she squealed, wrapping me in a damp hug. "This is so exciting, isn't it!"

I knew we'd get on brilliantly straight away. Despite the heavy, soggy atmosphere, her enthusiasm really lit up the room.

"So, have you scootered before?" I asked while waving the waitress over to order another coffee.

"Not since I was nine," she grinned.

"Me neither, but how hard can it be...?"

Sometime later, and with only a couple of misturns, we found ourselves heading out of Chepstow and up towards the Severn Bridge. This was a pretty big milestone in my journey. It would be my final return to England and a real step towards home.

We headed up on to the bridge and I felt apprehensive. Would they really let us scoot across the Severn Bridge? We *were* on the old bridge – the one supporting the M48 – but I still didn't think that this would be scooting territory.

As it turns out, there's a cycle path down one side of the busy motorway. Mind blown!

Excitedly, I scooted out over the river. Wind whistled down the Severn valley flinging raindrops in all directions at once. I was drenched through but smiling from ear to ear.

Safely back on English soil, Claire and I pushed on, eager to make it to Bristol before it got dark.

Still new to the scooter, I was happy to spend some time on relatively quiet and flat country roads, edging towards our rendezvous.

We arrived just as the sun was setting, and despite a bit of trouble navigating a busy city centre at rush hour (the pedestrians proving more of an issue than the traffic), travelling through Bristol on a push scooter was great fun.

As the sun set and the sky turned a deep blue, we were treated to one last descent down into the Avon Valley. "Wow!" I exclaimed. We'd rounded a corner and towering over our heads, spanning the great gorge like a spider's web, was the Clifton Suspension Bridge. One of the best things about not navigating myself was that relatively well-known landmarks like this one could creep up and surprise me.

*

The following morning, I woke to find myself surprisingly achy, but excited to get more distance under my belt. This was a Saturday, which meant that we had been joined by Jon and Alan (my other half and our dog), a massive boost to my motivation. Their arrival prompted a miraculous muscular recovery and I was keen to make the most of the next couple of days – as come Monday my emotional support team would be leaving me again.

Being my fourth and last week on the road, rounding off one thousand miles travelled under my own steam, I knew this final week would be mentally tough. By comparison the idea of travelling thirty miles (with support) today seemed perfectly pleasant. I thought this to myself during the drive back into Bristol city centre and was pleased to see that Claire's smile was matching mine as we jumped back on the scooters.

Our first stop today was to be in the car park for Goatchurch Cavern, at the entrance to the Mendips AONB. I had never been to the Mendips and the weather today was perfect, blue skies and brilliant bright sunshine. As I settled into my scooting rhythm, I pictured myself amongst the hills and found everything to be going well.

I was a little faster than Claire, but this didn't bother me. I was happy to stop every mile or so and wait for her to catch up. Claire is one of these people who is always wearing a smile and looking back to see her cheerily coming down the road was a joy in itself.

We carried on this way until we emerged in the shadow of some beautiful limestone hills, their bright green grassy tops decorated with patches of exposed rock. On we went through narrow roads until a dramatic gorge came into view, making us both stop and appreciate our surroundings. It was amazing that this morning we had gone from navigating city streets, to traversing remote country lanes and now faced sheer limestone cliffs. How privileged we were to be there, I thought to myself, before being interrupted by a tummy rumble. Thankfully, at the base of the cliffs was our support crew with a boiling camp stove and some tasty Super Noodles.

We headed away from the carpark on a smaller road and immediately began ascending. Sweat began to drip from our brows onto the track, which was becoming more of a footpath the higher we climbed. Soon, we were pushing the scooters over rocks and mud as scooting became an impossibility. It was glorious to be away from the tarmacked roads, the broad sky above, the woodland creaking in the slight breeze, birds darting and chirping about. Before we knew it, the track had spat us out onto an exposed hilltop. We carried on pushing to the very top.

Looking back from here we could see all of the countryside we had crossed that morning. In the near distance was the cityscape of Bristol and further away, the Severn Bridge.

I lifted my eyes slightly and could just about make out the shadows of the black mountains that I had run across just a few days previously. I felt an immense sense of pride looking back and knowing I had come all this way and allowed myself a moment or two to reflect.

Compulsory hilltop selfies captured, we pushed on to the road where we knew we could start having some fun and whizzing back down. The wind roared in my ears and rattled the straps of my helmet as I shot down the hill. At this stage I put Claire out of my mind and just let myself fly. I was moving so fast I daren't try the brakes or steer too much, I just blasted down the middle of the lane, eyes streaming, enjoying every minute. It lasted for about two miles and I have to say was one of the most fun experiences of the whole trip.

Later that evening, when we finally met our support team in the small village of Crickham, I noticed that my top speed for the day was over thrity-four miles per hour. On a kick scooter. I did not expect scooting to be so exhilarating and though we had fallen short of our planned mileage again I went to bed happy. Scooting was hard work, but it was still new and fun, and I felt very lucky to be there.

*

On Sunday morning, I was eager to see what the day would bring but was a little disappointed to find that these first few miles were to be completely flat and along small, relatively unremarkable roads. I found myself falling into a good rhythm and getting speedier and speedier, but our surroundings meant that this morning's miles really fell to just covering ground.

To make matters worse, the drivers we encountered seemed to have a real thing against scooters and our presence on the road. It was the first day we had really experienced hostility and there were a couple of times where I worried for Claire and myself, with 4x4's hooting and passing deliberately closely to try to prove a point. Needless to say, I had a few choice words that I threw their way (and maybe a few hand gestures too) but mostly I just tried to ignore them, put my head down and push on. This meant that I would often turn around and find that Claire was no longer behind me, leaving me feeling a little guilty.

Claire would still flash me that contagious smile as she caught up – but I got the feeling she wasn't enjoying this morning so much, something which probably encouraged her decision to call it a day at our lunch spot. With a long drive home and work in the morning I completely understood, and we said our goodbyes around midday. I was sorry to see her go. She'd been a huge motivation for me, always grinning despite what the weather, the hills and the inconsiderate drivers had thrown at us. I'll always be thankful for her input into the adventure.

The rest of the day remained pretty unremarkable, though with noticeably fewer angry drivers. There was a bit more excitement as I had to climb and skirt the edge of the Quantock Hills AONB, but by this point it was late in the day and I was too tired to appreciate the scenery. I just wanted to make sure I made it to the campsite before it got dark.

I pushed on and on and arrived just before the sun started to set, with another twenty five miles in the bag. Happy though I was to be closer to the finish, the evening was slightly tainted by the imminent departure of Jon and Alan, though at least I knew this was the last time they would be returning home without me.

I just had one more week to make it through to reach my goal of Land's End. Then for the first time in over a month I would get to go home and sleep in my own bed.

As I thought this to myself, I smiled once more. At home all I can do is dream of going out on adventures and seeing new parts of the world. Yet, here I was on the road and I found myself really missing home.

Luckily, Jon had bought some doughnuts to cheer me up before he left so I ate a doughnut in bed and promptly fell asleep on the rest of the bag. There is no way I would let myself do that at home. And just like that, adventure was winning again.

*

The next morning, following two or three cups coffee, I packed all my camping gear and stuff for the next few days into my rucksack and marvelled at just how big and heavy it was. I looked from the huge rucksack to the (now very small looking) scooter and wondered if I perhaps should have done a test run with the full gear before letting Jon drive away. The bag was almost as tall as the scooter. I was convinced that the moment I put it on the front it was going to make the scooter fall over. I felt like an idiot for not testing it first and resigned to the fact that I was likely to have to carry this big thing on my back for the next five days. Not good.

I should at least try to put it on the scooter, I thought. I heaved the bag up on to the carrying rack and waited for the scooter to fall. And to my surprise (and delight) it didn't.

Determined to make a serious dent in the remaining mileage, I scooted hard that morning. The bag made a huge difference to the handling, but the downhills and flats still seemed to be manageable.

From my campsite I cruised down the canal and into Taunton, where I initially enjoyed passing through the city centre like a tourist. After a few brushes with pedestrians, however, I changed my mind about the whole thing. I wanted to get out of town and back into the country.

Luckily, I didn't have to wait for long and was soon back on a narrow cycle path heading out of town. These paths shortly turned into country lanes and then, I was delighted to see, re-joined the towpath for several miles of beautifully flat, uncongested scooting.

Every now and then I would be disappointed to see Google directing me away from the towpath, making me fear that my traffic free section was coming to an end, before it would surprise me again by sending me back to the canal.

On one such diversion I happened to pass through a village with a very inviting pub. As it was nearing midday and I had already covered about eighteen miles I thought *why not?* And popped in for a burger. I may still have a long way to go but when one comes across an opportunity such as an open pub at lunchtime, what is one to do?

Burger consumed and feeling super heavy, I set off again, pleased to join the canal once more and head for the town of Tiverton. I had made the most of the Wi-Fi in the pub to see what I could expect from the rest of the day. I was due to follow the canal into Tiverton, then I would face a long climb that I was not looking forward to. There were twenty miles left to go and scooting off I started to worry.

My legs were stiffening up, I was tired, and this big hill was looming constantly in the back of my mind. I decided that the best option was to stop in a bakery in town and get a coffee and snack in order to power me up the hill. To make things more challenging, my throat had taken a disliking to something and felt like it was coated in a layer of broken glass. It seemed I was getting ill, which was not too surprising given how fatigued I was, but I had hoped any illness would wait until I'd finished.

I was feeling really quite miserable. Something which the seemingly endless uphill miles to the campsite did little to improve. I couldn't wait to just get into my sleeping bag, curl up and go to sleep. I nipped into the tiny campsite shop on my way in and browsed the shelves whilst waiting for the farmer to appear. When he did, his curiosity and enthusiasm made me forget how tired and ill I had just been feeling, and we had a long chat about the challenge. He was impressed that I had come so far and said during the summer he gets a lot of LEJOG cyclists. "What do you think of the hill out of Tiverton?" he asked in his thick West Country accent.

"It was a real killer," I croaked, thinking back to the seemingly endless incline.

"Folks round here call it the Long Drag," he muttered with a wry smile.

"I think I know why!" I laughed.

He offered me a camping pod for the same price as a tent - something which I happily accepted before purchasing a pint of milk and some biscuits. It was time for bed. It turns out that thirty eight miles on a scooter is pretty hard work.

*

Following a frosty sunrise, I set off again waving goodbye to the farmer as I left. I had struggled to eat anything the previous evening due to my sore throat and as a result was feeling really sluggish. Winding through quiet country lanes, I couldn't help but think I just wasn't in the mood.

I rounded a couple more bends and came face to face with two huge horses. The riders were as surprised as I was.

"Morning," I said with a grin.

"Morning. You look like you're going a long way."

"John o'Groats to Land's End," I said proudly, thinking of everything I had achieved so far.

"Wow!" they said, clearly impressed.

I explained that I had been feeling sluggish and they recommended a coffee in the next town. I thanked them for their advice and set off again. I hadn't realised until they said but I really needed some caffeine.

Following their instructions, I ended up at a small café run by community members. Everyone in the room was having a chat so I ordered a coffee and sat down where I thought I would be out of the way. Only I found I wasn't as inconspicuous as I thought. The interrogation starting at the next break in conversation.

"What's that thing I saw you riding?"

"Where're you off to then?"

"Doing it for charity, are you?"

I wasn't feeling pressurised or scared. I was thrilled to have the opportunity to discuss my journey and enjoyed the focused incredulity. "Yep. I'm raising money for International Aid for the Protection and Welfare of Animals."

"Here," said the lovely lady who had served me tea. "Instead of paying for your cuppa, put a few quid to your charity instead."

"Thank you so much," I grinned, sending a couple of pounds to my Just Giving page.

I thanked them for their hospitality and looked at my watch. It was time to get going or I risked having to scoot in the dark.

The rest of the day saw me travel on roads to Okehampton and then I was treated to a few miles along the Granite Way, a path which provided beautiful views of the desolate, rugged moorland as it skirted around the edge of Dartmoor. I felt so happy to be travelling in such a simple way through such beautiful scenery. This is what scooters were made for.

I carried on smiling for the rest of the afternoon and was even happier to be offered a place to camp for free when the owner found out what I was doing. My body was tired, my throat and lungs sore, and my kit was a bit gross, but I was having a great time. And what's more I had just ninety seven miles left to go.

*

Great as the day before had been, there was no masking my tiredness when I awoke the next day. Shivering in the misty morning and with achingly numb fingers, I packed up earlier than ever.

Down in the village I knew there was an inn that would be open for breakfast so I popped in, ate and warmed myself by the fire. When I set off again, I was feeling marginally more human.

I was going to meet with my good friend Becky this day (she had really kindly offered to bring me lunch) and I thought I should try and get as far as I could before then so she didn't have to travel as far to meet me.

I scooted for about ten miles and found myself outside another pub, a welcome fire roaring in the hearth. It looked too delightful to just pass by. Signal here was terrible, so I couldn't let Becky know where I was, but I wasn't expecting her yet anyway. Plus, my scooter was outside, and I was willing to bet that there weren't many people daft enough to be doing what I was doing.

I went in, ordered coffee and sat by the fire. Just as I was finishing it off, a lady and a tiny puppy came in. How sweet! I rubbed her head as I would have done with our puppy and she obediently rolled over so I could scratch her tummy.

"Er... Sophie! Hello!"

I looked up shocked. It was Becky! I hadn't even registered that it was her! I paused for a moment, unsure whether to carry on fussing the dog or talk to Becky, then kind of did both at once.

"Don't worry about it," said Becky as I apologised for ignoring her. "She always gets more attention than me."

I was thrilled to hear that not only was Becky bringing me lunch, but she planned to support me all day. And that she did. For the next twenty or so miles we played a game of leapfrog, with Becky feeding me and encouraging me all the way. She even listened to my fantasy of some coke and magically appeared with some a couple of miles down the road.

I had entered Cornwall that morning and it turned out the route was outrageously hilly. I was super tired, but it didn't matter because Becky was there to make sure I had everything I needed. At the end of the day she bundled me and the scooter into the back of her van and took me to her house.

I was really happy to see Becky's husband Paul (another old friend) and to join them for an amazing supper and an evening by the fire. It had been a challenging day crossing an exposed area of open moorland, with the price of this open and wild scenery surrounding Bodmin Moor being a lot of uphill scooter miles, but Becky had made it a (relative) breeze.

*

I was dropped off the following morning and began scooting south again. The notable marker in today's route was Truro, a city which I had heard a lot about but never visited. The miles covered in the approach to the city were very much done with my head down, eager to make it to the end of this day so that I could get on with the final day of scooting tomorrow.

I did suffer a few eventful miles, whereby Google led me down what was definitely a footpath (not a cycle path as it claimed). One that was definitely not welcomed by the people who owned the land. It was not maintained in the slightest and tricky to walk down let along lug a scooter down. But that only went on for a mile or two and by the end, after a beef sandwich, I was able to look back at it in a humorous way.

By the time I reached the city, I was less keen on looking around and decided a quick look at the Cathedral would suffice. It was a cold day and my chest was hurting so my enthusiasm was generally low. I parked up my scooter by the cathedral and had a wander round, then picked it up again and headed to the campsite. I passed a pizza place on my way there and whilst waiting for the lady in charge to answer I ordered a large pizza. I put up my tent, showered, and then ate in my sleeping bag, speaking to Jon just before drifting off, excited that I would see him tomorrow.

Getting to this point had been incredibly hard work, but there was only one more day (and thirty four miles) to go. I could do this. The end was well and truly in sight.

*

On my final scooting morning I did not wake to the conditions I had hoped for. Strong winds and heavy rain battered my tent. I ducked out and ran for the shelter of the campsite wash block carrying as much as I could and then returning for the rest. I had a shower to warm up and then packed everything away, the wet t-shirt I had just used as a towel being thrown in too as there was no need to wait for it to dry.

The tent was the last thing to go away and as I took the pegs out, I realised just how windy it was. I thought that it was a bit of a nightmare but that I just had to scoot on and hope it wasn't a headwind the whole way. I had been lucky with the weather so far, but it seemed horribly unfair that it should be so difficult on the last real day of distance. I just hoped that it would ease off as the morning went on, lifted my pack on to the scooter for the last time and pushed off out of the campsite.

I had scooted about ten miles before I rang Jon in tears. It was just so hard. The rain was cold and stinging my cheeks as the wind drove it constantly in to my face. Every now and a gust would catch my pack and force me out into the road.

"Jon, I don't think I can make it," I sobbed down the phone.

He just laughed and said, "Of course you can. It's going to be hard, no doubt, but you've already come so far. You can't possibly stop now."

I snivelled and muttered a few things about how he didn't know anything because he wasn't here, but deep down I knew he was right. There was nothing for it but to keep pressing as hard as I could towards my final destination on this leg, St Just. I said goodbye to

Jon and wandered across the road to a post office. I picked up a nutritious snack of a freshly baked jumbo sausage roll and a bottle of Lucozade, and sheltered behind a wall outside to eat it. This in itself was a bit of a pain, with gusts coming over the wall and swiping precious bits of pastry off into the air, but on the whole, it made me feel a bit better. I just had to keep repeating to myself that this was the last day. I now had less than twenty five miles to go and then I would never have to ride this scooter again.

I loved the scooter at the start and looking back I would say I love it now, but then and there, in my darkest moment, the scooter and I were not friends. Not even nearly friends. And at times during that final day I have to confess that I thought about throwing it in the sea and getting on a bus.

Following the sausage roll incident, things did actually start to get better. My route was descending to sea level and every now and then I would get a few hundred metres of shelter from tall hedges on the side of the road.

I excitedly whooped as St Michael's Mount came into view. It finally felt like I was nearly there. I now had to choose between following roads around the bay to Penzance or taking the coast path. The coast path had the perks of being shorter and flatter, but the downside of gale force gusts bringing spray in from the sea. The road was the sensible option. More sheltered, not too much longer and with no serious hills.

I stood in the full force of the wind, still being blinded by the cold rain, trying to think it through. The road was the only option really, yet looking at the waves racing in, hitting the rocks and jumping over the path I couldn't bring myself to take the sensible option. I made sure all my zips were done up tight and set off down the coast path, knowing that I would probably regret this decision, but equally knowing I couldn't forgive myself for not giving it a go.

A short while later I reached Penzance, soaked to the bone and desperate for a place to sit down and get a hot meal. I found both of these things in a small deli by the harbour and set about de-layering, apologising for my wetness as I did so. I had a hot lunch and a huge hot chocolate whilst sulking and looked at the last seven miles or so I had to cover on the map. I had a long hill to climb before the road flattened out and wound across to St Just.

I packed up once more, put on my soggy waterproofs and stepped outside for the final push. The first few miles were slow as expected, but I was grateful that the hill I was climbing sheltered me from the wind that I had been battling all day. As I reached the top and started to really close in on the finish line, I was delighted to find that my slight change in direction meant that at times the wind was battering me from behind and pushing me long at incredible speeds. This was good news because the light was rapidly fading and, though I had strapped a flashing camping light to my back so that vehicles could see me, I had no head torch and so would not be able to see where I was going if it were to get much darker.

A couple of hours later the lights of St Just came into view and a terrific relief fell over me. I cruised into town to find my Airbnb.

After eight long days of scooting I had successfully covered the 230 miles between Chepstow and St Just. Two seemingly unrelated towns that some people have never even heard of. But to me this was huge. I had just completed stage nine of my journey from Inverness, and all that lay between me and the finish was seven miles of dog walking along the coast.

I smiled. All that remained for me that day was to have a long, hot shower and a cold Cornish beer.

Instagram: @rooneysophie

Facebook: thesophierooney

DARWIN TO DURBAN: 10,000 KMS

Chapter 44

Under an Open Sail

By Josiah Skeats

The day I cycled into Sydney was one of the happiest moments of my life.

The next day, I slid into a slump.

Reaching Sydney was the culmination of three years of pedalling my bike around the world and two years of dreaming before that. A significant chunk of time had been devoted to a single purpose. But now it was over.

Post-expedition blues are well documented, and six months later, I was still battling them. I had stayed in Australia, working as a labourer and saving money, but for what I wasn't sure. I hadn't found purpose again. I seemed to be living in the shadow of my bike trip, and so I considered cycling further. But that was too easy an option. It wouldn't stretch my comfort zone like it once had because physically and mentally I was strong enough to ride anywhere in the world I wanted. If I tried to pedal from these problems, I'd be circling the globe forever.

Solutions can come from unexpected places. Mine came in an email from a stranger named Wyn. It was an invitation to help sail his yacht from Australia to South Africa. I had sailed once, several years before. It had been a pleasant afternoon off the Kentish coast that had left me seasick, frightened and swearing I'd never sail again. Now, bolstered by cycling success or just desperate for change, this invitation seemed to offer something I needed and I didn't hesitate to confirm my place aboard *Leia B*.

Friends said it was crazy, or a death wish, or that I should learn to sail first, but I remembered similar responses when I had left to cycle, and once again their words did little to arouse doubts. My enthusiasm was unwavering; I had found purpose again.

I stood outside Darwin Sailing Club inhaling the salty air with a blend of expectation and satisfaction. Children were learning to sail in small dinghies and a motorboat scooted between them as they capsized. Further out, thirty yachts were anchored, bobbing atop the sapphire water that rolled up and down. It appeared the ocean was breathing. One of those was my boat, destined for Africa.

A man asked if I was going sailing. I told him I was. He looked to the horizon and watched a flag flap in the wind. "You've got a great day for it," he smiled, before returning to his work.

I had only seen Wyn from the tiny photo beside his emails, but I recognised him instantly. Khaki shorts. Wide-brimmed hat. Leathery and weathered skin. Enormous smile. He strode towards me looking every bit like a modern-day adventurer, and younger than his sixty-three years. His first two attempts to sail around the world had ended in failure. He had started this third attempt from Cape Town two years before, so the Indian Ocean was the final hurdle to success.

The other member of the team was Anthony, a twenty-eight-year-old South African who had spent his life on boats. He arrived last and had put a beer in our hands and a smile on our faces within minutes. I would soon learn this was typical. He was generous, didn't take life too seriously, and had a good sense of humour - a valuable addition to the team.

I liked my crewmates instantly, which was a relief because the furthest I could escape them over the following months was eleven metres, the modest length of *Leia B*. Living and working in such confines would demand strong teamwork, and I relished this new challenge.

Years of adventure have taught me to fall asleep anywhere, however on that first night I was too excited by my novel surroundings. A rope clapped against the mast and water lapped against my cabin. I was intrigued by how thin the walls were, and placed a hand against their smooth surface. As the boat rocked me to sleep, my final view was to stars that appeared to rain down through the open hatch above my bed.

A weather window had been forecast several days ahead, but there was a frenzy of work and final checks to do before we could leave. A month's food was bought and the nine hundred-litre water tanks filled. We would be rationed to five litres per day per person, with an extra five for the cook. While Ant and I had been scrubbing and cleaning, Wyn was ensuring the technical things were in order. These were anxious moments; a problem here could delay us by weeks or months.

Wyn's final check involved scrambling to the top of the mast. He looked relaxed when he descended, "Well, everything's okay up there. Nothing can stop us leaving now," he beamed. Five minutes later, we cast off the bowlines and slipped away.

Setting sail that first time was like the moment a rollercoaster begins. You've strapped in and relinquished all control. No matter how frightening the next minutes are, you've just got to sit and endure it. Well, I had just surrendered control for several months, right down to the waiver I'd signed accepting the risk of piracy, freak weather, boat breakages and various other terrifying scenarios. If I hated sailing as I had that first time, or suffered seasickness, or disliked my crewmates, I would be hundreds (maybe thousands) of kilometres from help. I hoped Wyn knew what he was doing.

The safety of land shrank behind us, and we were swallowed into the empty horizon ahead. The grey smudge of Darwin vanished, replaced by a warm halo of light where it had once been. This jump from my comfort zone aroused familiar pangs of excitement, made my heart beat stronger and my eyes shine brighter.

During those first days I observed my new surroundings with the fresh eyes of a child. Everything awoke a giddying sense of wonder which seemed to amuse the hardened sailors of Ant and Wyn. While they sat inside reading books, watching films or working, I was glued to the helm's chair watching a view more addictive than any film I've seen or book I've read.

I saw a pod of dolphins flying through the clear window of water just beyond our boat. They chased each other, whirling and twirling, and unleashing geysers of water that erupted from their blowholes with a noisy hiss. "Did we provide some shelter and protection?" I asked Wyn, "or did we make their swimming easier?"

"I'm more spiritual than that," he replied with a wry smile. "I think they just came to say hello."

I watched a feeding frenzy; a school of tuna attacked from below, a ravenous flock of birds dived from above, and the fishy prey leapt in blind panic. We sailed through the middle of this captivating carnage as a thousand tiny battles for life and death unfolded around us.

While brushing my teeth one night, a flying fish crashed into my head.

In those early days, everything felt new and exciting. I was surprised every time I looked up from my book and there was still nothing to see. I felt imprisoned aboard *Leia B*, but my confinement was voluntary and there was nowhere else I'd have rather been. Even eating fresh fish for lunch and dinner was unique and hadn't yet become a daily tribulation. I almost convinced myself it would be easy sailing right to South Africa.

Wyn proved a patient instructor, and soon, I had learned my *ports* from my *starboards*, my *halyards* from my *topping lifts*, and my *tacks* from my *jibes*. I could tie a bowline knot in the dark and manage the lonely nightshifts without waking Wyn each time the wind changed direction or cargo ships seemed bound straight for us. Perhaps the greatest skill I learned, however, was to cook curry – fish, of course - tilting the pan over the flame to the rhythms of the sea while scooping up potatoes that had rolled onto the floor, slicing vegetables and holding on for balance.

One morning, a wall of grey storm advanced towards us. "This is going to eat us," Wyn said. There was no exaggeration or melodrama in his voice. Half an hour of stillness followed where I naively hoped we might evade nature's wrath, but this was the calm before the storm.

Finally, a huge wave slammed sideways through the boat and announced that the storm had arrived. It flung the cupboard doors open and the three of us flailed for something to hold onto. Wyn said the last thing in the world I wanted to hear, "I thought that one was going to tip us." We hadn't seen another boat in five days. We were over a thousand kilometres from land. We were alone.

Terrified and helpless, I retreated to my cabin, where the thin walls exploded with cannon fire as each wave crashed against us. The view from my side window seesawed between sky and sea. The hatch above my head, the one I liked to gaze at the stars and moon through... now I wondered how I would escape through it in the disorientating chaos if the boat capsized. How quickly would it fill with water?

My cabin felt claustrophobic, like a coffin. I stuffed my laptop, phone and hard drive into a waterproof bag and sat beside the emergency life raft with the same expectance you might wait for a bus. I was waiting for the inevitable wave that would sink us. Wind-whipped spray bit into my face, and the ocean's anger horrified and impressed me in equal measure. Each wave scooped us skyward, and for a second, I looked across an uneven desert of dunes that stretched to a distant vanishing point. Our speed doubled as we surfed down the wave. There was a deafening screech as the auto-pilot battled to maintain a straight course, resulting in giant, heart-stopping 'S' turns. Then, as we sunk into a trough, I craned my neck to observe a towering mountain landscape, snowy crests atop each wave, that rivalled the mightiest Himalayan peaks. This entire panorama was endlessly shifting, crashing and falling.

It felt miraculous when, after several hours, the storm began to wane. Above the creaking and roaring and noisy staccato of ropes slapping the mast, arose the soft melody of Wyn's accordion. Normally, his jaunty tunes transported me to a Parisian café on a spring afternoon or a mariner's bar where you might sing sea shanties, but now it felt like the scene from *Titanic* where the band continues playing even as the ocean swirls around their feet.

Ant came outside, beaming "Ha! Your face was amazing! You were so scared!" and soon we were both laughing and retelling our accounts of the storm with dramatic re-enactments. We watched the waves march to the horizon. It would still be eight days until any land appeared there. I had renewed respect for the power of the ocean, a deepened sense of comradeship, and I realised the boat felt like home. I chuckled when I eventually recognised the song Wyn was playing; *Somewhere beyond the sea.*

Laughter was a common sound echoing through *Leia B*. Normally it belonged to Ant and I as we fooled around like inseparable brothers. Our daily work was accompanied by karaoke singing and frequent dance breaks. He possessed remarkable patience when it came to hiding somewhere and jumping out on me, which I repaid by climbing through his hatch and locking him from his room or teasing him for running out of cigarettes. I think we both derived an evil pleasure from waking the other for their 1am night-shift; the more peacefully they were sleeping, the better!

If I viewed Ant like a brother, then I saw Wyn as a teacher, and his lessons encompassed far more than simply sailing. Morning coffee was always a discussion, ranging from topics of love to money to purpose to friendships. He shared stories from two years of sailing, listened to my stories of cycling around the world, and I got the impression he saw part of himself in me. For my part, I couldn't have wished for two better friends to share this trip with. I did detect occasional tension between the other two who couldn't have been more different in mind-set, but I hoped this wouldn't cause problems further on.

It was fortunate I had made these friendships for there was no escaping each other. One morning, I emerged from the toilet. "What have you been eating?" Ant exclaimed while feigning disgust. I thought he was joking, until moments later when Wyn asked if I was feeling unwell.

"No, why?" I replied.

"Well... you know, a boat is a small place... the smell..." he stammered, to my embarrassment.

The only time I spent alone was on the night watch while the others slept. These were magical moments, spent watching the boat cruise through a blanket of darkness and never deviating from its westward course. I found my awareness heightened by responsibility and loss of sight, so I would notice changes in the sound of the flapping sails or to the direction from which the wind stroked my face. With no light pollution for hundreds of kilometres, starlight sprinkled across the landscape and it was a rare night when I didn't spot a shooting star. Even more impressive than the stars was the phosphorescence in the water. Our wake sparkled like the embers of a campfire scattered in the breeze. I dipped my hand into the warm water and was hypnotised as it appeared to be dusted with glitter. I watched night soften through various shades of colour into a new dawn, eventually climaxing in a fiery sunrise that heralded the end of my shift.

As we approached Cocos Keeling, roughly a third of the way, we were eager to leave the boat. Ant was drooling at the prospect of a cold beer, Wyn had compiled a list of repairs and I couldn't wait for the ground to be stable beneath my feet. I struggled to focus on anything except checking the horizon for that first reassuring glimpse of land. An increasing number of birds suggested we must be getting close. When it eventually did appear, I was afraid to blink in case it vanished.

I was sceptical those postcard-perfect tropical islands existed, assuming every photo had a tacky resort and a dozen hungover tourists hidden just outside the frame, but Cocos Keeling proved me wrong. It is three thousand kilometres from Australia, measures just thirteen square-kilometres and only six hundred residents call it home. They live largely undisturbed by the rest of the world.

I had imagined sailing to be quiet, like soaring on the breath of the wind, but the sails flap, the ropes creak, the winds whoosh and the water roars against the hull and blasts against the sides. These noises are incessant and become background noise. The first thing I noticed as we dropped anchor was an overwhelming stillness. If we heard any water at all, it was the peaceful whirrs of water lapping against the side like a trickling stream. I felt my breathing slow down and begin to relax.

Upon arrival, a welcoming party of five black-tipped reef sharks began circling our boat. For a week they never left us, daring to venture closer to investigate our thrashing saucepan and collect food scraps as we washed up. Ant and I began each day swimming alongside them. At first, we pointed out interesting sights so neither missed anything, but we soon gave up as there was too much to see. Sea cucumbers sprawled on the sea-floor, graceful turtles soared oblivious to our presence and giant clams the size of dinner plates clapped shut as we drifted above them. Some fish rested in eddies behind colourful corals while others battled against the current and gulped morsels of food that it carried. A noisy chatter of fish nibbling chunks of coral provided a constant soundtrack to this underwater metropolis.

I had lost count of how many days it was since we had last touched solid ground, so we swam ashore and collapsed on the scorched sand in a state of complete contentment. Palm trees fanned above us like green fireworks and a treasure of fallen coconuts had collected around their base. We hacked them open and let fresh milk dribble between our lips, barely finishing one before cracking open the next. A local couple had been spearfishing, and they offered a piece of the fish to me, still in the banana leaf it had been barbecued in. The white flesh melted on my tongue. The couple had moved here a year ago, and she was one of the island's two doctors. I asked if they were going to stay, which made them both giggle and reply, "Why would we ever want to leave?"

We were required to register at the police station. It was unlocked but empty, so we waited in the tiny office, which had a single desk, a laptop left open and papers strewn across the desk. I wondered what type of crime, if any, existed here. I flicked through a few issues of 'The Atoll', the island's monthly newspaper which more closely resembled a school newsletter, congratulating the island's sports teams on recent victories, showing photos from the end of Ramadan 'Hari Raya' celebration and advertising a Beach BBQ. There were a few jokes, inspirational quotes and healthy living tips which imparted wisdom such as 'stop smoking'. It was a delightful read, bringing only good news. Perhaps there was only ever good news to share in Cocos Keeling.

The police woman arrived in a golf cart, signed us into immigration, and advised us to buy food now because the plane had just arrived and we might still find fresh food.

After a relaxing five days, I was surprised how normal it felt to hoist the sails and glide from heavenly Cocos Keeling, as though I had been doing it my whole life. The trepidation I had felt in Darwin was still there, it still felt counter-intuitive to leave land, but this was masked beneath the thrilling curiosity of what might be discovered ahead.

As we sailed through the shallow atoll, Ant and I threw a rope off the back of the boat, jumped in donning a mask and snorkel, and clasped the rope. Though the sandy seabed was twenty metres below, I saw it through the glassy water with a clarity so startling I could have been on land. I suffered vertigo wondering why I wasn't falling, then realised it was because I was flying. By contorting my body I could shift the water pressure and control the flight, banking left, right, and dipping deeper into the water. I had joked we were shark fishing, but this became less funny when I spotted a shark gliding nearby and swallowed a lungful of saltwater in panic.

Land dropped from the horizon behind us again, throwing us back into our own bubble. My mind travelled across the ocean to revisit bustling, full-of-life cities that had assumed a dreamlike quality. We looked forward to receiving a weather forecast and email through the satellite phone every few days for this was our only contact with the outside world. Sometimes a cargo ship appeared on the horizon. We often tried to communicate through the radio but the antennae had snapped in the storm and the only response was a lonely radio crackle. Though we couldn't speak to them, it was comforting to know they were out here and I felt a close bond with them.

Days began to merge into each other as I settled into a routine. The wind remained constant and we seldom had to touch the sails, so while there was general housekeeping work to complete, a bigger challenge was to stay occupied. This meditative period offered an opportunity for reflection, and at last, I began to process the cycling trip. It was a revelation that the key elements of the cycling trip – discovery, unpredictability, physical and mental challenge, purpose, and meaningful interactions with people – were also being fulfilled by the sailing trip. Perhaps the cycling trip was merely a chapter in a long and unfinished book, and I looked forward to reading further to find what came next.

The vast landscape encouraged these deep thoughts, however despite its apparent emptiness, when you looked closer, the Indian Ocean was ever-changing. The water was a giant mirror that recorded intricate details of the sky. On a cloudy day it appeared we were grinding across a slab of slate, but on a sunny day I was blinded by a dazzling reflection and intrigued by shafts of light sinking through the azure water. Sunrise and sunset were my favourite times as it became impossible to tell whether it was the sea mirroring the sky or the other way around; regardless, it looked like someone had cracked an egg-yolk into both. There were days when the only disturbance in the water was our furrowed wake ploughed through the middle of it and these ripples extended forever. There were days when uniform waves rolled towards us with even gaps between them, and others where tumultuous waters seemed to grow and shrink according to their own whimsy, leaping up like a drop of water on a beaten drum.

Over time cracks had begun to appear in the friendships as our inescapable confines taught us each other's frustrating habits and then squeezed us together. These conflicts were often trivial and short-lived; one morning I was aggrieved to realise Ant had prepared muesli three days in a row, while I had been forced to cook the time-consuming alternative of porridge. Tensions between Wyn and Ant, on the other hand, were increasingly problematic as it became evident they were very different people. While both were accomplished sailors, their styles and mind-sets were contrasting, and a middle ground became harder to find. There were no arguments or explicit frustrations – sailing required too much cooperation for that - but the laughter, music and conversation that had previously echoed through the cabins was lost.

This strain was exacerbated by several days of no wind. Progress dragged to a halt, and with no breeze the tropical temperatures grew stifling. The sea was so flat we appeared to be sat on a smooth tablecloth stretched across an impossibly vast table. We didn't bother to raise the sails and the respite of land got no closer. *Leia B*'s imprisonment became unbearable.

Craving freedom, I jumped into the ocean and swam towards the featureless horizon. In that barren and unforgiving environment, the boat is your tether to survival; it was unnerving to ditch that connection, but also exhilarating to escape its grasp for a few moments. When I turned around to swim back, the boat was exactly where I had left it, a pathetic sight swallowed by hundreds of miles of nothingness.

At last, a puff of air returned and we slipped towards the strange sight of land that shattered the horizon. Mauritius should have been a beautiful sight yet it also brought disappointment. I don't know whether Ant had volunteered to leave, or Wyn forced him off, but the outcome was the same. Wyn and I would embark on the final stretch to South Africa alone.

True to form, Ant insisted on buying a final beer before he left. He joked I should switch boats, for there was another headed to South Africa, captained by an ancient American sailor called Jim, who was completely deaf.

"Jim! Jim! There's a squall" I said.

"What! Your name's Paul?" Ant quickly finished my sentence, imitating the deaf sailor, and we erupted into hysterics. I would miss him. We embraced, I watched his taxi fade into the chaotic traffic and then I turned back towards the hushed marina.

The Indian Ocean had a climactic conclusion in store and provided a final test to ensure I earned the right to call myself an ocean sailor and Wyn a circumnavigator. The strength of our partnership and all my newly acquired sailing skills would be needed in order to pass. A frightening weather forecast had chimed onto the satellite phone, warning that hurricane winds would arrive one day before we were scheduled to arrive in Durban. Wyn adjusted the route to include a detour that would add three days but avoid the worst of the weather.

The wind arrived with gusto, as if making up for lost time. Our overpowered sails had to be lowered, so we scrambled onto the roof amidst a stinging rain that thrashed from the darkness. The boat bucked like a rodeo bull lurching into the trough of every wave. Water spilled over the bow, washing across the deck and around my knees. Several times, the force of it nearly swept me from my feet as the sea fought to pull me to her depths. Wyn and I were metres apart but screamed instructions at each other, trying to be heard over the cries of the ocean. Conditions were every bit as ferocious as the storm that had terrified me weeks before, but this time exhilaration and adrenaline surged through me. I trusted the boat and I trusted our teamwork. I felt alive.

As the winds abated, we studied the devastation around us and realised the ordeal wasn't over yet. We had a torn sail, a snapped rope, a broken rudder shaft, two overheated engines, flat batteries and exhausted crew. The broken rudder shaft was the most severe problem, because we had lost steering control.

While Wyn began building a makeshift rudder, I hand-steered and altered the sails. We worked tirelessly through the night and all the next day, until our new contraption was complete. It was the Frankenstein of rudders, bodged together from random blocks of wood, lengths of chain cut from the anchor, and a plastic chopping board, but it worked. We high-fived, laughed and cheered like only crazed men lost at sea can. We were back on track, and only a few days from South Africa.

As we limped towards Durban, Durban Sea Rescue had heard of our plight and warned us of large waves at the mouth of the harbour. They begged Wyn to let them tow us in, but Wyn, who stood on the verge of completing his circumnavigation, remained steadfast and rejected this offer. I was proud of this decision after we had come so far. We agreed to radio Sea Rescue every hour and they would remain on standby until we arrived.

I watched the sun dip into the Indian Ocean for the last time. It was as mesmerising as the seventy-one sunsets and sunrises before it.

Africa was only a hundred kilometres beyond that pastel-coloured panorama, but it wasn't visible yet. It could have been Australia a hundred kilometres away instead, and I would still have had no idea. It confused me; how could there be so much change but also so little?

First came the halo of light, so faint we strained to see whether it was land or the dying remnants of daylight. Then it was unmistakable; manmade lights were strung along the land like a pearl necklace hung around a jagged and moonlit silhouette of mountains. As we edged closer, things shifted into focus and those pinpricks of light, which appeared like the starry skies of my night shifts, transformed into skyscrapers and cars and a World Cup football stadium. These were my first intoxicating glimpses of Africa.

Durban is South Africa's busiest port. There was a constant stream of cargo ships that dwarfed us as they glided in and out of the harbour. A chatter of thick South African accents erupted from our radio, seeking to coordinate this frenzied traffic. We zigzagged across the channel, dodging larger boats and creeping towards the blinking green and red lights that marked the harbour entrance.

Volunteers from Durban Sea Rescue stood on the harbour walls, clapping and waving. Their boat was still lowered into the water ready to rescue us, but that was no longer necessary. I stood on the roof, fist-pumping the sky, singing and dancing with appropriate music blasting through my headphones. "*I bless the rains down in AFRICAAAA...*"

I was in disbelief we had made it. The spectacle caused bewildered fishermen to gaze up from their rods. We moored in the harbour and let the world quieten around us. I climbed into bed and stared at the stars through my hatch for a final time. There was something comforting about their constancy.

It was Sunday, the immigration and customs offices were closed and we were supposed to stay on the boat until they opened the following morning, but neither of us ever contemplated this. We leapt from *Leia B*, felt the reassurance of land beneath us and slipped into a café amidst a sea of lazy Sunday morning crowds. No-one took any notice of us, and I liked that. This had been a personal journey.

Wyn and I sipped our coffees in silence, no more lessons or stories to share. I gazed east towards Australia. The sun burned a streak of silver through the ocean and a gilded yacht with puffed out sails headed towards it.

The day I sailed into Durban was one of the happiest moments of my life. I didn't slump the next day. I understood that my life was a long and unfinished book, and the next chapter was just another 'Yes' away.

Website: **josiahskeats.com**

Facebook: **josiahskeats**

Instagram: **@josiahskeats**

Chapter 45

I'm Not a Morning Person but...

By Amelia Jane Thorogood

Flapping my arms in a most inelegant way, I looked across at the man who, in four months, was going to be my husband and asked with genuine concern, "How are we going to get out of here?"

Looking down at his rapidly disappearing feet, he laughed as he replied, 'I've no idea, I'm still trying to work out how we got here!'

'Here' was a very muddy and very wet field in Texas. We were just outside Amarillo, and before you ask yes, we did 'ask' someone if this was the way to Amarillo. Turns out, that joke is only funny in the UK!

We were eight days into our month-long road trip from Chicago to San Francisco. During our thousand miles on the road, we had already 'survived' the terror of joining the interstate leaving Chicago, a massive storm in Kansas with 'Danger to Life' warnings and had a near-miss with some very dodgy characters in a back street in St Louis.

We were now in a field to see one of the must-visit attractions of Route 66 - the Cadillac Ranch. An installation of ten Cadillac cars buried nose down in the earth. The Texas rain had been unusually heavy, and the vehicles now resembled an isolated archipelago of spray-painted islands.

"I don't think I can move."

"Stand still, stop splashing," he said, grabbing my backpack as I lost my footing. I think he was trying to stabilise me... it didn't. We both lost our balance and fell face down into the Texas mud.

However, this isn't a story about our road trip; it could be because it was such an incredible once in a lifetime adventure. This is the story of how I changed every aspect of my life to enable me to be able to live my best life and go on the trip. I did it by doing something very, very simple - choosing to get up early.

I need to go back in time a little for this to make sense... For most of my life, I have looked like someone who reasonably had 'it' together. I had a successful and stressful job as a middle leader in a secondary school. I had travelled a bit, had a few relationships and was doing a reasonably good job of appearing to be a well-rounded, useful contributor to society. I think, like a lot of people, I probably moved between about four and six on an entirely unscientific and totally made up by me happiness scale.

I was permanently exhausted and never felt on top of my work. My days were a fury of 'busy'. I was regularly late and spent more time on Facebook than I did face to face with my friends. I counted the hours in the school day, how many days until the end of the term, how many days holiday I had left - each external factor would influence the type of day I was having.

I made grand plans for adventures but somehow found excuses not to carry my ideas through. I wanted to lose weight. I would eat healthily and then have no willpower when confronted with the smell of pizza from the school canteen. I wanted to read more but lost hours of my day to social media or Netflix. This was the approach to my life for many years, a few brief moments of brilliance interspersed with a lot of getting in my own way. I knew I was capable of so much more if only I could get myself together.

October, two years ago, I had a nasty dose of flu and spent several nights awake and uncomfortable. There isn't a great deal to do at three in the morning, and I was feeling especially pathetic and sorry for myself. After establishing I wasn't likely actually to die from my symptoms, and I didn't have the first case of the plague in four hundred years, I began to think about all that was 'wrong' in my life. No one else was awake so I asked Google.

Google didn't tell me what was wrong. It's a computer programme, not a therapist! But Google did tell me that I needed routine and structure and commitment if I wanted to fulfil my potential.

I read stories about athletes, people who had set up businesses, done fantastic charity work and all manner of other beautiful things that set them apart from the ordinary. What they all seemed to have in common was not so much what they had done to be successful, but what they did every morning to set themselves up to be successful. Great mornings make great days, and great days lead to great lives.

By 7am I had a really, really long list of things I could do to live a better life. I was going to read classic works of literature and all the self-help books, start running, save pandas and do twenty-seven other incredible things before breakfast. Despite being still unable to breathe, I felt more energised and focussed than I had in a long time.

"Everything is going to be brilliant," I said excitedly after sharing the blueprint for my soon to be wonderful life with my partner over breakfast a few hours later. My bubble was somewhat burst when he very practically pointed out that I would need at least seven hours a day to fit all these activities in and had I forgotten that I had to leave home at 7.30am and that I quite liked to sleep! (He is the sensible one in our relationship. I'm all ideas, glitter and rainbows - we achieve balance. It works.)

"Then I'll get up at four thirty to fit it all in!" was my rather stroppy reply.

In my defence, I was still not feeling very well, and I honestly hadn't really thought it through. The last time I had voluntarily seen such an early time was many years ago when a night out actually meant a night out. Not like now when I'm all party, party until 9.30pm then I like to be in bed with a mug of tea!

I recovered from my 'plague flu' and went back to work and routine, but the idea that there was more continued to swirl around and refused to go away. I realised that I had a choice. I could continue to make excuses for not having and doing the things I wanted. Or I could get on and do something about it. If I wanted to change, I was going to have to change. And if getting up early was the way to make the time, then that's what I needed to do.

The first morning was genuinely hideous. I felt as if I had been asleep for about four minutes when the alarm buzzed. I wanted to cry. Every part of my rational brain told me to go back to sleep, to stay where it was warm. It was pitch dark, the proper inky darkness you only get in the middle of the night. Only the cats, foxes and possibly criminals were awake.

It sounds so simple. All I had to do was get out of bed. I wonder how many hours of productivity and brilliant ideas are lost through snooze button syndrome. I counted backward.

Five... in a minute... Four... it's too cold ... Three... you are nuts... yes, but think how good you'll feel... Two... you can do this... One.... Duvet flung back, and I was on my feet. Hurrah! I was up.

Staggering to the bathroom, I figured cold water was needed to shock my body into being fully aware of what my brain was asking it to do. Face splashed and teeth cleaned. I was feeling a whole lot more with it, so I pulled on the closest thing I had to exercise clothes. I have spent a lifetime believing sport was for someone else and don't own anything lycra or sporty - baggy joggers and an old t-shirt would have to do. My trainers may possibly have dated from the time when Rick Astley was in the charts the first time round!

I had read that Barack Obama began his day with exercise and decided that if he could still run the whole of America afterwards, then I could probably make it to work. So, all fired up by my getting out of bed success, I tied my hair up, pushed the coffee table back, and connected my laptop to the TV. I had high hopes. I was going to have the grace of a ballerina, the waist of a supermodel and the arse of J Lo by breakfast. And arms - obviously I already had arms, but now they were going to be amazing and not do that saggy waving thing anymore.

I am a curvy girl. Despite the many opportunities of Zumba classes, park runs and aqua aerobics, I had totally failed to make any physical progress and have to confess to largely neglecting my body for most of its adult life. It is possible I had once, many years ago, broken into a run when we put my friend Helen into a wheelie bin on a night out, but I feel the alcohol may have made the running seem more dramatic than it was. I have never run for a bus.

I had chosen to start with an online dance workout. Until my mid-teens, before I got boobs and found boys, I had loved to dance. It never crossed my mind then whether I was any good; it was just for fun. I wasn't the sporty type. I rarely made any connection between my hockey stick and the ball and, despite Miss Griffiths constant bellowing of 'pass' in netball, I'm reasonably sure I never did. But dancing was something that I had loved.

Autumn, my impossibly cheerful American coach, encouraged me to step touch, giddy-up, and ride the horse. I tried to honky-tonk turn in time with Kenny and the rest of the ridiculously toned class, all wearing impossibly tiny shorts and cropped tops. As I stepped and hopped, every fibre of my body told me this was stupid. My things jiggled, my boobs bounced (I didn't know about sports bras then) and my bottom that I was supposed to be toning quaked to a rhythm entirely of its own.

My neglected body was protesting, my lungs screamed and I was fairly sure that I was doing my heart some severe damage - surely it shouldn't be able to beat that fast! I hit pause and took a massive puff of Ventolin. The timer said I had been exercising for seven and a half minutes. I felt as if I had been run over by a bus. This was not fun.

But being overweight and self-conscious isn't fun either. I had come to hate the way I looked. I dreaded invitations to weddings and parties because of the inevitable angst that would come about what to wear. I'm not very good at 'dressing up pretty.' It started when I was fourteen when my grandmother had made me a dress for a family wedding. When I came to try it on, I had obviously put on weight as it didn't fit. I remember just how embarrassed I felt. The too-tight dress became a metaphor for feeling trapped inside my own body.

Sitting on the coffee table looking at Autumn, frozen mid-leap on the screen, all abs and arms and everything I wanted, I knew that there wasn't any secret to this. No one was going to get fit for me. The only way was to press play and drag myself through the next twenty-seven minutes of the workout. No one could see me, and I was unlikely to die.

That first-morning workout was probably one of the hardest things I have said yes to, but the feeling afterwards was terrific. The endorphins (or dolphins, as I now know, I was mistakenly calling them for years) had a sort of reverse hangover effect. A giddy, light-headed euphoria that I hadn't experienced in years. I couldn't actually climb the stairs afterwards, but I already knew I would be pushing play again tomorrow.

The broader impact of my regular morning leaping wasn't immediately apparent. I initially justified eating takeaway pizzas or bowls of pasta that were bigger than my head by saying I'd done a really tough work out and I had earned it. After a while, it started to feel a bit daft to be undoing my morning work with my evening meal.

I have been a lifelong vegetarian with vegan tendencies, but this does not make you healthy. But gradually, I found I was almost unconsciously choosing more wholesome options. A salad instead of chips, saying no to pudding, carrying a water bottle and actually drinking from it during the day. As my body became physically stronger, my desire to fuel it more consciously became stronger.

I've never dieted, but the weight started to come off. Two years later, I fit into a pair of jeans smaller than I wore when I was a teenager and am over four stone lighter. I don't have the waist of a supermodel, but I don't really care! What I do have is a confidence that I've never had before and physical strength that makes me unafraid to take on a challenge. I hadn't realised how much my weight had held me back. It was always in the background of every decision I made. Thirteen mile sponsored night walk, no problem, and I raised over a thousand pounds for charity. Walk a thousand miles in a year - try and stop me. And this year, my husband is sharing his love of walking in the Lake District with me. I was always too afraid to say yes before.

There is a lovely feeling of being up before the rest of the world. The day stretches ahead in a way that makes me think of snow before it has been walked on, perfect and unspoiled. I felt I had earned a cup of tea after my exercise efforts, and I sat with a blanket over me, watching the sun begin to lighten the sky. I am fortunate that, although I live in an urban area, I have a vast south-facing garden. We've worked hard to create a pleasant view from our patio doors, and I often spend time sitting here and thinking. That is until I get distracted by my phone or my laptop.

I've never really tried to meditate before. I'd been to a few yoga classes where visualisation and meditation had been part of the final relaxation. I usually fell asleep. The internet is full of wisdom as to why morning meditation is beneficial, and my research had suggested that this was another critical secret to conquering my day and, in turn, my life. I also rather shallowly thought sitting on my blanket and thinking of cosmic things would somehow make me a cool and interesting person. Sitting in silence - how hard could it be?

I settled cross-legged in front of the rising sun and felt all new age and at one with the universe. I even lit some incense which didn't impress the dog. Breath in and a deep breath out. My leg hurts. Deep breathe in, slowly out. I really must book a haircut. Oh, and nails too, blue would be nice this time. Deep breathe in. Is today Tuesday? What's for supper tonight? Bugger forgot to breathe out.

I'd planned to do ten minutes of silence; I lasted about four. I thought about what had already happened, what was going to happen or what might happen. While the first morning was not very successful, it did make me appreciate that my brain needed a rest from being always overloaded with worry. I had never talked to anyone about being anxious all the time. Still, stopping and thinking about it, I could see that my ability to find something to stress constantly was not doing me or anyone around me any favours. By this time, the dog had joined me on my blanket and was fast asleep and utterly unconcerned about what his bonkers owner was doing - a perfect example of living in the moment.

I persevered, and it took me three to four weeks of practicing every day before I felt competent at being in silence. Now, my 'meditation' is one of my favourite parts of the day. It feels like I am giving myself a gift, a little mini holiday from the world. If I miss a day, my brain feels smaller. I've since found that there are lots of ways of meditating and several apps lead you through guided meditations.

The decisions and problems I have to deal with and face haven't gone away, but I am calmer and better equipped to handle them. Work, home-life and social situations have become more comfortable because of the 'space' my morning meditation creates in my head.

I have what the Japanese call 'tsundoku.' It is a condition that has led to books gathering in piles waiting to be read. I cannot resist buying books and bookshops, and libraries are my happy place. I am, however, not very good at reading books I buy. In the dark, pre-smartphone past, I read regularly. I once missed my stop on the tube on my way to college because I was lost in a Jane Austen novel.

Now, I know where someone I went to primary school with (and haven't seen for thirty years!) went on holiday but haven't a clue how any of the best-sellers or must-read books of the past few years ended. Too much social media makes me anxious, and not reading makes me sad.

As my mornings were a time for self-improvement, an obvious place to start was with the library of personal development books I had accumulated. I read 'Feel the Fear and Do It Anyway' on a train about twenty years ago; I arrived in Wigan, a different person to the one who had left Watford Junction three hours earlier, so I knew that this stuff could blow your mind. I'd just forgotten everything I have read.

I just needed to say yes to reading one book. My first challenge was deciding what to read, did I want to learn how to create miracles, what the secrets of super achievers were, how to rise strong or how to get things done. I wanted to know all the things! I settled on 'You are a Badass' mostly because I liked the title (and my exercise was working on my ass already!)

It promised to make me stop doubting my greatness and help me start living an awesome life. Yes, please!

I set a timer on my phone, put my headphones on, and started to read. Almost two years on, I haven't stopped. I have now read over twenty-five books in bite-sized mouthfuls of fifteen minutes every morning. I wouldn't say that every single one has been life-changing, but I have learned an enormous amount from my reading.

I began with personal development books and worked on understanding my own behaviour and why I reacted the way I did to things. I then looked at productivity and decluttering. I've had a brief foray into faith and different religions. I've read about how to manage relationships and took an idea from my reading into my classroom on the same day and had massive success in dealing with a challenging student. I did a little happy dance in my cupboard after that lesson!

I have given myself the gift of time to read. Some of the books I have read are like having a chat with a friend. I've found that whatever it is I am struggling with or want to improve, someone else has already worked on it and worked it out.

I have gone to a couple of events where the authors have been speaking. I've met some lovely people both in the flesh and online and was ridiculously excited to be seeing Marie Forelo author of 'Everything is Figureoutable' speak. While I fangirled most embarrassingly, I also realised that these writers are not so different from most of us - they are just super focussed, clear on what they want and then get on with it.

'If I want to live a life I've never lived, I have to do things I've never done.' I can't remember whose words they were but when I read that one cold January morning I knew that I didn't want to be 'just' a teacher for the rest of my life. I have never been a teacher who moans about how much work they do and how little they are paid. I come from a family of educators; I saw whole Sundays disappear as my mother marked endless French exam papers. I heard stories of how my grandfather, a headteacher in the sixties, broke his heart over the terrible parenting he had witnessed. I knew what I was getting into and have always prided myself on doing as good a job as possible, but I have realised it isn't all I want to do.

Reading made me want to write again. I started my first newspaper when I was nine. 'The Foghorn' covered the excitement of the local agricultural show, the escaped cows and the life and times of Beatrix Potter! I published two editions and had a readership of seven!

On my bookshelf, there is a blue box that hasn't been opened in years. The box contains the chronicles of my teenage life and makes for totally cringe-worthy reading. I've recorded how much I hated Mr. Rowlands for his excessive homework setting, how much I fancied Mark in my German class and how cross I was that my Mum wouldn't let me go to London (from North Wales) to see Prince in concert. In hindsight, she made the right decision in saying no, and there is no way I would let a teenage girl do what I was proposing! At the time, it felt as if my social world was over. Diary writing is now called 'journaling' and is the mainstay of many personal development programmes.

Way back in 1991, before mobiles, pre-internet and when editing still meant that things ended up on the cutting room floor, I set off to university to study Media and Communication. I had a vague idea of becoming a journalist. After getting a bit lost and side-tracked, my first article was published in January last year. Thirty years later!

Late-night marking and the rest of life had ensured that I thought I was too exhausted to write. I read an article in a health magazine that had said that if a goal or plan is written down, then there is a 42% greater chance that it will happen. I have no idea if this statistic is real or not, but it seemed worth a go. So, on a post-it note, I wrote 'write something and be published.'

I added writing to my morning schedule. I armed myself with a new fountain pen and an empty notebook. The blank page stared back at me. This was much harder than I remembered it being. I must feel less angst than I did as a teen. So, I wrote a to-do list. It was massive - and ranged from things like buy more tea bags and calling my mother, to taking a year off work and traveling the world without flying. Eeekkk! I wrote things on my list I had forgotten that I wanted to do. Visiting places, catching up with old friends, trying new recipes. Writing the list was so simple, but the possibilities it created were so exciting.

I started small and called my mother that evening and bought the tea bags! I arranged to meet an old friend at the weekend. We visited a gallery and had afternoon tea and wondered why it had taken us so long.

I'd written 'start ballet' again. There was a class literally down the road. I dug my old dance shoes and shuffled around at the back of the first class. My vague notion that somehow muscles memory would kick in was totally misguided - and apparently, you can get cramp in your stomach muscles! Who knew? But from my reading, I knew 'done was better than perfect,' and I've kept going.

I surprised myself by putting singing onto my list. Again, a quick search found a local community choir. I'm not amazing and will never be a soloist, but I am better than I ever thought I could be. The community choir led to auditioning for the London Show Choir, which has allowed me to be part of some incredible experiences. I've sung at Wembley, recorded at Abbey Road, performed with West End Stars, and found myself dancing the Time Warp (complete with lab coat and purple hair) on the South Bank cheering runners on at silly o'clock on a Sunday morning.

Making friends as an adult is hard. Being brave and saying yes to the things that I wrote on my list has led to meeting some incredible people who have enriched my life beyond measure. I met my husband at choir. So if you have tried dating sites without success, try singing instead!

Once I had written my 'to-do list' I needed to find something else to write each morning. By the end of the first week, I had written a poem, my first in many years. It was about my drive to work each day, the people I noticed and the routines they followed. I knew if I was late or early by the human landmarks I passed each day. I found online some prompt for daily creative writing and soon had a head full of 'imaginary' friends and scenarios.

I don't know why I forgot to write, but writing makes me happy. I feel like I am emerging from a very thick fog. I also found that lots of places will publish your work - admittedly for free, but it's a start. I had over twenty articles published for the National Student, and the day I received an email praising my writing from the editor felt like being awarded an A* in an exam. I will never not be excited to see my name in print!

Six months after first saying yes to getting up early, I used the skills, confidence and self-awareness I have gained to say yes to a massive change in my career. I resigned from my middle leader role and stepped away from the potential of promotion to be a part-time 'ordinary' teacher. I realised a considerable amount of my identity was caught up in my work and 'being Miss Taylor' as I was then. My morning work meant I dared to redefine myself and reconnect with my lost creativity. I've started a Masters in Creative Writing, set up a website and I'm also exploring a possible venture into life coaching.

Someone recently said to me that I looked ten years younger than when they met me five years ago! They asked me what was different; my reply was I'm happy. The truth is that if something is important enough, you will find a way to do it. If not, you will find an excuse. I've got rid of the excuses, and it began with that first early morning.

And finally, back to the Texas field and one of the best moments of our entire trip. Mud splattered in every imaginable place. We drew quite a crowd as people laughed and photographed us, and I didn't care. The trip was our pre-wedding honeymoon. To drive Route 66 had been on my original to-do list. So we did it. Sitting in the Texas mud with the man I had finally said yes to, I knew that not only had I fallen in love with him, but I had also finally fallen in love with myself. This was one of those magical moments that happen when you feel truly 'alive'.

Website: **ameliathorogood.com**

Chapter 46

When I Said Yes

By Samantha Watts

It's been a funny year. If you had told me that I would one day give up work altogether to homeschool one of my own children one to one, I would not have imagined that possible or even sensible. But that's what I did.

On January 16th, 2019, I took the plunge and withdrew my son, Arthur, from mainstream school. At the time I had no plan in place, nothing formal worked out and no idea how I was going to manage.

Saying yes to this was more like saying no. I said no to mainstream education, who singled him out, isolated him and made him feel less than the rest of his peers. I said no to whole days of him running round the school field in a state of massive anxiety because no proper safe space was given to him when he needed it. Most importantly, I said no to my son feeling humiliated. He was embarrassed and could not cope any more. Enough was enough.

There are many stand out moments of stressful situations at school that led to this decision. Arthur had moments where he just could not cope with the other kids and the expectations of mainstream school. There were times when Arthur did not understand personal space. On one occasion he had touched a child's teeth because he was trying to straighten them. Another child was bitten and he chased another child with a stick. I was in a terrible state sat at home wondering what he might do next. It just wasn't working at all.

When he told me in an incredibly mature way for his age (only five) that he could not take any more school because everyone stared at him and he could not cope with it, I was left with very little choice. If you can take your child's pain away, you do it, simple as that.

As a trained teacher, I had already offered help to the school and had him for afternoons in his first year. That had helped as it seemed he struggled mostly with afternoons then. However, this was something different altogether. This was just me and him. No work in his school bag for me to try. No teacher for me to work with. No collaboration or scheme of work to support me. Just me and him.

I was elated... and absolutely terrified. On the one hand, I felt like I had no choice, but on the other hand the thought of spending endless days with my chatty sparky boy was exciting.

*

At this point it feels relevant to explain what Arthur is now diagnosed with. His current formal diagnosis is Autism. It sounds like such a friendly and non-threatening word, so simple. Arthur's behaviour is so complex and almost impossible to manage sometimes that I am amazed one word is supposed to capture or explain it.

I feel terribly disloyal ever selling autism as a negative. I love my son, as I tell him, 'with everything' and I have had some amazing experiences with him this year. I feel as I write this that I want to be honest and explain how saying yes to spending twenty-four seven with Arthur has been one of the most intense experiences in my life. It has its ups and its downs, but let's just say, I have never been bored!

The first month went by in a blur of determination from me. It wasn't difficult at all! I was going to turn him into a genius. We were going to learn together and it was going to be a wholesome and fulfilling experience for us both. This we will class as the honeymoon period. Arthur was so pleased to not be going into school he would do as much work as I threw at him. WE WERE NEVER GOING TO WATCH TV... EVER!!!

I had friends round for coffee and proudly showed them his work; look how much he is doing with me and how much more than he was doing at school. I worked through several different work books at once, all whilst balancing being a breastfeeding mum to a one-year-old and taking care of my ten-year-old around school. At the time, I think I was in a blind panic about how much I had taken on and how much responsibility homeschooling came with. If in doubt, I will throw myself one thousand percent into something just so I can say it's not my fault it went wrong!

I took him swimming, roller skating, running, horse riding and anything I could. I even hired a private yoga teacher to come to the house. Looking back it was hysterical. She would try to show him the usual moves but called them something fun and child friendly. All Arthur would do is agree to try one if she tried one of his moves. Usually this involved both of us yapping and running round on our hands and knees pretending to be puppies. Me and a grown woman being puppies... the things you do.

Roller skating at a homeschool club took a turn for the worst when Arthur tried to convince a little girl (who was clearly at home for similar reasons to Arthur) that Plants Vs Zombies was better than My Little Pony. I had to drag him away while he shouted from the car, "It is better, I tell you!" Once he was strapped in, he calmly turned round and asked me if she could come round for a play date next week!

*

March was a huge turning point for us as a family, and things calmed and settled slightly afterwards.

Arthur had been increasingly moody during the day. He would complete work some days but others he would argue and be very tired. The school had previously suggested his diagnosis was PDA Autism which is a very oppositional diagnosis and relies heavily on choices being given for success in schooling and parenting. I was finding increasingly he would choose not to work or to do something different to what I had planned. I was exhausted from trying to constantly adapt to his moods.

Bedtime, which had always been hard work for us, became unmanageable. Arthur would, at five years old, be bouncing off the ceiling at 10pm at night, and he was keeping my other children awake when they were shattered.

The breakthrough came when we had a disastrous night. He started getting really agitated at about 5pm when his dad came home. I was struggling to manage his disregard for my instructions on playing nicely outside. His dad went outside and removed a stick that had become a weapon. Within minutes he had completely lost it. He was attacking his dad with everything he could lay his hands on. Literally whole toy boxes were thrown full pelt across the house.

We did our best to calm him down whilst sheltering the other children. It became apparent that this was not going to stop. Rather, he was building up to some scary actions. When he threatened to get knives out of my cutlery drawer, enough was enough.

First of all, I rang the doctor. In my head he needed a tranquilliser to help him and us regain control. The doctor told me to ring an ambulance. This was not the response I was expecting. We weren't ill or injured or bleeding. However the doctor advised the help we needed in terms of possible medication would need to be a hospital and it was not safe to drive Arthur whilst he was attacking us.

Reading this back now, I can hardly believe he was this bad. It is one of the saddest moments of my life. I could see Arthur wanted to stop but he couldn't. We needed help and fast before he really hurt us or himself.

The ambulance, after much umming and arrhing, came two hours later, and Arthur spent the night in A and E shouting full on abuse at anyone who went near him. He was in a desperate panic about what they were going to do to him, totally terrified about needles and doctors touching him. He even hates his blood pressure being taken, which they tried to do and failed in the ambulance. Arthur is a big boy for his age and very strong, and he will only do things when he is ready.

After twelve hours in hospital, we finally got melatonin which has and still does rescue us. He takes a dose every night and is usually asleep within the hour. Without this, his brain rattles around into a state of total agitation, and he gets more and more angry looking for someone to pick a fight with.

This gave us, and most importantly me, some respite. Before then I might be in his room for two hours rubbing his feet with lavender oil and stroking his head telling him stories. I'd have to ignore a toddler crying for her mummy every night and I'd tell my ten-year-old, "Sorry, I won't be long." Because it was always me that had to put Arthur to bed, the other two automatically wanted me too. Daddy was always left juggling them and waiting it out for me.

Getting the chance to have a break and a rest was amazing. I felt more clear headed then I had been in ages. Suddenly saying yes to homeschooling seemed to be a less impossible task.

The family started to construct a new bedtime routine, and things calmed down so much. I began to look for more outside activities as I realised we both needed to get out of the house as much as possible now the light was coming back.

Around this time I began to notice Arthur's obsessive tendencies. Depending on what he had seen on the TV or YouTube he would suddenly have a need to see everything he could about that thing. This began with the sea. If I ever see another jellyfish or octopus again as long as I live it will be too soon! We watched documentary after documentary on them to the point where I was dreaming about the sea and seeing it in my head walking round supermarkets.

We moved from that obsession to many others, including monsters of the deep that don't exist and are clearly faked photos. A lot of his obsessions revolve around his Xbox. He would stop friends or their mums in the street to tell them uninvited all about them in such massive detail they would be bewildered. I recognised that this need to download became his release.

He had, and still does, have a long love affair with Godzilla. He can tell you things about Godzilla which no one else would know. In the lounge, I have had to sit through many hours of it on YouTube, and my other two kids just leave the room if he switches it on now. They know he will be there for hours telling anyone everything he knows even if he has already told you all of it before.

In a way, the days with the obsessions were the good days; they were days when he could verbalise himself in a way. The days when he was, and still can be, a closed book are much, much worse. On March 11th, I wrote in my teaching diary, 'Arthur is very distressed and refusing to work. It has taken us an hour to do seven sums.' Those are the days when I feel a failure. Those are the days when I phone my husband at work and cry. Those are the days when I question if I can do it anymore. An event that felt like another turning point for me was an Aldi shop. As stated, Arthur has suspected ADHD. This looks like a lot of energy in very uncontrollable outbursts. In shops he will run off, sometimes as soon as we get in there. I have to keep his attention on me, ask him to go and find me things and keep asking him questions. On this particular day he had been allowed to buy a rolled up poster for his bedroom. He was walking along tapping people with it. He was not hitting people hard or hurting anyone, it was more of him being a nuisance than anything. I was trying my best to talk to him about it, and urging him to stop whilst trying to be calm. He was listening to me, but I suspect he could not really hear me as he has selective hearing.

I was just trying to steer him towards the till when an older woman pulled me over. She said, "Your son just hit me."

I was about to explain his situation to her as best I could when she said, "If he is autistic, he should wear a jumper or a hat or something to tell people."

I was about to apologise again when she said, "Or you could just online shop. That would be a lot less stressful for people like me."

I didn't know what to say. I felt my cheeks flushing with embarrassment... or was it anger? I considered apologising again... but walked away instead. I got three steps. I couldn't leave the conversation like that. I turned back to the woman and, through gritted teeth, said, "It's really hard being a parent to a child with special needs, especially when people like you are so ignorant!"

I got to the car and sat in the driver's seat trying not to cry. Arthur had missed most of the exchange but could see his mum was upset. Luckily for me, Facebook proved to be a supportive tool this time. I ranted a massive post on there. It was that or I went and slapped the woman across the chops. How dare she be so rude about someone who could not help it? Would she be like this if he was blind and his dog got under her feet? I felt anger for my son, but also a pride grew in me. We had survived what I felt was a serious act of discrimination and lived through it. The amount of people who told us to carry on and we were doing great gave me the strength to brush off the woman's comments and get on with my day.

*

I tried several attempts to 'socialise' Arthur with mixed results.

People/friends/health professionals all ask, "So, how do you socialise him?"

Yessssss, that is a good question!

Arthur thinks he likes other children. He likes the idea of other children and would play with a tiny toddler in the park if he is bored. However, this is always an anxiety inducing waiting game. When will he do something stupid and impulsive? Not if, when? Every social engagement feels doomed.

We agreed to a birthday party once. Against my better instincts, I took him. He ended up in a whipping frenzy with some glow sticks stuck together. He could not cope and was taken home in tears. When mixing with others, he becomes a boisterous, over-excited Labrador crossed with a mean dictator who has zero tolerance for people who don't follow orders.

Homeschooling has its ups and its downs.

Before homeschooling, I would spend six hours in absolute anxiety. Would I get a phone call whilst food shopping today to tell me he had spent over an hour running barefoot around the school field (true story)? Would I pick him up and have him run off at the school gate similar to a champagne cork being released, only to have him run into the road and bump into every single person on the pavement (every day)? Would I be told by parents that Arthur had done something to upset their child by crossing their personal boundaries? Yes, nearly every day.

So, although homeschooling has its ups and downs, they are ours. We are not answerable to anyone else. I don't have to apologise to anyone for anything. I have given the space back to my boy to make mistakes and noise and a ruckus if he needs to, and no one else is there to tell us this is not acceptable. Of course, I talk to him about appropriate behaviour when he is rude to me (all the time) because he finds book work really stressful and it creeps out of him without him even knowing it.

The intensity of homeschooling lessened when we got our allotment.

We had been using a friend's allotment on and off for a few weeks in the spring and found we were spending more time there than she was. I enquired about some of the unused ones at her site and was rewarded with a half allotment that clearly no one else wanted. It was so wild I stood on my first viewing wondering what could be living in it. The weeds were literally higher than me and looked like they'd been there forever. This was it. My friends and family thought we were mental!

My first thought was, 'How the hell do I get to the soil?'

The next allotment holder along helpfully advised to throw weed killer on the lot and cover it up for six months. No, no, no. That was against everything I stood for. I like nature! Why would I throw a ton of nasty chemicals on the land my children were going to be working with? And kill everything living in the space? No!

I encountered some funny looks off the elderly chaps on my allotment the first few weeks of visiting the allotment. Arthur was given (after some hesitation) some shears and cutting secateurs. I watched with trepidation as he hacked away with us at the weeds. After five concerted minutes of chopping back brambles, he disappeared into a thicket only to appear moments later with a ladybird balanced on his finger. He was stood so still staring intently at the little insects movements as it travelled across his hand. I knew from homeschool time how much he loved being outside, but this was different. He lost himself in each moment and spent most of his time looking for spiders and snails and slugs.

Slugs in particular deserve their own moment here. They have become a sensory experience for him. Despite being brought up to love all of God's creatures by two animal loving parents, Arthur seems to have a fascination for dismantling bugs and beasties. When I say dismantling, I mean pulling apart and fiddling with the insides even if this is stomach churning and slimy. He once carried a dismembered slug around a local park for two hours and named it 'Wet Wet'. The poor thing was not in great shape afterwards despite me pleading with him to put it down.

*

Another huge sensory input for Arthur is mud. I could talk about mud and how much he loves it but I think the best way to sum it up is to describe my favourite photo from October of last year. He is stood bare foot in the mud with his legs completely covered. We tried and failed to dig a nature pond at the allotment. The moulded plastic we put in to hold water just floated and refused to sit in the hole we had dug for it.

When I removed the plastic pond, I discovered that we had just dug a muddy hole that became fondly known as 'the swamp'. At first Arthur wore shoes which were ruined and then wellies which his autistic toes hated. Finally, when he took all footwear off and went barefoot, he got the sensation he had been craving all along. Even after I had sat all night with tweezers pulling thorns out of his feet, he still wanted shoes off. I would watch his face relax in the pleasure of the mud oozing over his skin. He even told me that mud is good for you, and he would rub it on cuts on his knees.

Passersby and dog walkers would make comments about my washing machine and my house began to resemble a dry swamp with drifts of mud collecting in corners. I would have to bring him home and put him in the bath every day, and would then I'd spend half an hour cleaning my bathroom after he had romped muddy water everywhere. But… it was all worth it. My boy was at peace in those muddy moments like an animal wallowing.

*

I began to rush through bookwork, desperate to get him down to the allotment where he would relax and not be angry all the time.

I tried to build (or at least planned to build) all sorts of fancy homeschool classroom equipment down there. In my head, this was the perfect place to sit and draw or maybe attempt some maths. However Arthur had different ideas. The allotment was his downtime. He would not be taking work there. There was mud and wild, and that was the way he liked it.

We had a very to-the-point conversation about it quite recently when I tried to get him to help me build a shelter to work in. He said, "Don't change a thing here, Mummy. It's perfect the way it is."

He doesn't want a sand pit because it would get muddy! Says he! I tried to fit a blackboard. "No Mummy. We don't need it." I did bring in a mud kitchen. I got away with this because he said, "Fine. It's for Ivy (his sister) who is two. But I am not using it!"

He is so set in his ways. Things have a very defined space and purpose, and he will not be persuaded away from his ideas. If he thinks you are trying to change his mind, he gets really agitated.

*

Sometimes if we are lucky we have a visitor to take there with us. Although as I am writing this now in February in the middle of one of the worst storms (Ciara) we have had in a while, no one wants to come and sit in our mud patch right now! Arthur does respond really well to adults. I think because they make allowances for his cantankerous ways and ignore his moods. He also talks really, really fast and is engaging if adults do respond to him. He has an endearing way of stopping suddenly in the middle of a conversation and stroking my hair, or if he knows them and they are female, stroking the adult's hair. He loves hair so much.

My brother's girlfriend came down a lot when we first got our allotment, and she would become his sounding post for all of his waffle about his computer games. It was like the allotment became his safe space to share all of his gaming knowledge. It was a release for him to tell someone how to defeat the Endor Dragons or which was the best Fortnite skin to wear.

It would also be a relief for me. Someone else to share his endless chatter with. If it's just us, he talks at me non-stop, which is literally exhausting. And besides, my brother's girlfriend does have amazing hair!

Spending time with your own child makes you really evaluate your own parenting but also yourself. I have spent some serious amounts of hours debating if I could be autistic and/or ADHD. And if I am, what does that mean for me? Do I need to work on anything with that knowledge? Does it answer any lingering questions for me about myself? I would say that after over a year of having to compromise and bend myself around someone else, I have come to the conclusion that having a diagnosis doesn't make a difference. I am still me just as Arthur is still my little boy.

I have been quite a perfectionist for most of my life, and I'm a qualified teacher trained to get the most out of eleven to fourteen-year-olds writing essays. But I have had to re-evaluate what I think is 'enough' and that has been one of my biggest challenges. Even when visitors who come to my house to see and assess Arthur have said he will have down days and days when he does not work. They told me to not fret and to do my best. I still have had a lot of panics.

The 'have we done enough today?' question haunts me long after we put the pens and books away. What if I had been more patient today? What if I had chosen different work to show him first? Should I have given him a different breakfast cereal or more water when he woke up? Being wholly responsible for someone's welfare and education twenty-four seven is not for the faint-hearted. Being a homeschooler to a child with difficulties has redefined my definition of perfect and my definition of what is acceptable. I feel that my job, which is to get the best out of my boy, is mixed in with protecting him and allowing him to grow. Does it make sense to spend all day lecturing him on things he is too stressed to listen to? Or is it better to just watch and listen and try to pick what he needs that day to be happy and try to meet those needs? Or is it a balance of the two? It's really hard to find that balance and even harder to explain to others how we got there.

*

If someone else is looking to homeschool their little one (or bigger one)... I would urge them to think it over very carefully. Have you got the energy to do it? Do you have some supportive and helpful relatives or friends who can relieve you every so often?

Homeschooling very different to parenting. It's impossible to not cross the two over, so the teaching changes your parenting too. Where does the parenting stop and the teaching begin?

And think about your other dependents; how will they feel about it? I have dealt with jealousy from the other two kids on a huge scale. This is something to factor in.

Lastly, factor in the effect on your relationship with your partner. They may not experience or understand the emotional drain that homeschooling is on you. If they do, they will send you off on spa days like mine does, but I think that is only because he works from home and witnesses my battles first hand.

Homeschooling Arthur is the most rewarding thing I have ever done, and if could I go back a year, I would choose it all over again. The only thing I would change is how hard I have been on myself. I would have not stressed so much about trying to achieve everything every day. I would have gone with the flow a lot more and just accepted the bad days and the good. I would also have had more days in green spaces to recharge for when bookwork seemed like a monster we had to tackle together.

But we fought those battles as a team and I am proud, so proud of us. We did it and we still do it, every single day.

Chapter 47

In the Footsteps of a Saint

By Morwhenna Woolcock

This was it. It was finally happening. I was about to take the first few steps (well, pedals in this case) following roughly in the footsteps of the 5th century Saint Morwenna. From the Brecon Beacons in Wales to Morwenstow in North Cornwall by bike, boat and foot. A journey of 190 miles over twenty-one days.

Me, an unfit forty-year-old stroke and mental health survivor, who'd never attempted a trip like this before. Could I really do this?

*

On the 17th August, 2011, I'd had an idea.

I'd been signed off work with severe depression and everything was crashing down around me. It felt as though my foundations had been knocked out by a wrecking ball, and my life had become a pile of rubble that I was buried beneath. I felt trapped. I couldn't function. I started to wonder who I was and how I'd get better.

During this turbulent time, I read an article explaining how our names can determine the kind of life we have. Intrigued, and rather bemused by this, I searched for more information about my name and what it meant. At first there wasn't much, but then, I discovered a saint. A Saint with my name (well almost as I've got an 'h' in mine) who had a church in Morwenstow on the rugged North Cornwall coast.

Intrigued, I drove down from Bristol, and when I arrived, stood quietly in the church gazing up at the rounded wooden roof beams that looked exactly like an upturned boat. Shafts of light shone through a stained-glass window creating dappled patterns on the flag stone floor.

Taking a step closer to the window, I studied the image of St. Morwenna. With a crown on her head, a model church in her hands and a faraway look in her eyes, she looked ethereal. Was this really what she was like?

I already knew she was the daughter of Brychan Brycheiniog, a Welsh 'King' who was a Celtic Spiritual Teacher. He'd lived in the Brecon Beacons and is said to have had twenty-four children, all of which became saints! St. Morwenna was born around 480AD and was the saint of reading and learning, which I liked the sound of. But how did she end up here? In Cornwall?

So many questions buzzed around my head; How would she have travelled? What would she have eaten? Then one really stood out. What would it be like to follow in her footsteps? A seed of an idea had been planted…

It wasn't until 2015, the year of being forty, that I finally said YES to this adventure. It's been one of the best things I've ever done.

This was going to be a big challenge. Along with my fragile mental health, I'd had a brain haemorrhage when I was twelve. Paralysed down my left-hand side, I'd relearnt how to walk. I have a condition called Drop Foot and have never really been much of a walker.

One thing would help though. In 2008, I was fitted with a walking implant, a STIMuSTEP. Embedded into the nerves that control the up and out movement of my foot, it works by sending an electrical current through a control box that sits on the skin, activating the muscles that don't work and lifting my foot, making walking easier. Even being bionic-ish, this trip was something I'd really have to train for.

I trained for nearly a year before I was fit enough to set off. I was ready. Or so I thought.

Bike – Brecon to Cardiff – 55 miles [Day 1]

It was at this moment that I realised I'd not done nearly enough cycling training. I'd cycled to the next village, once, which was about a three-mile round trip. I'd been focusing on the walking. Too late to worry about that now.

I glanced at my partner, Richard, who was on his bike next to me. He smiled. "Don't worry. You got this!" I didn't feel like I had 'this'!

We wound our way along the trail next to the Taff river and I thought, 'Hey, this isn't so bad. It's flat and pretty and nice to cycle on...'

As soon as I'd had that thought, the track ended. We were on the road. And there were hills. Lots of hills.

"My original idea of travelling by donkey wouldn't have been so crazy after all," I said through gritted teeth.

"Your bike is your modern-day version of a donkey. Pedal harder!"

When considering how St. Morwenna would have travelled, donkey had come up as a possible option. Well donkey or horse.

When I'd inquired about this at a donkey sanctuary, I was politely informed that I'd be a 'bit too heavy'. So, bike it was. I'm glad really, as bikes don't tend to have a mind of their own, need feeding, or produce lots of poo.

Coming off the road, we started to climb alongside a reservoir. "Why... is... it... so... tough?" I puffed.

"We're going uphill," said Richard over his shoulder. Why wasn't he as out of breath as me? Why wasn't he beetroot red with sweat exuding from every pour like I was? I bit back any retort that I had.

The track was covered in a mix of wood chip and rough stone, soft and difficult to get traction under our tyres. It was challenging. I took a tortoise approach and said to myself, "Just to that nettle. Just to that thistle."

At this slow pace, would we actually get to Cardiff before it got dark? We'd not packed any lights.

We kept going as the sunlight started to fade, and soon we were cycling by the light of the moon. Bats flitted and wheeled around us in the semi-darkness, and the only sound was the crunch of gravel under our wheels.

Riding through the streets of Cardiff at nearly midnight, we couldn't avoid stopping at a corner shop to buy some celebratory beers. They clinked joyfully in our back packs as we cycled thought the still, crisp night. In the early hours we finally made it to the Cardiff YHA, our bed for the night.

We'd done it. We'd completed the first stage of the journey.

Physically exhausted and a little bit tipsy, we collapsed into our bed, smiles spread over our faces.

Boat - Barry to Watchet - 13 Miles [Day 2]

Will it happen or won't it? That was the question on my mind.

Ping – an email. It was Adam the Harbour Master; We were to get to Barry Docks Lifeboat station for 4pm and they would come and pick us up in a twenty-seven-foot boat with a dark blue hull.

OH. MY. GOODNESS!! It was really going to happen!

We'd taken a quick train ride to Barry Docks to meet our impromptu ferry. In the swelteringly heat, I suddenly realised how heavy my suitcase was. What on earth had I packed? Dragging our luggage behind us, we headed to the waterfront to look for the Lifeboat station. It's bright orange so should have been easy to spot.

No sign of it.

Could we see it? No.

slight panic

"I'll go ask in that big building," I said to Richard. "Looks like that's the dock office." Off I trundled.

"I'm looking for the RNLI life boat station. Can you tell me where it is please?" A blank look crossed the face of the receptionist.

"Oh, I don't know," she replied. "Let me have a look on Google." This was not promising. How can they not know where it is?

"It's right over the other side," said another lady. "You'll need to go all the way around. There isn't a direct way across." They showed me on the map. It would take about two hours to walk it.

I went and told Richard the good news. My face was starting to turn a delightful shade of scarlet as the day became warmer. I could feel the sweat on my brow and the annoying tickle of it as it ran down my face, making my glasses constantly slide down my nose. We were both starting to flag.

We kept walking, but the Google Maps kept changing the route as we scanned the seafront looking for something orange.

We made it as far as ASDA but I'd had enough. I was hot from the inside out, sweaty and slightly panicky that, after being so close to actually crossing by boat, we might not get there in time. Would my journey end here? "I'm calling a taxi!"

This was a 'modern' pilgrimage after all. It was more important to get to the lifeboat station than worry about, 'Oh, that's not how you do a pilgrimage!'

Within ten minutes, a lovely taxi man turned up. Red faced and slightly out of breath, I must have looked like a crazed woman as we bundled into the back of his cab.

Finally, we came to a steep lane and at the bottom was the lifeboat station.

While we waited for our 'ferry', we ate our lunch and were given a tour of the Barry Island Life Boat which can hold up to 150 people. Dave, one of the lifeboat volunteers who looked after us, showed us clips of the weather he'd been out in – waves so powerful and high that they went completely over the 11.6 metre high lighthouse. You really need a strong stomach for this.

Dave's 'day' job? He works in a bank.

Eventually, we spotted a little boat on the horizon. How would St. Morwenna have travelled? From the research I'd done, it seemed that boats similar to the Irish *currachs* were used. These smallish rowing boats were made of a wooden frame, over which animal skins or hides were once stretched. I wondered how my crossing would compare. For a start. This boat had an engine.

The part I'd had no idea how it would happen – was happening. We were on a boat. Crossing the Bristol channel. I felt the emotions of the moment well up inside me like a bubbling fountain of joy. Adam, the Harbour Master who had sent me the email, was retiring the following month. Had I asked any later, this probably wouldn't have been happening.

"This is as good as it gets," said Dan the Skipper, as we glided across the water in his small fishing boat *The Reel Deal*. The sea was calm and still. The sunlight danced on the smooth surface. It was millpond flat.

"It's never been like this before," said Adam. "St. Morwenna must be looking over you." I felt a twist in my stomach and a small leap of hope that I'd actually be able to make this journey after all.

After a blissful few hours, Watchet appeared in the distance. Due to the tides we had to disembark here rather than Minehead. This was fine, as hearing about my journey, a lovely friend had offered to pick us up and drive us to Minehead.

Turns out where we were staying was where Adam's wife worked….! Oh, the serendipity!

Foot – The South Coast Path 122 miles. [Days 3 – 21]

Day 3 – Minehead to Porlock Weir (9.5 miles)

Today we started the long walk. There was only one small detail. We'd left the car in Newport with the bikes, and Cerys, our dog, needed collecting from Bristol. This was where Richard popped off, no point in us both going. He'd be back in while so we could walk the first few days together… Wouldn't take long…

It was 5pm by the time I saw the car driving down the street towards me. "It's a surprisingly long way to Newport," said Richard as he stepped from the car and Cerys bounded out behind him.

Everything was finally sorted and the three of us stood looking up at the large sculpture of two hands holding a map, the official start line of the South West Coast Path (SWCP). Gripped with a feeling of excitement, I squeezed Richard's hand, bent down to pet Cerys and took the first few steps heading in the direction of Cornwall.

By the time we arrived In Porlock, it was dark. As our eyes adjusted to the darkness, I noticed the ghostly outlines of figures appearing to loom out at us from the shore. Fear seized my heart and in gulped breaths I said, "Whaaat are they...?"

"Ah, just dead trees," said Richard. "They must be what's left of the forest. I read about it. Apparently, it was submerged by the sea about seven thousand years ago."

Feeling slightly calmer on hearing this, we clambered over the massive boulders that we were suddenly faced with, all the while glancing at the trees in case they moved.

It was about 10.30pm by this point and I'd not been able to get hold of the pub where we were staying. Walking along the road, we put the torch on so anyone else out and about would see us.

One car drove past. That was it. It was so still and quiet, like a ghost town.

Eventually we got to Porlock Weir, but the signs of it having been abandoned persisted. Thoughts of dystopian films sprung to mind. There wasn't a soul around. Were we the last survivors of some kind of apocalypse we'd missed as we'd been meandering along the marshes? There was no mobile reception. Worst of all, the pub we were staying at was closed.

I banged on the door, calling out as I did so, but got no response. I looked at Richard who stood in the spotlight of my torch. He just shrugged.

A smartly dressed gentleman came out of the hotel next door and asked us if we were ok. "You need to call the other pub," he advised.

There's another pub?!

Giving us the number, we went inside the hotel to call. Turned out, the car that'd passed us was the landlady. She got out of bed, got dressed and came back to let us in.

Tomorrow we'd do better and a) try to arrive during daylight and b) have a proper dinner...

*

Day 4 Porlock Weir to Lynmouth harbour (12 miles)

Today we were walking to Lynmouth, a twelve-mile walk through woodland and over clifftops, the furthest I'd walked so far. This trip wasn't a race and I was keen to try and savour as many moments as possible, especially as it had taken me so many years to actually get to the point of actually doing it!

This part of the SWCP was full of colourful rhododendrons. The vibrant magenta flowers looked impressive and disguised their poisonous and invasive behaviour. The flower-heavy branches danced on the light breeze as if nodding whispers of encouragement to us as we walked beneath them.

We tramped along the quiet lanes with only glimpses of the glittering sea between the towering and dense shrubs. Between Culbone and Countisbury we stumbled upon Sister's Fountain. Reputed to be where Joseph of Arimathea once stopped, was this spring somewhere St. Morwenna had drunk from on her journey? I dipped my hand into the cool water and closed my eyes hoping to conjure up an image of her in my mind's eye.

The elaborate stone structure and rough-cut cross that sits over the spring, an early 19th century addition, jarred with the softness of the surroundings giving it an air of a scene from The Blair Witch Project. I was keen to leave.

Soon afterwards, I needed a wee stop. We'd only seen one other person so far so figured it would be safe to go just off the path...

No sooner had I unzipped my trousers did I hear a friendly hello, and two ladies appeared. They were excessively smiley and jolly despite seeing me with my trousers on their way down my thighs. 'Typical!' I thought as I quickly pulled up my trousers, and giggling nervously, tried my best to chat to them as if this was the most normal thing in the world.

With a few miles still to go to reach Lynmouth, I noticed my walking was becoming more laboured than usual and I was dragging my leg. It felt heavy and I was beginning to stumble. Something wasn't right. I stopped. STIMuSTEP, my walking implant, wasn't working. I checked it, repositioned it. I turned it off and on again. No lights came on, no reassuring buzz or the slight tingle I feel, as the electrical current passes through my skin. Nothing. It had run out of power. Getting into Porlock so late the night before I'd totally forgotten to charge it.

The light was fading and my lower back ached. We could see the twinkling of lights starting to come on at Lynmouth below and the path stretching out in front of us. I was close to the edge in more ways than one, and there was still at least two miles to go.

I had to stop as my legs felt like jelly. I squashed myself right up against the wall, sat down and closed my eyes. I felt the warm, salty air caress my cheeks and listened to the sound of the sea and the birds to help calm my nerves. You wouldn't want to be walking along this stretch of the coast on a very windy day; you could easily be lifted like a leaf and be blown out to sea.

We cut across the fields to the main road hoping for a straighter path. This turned out to be a very steep road into Lynmouth. We could see the road disappearing down the hill. My back was shot.

My knees ached. Time to call for reinforcements. I dialled for a taxi.

Turns out, we aren't the only ones to call for a taxi at this point. Gary, the taxi driver, was brilliant at working out exactly where we were from our rather vague description.

We bundled in and chatted away. Gary called one of the pubs to see if they would feed us. YES! We were dropped off at the front door.

It was rather lively in the pub and I overhead one of the barmen saying, "We are closer to another country than we are to a major supermarket. If you put a search in on Google – it shows Wales as the nearest. It's just across the water!"

My shoulders relaxed and I let out a long sigh of relief as our fish and chips were delivered to the table. Thank goodness I'd factored in some rest days, and tomorrow was one of them.

*

Day 8 – Illfacombe to Woolacombe – 13 miles

Richard was leaving today, which made me feel both apprehensive and excited. We'd really enjoyed the last few days rambling along the Devonshire coastline. I was going to miss him by my side. Worst of all, I was losing my chief encourager. Who was going to cheer me on when I felt like stopping or giving up?

My thoughts slipped to St. Morwenna. Did she travel alone or with others? What kept her going when things got tough? From what I'd read about life in the 5th century and being a Celtic Saint, life was challenging pretty much all of the time. There were no taxis, no battered fish and chips to enjoy or warm beds to sleep in.

Did she ever feel like throwing it all in and giving up? I'll never know, but having an inkling of her resilience helped spur me on. I decided to keep those thoughts in my pocket for when I *really* needed them.

I wouldn't be alone for long as various friends joined me at different stages of the walk. I liked the idea of having some time with Richard and Cerys, some on my own and some with friends. It was a good mix – the solo days challenged me and the days with others encouraged me.

*

Day 10 Woolacombe to Saunton – 8 miles

My first day walking alone. Would I get lost? Would I struggle with the mileage? I had no idea.

It was the hottest day so far and I melted like a Salvador Dali painting. It was slow going and I had to reach into my pocket of resilience on many occasions. I was determined to get to Saunton under my own steam and arrive earlier than previous days if I could. I didn't relish the thought of walking on my own after dark.

The relief I felt on reaching my bed for the night that day was palatable. Once checked in, I had a cold bath. I heard my skin 'hiss' as I got into the icy cold water. I lay there for a very long time thinking about how incredible and unexpected some of the journey had been so far and how much of it, if any, was anything like St. Morwenna's.

*

Day 11 – Saunton to Barnstaple - 12.8 miles

Deciding it was time for a break from walking, I perched on a tree stump on a grassy hillock not far outside Saunton. From my vantage point, I could watch people walking their dogs, enjoying the sunshine and... wait – did that hedge just move?

Appearing out of the dunes in full camouflage gear was a platoon of soldiers all heading in my direction. I sat and watched, my eyes almost popping out of my head. They marched past a gentleman wearing pink shorts walking a small white dog on a lead. All rather surreal.

It was a totally different environment as I walked alongside the river Taw. Gone were the dramatic cliff paths and blue sea to be replaced by grassy banks and a wide river. An array of boats lay stranded on the large mud flats.

Around this point I noticed that a swallow had started to follow me. It darted up and down and around me and stayed with me for quite a few miles. Was it a sign from above? Was St. Morwenna looking down on me?

I reached the Tarka Trail which is flat all the way to Barnstaple. I passed a woman pushing a poodle in a pushchair.

My feet throbbed from pounding the tarmac, and my legs itched terribly. An annoying heat rash had appeared just above my sock line, and the strap that holds my STIMuSTEP around my leg kept slipping due to the heat. All I could see in front of me was miles of straight, grey, hard tarmac.

Once in Barnstaple, I treated myself to a cream tea in a smart looking café. My legs, feet and newly forming blisters were grateful for the rest.

*

Day 13 Westward Ho! to Clovelly (11 miles)

Some stretches along this part of the path felt prehistoric and I expected to see dinosaurs in the foliage. It felt like I was on an expedition to a forgotten land. I loved it. Walking the path like this gave me a totally different perspective on time and location. It's magical!

When I reached Clovelly, the picturesque village with no cars and no individually-owned houses as it's all owned by one family, I was greeted with a steep shiny cobbled street – a personal nightmare! I took in the uniqueness of the surroundings as I inched my way slowly, slowly down the cobbled street. I marvelled at the sledges propped up outside people's houses.

I met a couple fixing their sledge. They'd moved to Clovelly in April and had been getting used to life on these cobble streets. I asked them what the sledges were for. "Without your sledge you're really stuck. This is how we bring everything up to our home. It used to be donkeys, but not anymore. That's seen as being animal cruelty now."

*

Day 21 Elmscott to Morwenstow (8 miles) – The Last Leg

The days between Clovelly and Elmscott were filled with many moments of thinking 'Who's idea was this trip? Oh yes mine' to 'Why am I doing this?' as I hobbled my way down the hundredth steep valley, only to have to go up the other side and then down again.

The walk had been a constant up and down-ness both mentally and physically. Had I *really* known this before I'd set off, I doubt I would have considered doing it. My naivety and excitement about the 'story' of St. Morwenna, her journey, and trying to feel some that, had buoyed me over the reality of actually how challenging this was going to be. I was truly elated and surprised at my determination and physical ability to have actually made it to this point – the last day of walking.

I woke up really early with mixed emotions – the excitement of this being the final part of the walk as well as a sadness that this adventure would soon be over. I wanted to make this day last and savour each and every moment. My target was to get to Morwenstow by 4pm as I knew a) it was due to rain after that and b) Duncan from The Stroke Association would be there to greet me with a finishing line.

By 7.45am I was on the path and headed to Morwenstow. This was it. The last day of walking. The sun shone and the sea glistened. My lack of sleep couldn't bring me down.

On this particular stretch, I noticed an abundance of grasshoppers. They helped distract me from the pain I was feeling. My right knee was extremely sore and I had to work out a way of getting down the endless steps without putting too much pressure on my *good* leg. I developed a kind of lopsided hop, that must have looked bizarre to anyone who saw me. But it worked.

I stopped and leaned on my walking poles to take a breath. Below me was a bridge.

Excited, I pressed on, and finally, on reaching the wooden bridge, I could see the Kernow (That's Cornish for Cornwall) sign! I stared at it for a moment through bleary eyes. I was crossing the border from Devon to Cornwall. I went back and forth a few times, just for the sheer novelty of it, and then continued on my way with a slight spring in my step.

Reaching a bench with an expansive view, I paused and looked around me. The rough craggy black rocks, the birds swooping and the sea. The crashing waves were loud yet calming, and I felt very happy. I thought about all that had happened to have gotten to this moment. "This," I said to myself, "is a big deal. This is an achievement. I need to remember this and feel proud of it."

I looked out to sea and something caught my eye. Is it? Could it be? My heart skipped a beat as I realised YES it was – Dolphins! A pod jumping and frolicking in the waves. I stood and watched them for as long as I could before they disappeared from view.

'How much further?' I thought to myself. On the horizon a figure appeared. I stopped – is it Richard? He saw me and started waving!

YES! I started to trot towards him. I threw my walking poles to the ground, and in true Hollywood movie style, we embraced laughing!

There were a few sheep watching us.

"It gets *really* tough the last few miles," he said.

The path was so steep and slippery due to the loose stones, it was the hardest part of the whole walk. A couple of times I lost my footing and ended up on my bum. Now I had bruises and pain pretty much everywhere.

All of a sudden, we could see St. Morwenna's Church in the distance. I paused to take it in. My breath caught in my throat and I felt tears pricking at my eyes. I was nearly there. Nearly at the end.

It was a funny feeling. Part of me didn't want to finish, for it to be over. St. Morwenna had apparently chosen this spot for her church, as on a clear day, she could see her homeland of Wales.

I turned, and raised my hand to shield my eyes from the glare of the sun. Squinting, I looked out to sea, trying to glimpse what St. Morwenna had once seen and close the gap in time between us.

The last few steps took us down into a valley again and then up along the side of a steep hill until we reached the path leading to the church. This was it. The end of the journey.

We walked towards the spot where Duncan (the man from the Stroke Association) said he would be and… nothing. There was no one there. "I wonder where he is?" I said, "Is this the right spot?"

I had no mobile service so couldn't call him. Just as we were going to go into the church, a white car pulled up. The driver's window was down and a man was pointing at us. Duncan!

He parked up and we rushed over. "I thought I'd missed you," he flustered. "When I got your text, I panicked and rushed down to the site at around 2pm, set up the finish line and waited. You didn't show so thought you'd already finished. I packed up and started to drive back to Ilfracombe. Then, at the top of the hill all your messages suddenly came through. I turned around and came straight back."

Laughing, we re-set up the finish line so I could cross it. Then packed it up again and went to the tearooms for a celebratory cream tea. What an amazing cream tea it was.

The End – A 190-mile journey. Completed.

Website: **morwhenna.com**

Instagram: **@morwhennawoolcock**

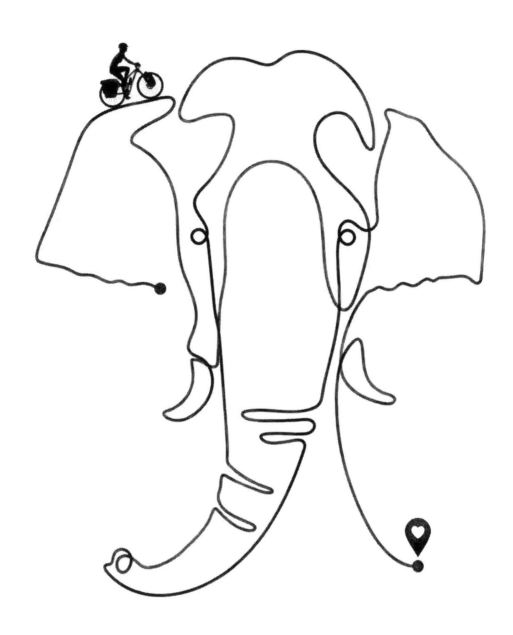

Chapter 48

Under an Elephant's Belly

By Esther Zimmer

I'm standing on the upstairs balcony of the main house, a simple wooden structure surrounded by trees. I notice the way their branches reach towards the sky like long, contorted arms. Two elephants saunter past, their trunks swaying, and I experience the intoxicating pull that so many of us feel in the presence of these four-legged giants: a desire to be close whilst simultaneously awed by their power and size.

The sky and surrounding hills are thick with the smog caused by fires as nearby forest is cleared. It burns my eyes and sits in my throat. I feel a tightening sensation in my chest, as if my heart's constricting, as I imagine the trail of death and destruction the fires are leaving in their wake. I force my mind away from the image and look towards the river that runs along one side of the property's perimeter. I watch as the two elephants lower their large, rotund bodies into the flowing water and as they exhale and relax, so do I.

I'm looking for Faa Mai, the first elephant born at Elephant Nature Park (ENP). I'm holding a wooden carving of her in my hand – a surprise gift for David, my husband – but also a keepsake to remind us both of what can happen when you're willing to, 'Keep some room in your heart for the unimaginable', as the poet Mary Oliver once wrote.

I could never have imagined this.

I thought leaving everything that felt comfortable, familiar and safe in London almost a year ago to embark on a cross-continental cycling expedition had transported me beyond the limits of my imagination. Then it led us here, to working as volunteers with rescued elephants in Thailand.

To my left, a burst of movement from the trees grabs my attention. I turn to see Faa Mai running towards the house. I can't help but laugh at the loose pile of corn stalks piled atop her head, the top ends fanned across her face like a fringe. I've learnt it is not unusual for elephants to adorn themselves this way. Her chubby legs, not dissimilar to those of a toddler's, pump up and down as she propels herself across the cracked earth, dry from a lack of rain.

On the platform below, day visitors jostle one another excitedly as a herd of elephants make their way towards the house and a rainbow buffet of fruit on offer. I look back at Faa Mai. It's obvious from her expression that she's determined to be first in line for the food.

Faa Mai is ten years old, no different from a child, and she endears herself to everyone she comes into contact with, animal and human alike. She's curious, intelligent, playful and *very* social. She regularly leaves her mother and herd to pay visits with the elephants that have been rescued by ENP's founder, Lek Chailert and her husband, Darrick Thomson. They've been rescuing captive service elephants ever since the sanctuary was founded in the 1990s. It's since become a mix of hospice, rehabilitation centre, orphanage and most importantly, a safe and loving home for almost a hundred elephants.

While Faa Mai will never be truly wild, knowing that her life won't follow the same trajectory as many of the roughly 3,800 captive elephants in Thailand - not to mention the thousands more held captive throughout Asia - gives me reason enough to close my eyes, put a hand on my heart and send a prayer of thanks to the Universe. Faa Mai will never have her spirit cruelly broken in order for her to work as a captive service elephant.

In order to break an elephant's spirit, it's tortured.

*

I desperately want to avert my eyes from the screen, but I steel myself not to. It's our first full day at ENP and seeing this documentary is required viewing as volunteers. It's scheduled early in the week for a reason: so we truly understand what captive service elephants - that is, any elephant working in the logging or tourism industry, or any elephant who provides entertainment or plays a part in religious activities - goes through.

What we learn is the most critical lesson of our entire volunteer experience.

We're watching a baby elephant being put through Pajan, the barbaric process used to render a wild elephant docile, also called the 'crush box'.

I'm sickened by the gruesome scene playing out before us; the elephant stands in a cage, chained and roped and surrounded by a dozen or so men of various ages. It's obviously distressed. It's unable to move or lie down but it fights bravely against its restraints and I watch in horror as it's beaten with chains, clubs and sticks and blood runs from its body, ears and feet as they're stabbed repeatedly with hooks and nails.

I learn that it will be tortured this way, hour after hour, for up to ten days. It will also be deprived of food, water and sleep during this time in an effort to speed up the 'crushing' process.

I lean into David for comfort, which does nothing to stem the flood of tears I have no power to stop. I imagine how much that baby must be yearning for the comfort of its mother. It could be anywhere between just one and three years old. If captured in the wild then there's a high chance the mother was killed, otherwise it was most likely conceived through forced mating - a common practice that's tantamount to rape. Whatever the situation, after Pajan it will never be a baby elephant again.

Every single captive service elephant across the world has been through some form of Pajan.

The goal of Pajan is 100% submission.

*

I was aware that almost a hundred African elephants lose their lives every day as a result of human-elephant conflict and poaching. I'd seen numerous gruesome images of their mutilated bodies. I'd go so far as to say I'd almost become desensitised to these images, much to my shame. The problem just felt too big and too far outside of my realm to help solve.

It's far too easy to turn away when a problem feels overwhelming or it feels impossible to make a difference. It's easier still to simply ignore an issue when it's difficult to comprehend the impact because you can't actually *feel* it, when it's someone else's problem that you're watching on TV from the comfort of your couch.

However, travelling by bike brought me face-to-face with blackened countryside, ravaged by fire and cleared for agriculture and development. I traversed through hundreds of kilometres of drought-stricken land, the soil overexploited through human activities such as grazing and growing. In gorgeous locations so remote that the only thing connecting us with the outside world was a satellite phone, I opened my tent on the side of a mountain one morning to witness a spectacular sunrise, and much to my distress, wet wipes fluttering past in the breeze.

Each experience led to many dark moments questioning if there's any place on Earth left untainted by humans. I was no longer watching 'someone else's problem' from afar. Instead, cycling had immersed me in the truly bleak reality of some of the issues faced by this beautiful planet we call home.

Then cycling brought me, quite literally, face-to-face with Asian elephants.

I stand amongst them and I hear their personal stories. I cry and I rage against what they're forced to endure and how they're exploited for human entertainment and pleasure.

Simultaneously I learn, no – I *witness* – how they're sentient, empathetic beings, with an emotional IQ not far removed from our own. I watch an able-bodied elephant use its trunk to assist one who's disabled, elephants who can see being the 'eyes' for elephants who are blind, how mothers and nannies rush to help the babies climb up steep river banks and a fortnight after leaving ENP, I sob all over my laptop while watching a video which shows the body of an elephant who has died of old age laid out for burial. It's not his mother, yet one of the babies has draped himself across the dead elephant in grief. The herd surrounds them both and they mourn together in chorus. Their cries echo across the surrounding hills and into the deepest recess of my heart. Their sorrow is *palpable*.

I've not been at ENP long when I realise how horribly ignorant I am. I'm shocked to learn of the Asian elephants' near-extinction; there are only 45,000 left. I'm even more shocked to learn of the horrific lives one-third of those elephants live in captivity.

The cruelty doesn't end with Pajan – it continues daily as they work as slaves, carrying tourists and unable to drink, forage, play or socialise the way a wild elephant would. Brutally controlled by the prodding of a bull hook or a nail discreetly pressed into their skull. Despite their imposing size, they're not physiologically designed to carry weight, which causes pain. There's no acceptable reason for riding an elephant, but ignorant tourists create the demand.

Once your eyes are opened you can't *not* see the cruelty: elephants forced to be 'painters', or to perform demeaning tricks in circuses or shows, or on busy city streets. What torture that must be for these magnificent, wild beings. And those elephants that stand so patiently outside of temples? They're often held in place with spiked shackles that eat into their flesh if they move. While festivals and religious ceremonies may look like the perfect photo opportunity, consider how that pretty procession of elephants are being made to walk for miles on a burning hot tar road, often transported from one event to another, as if a single procession with noisy crowds wasn't terrifying enough for a creature whose home is in the forest. So many of these activities appear harmless, but there's a dark side to animal tourism that far too many of us simply aren't aware of.

It occurs to me that while I don't play a role in supporting any of these activities, by doing or saying nothing, I'm effectively refusing to play a role in the solution.

*

A day that was remarkably clear of smog and has turned into one of those beautiful evenings when the sky turns an increasingly deeper shade of blue as the sun begins to set. Sultry cedars swing lazily in the breeze. David and I are sitting amongst our fellow volunteers on lounge chairs scattered along the balcony of the main house. I look at their faces and think about how I'm going to miss these new friends. They've come from all over the world and everyone's lives are different, but we've bonded over this shared experience.

It's such an odd thing to meet strangers and connect over so much suffering, but there's so much beauty and hope here, too. We've held one another and we've cried, but we've also laughed as we've worked side-by-side, and willingly shared intimate details of our lives in a short space of time. Perhaps learning each of the elephants' personal stories has made us less reticent about sharing our own.

I ponder the way humans are drawn to one another while everyone else remains unusually quiet, either reading or writing. I'm vaguely conscious of a sprinkler coming to life and its clackety-clack adding to the sounds of an evening unfolding. What we're all hoping to hear is the dinner bell, except we're suddenly treated to another, far more appealing sound: the trumpeting of an elephant.

I leap to my feet. An elephant's trumpeting never fails to evoke a soaring feeling in me. It's the sound of the wild and I feel my own wild within being summoned too.

The others aren't far behind me, we're all eager for a front row view. We've been here long enough now to know who plays this particular solo. Chana is a nine-year-old orphan who, after being put through Pajan, was forced to work performing circus-style tricks and begging for money from tourists on the streets. It's unknown how the injury occurred, but her leg was broken in two places and left untreated. As Chana was unable to work, she was of no further use to her owner.

Chana's injuries are still too serious for her to be able to roam and play with the other elephants without the risk of being further injured by accident. So, she stays in a separate area within the sanctuary during the day. However, when the other elephants are bedded down in their sleeping enclosures for the night, Chana is given the run of the park.

We watch with delight as she runs as best she can towards a dirt pile where she sits on her bottom before slumping with a flop onto her side, causing fine dust to rise and envelope her in a red cloud. Minutes later she's working hard to get back on her feet, but you can see the determination in her eyes and soon she's lumbering by and trumpeting away again. She's such a joyful sight and Chana's trumpeting is a way of expressing her excitement at being free to explore and play. I can't help but think of my three little nieces who start shrieking the moment they get home from school and are finally allowed to go outside and let off steam. Chana's excitement is no different.

Until my time at ENP I had no idea how playful and social elephants are, *how human-like.* I've passed many happy hours watching them swim and play together in the river, often plunging at speed into deep channels of water. Who knew an elephant could completely disappear right in front of your eyes? That's until trunks appear above the surface like snorkels, allowing them to remain fully immersed for as long as they wish. It's impossible not to get the giggles as they splash about. Due to their sensitive skin, they take mud baths to protect it, but a large amount of comedy-like wrestling also takes place in those baths. If you've never seen a bunch of elephants covered in mud and wrestling, I'm not sure you've really lived.

Gingerly following Chana is Kabu, a twenty-nine-year-old female elephant. Chana's story is sad enough, but Kabu's story is the one that keeps me awake at night, tears pouring down my face as I try to bend my mind around the complexity of the Asian elephant's predicament. This isn't a black and white issue based only on cruelty and greed – although it is tourists who drive the abhorrent demand to be carried and entertained by elephants. Yet, there are cultural and long-held traditions to consider and many elephant owners have families to provide for and very few options. To believe the problems - and therefore the solutions - are simple is a naïve way of thinking that risks creating further barriers, rather than breaking them down. However, I still struggle to comprehend how the human race can be so callous to animals, how we're so quick to discredit their pain and suffering simply because they're just that, an animal. And there's something I find particularly pitiful about how we wield our power over elephants.

Kabu came to ENP after she was crippled following a logging injury. Logging was banned in Thailand in 1989 but still takes place illegally or in border areas. Elephants doing this work are at risk of having their legs snapped under the weight of chains or logs and many are forced to continue working well before their injuries have healed.

Not only was Kabu crippled, she had two babies torn away from her and put through Pajan. As is often the case when an elephant is forced to live a life of fear, hardship and misery, Kabu was so emotionally traumatised when she arrived at ENP that she shunned other elephants and preferred to be left alone.

That is, until Chana arrived and Kabu immediately adopted her.

A motherless baby and a mother who had her children torn away from her, both elephants were psychologically and physically traumatised but have formed a bond that will last their lifetimes. It's a critical bond that also plays a key role in helping them to heal. Elephants are highly sensitive, social, loving beings. They recognise and will run to greet one another and even hug with their trunks.

An elephant that prefers to be left alone has forgotten how to be an elephant.

As I learn the ways of a wild elephant, it's excruciatingly obvious how torturous it must be not to be free to roam far and wide, foraging throughout the day led by instinct and memories. How hydrating via a trough and hose is a far cry from being able to suck water when needed from a cool river, or a watering hole. How maddening it must be not to be able to protect sensitive skin with dust or mud. Living instead, *if it can even be called living*, constrained in shackles for *decades*, forced to exist according to a human's wants and way of life.

Yet what inflicts the deepest wounds of all is how elephants' complex emotional lives are virtually held in contempt, even used against them to further break their spirit. Just like us they crave connection and love but their social structures are even more complex. In the wild a female elephant will spend its whole life living in a tightly knit family group, led by the matriarch. They care for and protect one another, and work together to raise one another's babies. We could learn so much from their example.

While humans consciously seek to form deep bonds outside of family, an elephant's desire to be with theirs is deeply innate. Take that capability away from them and tear their families apart and you've removed an intrinsic part of what makes an elephant an elephant.

Kabu was fortunate. Many elephants never recover from the trauma of being torn apart from their loved ones.

*

"I don't want to leave," says David, looking at me intensely.

It's evening and we're back in our room getting ready to turn in for the night. We've only been at ENP a few days and the plan had been to volunteer for seven then make our way to and through Myanmar by bike, before concluding our travels. If we stay any longer, that plan will become obsolete.

"Me neither," I reply.

We stand facing one another for a moment as the ceiling fan hums above us and colourful geckos crawl up the walls. I'm holding a pair of earrings in the palm of one hand, two gold spheres engraved with Sanskrit. I bring them up to my face and study them for a moment, as if I'm searching for a clue.

"What do you want to do?" I finally ask, confident I already know the answer.

I'm not the only one who's been affected by the elephants. In the fifteen years we've been together, I've only seen David cry on a couple of occasions. As my gentle husband has interacted with these equally gentle giants, I've seen tears dampen his cheeks several times. I'm watching the person I love the most change in positive, powerful ways right in front of my eyes, simply from being in their presence.

"Let's see if we can stay for longer," David suggests.

When David and I wobbled out of Istanbul almost a year ago, we didn't entirely know what we were doing. I'd suggested we cycle a route we'd originally planned to drive, despite not having an iota of cycle touring experience between us. We'd frequently giggled together about the ambitious, cross-continental path we'd chosen for our first expedition. Yet the trip had far exceeded any expectations either of us may have had, and we'd adapted easily and quickly to life on the road.

It would have been so easy to keep going beyond the year we'd planned to spend travelling, but David had recently accepted a job offer in London. It's no secret I was hoping we wouldn't return to the city we'd left, at least not to live.

As I step out of my clothes I contemplate the end of our journey and I know I'm not the same person who left London all those months ago. I've changed in ways I could never have anticipated and I want the life I live there to change too. I'd been so sure that by the end of this trip I'd have a clear sense of direction, but I'm still not entirely sure what I'm going to do in the next chapter of my life.

However, despite my reluctance to return, I can't shake the feeling that our journey was always going to lead us to ENP and that we were always going to return to London. I can feel the elephants altering the course of my life, even if I don't quite know how.

*

"Welcome to my office!" says Lek with a giggle as I get down on my hands and knees and crawl underneath Faa Mai's belly to sit with her. I'm having a serious 'pinch me' moment. I didn't expect to be sitting under an elephant with a world-renowned Asian elephant conservationist today – *or any day, for that matter.*

It's the first time I've met Lek. She recently returned from an educational tour and has come to see Faa Mai and one of the herds. She has a close relationship with every animal she rescues and yet it's her bond with Faa Mai that's the strongest. Faa Mai's chubby legs couldn't move fast enough when she spotted Lek, the elephant's reaction is reminiscent of that of a child's who's just seen an ice cream truck. There's definitely a moment when I'm convinced we're both about to be devoured. But Faa Mai comes to a stop, ears flapping with pleasure and pushes Lek gently into a crouch so she can fit between her front legs, as if Lek were a baby elephant in Faa Mai's care.

Which is how I come to be sitting opposite this tiny Thai woman and the formidable driving force behind so many of the projects we've been learning about. From rescuing captive service elephants to running educational programmes and helping elephant-related tourism attractions and camps convert to an ethical business model, and so much more.

I'm surprised when Lek shares her frustrations with me, a stranger. But she's been doing this work for decades and has witnessed so much cruelty and is keen to educate others. I wonder how much she must suffer; it must break her heart repeatedly, knowing that for every elephant she helps, there are far more she must leave behind.

She shares her dreams, too. Of semi-wild projects that allow a number of elephants to live with minimal human intrusion, even though that's sadly not what most tourists want. Lek knows that even ethical businesses aren't the perfect solution for the elephants, but they can be a way to educate and therefore a stepping-stone to something better.

And without tourism, businesses risk running out of money to provide even minimal care for elephants. At the time of writing, all elephant-related businesses in Thailand are closed due to COVID-19 and at least a thousand elephants are at risk of starving to death. The forest may be the elephant's home, but the ugly reality is that there's not enough forest left to sustain the wild population, let alone a large number of elephants that have previously been held captive.

What strikes me the most about our conversation though is that despite everything Lek's seen, everything she's been required to sacrifice and for all the work that still needs to be done, there's no judgement of others, no shaming. Lek tells me she believes that true change comes when we lead by example and show compassion and love. She's a living example of how successful that approach can be.

As she talks, I experience a moment of realisation. The elephants may have started to change the course of my life, but meeting Lek was the final push I didn't even know I needed.

*

The herd approaches and as we stand to greet them the elephants eagerly reach for Lek, reminding me of when I return to my family after being away. Everyone wants to hug and be hugged at once and there's that wonderful feeling when one embrace ends and another immediately begins. Only this time arms are trunks.

It's obvious Faa Mai isn't the only one who's devoted to her. The herd express their delight at Lek's presence with low, guttural sounds, nuzzling her hair, face and body with their trunks, smearing her face and clothes with red mud from the baths they'd been playing in moments earlier. I watch, entranced, as Lek turns towards the river and as she does so, Faa Mai winds her trunk gently around Lek's wrist and they walk side-by-side. It's such a natural, almost *intimate* movement that makes me think of a child slipping her hand unthinkingly into her mother's.

The more time we spend with the elephants, the more at ease they become in our presence. Soon they begin to nuzzle our hair, faces and bodies too. Lek takes my hand and directs me to stand right in front of Faa Mai - I'm literally tucked under her chin - and then she verbally guides me to place a hand on either side of Faa Mai's head and up behind her ears. I run my palms across thick, furrowed skin, which is surprisingly soft in this shrouded place, out of sight from the sun. I close my eyes and I breathe her in.

After a while I step back so I can look into Faa Mai's eyes. She lifts her trunk and gently caresses my face and I'm so choked with emotion that all I can do is stand there, tears streaming down my grubby cheeks. To stand eye-to-eye with an elephant at peace is to feel its extraordinary healing power.

As we walk back towards the house, I feel profoundly affected. I'm astounded by how these magnificent animals have been so horribly abused by humans, and yet they're so willing to forgive the unforgiveable and share their deep sense of loyalty for family with the people who love them.

As for Lek, I'm in awe of the incredible work she does but I'm even more in awe of who she is as a person and how she goes about that work. The elephants have shown me what I want to do next, but it's Lek who's shown me how to do it. I needed to see activism and advocacy conducted in a way that reflects my values. I can see my next step.

*

Since returning to London David has often joked that, "Rather than cycling across the biggest land mass on the planet, all I really needed to do to get a little perspective was to hug an elephant." But we both know that's not true. We wouldn't have been the same people without all the experiences we'd had as we unknowingly cycled towards ENP.

We left everything that felt comfortable, familiar and safe behind and in doing so, we expanded our perception of how much more we're capable of, as a couple, but as individuals too.

I needed to wobble out of Istanbul on my bike with no idea about what I was doing, to leap into the unknown, in order to truly understand that you don't need to have all the answers before you start something. You just have to take the first step.

Yet I spent far more time on that journey than was necessary trying to figure out what I was going to do once it was over. What I learnt is that answers rarely arrive the way you may expect or even want them to. I didn't expect to reach the end of our trip with no clear sense of direction, only to take a final road that literally led me to a herd of elephants and a woman who would change the course of my life. I didn't expect to become an activist and advocate for elephant conservation.

Now when I talk about elephant conservation people ask, "Why elephants? There are so many causes that could use your attention," and that's true. But in a world that constantly asks, "What's your why?" I don't believe we always need one. Sometimes you feel a calling so strong you respond without question. I still can't explain why I suggested we cycle a route we'd originally planned to drive. I just know it's what my heart wanted.

It's no secret that I was hoping I wouldn't return to London, at least not to live. Yet it's the elephants that made returning so much easier and I believe it's exactly where I'm meant to be, for now. I'm using my voice to stand up for what I believe in and I do so following Lek's example. I also know now that a problem is never too big or too far away to help solve.

Take the leap, take your time and be willing to believe that, 'What you are seeking is seeking you', as Rumi says. And always, always keep some room in your heart for the unimaginable.

Esther and David Zimmer are UK Ambassadors for Elephant Nature Park.

Websites: **www.estherzimmer.com** and **www.elephantnaturepark.com**

THE PAMIRS

KHOROG : TAJIKISTAN TOWARDS OSH : KYRGYSTAN

1 : 500 000

Chapter 49

Act Big. Live Small.

By David Zimmer

"It's dengue fever."

With those three words, the doctor confirms what I know already – I'm seriously sick.

I've been on my back in a little hotel in Cambodia for three days with a 40°C (104°F) temperature, losing it from both ends and so achy I can't move from the bed except for the regular painful sprint to the toilet. Because my sodium levels are tanking, my brain is swelling inside my skull, giving rise to a constant debilitating headache that could drop an elephant. I haven't slept in those three days.

It'll be ten days before the fever breaks and I can take comfort that I've escaped the worst that dengue can throw at you – the bleeding-from-everywhere haemorrhagic fever that half a million people develop and 25,000 die from every year.

It's another month before I can get back on my bike. A visceral reminder of a principle that has guided my wife and I since we set off on a bicycle journey from Istanbul to Singapore: don't be in a hurry. If I've learned one thing on this, my first big adventure, it's the importance of time and toil. Just about anything can be accomplished with them, and nothing truly great is accomplished without them.

As I try to keep a warm, de-fizzed can of Sprite and a few crackers from rapidly exiting one or more orifices, I think about the significance of time. It's ultimately what this trip is about; a chance to slow down. A chance to strip my life bare of the complexities I've saddled it with – career, money, house, relationships, hobbies... stuff – and pare down every day to its simplest elements: water, food, shelter and turning the pedals. It's a chance to live, on the bicycles, at the speed of life.

While I sit in bed sweating like a pig, I cast my fevered brain back over a journey that so far has covered eleven thousand kilometres, eight countries and eight months. Slowly, over days, an idea starts to form from these seemingly disconnected memories of my trek and my thoughts about time. A simple idea about not just getting more out of my time, but doing more with it:

Act Big. Live Small.

It sums up for me the lessons learnt on the road. It's about getting more out of life by increasing the effects of how I act, while reducing the impact of how I live on the world around me. I flash back to moments in time that form the building blocks of this little epiphany; the first being the day the seed of this journey was planted eleven years ago.

Like many big ideas and great adventures, it starts with a trip to Ikea...

*

My wife, Esther, and I bought our house in London in 2007. As you do when you have no stuff, we made the slog to Ikea to buy lots of it. Nearing the end of the Nordic retail labyrinth, thinking we couldn't possibly need another Swedish thing in our lives, we spied a six-foot map of the world. We stood in front of it, open-mouthed, like kids glimpsing the bounty under the tree on Christmas morning. *This* is the kind of random stuff we needed.

Once up on the wall, the Big Bloody Map's Mercator format made Asia look even more massive; trust me, it is. There might as well have been a huge neon sign on it blinking,

Go there...

Go there...

Go there...

From its modest beginnings in Scandinavian homewares, the idea of taking a Big Asian Trip, ebbed and flowed through our day-to-day lives. Sometimes thinking about it was almost orgasmic, like an injection of adrenaline. Some days it was like Nelson from The Simpsons, pointing and taunting me with a "Hah hah!" as I sat, adventureless, in an office. For long periods – years – it barely got a thought, like that bit of damp on the bathroom wall you know you should do something about, but don't.

In the end, Esther lit the adventure touch paper with a simple yet bold question. One grey January night in 2017, ten years after hanging the Big Bloody Map, she came home and said,

"Don't feel you need to answer right now, but how about riding bicycles across Asia?"

The bikes we'd bought years ago on a cycle-to-work programme saw more action as drying racks for my underwear. Esther probably didn't expect me to quickly say, "Why the #@&! not?"

It's like when you dare your brother to jump off the roof of your parents' house with you, not expecting him to actually take you up on it. At that point we were both committed.

*

Dr. Kosal – a charming Cambodian man with delightful cartoon mannerisms – interrupts my reminiscing to hang a sodium IV. Mercifully, it keeps my brain from feeling like it's going to explode through my eye sockets. Esther and I laugh about how this knee-jerk 'Say Yes' moment brought us from London to this moment – a doctor searching for a vein in my arm in a Cambodian guesthouse. Circumstances we could never have predicted, surroundings we never could have imagined. We felt the same when we first cast our eyes on the mountains, and our legs strained to push us thousands of metres up into their lofty peaks…

*

It's the mountains that rekindled a long-standing reverence for and connection with nature which is at the core of 'act big, live small'. John Muir said, 'The mountains are calling, and I must go'.[1] And despite growing up in Pennsylvania, where the highest point is 979 meters, the mountains called me out on this adventure. It's no mistake that the routes I plotted took in some of the highest roads and trails in Asia. I wanted to see the mountains up close. Esther was less convinced at first. As we painfully built our climbing legs on the up-and-down hills of central Turkey, she googled 'world's flattest country'. It's the Maldives, but much less conducive to long-distance cycling.

As we approached the Zagari Pass in the Georgian Caucasus a few weeks later, the yearning for flatness was forgotten. We climbed to 2,600 metres – it felt like I could reach my fingers into the cold snow permanently sat on the astonishingly elegant, elongated peak of Shkara, Georgia's highest mountain at 5,193 metres. Rainbow-hued swaths of wildflowers coated her base. She ignited a torrid love affair with a mountain range that runs the length of the Eurasian continent – from the Taurus, the Caucasus, the Pamir and the Hindu Kush, to the Altay, the Tian Shan, the Karakoram and the Himalayas.

The draw isn't just their sheer size or beauty. Legendary mountaineer Anatoli Boukreev said, 'Mountains are not stadiums where I satisfy my ambition to achieve, they are the cathedrals where I practice my religion.'[2] I understand Boukreev's adoration – nature

---

[1] Letter from John Muir to Sarah Muir Galloway, University of the Pacific, ©1984 Muir-Hanna Trust

[2] Anatolie Boukreev & Linda Wylie, *Above the Clouds* (New York: St. Martin's Griffin, 2002)

is my divine, too, and the mountains taught me that what's important is *out there*, not behind my desk.

As we cycled the lunar landscape of Tajikistan's 4,655 metre Ak-Baital Pass, the thin air created a backdrop of the deepest blue to the rusty and blood-red shades of the Pamir Mountains. I was awe-struck despite the lung-busting climb and the sometimes un-cyclable 'path' of rubble oatmeal. And I understood the adoration a little more.

Because the mountains made us. Seventy million years ago the Arabia and India landmasses collided with the Eurasian mainland, violently thrusting up these ranges. These in turn created new weather patterns, bringing huge rainfalls to their slopes that transported sediment to fertile plains like those we cycled through in the Wakhan Corridor which have supported human life for millennia.

And sometime in the next 100 or 200 million years, the continents as they exist today will come together again. New oceans and new ranges will form, long after the highest mountains we cycled through are eroded to nubs. I see a responsibility and purpose in considering what faint memories we will leave in the rocks.

*

Dr. Kosal interrupts my mountain reverie to stick another IV in my arm. Potassium? Magnesium? I've lost track. As I contemplate popping one of the Valium he's casually tossed me, I think about 'running away' on the bikes at forty-four. It's a lot flipping harder than I thought it would be.

It's not like when I was seven and I threw a few Oreos and a pair of Superman Underoos in my Speed Racer lunch box and ran out the back door. I made it about a hundred metres into the woods for a few hours until I started to wonder what Mum was cooking for dinner.

It takes us a second to commit to cycling across the earth's largest landmass; it takes us months to strip away years of accumulated commitments, like layers of varnish. At one point our local Oxfam charity shop in Tooting had most of the contents of our lounge artfully arranged in the shop window, a museum exhibition on the Zimmers.

We haven't missed much on the road, bar the odd ice cube, the Sunday papers and the football. We get more and more out of every day with less and less. 'Less is more' has become comfortable, normal. It's an adage made real for us by the story of Mom and Michella…

*

It was toffee pudding weather – hot and sticky. 'Tarzan couldn't take this kind of hot', as Neil Simon wrote[3]. Our train from the crumbling Art Deco station in Kampot, Cambodia was three hours late. Food and cold beer were fast becoming priorities.

I heard a woman in French-accented English explaining to a few other tourists what the local women were selling on the platform. I started talking with her about some of the other funkier things available – fetal eggs, alien fruit.

"I'm Mom, like short for 'mother'," she said as we introduced ourselves over a few crunchy fingers of green mango. "You dip them in the little bag of chili and salt," she explained.

I asked where she was from, assuming that, despite Asian features, her excellent French and English meant she'd come from elsewhere.

"We left Cambodia in 1975 when I was seven on the day the Khmer Rouge captured Phnom Penh. We've lived in Paris most of our lives. I've returned since, but this is the first time Michella [her sister at her side] has been back since we left forty-four years ago."

Esther and I were stunned for several seconds – we'd heard about the emptying of Phnom Penh but never met anyone who'd lived

---

[3] Simon, *Biloxi Blues (New York: Samuel French, 1986)*

through it. The day the Khmer Rouge took the city, they walked the streets telling every resident to leave because the Americans were going to start bombing. The motive behind the lie was to drive people into the country to work the newly collectivised farms. Phnom Penh lay abandoned for the next four years.

"I just have flashes of pictures, but I was only eight," Michella said, sometimes looking to Mom for a word. "I can't remember the horror of that time as people describe it."

"I do remember the soldiers saying we had twenty-four hours to leave," said Mom. "There were six children in our family – my mother had lost another four children at birth."

Their mother was a cousin of King Sihanouk, deposed shortly before the civil war, so they had been raised in a position of some privilege.

"At that point, my mother had never given me a bath. Each of us had our own nanny – and when it was bath time, we were handed over to them."

I can't fathom what went through their mother's head at that moment. She had lost four children and never fully raised the other six without a team of nannies. Now she was told she had a day to leave their entire lives behind. But I imagined a determined woman – a formidable woman – similar to the two standing on the platform with me.

"Even after we left Cambodia, she didn't bathe us. My older sister raised us mostly while my mother did business, selling jewellery and family things to provide for us. My mother is now seventy-eight and still smokes twenty cigarettes a day."

She didn't bathe her kids, but she dragged six of them through an unfathomable hell to a new life. Mom and Michella's mother may lack certain old-fashioned ideals of maternity, but in my opinion, she's an effing bad-ass. In less than twenty-four hours, she started the family on a three hundred-kilometre walk to Saigon.

"We had a small car, but the family pig rode in the back while we walked alongside," said Mom with a giggle.

I can picture the family marching out of Phnom Penh, their mother with a cigarette clamped firmly between her lips, and the pig's head poking out of the car window like a Far Side cartoon. An illusion of humour amidst a life-or-death predicament. They made it to Vietnam – where their father was imprisoned as a Cambodian air force officer – and eventually immigrated to France three years later.

There wasn't a hint of sadness in Mom's voice even as she described their return to their old house. They asked the current owners if they could look around. When Phnom Penh was liberated they were a world away, unable to reclaim their home.

"We remembered where we slept," Mom said simply.

I got the impression this is a situation many Cambodians have come to terms with – uprooted families, lost homes, lost loved ones. But Mom surprised me and drove the lesson home when she said she was going to sell her Paris flat and move back to Phnom Penh.

"My children are here. And you don't need things here – you don't need much to live and enjoy life. In Europe, you need lots of things to live. In Cambodia, you need a room to sleep in. Everything else is outside. Easy."

*

The fever finally breaks. I breathe a wheezy sigh of relief that the Internet images of Ebola-like bleeding haven't become reality. I get back on my feet, slowly – the Mekong is an ideal environment for sluggish convalescence. I walk along languid stretches of the river, evocative of a different time, slowing my stride to match the pace of life in Cambodia and Laos, where I spent several weeks recovering in Vientiane. I find myself slowing down more and more to absorb what's in front of me.

The impetus for taking to the bikes wasn't about seeking a life-changing experience. It was about seeking a perspective-changing experience. Adventure, at the end of the day, is simply doing something that's out of the ordinary for you, whether big like cycling Asia or small like spending a few hours in the woods as a kid with my lunchbox. In trying something out of the ordinary, we challenge our point of view.

Getting on the bike allows me to see the world at a human pace, rather than it whizzing by through a grimy windscreen. And it's the perspective shift that lets me empathise with things outside my frame of reference. We're inundated with references to environmental crises and social breakdown. It's easy to become numb to it. But on the bike I can see, intimately, the impact of the life I'm leading, a realisation delivered to me like a punch to the gut as I cycle through some of the most striking landscapes on earth…

*

It wasn't until vomit rose in my throat from the stench of household rubbish dumped down the greenest of green hillsides in the Vietnamese jungles that the realisation hit me.

It wasn't until my eyes burned and streamed from the nuclear winter-style smog in northern Thailand – caused by fires lit to clear forest for grazing – that I understood the giant bloody pickle we're in.

It wasn't until I saw the hundreds of artificial limbs lining a wall in a museum in Laos, the legacy of 100 million unexploded bombs from America's undeclared war on the country, that I wondered when we were going to get our heads out of our collective butts.

It wasn't until I cycled the streets of Sihanoukville – where the unfettered, corruption-fuelled pursuit of economic growth has driven the construction of over a hundred Chinese casinos, turning a once-sleepy coastal Cambodian town into a polluted wasteland – that I thought,

"Damn. I don't think we're going to turn this around." But a simple handshake in Georgia helped me understand that individual actions can build to something bigger.

As we pedalled through the Caucasus – a landscape that would send the average Instagram junkie into a sexual euphoria – we stopped to fill our bottles at a small mountain spring far from anything. Rubbish was scattered everywhere – bottles, bags, wrappers, cans. In that moment, I saw Esther's heart break a little. Without thinking, we started picking up a few things. Soon we'd filled an old concrete sack with several hundred bits of discarded rubbish. A 4x4 stopped a few metres ahead and a Georgian man walked up to us. With a leathery, sun-creased smile, he looked us each in the eye and shook our hands slowly. Lacking a common language, his modest 'thank you' was a lightning bolt.

His validation of our actions hit home – how I act can make an impact, even if for one person. At times, when the pollution, poverty and inhumanity seemed like the constant background noise to otherwise intoxicating people and landscapes, the challenge felt insurmountable. We loved every minute of every day on the bikes, but the journey pointedly brought to life the knife-edge we seem to be balanced on.

*

My recovery continues – fortified by cold Beer Laos, one of the world's great hot weather beers – under a sultry haze in Vientiane, a sleepy gem of a city. It's surprising how completely comfortable I feel as part of the Vientiane furniture. But if I'd have followed others' advice, I would've never got on the bike in the first place, let alone found contentment a world away...

*

As we shared plans for our trip and sought advice from other adventurers, an American cyclist on a touring forum wrote:

"You're brave to be going to the 'Stans. Especially your wife."

It's the ignorance that got me – the assumption that anything 'different' equals 'worse' or 'dangerous'. It's vanity and insecurity that blocks us from divorcing a government from its people, a religion from its practitioners. All Americans aren't narcissistic, ego-maniacal morons. So why assume someone from a 'Stan is anything like their autocratic leader?

My parents taught me the 'all are created equal' ethos from the moment I could think for myself, so I was surprised that getting them to 'sign the permission slip' for my trip ended up being the hardest bloody part of the whole odyssey. When we told Esther's seventy-eight-year-old mum about our adventure, she asked, "Can I come?"

She was serious. My parents, two very well-educated and liberal people, took the express train to, "Are you nuts?"

They assumed that people would treat Americans with the same disdain that the current insular American government now treats the rest of world, so traveling through the 'Stans on bicycles invited a kidnapping scenario out of some crappy Steven Segal movie. I was angry that I had to rationalise the trip. I also came to appreciate their perspective, fuelled by the constant barrage of alarmist media.

With regular phone calls, an expensive personal locator beacon and my patience-of-a-saint sister who taught them to follow us online (neither Mum nor Dad had ever turned on a computer), we got them on board.

Then, two weeks before we were due to cross the border into Tajikistan, four cyclists were killed along our planned route by a lone ISIS fanatic. As the murders hit the front page of the New York Times, Dad dictated the equivalent of a 'cease-and-desist letter' – his lawyerly habits die hard – to my sister begging us to return. We didn't think twice about continuing.

*

I gradually rebuild my strength in Vientiane – if you're looking to eat yourself back to good health, you can't do much better than Laotian cooking. As I shove another handful of sticky rice in my mouth – dipped in a bowl of jaew, a fiery tomato dip – I reflect on what made continuing our journey a foregone conclusion despite the deaths of our fellow cycling adventurers. It's not the bikes or the food or the landscapes. It's the many random acts of humanity that made staying in the saddle an easy decision – and two in particular remind me that goodwill is a universal language, no matter where you go....

*

We left Istanbul at the beginning of Ramadan, having no idea what to expect of the places we'd see or people we'd meet. We hadn't even ridden our bikes with the panniers on and loaded until that point.

Within a few miles of Istanbul, the first of many people pulled over to pop their trunks and hand us wobbly cyclists a bag of freshly picked cherries. After a hot morning drinking tepid water, they were like ambrosia. Our handlebars and panniers soon groaned under the weight of greengages and mulberries as fruit sellers regularly flagged us down. The women often took pains to tell us, proudly, that they did the picking.

In the Ottoman town of Tarakli, we walked down an old market street looking for a place to eat. We tried to respect our Turkish hosts and not eat in plain sight while they fasted, so some days we were famished by sundown. We passed an open door with tables out front and peeked in. Before we could decide if it was a home or restaurant, a Lovely Old Woman, as she will forever be known, motioned us in.

If there is an idyllic example of the Lovely Old Woman, it was her – from the wise, twinkly eyes to the beautiful, round, crinkly face and the simple scarf framing it, to the way she tut-tutted about us and the warm, weathered hand she used to pull us here and there.

She guided me to the table out front and pointed Esther inside. We were confused until I realised that I was to eat with the men and Esther was to eat inside with the women. I heard a chorus of friendly laughs and chirping as Esther entered. I later learned that these were sounds of welcome and approval. We were conscious to dress to the local norms, and the Lovely Old Woman, seeing Esther's effort, made a big fuss to show her off to the other women. They whole-heartedly approved of Esther's shawl and long skirt, welcoming her like an old friend.

A hugely satisfying meal of lentil soup, salad, rice pilaf, beans and trays of fruit – a typical Ramadan meal – was laid in front of me and other guests, some who seem familiar to our hosts and some strangers. The local mosque fired the cannon signalling 8.21pm – sunset – and we tucked in with relish. By 8.27pm, plates were licked clean.

Eventually Esther was released to join me outside for the mandatory cups of tea – but not before the women hugged the stuffing out of her. At some point I tried, using my Google Turkish, to pay for our meal, but the Lovely Old Woman quickly made it clear that it was her pleasure – if not duty – to welcome strangers to break the Ramadan fast. She sat between us with her arms on our shoulders, like we were children returning home from a long journey.

*

Another bottle of cold Beer Laos cools the jaew's chili fire, but the warm glow of that night with the Lovely Old Woman remains, a glow that subsequent Turks, Georgians, Azeris, Uzbeks, Tajiks – and one truly wonderful Kyrgyz grandmother – would only intensify…

*

We were fifty kilometres from Osh, on the home stretch of four weeks cycling the unforgettable Wakhan Corridor and Pamir Highway – high passes, 360-degree mountain views, lives lived above the treeline. We were setting up our tent along a roadside stream when a determined looking Kyrgyz woman – Apa was her name – marched purposefully our way, pushing a pram. We expected to get an earful from her for maybe camping where we shouldn't. If she'd been my grandmother, Naomi, she'd have had a wooden spoon in her hand, ready to crack it across my bum – she had that look on her face.

We got the earful, but not quite for the reason we expected. We managed to figure out with a couple of Russian words that she was saying,

"You can't sleep here – it's too cold."

We told her we'd been camping for months across Central Asia, but she wasn't having it. We had no choice but to repack our gear – she had a force of character that demanded compliance – and follow her up the hill to the house she shared with her son, his wife and the world's most adorable baby granddaughter.

She showed us to a simple, warm room, and we watched her issue orders to her daughter-in-law like a field commander. Tea appeared in seconds, a hearty dinner of soup and dumplings shortly after.

We spent some time 'chatting' with Apa – she'd say something to me in Kyrgyz and when I'd apologetically shrug my shoulders, she'd put her hand on my arm and laugh hysterically. Esther was sure she was flirting. We also tried subtly but desperately to finagle a cuddle with the baby. Apa held onto her with some sort of grandmother tractor beam that even Obi Wan couldn't breach.

In the morning, fresh bread and homemade jam awaited us. I offered a small thanks to the gods (and to Apa's imperturbable daughter-in-law) for a break from the standard breakfast Esther and I made ourselves – paper-paste porridge.

As I loaded up our bikes, Esther achieved the unthinkable as the baby was passed to her; she looked at me like Indiana Jones securing the golden idol.

We tried to give Apa the going rate for room and board; I didn't need to speak Kyrgyz to understand her response. I'm surprised she didn't give me a slap on the hand. We did sneak a note and a few dollars under our pillow; I've always wondered if my shaky Cyrillic printing made any sense.

The moral of my time in these 'no go' countries was an affecting one – that the most basic act of humanity is to show hospitality to another. A roof under which to rest road-weary bones, a cup of tea, a bag of cherries. I wondered if, on seeing a stranger in my city, I'd be so quick to invite them into my home before even knowing their name?

*

My time in Vientiane has me feeling recharged. Esther and I sit in our 'happy place' – a little street stall selling heaping bowls of spicy noodle soup – and decide I'm ready to get back on the bike. I miss the daily routine of the bikes. Esther thoughtfully suggests we restart with a route up some of the steepest climbs in Laos. Thanks for that, Sweetpea.

For the first time, there is some urgency in our planning; as we plan our first ride in a month, we're also contemplating the end of our journey. I could easily cycle for another year or more, despite coughing up a lung on the first Laotian hills. A streak of practicality runs through our thinking – we've had a glorious run of good fortune (barring dengue) and a job offer has come up back in London; an offer that allows a big step towards the life we want to live. We're still working to define what that is; but we're 100% certain, after a year on the road, that it's something dramatically different.

As with the start of our journey, a random question provides a jolt to the system at the end...

*

I'd been following a few long-distance cycling groups online. Not knowing my elbow from a Rohloff hub a year ago, I used them for research. Now I'm enjoying answering questions posed by others about to take to the road. Close to passing out after my first post-dengue rides, I see a post from a cyclist about to return from his own year-long journey. He asks the group:

"What should I expect when I return home, and what will it be like settling back into normal life?"

His question immediately makes me feel mentally queasy – but I can't place why. I read it to Esther; her reply clears my unease like some sort of brain enema.

"That's the wrong bloody question," Esther says. "You should ask yourself, 'What do you want your life to be like when you return?'"

She's instantly turned the question from a passive one to an active one. We made the big decision to take to the bikes to challenge our way of living – why the hell would we want to go back to things as they were? What I left is not what I want to return to. So I had to take the initiative, apply what I learnt on the bike and make my life what I wanted it to be.

When you confront things – people, places, ideas – that make you a little uncomfortable, you learn. When you do things that are out of the ordinary, whatever your definition of ordinary may be, you learn. And 'when we know better we tend to act better', as conservationist Darrick Thomson said to me once.

What I learnt on the road, with a bit of dengue-facilitated introspection, was as important as the journey itself. Discovering that I don't need much to be happy. How a reverence for nature made me rethink the impact my lifestyle was having on the world around me. Recognising that every small positive action matters. Understanding that goodwill is a universal language. If I read these thoughts to a few friends, they'd probably say, "Zim, don't be a wuss." But these pedal-bound bombshells crystallised an idea painfully obvious to my now forty-six-year-old self that I wouldn't have appreciated in my twenties:

Act Big. Live Small.

I got off the bike thinking that I didn't just want things to be different when I returned – I wanted to, for once, *be* the difference, even if in my own small way. Now I know how.

Website: **everythingaheadofyou.com**

Facebook: **davidhzimmer**

Epilogue

Teddington Trust

by Nicola Miller

Adventures for adventures! I cannot think of a more fitting proposition for the Biggest Book of Yes!

If you are reading this as a newcomer to the Big Book of Yes series, then hello and welcome. And if you are reading this for a third dive into the world of saying YES, then hello and thank you for your continued support!

As of June 2020, the preceding two editions have raised over £2,500 for our small charity, Teddington Trust. As a small charity run entirely by volunteers, a sum like this goes a long way. What we do with this particular money is very special indeed...

Living with the ultra-rare disease of xeroderma pigmentosum (XP) means adapting to a very particular lifestyle. You must ensure complete protection from all ultra-violet light. This means ALL daylight and most types of artificial sources of lighting.

You see, individuals with XP lack the ability to repair damage done by UV rays. They are ten thousand times more likely to develop skin cancer.

Avoiding daylight is often a concept too big for many people to even comprehend. In light of this year's life-altering global coronavirus pandemic, the world has inadvertently had a fleeting insight into the XP way of life — one of isolation, mask wearing and shielding.

So, as you can imagine, a life of adventure on the open road or high seas may, for our community, be entirely out of reach. But that is not to say that adventures cannot be had. At Teddington Trust we are passionate about giving our community of children and adults the tools and education to be inspired to live their best life.

Two years ago, we held our first ever Teddington BIG Adventure Sleepover, which brought together eleven families from across the UK to enjoy high adventure while we took care of the rest. We funded the adaptation of an accommodation block at an activity centre in the heart of the Dearne Valley. We made safe a yurt and sports hall, providing UK protective safety helmets for all – all in readiness for the families to come and enjoy one night of friendship and high octane fun. We rock climbed together, did archery and fencing, laser quest and crafts, and enjoyed lots of giggles along the way.

Building on the success of our first year, and just like the Big Book Of Yes, we were back, bigger and better the following year, this time for two nights and with more families and more activities.

To date the funds from the BBOY have helped fund nearly thirty of our guests, meaning that more families can benefit from this free activity weekend.

So whether it's the incredible authors and artists who have given generously of their time, or you the readers for buying this book, your support has meant that these adventures are helping end isolation and fear for children and adults living with the life-limiting condition of XP.

You are bringing families together to have their own adventures. Thank you.

With much love

Nicola Miller x

Chair of Trustees for Teddington Trust

www.teddingtontrust.com

Follow us on Facebook and Twitter **@TeddingtonTrust**

List of Illustrators

All the wonderful illustrations throughout the book have been drawn, crafted and designed by the following artists. If you liked their work, please find out more by following their links (@ contacts are for Instagram).

Chapter 1 – Tom Napper **tomnapperdesign.co.uk**

Chapter 2 – Hattie Suttard Parker **hattieparker.co.uk**

Chapter 3 – Lizzie Sullivan **@sunnysullie**

Chapter 4 – Samantha Elizabeth Allen **linkedin.com/in/samantha-allen-096a8677**

Chapter 5 – Victoria Galitzine **victoriagalitzine.com**

Chapter 6 – Nicola Hobbs **sparkleice.me**

Chapter 7 – Henri Renard **@henrirenard**

Chapter 8 – Angela Chick **angelachick.com**

Chapter 9 – Anne-Laure Carruth **anne-laurecarruth.com**

Chapter 10 – Leanne Rutter **@pangolintattoos**

Chapter 11 – Sarah Day **beardrawing42@gmail.com**

Chapter 12 – Alice Boydell **wonderwagon.co.uk**

Chapter 13 – Tanya Noble **@tanyanoble**

Chapter 14 – Alejandra Eifflaender-Salmón **our-tribe.co.uk**

Chapter 15 – Ellie Stevens **@elliegraceillustrates**

Chapter 16 – Michelle Robyn **@michellerobyndesigns**

Chapter 17 – Jaeden Harris **andreaharrisuk@aol.com**

Chapter 18 – Rion Badenhorst **facebook.com/sinssaintstattooparlour**

Chapter 19 – Katie Hammond **@scribblingsstudio**

Chapter 20 – Katie Hammond **@scribblingsstudio**

Chapter 21 – Rachel Tomasardottir **facebook.com/spirographgirl**

Chapter 22 – Rachel Fitch **@rachelfitch_design**

Chapter 23 – Zoe Langley-Wathen **headrightout.com**

Chapter 24 – Helen Proudfoot **@proudfootforward**

Chapter 25 – Jo Vincent, Bryony Wildwood and Geoff Long **jovincentart.com, bryonywildblood.com, geofflong.co.uk**

Chapter 26 – Michelle Robyn **@michellerobyndesigns**

Chapter 27 – Erika Manning **@erimanning**

Chapter 28 – Lynda Brown **@lyndambrown.lb**

Chapter 29 – Rebecca Nunn **@rexiraptor**

Chapter 30 – Joanna Langdon

Chapter 31 – Lynette Marshallsay **facebook.com/lynette.hall.921**

Chapter 32 – Katrina Williamson **katwilliamsonart.com**

Please Leave a Review

We really hope you enjoyed reading our stories. If you have a minute it would be absolutely amazing if you could head over to Amazon and leave an honest review. Every review makes this book more visible to the general public, so just by tapping a few words and selecting a star rating, you are potentially raising even more money for charity. Good on you!

Please search on Amazon for The Biggest Book of Yes. Near the bottom of the page you will find the 'WRITE A CUSTOMER REVIEW' next to all the other reviews. Hit the button and leave an honest review and we'll be eternally grateful.

Thanks, you wonderful human being!

The Biggest Book of Yes team

So you've finished reading the Biggest Book of Yes. Now what?

Well, maybe you'll go off on your own adventure. Maybe you'll be the next one saying, "Yes!"

In the meantime, if you're still looking for more inspiration, head over to Amazon right now and buy the predecessors to this book, **The Big Book of Yes** or **The Bigger Book of Yes**.

Same deal.

100% of the authors' and artists' time was given for free.

100% of the royalties go to Teddington Trust.

100% of the stories will inspire you to find your own YES moment!

Printed in Great Britain
by Amazon